D0857440

The End of Empathy

Why White Protestants Stopped Loving Their Neighbors

JOHN W. COMPTON

OXFORD
UNIVERSITY PRESS

OXFORD
UNIVERSITY PRESS

Oxford University Press is a department of the University of Oxford. It furthers
the University's objective of excellence in research, scholarship, and education
by publishing worldwide. Oxford is a registered trade mark of Oxford University
Press in the UK and certain other countries.

Published in the United States of America by Oxford University Press
198 Madison Avenue, New York, NY 10016, United States of America.

© Oxford University Press 2020

Library of Congress Cataloging-in-Publication Data
Names: Compton, John W., 1977– author.
Title: The end of empathy : why white protestants stopped loving their
neighbors / John W. Compton.
Description: New York, NY, United States of America : Oxford University
Press, 2020. | Includes bibliographical references and index. |
Identifiers: LCCN 2019044729 (print) | LCCN 2019044730 (ebook) |
ISBN 9780190069186 (hb) | ISBN 9780190069209 (epub) | ISBN 9780190069216 (online)
Subjects: LCSH: Christianity and politics—United States. |
Empathy—Religious aspects—Christianity. | United States—Church
history—19th century. | United States—Church history—20th century.
Classification: LCC BR516 .C687 2020 (print) | LCC BR516 (ebook) |
DDC 280/.409730904—dc23
LC record available at https://lccn.loc.gov/2019044729
LC ebook record available at https://lccn.loc.gov/2019044730

1 3 5 7 9 8 6 4 2

Printed by Sheridan Books, Inc., United States of America

Contents

Introduction

Seemingly every day, a new poll finds white evangelicals—by far the largest subset of American Protestants—espousing views that would appear difficult to reconcile with the golden rule. For example, evangelicals are *more* likely than members of other religious groups to favor drastic cuts to foreign aid and domestic social welfare programs. They are *less* likely than other believers—or nonbelievers, for that matter—to say that the United States has a duty to accept refugees displaced by violence or natural disasters in their home countries. They are *more* likely than others to favor sharp reductions in legal immigration, as well as the deportation of undocumented immigrants, including children, who have entered the United States illegally. They are *less* likely than others to view systemic racism as a serious obstacle to the socioeconomic advancement of racial minorities. They are *more* likely than others to favor harshly punitive approaches to criminal justice, including the death penalty. The list goes on and on.[1]

These findings were fairly well established by the time of the 2016 presidential election. Still, the news that most evangelicals cast their ballots for Donald Trump caught many commentators off guard. In part this was because what was known of Trump's personal life was sharply at odds with evangelical teachings. But it was also because Trump, in contrast to previous Republican nominees, made no effort to square his conservative policy positions with the Christian ethic of love and compassion. In fact, his chief calling card was his promise to show no mercy to those on the margins of American society.[2] And yet, evangelicals, far from balking at Trump's proudly amoral agenda, awarded him more than 80 percent of their votes. Significantly, Trump also fared reasonably well with white *mainline* Protestants, traditionally the more liberal branch of American Protestantism, capturing over 50 percent of their votes.[3] Perhaps most surprising of all, devout white Protestants—those who reported attending religious services on a weekly basis—were the most enthusiastic Trump supporters of all.[4]

The news of Trump's strong showing with white Protestant churchgoers soon sparked a broader debate concerning the relationship between religiosity and liberal democracy. For many commentators on the Left (as well as a few on the Right), the 2016 election returns confirmed a long-held suspicion that religious citizens—or at least white Protestant ones—are less than fully committed to the egalitarian norms of toleration and mutual respect that are often said to undergird the American constitutional system. How else to explain devout evangelicals' enthusiastic support for a proudly irreligious candidate whose chief campaign strategy was to stoke irrational fears of immigrants, refugees, and non-Christians?[5] But not everyone agreed with this line of analysis. Other commentators, including many who were deeply troubled by Trump's victory, looked to history to show that Protestant Christianity was not an inherently reactionary force. In earlier eras, these writers pointed out, religious ideas and institutions had often functioned as engines of social reform, providing much of the grassroots energy behind the movements to abolish slavery, enfranchise women, prohibit child labor, establish a rudimentary social welfare state, and enact the transformative civil rights laws of the 1960s. Twenty-first-century Protestants may have been hoodwinked into supporting a candidate whose views were at odds with core Christian teachings. But to claim that this single incident was illustrative of Protestant religiosity's broader impact on American political development was simply wrong.[6]

A glance at the historical record suggests that the second group of writers had a point: whatever else may be said about the relationship between Christianity and liberalism, it must be acknowledged that, at least in the American case, advocates of egalitarian reforms have often employed religious ideas and symbolism to great effect (as have their opponents). But to highlight the religious reform movements of the past is to raise a more fundamental question: what happened to this more tolerant and empathetic faith tradition? How, in other words, did the connection between Protestant religiosity and concern for the marginalized become so attenuated as to allow a candidate like Donald Trump to win the churchgoing vote in a landslide?

The most common way of answering this question is to point to the relatively recent rise of evangelicalism as the dominant strand of American Protestantism. For most of the nation's history, the bulk of American Protestants were not evangelicals but rather *mainline* Protestants—a category that includes the Congregationalists, Episcopalians, Methodists, Presbyterians, Disciples of Christ, and some branches of the Baptist and Lutheran faiths. During the first half of the twentieth century, most of these denominations experienced strong growth, even as their leaders adopted left-of-center positions on issues such as child labor and civil rights. This changed during the late 1960s and 1970s, when the mainline churches began suffering serious declines in membership and giving, and when evangelical churches and denominations, such as the Southern Baptist Convention (SBC), began experiencing strong growth. By the end of the 1970s the balance of power in American Protestantism had shifted to the theologically conservative evangelical churches, though it was initially unclear how (or whether) this would affect the political realm. But then came the presidential election of 1980, when a series of large and well-funded conservative religious groups, led by Jerry Falwell's Moral Majority, entered the political arena in support of former California governor Ronald Reagan. The new groups, which were dominated by evangelical and fundamentalist clergymen, adopted hardline conservative positions not only on issues such as abortion and school prayer, but also on such seemingly secular subjects as welfare, defense spending, and taxes. And while no one could have predicted at the time of Reagan's presidential victory that evangelical elites would one day enter into a strategic alliance with a playboy real-estate tycoon, it was then that evangelicalism, a faith tradition based on *theological* conservatism, became firmly wedded to the newly conservative political agenda of the Reagan-era Republican party.

Answers to why this shift occurred are more varied, but one popular theory holds that the politicization of evangelical religiosity was fueled by a sense that believers were losing, or had already lost, control of the wider culture. In some versions of the story, the sexual revolution—including the advent of legalized abortion and the movements for women's and gay and lesbian rights—takes center stage as the event that launched the Religious Right.[7] In other versions it is the nation's growing religious and ethnic diversity, together with the federal government's increasingly aggressive actions in defense of African American civil rights (which often entailed greater oversight of religious entities, such as private schools).[8] Still other commentators stress the entrepreneurial role of the conservative business community, which sensed that evangelicals' alienation might serve as the basis for a new and powerful political coalition based on shared enmity toward the modern Democratic party.[9] Whatever the immediate trigger, the underlying cause in most accounts is a growing sense of alienation, together with the conviction that aggressive political action was needed to prevent further erosion of traditional Protestant (or in some versions Judeo-Christian) values and prerogatives.

Without question, each of these narratives contains a grain of truth. Yet upon closer inspection, a focus on cultural alienation alone cannot fully account for the increasingly strident conservatism exhibited by white Protestants over the past half-century. The most serious problem with the conventional story is that it cannot explain the long history of Protestant social activism that preceded the Reagan Revolution. After all, during the 1910s, the 1930s, and the early 1960s—also periods of increasing diversity and unprecedented social change—millions of white middle-class Protestants channeled their anxieties into progressive reforms, helping to abolish child labor, establish reasonable workplace regulations, construct the social safety net, and enact civil rights laws that transferred resources and political authority to minority groups. Nor can strategic outreach from conservative businessmen or political operatives fully explain the shifting political valence of Protestant religiosity. For while it is true that conservative executives and libertarian activists succeeded in forging close ties with leading evangelicals during the 1970s and early 1980s, the more interesting question is why previous efforts to cement an evangelical-business alliance met with virtually no success. As we shall see, postwar conservatives spent a small fortune attempting to foment religious opposition to the New Deal–era welfare state—but to no avail. Why did such efforts suddenly gain traction in the 1970s and 1980s?

A final hole in the conventional story stems from the questionable assumption that theological conservatism and political conservatism are natural allies. To be sure, the theologically conservative wing of American Protestantism has always featured its share of outspoken political conservatives—from the early twentieth-century revivalist Billy Sunday to mid-century radio preachers like Carl McIntire and Billy James Hargis. And yet, as late as the mid-1970s many of the most powerful actors in the evangelical movement placed themselves either in the center or on the left of the political spectrum. If leading evangelical thinkers like Carl Henry and Francis Schaeffer were disturbed by the sexual revolution, they were also disturbed by environmental pollution, economic inequality, and Americans' often reflexive support for militaristic approaches to foreign policy (as were many of the nation's best-known evangelical politicians, including Oregon Senator Mark Hatfield and Illinois Congressman John B. Anderson). What explains the disappearance of this centrist strand of evangelicalism in the years around 1980?

To sum up the problem: if Protestant religiosity was for many decades associated with moderately progressive policy views on issues such as race relations and economic redistribution (as will be demonstrated in much more detail below), then accounts that begin the story of the Religious Right in the 1970s are necessarily incomplete. In order to explain how devout white Protestants ended up on the far right of the political spectrum, we must first identify the forces that in an earlier era pulled so many of them toward the center left. And we must examine why those forces ceased to operate in the years around 1970. Identifying these moderating forces, and explaining why they collapsed, are the central tasks of this book.

Toward a Theory of White Protestant Social Concern

In the pages that follow I develop a theoretical framework capable of explaining both the rise of white Protestant social concern at the end of the nineteenth century and its sudden decline at the end of the twentieth. The theory proceeds from two simple premises, neither of which has any claim to originality. The first, which will come as no surprise to readers of James Madison (or John Calvin), is that religious believers are on average much like similarly situated secular citizens when it comes to their behavior in the political realm. Like their secular neighbors, believers routinely base their political decisions on self-interest or ingrained prejudice rather than careful and disinterested study of sacred texts or deliberation about the will of a higher power. Nor are believers likely to hold views about the proper ordering of society that are radically different from those of nonbelievers who are similarly positioned in terms of race, class, gender, and other well-known predictors of political behavior.[10] In short, believers are typically no more likely than anyone else to engage in costly or self-denying forms of political behavior, such as supporting programs that, in the name of justice or fairness, transfer resources or political authority to other citizens or groups within society.

Of course, it is also true that American history is replete with episodes in which large numbers of believers have indeed acted in ways that neither self-interest nor in-group prejudice can readily explain. This leads to my second premise, which is that whenever members of a particular faith do engage in apparently empathetic or otherwise costly forms of political behavior, it is typically because strong religious institutions have compelled them to do so. Stated otherwise, religious convictions are more likely to shape individual behavior when the believer is enmeshed in a congregation or other body that is capable of interpreting and (at least to some degree) enforcing the doctrines in question.[11] There is little reason to expect that, absent religious authority, believers would behave differently from similarly situated secular citizens.[12]

Both premises require some elaboration. Note that I have limited my claim about political behavior to the modern era. In earlier periods—early Puritan New England, for example—when belief in a future state of rewards and punishments was a more pervasive presence in the mental lives of average citizens, it is likely that costly, religiously motivated forms of behavior were more common (though even here it can be difficult to sort out which behaviors flowed from genuine religious conviction as opposed to group pressures and legal sanctions). And even in the modern era one can find exceptional cases of believers engaging in striking acts of self-sacrifice without the impetus of external group-related incentives (think of the more extreme present-day opponents of abortion and nuclear proliferation, for example). My claim is not that such behavior is impossible but that it is exceedingly rare. At least in the United States, and limiting the discussion to white Protestants, the number of believers who adopt political views that are radically at variance with those of similarly situated nonbelievers, or who routinely sacrifice significant quantities of time, energy, or money on behalf of their stated religious convictions, appears to be quite small.

How, then, do religious institutions compel empathetic or otherwise costly forms of political behavior? They do so in two ways. First, authoritative religious institutions typically provide the believer with a set of what might be termed mediating doctrines—rules of conduct that connect the often abstract commands of the sacred texts to the business of everyday life. The Christian who remains aloof from organized religion may very well believe that the golden rule (for example) is a legitimate and binding tenet of the faith, but the abstract nature of the command will typically allow her to avoid applying it too rigorously in situations that seem to require inordinate sacrifices. Confronted with a friend or neighbor (let alone a stranger) in dire financial need, she may well succeed in convincing herself that it is in the friend's best interest *not* to offer assistance, perhaps because doing so would cause the friend to become dependent on the largesse of others, or because the money is urgently needed for some other purpose. Authoritative mediating doctrines make this sort of self-serving rationalization more difficult by telling the believer precisely what the general tenets of the faith demand in a range of specific situations. Some believers may still manage to rationalize selfish or prejudicial conduct as consistent with the doctrines of their faith tradition, or they may decide that a particular mediating doctrine results from a misreading of the sacred texts, but in either case they must be willing to accept the consequences of being labeled an iconoclast.[13]

The second way in which religious institutions (sometimes) compel altruistic or otherwise costly forms of behavior is by imposing significant costs on those who would otherwise pay lip service to religious teachings. These negative incentives may take different forms. Some religious sects rigorously police the conduct of their members, penalizing those who fail to adhere to the tenets of the faith. Others make such exacting and well-known demands of their members (in terms of time, money, or alienation from secular society, for example) that potential "free riders" are discouraged from joining in the first place.[14] Whatever form institutional incentives may take, their end result (in the case of strong institutions) is to discourage individual believers from backsliding, freeriding on the efforts of others, or otherwise failing to abide by religious edicts in their day-to-day conduct.

The question, of course, is why anyone would willingly join a religious body that makes such strong demands of its members. The answer, typically, is that the group offers some benefit that can only be obtained by submitting to its authority.[15] Examples range from the purely spiritual (such as a more intense or satisfying religious experience) to the largely material (such as the opportunity to perform in the choir). Speaking historically, however, the most compelling selective benefits associated with membership in an American Protestant congregation were often socioeconomic in nature. As the sociologist Max Weber pointed out more than a century ago, sects like the Baptists and Methodists imposed innumerable restrictions on their members' personal lives, but they also gave them something very valuable in return: access to the middle and upper echelons of American society.

Weber's argument proceeded from two firsthand observations concerning the nature of religious and group life in the United States. First, he noted that

American Protestant congregations were typically organized in the manner of sects rather than churches. Whereas a church, as Weber defined it, assumes the responsibility of ministering to every person, no matter how irreligious, within a given jurisdiction (e.g., a parish, town, or nation), a sect is "a free community of individuals" who are admitted to "membership on purely religious grounds." Sect members must submit to rigorous inspection of their beliefs and past conduct, and those admitted to fellowship are expected continually to prove their worth (and confess their failings) to the community upon pain of excommunication. It was for this reason, Weber observed, that American Protestant congregations were typically kept small enough so that their members could "know each other personally."[16] Only in this way could they engage in the mutual scrutiny of conduct and character that provided "the exclusive foundation for the social cohesion of the organization."[17]

Weber's second observation was that membership in a sectlike religious group conferred a very specific real-world benefit that few upwardly mobile Americans could afford to go without. In short, it publicly testified to a person's character. In a highly mobile society where citizens routinely relocated to new cities and even changed occupations, ascertaining whether an individual was likely to prove reliable in a business or social transaction was no simple matter. But if the new doctor, banker, or eligible bachelor in town carried a letter of membership from a reputable Protestant congregation, one could be reasonably certain the man was at least not a charlatan. Sect membership thus served as an invaluable stepping-stone to the middle and upper classes. Those who could claim it were well positioned to improve their lot in life, while those who lacked it were relegated to the margins of polite society. Indeed, Weber observed that citizens excluded from church (sect) membership often fell "victim to a . . . social ostracism" so severe as to be effectively "deprived of social contacts."[18]

Weber offered several memorable anecdotes from his 1904 American sojourn to illustrate the social—and, indeed, monetary—value of Protestant sect membership. He met a German American doctor who had once asked a patient to describe his symptoms, only to be told: "I am from the Second Baptist Church in X Street." The doctor was puzzled by the disclosure of this seemingly irrelevant information until he realized that the patient was conveying an implicit message "which was not without interest for the doctor"—namely, " 'Don't worry about your fee!' "[19] During a visit to Oklahoma he encountered a manufacturer of iron tombstone lettering who claimed to be indifferent to the niceties of theology ("as far as I'm concerned, everyone can believe what he likes") but who refused to do business with any man who was not a member in good standing of a local church.[20] Finally, he provided a vivid account of an outdoor baptism witnessed while visiting relatives in North Carolina. Puzzled as to why an "intelligent-looking young man" would consent to being dunked, fully clothed, into the "icy water of a mountain stream," he inquired into the man's background, ultimately discovering that he was new in town, and needed a loan to open a bank. Further examination

> revealed that admission into the Baptist church was so important not so much on account of the potential Baptist clientele but rather to attract non-Baptist clients. This was because the *thorough scrutiny* of the candidate's moral and business conduct that preceded admission . . . was regarded as by far the most rigorous and reliable of its kind. The slightest unpunctuality in the payment of a debt, careless expenditure, frequenting the tavern—in short, anything that cast a shadow on the business qualification of the man in question—would lead to his being rejected by the local church community. Once he has been voted in, the sect will accompany him for the rest of his life in everything he does. If he moves to a different town, it will provide him with the testimonial without which he will not be accepted in the local church of his "denomination."[21]

To be sure, Weber acknowledged that both the rigors of church discipline and the significance of church membership as a professional credential had declined somewhat by the early twentieth century. In the nation's larger cities, fashionable congregations had expanded to such a size that careful oversight of members' personal lives was no longer possible (though individuals whose sins had become public knowledge were still regularly, if quietly, purged from church membership rolls).[22] Hence, while church (sect) membership remained a fairly reliable proxy for good character, it was now often supplemented by membership in nominally secular organizations that (perhaps because they were typically populated by devout Protestants) exhibited all the classic features of religious sects, including rigorous screening of applicants and the requirement that members constantly "prove themselves" by sacrificing time, energy, and money to advance group aims. (As we shall see, Weber probably overestimated the extent to which nominally secular membership groups had taken over the traditional character-vouching function of the Protestant congregation; in fact, both types of membership would remain essential to socioeconomic advancement through the middle decades of the twentieth century, and many nominally secular groups were closely linked to religious bodies.)[23]

Though Weber mostly limited his discussion to the character-vouching function of church and group membership, his basic point can be extended to other types of selective benefits that facilitate socioeconomic advancement. Church membership may permit access to elite social networks, for example, or it may publicly testify to the fact that a person has already reached the upper echelons of society. Both of these dynamics seem to have been at work in the mid-twentieth-century United States, since sociologists routinely observed that upwardly mobile white Protestants were more likely than other citizens to abandon "low status" churches in favor of more prestigious denominations (typically the Episcopalians, Congregationalists, Presbyterians, or Unitarians).[24] Membership in a prestigious denomination was valuable not so much because it meant that a person had passed a rigorous character test—by this point, the most prestigious Protestant denominations had largely abandoned efforts to police the personal conduct of their members—but because, like the country club, it both signaled admission to "the establishment" and offered opportunities for further socio-economic advancement. (The same studies showed that CEOs and highly paid professionals were overwhelmingly clustered in these four denominations.)[25]

Whether derived from Weber's sect dynamic in its classic form or from the related but distinct desire to confirm (or signal) one's elevated position in the social order, the socioeconomic "pull" of mainline church membership conferred a somewhat nebulous but nonetheless real form of authority on church officials. Citizens who sought the socioeconomic benefits of Presbyterian church membership (for example) naturally found it advisable to immerse themselves in the organizational life of the denomination, which necessarily entailed subjecting oneself to a broader religious culture that emphasized the importance of aiding those on the margins of society. As with any democratically governed entity, the policy commitments of the mainline denominations were open to challenge and debate. But to openly criticize, say, denominational leaders' support for foreign aid programs was not simply to make a political point; it was to reject one of the longstanding commitments that gave Presbyterianism its substance as a social identity.

Applying this insight to the case of mainline Protestants more generally, we shall see that, from the mid-nineteenth century through the 1960s, most non-Southern Protestants not only professed to believe that Christian principles, properly understood, favored government efforts to aid the downtrodden; they were also embedded in religious networks that were capable, at least on occasion, of focusing attention on specific social problems and incentivizing the faithful to take responsibility for correcting them.

So what changed in the 1960s and 1970s? The answer, obviously, is "quite a lot." But the most important change, I shall argue, was the rapid erosion of religious authority within the mainline Protestant churches, denominations, and ecumenical bodies—a development that was at least partially independent from the contemporaneous social upheavals that continue to define these decades in the popular mind. If white Protestants were more inclined to adopt far right policy positions in 1980 than in 1950, it was not only because of alarm at the rise of feminism, legalized abortion, and no-fault divorce. It was also because the institutions and social dynamics that had traditionally channeled believers' anxieties into egalitarian reform movements had largely collapsed.

A Brief Sketch of the Historical Argument

Employing a combination of archival evidence and public opinion data, *The End of Empathy* traces this story across three historical epochs. Part I ("The Age of Stewardship") examines the period from the mid-nineteenth century to the 1930s, when a combination of theological conviction and socioeconomic incentives led millions of Protestant believers to view the creation of a more just society as a divine imperative. Part II ("Why the Center Held") highlights the role of mainline Protestant institutions both in constructing the mid-century welfare state and in defending it against attacks from well-funded interest groups and politicians on the Right. Part III ("From Revelation to Rationalization") documents how the collapse of mainline religious authority in the late 1960s both exacerbated the nation's ideological divisions and paved the way for the rise of a new strand of Protestantism that offered middle-class white believers the assurance of salvation while simultaneously liberating them from the biblical injunction to care for the widow and the orphan.

The central theme linking the three sections—the independent variable, so to speak—is the evolving nature of Protestant religious authority. In brief, citizens from the mid-nineteenth century to the early 1960s faced strong incentives to join and become active in churches and membership groups affiliated with the large mainline Protestant denominations. The mainline churches and membership groups, in turn, instilled in their members a profound sense of religious duty toward the less fortunate. That average churchgoers took these lessons to heart was due, initially, to the sect dynamic chronicled by Max Weber. But even after American churches began to shed many of their sectlike characteristics, the enduring importance of membership as a marker of social respectability, together with the access it provided to elite social networks, vested religious elites with considerable sway over their upwardly mobile parishioners. At the same time, the religion boom of the late 1940s and early 1950s—and the financial windfall it produced—allowed mainline leaders to expand their institutional reach by, for example, constructing an expansive network of state and local church councils. That Northern white Protestants remained generally supportive of Democratic social welfare and civil rights programs, even as they tended to cast their presidential ballots for moderate Republicans, testifies to the influence of the churches' educational efforts on behalf of the postwar welfare state.

This state of affairs endured through the early 1960s, when two relatively new social dynamics began to undercut the authority of the mainline churches and ecumenical groups. First, developments in higher education and the labor market greatly reduced the social and economic significance of church membership (as well as other forms of group membership), thus sounding the death knell for what Weber called the "sect spirit." As college enrollments skyrocketed, as more and more students pursued degrees in the sciences and engineering, and as massive corporations employed an ever larger percentage of the labor force, informal social networks became much less important as stepping-stones to the middle and upper classes.[26] Having secured jobs with large corporations on the basis of their educational qualifications and technical expertise, white suburbanites had little reason to fear that leaving—or even failing to seek out— the local Presbyterian or Episcopal church would seriously diminish their social standing or economic prospects. By the same token, those who remained in the mainline flock had few incentives to heed their purported leaders' advice on the burning questions of the day.

Second, the postwar period witnessed an unprecedented surge in residential mobility. The great winner in the relocation sweepstakes—thanks to a government-financed boom in the defense, aviation, and technology sectors— was the western Sunbelt, a region with comparatively low levels of religious commitment and an unusually weak religious infrastructure. California's ratio of mainline Protestant churches to Protestant residents was roughly half that of the Midwestern states in the late 1930s, and it fell even further behind as a result of the postwar relocation boom. The millions of white middle-class Americans who moved westward in the postwar years thus found themselves in an environment where religious authority was stretched unusually thin, and a significant number of them drifted away from organized religion as a result. Others were drawn to politically conservative religious entrepreneurs whose calls for tax cuts and increased defense spending dovetailed nicely with the material interests of the state's burgeoning population of young suburban professionals.

By the late 1960s the mainline denominations were in crisis: attendance was down, budgets were stretched thin, and ecumenical bodies were laying off hundreds of employees. Popular and academic commentators blamed it all on the churches' increasingly "radical" stances on civil rights, the Vietnam War, women's rights, and economic justice.[27] As we shall see, however, this familiar story gets the causal relationship between the decline of mainline Protestantism and the conservative political backlash of the late 1960s and early 1970s exactly backward. The mainline churches did not suddenly discover politics in the late 1960s; nor, with the notable exception of gender equality, did they move appreciably to the left over the course of the decade. What happened, rather, was that the collapse of religious authority over the course of the late 1950s and early 1960s liberated large numbers of upwardly mobile white Protestants from the normative commitments that had bound their forebears. Now free to follow their own inclinations and interests—not only in their personal lives, but also in their thinking about politics and society—many of them discovered a sudden aversion to talk of entrenched inequality and economic redistribution. Their objection was not to clerical political activism per se, but rather to the "prophetic" policy vision the mainline denominations had faithfully espoused since the turn of the twentieth century.

Needless to say, this history casts the rise of the Religious Right in a new light. In particular, it suggests that evangelicalism rose to prominence at least in part because it was well suited to an environment in which religious authority in the traditional sense had all but ceased to exist. In the new age of personal autonomy, the leaders of the Religious Right flourished by reshaping the Christian message to comport with the prejudices and material self-interest of their target demographic. Focused on personal salvation and stripped of any concern with social justice, post-1970s evangelicalism struck a chord with white middle-class Protestants who now had little reason to concern themselves with the plight of the less fortunate. Contrary to popular belief, its chief spokespersons, including Jerry Falwell and Pat Robertson, possessed neither the intrinsic religious authority nor the institutional structures necessary to shape their supporters' views on important questions of public policy. Instead, they rose to national prominence by being among the first religious figures to endorse the conservative political backlash of the late 1970s. Realizing that the white electorate *as a whole* was tracking rightward on issues ranging from civil rights to taxes and abortion, they placed early bets on the conservative insurgency and were rewarded with brief but successful careers as Republican power brokers.

At the same time, this book's thesis challenges many cherished assumptions of the secular Left, including the widespread belief that religious authority is the eternal enemy of movements for human dignity and equality. In fact, for much of the twentieth century religious authority was among the forces most responsible for building white middle-class support for social welfare and civil rights programs. When it suddenly collapsed in the closing decades of the century, the end result was not the flowering of a more enlightened or empathetic society (as much popular commentary might lead one to expect), but rather the rise of popular ideologies that dismissed almost all state-sponsored efforts to aid the downtrodden as wasteful, counterproductive, or sinful. In the case of well-off citizens, this novel *Weltanschauung* was obviously self-serving; for those closer to the bottom of the socioeconomic ladder, less rational motives were probably at work. Either way, the end result would not have surprised the theologian Dietrich Bonhoeffer, who once observed that the erosion of religious authority had a tendency to unleash "the vigilant religious instinct of man for the place where grace is to be obtained at the cheapest price."[28] Left entirely to their own devices, Bonhoeffer knew, most citizens will prefer ethical and religious perspectives that conform to their preexisting interests and prejudices rather than challenging them.

A Brief Note on Definitions and Methodology

Before proceeding to the main argument of the book, it may be helpful to specify in advance the terms that will be used to describe the various religious groups that appear in the following pages. The careful reader will note that I have to this point been somewhat haphazard in this regard, often using such terms as *evangelical, white Protestant*, and *religious voters* more or less interchangeably. Going forward, I will attempt to use these and other terms only in ways that contemporaneous historical actors would have understood. For example, when discussing theologically or politically conservative Protestants in the early 1900s, I will use the term *fundamentalist*—the term that the thinkers and groups in question coined to distinguish themselves from liberal or modernist Protestants, who had abandoned the principle of biblical inerrancy, as well as some traditional doctrinal tenets of the faith. I will use the term *evangelical* to refer to the ecumenical-minded conservative Protestants who, beginning in the 1940s, began to distance themselves from the fundamentalists (whose rigid separatism and tendentious eschatological theories they deemed counterproductive to the ultimate goal of saving souls). It was at this point—and not before—that the term *evangelical* became attached to a concrete group of believers, namely, the churches and denominations that came together under the umbrella of the National Association of Evangelicals (founded in 1942), as well those that clustered around Billy Graham and his various enterprises, including the Billy Graham Evangelistic Association.

My only conscious exception to this approach involves the term *mainline*— a label I will use to denote the large Protestant denominations (including the Methodists, Northern Baptists, Presbyterians, Episcopalians, and Congregationalists) that in 1908 came together under the banner of the Federal Council of Churches. Although this term did not come into widespread usage until the 1960s, it is nonetheless helpful to have some way of referring to the vast majority of American Protestants who were members in good standing of these denominations, and who either subscribed to or acquiesced in the positions adopted by denominational leaders.[29] (If no contemporaneous term exists, it is likely because these denominations claimed an overwhelming percentage of the Protestant population as members; only groups that were attempting to separate from the main body of American Protestantism had reason to adopt qualifying labels like "fundamentalist" and "evangelical.")[30]

A brief word concerning methodology is also in order. Although this book relies extensively on archival research to support its main arguments, it is not in any sense a comprehensive history of American Protestantism in the twentieth century. Nor should the reader expect a broad history of the rise and fall of the post–New Deal liberal order. Rather, my aim—and what I hope is my unique contribution—is to complement the many existing studies on these subjects by showing how a very specific set of Protestant religious ideas and institutions contributed to the construction and maintenance of the American social welfare state, and how their collapse rendered the welfare state suddenly vulnerable to attacks from the Right.

To this end I draw extensively on two types of archival sources: (1) the records of national religious bodies, such as the National Council of Churches and the large mainline denominations; and (2) the records of local religious bodies, such as state and local church councils, that worked to build popular support for the policy priorities of national religious leaders. Armed with this evidence, I revisit several well-known historical episodes, showing how the support of religious leaders and lay people—at both the national and local levels—either contributed to significant liberal policy achievements, such as the New Deal and the Civil Rights Act of 1964, or else helped foil the efforts of conservative activists to mobilize popular opposition to these programs. Finally, in some of the later chapters, including the chapters on the Civil Rights Act and the rise of the Religious Right, I rely on public opinion data to supplement evidence from these archival sources. The end result, I hope, is a comprehensive picture, not of the rise and decline of the Protestant mainline, nor of the rise and decline of twentieth-century liberalism, but rather of the most important points at which these two stories intersect.

PART I

THE AGE OF STEWARDSHIP

1

The Road to Armageddon

We ask that those of our people to whom fate has been kind shall
remember that each is his brother's keeper, and that all of us . . . shall
feel our obligation to the less fortunate who work wearily beside us.
—Theodore Roosevelt, "Who Is a Progressive?" (1912)

In the early years of the twentieth century, an army of devout middle-class
Protestants entered the political arena, determined to transform American society. The nation had witnessed sporadic bursts of grassroots religious activism
in the past, but this time was different. In contrast to the nineteenth-century
reform crusades, which tended to be narrowly focused on particular sins (e.g.,
intemperance and slavery), this one targeted multiple social problems simultaneously. Perhaps even more surprising, the social problems of greatest interest
to the reformers mostly affected the working class—a group whose pleas church
officials had long ignored. Finally, where previous crusades were often elite-led
affairs and limited to members of one or two Protestant denominations, this one
spilled across the usual divisions of class, church, and region: it united working-
class Methodists and upper-class Congregationalists, ministers and laypeople,
men and women, Easterners and Westerners (and even many Southerners) in
an ambitious campaign to create a fairer and more democratic political order.
And, in part for this reason, it culminated in a nearly unbroken string of legislative triumphs: pure food and drug laws, a federal child labor ban, women's
suffrage, a national prohibition on alcohol, a federal income tax, federal child
and maternal health programs, mothers' pension programs, and protective labor
laws for women, to name a few. All these reforms and many more were put into
the state and federal statute books (or the Constitution) in quick succession, and
most of them benefited from the backing of the major Protestant denominations
and parachurch groups.

With the benefit of hindsight, this remarkable outpouring of religious activism can be described as simultaneously ephemeral and enduring: ephemeral in the sense that many of the landmark Progressive Era reforms would
be repealed or scaled back during the 1920s, but enduring in the sense that it
birthed a religious worldview that would shape the course of American political
development for decades to come. For even as conservatives gained ground in

the years following World War I, the nation's largest Protestant denominations and ecumenical bodies remained firmly committed to the principles articulated in their Progressive Era pronouncements. Over the next half century the leaders of this informal religious coalition would attempt to serve as the nation's collective conscience. Whether the subject was immigration, unemployment insurance, or civil rights, they placed themselves on the side of the downtrodden, the forgotten, and the marginalized, even as they cultivated close ties with economic and political elites. In so doing, they offered critical support for a range of novel government programs that promised to increase economic opportunity and civic participation. From the perspective of the present, their efforts were sometimes marred by painful blind spots, including a naïve faith in the power of dialogue to address evils, such as the nation's racial caste system, that ultimately required massive intervention on the part of the state. Yet whenever the Protestant establishment chose to speak unequivocally on pressing social issues (as it eventually did in the case of civil rights), it spoke with authority. Lawmakers ignored its pronouncements at their peril.

If we are to explain the ideological evolution of American Protestantism over time, then, we must begin by examining the ideas and social forces that paved the way for the landmark reform crusades of the Progressive Era. In this chapter I argue that three developments were particularly crucial. The first was the mid-nineteenth-century revival of a strand of Protestant social thought that stretched back to the Puritans—a *prophetic tradition* built on the interconnected ideas of stewardship, providential duty, and collective accountability for sin. The second was the *sect dynamic* observed by the sociologist Max Weber during his early twentieth-century visit to the United States—a social dynamic that incentivized upwardly mobile citizens to seek membership in Protestant churches and membership groups while also endowing church and group leaders with considerable influence over the beliefs and behaviors of their members. The third was the rise of an *ecumenical infrastructure* that promoted cooperation between elite reformers and average citizens, and also between believers of different social and denominational backgrounds. The widespread use of federated group structures in particular allowed reform-minded elites to disseminate information to large numbers of Americans while simultaneously cultivating trust that proposed reforms would be implemented in good faith. Together, these three forces—the prophetic tradition, Weber's sect dynamic, and an ecumenical infrastructure of interconnected church and parachurch groups—would underpin mainline Protestant social activism through the 1960s. It perhaps goes without saying that each of these supports underwent subtle changes over time. Yet for the better part of a century their core features remained intact and recognizable; and so long as this was the case, churchgoers were well represented in egalitarian reform movements.

The Recovery of the Prophetic Voice

The Progressive Era reformers were profoundly influenced by an inherited religious tradition—call it a popular theology—that stressed the duty of reforming society in preparation for Christ's return. At its core were three convictions: the belief that the United States had succeeded ancient Israel as God's agent in history (providentialism); the belief that widespread immorality, whether in the form of personal vice or systemic oppression, was a collective failure for which all Americans were ultimately responsible (collective accountability for sin); and, finally, the belief that property holders and other economic actors were but temporary stewards of resources that were intended for use in the building of the Kingdom (stewardship). Not all of the period's progressive activists were orthodox Christians, by any means. But even those who were not routinely invoked the signs and symbols of the Protestant reform tradition. Steeped in the lore of religious abolitionism, figures such as Teddy Roosevelt, Jane Addams, and Florence Kelley still inhabited a world of good and evil, of national destiny, of sacred obligations. The language of providential duty thus served as the lingua franca of progressive reform—a shared moral vocabulary that connected even agnostic elites to millions of average believers, allowing them to frame policy debates in ways that spoke to middle-class citizens' innate sense of right and wrong.[1]

The conviction that Americans were duty bound to remake society in preparation for the coming of the Kingdom predated even the abolitionists, however. It arrived on the shores of New England with the first Puritan settlers, who believed they had been commissioned to build a model society that would inspire repentance and reform in the mother country and, ultimately, the wider world. This sense of divine calling—embodied in the idea of the covenant—was the cornerstone of New England's religious culture. It was also the source of tremendous anxiety. For the Puritans knew that, should they fail in their mission, they would cause the Almighty to "break out in wrath against us, and be revenged of such a people, and make us know the price of the breach of such a covenant."[2] When catastrophe struck the Puritan colonies, whether in the form of a crop failure or an Indian attack, it inevitably triggered a nagging fear that the community had strayed from the path of righteousness. Such anxieties, in turn, gave rise to the venerable rhetorical tradition of the jeremiad: ritualistic sermons in which ministers enumerated the sins of their congregants, reminded them of the terms of the covenant, and called them to repentance and reform.[3]

In Puritan New England, virtually any sin, if widespread enough, could invite the disciplining hand of the Almighty: drunkenness, disobedient children, Sabbath breaking, swearing, idleness, and even such hard-to-pin-down transgressions as "contentiousness" and "hypocrisy" were, at various times, blamed for courting disaster. At least through the middle decades of the seventeenth century, however, economic sins were particularly popular targets of clerical scorn. Citing John Calvin's commentary on Genesis 2:15, Puritan divines insisted that property owners were but temporary stewards or trustees of resources on loan from God.[4] This conviction inspired a host of laws and practices designed to ensure that the region's resources were used in ways that furthered the long-term well-being of the community, as opposed to the short-term interests of property owners. Puritan leaders imposed tight controls on land sales and the timber trade, for example, and they also kept a close eye on everyday commercial transactions. Instances of oppression (price gouging) and usury (charging interest) were punished as criminal acts on the theory that the prosperous should not be permitted to "grind the faces of the poor."[5] As late as 1676, Increase Mather interpreted the wave of devastation unleashed by the Wampanoag chief King Philip as evidence of God's displeasure with merchants who were setting "excessive [prices] . . . upon their goods" and unapologetically committing "that odious sin of Usury."[6]

But if stewardship and collective accountability were fixtures of early New England culture, they lost much of their luster—or at least much of their critical edge—in the decades around the turn of the eighteenth century. To be sure, clergymen continued to interpret current events, particularly disastrous ones, in light of the region's providential mission. But the former emphasis on economic wrongdoing gradually disappeared as most ministers came to accept that prosperous merchants—even ones who relied on complex credit instruments and sued to enforce debts in the civil courts—should not be regarded as sinners, assuming that they lived otherwise upright lives and gave generously to religious and charitable causes.[7] Just as important, the original focus on the shortcomings of the faithful gave way to a new concern with the threats posed by outsiders. During the 1760s and 1770s, many New England divines saw the hand of God in the region's bloody conflicts with France and its Indian allies, and later in the escalating tensions with English colonial authorities. Yet the resulting jeremiads—if one can call them that—rarely focused on probing the moral character of the audience; rather, they tended to assure listeners that these unsettling events were, in fact, part of God's larger design.[8]

Not until the 1820s would the more traditional jeremiad, with its emphasis on stewardship and collective accountability for sin, begin to regain some of its lost cultural influence.[9] Attempting to isolate a single factor that led to its revival is probably a fool's errand. What can be said with certainty is that its recovery was closely connected to a series of reform movements that emerged from the national wave of religious revivals known as the Second Great Awakening. Under the tutelage of Lyman Beecher, Charles Grandison Finney, and other celebrity preachers, American Protestants learned that they were complicit in a range of national sins that threatened the young republic's future. Heeding the revivalists' call, hundreds of thousands of believers joined voluntary societies that targeted particular sins, including slavery, intemperance, gambling in lotteries, and Sunday commerce.[10] Yet the reformers soon encountered a problem: many of these sinful industries were protected by entrenched legal precedents—and in some cases by the Constitution itself. Stung by a series of adverse court decisions, the activists appealed to a higher power. No amount of legal precedent, they argued, could justify a breach of the nation's special covenant.[11]

The sin most responsible for reviving the prophetic strand of Protestant social thought was, of course, slavery. Confronted with the objection that the Constitution prohibited interference with the South's "peculiar institution"—and that slavery was, in any case, a regional problem—antislavery activists reminded Northern audiences that an avenging God was unlikely to be persuaded by such arguments. For if slavery was a sin, then it stood to reason that all Americans were complicit in evil, not only because of the myriad economic ties between North and South but also because republican citizens were the ultimate authors of their own political institutions.[12] As Leonard Bacon, pastor of New Haven's Center Church, informed his congregation, the severe economic depression of 1837 appeared to be "Providence['s]" way of "teaching a lesson." New Englanders who were previously unaware of the

> tie of brotherhood, that binds them alike to the lordliest oppressor and the meanest of his slaves, [are] be[ing] touched where they can feel. Ask the merchant and the manufacturer, whose drafts come back dishonored, and who are themselves made bankrupt, because slaves have fallen to one sixth of their last year's price—ask them, and ask their creditors, if we have no concern with slavery.... The first strokes of [God's] chastisement fall, as is meet, upon all the land. The merchant princes of New England share in adversity, as they have shared in prosperity and sin.[13]

Here was the old Puritan formula in all its glory. Because all Americans were members of a single covenanted community, the consequences of sin, no matter where it occurred, would be visited on all citizens alike. Decisions in the economic realm, no less than in other spheres of life, were subject to the scrutiny of the Almighty. And those who, in the blind pursuit of profit, chose to do business with slaveholders—which was to say, virtually all Americans—stood in danger of hellfire.

A similar logic underpinned the antebellum temperance movement. Launched in the late 1820s, the movement was initially powered by a widespread fear that a sudden spike in alcohol consumption—fueled by surplus grain production on the frontier—was breaking up families and filling poorhouses.[14]

When prayer and moral suasion failed to remedy the problem, groups such as the million-member American Temperance Society (ATS) began advocating statutory restrictions on the sale and manufacture of alcohol, and from this point forward they confronted roughly the same legal and constitutional obstacles as their allies in the antislavery movement.[15] Faced with claims that restrictive liquor laws violated the rights of property holders, the ATS and like-minded groups changed the subject, shifting the discussion from black-letter law to the higher authority of the covenant. As Lyman Beecher explained in his highly influential *Six Sermons on Intemperance* (1827), if the nation's material abundance was a gift from God, it followed that property owners were under an affirmative "duty" to "serve [their] generation in some useful employment."[16] The liquor business, which consumed "a vast amount of capital" while producing no larger social "good" that might counterbalance the "enormous evils" that were "inseparable from the trade," clearly did not meet this standard. And any nation that sheltered such an industry, Beecher insisted, was due for a divine reckoning.[17]

If the antislavery and temperance movements helped spark a revival of the older, prophetic strand of Protestant social thought, the Civil War cemented its place in the mainstream of American public discourse.[18] Abraham Lincoln, in his second inaugural address, famously declared that Americans would have no cause for complaint if the conflict continued "until all the wealth piled by the bondsman's two hundred and fifty years of unrequited toil shall be sunk, and until every drop of blood drawn with the lash shall be paid by another drawn with the sword," for "it must be said 'the judgments of the Lord are true and righteous altogether.'"[19] Although Lincoln never claimed that the hand of Providence would guide the Union forces to victory—the motives of the Almighty were in his view beyond human comprehension—many Northern ministers reasoned that if the war reflected God's judgment on a slaveholding nation, then he would surely see it through to a successful conclusion.[20] Many of them drew on this providential understanding of the conflict to build support for the Reconstruction-era constitutional amendments that abolished slavery and (briefly) granted a modicum of legal protection to the former slaves. As the Congregationalist minister Horace Bushnell informed the Yale graduating class of 1865, the same God who had aided the Union cause now expected Americans to cleanse the Constitution of its Founding-era impurities. To fail in this task would be to risk his wrath a second time.[21]

The Rise of the Social Gospel

The antislavery and temperance movements thus demonstrated that religious appeals were more than capable of mobilizing popular opposition to even the most entrenched of inherited institutions. Yet there was at least one realm in which Protestant religiosity seemed more likely to blunt serious ethical reflection than to foster it: For most of the nineteenth century, leading Protestants steadfastly resisted any suggestion that the titans of "legitimate" industry should be held accountable for the terrible human cost of industrialization.[22] Although celebrity revivalists such as Lyman Beecher sometimes expressed concern for *European* peasants who were being herded "into manufacturing establishments to wear out their days in ignorance and hopeless poverty," they insisted that American industrial laborers enjoyed two critical advantages over their Old World counterparts: freedom from feudal obligations and access to an abundance of cheap land.[23] In America, the thinking went, any citizen who was reasonably industrious would soon find an employer who compensated him fairly for his labors and would in time ascend to the upper rungs of the socioeconomic ladder. And if a man was unlucky in his choice of employers, he could always relocate to the frontier, where land was virtually free for the taking, and begin a new career as a yeoman farmer.[24]

But the belief that the United States was an exceptional land of boundless economic opportunity became increasingly untenable as the nineteenth century drew to a close. The roots of its decline can be traced to the late 1880s and early 1890s, when the pioneers of what came to be known as the Social Gospel movement discovered that their parishioners were falling ever deeper into poverty, even as many of them observed the classic Calvinist virtues to the letter.[25] These ministers, most of whom pastored working-class churches, pointed out that the urban poor were subject to a host of physical dangers and temptations—from unsanitary living conditions to the ubiquitous corner saloon—that were largely absent from middle- and upper-class neighborhoods. Together with the leaders of the burgeoning settlement movement, they collected hard data on working conditions, which led to the discovery that many industrial workers labored for seventy or more hours per week, leaving little time to tend to their families or pursue educational opportunities. Social surveys also suggested that language barriers and lack of access to formal education, not an aversion to hard work, were responsible for the alarming poverty rates among immigrant laborers. Then there was the work itself, which was not only dangerous and physically draining but also mind-numbingly dull, a far cry indeed from the Calvinist calling. As Walter Rauschenbusch, the movement's intellectual leader, put it, there was little in the modern industrial system that could be expected to "produce in the common man the pride and joy of good work."[26]

The closing of the frontier—the discovery, extrapolated from the 1890 census, that most western lands suitable for settlement had already been claimed—dealt a fatal blow to the theory that America alone had been spared the curse of systemic poverty. Indeed, if the supply of cheap land had been exhausted, it was no longer clear how the relationship of the industrial magnate to his workers differed from that of the feudal lord to his serfs. Increasingly, mine and factory workers were housed in company towns that bore an uncanny resemblance to feudal manors.[27] And even those who escaped this fate were subject to the arbitrary authority of company officials, who could fire them at a moment's notice but were under no obligation to compensate them if they lost a limb on the job. Here, wrote the minister and social reformer Josiah Strong, was a "despotism vastly more oppressive . . . than that against which the thirteen colonies rebelled."[28]

With the discovery that American workers were not, in fact, freer than their European counterparts, the chain of reasoning that had long shielded the labor relationship from religious and ethical scrutiny suddenly collapsed. For if workers faced real and durable obstacles to economic advancement; if many of them were trapped in dangerous and physically taxing jobs from which there was little hope of escape; if industrial wages were too low to keep even a small family clothed and fed; and if the length of the typical workday made a mockery of the ideal of the "Christian home"—all these facts suggested that the titans of "legitimate" industry, no less than slaveholders or liquor dealers, should be held to account for their poor stewardship of God-given resources.[29] Hence, Washington Gladden, widely regarded as the father of the Social Gospel movement, justified his support for progressive economic reforms by proclaiming that every "possessor of wealth" was merely "as a steward or a trustee," "bound" to use his property for the "Christianizing" of "the society in which he lives." Rauschenbusch, citing the parable of the talents, likewise reminded America's industrialists that "our resources are a trust, and not absolute property. We manage and control them, but always under responsibility. We hold them from God, and his will has eminent domain."[30]

In later years, after the Social Gospel movement had effectively permeated the institutions of mainline Protestantism, politically conservative religious leaders often accused thinkers like Rauschenbusch of devising a purely materialistic theology—one that, by refocusing the believer's attention on the evils of this world, effectively subordinated religion to social ethics, and divine revelation to human reason. In reality, Social Gospel thinkers were not indifferent to questions of personal sin and salvation. Rather, they argued that if the church was serious about saving souls, it had no choice but to concern itself with the social and economic forces that were hardening entire classes of citizens against the message of the Gospel. Workers who were forced to labor seven days a week, or who were too exhausted to rouse themselves for Sunday worship, or who saw exploitative employers installed in positions of leadership in the church were understandably more likely to seek answers from radical labor organizers than from men of the cloth.[31] In the second place, as revivalists had been pointing out since the days of Beecher and Finney, an authentic conversion experience necessarily alerted the new believer to social injustices in the surrounding society. How could citizens who for the first time truly loved their neighbors as themselves not exhibit "the spirit of the reformer" as they contemplated the extent of "organized evil" in the world?[32] Finally, in an age when fewer and fewer Americans were able to find spiritual meaning in their occupations, Social Gospel thinkers argued that a new form of labor—the work of building Christ's Kingdom—was needed to fill the void once occupied by the Calvinist calling. In joining the struggle to purge American society of entrenched inequality, exploitative labor practices, and other social evils, a man "set his hands to a task that will never end and will always expand," one that "ke[pt] him growing" in faith by making "ever larger demands on his intellect, his sympathy, and his practical efficiency."[33]

Initially dismissed as dangerously radical, the idea that God expected Christian citizens to cooperate in the construction of a fairer economic order would by the early 1900s achieve the status of orthodoxy within wide swaths of American Protestantism. One after another the mainline denominations created departments, commissions, and bureaus dedicated to investigating the causes of poverty, industrial strife, and other social problems (as summarized in Table 1.1).[34] Equally important, church officials added social-ethics courses to the standard seminary curriculum, with several prestigious schools—Union

Table 1.1 Social involvement of the mainline Protestant churches

Denomination	Membership (1906)	Primary social-service body (date created)	FCC member?
Congregational	700,000	Department of Labor and Social Service (1910)	Yes
Disciples of Christ	983,000	Social Service Committee (1911)	Yes
Methodist Episcopal Church	2,986,000	Methodist Federation for Social Service (1907)	Yes
Northern Baptist Convention	1,052,000	Social Service Commission (1907)	Yes
Presbyterian Church in the U.S.A.	1,179,000	Bureau of Social Service (1903)*	Yes
Protestant Episcopal Church	886,000	Joint Commission on Social Service (1911)	Yes

* Originally named the Department of Church and Labor.

Sources: Federal Council of Churches of Christ in America, *A Record of Development and Progress* (pamphlet), NCC, RG 18, Box 81, Folder 20; *Religious Bodies: 1906* (Washington, DC: Government Printing Office, 1910), 25–29.

Theological Seminary, the University of Chicago, the Episcopal Theological School—going so far as to require students to work several hours per week at local settlement houses or missions.[35] Once installed in pastorates, many new seminary graduates, often inspired by the example of Jane Addams's Hull House, transformed their congregations into "institutional churches" whose libraries, drama clubs, cooking schools, English classes, and free medical clinics aimed to "provide a material environment wherein the spiritual Christ can express Himself, and be felt among men as when He was here in the flesh."[36]

Two events in particular signaled the Social Gospel movement's emergence as the dominant strand of Protestant social thought. The first occurred in early December 1908, when the Federal Council of the Churches of Christ in America (FCC), a newly formed umbrella group representing thirty-two denominations of American Protestants, adopted a "Social Creed of the Churches" that made an explicitly Christian case for the eight-hour day, the six-day workweek, the living wage, the abolition of child labor and sweatshops, and state supervision of working conditions.[37] According to press accounts, the speech introducing the Creed was the emotional "high point" of the FCC's inaugural meeting. Deeply moved by the Methodist minister Frank Mason North's call for clergymen to leave "the cloister" and apply themselves to building a "new social order" in which Christ's "law of love" would reign supreme, the delegates promptly endorsed North's proposed program of industrial reform, greeting its passage with "loud and long applause."[38]

The second symbolic triumph occurred in 1912, when former President Teddy Roosevelt, a man deeply influenced by the ideas of Rauschenbusch, Gladden, and other Social Gospel thinkers, launched a third-party bid for the presidency as the nominee of the newly formed Progressive Party.[39] Although Roosevelt would ultimately finish second to the Democratic nominee, Woodrow Wilson, his scathing critique of "special privilege" and his uncompromising stance on behalf of workers' rights had the effect of pulling both major parties significantly to the left on economic issues. As important, Roosevelt's campaign marked a major shift in American political rhetoric—a shift away from the language of laissez-faire individualism and toward the ideals of stewardship and collective accountability that animated the Social Gospel.

As early as 1910, in the speech that announced his return to the political arena, Roosevelt likened unscrupulous industrial employers to the antebellum plantation class, declaring that the time had come for "the man who wrongly holds that every human right is secondary to his profit must now give way to the advocate of human welfare, who rightly maintains that every man holds his property subject to the general right of the community to regulate its use to whatever degree the public welfare may require it."[40] He further developed this theme in "Who Is a Progressive?," the most philosophical of his 1912 campaign speeches, in which he defined a progressive as any citizen who believed that men in positions of economic power—whether a "slave-owner . . . or [the] multi-millionaire owner of railways and mines and factories . . . or . . . the owner of a foul little sweatshop"—should not be permitted to "gr[i]nd down" their workers, forcing them to "lead starved and sordid lives so that their souls are crippled like their bodies and the fine edge of their every feeling is blunted." A progressive, in other words, was anyone who believed that "each must be his brother's keeper, and that all must feel their obligation to the less fortunate who work beside us in the strain and press of our eager modern life."[41]

That the founders of the Progressive Party viewed their movement as fundamentally religious in nature was made crystal clear at the party's nominating convention, held in August 1912. As more than one reporter noted at the time, the scene at the Chicago Coliseum more closely resembled a religious revival than a typical political convention. For one thing, the auditorium was packed with ministers, social workers, and women's-club leaders—and machine politicians were conspicuously absent. Also, the speakers referenced the Almighty at seemingly every opportunity. The opening session began with an invocation, followed by a joint recitation of the Lord's Prayer (something seasoned reporters claimed never to have witnessed at a political gathering). Then, after adopting a platform stuffed with radical (for the time) policy proposals—the eight-hour day, the living wage, old-age pensions, the abolition of child labor—the delegates marched through the convention hall to the tunes of "Onward, Christian Soldiers" and the "Battle Hymn of the Republic." When Roosevelt finally mounted the stage, it was to deliver an acceptance speech entitled "A Confession of Faith." Declaring that the new party stood for "the eternal principle of righteousness," the former president ended his address with a line that had recently proved popular on the campaign trail: "We stand at Armageddon, and we battle for the Lord!" Their official business finished, the delegates then "stood, and for the last time that chorus of thousands sang. The trumpets and trombones sounded . . . and the voices joined them with the words: 'Praise God from whom all blessings flow.' Still standing, with bowed heads they received the benediction."[42]

The Sect Spirit and the Rise of the Protestant Establishment

The Progressive reform agenda did not lack for organized opposition. If figures like Teddy Roosevelt, Florence Kelley, and Jane Addams had a special fondness for martial metaphors, it was because they believed, with some justification, that they were locked in a life-and-death struggle with a formidable coalition of reactionary interests, including conservative industrial titans, the liquor traffic, and the urban political machines that held a controlling interest in both major parties. In the progressive imagination, this unholy triumvirate was guilty of conspiring to keep workers—particularly those who were recent immigrants—poor, illiterate, and financially dependent on the largesse of machine bosses. Industry needed cheap labor, the saloons needed a class of miserable men who would seek solace in the bottle, and the ward heelers needed a reliable voting bloc.[43]

Although the notion of a vast reactionary conspiracy had little basis in reality, it was true that machine politicians and conservative businessmen were seemingly well positioned to slow the march for reform. Acting through the National Association of Manufacturers (NAM), textile manufacturers spent heavily to oppose new restrictions on child and female labor. Liquor producers, who made up the nation's fifth-largest industry, invested large sums opposing both prohibition and women's suffrage (on the theory that women would inevitably vote dry). And food processors, drug makers, and the liquor interests formed a united front against state and federal food and drug purity standards.[44] Beyond their vast resources, these groups benefited from the fact that conservative Southern Democrats and "stand pat" Republicans were overrepresented in congressional leadership posts.[45] And yet, in the end, none of this seemed to matter. After some initial foot-dragging by skeptical party leaders and committee chairs, many landmark progressive reforms—including the first federal child labor law, the suffrage amendment, the Pure Food and Drug Act, the federal Children's Bureau, the Sheppard-Towner child and maternal health program, and even national liquor prohibition—sailed through Congress with only token opposition.

How did the progressives manage to achieve so much in such a short span of time, and over the objections of such formidable opponents? It was not by the force of their ideas alone. Rather, the progressive juggernaut derived much of its power from the fact that Social Gospel ideas were by the early 1900s embedded in scores of formal organizations, many of which were capable of mobilizing large numbers of Americans on behalf of specific reforms. Table 1.2 contains a list of the largest reform-minded membership groups in the years between 1900 and 1920. Broadly speaking, these groups can be divided into three categories: nominally secular women's organizations, evangelistic associations, and denominational auxiliary groups.

The major women's groups—such as the Women's Christian Temperance Union (WCTU), the General Federation of Women's Clubs (GFWC), and the Congress of Mothers—pursued an array of policy reforms that were intended to advance "the external and internal interests of the home." The first such group to achieve national prominence, the WCTU initially confined itself to battling the liquor traffic, using both political pressure and what would today be called direct action tactics (such as invading saloons en masse to pray for their patrons and owners). By the late 1880s, however, the group's dynamic president, Frances Willard, had won approval for a multifaceted program that included support for

Table 1.2 Social involvement of selected membership groups, 1900–1920

Organization	Approx. peak membership	Child labor	Liquor prohibition	Mothers' pensions	Pure food	Women's labor laws	Child and maternal health
Baptist Young People's Union	275,000		X				
Epworth League	600,000	X	X				
General Federation of Women's Clubs	1,700,000	X		X	X	X	X
National Congress of Mothers	200,000	X		X	X		X
Woman's Home Missionary Society	250,000	X	X				X
Woman's Missionary Union	500,000	X	X			X	
Women's Christian Temperance Union	200,000	X	X	X	X	X	
Young Men's Christian Association	700,000	X	X				
Society of Christian Endeavor	1,000,000	X	X	X		X	
Young Women's Christian Association	400,000	X	X	X	X	X	X

pure food and drug laws, women's protective labor legislation, and similar social reforms. The General Federation of Women's Clubs (GFWC), which sometime around 1900 surpassed the WCTU as the nation's largest women's organization, shared the older group's maternalist philosophy and advocated for an equally broad range of reforms (while placing less emphasis on the liquor question). The GFWC was particularly instrumental in securing state and federal child labor laws, pure food and drug legislation, protective labor legislation for women workers, comprehensive birth registration, civil service reform, and federal environmental conservation programs. A third group, the Congress of Mothers (which would soon be renamed the Parent-Teacher Association), frequently partnered with the WCTU and the GFWC in efforts to promote the physical and spiritual well-being of mothers and children. In addition to opening maternal health clinics and aiding local public schools, its leaders advocated legislative action to abolish child labor, create pension systems for mothers, promote child health and nutrition, boost education spending, reform the juvenile justice system, and censor immoral films and literature.[46]

Evangelistic organizations such as the Young Men's and Women's Christian Associations (YMCA and YWCA) and the Young People's Society of Christian Endeavor made up a second major category of reform-minded membership groups. Although these ecumenical groups are sometimes described as apolitical, they were in fact deeply involved in a range of reform campaigns. Indeed, the YWCA, whose ranks included tens of thousands of female factory workers, generally marched in lockstep with the progressive opinion leaders of the mainline churches, declaring support for child labor laws, wage and hours regulations, and the right of workers to organize. The YMCA was less outspoken on industrial questions, though the group did adopt a social ethics curriculum drafted by the pioneering Social Gospel theologian Graham Taylor, and its publishing arm, the Association Press, published several of Rauschenbusch's bestselling works.[47] The Christian Endeavor movement, while ostensibly focused on its members' spiritual development, also encouraged local chapters to form Christian citizenship committees to study problems of state and local government, as well as temperance committees to combat the liquor traffic. Discussions at the group's national conventions covered topics ranging from international arbitration through municipal corruption to the menace of the saloon. In 1907 the group formed an offshoot known as the Patriots' League for the explicit purpose of promoting political activism in areas such as child labor and municipal government reform; its honorary chairman was none other than President Teddy Roosevelt.[48]

Finally, most of the major Protestant denominations had by the late nineteenth century spawned auxiliary groups that offered laypeople the opportunity to work hand in hand with church leaders to advance a variety of social reforms.[49] Of these, the largest were probably the Epworth League (a youth group affiliated with the Northern Methodists), the Baptist Young People's Union (affiliated with the Northern Baptists), the Woman's Missionary Union (affiliated with the Southern Baptists), and the Woman's Home Missionary Society (affiliated with the Northern Methodists). As a general rule, the Baptist groups tended to focus their social activism primarily on prohibition, while the Methodist, Presbyterian, and Congregationalist groups also joined campaigns for child labor laws and other forms of protective labor legislation.[50]

All of the groups listed in Table 1.2 were primarily populated by middle-class churchgoing Protestants. For this reason it is useful to think of these groups, together with the mainline churches and ecumenical bodies, as forming a kind of informal national religious establishment—the "Protestant establishment," for short.[51] Certainly, the leaders of the Protestant-dominated membership groups thought of themselves in these terms, as did their opponents (who regularly complained about the inappropriateness of "the church" involving itself in politics). Moreover, the concept of an establishment accurately reflects the fact that these groups were interconnected in a variety of ways: they regularly joined forces to promote specific reforms; their leaderships (and membership rolls) overlapped to a significant extent; and, most important, they shared a common worldview centered around the ideals of stewardship and providential duty. No less than the founders of the FCC, members of nominally secular membership groups such as the GFWC and the Congress of Mothers believed they had been called by God to "regenerate" American society in preparation for "the coming of the kingdom."[52]

But to point out that churches and membership groups were important carriers of Social Gospel ideas raises an even more fundamental question: Why were millions of Americans buying what these groups were selling? The mystery only deepens when one considers that most early twentieth-century membership groups, in contrast to their present-day descendants, expected members to carry out most of the labor necessary to implement their agendas, including such unpleasant and time-consuming tasks as inspecting factories and prisons, attending juvenile court hearings, and personally petitioning state and federal lawmakers.[53] What explains the popularity of religious and quasi-religious organizations whose policy objectives were of little direct benefit to their middle class members?

For some believers, religious conviction alone may well have sufficed to motivate costly forms of civic engagement.[54] Yet there is much evidence to suggest that religious motives were buttressed by socioeconomic pressures of the sort observed by Max Weber during his 1904 visit to the United States. Weber's argument, as we have seen, stressed the character-vouching function of church and group membership. He noted that most of the nation's Protestant congregations and membership groups were organized in the manner of sects, meaning they rigorously scrutinized the beliefs and past behavior of potential members and zealously policed the conduct of those admitted to fellowship. Where the Methodists had "class meetings"—small groups in which church members engaged in the mutual confession of sins—the Baptists had congregational covenants that defined the rights and responsibilities of membership in minute detail.[55] For their part, ecumenical membership groups such as the YWCA and the Society of Christian Endeavor enforced standards of personal conduct that were hardly less stringent than those of a Methodist class meeting.[56] As a result, membership in a sectlike Protestant congregation or group publicly testified to an individual's reputation for honesty, sobriety, frugality, and the like. And in a nation of peripatetic strivers, such testimony was indispensable for citizens who hoped to climb the socioeconomic ladder. This explains why the businessmen and professionals who advertised their services in *Who's Who* volumes regularly listed their church affiliations and leadership roles alongside educational degrees and professional society memberships.[57] It also probably helps to explain why, as Weber observed, so many upwardly mobile Americans wore group pins or badges on their lapels: they knew that the typical employer or boardinghouse owner was likely to view someone sporting a YWCA or Christian Endeavor emblem as a reasonably safe bet.[58]

Of course, not all late nineteenth-century "joiners" were seeking immediate socioeconomic benefits such as employment or housing. Some of the period's largest membership groups, including the GFWC, were largely (though not entirely) populated by married women who had little interest in joining the workforce, and who were in any case effectively barred from most professions. Even here, however, there is reason to believe that the character-vouching function of sect membership was an important part of the story. Indeed, it is noteworthy that federated clubwomen, when asked to explain the explosive growth of their movement, routinely invoked a service-oriented conception of citizenship that all upstanding women were presumed to share. The standard narrative held that the invention of time-saving technologies, such as the sewing machine, had given birth to a new middle class of "earnest, eager women who are neither forced by the exigencies of their fortune to add to the wage-earning capacity of their families nor . . . willing to give themselves up to a life of personal indulgence." Women's newfound free time, in other words, was not something to be wasted on selfish or frivolous pursuits, nor even on providing additional care for one's immediate family. Rather, as one GFWC officer explained, American women knew in their bones that with "every added moment of leisure time" came an "added [measure] of responsibility" to work toward the betterment of humanity.[59] The upshot was that the decision of whether or not to seek membership in a reform-minded women's group was anything but a personal matter;

it was a test of character—one that any woman concerned about her (or her family's) social standing would not want to fail.[60]

If economic pressures and social expectations worked to push average citizens *into* churches and quasi-religious membership groups, it also mattered a great deal that these organizations were structured in such a way as to ensure that their members' energies were immediately redirected *outward*, toward large-scale projects of social reform. A new member of a local GFWC or WCTU auxiliary, for example, would quickly find herself assigned to one of twenty or more functionally differentiated departments or committees, each dedicated to combating a specific sin or injustice.[61] Ecumenical groups such as the YMCA, the YWCA, and the Society of Christian Endeavor were modeled on a similar pattern. In 1914 a typical YWCA in a midsize Midwestern city featured no fewer than twenty-four standing committees, the vast majority of them focused on community work of one sort or another.[62] Similarly, in 1910, at a time when one in seven college students was a dues-paying member of the YMCA, new recruits to the University of Pennsylvania college association chose from a list of assignments that included conducting weekly Sunday morning religious services for students; holding a weekly vespers service for hospital patients and staff; operating a settlement house with twelve full-time residents and a working farm; running summer camps for poor children; organizing religious discussion groups and Bible studies in the university's dormitories, fraternities, and department buildings; overseeing a program of university-wide lectures by distinguished academics and clergymen on "social, moral and religious subjects"; and, last but not least, funding and staffing a hospital in China.[63]

New recruits to Protestant membership groups, if they hoped to remain in the good graces of their fellow group members, had to "prove themselves"—to borrow a phrase from Weber—by working diligently to advance the mission of the particular committees or departments to which they were assigned. And because local Y associations, WCTU auxiliaries, and federated women's clubs typically kept meticulous records, we can safely say that most members rose to the challenge. By way of illustration, consider that in 1908 WCTU members from the Kennebec County, Maine, department of Prison and Jail Work—to pick a department more or less at random—held 48 meetings with local prisoners, during which they distributed 75 articles of clothing, 50 bouquets of flowers, 200 magazines, and 25,280 pages of religious and temperance literature.[64] Or that in 1916 the women of the Home Department of the Dayton, Ohio, YWCA arranged lodging for 302 female industrial workers and 1,108 "transient guests," while also serving 161,683 meals to hungry laborers and others.[65] Or that between 1909 and 1911 members of the Prison Reform Committee of the Chicago Woman's Club personally inspected forty-five of that city's police stations, thirty-nine of which were deemed unfit for human habitation owing to "dampness, darkness,

dirt, vermin [or] bad sanitation."[66] In addition to making clear that the books
were in order, such careful recordkeeping was intended to document for pos-
terity each group's incremental contribution to the regeneration of American society. As one local YWCA secretary explained in an introduction to an annual
report, the facts and figures contained in the volume would provide readers with
"a back-ground from which to estimate how successfully" the group was carrying out its mandate to act "as a social force for the extension of the Kingdom of
God."[67]

Once its core components were in place, the Protestant establishment provided elite reformers with an invaluable communications network—one that
allowed them to bypass the era's highly partisan press and disseminate facts
and information directly to millions of average Americans. Any woman who
attended a state or national convention of the GFWC or the Congress of Mothers,
for example, could expect to hear from settlement workers, social scientists,
medical professionals, factory inspectors, and countless other reform-minded
professionals who were well positioned to report on the extent of specific social problems and propose remedies. And in the months between conventions,
these groups' national offices did a brisk business filling requests from local clubs
for educational tracts and model laws prepared by elite-dominated groups like
the National Consumers' League (NCL), the National Child Labor Committee
(NCLC), and the federal Children's Bureau.[68] As scholars including Theda
Skocpol and Landon Storrs have pointed out, the cross-class linkages that
resulted from these efforts were mutually beneficial: Elite groups such as the
NCL, the NCLC, and the American Association for Labor Legislation (AALL)
were willing and able to supply the statistics and model statutes that broad-based
membership groups such as the GFWC and the Congress of Mothers needed
in order to carry out the "hard work" of "arousing public interest, shaping
public opinion, [and] arguing before legislators."[69] The women's groups, in turn,
supplied a level of grassroots lobbying power that no elite group could hope to
match.[70]

The nation's mainline Protestant churches provided elite reformers with a
second, less celebrated point of connection to millions of average citizens—one
whose influence arguably rivaled that of the women's groups. By the early 1900s,
as we have seen, all of the mainline denominations had formed social service
departments or commissions that were tasked with integrating discussion of industrial and other social problems into the everyday life of the church.[71] After
about 1910, the FCC's Commission on the Church and Social Service increasingly took the lead in coordinating the educational efforts of the various denominational social service agencies. Although not exactly flush with resources,
the Commission proved its worth by providing a forum in which representatives of the social service agencies could come together to share ideas on how

best to stimulate public interest in child labor and other social evils.[72] One innovative idea that emerged from this period was to designate specific Sundays when American Protestants would simultaneously contemplate a specific social problem in the light of the Gospel. The most popular "Social Sundays" were probably Labor Sunday and Child Labor Sunday, observed in early September and late January, respectively. Both days were designed to draw attention to the plight of industrial laborers, and in order to facilitate their observance FCC officials, in conjunction with nominally secular reform groups like the NCLC, supplied the nation's Protestant ministers with a suggested order of service, complete with Scripture passages, responsive readings, and service-oriented hymns.[73] Although hard data on the number of participating churches is lacking, both days seem to have been widely observed, at least in the nation's larger cities. In 1910 around 2,000 ministers wrote to the NCLC to report on their Child Labor Sunday observances, and by the 1920s the FCC claimed to be distributing as many as 30,000 copies of its Labor Sunday program every year.[74]

Social Sunday observances served a dual purpose. On the one hand, by acknowledging the ethical and religious dimensions of industrial employment, they extended an olive branch to the many urban laborers who had long ago written off organized religion as a tool of capital. But the larger objective was educational—that is, to provide middle- and upper-class churchgoers with an accurate picture of the appalling conditions in which less fortunate citizens lived and worked. In 1918, when the theme of Labor Sunday was "The Church and Women in Industry," the FCC's printed sample program opened with a message obviously aimed at the local minister: "The information contained [herein] is gathered from authoritative sources and is up to date. . . . You can use it with entire confidence. . . . We think you could do no better than to build these facts into your message of the day."[75] Upon opening the brochure, the minister would encounter a wealth of information on the size of the female workforce, the impact of the war on the labor market, industrial regulations in England and America, and the health risks posed by long hours and unsanitary working conditions. He would learn that many working women lacked such basic necessities as "sanitary provisions relating to rest periods, time and place for meals, suitable toilet facilities, with abundance of water and towels for washing . . . pure air, light, freedom from dust." And he would be urged to remind his parishioners that "no more helpful work can be done by citizens, especially women who have a serious interest in their industrial sisters, than the frequent inspection of conditions of employment in their communities."[76]

Yet the story of the Progressive Era is not a story of average citizens blindly following the policy recommendations of elites. To the contrary, as Skocpol has pointed out, early twentieth-century civil society was structured in such a way as to promote a cooperative, give-and-take relationship between middle-class group members on the one hand and elite reformers on the other.[77] More specifically, Skocpol observes that nearly all of the period's large membership groups—and even many smaller, elite-dominated groups—were organized as multi-tiered federations consisting of local, state, and national units.[78] The preference for federated organizational forms sprang from principled as well as pragmatic motivations. Organizers assumed that groups attempting to influence public policy ought to be genuinely reflective of the public will—something that was only possible if authority (and opinions) flowed upward from local groups to state federations and thence to the national headquarters. At the same time, because federated organizational structures mirrored the nation's decentralized political system, they enhanced a group's political effectiveness, allowing it simultaneously to bring pressure to bear on officeholders at multiple levels of government.

Arguably the form's greatest benefit, however, was its ability to foster trust between local "joiners" and the distant officers who staffed a group's national headquarters. To take a single example, the leaders of the NCLC sat atop a superstructure of dozens of state and local child labor committees that monitored working conditions and child labor law enforcement in cities from coast to coast. These local bodies were purposely designed to include a remarkably broad cross-section of citizens; entities represented on the Minneapolis committee included "the Woman's Club of Minneapolis, . . . whose president is our vice-president; the State Federation of Women's Clubs, whose president is a member of our executive committee; the Associated Charities, . . . social settlements, labor unions, the ministry, represented by a Protestant minister, Catholic priest, and Jewish rabbi on the executive committee; the juvenile court, by one of its judges, and the State University, by the professor of economics." By organically linking the NCLC to hundreds of women's clubs, churches, and synagogues, the group's federated structure ensured that average citizens would view the organization not as a distant cabal of out-of-touch elites, but as the ideal vehicle for addressing intensely local concerns.[79]

The Protestant Establishment at High Tide

That elite policy groups such as the NCLC had entered into a "close and symbiotic" relationship with the nation's largest Protestant denominations and membership groups did not escape the notice of prominent political observers.[80] By 1910, if not before, political commentators were openly speculating that this loose aggregation of religious and quasi-religious activist groups represented a new and potentially enduring "third force" in American politics. Teddy Roosevelt's strong second-place showing in the 1912 election in particular seemed to signal the emergence of a bloc of moralistic citizens whose passion for battling what they regarded as unjust institutions trumped preexisting partisan allegiances. And because women were believed to be particularly sympathetic to the Progressive agenda, the sense that "the church" and its allies were on the march waxed in tandem with the rising fortunes of the suffrage movement.[81] Male lawmakers speculating on the repercussions of adding millions of female voters to the rolls gave particular weight to two highly speculative pieces of conventional wisdom: first, that women would tend to vote as a bloc; and second, that women's policy concerns were largely confined to issues affecting children and family life.[82] Needless to say, these widely shared assumptions worked to the benefit of large female membership groups like the GFWC and the National Congress of Mothers, who had long claimed to represent the views of "organized womanhood." To many lawmakers, it now seemed clear that defying the combined forces of the churches and women's groups was a riskier proposition than defying industry.

Three very brief examples will suffice to illustrate the point. Consider, first, the female-led campaign to secure federal funding for child and maternal health programs—an effort that culminated in the creation of a major new federal agency, the Children's Bureau, as well as the passage of the Sheppard-Towner Act, a pioneering federal program that offered matching funds to states that agreed to treat and promote awareness of medical problems affecting new mothers and infants. Both initiatives faced stiff opposition from congressional conservatives, who argued that they impinged upon the constitutional authority of the states. Yet no more than a handful of lawmakers proved willing to oppose the combined forces of the nation's female membership groups, and in 1912 Congress overwhelmingly approved the creation of the Children's Bureau, arming it with a sweeping mandate to report on "questions of infant mortality, the birth-rate, orphanage[s], juvenile courts, desertion, dangerous occupations, accidents and diseases of children, employment, [and] legislation affecting children in the several states and territories."[83]

Determined to put the new agency on a secure footing, the Bureau's first leader, Julia Lathrop (herself a GFWC member), wisely relied on female group members to implement most of her flagship programs. Lathrop's first official act was to travel to the GFWC's biennial meeting in San Francisco, where she enlisted the nation's clubwomen in a campaign for universal birth registration.[84] Over the next few years hundreds of federated women's clubs and local affiliates of the Congress of Mothers canvassed their communities, documenting discrepancies between official records and actual births—information Lathrop used to lobby for legislation to improve registration procedures.[85] Even as the Children's Bureau began to undertake more controversial activities, such as reporting on child labor practices and lobbying for large-scale federal health programs, the high levels of trust between rank-and-file "joiners" and Bureau officials largely insulated Lathrop's agency from the hostility directed at other federal agencies in the immediate aftermath of World War I. To contemporaries, the reasons for the discrepancy were not hard to fathom. As the GFWC's Corrine S. Brown explained to a congressional committee in 1920, "The women of the country trust the Children's Bureau. It has become known in every state and city. It has established cooperation with state health authorities and with countless agencies working for children. Women's clubs and committees are accustomed to cooperating on health campaigns under its guidance."[86]

Lawmakers, for their part, increasingly feared the nation's clubwomen. In the early 1920s the adoption of the suffrage amendment, coupled with the formation of a powerful umbrella group known as the Women's Joint Congressional Committee (WJCC), briefly elevated women's groups to the front rank of organized interests. So pervasive was the notion of a monolithic "woman vote" that the WJCC managed to secure the endorsements of no fewer than thirty-four governors for the Sheppard-Towner bill.[87] Once again a small but influential cohort of conservative lawmakers objected that the legislation impinged upon the states' "reserved" powers, and this time they were joined by the American Medical Association (AMA), which increasingly perceived federal health programs as a threat to the autonomy of the medical profession.[88] In the end, however, most lawmakers elected to honor the apparent wishes of the nation's newly enfranchised female voters. Sheppard-Towner easily passed the House (279 to 39) and Senate (63 to 7), and supporters and critics alike cited women's groups as the driving force behind its passage. As one senator explained, "If the members could have voted on [the Act] secretly in their cloak rooms it would have been killed as emphatically as it was finally passed in the open under the pressure of the [WJCC]."[89]

Women's groups were also in the vanguard of the campaign for a federal child labor ban (as was the Children's Bureau), though in this case they benefited from the monolithic backing of the mainline Protestant churches. The churches, as we have seen, had been actively promoting state and federal child labor regulations since the first Child Labor Sunday in 1905. By the early 1910s thousands of churches were setting aside a Sunday morning in late January to draw attention to the problem of child labor. During the remainder of the year, Owen Lovejoy and the other leaders of the NCLC (many of them ordained ministers) traveled constantly, often addressing several congregations per week.[90] By 1915, when the original version of what would become the first federal child labor law was introduced in Congress, virtually all of the nation's largest churches and female membership groups had endorsed to the measure; supportive petitions poured in from the FCC, Protestant denominational bodies, and state federations of churches, as well as the GFWC and many of its state and local auxiliaries.[91] Confronted with this show of force, most lawmakers not directly connected to the textile industry brushed aside the constitutional objections of conservative business groups such as the National Association of Manufacturers. The Keating-Owen Act, as the final version of the bill was known, won overwhelming support in both the House and the Senate, passing by tallies of 337 to 46 and 50 to 12, respectively.[92]

The first federal child labor ban was short-lived, however; in 1918 the Supreme Court struck it down as exceeding the scope of Congress's interstate commerce power. At this point the Protestant churches and membership groups closed ranks in support of a prohibitive federal tax that would effectively eradicate child labor without (it was hoped) running afoul of the Court's federalism jurisprudence.[93] When this law too was struck down, child labor opponents turned to the constitutional amendment process.[94] Among religious bodies, the FCC led the way, dispatching Dr. Worth Tippy, executive secretary of the Commission on the Church and Social Service, to Washington to form a broad-based coalition including Jewish and Catholic religious leaders, the GFWC, the WCTU, the National Congress of Mothers, the League of Women Voters, and a number of other women's groups.[95] Not to be outdone, most of the mainline churches went on record in support of the amendment, as did the YWCA.[96] Yet again the National Association of Manufacturers proved no match for the combined clout of the nation's informal religious establishment. The Child Labor Amendment sailed through Congress, easily winning the supermajorities required by Article V (though the ratification effort, as we shall see, ultimately stalled in the states).[97]

The successful campaign for the national prohibition of alcoholic beverages presents a final case where the combined backing of the churches and membership groups proved more than sufficient to overcome the opposition of a large and profitable industry. Although some women's groups, including the WCTU, devoted significant resources to the dry crusade, the major force behind the Eighteenth Amendment was the male-dominated Anti-Saloon League (ASL). The ASL was not a broad-based membership group in the mold of the GFWC or the YMCA; its members were almost entirely clergymen (mostly Methodists), and the precise size of its membership was a closely guarded secret. Yet the group enjoyed close ties to sympathetic women's and evangelistic groups, and by 1910 some twenty thousand churches were allowing its agents to make fundraising appeals during Sunday services (by 1915 this figure would top forty thousand).[98] The League, which publicly billed itself as "the church organized against the saloon," could therefore credibly claim to represent the views of a large bloc of Protestant churchgoers, and—more to the point—it proved capable of delivering their votes in closely contested elections.[99] Fearing they would find themselves facing a well-financed opponent or else be singled out in League propaganda as a shill of the liquor interests, Republican and Democratic lawmakers alike fell in line behind an escalating series of restrictive liquor laws. In 1909 Congress banned C.O.D. shipments of liquor; in 1912 it severely restricted liquor sales in the District of Columbia; and in 1913 it criminalized the interstate transportation of liquor from wet to dry states, overriding a presidential veto in the process.[100] By 1913 a majority Americans resided in "dry" territory, thanks to a combination of League-backed statewide prohibition laws (in effect in nine states) and local option laws that were in effect in much of rural and small-town America.[101] The League then turned its attention to the U.S. Constitution, securing a constitutional amendment prohibiting the sale and manufacture of alcohol as well as a draconian enforcement statute—the Volstead Act—that defined as "intoxicating" any beverage with an alcohol content above 0.5 percent. So powerful was the ASL's lobbying operation that when President Woodrow Wilson vetoed the Volstead Act in an attempt to secure minor technical changes, the League refused to consider revisions; instead, it easily secured the necessary supermajorities to override his veto.

Whither the Fundamentalists?

To say that an informal "Protestant establishment" was a major force in Progressive Era politics is not to deny the existence of serious schisms within the Protestant ranks. In fact, the period from the early 1900s to the mid-1920s was marked by intense theological infighting. The most serious disagreement pitted fundamentalists against liberals (or modernists), the former insisting on biblical inerrancy and a literal reading of Scripture (including the Genesis account of creation), the latter open to updating the Christian message with insights gleaned from modern science and hermeneutical techniques borrowed from the humanities. Because a few well-known fundamentalists were staunch foes of the progressive economic agenda, it is often assumed that this theological cleavage mapped neatly onto the political divide between reformers and defenders of the regulatory status quo. But nothing could be further from the truth. At least prior to the 1920s, the vocal fundamentalist opponents of progressivism were a small minority. Most fundamentalists were either indifferent to politics or else happy to make common cause with progressives when it suited their interests, as it did in crusades against liquor, gambling, vice districts, and urban political corruption.

Perhaps the most outspoken fundamentalist critic of progressivism was the wildly popular revivalist Billy Sunday, who was known to refer to the Social Gospel movement as "godless social service nonsense."[102] Like many fundamentalists, Sunday drew a sharp distinction between saving souls and regenerating society, arguing that the latter was beyond the church's purview. In practice, however, this proposed division of labor was ignored more often than it was honored. Sunday himself was a staunch supporter of the ASL, and many of his allies were as deeply involved in politics as the most ardent Social Gospel theologians. For example, William Bell Riley, arguably the most influential fundamentalist of the early twentieth century, spent the early years of his ministry waging holy war against Minneapolis's notoriously corrupt city government, and Mark A. Matthews, the fundamentalist pastor of the nation's largest Presbyterian church, played a similar gadfly role in Seattle.[103] The early leaders of Chicago's Moody Bible Institute (MBI), another pillar of the early fundamentalist movement, embraced a wide range of reform causes, declaring that Bible-believing Christians were duty bound to "execute the laws, close the dram shops, exterminate the gambling hells, sanctify one day in seven as a day of rest, and make in every way for the betterment of the poorer classes."[104]

Nor were most fundamentalists great fans of the profit motive. While it is true that Sunday and the MBI were known to lionize big business, other giants of the movement, including Riley and John Roach Straton, regularly inveighed against "growing and grasping corporations" and "covetous, Mammon-worshipping" businessmen who lined their pockets by appealing "to the lower instincts of the race."[105] Many prominent fundamentalists, including Straton, Matthews, and J. Frank Norris hailed from the South, and they tended to exhibit their home region's instinctive distrust of Northeastern bankers and concentrated economic power. If their complaints about Mammon worship were directed at liquor producers more often than textile manufacturers, they nonetheless shared their theological adversaries' conviction that government had an important role to play in checking the baser tendencies of the nation's increasingly freewheeling capitalist economy.[106]

This conviction created an unbridgeable chasm between the leading lights of American fundamentalism and the major political opponents of progressive reform. Broadly speaking, big business's political allies—whether Northeastern "stand pat" Republicans or conservative Southern and border-state Democrats—tended to be proto-libertarians who sought to hobble regulatory authority across the board.[107] Needless to say, the notion of making common cause with outspoken "wets" was for most fundamentalists a nonstarter. Another factor that fueled mutual distrust between the two groups was that many leading congressional conservatives, including Senators James A. Reed and Boies Penrose, were products of the very political machines that the fundamentalists blamed for transforming America's cities into dens of iniquity. Finally, most fundamentalists were (it almost goes without saying) deeply serious about matters of theology—so much so that the orthodoxy of a candidate's religious views was often a more important consideration than the specifics of his party's platform. This was why Lyman Stewart, the politically (and theologically) conservative oil baron who financed the hugely influential book series *The Fundamentals*, regretfully announced that he could not support the Republican nominee, William Howard Taft, in the 1908 presidential election. Although Stewart was "in sympathy with

Mr. Taft politically," he also knew that Taft was a Unitarian, and he could not in good conscience cast a ballot for "an enemy of the cross of Christ."[108]

No single figure better illustrates the complex and crosscutting nature of the period's religious and political allegiances than William Jennings Bryan, the Nebraska congressman and three-time Democratic presidential nominee. Bryan, a devout Presbyterian, was a biblical literalist who is today best remembered for defending the Genesis account of creation at the 1925 Scopes Monkey Trial. But "the Great Commoner" was also a staunch critic of big business, a friend to organized labor, and an enthusiastic proponent of the Social Gospel who believed that human agency had an important role to play in ushering in Christ's Kingdom on Earth.[109] And no less than Rauschenbusch and Roosevelt, he insisted that citizens in positions of economic power were under a divine obligation to act as stewards of the resources in their possession.[110] Bryan thus shared a great deal in common with both the leading fundamentalists and the leading liberals or modernists of his era. If his postmillennial faith in the possibility of moral progress distinguished him from such orthodox, premillennial fundamentalists as Riley and Straton (who anticipated an imminent Second Coming), his uncompromising faith in the inerrancy of Scripture, together with his burning hatred of the Darwinian theory of evolution and the liquor traffic, kept him in the good stead of the fundamentalist camp, ultimately earning him the sobriquet "Mr. Fundamentalist." And so long as Bryan was the public face of American fundamentalism, an alliance between biblical literalists and big-business conservatives was, to put it mildly, highly unlikely.

2

The Brief Reign of Whirl

No city has a more wonderful bunch of churches than Middletown. Select one and make it your Church—the place where you can worship God, learn of His world program, become associated with the best people, and where you will find a glorious opportunity for service.

—Newspaper advertisement, quoted in Robert S. Lynd and Helen Merrell Lynd, *Middletown* (1929)

As late as 1920 Protestant elites could credibly present a united front on most questions of morality and public policy—a fact that was on full display on the night of January 16, when believers across the country staged celebrations to mark the moment when the Eighteenth Amendment and its enforcement statute, the Volstead Act, would take effect.[1] By the middle of the decade, however, the picture looked very different. By that point believers were bitterly divided over the wisdom of continued prohibition enforcement; the large Protestant denominations were wracked by infighting between fundamentalists and liberals; a revitalized Ku Klux Klan was busy waging holy war against Jews, Catholics, and racial minorities; the nation's largest women's groups were in disarray, having been tainted by allegations of Bolshevism; and long-standing moral prohibitions—for example, against the use of birth control—were everywhere falling by the wayside.

Analyzing the collapse of the Progressive Era's moral consensus from the perspective of 1929, Walter Lippmann famously concluded that the "acids of modernity" were to blame. Religious dogma was everywhere crumbling under the relentless scrutiny of modern science; and inherited ethical doctrines, most of which had originated in the churches, were faring no better. The problem was not so much that the conventional beliefs had been true; it was that American society seemed rudderless in their absence. Lippmann lamented that many prominent religious leaders and would-be public moralists no longer seemed to believe in much of anything; worse, those who still clung to the old certainties were becoming increasingly fanatical, in some cases violently so. What the future held in store was unclear, but a return to the spiritual and intellectual comforts of the past was out of the question. The "modern world" was therefore haunted by a dilemma: it was "impossible to reconstruct an enduring orthodoxy, and impossible to live well without the satisfactions which an orthodoxy would provide." Quoting Aristophanes, Lippmann concluded that "Whirl was King, having driven out Zeus."[2]

Lippmann's *A Preface to Morals* remains required reading for anyone hoping to gain a better understanding of the social and intellectual climate of the 1920s. And yet, with the benefit of hindsight, what is perhaps most remarkable about his thesis is how quickly it went out of fashion. Indeed, the major claim of *A Preface to Morals*—that broadly shared moral convictions were a thing of the past—would seem hopelessly out of date within two decades of its publication. By the early 1950s a new generation of social critics would be describing a congenial consensus culture in which average citizens seemed all but incapable of thinking differently from their peers. In *The Lonely Crowd* (1950), for example, the sociologist David Riesman and his co-authors Nathan Glazer and Reuel Denney lamented the rise of an "other-directed" personality type that took its moral bearings from friends, neighbors, and coworkers. The substance of a given individual's convictions depended on the nature of the peer group, but for members of the growing middle class a vague ethos of concern for the less fortunate seemed to predominate. Even wealthy corporate executives, who would in the past have been expected to prioritize profits above all else, now expressed genuine sympathy for the goals of the labor movement—apparently because they thought this was what the public expected of them.[3] The journalist William Whyte, in *The Organization Man* (1956), likewise described a society in which even religious disagreements had been muted to the point of insignificance. Based on interviews with hundreds of suburban churchgoers and ministers, Whyte concluded that what American Protestants wanted most from organized religion was a "sense of community." What they emphatically did not want, he found, were battles over theology and denominational dogma. Hence, the messages and programs of the nation's thriving suburban churches were becoming increasingly indistinguishable—a bland, if cheery, mélange of appeals to fellowship, service, and civic duty.[4]

How did the apparent moral anarchy of the late 1920s evolve into the consensus culture of the 1950s? Any comprehensive answer to this question would have to grapple with such intervening events as the Great Depression, the Second World War, the baby boom, suburbanization, and the dawn of the Cold War. We will touch on all of these developments in later chapters. The aim of this chapter is to highlight a little-noted point of institutional continuity between the 1910s and the 1950s. My argument, in brief, is that the mainline Protestant churches and ecumenical bodes—though not the large secular membership groups—survived the turmoil of the 1920s with their authority *and ideals* more or less intact. Although the prohibition debacle and the rise of nativist groups such as the Ku Klux Klan posed serious problems for denominational leaders, the twin crises ultimately led Protestant officials to reaffirm their commitment to the egalitarian convictions that had guided the ecumenical project since the early years of the twentieth century. During a decade when American politics turned conservative and secular membership groups entered a period of decline, the ideals of the Social Gospel movement remained very much alive in the churches—that is, in the large mainline denominations, in the Federal Council of Churches (FCC), and in a burgeoning network of state and local church councils that took shape under the FCC's direction. And as we shall see, the ethical convictions of religious elites were of more than academic interest. By keeping the stewardship ethic alive during the 1920s, the churches were unknowingly helping to lay the groundwork for the transformative economic policy initiatives of the 1930s.

Trial by Fire: Prohibition and the Second Coming of the Klan

On September 14, 1925, the *New York Times* published the first of a series of stories on a rigorous new study that seemed to show that prohibition was creating more social problems than it was solving. The study provided evidence that crime rates, instead of plummeting, had experienced a "sharp rise" in the period between 1920 and 1923. Alcohol consumption, too, was on the rise, at least among younger Americans, and deaths resulting from alcoholism had also increased. If the *Times* series contained a silver lining for the prohibition forces, it was that business productivity was up, and social workers were reporting a decline in domestic problems stemming from alcohol. But these glimmers of hope were overshadowed by survey data indicating that both employers and workers strongly favored repealing the Volstead Act, or at least modifying it to permit the sale of light wines and beer. Arguably the most shocking fact contained in the entire study, however, was the name of the organization that had sponsored it: the Federal Council of Churches.[5]

The question of how to respond to the Volstead Act's shortcomings, or whether even to acknowledge them, drove a wedge through the ranks of organized Protestantism. The FCC's highly detailed report—which, for all the ammunition it provided the wet forces, actually came down in favor of education and reform rather than outright repeal—was met with disbelief by religious activists who had devoted their professional lives to the battle against demon rum. Clarence True Wilson, general secretary of the Methodist Board of Temperance, Prohibition and Public Morals, denounced the study as "biased," "partisan," and "one-sided," though he was unable to say precisely why FCC officials had undertaken to sabotage a policy they had long supported.[6] The Reverend Charles Scanlon, secretary of Moral Welfare for the Presbyterian Board of Christian Education, agreed that the report was little more than "verbose nonsense." Wilson, Scanlon, and many other religious officials who had eagerly marshaled empirical evidence in the reform struggles of the 1910s now blasted the Council's research department for its shortsightedness in publishing data that gave "aid and comfort to the enemy." Trying times, they insisted, required "faith," not statistics. Or, as Scanlon put it, "One may state the facts and miss the truth."[7]

The FCC, for its part, spent the late 1920s trying out a variety of more or less irreconcilable positions on the liquor question. In the weeks following the release of the study, the Council issued a statement reaffirming its "unequivocal" support for the Volstead Act and calling for a "renewed moral crusade to strengthen the hands" of law enforcement.[8] Two months later, however, the Council's Executive Committee voted down a resolution that would have devoted significant resources to the enforcement struggle.[9] The following year FCC officials advised a Senate committee against repeal, declaring that "no plan less thoroughgoing than prohibition [was] sufficient to eradicate the evils of the liquor traffic."[10] Then, in 1927, allegations of corruption in the ranks of the Anti-Saloon League led the FCC to begin publicly distancing itself from the organization that had long enjoyed de facto control over the federal enforcement apparatus.[11]

Although the Council's half-hearted commitment to national prohibition undoubtedly irritated many mainline denominational officials, the underlying disagreement concerned means rather than ends. The question, all agreed, was whether the Volstead Act was proving effective at moderating alcohol consumption and, by extension, protecting American families from the ravages of the saloon. Men like Wilson and Scanlon consistently answered in the affirmative—notwithstanding mounting evidence to the contrary—while the FCC seemed, at least on occasion, to entertain the possibility that educational efforts were preferable to criminalization.

The more serious rift in American Protestantism, it soon became apparent, was between those who supported prohibition as a means of curbing domestic abuse and other social problems and those who viewed it as a single front in a much broader war against Catholics and other "foreign" invaders. To be sure, many of the nation's early dry crusaders, including Frances Willard, had promoted both objectives simultaneously. By the early 1920s, however, a clear division had emerged between an ecumenical wing of American Protestantism, which viewed explicitly nativist policies as antithetical to the message of the Gospel, and a nascent and rather loosely organized fundamentalist wing, which used the terms "Americanism" and "Protestantism" more or less interchangeably. The FCC and other entities affiliated with the ecumenical wing, while not entirely immune to the lure of anti-Catholicism, were nonetheless resolutely opposed to immigration restrictions and other measures that sought to define American citizenship in explicitly racial or religious terms.[12] The same meeting of the FCC's

Executive Committee that divided bitterly over the question of funding prohibition enforcement, for example, unanimously approved a resolution condemning
the 1924 Johnson-Reed Act, which effectively barred immigration from Asia.
How were American missionaries supposed to "talk [of] Christianity" in Japan
and India, it asked, rhetorically, when Congress had put a "sign on the Pacific
door, which says: 'No yellow and brown men wanted' "?[13]

The Protestant leaders of the resurgent Ku Klux Klan, in contrast, viewed
the rising crime rates of the 1920s as evidence that the nation had already
permitted far too many foreigners to pass through its gates. In contrast to its
Reconstruction-era predecessor, the 1920s iteration of the Klan was more
concerned with suppressing immigration, harassing parochial schools, and
enforcing liquor restrictions than with policing racial segregation in the South
(where Jim Crow appeared to be solidly entrenched). It drew much of its support from rural and small-town WASPs who saw in the proliferation of speak-
easies and celebrity mobsters—many of them Catholic or Jewish—evidence that
the millions of non-Protestant immigrants who had entered the country in the
early years of the twentieth century had embarked on a coordinated campaign
of subversion. At the height of its power, the group succeeded in infiltrating
police departments and city halls from Southern California to New Jersey, all
in the name of preserving law and order.[14] And in many of these same areas,
Protestant clergyman applauded the Klan's efforts—when they did not don
hoods themselves.

Prominent fundamentalist preachers were particularly enthusiastic about
the secret order. In 1923 Los Angeles's Robert P. "Fighting Bob" Shuler, an ar-
chetypical fundamentalist who held Jews, Catholics, liquor, and modernist theology more or less equally responsible for America's ills, penned a letter to the
Moody Monthly praising the Klan as a "positive and active friend of Protestant
Christianity." Oscar Haywood, the Klan's chief lecturer in New York City,
expressed similar sentiments while simultaneously serving as an associate
minister at John Roach Straton's Calvary Baptist Church. And J. Frank Norris,
pastor of the First Baptist Church of Fort Worth, Texas, and founder of the
nation's first radio ministry, allowed the Klan to run advertisements in his religious newspaper. Norris also promulgated Klan themes from the pulpit, using
a 1926 sermon entitled "Rum and Romanism" to allege that his city's Catholic
mayor was both soft on prohibition and actively diverting taxpayer dollars to
the Vatican. When a friend of the mayor's arrived, unarmed, at Norris's study to
contest the charges, the pastor pulled a revolver from his desk and shot the man
four times, killing him. Norris's legend only grew when a sympathetic jury—one
almost certainly devoid of Catholics—found that he had acted in self-defense.[15]

But while the Klan drew members from all branches of American
Protestantism, including the mainline churches, the elites who staffed the upper

echelons of the mainline denominational and ecumenical bodies were uniformly hostile to its nativist brand of Christianity. As early as October 1922 the FCC's Executive Committee issued a statement expressing alarm at the "recent rise of organizations whose members are masked, oath-bound and unknown, and whose activities have the effect of arousing . . . religious antipathies."[16] A long list of prominent mainline ministers, including the Baptist Harry Emerson Fosdick and the Methodist Bishop Francis J. McConnell, quickly followed suit, as did their denominational hierarchies.[17] The mainline religious press—North as well as South—was virtually monolithic in dismissing the Klan's views as incompatible with the message of the Gospel, with some publications going so far as to back a federal investigation of the organization.[18] The Klan, naturally, responded to all the negative attention by adding "liberal" and "modernist" ministers to its enemies list; modernist theology, its official publications now alleged, was almost as bad as Catholicism.[19]

At first, mainline religious leaders' anti-Klan pronouncements did little to curb the KKK's surging popularity.[20] But religious authority eventually reasserted itself. In the mid-1920s, a rising chorus of denominational resolutions, coupled with a handful of disciplinary actions against Klan-aligned ministers, sent a clear signal that clergymen tainted by KKK involvement were unlikely to ascend to prominent mainline pulpits or climb the ranks of the denominational hierarchies.[21] At around the same time, the Klan began to suffer the consequences of a weak—one is tempted to say nonexistent—organizational infrastructure. Some historians, citing the 1920s Klan's use of Protestant religious themes and imagery, its sponsorship of civic initiatives, and its opposition to drinking, gambling, and other vices, have characterized the secret order as a successor to the large, Protestant-dominated membership groups of the early 1900s.[22] But the resemblance was mostly superficial, since the Klan lacked the characteristics most responsible for the flourishing of groups like the General Federation of Women's Clubs and the Society of Christian Endeavor: namely, a viable federated organizational structure and organic links to the major Protestant denominations. Without strong intermediate institutions, or really any kind of systematic leadership at the grassroots level, the 1920s KKK was overly reliant on the seat-of-the-pants strategizing of a small and factious circle of shadowy national leaders who had tapped into a powerful vein of nativist resentment, but who were incapable of translating the resulting movement into a lasting and consequential organization (and who were in any case probably more interested in lining their own pockets). The order suffered a spectacular implosion in 1925 when a prominent Grand Dragon was convicted on rape and murder charges, and when opponents began infiltrating klaverns and publishing their membership lists. Politicians and civic leaders who had once welcomed the Klan's endorsement now ran for cover, depriving the group of an elite base of support. Young men on the make—like their ministers—increasingly shunned the organization, viewing it as a serious obstacle to socioeconomic advancement. By 1927 an order that had claimed perhaps four million members at its peak had shrunk to less than 350,000.[23]

Thus, while the 1920s Klan resurgence is rightly remembered for the reign of terror it inflicted on religious and ethnic minorities, arguably its most significant long-term consequence was that it forced mainline denominational leaders to stake out a clear position in opposition to those who would define American citizenship in terms of religion or ethnicity. Whereas mainline elites had in the past made common cause with racists when it served their purposes—as it did in the fight for prohibition—the emergence of an unabashedly nativist version of the Gospel, coupled with prohibition's evident failure as a matter of policy, pushed mainline leaders significantly to the left on issues such as immigration, interfaith cooperation, and African American civil rights (as we shall see in more detail hereafter).[24] At the same time, the prohibition debacle taught mainline leaders the valuable lesson that large numbers of their fellow citizens resented being asked to assent to the legal entrenchment of specifically Protestant mores at a time when the Protestant share of the population was shrinking.[25] To be sure, the stewardship ideal, with all of its paternalistic implications, remained integral to mainline popular theology, but after the early 1920s it was gradually severed from the providential—and distinctly Protestant—conception of nationhood that was so central to the reform campaigns of the early 1900s. Increasingly, mainline leaders framed efforts to aid the less fortunate not as a surefire way of ushering in the Millennium, but as simply the right thing to do. Christ's command to care for the hungry and displaced was now to be obeyed for its own sake, not because of any bargain the Almighty might have struck with the New England Puritans. And from this it followed that if other religious groups wanted to join in the struggle for a more just society, they should be welcomed with open arms.[26]

The Collapse of Organized Womanhood

If the prohibition debacle dealt a serious blow to the mainline churches' prestige and sense of unity, the nation's women's groups were hit even harder. Although the level of commitment varied greatly from group to group, prohibition was widely perceived as a "women's issue," and antisuffrage activists were among the first to gloat when it proved both unworkable and unpopular. The *Woman Patriot*, the house organ of the National Association Opposed to Women Suffrage (NAOWS), reinvented itself in the early 1920s as a champion of limited government and constitutional liberty, chastising progressive women's groups for "diminishing the reserve legislative powers of the State[s]" and "establishing a precedent for the adoption of other Amendments in the future by means of which all the legislative powers of the States may be taken away."[27] If the NAOWS could not roll back the Nineteenth Amendment, the magazine's editors seemed to suggest, it could at least cast doubt on the constitutionality of the many progressive reforms that bore the stamp of female activism.

Criticism from more credible entities, including the Federal Council of Churches, convinced many women's groups to begin distancing themselves from the dry cause. This in turn created a rift between groups like the Women's Joint Congressional Committee (WJCC), for whom prohibition had never been a central focus, and those like the Women's Christian Temperance Union (WCTU), who viewed it as the linchpin of the entire reform program. In 1927 the WCTU, the first broad-based women's group to concern itself with industrial issues, formally cut ties with the WJCC, citing the latter group's indifference to the dry cause.[28] Two years later the founding of the Women's Organization for National Prohibition Repeal (WONPR) by the New York socialite and Republican party activist Pauline Morton Sabin exacerbated what was already a serious schism. In less than a year the WONPR gained 100,000 dues-paying members, thus shattering the myth that American women were monolithic in their hatred of demon rum.[29]

Prohibition was far from the only corrosive force eating away at the fabric of female civil society, however. In 1924 Henry Ford's *Dearborn Independent* published a widely reprinted series of articles claiming that the nation's largest women's groups were run by an "interlocking directorate" of communist partisans who took orders from Moscow. As evidence, the *Independent* supplied the original "spiderweb chart," which graphically linked dozens of female activists to Bolshevik front groups. Most of the allegations were utterly spurious, and in any case the chart's reasoning was circular, since a woman's membership in one allegedly communist-friendly front group was presented as irrefutable proof that all of the organizations to which she belonged were under Bolshevik control. As fanciful as the charges may have been, they struck a chord with a nation still reeling from the Russian Revolution and the alleged discovery of secret anarchist cells operating in the United States. Almost overnight large numbers of Americans began seriously to entertain the possibility that such previously beloved groups as the GFWC, the Congress of Mothers, and the YWCA were secretly working to subvert the American way of life. A poem appended to the bottom of the infamous spiderweb chart put the matter starkly:

> Miss Bolsheviki has come to town,
> With a Russian cap and a German gown,
> In women's clubs she's sure to be found . . . [30]

The controversy over the spiderweb chart launched a proxy war between women's groups who remained committed to traditional ideals of stewardship and those who, in the conservative political environment of the 1920s, preferred to leave big business free to run its own affairs (and, by extension, those of its workers). To some extent, the battle was fought *between* organizations, as when groups like the Daughters of the American Revolution (DAR), which had once championed child labor laws and other progressive reforms, turned against former allies, including the WJCC and the League of Women Voters, denouncing them as communist fronts.[31] By the mid-1920s, however, the ideological divide increasingly ran through the Red-tainted groups themselves, as conservative activists took aim at the very principles and policy positions that had long provided "organized womanhood" with its strong sense of unity and purpose. In 1923, for example, a group of delegates to the national convention of the Parent-Teachers Association—as the Congress of Mothers now called itself—caused a stir by introducing resolutions denouncing child labor laws and arms control initiatives as contrary to American ideals (both were ultimately defeated). Around the same time, a conservative GFWC faction under the leadership of the Kentucky writer Georgia May Martin began publicly denouncing such long-standing group priorities as child labor reform as "pure socialism and Communism—the nationalization of children." Remarkably, Martin and her supporters argued that the GFWC's original raison d'être—bringing the unique insights of women to bear on social problems—was fundamentally misguided in that it impinged upon male lawmakers' freedom of action. Henceforth, they argued, clubwomen should eschew lobbying entirely—though apparently not before working to repeal child labor regulations and the other "socialistic" measures they had once championed.[32]

A final force that chipped away at the foundations of female civil society—one not entirely unrelated to prohibition and the Red Scare—was an emerging divide over the ultimate *aim* of female activism. Politically active women divided into two camps following the enactment of the Nineteenth Amendment. An egalitarian group, led by Alice Paul's National Woman's Party (NWP), promoted measures such as the Equal Rights Amendment (ERA), which promised to end all legal distinctions based on gender. American women, these activists argued, would never become full citizens until they were freed from paternalistic regulations that treated them as wards of the state. Such proposals drew fierce opposition from the Women's Joint Congressional Committee and other "protectionist" groups that favored the continuation of measures that promised to shield vulnerable female workers from exploitative employers. The end goal of the protectionist wing's leaders—including Florence Kelley, Grace Abbott, and Julia Lathrop—was not to entrench a system of gender-specific state oversight, but rather to secure wage and hours protections for all workers, men as well as women. And yet, the protectionists also believed that differential treatment was justified in cases where women faced obstacles that were unique to their sex. A case in point was the Sheppard-Towner Act, which, in Kelley's words, addressed an "inequality by reason of sex, in favor of women—maternity not applying alike to both sexes."[33]

There could be no doubt about which faction big business preferred. As the historian Jan Doolittle Wilson has written, the "NWP's . . . support of the [ERA] made the organization less objectionable to [the] manufacturers," who were footing the bill for much of the period's Red-baiting propaganda. Well aware that the ultimate aim of groups like the WJCC was to establish a comprehensive regime of workplace oversight, the National Association of Manufacturers (NAM) and its allies trained their fire on the WJCC and its affiliates "while often sparing the members of the NWP," who "tended to support the elimination, rather than the promotion, of sex-based industrial legislation." (Indeed, it is noteworthy that Paul's NWP was one of the few women's groups that never had to fend off charges of Bolshevism; it was not included in the spiderweb chart, even though its leaders were among the most radical feminists of their day.) In addition to covertly financing attacks on leading female reformers, NAM plied women's groups with "educational" materials and pro-business speakers—a tactic it would repeat to good effect in the post–World War II period. To head up the effort, it formed a Women's Bureau whose director, Marguerite Benson, traveled the country warning women's clubs and chambers of commerce of the dangers of "extreme measures," like child labor laws, that appeared to improve the lives of poor Americans but were in reality designed, or so Benson claimed, to subvert the nation's capitalist economy and usher in Soviet-style despotism.[34]

By the fall of 1924, when state legislatures around the country began debating the Child Labor Amendment, the idea of a monolithic "woman vote" lay in shambles. As a result, lawmakers no longer feared that opposing the measure would trigger an electoral backlash. If anything, supporting ratification was probably the bigger gamble, as this risked provoking the ire of deep-pocketed trade groups such as NAM. To make matters worse, the prohibition debacle proved a godsend for the amendment's opponents. As NAM and its allies were quick to point out, many of the same groups now pushing a constitutional ban on child labor had earlier promised that prohibition would usher in an era of domestic peace and prosperity. Given that the Eighteenth Amendment had instead launched a decade of lawlessness—and birthed an incompetent and patently corrupt bureaucracy (the Bureau of Prohibition) that was becoming well-known for its callous indifference to basic civil liberties—claims that federal bureaucrats were capable of policing child labor, and that their efforts would not disrupt the rhythms of family life, were no longer an easy sell.[35] A League of Women Voters volunteer who lobbied on behalf of the Child Labor Amendment in Indiana recalled that the group's arguments were everywhere met with the same rebuttal: "Look at the Volstead Act!"[36] By 1930 an amendment that had once seemed destined for ratification was effectively dead, as only six states had approved the measure.

The Sheppard-Towner Act met a similar fate. On the level of policy, the law was a smashing success: in states and localities that participated in the program, infant mortality rates plummeted.[37] Yet its opponents never abandoned their goal of repealing a measure they deemed an affront to American ideals of limited government. In 1927, when the law came up for renewal, ideologically conservative groups such as the Woman Patriots and the Sentinels of the Republic launched a public relations offensive against the federal Children's Bureau, tarring the agency as a Bolshevik front group run by "old maids" who were less interested in helping families than in overthrowing the American constitutional system.[38] With the nation's major women's groups in disarray, these and other arguments that had fallen on deaf ears in the early 1920s now gained a serious hearing from lawmakers. The Bureau's supporters managed to secure a two-year appropriations extension, but this would be their final legislative victory. Although several bills were introduced to extend Sheppard-Towner beyond this period, none emerged from committee, and the program that was arguably the signal achievement of "organized womanhood" expired in 1929.

The Sect Spirit in the Jazz Age

By the end of the 1920s most of the broad-based membership groups that had powered the great reform crusade crusades of the early 1900s had drastically scaled back their political activities or else faded from the scene entirely. Yet there was more than one segment of American civil society that remained surprisingly vibrant and at least nominally committed to combating social injustice: the mainline Protestant churches.

In one sense, of course, the 1920s were trying times for the mainline. In addition to the prohibition controversy and the rise of the Klan, several large denominations, including the Presbyterians and Northern Baptists, were racked by infighting between fundamentalists and modernists. And the controversies over evolution, dispensationalism, and biblical inerrancy would grow ever more heated as the two sides struggled for control of the denominational machinery.[39] Yet, through all the drama, average Americans kept showing up for church—often several times per week. A 1922 survey of sixteen thousand Protestant church members found that the median respondent spent an average of nine and a half hours per week inside a church building. Remarkably, around half of this time was spent *outside* of formal worship services, with Sunday school consuming a little over one and a half hours per week and other

"subsidiary" activities—women's groups, mission societies, youth groups, social service activities—taking up more than three hours.[40] Other studies confirmed that religious civil society, at least, was as vibrant as ever. For example, the
Census Bureau's 1926 survey of religious bodies found that the number of children enrolled in Sunday schools (21 million) was almost as high as the number
enrolled in the nation's public schools (24.7 million). And thanks to a booming
economy, the nation's churches were enjoying a period of robust financial health,
with annual expenditures rising nearly 150 percent between 1916 and 1926. (For
purposes of comparison, the $817 million spent by American churches in 1926
was about 40 percent of the total amount expended by all levels of government
on public education.)[41]

If Americans continued to devote considerable time and money to church
activities, even as they cut back on other forms of civic engagement, it was at
least in part because of the continued vitality of what Max Weber called the "sect
spirit." Church involvement, in other words, remained deeply important as a
marker of social respectability. As in earlier periods, *Who's Who* volumes and
social registers remained filled with men and women who proudly proclaimed
their memberships in mainline Protestant churches, and young men embarking
on business or professional careers were strongly encouraged to seek membership in a respectable church, both as a way of cultivating social contacts and in
order to establish a reputation for upright behavior.[42] "Go to church even if it is
hard to take," was the advice that the president of the American Bar Association
gave a graduating class at Harvard Law School. "You'll meet a lot of nice people
there. It isn't so important for you to see them as for them to see you. Now that's
called the church racket, but what of it, as long as you're getting business in a
quiet genteel way."[43]

Many urban churches offered more concrete forms of assistance to citizens hoping to ascend from points further down the socioeconomic ladder.
Prominent congregations in New York City, Chicago, Detroit, and elsewhere
maintained lists of reputable rooming houses, offered literacy classes and other
educational programs, and organized men's and women's clubs that provided
uprooted rural and small-town citizens with opportunities for socializing and
a sense of community. As one historian, in a study of a prosperous Chicago
Presbyterian church's 1920s outreach efforts in that city's rooming-house district, has explained, mainline church membership announced a "transformation of one's social and cultural habits; that is, one became an active participant
in . . . middle-class culture."[44] In firsthand accounts, new church members were
more likely to describe themselves as seeking "friendship and advice," "Christian
fellowship," or opportunities for "mental and physical upbuilding." But the implicit message was the same: church membership and auxiliary activities continued to serve as one of the most reliable points of entry to the middle class.[45]

To be sure, some prominent contemporary observers described the 1920s as a period of declining religious authority. In their landmark study of "Middletown" (Muncie, Indiana), for example, the sociologists Robert and Helen Merrell Lynd argued that the significance of religious institutions in the life of a typical Midwestern city had diminished markedly since the 1890s. Based on extensive firsthand observations and interviews, the Lynds noted that Sabbath observance was on the wane; that many prominent citizens had ceased to believe in the literal truth of heaven and hell; that ministers were no longer ranked among the city's most important civic leaders; that church attendance was down slightly (though Sunday school attendance had held steady); that ecumenical cooperation was less common than in the past; and that busy executives now resented the time-consuming nature of church leadership positions (while apparently preferring to devote their limited free time to fraternal and civic club activities).

And yet, looking back from the perspective of the present, what comes through most clearly in *Middletown*'s chapters on religion is the enduring force of Weber's sect dynamic. The Lynds noted, for example, that the town's most prestigious churches continued to shun potential members, including prominent citizens, who were believed to be deeply in debt or whose private lives were not in order; that the same busy executives who were spending more and more time in secular clubs nonetheless held a virtual lock on church leadership positions; and that church advertising campaigns frequently touted the benefits of associating oneself "with the best people"—which was more or less the same thing working-class parents said when queried about their reasons for sending their children to Sunday school.[46] Perhaps most telling, the sociologists documented the "widespread" tendency of new Middletown residents to select their churches based in part on "instrumental" considerations. Asked how he had decided to join his present church, one "young businessman" explained: "The ___ church has done a lot for me; when I first came here it got me to know ___ and ___ and ___, and there aren't keener businessmen in town."[47] Although it was probably true that the average Middletown resident was less devout than in the late nineteenth century, there was much evidence to suggest that the authority of formal religious bodies vis-à-vis individual citizens remained quite robust.

The Churches as Repositories of Progressivism

Perhaps because they saw few signs that their cultural position was slipping, mainline church officials generally resisted the wider nation's ideological trek from the progressive idealism of the 1910s to the pro-business conservatism championed by Republican Presidents Warren G. Harding, Calvin Coolidge, and Herbert Hoover. Indeed, most mainline elites held firm to the ideals of the

Social Gospel, insisting on a version of Christianity in which social justice and spiritual well-being were inextricably linked. Well into the 1920s the Methodists, Northern Baptists, Presbyterians, Congregationalists, and Episcopalians continued to issue denominational pronouncements urging new federal laws to prohibit child labor, improve working conditions for women, and protect the right of workers to organize.[48] Similarly, most mainline seminaries remained firmly committed to educating aspiring ministers in the practical business of social reform even as their faculties divided over matters of theology.[49] And Protestant religious periodicals, such as *Christian Century*, spent the 1920s proclaiming an unreconstructed progressive vision of a society in which the application of Christian principles would bring an end to such evils as alcohol abuse, child labor, and even war.[50]

No mainline body, however, remained more devoted to the ideals of the Social Gospel than the Federal Council of Churches. Indeed, for all its waffling on the prohibition question, the FCC continued to churn out a steady stream of reports on labor disputes and working conditions in the nation's major industries, few of which cast employers in a positive light. The Council also embarked on significant new initiatives in the areas of race relations and interfaith cooperation.[51] Under the leadership of George E. Haynes, an African American scholar with a doctorate from Columbia, it launched a Commission on the Church and Race Relations that worked to educate white churchgoers about the evils of lynching and segregation.[52] Moreover, in a direct response to the rise of the Klan, the Council joined with national Jewish organizations to found the Committee on Goodwill Between Jews and Christians—later renamed the National Conference of Christians and Jews (NCCJ)—which sponsored dozens of interfaith conferences in an effort to bring Protestant churchgoers into closer communion with their Jewish neighbors.[53] Having learned a valuable lesson from the prohibition debacle, the FCC would henceforth make every effort to issue its social pronouncements in conjunction with like-minded Jewish and Catholic bodies, such as the National Catholic Welfare Conference and the Central Conference of American Rabbis.[54]

Predictably, fundamentalist preachers and conservative industrialists saw in the FCC's left-leaning policy pronouncements clear signs of Bolshevism. And yet, in contrast to the many women's groups that were seriously damaged by spurious allegations of communism, the Council always seemed to land on its feet. One reason the FCC fared better in the public relations department was because of residual goodwill stemming from its popular and widely publicized role in organizing relief efforts and a Protestant chaplaincy corps during World War I.[55] A second—and probably more important—reason was that many moderately conservative elites remained firmly committed to the larger ecumenical project, even as they disagreed with some of the policy stances staked out by the Council's leaders. Indeed, business-friendly Republicans regularly rode to the FCC's defense when it was accused of adopting "un-American" positions. In 1921 Robert J. Caldwell, a Connecticut businessman and party official, rallied a dozen prominent executives to sign a joint statement rebutting a Pittsburgh industrialist's claims that the Council had been infiltrated by "radical and Bolshevik elements."[56] Three years later, when xenophobic members of Congress took to the House floor to attack the Council's stand against the racially restrictive 1924 immigration law, President Coolidge himself calmed the critics by inviting the FCC's president to dine at the White House and publishing a letter expressing his "deep appreciation of the service of the Council in international relations."[57] And as late as 1930 the FCC received financial backing from a long list of prominent businessmen (or their foundations), including the accounting firm founder Arthur Andersen, the copper magnate Cleveland Hoadley Dodge, the publishers Maxwell Geffen and Gardner Cowles, and the vacuum-cleaner entrepreneur William H. Hoover.[58]

By the end of the decade the Council had clearly become, in the words of one historian, "the most influential organization in American Protestantism, or indeed, in the entire American religious scene."[59] Still, the FCC's leaders were highly sensitive to claims that the group's "prophetic" pronouncements on behalf of workers and minorities bore no relation to the views of rank-and-file churchgoers. In part for this reason, they strongly encouraged the formation of state and local councils of churches—intermediate bodies that, while fully under the control of local clergymen and lay leaders, were intended to provide FCC officials with an organic link to the men and women in the pews. Although local councils (or federations) of churches were not unheard of in the nineteenth century, the idea grew in popularity after the FCC began promoting it in the 1910s. A pair of Council officials, Roy B. Guild and Fred Smith, headed the effort. The duo traveled incessantly, sometimes addressing clergymen and lay leaders in as many as forty cities per month. They provided advice on fundraising and organizational structures while also compiling a do-it-yourself manual to guide religious leaders in locales they were unable to visit in person.[60] By the late 1920s the effort had born significant fruit: at least forty-nine cities had formed professional councils staffed by paid administrators, while hundreds of smaller communities had launched volunteer councils.[61] The largest local councils, such as those in New York and Chicago, employed ten or more full-time staff members and controlled annual budgets of as much as $100,000.[62] And although not all Protestant churches participated in state or local councils—efforts to incorporate black churches were half-hearted at best—contemporaneous studies found that participation rates in the nation's larger metropolitan areas were often above 50 percent, and in some cases as high as 90 percent.[63]

Many of the functions performed by local church councils were purely ecclesiastical in nature. The first task undertaken by those that followed the FCC's
suggested program was to conduct "a scientific and thorough going survey of
moral and spiritual needs" of their respective communities.[64] This meant,
among other things, canvassing the entire city to identify neighborhoods where
Protestant churches were in short supply, or where the percentage of residents
attending Sunday school or church had dipped below the norm. Most councils
also featured a comity committee whose primary function was to adjudicate
disputes over the location of Protestant churches. When an existing congregation sought to move to a new neighborhood or when a newly formed congregation proposed to build a church, it would present its case to the committee, which
would conduct a study to determine whether the population of unchurched individuals was large enough to support a new congregation. If the committee judged
the proposal undesirable, it would attempt to arrange a compromise, such as a
move to a neighborhood where the supply of churches was smaller and demand
greater. In addition, councils typically aided in the design of Sunday school cur-
ricula, provided a course of training for new teachers, and organized a "pulpit
supply"—a sort of speaker's bureau that provided ministers for Sunday services
whenever a congregation's usual minister was indisposed.[65]

State and local councils did not limit themselves to saving souls and filling pulpits, however. Arguably their most important function was to serve as
a mouthpiece for Protestant clergymen and lay leaders who wished to express
their views on issues of public concern. A study of twenty-nine local councils
conducted in the late 1920s found that 86 percent had recently "agitated for reform on specific issues," and more than two-thirds had formally endorsed or
opposed a particular piece of legislation. In cities such as Detroit, Pittsburgh,
and Chicago, as much as 50 percent of the local council's communication with
member churches concerned public affairs; popular subjects included Sabbath
observance, drinking, and gambling, but systemic questions of economic justice
and race relations also occupied a prominent place on the agendas of these and
other councils.[66]

Deciding exactly when it was appropriate to issue political pronouncements
on behalf of "the church" was, of course, a tricky business. Most councils adopted
guidelines that limited their political involvement to issues that involved "a clear
principle of moral or religious welfare," and to cases where religious leaders
were "practically unanimous" in their judgments about the proper course of action.[67] In practice, many councils resorted to conducting referenda to determine
whether official pronouncements were warranted. In 1927, for example, the
Massachusetts Federation of Churches asked the state's clergymen for their views
on abolishing the death penalty, jury service by women, U.S. participation in the
Permanent Court of International Justice, and U.S. membership in the League of

Nations. Because support for the last two proposals was virtually unanimous, the Federation went "on record as favoring these measures." Jury service for women and abolition of the death penalty, in contrast, garnered the support of only two-thirds of responding clergymen, leading the council to issue a statement that, while stopping short of a formal endorsement, nonetheless indicated that "a clear majority" of the state's ministers favored both proposals, while also urging individual churches to undertake "a careful study of both issues."[68]

A final critical function of the local church council was, in the words of one of the conciliar movement's organizers, to serve as a "clearing-house of information within its own community."[69] Among other things, this meant acting as a conduit for educational and other materials generated at FCC headquarters. Indeed, the FCC's various department heads viewed the growing network of state and local church councils as an invaluable link to the hinterlands, and they were not shy about using it for their own purposes. In a typical year, Council department heads bombarded their local counterparts with dozens of communiqués, many of which touched on such sensitive issues as race relations, industrial reform, and war and peace.[70] Although some councils were more receptive to the FCC's pleas than others, surveys of local executives conducted during the 1920s indicated that a considerable portion made more than token efforts to advance the Council's policy priorities: for example, about half had promoted observance of Labor Sunday, almost 40 percent had distributed information regarding the Council's broader industrial program, and 25 percent had recently organized an industrial conference. In the area of race relations, around 40 percent of local councils reported having participated in the FCC's Interracial Sunday program, the same percentage claimed to have followed up on the Council's suggestion of organizing pulpit exchanges between black and white churches, and 30 percent had taken the further step of organizing an interracial religious conference.[71]

The question of precisely what impact all this activity had on average ministers and churchgoers is difficult to answer. H. L. Mencken, in his inimitable acerbic style, dismissed the church federation movement as the creation of "well-heeled and mainly elderly men and women, all of them eager to do good by force," even in cases where most churchgoers were indifferent or opposed to the causes in question.[72] What limited contemporaneous evidence exists, however, paints a more complicated picture. For example, some (admittedly primitive) surveys found that most ministers and lay leaders strongly supported their state and local councils' political activities.[73] And on at least a handful of occasions, local councils proved capable of mobilizing large numbers of churchgoers on behalf of specific causes. In 1928, for example, Massachusetts Senator David Walsh estimated that a state federation of churches' letter-writing campaign on behalf of the Kellogg-Briand Pact was responsible for one-third of all the mail received by his office; in Michigan, a similar campaign sponsored by the Detroit Federation of Churches convinced more than a thousand congregations to petition their representatives.[74]

That lay interest in social problems not related to prohibition declined markedly over the course of the 1920s seems undeniable. And yet, the arguably more important point is that the major institutions of mainline Protestantism—the clergy, the local church councils, the denominational hierarchies, the FCC—remained firmly committed to the ideals of the Social Gospel, even as the men and women in the pews seemed increasingly skeptical of large-scale social reform. This disjunction is puzzling until one remembers two facts. First, American clergymen remained, on the whole, far better educated than their parishioners—at a time when only about one in five Americans had graduated from high school, more than half (59 percent) of Protestant clergymen in the mainline denominations had graduated from college, seminary, or both—and they were overwhelmingly products of seminaries that continued to stress the necessity of confronting social injustice.[75] Having studied the religious and ethical dimensions of industrial conflict, race relations, and foreign policy in the classroom, ministers saw no reason why they should fall silent on these issues once installed in a church.

Second, in an age when religious authority—meaning the pull of the institutional church over the individual believer—was still quite robust, rank-and-file churchgoers were generally tolerant of clergymen weighing in on political matters, even when they did not fully agree with the positions adopted. Indeed, notwithstanding the intense theological debates that shook the mainline denominations in the late 1910s and early 1920s, reports of churches ousting ministers over specifically *political* stances are surprisingly rare. (Nor was firing even an option for churches, such as the Methodists and Episcopalians, whose ministers were appointed by a central body.) Even during the decade normally regarded as the nadir of American progressivism, then, most Protestant churchgoers remained at least partially integrated into a growing and interconnected network of religious bodies that stressed the religious duty of social reform. And in 1929, when economic conditions suddenly changed, that network would play a critical role in mobilizing Protestant support for a fundamental rethinking of the American economic order and its relation to the state.

3

The Churches Do Their Part

My friends, the ideal of social justice of which I have spoken—an ideal that years ago might have been thought overly advanced, is now accepted by the moral leadership of all the great religious groups of the country.
>   —Franklin D. Roosevelt, "Address at Belle Isle Bridge Naval Armory" (1932)

In October 1932 the presidential candidate Franklin D. Roosevelt made headlines by declaring that his calls for a concerted program of government intervention to combat the Great Depression were no more "radical" than the views "of the Federal Council of Churches." Some conservative commentators described FDR's campaign-trail reference to the Federal Council as a borderline gaffe, believing that the New York governor had unintentionally—but tellingly—linked his own economic agenda with that of an organization that had in the past battled accusations of harboring communist sympathies.[1] In fact, the remark was neither spontaneous nor a political blunder. It came near the end of a Sunday afternoon campaign address, delivered before an audience of more than six thousand at the Detroit naval armory, in which FDR and his speechwriters deliberately framed the candidate's program as an authentic embodiment of the social teachings of the nation's three largest faiths.

Roosevelt began his remarks by describing two competing political philosophies: the first held that economic suffering was no concern of government, that even in the face of widespread poverty and hunger lawmakers should simply "let things alone." The second strove "for something new, something that the human race has never [yet] attained," namely, "social justice through social action." This was followed by an overview of several relatively recent reforms, including worker's compensation laws and restrictions on child labor, that embodied the spirit of the newer philosophy—reforms that had once been denounced as "socialist" or un-American but were now widely accepted as having contributed to the creation of a fairer society. Only at this point did Roosevelt directly address the claim, recently popular in Republican circles, that his own economic program was too radical for the American electorate to accept.[2] Not only were his ideas not particularly unorthodox from the standpoint of economics, Roosevelt insisted; they were also in keeping with principles that had guided Protestant, Catholic, and Jewish social involvement for the better part of three decades.

Far from an afterthought, the reference to the Federal Council of Churches was followed by a lengthy quotation from its 1932 Labor Sunday message, which was in turn followed by quotations from a papal encyclical and a pronouncement of the Central Conference of American Rabbis. A single theme linked the three passages: that concentrated and unaccountable economic power posed a serious threat to both democratic government and human dignity. The public, Roosevelt insisted, was not only within its rights but positively obligated to intervene in the economy when dominant actors ignored the "dictates of social conscience" in favor "of the spirit of the god of Mammon." The religious impulse to aid the suffering had served the country well during the Progressive Era, he argued; and assuming voters chose "the path of faith, the path of hope, the path of love toward our fellow man," it would do so again. At this, the audience erupted into prolonged applause.[3]

Roosevelt would soon prove that his campaign references to the social ideals of the churches were more than empty rhetoric. Like his advisors Harry Hopkins and Frances Perkins, both of whom began their careers in the settlement house movement, FDR was steeped in the Protestant reform tradition. An Episcopalian, he attended religious services frequently as a child, was an active participant in Protestant social service organizations during his student days, and occupied the surprisingly time-consuming post of senior warden at his home church in Hyde Park for the duration of his time in the White House.[4] Over the course of his presidency he would sign into law a series of groundbreaking economic reforms—old-age and disability pensions, unemployment insurance, federal wage and hours laws—that must have seemed like pipe dreams when they were written into the 1908 "Social Creed of the Churches." And his efforts did not go unnoticed by religious elites. One after another, the mainline denominations issued proclamations endorsing FDR's domestic agenda as an authentic step toward the creation of an economic order that would protect vulnerable citizens instead of exploiting them. Though these resolutions rarely mentioned the president or his signature initiatives by name, they left no doubt about where the churches stood in relation to such core New Deal programs as Social Security.[5]

Until recently, however, historians of the New Deal have had relatively little to say about the Protestant churches' contributions to the landmark economic reforms of the 1930s and early 1940s.[6] In fact, it is widely assumed that FDR's legislative triumphs were underwritten not by moralistic Protestants, but by a coalition of previously marginalized voting blocs and interest groups, including Catholics, Jews, organized labor, and eventually African Americans. And there is a grain of truth in this claim: in his four campaigns for the White House, FDR consistently won the Catholic and Jewish votes by overwhelming margins while typically winning only around half of the non-Southern Protestant vote. Moreover, most of the Jews, Catholics, and union voters who backed FDR in his campaigns for the White House became permanent members of a new Democratic coalition that would dominate American politics through the late 1960s. In light of these facts, it is no wonder that the New Deal is often described as a defeat for the well-heeled WASPs who filled the nation's mainline churches— described, that is, as the pivotal moment when resources and authority began to be wrested away from the traditional governing class and redistributed to those who had long been relegated to the margins of the nation's political and cultural life.[7]

And yet there is an important sense in which the mainline churches were critical not only to the success of the New Deal, but also to the larger project of constructing a viable social welfare state that would occupy Democratic leaders through the Kennedy and Johnson administrations. For while Northern mainline churchgoers leaned Republican and were therefore lukewarm in their support for FDR and subsequent Democratic presidents, many of them strongly sympathized with the goal of constructing a fairer economic order—no doubt in part because their own denominations had been preaching it for the better part of three decades. When it came to specific policy problems, ministers found that their parishioners were more than willing to consider progressive reforms and, if convinced of their merit, to work toward their enactment. In the case of the New Deal, Protestant clergymen and lay leaders offered the Roosevelt administration several tangible forms of assistance—from local educational sessions to letter-writing campaigns to "NRA Sundays"—that went well beyond their public expressions of support. Arguably the churches' greatest contribution to the construction of the American welfare state, however, was to serve as a bulwark against attacks from a growing cadre of proto-libertarian entities on the far right. So long as most Protestants attended mainline churches, and so long as mainline leaders were monolithic in their support of social welfare programs, claims that there was something fundamentally un-American about redirecting resources to aid the downtrodden would remain an exceedingly tough sell.

New Strategies for a New Deal

Religious leaders were no less surprised than economists when the U.S. economy plunged into depression in late 1929 and early 1930, throwing millions of Americans out of work and spawning breadlines from coast to coast. But unlike the economists, who needed time to analyze the root causes of what came to be known as the Great Depression, the clergymen who staffed the upper echelons of the mainline denominations and the Federal Council of Churches knew immediately what had happened: Americans were being judged for their misuse of God-given resources. During the 1920s a decade of unprecedented corporate profits and government surpluses, politicians and business leaders alike had ignored calls by the FCC and other religious bodies to invest in a more robust social safety net, choosing instead to engage in an orgy of profit taking and extravagant living. Handed a golden opportunity to translate the social ideals of the Protestant churches into a concrete policy program, the nation had taken the opposite path, rejecting the Child Labor Amendment and even rolling back many of the novel social programs, such as the Sheppard-Towner Act, enacted during the heyday of the Progressive movement. And now the bill for America's decade of excess had come due. As the FCC explained in its 1930 Labor Sunday message, any believer seeking to understand the origins of the crisis need only examine the values exhibited by American elites over the previous decade—a generation of leaders "so blind and morally callous that it has been unwilling to divert sufficient profits of modern industry to stores of reserves for the protection of the unemployed and the aged," a generation that "insisted on the rights of property to dividends but . . . concerned itself too little with the rights of workers to security of employment and to protection in old age."[8]

From this perspective, formulating a plan to reverse the catastrophic downturn of the early 1930s was as simple as tracing its causes. Clearly, God expected the nation to abandon its prodigal ways and start taking the long view: to begin prioritizing the well-being of workers and families over boosting corporate profits, to use the levers of official power to counterbalance the unchecked authority of employers over workers, and to create a social safety net that would make life bearable for the millions of Americans who, despite their best efforts, were suddenly unable to find gainful employment. Much to the chagrin of religious elites, however, President Herbert Hoover largely rejected this line of analysis, preferring instead to promote voluntary recovery programs and charitable efforts to aid the unemployed. For a time the churches deferred to the president, responding to his initiatives in a spirit of patriotic cooperation that seemed to befit the gravity of the nation's plight.[9] In the end, however, Hoover's unyielding opposition to new forms of state intervention in the economy convinced church officials that he was poorly suited to the task of reversing the nation's economic fortunes.[10]

Roosevelt seemed like a better bet. By the time of his landslide victory in the 1932 presidential election, mainline leaders were cautiously optimistic about his domestic program, which—although the details remained murky—seemed likely to include such Council-backed initiatives as public works programs, old-age pensions, unemployment insurance, and even moderate forms of centralized planning, including trade associations that would be tasked with coordinating production and stabilizing employment in specific industries. And yet, any effort to mobilize rank-and-file churchgoers in support of these programs would be complicated by the withering of the large parachurch groups that had done so much to build support for the economic reforms of the Progressive Era. Aside from the General Federation of Women's Clubs, which did generate some regional support for aspects of the New Deal, and the Townsend Clubs, which used religious appeals to help mobilize grassroots backing for a system of old-age pensions (though not the one eventually endorsed by the Roosevelt administration), the broad-based membership organizations that might have been expected to build grassroots support for the New Deal were now either too small or too racked by infighting to be of much assistance.[11] To make matters worse, the churches were themselves confronting an increasingly dire financial situation: by 1932 contributions to Protestant denominations and ecumenical bodies had fallen to 60 percent of their 1929 levels.[12] Hence, if mainline officials were to have any hope of orchestrating an effective lobbying campaign on behalf of their long-standing social ideals, it would have to be a very different sort of campaign than the ones they had overseen in the early years of the twentieth century.

One church leader was particularly influential in pioneering a top-down style of mobilization appropriate to the transformed civil society of the 1930s. James Myers, a gaunt, stern-faced, balding man with wire-frame glasses, served as the FCC's industrial secretary from 1925 to 1947. A tireless crusader for workers' rights, he maintained a punishing schedule of long workdays and constant travel, dividing his time between mediating strikes, lobbying for union organizing rights, procuring food and clothing for striking workers and their families, and presiding over the funerals of men and women killed on the picket lines. More to the point, he displayed a genius for mobilizing grassroots religious support—or at least the appearance of such support—for left-leaning economic initiatives. When his department budget was slashed, he relied on elite advocacy groups such as the American Association for Labor Legislation (AALL) to supply research and educational materials while also cultivating wealthy donors to make up for the sharp decline in denominational contributions to the Council. To compensate for the erosion of "secular" civil society, he relied on sympathetic state and local church councils to disseminate information and mobilize ministers on behalf of New Deal programs. To reach those who had drifted away from the faith, as well as those who were skeptical of the need for new federal programs, he placed articles in popular magazines, describing in excruciating detail his heartbreaking encounters with child laborers, starving coal miners, and striking workers bludgeoned into submission.[13] Perhaps most important, he formed close bonds with his counterparts in the Jewish and Catholic social service agencies, realizing that in an age of growing religious diversity the impression of a monolithic "Judeo-Christian" religious establishment would carry far more weight than Protestant pronouncements alone.

Myers's first Depression-era foray into the world of lobbying was not entirely successful, but it provided a trial run for many of the techniques he would later use in support of the New Deal. In 1930, as the ranks of the unemployed continued to swell, many elite reformers seized on the idea of unemployment insurance as a way of reducing the severity of future downturns. Although there were several competing proposals in circulation—England, in fact, had enacted such a system in 1920—most called for states to require employers and/or workers to pay into an unemployment reserve fund from which laid-off workers would be entitled to draw benefits for a limited period of time. Proposals were introduced in several state legislatures in 1931, and in early 1932 Wisconsin became the first state to enact an unemployment insurance law.[14]

For Myers and like-minded religious advocates, the push for unemployment insurance was a logical extension of the stewardship ideals that had guided the progressive economic reforms of the 1910s and early 1920s. Never again, they argued, should wealthy Americans be permitted to game the business cycle by hoarding the profits of the boom years while disavowing responsibility for those thrown out of work by the inevitable bust. As Grace Abbott, Lillian Wald's successor as head of the U.S. Children's Bureau, explained to the readers of a Congregational periodical in early 1931, the "richest country in the world" now found itself, "as in previous periods of industrial depression, entirely unprepared [to care for] for its victims"—namely, the families and children of the unemployed. The time had come to abandon "temporary expedients" and adopt a permanent system of unemployment compensation to ensure that the negative consequences of reckless speculation would never again land squarely "upon the backs of little children."[15]

Myers fully shared Abbott's sentiments, and he was determined to use what remained of the ecumenical infrastructure to awaken middle- and upper-class Americans to their responsibilities toward the unemployed. In February 1932, as the unemployment rate climbed to nearly 20 percent, he wrote to 178 local ministers' associations urging them to go on the record in support of unemployment insurance and a joint state-federal unemployment bureau.[16] Around the same time, he began corresponding with state and local unemployment insurance "committees" and "conferences"—groups of prominent citizens who publicly backed some version of the Wisconsin plan—with the aim of ensuring that prominent clergymen were included in their ranks.[17] By early 1933 he was fully engaged in the push to create a state unemployment insurance system in New York, an effort spearheaded by the New York Conference for Unemployment Insurance Legislation. In late February, as the state legislative session was entering its final frantic weeks, he wrote to a self-curated list of 150 "liberal" ministers scattered across New York state urging them to mobilize their congregations in support of a pending unemployment insurance bill.[18]

Several ministers responded enthusiastically, even going so far as to mail Myers copies of the letters they had sent to Albany.[19]

But despite Myers's best efforts and the support of Governor Herbert Lehman and state Democratic party leaders, the New York legislature failed to enact an unemployment insurance bill in 1933. Although the plan passed the state senate, it was ultimately bottled up in the lower chamber of the state legislature. At this point, instead of giving up the fight, Myers turned his attention to the U.S. Congress. As usual, he was aided by a wealthy donor—in this case, Elizabeth Brandeis Raushenbush, the daughter of Supreme Court Justice Louis Brandeis and daughter-in-law of the late Social Gospel pioneer Walter Rauschenbusch.[20] An accomplished academic and activist in her own right and one of the principal authors of Wisconsin's first-in-the-nation unemployment insurance law, Raushenbush wrote Myers in February 1934 with the news that New York Senator Robert F. Wagner had introduced legislation that would incentivize "every state" to adopt an unemployment insurance system within the "next year." Although the president's Labor Secretary, Frances Perkins, was prepared to back the Wagner-Lewis bill, Raushenbush reported that FDR was "waiting to see how the country responds to the proposal. If it seems to get strong support he will push it."[21]

Sensing that the support of church leaders might be enough to sway the president, Myers sprang into action. With Raushenbush footing the bill, he authored a form letter urging support for the Wagner-Lewis legislation and arranged to send it, along with an article by the economist Paul Raushenbush (Elizabeth's husband), to a long list of religious leaders, including 200 editors of religious periodicals, 200 local church council officials, 25 heads of denominational social service agencies, 150 "liberal" ministers in New York state, 200 "liberal" ministers in "all parts of the country," and, finally, a mailing list of 3,000 "ministers, Y.W.C.A. secretaries, college professors" and others who had in the past requested to receive the Council's newsletter, *Information Service*.[22] Recipients were encouraged to write "at once to President Roosevelt and your congressman and senators" and urge them to "help realize another one of [the social ideals of the churches] in the actual life of the nation."[23] Secretary Perkins, for her part, made the rounds of the denominational social service agencies, pressing the case that the Wagner-Lewis bill, or some similar program, was desperately needed to prevent a recurrence of the hardships of the early 1930s.[24]

Perkins's and Myers's crusade to mobilize the nation's Protestant ministers on behalf of Wagner-Lewis bill benefited from the fact that all of the large Northern denominations had by this point adopted resolutions calling for some form of action to help families weather prolonged periods of sickness, disability, or systemic unemployment. As early as 1931 Episcopalian leaders had called for the creation of a voluntary program of "reserve [funds] to ensure regularity" of income during economic downturns. The following year delegates to the national gatherings of the Methodist and (Northern) Presbyterian Churches endorsed state-sponsored unemployment and disability insurance, as well as old-age pensions, as (in the words of the Methodists) consistent with the Christian principle that all citizens should "have [the] opportunity to develop their capacities to the fullest possible extent." In 1933 the Disciples of Christ—traditionally the most reticent of the mainline denominations on matters of labor and industry—declared their support for "guarantees against unemployment, . . . accident and health insurance . . . [and] old age security."[25] Finally, in the spring of 1934, Bishop William T. Manning, the top Episcopal prelate for New York City and a man well-known to the Roosevelts, lent his support to a resolution that would put the president's own denomination on record as supporting a federally sponsored program of unemployment insurance. (Manning's resolution would eventually be adopted by the Episcopal House of Deputies in late 1934.)[26]

It is difficult to say with certainty whether these church pronouncements, or for that matter Myers's letter-writing campaign, shaped FDR's thinking on the unemployment insurance question. Still, it is worth noting that only a few months after Myers and Raushenbush hatched their plan, Roosevelt launched the President's Committee on Economic Security, a body tasked with devising "means . . . to provide . . . security against several of the great disturbing factors in life—especially those which relate to unemployment and old age." The Committee's Advisory Council included a number of individuals with close ties to Myers and the Federal Council: Grace Abbott was a member, as was New Hampshire Governor John G. Winant, an active Episcopalian and YMCA leader with a reputation for championing progressive economic reforms in his home state. Moreover, the group's executive director was Edwin E. Witte, a Wisconsin native and close associate of the Raushenbushes who was well connected in mainline denominational circles.[27] Few could have been surprised when, six months later, the Committee presented the president with a list of recommendations that included unemployment insurance as "a front line of defense" against the financial hardships of unemployment.[28]

Just as Myers and Elizabeth Raushenbush had hoped, a system based on the Committee on Economic Security's recommendations was incorporated into the Social Security Act—the centerpiece of the New Deal-era social welfare state—which FDR signed into law in August 1935. Shortly thereafter Roosevelt nominated Winant, who was rumored to be mulling a presidential bid, to head the newly created Social Security Board. The Republican accepted the post, effectively ending his own political career (though FDR would later name him ambassador to Great Britain), and immediately began working to translate the Social Security Act's complex provisions into terms average Americans could understand. Realizing that religious leaders were uniquely well positioned to help dispel the cloud of mystery surrounding the law, Winant wasted little time in seeking their assistance. In March 1936 he convened a meeting with Protestant, Jewish, and Catholic representatives, with each set of faith leaders agreeing to disseminate information about the Social Security program through their respective periodicals.[29] (Myers, who attended the meeting, subsequently devoted an entire issue of *Information Service* to fleshing out the eligibility criteria for the law's various benefit programs, as well as the intricacies of its funding mechanisms.)[30] In addition, the group agreed to undertake "cooperative activities" for the purpose of publicizing the law's provisions.[31]

Winant next focused his attention on the nation's most prestigious seminaries, hoping to convince future Protestant clergymen, in particular, that Social Security's pension, disability, and unemployment insurance programs were in keeping with the social teachings of their respective denominations. It was not a hard sell. Following Winant's February 1937 appearance at Union Theological Seminary, the school's president, Henry Sloane Coffin, wrote with assurances that the Social Security Board would "have the thorough co-operation of this group of ministers in what you are trying to do."[32]

The Cross and the Blue Eagle

But for all the energy that Myers and other mainline clergymen poured into the fight for unemployment insurance, it was the National Industrial Recovery Act (NIRA), the administration's ambitious plan to revive the nation's moribund industrial sector, that absorbed the bulk of their time and energy during 1933 and early 1934. In this case the problem was not one of prodding cautious legislators into action—the NIRA had sailed through an overwhelmingly Democratic Congress in the spring of 1933—but of mobilizing the broad base of public support that would be necessary for the law to meet its ambitious goal of stabilizing prices, production, and employment across the nation's major industries. One of the most complex federal regulatory measures ever conceived, the NIRA depended heavily on the voluntary compliance of private actors, including large employers, small businesses, and unions, all of whom would be tasked with helping to devise industry-specific regulatory codes that the federal government would then be empowered to enforce. Among other things, those charged with creating the codes were instructed to guarantee fair competition within industries, protect the right of workers to join unions, and establish minimum wages and maximum hours of employment.

Businesses that complied with the law's industry-specific codes were awarded a Blue Eagle poster bearing the slogan "NRA Member. We Do Our Part." The hastily devised symbol soon took on religious overtones. General

Hugh S. Johnson, who was tapped by Roosevelt to head the National Recovery Administration (NRA), regularly likened it to well-known Christian symbols. "Those who are not with us are against us," he declared, "and the way to show that you are part of this great army of the New Deal is to insist on this symbol of solidarity [the Blue Eagle] exactly as Peter of the Keys drew a fish on the sand as a countersign and Peter the Hermit exacted the cross on the baldric of every good man and true. This campaign is a frank dependence on the power and the willingness of the American people to act together as one person in an hour of great danger."[33] Mainline religious entities were quick to choose sides. By the fall of 1935 the Blue Eagle could be found stamped on the inside cover of the *Christian Century*, for example; and more than a few supportive ministers displayed it on the doors of their studies.[34]

In response to Johnson's call, Myers took it upon himself to secure public expressions of support for the NRA from religious leaders across the country. Unlike Johnson, however, Myers insisted on framing the effort as an exercise in interfaith cooperation. His first move was to contact his Jewish and Catholic counterparts—Rabbi Edward L. Israel of the Social Justice Commission of the Central Conference of American Rabbis, and the Reverend R. A. McGowan and Monsignor John A. Ryan of the National Catholic Welfare Conference—to suggest a joint statement of support for Roosevelt's recovery program. In a June 1933 letter to McGowan, he proposed that

> the national religious organizations might function in some helpful and definitive way to help make the most of the [NIRA], possibly through a national statement of some kind calling upon church people in the community to cooperate heartily in the provisions of the bill, and possibly by setting up joint local committees in various cities and sections which might issue such statements for their own communities and might supply speakers at both . . . employers' meetings and union meetings, and might keep in touch with local conditions, and bring as much public opinion as possible to bear on the actual functioning of the best provisions of this act.

McGowan, Israel, and Meyers agreed to meet in the nation's capital on June 26, a day when Myers was already scheduled to be in Washington for meetings with Secretary Perkins and the presidential advisor Harry Hopkins.[35]

Just as Myers had hoped, his Catholic and Jewish counterparts eagerly signed onto a joint statement—released to the press in July—announcing that the leaders of "national Protestant, Catholic, and Jewish organizations" had blessed the Recovery Act as consistent with "the social ideals and principles for which our organizations have stood for many years." Although it "remain[ed] to be seen" whether the Act would accomplish all of its ambitious goals, the men nonetheless deemed the law sufficiently "forward looking . . . in intent as to merit the heartiest cooperation of all in realizing the maximum social justice and economic cooperation made possible under its provisions." The missive further urged ministers and lay leaders to "take an active part in developing an informed public opinion in regard to the actual provisions of the [Act] . . . in order that in every community the greatest possible cooperation may be assured and the most substantial progress may be made toward a better social order."[36] The public-relations blitz was capped off by a photo op of the religious leaders surrounding General Johnson at his desk, all of the men deep in thought as they examined a stack of documents. "Religious leaders of all faiths came to Washington yesterday to pledge their aid to NIRA toward recovery," read the caption in the *Washington Herald*.[37]

Having engineered an expression of "Judeo-Christian" support for the recovery effort, Myers turned his attention to holding up Protestantism's end of the bargain. The day after the statement's release, he dispatched a mailing to the head of every council of churches, ministers' association, and denominational commission in the country outlining a "concrete program" designed to "stir" the "public conscience" in support of the NRA. To ensure that ministers had accurate and up-to-date information on the subject, he referred them to the joint statement as well as a special issue of *Information Service* that was "entirely dedicated" to spelling out the details of the law's complex provisions. In addition, he suggested that local councils of churches and ministers' associations organize speakers' bureaus staffed by "ministers and church leaders who are especially qualified to inform themselves thoroughly with respect to the [NIRA's provisions] both 'on paper' and as they are actually working out in national and local situations." Finally, he proposed that "in every city a conference be held at which addresses would be made by representatives of various groups and interests, for example, employers, labor unions, farmers, government officials, ministers and social workers." The Federal Council of Churches, he reported, stood ready to "help . . . in every possible way with information, counsel on setup of conferences and suggestions as to speakers."[38]

Myers's hope was that the Protestant churches might function as a sort of mediating institution, one capable both of connecting average Americans to the massive institutions—labor unions, corporations, the federal government—that were the primary focus of the NIRA, and also of fostering meaningful dialogue between all concerned parties. That he considered the churches capable of this herculean task indicates the extent to which he shared his progressive forebears' almost mystical faith in the power of reasoned deliberation to resolve even the thorniest of policy dilemmas. And remarkably, at least in the early months of the New Deal, his optimistic vision found some support in reality.

Within a month of receiving Myers's letter, several church councils wrote to report that they were cooperating with federal officials "in developing the N.R.A. sentiment." The Rochester Council of Churches informed Myers that it had designated September 17 as "N.R.A. Sunday," a day when the city's ministers would educate their flocks on the president's signature initiative.[39] The Connecticut Council of Churches announced that it had organized an NRA conference featuring "speakers representing both [sic] the government administration, employers and labor, and the church." Similar accounts arrived from church councils in Elizabeth, New Jersey, and Buffalo, New York, the latter enclosing a stack of newspaper clippings concerning its NRA-related activities.[40] A number of parish ministers, who may well have been spurred to action by their local church councils, wrote directly to the White House to report that they too were working to build support for the NRA, many of them requesting statements of support from the president.[41]

Arguably the most ambitious educational effort of all took place in California, where a group of prominent Los Angeles ministers, aided by Jack Warner, the legendary studio boss who had recently agreed to head the state Recovery Board, organized a "Golden Rule Army." The basic idea was to encourage all of the state's church members to sign cards pledging to "carry the spirit of the Golden Rule into my private, social and business life"—a pledge that, for business owners, clearly implied fidelity to the relevant NRA code. Within a week, hundreds of Protestant churches had agreed to participate in the program, including forty-eight in the city of Long Beach alone. Warner confidently predicted that there would soon be "3,000,000 churchgoers in the state . . . banded together in the California battalion, and that in due time every church member in the United States will be enlisted in this spiritual movement in support of the President's recovery program."[42]

Myers's year of frenzied activity in support of the NRA reached its climax in early December, when FCC officials arranged for President Roosevelt, Agriculture Secretary Henry Wallace, and a slew of other dignitaries to address a special Council session in the nation's capital. Ostensibly called for the purpose of commemorating the FCC's twenty-fifth anniversary, the gathering was largely dedicated to sanctifying the New Deal as an authentic embodiment of the social teachings of the mainline churches. Only a few months before the special session, the FCC's general secretary, Samuel McCrea Cavert, had used his Labor Sunday message to inform mainline churchgoers that "almost overnight a number of the social ideals of the churches have been incorporated into law and made the basis of a new deal in political and economic relations in this country."[43] Three weeks later the Executive Committee—the only body empowered to speak for the entire Council—issued a lengthy pronouncement praising the Roosevelt administration for pursuing a "national recovery program" that "endeavor[ed] to establish on grounds of economic stability and progress" the very principles of economic fairness that "the churches [had] been advocating on spiritual and humanitarian grounds" for "many years."[44] Now, Myers and other mainline leaders were hoping to hear the president draw these same connections himself—and in a nationally broadcast speech, no less. They would not be disappointed.

Speaking to a packed house at Washington's Constitution Hall, Roosevelt, not for the first time, framed the Depression and his administration's response to it as a straightforward morality tale—a story of sin and redemption that was by this point familiar to his audience. The nation, he declared, had recently emerged from an era "controlled by the spirit of conquest and greed." The task now before it was to replace the "pagan ethics" that had spawned the crash with the spirit of "social justice." Realizing this goal would require a joint crusade of the "churches—gentile and Jew" and "that human agency we call government," the one working through "social and economic means" and the other through "social and spiritual means." The administration and the churches "were rightly united in [the] common aim" of building a fairer economy, the president concluded, and with "the help of God, we are on the road toward it." As if to prove him correct, the delegates closed the session by issuing a special encyclical to the nation's churches, asking them to join in a "program of moral and spiritual strengthening" designed to ensure that the "superstructure" of the nation's new economic order would "rest not upon the sand but upon the rock."[45]

Labor's Magna Carta

For all the soaring rhetoric of the FCC's twenty-fifth anniversary gathering, many FCC leaders, including Myers, privately harbored doubts about the National Recovery Administration's ability to reshape labor relations. By early 1934 they were forced to acknowledge the mounting evidence that the NIRA's vaunted Section 7(a) was more bark than bite. For example, the law guaranteed the right of workers to organize but was generally powerless when it came to forcing employers to engage in collective bargaining with their unionized workers. And while it held out the promise of reasonable hours, wages, and working conditions, it lacked adequate enforcement mechanisms with which to punish recalcitrant employers. By the summer, *Information Service* was churning out a steady stream of complaints about the law's lax enforcement, even going so far as to express sympathy for striking workers at a time when a wave of violent labor unrest was sweeping the nation. With so few of the NIRA's promised benefits having been realized, was it any wonder that dockworkers along the West Coast were refusing to unload ships, or that Minneapolis Teamsters had effectively shut down commercial traffic in that city, allowing only drivers holding union passes to travel the streets? Clearly these men had "lost confidence in the ability of the government to apply the New Deal to them and [were now] taking matters into their own hands."[46]

Two events in 1935 caused Myers and other Council officials to transfer their energies from cheerleading for the NRA to advocating for a new and improved federal labor law. First, the Supreme Court, in a move that some Roosevelt advisors greeted with relief, ruled the NRA's complex code-making scheme unconstitutional.[47] Second, Senator Robert Wagner began drafting legislation that, if enacted, would transform Section 7(a)'s parchment guarantees into concrete legal protections for organized labor. Among the most important features of Wagner's bill were a detailed list of election procedures designed to ensure transparency and fairness in union elections, a prohibition on company-controlled unions, and a ban on various "unfair labor practices" that employers had traditionally used to undercut unionization drives. Finally, the proposed legislation created a powerful new administrative body, the National Labor Relations Board (NLRB), to investigate violations of the law and adjudicate disputes involving the law's provisions. But if organized labor was far from pleased with the status quo under the NIRA, neither was it uniformly enthusiastic about Wagner's proposal to strengthen federal oversight of the collective bargaining process. Although the American Federation of Labor's (AFL) William Green strongly backed the bill, other prominent labor supporters worried that the federal government could not be trusted to administer the new rules, and that employers would soon find a way to game the system, just as they had the NRA codes. The American Civil Liberties Union's (ACLU) Roger Nash Baldwin, for example, argued that the best thing the federal government could do for organized labor was to leave it alone to fight its own battles—in the streets if necessary.[48]

One person who was not conflicted about the need to bolster the NIRA's enforcement provisions was James Myers. As early as May 1934 he wrote to Wagner and other prominent senators to propose that "the present labor provisions of the [NIRA] . . . be strengthened and made permanent."[49] In February 1935, having spent much of the previous summer and fall in a futile attempt to negotiate an end to a massive strike in the Southern textile mills—and having delivered yet another funeral oration, this time for six striking workers slain by sheriff's deputies in Honea Path, North Carolina—he redoubled his lobbying efforts.[50] As he had for the NIRA, he began his push for passage of the Wagner Act by proposing an interfaith statement of support. By late February 1935, Myers, Monsignor Ryan, and Rabbi Sydney E. Goldstein—the new head of the Social Justice Commission of the Central Conference of American Rabbis—had hammered out a joint letter to Senator David Walsh, head of the Senate Education and Labor Committee, requesting that he act quickly to move Wagner's bill through the committee.[51] The statement stressed three themes: employer-controlled unions could never effectively represent workers and should be outlawed; the principle of majority rule should govern union elections; and a new administrative body should be created and endowed with sufficient authority to police the collective bargaining process. All three positions, the men emphasized, were consistent with previous policy pronouncements of their respective religious bodies.[52] After clearing the statement with the Federal Council's Executive Committee, Myers set to work promoting it in the press.[53] On March 21, the day before its official release, he sent a copy to Arthur Hays Sulzberger, publisher of the *New York Times*, with a request that it be prominently featured in the paper.[54] Sulzberger complied with a full-column story headlined "Three Faiths Back Wagner Labor Bill: Collective Bargaining Power Is Vital to Workers, Church Welfare Leaders Declare." That the divines did not technically speak for the entirety of their faiths, but only for their respective social service agencies, was buried in the eighth paragraph.[55]

As Wagner's bill gained momentum, Myers made arrangements for himself, Ryan, and Goldstein to testify before the Senate Committee on Education and Labor.[56] Myers used his appearance before the Committee not only to stress the importance of securing fair elections and truly independent unions, but also to propose that the bill be amended to require unions to accept all "competent workers without distinction of nationality or race"—a suggestion the Southern-dominated body rejected.[57] Nonetheless, the combined backing of the nation's largest unions, representatives of its major faiths, and the Roosevelt administration—which endorsed the bill after the Supreme Court's decision striking down the NIRA's Section 7(a)—was more than enough to secure Senate passage. On May 16 the upper chamber passed the Wagner Act by the lopsided tally of sixty-three to twelve. "[Senate puts] new claws in the Blue Eagle's collective bargaining guarantee," read the opening sentence of the *Times*'s front-page story.[58]

With the bill's fate now resting with the House of Representatives, Myers went immediately to work enlisting the nation's church councils in the struggle. On May 17, the day after the bill passed in the Senate, he sent two hundred local council heads a copy of the interfaith statement, together with a letter suggesting that Protestant clergymen, preferably in cooperation with their Jewish and Catholic colleagues, write their respective House members and issue their own "public statement[s]" in favor of what was "probably the most important single measure before Congress so far as the freedom of our working people goes."[59] Reaction to the appeal was less uniformly positive than in the case of unemployment insurance or the Recovery Act—hardly surprising when one considers that industry, which had largely acquiesced in the enactment of the NIRA, was monolithically opposed to Wagner's labor bill. Three letters that reached FCC headquarters on a single day in late May illustrate the range of responses. The head of the Toledo Council of Churches was the most enthusiastic, writing to say that he was organizing a letter-writing campaign among local ministers. The head of the Hartford Federation of Churches, while agreeing that the Wagner Act represented "the only possible next step toward a better industrial future" and promising to raise the issue at his group's next meeting, doubted that "it would be possible to get anything like unanimous approval of this point of view." Finally, the Philadelphia Federation of Churches reported that, after discussion of the proposed law, it had elected not to issue a pronouncement, citing the "wide difference of opinion among people who have made a study of the matter."[60]

Even without the unified backing of Protestant church officials, the House passed a version of Wagner's bill on June 19, though not before engaging in seven hours of "stormy" floor debate.[61] At this point the action shifted to a conference committee, which in late June reported a bill that preserved the core of the original. On June 28 both Houses approved the conference report on voice votes and without recorded debate, and on July 6 President Roosevelt signed what was now known as the National Labor Relations Act (NLRA) into law, describing it as "an important step toward the achievement of just and peaceful labor relations in industry."[62] The AFL's William Green went further, hailing the Act as "Labor's Magna Carta." [63]

That was not hyperbole. Between 1936 and 1939 five million American workers joined unions, more than doubling the 1934 union membership figure of three and a half million. By 1939 the Congress of Industrial Organizations (CIO) alone claimed as many members (four million) as the total unionized workforce of a decade earlier—and this at a time when nine million American remained out of work. The AFL, from which the CIO broke off in 1936, likewise swelled to more than four million members by the end of the decade.[64] Hence, in addition to being, as Myers called it, the "most important single measure" taken up during the 74th Congress, the Wagner Act was likely the most significant piece of labor legislation enacted during the twentieth century.

Mainline Protestant Elites and the New Deal: Toward a Fuller Picture

The relationship between mainline Protestant leaders and the Roosevelt administration was not without the occasional rough patch. In the spring of 1936, for example, many moderate church leaders balked when the Roosevelt campaign, in a ham-fisted play for the Northern "church vote," announced the formation of a new membership organization called the Good Neighbor League.[65] Although the League would eventually recruit about three thousand clergymen as dues-paying members, its publicity materials, which often implied that denominational leaders had formally endorsed the Democratic ticket, prompted sharp rebukes from a number of prominent religious officials, including the FCC's Samuel McCrea Cavert.[66] By Election Day it was clear that the group was doing the Roosevelt campaign more harm than good, and the president soon disavowed it.[67]

Another sore spot involved the vexed question of racial segregation. Black church leaders understandably criticized the FCC for blessing recovery programs that, particularly when administered by local officials in the South, implicitly sanctioned Jim Crow. (In response, the FCC's George Haynes helped organize the Joint Committee on National Recovery, which worked to combat discrimination in the NRA, the Agricultural Adjustment Administration, and other New Deal agencies.)[68] Finally, a handful of far-left church officials, led by the Methodist Federation for Social Service's Harry Ward, were convinced that the New Deal's architects were secretly in league with big business, and they urged ministers not to cooperate with what they regarded as a thinly "disguised attempt of Capitalism to save itself now that it is on the skids."[69]

But these were the exceptions. On the whole, both denominational elites and rank-and-file clergymen appear to have been strongly supportive of the New Deal.[70] One valuable source of information concerning the views of average ministers is a remarkable trove of thirty thousand letters that arrived at the White House in late 1935 and early 1936. In the summer of 1935 Roosevelt aides gleaned from public sources the addresses of 121,700 ministers, priests, and rabbis—or about 60 percent of all American clergymen.[71] In late September every person on the list received a letter, signed by the president (or an autopen), asking for information about how the administration's relief programs were affecting "your own parishioners" and "people generally in your community." The letter mentioned two programs by name: the "new Social Security Legislation . . . providing for old age pensions, aid for crippled children and unemployment insurance," and "the Works Program . . . provid[ing] employment at useful work" for those unable to find jobs in the private sector.[72] Perhaps flattered to have their views solicited by the president, nearly one in four recipients took the time to reply, and many of their letters ran to three or more pages. A Commerce Department official tabulated the responses, grouping them as either supportive, supportive but with criticisms, or generally critical. This preliminary tally—based on the first twelve thousand letters received—found that 48.5 percent of the responses fell into the first category, 35 percent into the second, and only 16.5 percent into the third.[73]

Modern analyses of the letters, which are preserved at the Roosevelt Presidential Library in Hyde Park, have generally confirmed the administration's findings.[74] And yet, because scholars have often lumped Protestant responses together with those of Jewish and Catholic religious leaders, it is possible that the Protestant response to the New Deal was less positive than the top-line figures would suggest.[75] In an effort to remedy this potential problem, I conducted my own analysis of Protestant responses from four states: Alabama, Arizona, Connecticut, and Illinois. (The states were selected to account for regional differences in partisanship between the South, West, Northeast, and Midwest; each comes first in an alphabetical list of the states in its region.) Together these states produced 494 letters in which the author revealed a denominational affiliation, either in the letterhead or below the signature. Following the procedure employed by the Roosevelt administration, each letter was coded as giving a positive, mixed, or negative assessment of the New Deal. I then tabulated the number of letters referring to specific programs (e.g., Social Security, the public works program), noting whether the author's evaluation of the program was positive or negative.

My principal finding is that Protestant support for the New Deal was roughly in line with the overall tallies produced by the White House and later historians. As can be seen in Table 3.1, 52 percent of Protestant ministers rated the New Deal favorably, while 35.8 percent offered mixed evaluations and 12.1 percent negative ones. Among the mainline Protestant denominations, Christian or Disciples of Christ, Episcopal, Congregational, and Lutheran clergymen were

Table 3.1 Clergy support for New Deal by state and denomination

State (N)	% Positive	% Mixed	% Negative
Alabama (110)	60.0	30.9	9.1
Arizona (18)	27.8	50.0	22.2
Connecticut (87)	52.9	33.3	13.8
Illinois (279)	50.2	37.6	12.2
Denomination (N)			
Baptist (99)	48.5	33.3	18.2
Christian/Disciples (28)	78.6	21.4	0
Congregational (58)	58.6	27.6	13.8
Episcopalian (51)	64.7	31.4	3.9
Lutheran (43)	60.5	32.6	7.0
Methodist (99)	35.4	52.5	12.1
Presbyterian (75)	46.7	37.3	16.0
Other Protestant (41)	59.5	32.4	8.1
TOTAL (N = 494)	52.0	35.8	12.1

particularly supportive, while Presbyterians were more evenly divided. The least supportive mainline denomination was the Methodists, primarily because many Methodist ministers had yet to forgive FDR and the Democrats for bringing back the "liquor traffic." Support also varied somewhat by region, with Alabama clergymen viewing the New Deal slightly more favorably than clergymen from Connecticut and Illinois. Still, it is noteworthy that even in heavily Republican Connecticut—a state carried by Herbert Hoover in 1932—a majority of ministers expressed support for the administration's recovery effort. Only in Arizona did the administration fail to earn positive marks from a majority of clergymen (a fact that may be due in part to a small sample size).

The major takeaway from Table 3.2 is that most ministers were strongly supportive of core New Deal programs, even if some raised concerns about their implementation or about unrelated issues such as prohibition. The two most commonly mentioned subjects, Social Security and the public works program, appeared in 57.3 and 35.5 percent of letters respectively, and both programs earned overwhelmingly positive reviews. The Civilian Conservation Corps (CCC) and the Tennessee Valley Authority (TVA)—the latter particularly important to Alabamians—likewise earned strongly favorable reviews, though these were mentioned in a relatively small percentage of letters. Prohibition repeal, in contrast, appeared in nearly one in four letters, with more than 97 percent of correspondents faulting FDR for the repeal of the Eighteenth Amendment. The administration's efforts in the areas of agriculture and foreign policy, which were mentioned in 16.8 and 10.8 percent of letters respectively, earned middling grades. (Many ministers with pacifist leanings criticized FDR for increasing, or at

Table 3.2 Clergy support for specific New Deal programs

Issue	% Mentioned	% Positive
Social Security	57.3	85.7
Public Works Program	35.5	68.9
Prohibition Repeal	24.6	2.4
AAA/Agriculture	16.8	41.7
Relief / "Dole"	19.4	12.4
Foreign Policy / Military	10.8	31.5
Spending / Debt	7.5	0
CCC	3.8	94.7
TVA	2.6	92.3

least failing to reduce, military spending.) Finally, 7.5 percent of letters expressed concerns about the long-term costs of FDR's efforts to stimulate the economy.

Perhaps the most noteworthy feature of the letters, however, is how often ministers linked specific New Deal programs to the social teachings of their respective churches. A Baptist minister from Danville, Illinois, heaped praise on the "Social Security Legislation, providing for old age pensions, aid for crippled children, and unemployment insurance," noting that "the churches throughout the centuries have prayed and labored to bring about such measures," which embodied the "principles of Christianity."[76] A Congregational minister from the same state recalled attending the national convention at which his denomination had formulated its Social Creed, observing that he was "very encourage[ed] to see [the] President and Congress speaking in similar terms and working along the same lines."[77] A plainspoken Baptist minister from Connecticut wrote to assure the president that he placed no stock in opinion columnists who tarred FDR as a socialist, declaring: "I'm not afraid of Socialism if the basis of that Socialism be the Golden Rule: 'Do unto others as you would have them do unto you.'"[78] An Alabama Methodist likewise judged the "Social Security Measure . . . one of, if not the greatest statutes . . . any Government has ever produced. It carries out the gist of the Social Creed of the Churches of America, some things the Christian organizations of the world have urged and stood [for] through the centuries."[79] Several ministers included clippings of letters to the editor or sermons in which they had expressed support for particular aspects of the New Deal.[80]

To be sure, the clergy letters of 1935 should not be taken as a perfectly representative sample of Protestant religious leaders. It is possible that ministers opposed to the New Deal were more likely to view the president's letter as a political stunt and thus more likely to refrain from responding. Still, there are good reasons to believe that the views expressed in the letters were roughly in line with clerical opinion writ large. For one thing, nearly 48 percent of ministers offered criticism of at least one administration initiative, suggesting that skeptical ministers were not averse to expressing their views to the president. A still more important consideration is that the center-left economic perspective reflected in most of the responses is consistent with the findings of more sophisticated clergy opinion polls that were conducted about a decade later (as we shall see in chapter 4).

The Stillborn Alliance of Fundamentalism and Big Business

But if mainline ministers tended to approve of the Roosevelt administration's domestic agenda, the same cannot be said of fundamentalist Protestants. Although the number of diehard fundamentalists was small relative to the total population of Protestant ministers, fundamentalists were well-represented in the burgeoning radio industry, and many of them used the new technology to condemn the New Deal as the work of the devil. Some even went so far as to suggest that the omnipresent Blue Eagle was the "Mark of the Beast" described in the Book of Revelation.[81] By 1935 the fundamentalist reaction against the New Deal was sufficiently intense as to capture the attention of FDR's aides. An internal White House memo from that year observed that "the opposition of what one can call the evangelical churches"—the terms *evangelical* and *fundamentalist* were used interchangeably at the time—was "growing steadily more bitter and open."[82]

The list of fundamentalist grievances against FDR was long. It began with the president's role in repealing prohibition. The colorful J. Frank Norris, pastor of Fort Worth's First Baptist Church, complained that Roosevelt had broken all of his campaign pledges save one: as promised, he had turned "the rivers of liquor back on the homes of the American people."[83] Other prominent fundamentalists, including Gerald B. Winrod and Gerald L. K. Smith, faulted FDR for joining forces with the "foreign" hordes. Winrod saw great significance in the fact that Jews were overrepresented in the president's "Brains Trust," and he launched a radio broadcast and newspaper to warn Americans about the perils of the "Jewish New Deal." Smith, a peripatetic Disciples of Christ minister and close ally of Louisiana Governor Huey "Kingfish" Long, was an equally virulent anti-Semite who regularly issued vague warnings about the sinister machinations of the president's advisors.[84] Although Winrod and Smith were somewhat marginal figures in the broader fundamentalist movement, both men commanded substantial followings, at least for a time. In 1938 Winrod, fresh from a whirlwind tour of Nazi Germany, announced his candidacy for the U.S. Senate; he lost the race, but only after Kansas Republican party leaders coaxed a popular ex-governor out of retirement to run against him in the primary. Four years later Smith polled more than 100,000 votes in his own unsuccessful bid to represent Michigan in the Senate.[85]

Mainstream fundamentalists were more likely to attack the president for his expansive conception of federal power, though they, too, frequently dabbled in anti-Semitism. The Baptist William B. Riley, who oversaw a large fundamentalist network in the upper Midwest and would later serve as a mentor to the young Billy Graham, complained that Roosevelt was "painting America red," likely with the aid of Jewish conspirators. Indeed, Riley speculated that the plans for the diabolically complex agencies at the heart of the New Deal—the NRA, the Agricultural Adjustment Administration (AAA), the Works Progress Administration (WPA), and the like—had been drawn up in Moscow as part of a deliberate scheme to bring about "not alone the fall of the American Government after the manner of Russia's collapse, but the overthrow of every civilized government in the world."[86] Norris was even more creative. His 1935 book, *New*

Dealism (Russian Communism) Exposed, offered readers a glimpse inside the CCC camps, where unsuspecting young recruits were being trained for the inevitable imposition of martial law.[87]

In the end, the notion that fundamentalist opposition posed a serious threat to Roosevelt's 1936 reelection bid proved illusory. Notwithstanding the vigorous protests of preachers such as Norris, Smith, and Winrod, FDR ultimately defeated his Republican opponent, Alf Landon, by more than five hundred electoral votes. To be sure, the president captured only a bare majority of the white Protestant vote (as compared to some 90 percent of the Jewish and Catholic vote). And yet he fared somewhat better with this demographic than had previous Democratic nominees.[88] Indeed, FDR won by healthy margins, not only in areas with large Catholic and Jewish populations, but even in predominately rural states, such as Winrod's (and Landon's) home state of Kansas, where non-Protestants were few and far between.

One likely explanation for the fundamentalists' impotence at the polls is that they labored in isolation. That is to say, they never succeeded in forging an alliance with the well-funded, business-backed groups, such as the American Liberty League and the National Association of Manufacturers (NAM), that were simultaneously working to derail the New Deal. The underlying problem, as in the Progressive Era, was that most fundamentalists were enthusiastic supporters of state power when used for the purpose of policing morality, while the major backers of the Liberty League—Irénée du Pont and his brothers, J. Howard Pew, John J. Raskob, William H. Stayton, Jouett Shouse, James Wadsworth—were essentially libertarians (though the term was not yet in common usage).[89] Almost to a man, the pro-business conservatives believed that individuals—at least ones who were wealthy, white, and male—should be left free to conduct their personal and economic affairs with as little state oversight as possible. Indeed, the Liberty League was born from what remained of the du Pont-funded Association Against the Prohibition Amendment (AAPA), and for many fundamentalists this fact alone was reason enough to oppose it.[90]

There was also the small matter of party allegiance. Although fundamentalist congregations could be found in all parts of the country, many of the movement's leaders were Southerners who distrusted both Republicans and Northeastern financial interests. Hence, while they shared the Liberty League's hatred of the man in the White House, they could not ignore the fact that the League's ultimate aim was to replace FDR with a Northern Republican.[91] (Nor did it help that the League's most prominent Democratic supporters, including John J. Raskob, had strong ties to the Northeastern financial establishment.)[92]

And yet, while most of the nation's leading fundamentalists remained suspicious of FDR's corporate critics, there were at least two joint ventures between conservative ministers and businessmen that moved beyond the planning stages. The first was Spiritual Mobilization—an organization cofounded in 1935 by James W. Fifield, the charismatic senior pastor of the First Congregational Church of Los Angeles. Fifield benefited from the fact that his congregation was one of the wealthiest and most fashionable in the city, with a membership that included a number of well-connected conservative activists, including Leonard Read and W. C. Mullendore, and such cultural luminaries as the *Los Angeles Times* publisher Harry Chandler, the Caltech president and Nobel laureate Robert A Millikan, and the filmmaker Cecil B. DeMille. Catering to his audience, he preached that the aims of the New Deal were directly antithetical to the message of the Gospel, and he initially envisioned a relatively modest organization that would disseminate this message in pamphlet form. (A frequent theme of the group's early publications was that the Eighth Commandment—"Thou shalt not steal"—expressly forbade redistributive programs that redirected resources from the wealthy to the less fortunate.)[93]

Fifield's labors on behalf of America's put-upon millionaires did not go unnoticed, however, and by the late 1930s his organization was drawing praise from a wide range of prominent conservatives. Former President Hoover was a frequent correspondent and advisor, as were the heads of the Los Angeles Chamber of Commerce (Read) and Southern California Edison (Mullendore). Buoyed by their support, Fifield set his sights on corporate donors. In 1940, he secured an invitation to speak at the national convention of the National Association of Manufacturers (NAM), where he addressed five thousand business owners and executives on the perils of unchecked federal power, urging his audience to be on its guard against "the menace of autocracy approaching through bureaucracy."[94] The speech struck a chord with the anti–New Deal crowd. With the disaster of 1936 still fresh in their minds, conservative corporate heads were casting about for alternatives to the Liberty League and its kin, which FDR had succeeded in tarring as front groups for industry. They needed an organization that could articulate a principled case against the New Deal but was not obviously connected to corporate interests, and Spiritual Mobilization fit the bill. Within a few years Fifield would be pulling in large contributions from U.S. Steel, Sun Oil, Republic Steel, National Steel, Gulf Oil, General Motors, Firestone Tire & Rubber, Chrysler Motors, IBM, Shell Oil, Sears & Roebuck, and many more corporate behemoths. And by the end of the 1940s he would possess sufficient resources to launch a multipronged assault on the welfare state, including a brisk pamphlet business, a widely distributed newsletter, and a nationally syndicated radio program.[95]

But while Spiritual Mobilization offers an example of fruitful cooperation between business and the clergy (or at least one clergyman), it is also the exception that proves the rule. That is to say, the group owed its success in no small part to Fifield's highly unorthodox conception of Christianity—a quasi-theological worldview in which the teachings of Jesus were more or less indistinguishable from those of Friedrich Hayek and the other libertarian economists who would soon be grouped together as the Austrian School. (Fifield kept a large stock of Hayek's 1944 best seller *The Road to Serfdom* on hand to distribute to interested clergymen.)[96] An avowed theological liberal, Fifield had little interest in questions of sin or salvation, and little patience for those who insisted on a literal interpretation of the Bible. The theological warrant for his economic views, such as it was, originated in the idea that human beings were endowed by God with inalienable rights, including the right to be free of government coercion in matters that did not involve direct harm to third parties.[97] If he succeeded where others did not, it was because he believed what almost no else believed: that Christian principles, properly understood, prohibited the use of official coercion to improve society, whether by regulating morality or aiding the widow and the orphan.

The second example of organized Protestant opposition to the Roosevelt administration was initially less concerned with rolling back social welfare programs than with ensuring that conservative religious groups were treated fairly by federal regulators. More specifically, the early leaders of what would become the National Association of Evangelicals (NAE) were convinced that an unholy alliance of liberal politicians and clergymen had conspired to seize control of the nation's religious life. They noted, for example, that the State Department relied on the Federal Council of Churches to help vet the visa applications of Protestant missionaries, and they saw signs that theological considerations were being unfairly inserted into the decision-making process.[98] But the major bone of contention was access to the airwaves. In 1928, the National Broadcasting Company (NBC), alarmed by the rise of Bible-quoting hucksters who lined their pockets with their listeners' donations, ceased selling airtime for religious programs. The network continued to air unpaid religious broadcasts, however, as part of its federally mandated responsibility to provide public service (or "sustaining time") programming. CBS adopted a similar policy in 1931, and both networks relied on the Federal Council of Churches to allocate the broadcast time set aside for Protestant programming (national Jewish and Catholic organizations performed the same role on behalf of their respective faiths). The Council, for its part, used its relationship with NBC and CBS to ensure that only mainstream preachers gained access to the nation's airwaves, and many local church federations performed a similar function with respect to local religious programming. Thus, the only available outlet for fundamentalists who hoped to reach a national audience was the Mutual Broadcasting Corporation, which continued to accept paid religious programming. By 1940, however, rumors were swirling that the two FCC's—the Federal Council of Churches and the Federal Communications Commission—were pressuring Mutual to adopt a version of the NBC policy, with the result that several popular fundamentalist programs, including Charles Fuller's wildly popular *Old Fashioned Revival Hour*, would be forced off the air.[99]

These were the considerations that led a small group of conservative clergymen and lay leaders to a 1942 convention in St. Louis, where they formally launched the National Association of Evangelicals (NAE).[100] Most of the group's organizers were fundamentalist ministers or wealthy laymen from the Northeast and upper Midwest, though a handful of Southerners also joined the effort. Their denominational affiliations ran the gamut of American Protestantism, but they were unified by a shared conviction that the Federal Council of Churches had become, in the words of one Michigan minister, "a serpentine octopus . . . which is strangling the churches of America."[101] The Boston Congregationalist minister Harold Ockenga, who was elected to serve as the NAE's first president, used his convention address to denounce the Federal Council as "the citadel" of "liberalism," and the "local council[s] of the churches" as its faithful minions.[102] (Ockenga nursed a particular grudge against the Boston Council of Churches, which tightly controlled access to station WBZ, the city's NBC affiliate.)[103] The group concluded its inaugural meeting by adopting a plan of action that stressed equal access to radio time, cooperation in mission efforts, establishing better "relations with government," and ensuring the continued "separation of church and state"—the last point being code for ensuring that no taxpayer dollars found their way to Catholic institutions.[104]

But for all their talk about ensuring equal access to the airwaves and the mission fields, Ockenga and the other early leaders of the NAE did little to hide the fact that they shared a common political vision. Indeed, from its inception the NAE defined itself in opposition to "liberal" Protestantism, a term that encompassed all church officials who believed that government had a moral obligation to protect citizens from unscrupulous employers and the vicissitudes of the market. In this sense, the group's ideological commitments resembled those of Fifield and Spiritual Mobilization, yet there were critical differences in how the two groups viewed their missions and framed their messages. In contrast to Fifield, the NAE's leaders, at least during the 1940s, rarely claimed a biblical warrant for dismantling the welfare state; nor did they contend that Christian principles expressly forbade state intervention in the economic realm. Rather, they insisted that the Bible had nothing to say about the proper ordering of the nation's economic life, and that mainline leaders were reading into the scriptures a "social gospel" that was not to be found in the text. J. Elwin Wright, another principal founder of the NAE, undoubtedly spoke for the bulk of the group's members when he lambasted the Federal Council for neglecting "spiritual issue[s]" in favor of "secondary matters such as social legislation, reform movements, and . . . kindred objectives."[105] (As with most conservative Protestant bodies, however, the NAE was never quite consistent on this point; it regularly inserted itself into political controversies, from the McCarthy-era investigations into communism to battles over state funding of parochial schools, all while disavowing any interest in "lobbying.")

Perhaps because of the less combative way in which it framed its policy positions, the NAE attracted a considerable following among conservative churches and clergymen during the 1940s and 1950s. It also drew financial support from several prominent Midwestern businessmen, though none who were capable of matching the largesse that IBM, General Motors, Shell Oil, and other corporations showered on Spiritual Mobilization.[106] Yet, in the end, the NAE never really established itself as a bona fide counterweight to the FCC. Nor did its formation inspire anything like the mass exodus from the mainline ecumenical bodies that its founders had hoped to set in motion. By the end of the 1940s, the organization claimed barely 750,000 members, and this figure was achieved only by the inclusion of several Pentecostal and Holiness denominations—highly decentralized groups whose members likely remained mostly unaware of the new organization. (The nation's largest theologically conservative Protestant denomination, the Southern Baptist Convention, declined repeated invitations to join the NAE.)[107]

Much to the chagrin of ministers such as Wright and Ockenga, relatively few white middle-class believers seemed much concerned by the "serpentine octopus" that was the Federal Council of Churches, nor were they particularly alarmed by the Roosevelt administration's embrace of "social legislation." Indeed, many citizens seemed downright pleased by the new programs—Social Security, unemployment insurance, federal wage and hours laws—that James Myers and other mainline church officials had helped push through Congress. But if conservative Protestants opposed to the New Deal made little headway during the 1930s and early 1940s, they would fare somewhat better in the aftermath of World War II, when a combination of Cold War anxieties, economic uncertainty, and labor unrest combined to fuel a new round of attacks on the welfare state's religious foundations.

PART II
WHY THE CENTER HELD

4

The Battle for the Clergy

Unless we can show to the ministers of the country that the American free enterprise system is sound and ... in harmony with the spirit of Jesus Christ, I am inclined to believe that the church will become an active, influential agency against this system in which we believe....
—Norman Vincent Peale to J. Howard Pew (1948)

In early February 1947 a group of National Association of Manufacturers officials converged on Pittsburgh, Pennsylvania, where the Federal Council of Churches was sponsoring a conference on the theme of "The Church and Economic Life." At first glance it may seem puzzling that the delegation, which included three former presidents of the organization, was not headed for Washington, D.C. That, after all, was where a Republican-led Congress—the first in sixteen years—was mobilizing for action on a host of issues that were at the core of NAM's policy agenda, from the president's annual budget (whose spending provisions NAM deemed far too generous), to efforts to combat inflation, to proposals to strengthen the Federal Trade Commission's anti-monopoly enforcement powers (which NAM opposed). Particularly crucial, from NAM's perspective, was the effort, already under way in the offices of Senator Robert Taft and Representative Fred Hartley, to draft legislation that would reverse the most labor-friendly provisions of the New Deal–era National Labor Relations Act—by, for example, giving employers more room to influence unionization elections and authorizing states to pass so-called right-to-work laws that effectively banned union security agreements.[1]

But instead of decamping for the capital, the NAM officials headed for Pittsburgh's William Penn Hotel. Poised on the cusp of a series of major policy victories, the executives worried that the FCC conference, if it came out strongly against NAM's agenda, might give lawmakers in Washington and elsewhere cold feet. With Congress now controlled by ideological allies, the last thing NAM needed was for the Council to proclaim that thirty million American Protestants stood firmly behind Truman's domestic agenda, with its promises of full employment and universal health insurance, all paid for by steeply progressive rates of taxation. In the words of Alfred P. Haake, a NAM member who was also briefly on the payroll of Spiritual Mobilization, the mission of the management men would therefore be to prevent "the socialistic forces" in the FCC from passing any resolutions that would tend to "undermine the idea of freedom itself with demands for increased security"—"freedom itself" being shorthand for NAM's legislative agenda for 1947.[2]

Only a decade before, the idea that a group of well-connected conservative activists would expend such energy attempting to influence the results of an FCC study conference would have seemed absurd. To be sure, the New Deal years had been good ones for mainline Protestant leaders, in the sense that the electorate had endorsed, or at least acquiesced in, the creation of a nascent welfare state— something that mainline leaders had long supported but that few of them had deemed possible in the years before the Great Depression. Viewed from another angle, however, the Depression years were trying times for the mainline—and for organized religion in general. Partly as a result of declining birth rates, a handful of denominations, including the Methodists and Presbyterians, began to suffer net losses in membership. Rates of attendance at religious services declined, too. Whether because they were exhausted from weekdays spent trying to scrape together money for food and rent, or perhaps because they couldn't afford a new suit or dress, many nominally Protestant citizens simply stopped going to church. Contributions to religious bodies plummeted as well—no surprise, since one in four Americans were out of work, and many more had watched their savings evaporate in the stock market crash of 1929 and the subsequent wave of bank failures. One might have expected Americans to turn to religion for solace, but many of them apparently looked instead to secular forms of popular entertainment, such as films and novels. Between 1931 and 1935 sales of religious books—as a percentage of all books sold in the U.S.—dropped by a remarkable 45 percent.[3]

By the mid-1940s, however, the trends of the Depression years had begun to reverse themselves, and by the end of the decade the nation would be on its way to a full-blown religious revival. The story of how the religious depression of the 1930s turned into the religion boom of the 1950s begins after World War II with the return of millions of American GIs from the European and Pacific theaters. With the war behind them, Americans began gradually readjusting to the rhythms of peacetime life. For many of them, the first step was to find a spouse and purchase a home in the suburbs, the second was to start a family, and the third was to join a church or synagogue. Although suburban communities were hardly a new invention, those that arose in the late 1950s were "qualitatively different from earlier eras" in the sense that "millions of Americans in the same stage of the family life cycle now lived in close proximity to one another. A suburban culture was a byproduct. Families with children were normative and pervasive, and part of normal family life was the church."[4] When asked why membership in a formal religious body was so important, the new suburbanites cited practical considerations as often as spiritual ones: they wanted Sunday schools that would teach their children right from wrong; they wanted ministers who were trained in the relatively new art of family counseling; and most of all they wanted what William Whyte, in his best-selling 1956 book *The Organization Man*, called "a sense of community."[5]

The end result of these converging social dynamics was a dramatic spike in church membership and attendance that was driven almost entirely by the behavior of men and women in their twenties and early thirties. As Robert Putnam and David Campbell have pointed out, weekly church attendance by Americans in their twenties increased from 31 percent in 1950 "to an all-time record for young adults of 51 percent in . . . 1957, an astonishing rate of change in seven years, implying millions of new churchgoers every year."[6] By the mid-1950s nearly three-quarters of Americans would claim membership in a specific church or synagogue, and nearly half would report attending services on a weekly basis.

For upwardly mobile Protestants, the pull of the "prestige" denominations was particularly strong. Studies of church switching in the 1950s and early 1960s found that men who exceeded their fathers' level of educational or professional attainment were regularly moving "up" the denominational ladder, abandoning their fundamentalist or Baptist roots in favor of membership in elite-dominated Presbyterian, Congregationalist, or Episcopal congregations.[7] As a result, the growth rates of the mainline churches, with the sole exception of the Methodist church, far surpassed that of the general population.[8]

That the Federal Council of Churches was enjoying a return to national prominence was due in large part to the surge in mainline church attendance. But the FCC's revival was also fueled by an unanticipated shift in the political landscape: With the advent of the Cold War, ecumenical projects came to be viewed less as a threat to particular denominational traditions and more as a bulwark against the spread of "godless" communism. Eager to sell the public on the Marshall Plan and U.S. membership in the United Nations, foreign policy luminaries including John Foster Dulles and General George Marshall turned to the nation's largest ecumenical body for help. Prominent FCC leaders, including the Methodist Bishop G. Bromley Oxnam, eagerly answered the call, endorsing the United Nations and organizing petition drives and rallies in support of U.S. aid to war-torn European nations.[9] Oxnam and like-minded religious leaders reasoned that major milestones in the Protestant ecumenical movement were by definition defeats for global communism, since they demonstrated that Americans would never submit to an ideology that denied the existence of the Almighty. Polls showed that average Americans were similarly enthusiastic about the idea of greater cooperation between the Protestant denominations, at least when ecumenical projects were framed as a critical weapon in America's Cold War arsenal. In 1950 the percentage of Americans favoring the creation of a unified Protestant church reached an all-time high of 50 percent.[10]

For Albert Haake, James Fifield, and other devout conservative activists, the postwar revival posed an obvious dilemma. On the one hand, as devout believers, they could hardly complain about the fact that Americans were once again filling the pews on Sundays. On the other hand, they were well aware that many clergymen—and certainly most denominational and ecumenical leaders—were not great fans of the profit motive. Only a few weeks before the Pittsburgh conference, an interfaith group of clergymen affiliated with the FCC, the Synagogue Council of America, and the National Catholic Welfare Council had issued a joint statement declaring that economic resources had been "given in trust to man to be administered, under God, for the temporal welfare of all, and not for the exclusive benefit of the few."[11] Almost simultaneously, the FCC produced a study document—denounced in the pages of *U.S. News* by the conservative publisher David Lawrence—that criticized large employers for ignoring the "deadly" effects of mind-numbing work routines, arbitrary personnel decisions, and the ever-present threat of layoffs.[12] The notion that economic resources came with ethical strings attached was of course deeply rooted in American Protestant thought, and also in Jewish and Catholic teaching. But to Haake and Fifield, such pronouncements smacked of nothing so much as godless collectivism. They could not be allowed to stand unchallenged.

Back in Pittsburgh, Haake and the NAM delegation sensed a setup. The conference agenda called for attendees to discuss a series of ethical dilemmas arising from the American economic system, from the dangers of concentrated economic power to potential holes in the social safety net. The existence of a predetermined agenda was nothing out of the ordinary, but this one was deeply problematic, according to Haake, in that it began from the false premise that American capitalism was ethically compromised, putting the onus on "the management men" to disprove the charge.[13] Things went from bad to worse when the delegates broke into small groups to begin their deliberations. The problem, Haake informed Pew, was that everyone "had special axes to grind. They had apparently come for the purpose of harnessing God to their wagons instead of merely serving Him. Some wanted the conference to endorse the closed shop, others wanted the guaranteed annual wage, still others wanted endorsements of consumer cooperatives, the fair employment practice bills, and so on including equal rights for negroes." Summing up the conference's first day, Haake lamented—without a hint of irony—that "every group there, except management, came to get something for itself."[14]

That night Haake met with Fifield, the NAM's Noel Sargent, Congressman Ralph Gwinn, and a handful of other business-friendly delegates to discuss how best to right the ship. The plan they eventually arrived at was remarkably simple: they would demand that the "radical" delegates tone down their critique of free-market policies. Failing that, they would embarrass the FCC by issuing a scathing minority report highlighting the interdependence of spiritual, political, and economic freedom—"when one fails all must fail"—and denouncing "modern collectivism" as the work of the Devil.[15] Events came to a head when Haake and his allies confronted the FCC's newly elected president, Charles P. Taft, with their threat to split the convention. In an effort to quell the insurgency, Taft promised to ensure that "there would come no affirmations out of the session, and that the various questions raised would appear [in the final report] only as questions to be considered, without any conclusions." The free market faction found Taft's suggestion "very fair and reasonable." Still, Haake let it be known that he would be carrying the draft minority report in his pocket and would not hesitate to "jump up at any moment" if the "radical group" should attempt to undermine the bargain via the amendment process.

In the end, this step proved unnecessary. Taft was true to his word, and the "radicals" were kept in check by the strategic positioning of three present or former NAM officers on the reporting committee. Although the final report of the conference leaned "somewhat to the left," Haake judged it "not bad." It declared that "property" represented "a trusteeship under God," but, crucially, it did not condemn the "excessive concentration of wealth"—an amendment to that effect was defeated by a single vote—and it urged labor unions to cease all forms of protest that ran counter to "the welfare of the entire community." *Time* magazine thus described the Pittsburgh gathering as a "watered-down version" of "England's famed Melvern Conference," the 1941 religious conclave in which prominent Anglican leaders had endorsed the welfare state and condemned economic inequality on biblical grounds.[16]

Haake, for his part, gleefully reported that the "radicals"—whose ranks included Bishop Oxnam and J. Kermit Eby, a minister employed by the CIO— "were disgusted with the report . . . and said they had failed to get anything for the people."[17] But while disaster had been narrowly averted, he warned anyone who would listen that the Pittsburgh conference should serve as a wakeup call for business. If the nation's corporate leaders were to have any hope of blocking Truman's domestic agenda, they would have to find some way of blunting the influence of the left-leaning clergymen who were preaching to millions of American churchgoers every Sunday—or, better yet, some way of reeducating them so that they appreciated the benefits of unregulated markets.

A Damned Hard Job

Thanks to the dramatic confrontation in Pittsburgh, and also to the arrival of the first hard data concerning the political and economic views of the clergy, Haake would soon gain a number of powerful allies in his struggle to recruit religious leaders to the libertarian banner. Three men in particular would spend much of the 1950s overseeing various projects aimed at creating a more pliant clergy: J. Howard Pew, the wealthy head of Sun Oil; Jasper Crane, a retired DuPont executive and head of NAM's clergy-industry program; and Noel Sargent, an Episcopal lay leader and NAM official.

Pew was among the first people Haake contacted to share his concerns about the Pittsburgh Conference. His decision to send the oil executive a lengthy overview of the proceedings may be explained by the fact that the two men were natural ideological allies; both were lay leaders in their respective mainline denominations (Pew was a Presbyterian), and Pew was, if anything, even more radically libertarian in his economic views than Haake. But there was another reason Haake chose to confide in Pew: he was one of the wealthiest men in America, and having recently announced his retirement as head of Sun Oil, he would soon have both time and money to devote to other projects. Clearly, it was Haake's hope that Pew would pour at least part of his $100 million fortune into a campaign to combat "the anti-religious communistic teachings [of] the church people."[18]

The sixty-five-year-old Pew was by this point well-known for funding attacks on the New Deal and its progeny. In the 1930s he had been a major financial backer of both the Liberty League and NAM, and he had just finished a term as chairman and chief fundraiser for NAM's National Industrial Information Committee, a propaganda arm whose principal aim was to convince the public that the economic problems of the immediate postwar years—high inflation, frequent labor stoppages, and the like—could be laid squarely at the feet of organized labor and its allies in the Truman administration.[19] In an effort to awaken American voters to the perils of social legislation, he would soon begin funding a number of influential libertarian think tanks, including Leonard Read's Foundation for Economic Education (FEE) and the American Enterprise Association (AEA), frequently cutting checks as large as $100,000 or more when he believed that the group in question was successfully sowing doubts about the legitimacy of the welfare state.[20,21]

Like Haake, Pew was convinced that mainline religious leaders represented one of the most formidable obstacles to rolling back the various New Deal–era programs that were currently "stealing from those who have and giving to those who have not."[22] And on this score, at least, the aging oilman was not blinded by paranoia. A series of surveys conducted in the late 1940s with input from Pew and other NAM officials showed that mainline clergymen were indeed overwhelmingly hostile to Pew's brand of libertarianism.[23] The most sophisticated attempt to discern the economic views of the nation's religious leaders took place in 1949. Under the direction of its politically conservative founder, Claude Robinson, the Princeton-based Opinion Research Corporation (ORC) contacted fifteen hundred randomly selected Protestant, Catholic, and Jewish clergymen, their names and addresses drawn from church yearbooks, city directories, and other publicly available sources. Respondents were asked a battery of questions concerning the ethics of capitalism, the state of labor relations, and whether corporations and business leaders were meeting their ethical obligations to the community. From the perspective of the study's sponsors, the poll's most troubling finding was that the nation's clergymen were fixated on "the human factor in the industrial equation"—that is, the question of whether industry was meeting its obligation to provide average Americans with "good working conditions, fair and just wages . . . and honest products." Although Jewish and Catholic clergymen were the most consistently negative in their assessments of the "American business system," most Protestant ministers—or at least a solid plurality of them—agreed that the nation's corporations were falling short of the mark. For example, 58 percent of Protestant respondents agreed that there was an "inherent conflict between business as it exists in this country and Christian . . . ideals and principles" (compared to 36 percent who disagreed with the statement); 45 percent believed there was "little economic justice in the way our business system distributes wealth" (compared to 39 percent who disagreed); 53 percent agreed that American corporations were guilty of wasting natural resources (compared to 37 percent who disagreed); 64 percent expressed either strong or moderate support for raising taxes on corporations (with 24 percent opposed); and 62 percent favored raising the federal minimum wage (with 29 percent opposed). Nor were Protestant ministers keeping these views to themselves. Fully 58 percent reported that they had recently addressed "business or economic problems" in their sermons.[24]

The deeper one dug into the findings, the bleaker the picture became. In only one region of the country, the South, were clergymen convinced that big business was meeting its ethical obligations.[25] (Ironically, the nation's poorest region was also the only one in which a plurality of clergymen believed that the American economic system was currently achieving "a high degree of economic justice in the distribution of wealth.") Even more worrisome were the discrepancies between younger and older ministers. The youngest respondents—those under thirty-four—were the most vociferous critics of big business. Fully 70 percent of them favored higher taxes on corporate profits; 56 percent judged the current distribution of wealth unjust; and a remarkable 50 percent *strongly* favored increasing the minimum wage (an additional 20 percent reported moderate support for the idea). The findings must have been particularly galling for Pew, who had asked Robinson—apparently in all seriousness—to include a question asking what ministers "think about taking money from the capitalistic system and at the same time preaching against it—whether that is ethical or not."[26] Although Robinson ignored the suggestion, the answer was easy enough to discern.

At roughly the same time that the ORC was gathering the first reliable data on the political views of the clergy, a different group of social scientists was uncovering evidence that the nation's leading citizens were increasingly concentrated in the most liberal of the mainline denominations. To be sure, the popular perception that the wealthy and well-educated were clustered in a handful of denominations—by most accounts, the Episcopalians, Presbyterians, Congregationalists, and Unitarians—dated to the nineteenth century. In the 1940s and 1950s, the arrival of more sophisticated polling techniques allowed academic sociologists and political scientists to confirm the conventional wisdom: by one count, the percentage of college graduates in the nation's Episcopal, Presbyterian, and Congregationalist congregations was more than triple that of the Baptists and nearly twice that of the Methodists.[27] The new academic studies also complicated popular perceptions by showing that the relationship between church and class was anything but static. Upwardly mobile citizens, it became clear, tended to switch denominations as they climbed the socioeconomic ladder (or in anticipation of climbing it). And with few exceptions, they switched into churches populated by the sorts of people they hoped to become. Typically, this meant leaving behind the fundamentalist, Pentecostal, or Baptist churches of one's youth in order to seek membership in a more fashionable Episcopalian or Presbyterian congregation.[28] The journalist Vance Packard, after interviewing several upwardly mobile church switchers, summed up the basic pattern: "For the majority of Americans . . . going to church is the nice thing that proper people do on Sundays. It advertises their respectability, gives them a warm feeling that they are behaving in a way their God-fearing ancestors would approve, and adds (they hope) a few cubits to their social stature by throwing them with a social group with which they wish to be identified."[29]

From the perspective of conservative activists like Pew and Haake, these were deeply troubling findings. For while Packard's church switchers may have been less interested in dogma than their ancestors, the upshot of the new sociological research was that the nation's future CEOs, elected officials, and civic leaders were heavily concentrated, and were likely to become even more concentrated, in churches which taught that Christian stewardship principles not only permitted but actually demanded some form of social welfare state to protect vulnerable citizens from the vicissitudes of the market.

Even before seeing the results of the ORC poll or the new academic studies of religion and class, however, Haake was well aware that any attempt to transform the mainline churches into champions of free enterprise would face long odds. And, to his credit, he made no attempt to sugarcoat this fact in his correspondence with his potential benefactor. "I shall not beautify the thing by calling it a 'task,'" he wrote to Pew after the Pittsburgh conference; "it is a plain, damned hard JOB." A job so hard, in fact, that it could only be carried out by a well-funded and competently run organization without obvious ties to business—a group other than NAM, in other words. And Haake was not shy about suggesting an already up-and-running organization to lead the charge. "There is now need for SPIRITUAL MOBILIZATION," he wrote.[30]

Spiritual Immobilization

By early 1948 Pew had agreed to bankroll a plan that, if successful, would transform the Reverend James Fifield's anti–New Deal organization, Spiritual Mobilization, from a one-man operation into a major player in debates over the ethics of the welfare state—a veritable counterweight to the liberal voices in the mainline denominational hierarchies and the Federal Council of Churches. On paper Fifield's group seemed to be doing quite well, even without Pew's financial backing. In 1948 alone the group secured $5,000 donations—the maximum amount allowed under its charter—from U.S. Steel, Sun Oil, Republic Steel, National Steel, Gulf Oil, General Motors, Firestone Tire and Rubber, Chrysler Motors, and American Rolling Mill. Other large companies, including IBM, Ohio Oil, Sears and Roebuck, Shell Oil, Standard Oil of Ohio, Standard Oil of California, and Youngstown Sheet and Tube cut checks of at least $1,000. As his budget expanded, Fifield began to experiment with diverse ways of transmitting his antiregulatory message to America's clergymen and their parishioners. Every month he distributed 125,000 copies of a newsletter containing a fresh batch of dire warnings about leftist politicians and their plans to extinguish the free enterprise system. He also sponsored wildly popular sermon contests, handing out $5,000 in prize money to the best entries—out of 24,000 submissions—on such themes as "The Perils of Freedom." And in 1949 he launched *Freedom Story*, a nationally syndicated radio program featuring thinly veiled critiques of the welfare state.[31]

Yet there were problems. For one, the group's myriad activities were expensive, and even with reliable corporate backing Fifield struggled to keep it afloat. Moreover, there was precious little evidence to suggest that the group was having a measurable impact on clerical opinion. It surely didn't help that its newsletters were both hilariously ham-handed in their treatment of ethical questions and nakedly partisan. Fifield, not a subtle thinker, used his monthly editorials to lay out a Manichean dichotomy in which any minister who was not unalterably opposed to the welfare state was guilty of aiding and abetting the Soviets. ("How much worse must things get before YOU get into action in behalf of Freedom?" he asked on the front page of a 1948 monthly bulletin. "On which side is YOUR influence? Do your parishioners understand your attitude toward pagan collectivism?"—"pagan collectivism" being, of course, shorthand for the New Deal/

Fair Deal agenda.)[32] Then there was the fact that the group's printed materials were virtually devoid of religious content, aside from the occasional reference to enigmatic Bible verses about thrift and self-reliance. If the goal was to convince ministers that there were specifically *theological* problems with the current drift of domestic policy, the precise nature of those problems remained curiously unspecified.

What was worse, the group's image took a serious hit in February 1947 when the *Nation*'s Carey McWilliams published a scathing investigative piece entitled "The Battle for the Clergy." The article's thesis was that Spiritual Mobilization was simply a front group for NAM and the nation's largest corporations, an attempt to deceive unsuspecting ministers by cloaking industry's antiregulatory agenda in religious garb. Why else, he asked, would the group refuse to disclose its financial backers? And why else would it use such dubious methods to distribute its propaganda, reeling in ministers with innocuous-sounding advertisements in left-leaning religious periodicals, such as the *Christian Century*, and then inundating them with economic tracts from conservative and libertarian polemicists, including Friedrich Hayek, Ludwig von Mises, and John T. Flynn? Adding insult to injury, McWilliams had uncovered old sermon transcripts in which Fifield had revealed himself as a bigot, railing against fair housing laws and warning his largely white congregation "not . . . to turn the town [of Los Angeles] over to Jews, Mexicans, and Negroes."[33]

Pew's ambitious plan aimed to solve Spiritual Mobilization's problems in a single stroke. He would agree to lead a major fundraising initiative on the group's behalf, but only on the condition that Fifield hand over the organizational reins to Norman Vincent Peale, pastor of New York City's Marble Collegiate Church. (Fifield, who complained constantly about the stress brought on by his two full-time jobs, was generally amenable to the idea of transitioning into a figurehead role.) Aside from his libertarian economic views, Peale's chief attribute was that he was a far less polarizing figure than Fifield—a man known less for conservative political diatribes than for his sunny demeanor and mastery of pop psychology. And it certainly didn't hurt that he was rapidly becoming a national celebrity, thanks to the recent publication of a best-selling self-help book, *Guide to Confident Living*, and a series of glowing magazine profiles. (In 1952 an even more successful book, *The Power of Positive Thinking*, would begin its remarkable run of 186 consecutive weeks on the *New York Times* bestseller list.) Peale was also well connected in the corporate world. He addressed dozens of trade groups and men's clubs every year, commanding $400 to $500 per appearance, and several prominent executives served on the advisory board of his devotional magazine, *Guideposts*. (Many of them ordered bulk subscriptions for their employees, hoping to substitute the power of prayer for the power of union organizing).[34]

Here, it seemed, was a man with all of Fifield's strengths and virtually none of his limitations—a man who could, as Pew put, "get the ear of the liberals."[35]

The ability to get the ear of the liberals was, perhaps surprisingly, the sole criterion by which the theologically conservative Pew seems to have judged potential clerical allies. Indeed, he repeatedly referred to Peale as "the greatest minister in America," notwithstanding the fact that the Reformed minister's theology, such as it was, was about as far from John Calvin's *Institutes* as it was possible to imagine.[36] Whereas ministers in the Reformed tradition had traditionally foregrounded the vast chasm separating even the most virtuous of human beings from their perfect Creator, Peale viewed Christianity as a commodity that was best marketed by sanding down its harsher edges. Indeed, the cherub-faced Midwestern transplant, who had little to say about matters of sin or salvation, urged his listeners (and readers) to focus on religion's "practical uses"—its ability to help believers "overcome fear and worry, hate and selfishness," to "withstand disappointments, illness, sorrow, and any other blows which may lie in store for you." Admirers described his sermons as a kind of "spiritual therapy" that worked "better than medicine," and several New York doctors were said to prescribe his Sunday morning services as a form of stress relief. A reporter who attended a 1948 service at Marble Collegiate recounted that Peale began the service by instructing audience members to "relax in their seats with their feet flat on the floor.... They should completely relax mentally as well as physically. They should empty their minds of worldly harassments, anxieties, and resentments. They should let worry and tension flow out of them. . . . When he got through preaching everybody was beaming and happy."[37]

Peale was enthusiastic when presented with Pew's plan to revamp Spiritual Mobilization. In fact, a tentative "statement of purposes" for the new organization, composed in September 1948, revealed that the genial Peale, like Fifield, harbored deep resentments toward his fellow ministers and the misguided economic ideas that they inevitably passed along to their unsuspecting parishioners. "When you realize," he wrote, "that from fifteen to twenty million people worship in American churches every Sunday, and that their ministers have an enormous influence with them, giving the sanction of religious faith to economic opinions, it is not difficult to be persuaded as to the immense power of clergymen as an opinion making force. Unless we can show to the ministers of the country that the American free enterprise system is sound and designed to best minister to the welfare of the average man, and unless we can further show that it is in harmony with the spirit of Jesus Christ, I am inclined to believe that the church will become an active, influential agency against this system in which we believe. . . . It is an open question in my mind whether we can arrest this drift but I for one would like to try." After receiving assurances that the organization would be adequately staffed and funded, and that he would be allowed to continue in his position at Marble Collegiate, Peale signed on.[38]

At the core of the revamped organization would be two committees of right-thinking Americans. Peale would organize a group of prominent ministers to serve as Spiritual Mobilization's public face, while Pew would focus on creating an informal finance committee, made up of corporate executives, that would supply at least $250,000 in funding while also ensuring the doctrinal purity of the group's missives. These men were to be "church members . . . who believe[d] in the philosophy that Christianity and American liberty are inexorably tied together, and if one falls, they will both go down."[39] Yet finding such individuals, whether ministers or laymen, turned out to be easier said than done. Even before Peale officially signed on to the project, friends began writing to express concerns that Spiritual Mobilization was "far more political than most people think and cannot be referred to under the general head of good citizenship."[40] Many of the clergymen Peale approached on Spiritual Mobilization's behalf apparently had similar reactions. In late October Pew wrote Fifield to report that Peale was "having some difficulty in getting his committee together. He has no difficulty in finding ministers who are sympathetic, but he has a problem in getting men who are willing to stand up and take the responsibility."[41] H. C. Stockham, a businessman and frequent Pew correspondent who was briefed on the project, was not surprised. In his own Methodist denomination, Stockham wrote, none of the clergy "would dare to take issue publicly with [Bishop James Chamberlain] Baker, [G. Bromley] Oxnam or their ilk. . . . Dissenters are liable to be sent to 'Siberia,' so to speak. Frankly, I am stumped as to a solution."[42]

To Pew's great surprise, many of the men in his circle of corporate executives were similarly ambivalent about joining a crusade to instruct American clergymen in the glories of the free market. To be sure, his friends Jasper Crane and James Francis (president of the Island Creek Coal Company) signed on right away, as did Don Mitchell, president of Sylvania Electric.[43] But momentum stalled when Pew dispatched Mitchell to recruit William Robbins of General Foods, a man Pew judged to be one of the "most promising younger" executives in the country. Reporting back to Pew, Mitchell wrote that "Bill Robbins was violently opposed to the idea, especially to the idea that business men should have any part in raising money for such a promotion. His feeling was that it is sure to be dubbed 'propaganda' and business will be charged to have ulterior motives in attempting sell the American Way of Life through Ministers of the country." And Robbins wasn't alone. Mitchell "subsequently . . . talked with one or two other business men and [found] their reaction very similar to Bill Robbins'—so much that I have come to the conclusion that, at least among business men of my acquaintances [sic], it will be most difficult to get a committee willing to assist in raising money for [Spiritual Mobilization]."[44]

Peale's advisory committee of ministers did eventually come together in late 1948, though it was hardly the all-star panel he had originally envisioned. The group consisted of about a dozen people, most of them mainline clergymen who were already on record as critics of the Truman administration.[45] Perhaps the most noteworthy recruit was the Quaker journalist Howard Kershner, a man well-known in church circles for his European relief work with the American Friends Service Committee and the United Nations International Children's Fund.[46]

With Pew picking up the tab, the committee convened for the first time on January 12, 1949, at New York City's Union League Club. It met again in March at the church pastored by Lester Clee, a Presbyterian and Republican party activist who had recently lost a bid for governor of New Jersey. The only concrete achievement to emerge from either conclave was the creation of a subcommittee that would draft a "statement of conviction" and come up with a plan for staffing the proposed organization. Nonetheless, Peale insisted that the meetings themselves marked a major milestone in the struggle to reorient the economic worldview of American Protestantism. "As I have been thinking over the matter," he wrote to Pew after the March meeting, "it appears . . . that one of the values of this movement might be simply in having such meetings where ministers may gather and become aware that there are other ministers of similar point of view. From this fact I believe they will take new courage."[47]

And then, just when things seemed to be falling into place, Peale suddenly backed out. Although he never committed his reasons to writing, he may well have sensed that heading an overtly political organization would adversely affect his burgeoning reputation as the nation's foremost prophet of positive thinking. Whatever the reason, Peale gradually distanced himself from Pew's plan, but not before suggesting a replacement candidate: Howard Kershner. In the spring of 1949 he began forwarding Pew glowing reports of Kershner's uncanny ability to speak economic truth to clerical power, including an account of a recent conference at which Kershner had won over a group of left-leaning Rochester ministers with his "good message . . . and unanswerable logic." Kershner had even agreed to take questions from the "crackpot" clergymen and had "answered all of [them] with dispatch and clearness, and [had] not evade[d] the most subtle of the questions."[48] By early June Pew too had become convinced that Kershner was "peculiarly fitted to work with ministers because he has made a profound study of the Gospels, our economy, and their relationship one to the other."[49]

Pew was so impressed with Kershner, in fact, that he abandoned the original plan to refurbish Spiritual Mobilization and instead set the journalist up as the head of a new organization, the Christian Freedom Foundation (CFF). From 1950 on, the CFF would become the primary vehicle for Pew's outreach to the clergy (though Sun Oil would continue to make small contributions to Spiritual

Mobilization through the end of the 1950s). Indeed, Pew lavished money on Kershner's organization, covering most of its first-year operating budget of $430,000, and contributing annual donations of around $300,000 for the next twenty years.[50] Pew's generous donations funded a variety of "educational" activities, including conferences at which ministers were introduced to the ideas of libertarian economists, the production of a syndicated newspaper column, and *Howard Kershner's Commentary on the News*, a radio program that aired on more than 150 stations.[51] But the bulk of the group's budget went to fund the publication of *Christian Economics*, a new journal that promised to flesh out the ever-elusive theological connection between Christianity and free-market capitalism. Each issue featured an editorial by Kershner, along with guest columns by prominent conservative thinkers, occasional news items, and regular columns by Percy Greaves, a well-known libertarian polemicist, and Orval Watts, chief economist at the Foundation for Economic Education. The masthead summed up the publication's philosophy: "We stand for free enterprise—the economic system with the least amount of government and the greatest amount of Christianity."

For several years Pew made *Christian Economics* his pet project. He monitored the magazine's content carefully, frequently writing or telephoning Kershner when he sensed that a contributor harbored a soft spot for "collectivist" policies. He also likely aided Kershner in obtaining the mailing list of the American Economic Foundation (AEF)—a libertarian group Pew had helped found in the late 1930s—which, together with Kershner's dogged solicitation of denominational mailing lists, allowed *Christian Economics* to reach ninety thousand readers by 1951.[52] Beyond this, however, Pew did his best to stay out of the spotlight, allowing Kershner and the Protestant ministers who dominated the group's executive committee to serve as CFF's public face. Indeed, Pew insisted that his name be omitted from the executive committee minutes, even though he was regularly in attendance.[53]

James Fifield soldiered on as head of Spiritual Mobilization, though he never quite got over the loss of Pew's financial backing. During the early 1950s he focused the bulk of his energies on his radio program, *The Freedom Story*, and ad hoc national campaigns such as "The Committee to Proclaim Liberty," an offshoot of Spiritual Mobilization that marked the 175th anniversary of the Declaration of Independence with yet another sermon contest—this time the theme was "Freedom Under God"—and a star-studded national radio broadcast, overseen by Cecil B. DeMille, in which A-list celebrities including Jimmy Stewart and Bing Crosby urged listeners to remain on their guard against the march of totalitarian tyranny, both at home and abroad.[54] Spiritual Mobilization also launched a new journal, *Faith and Freedom*, which soon garnered a small but devoted following among libertarian-leaning ministers and laymen. Like *Christian Economics, Faith and Freedom* focused on illuminating the Christian foundations of capitalism, and it featured guest columns from an emerging cadre of libertarian commentators, including Frank Chodorov, Felix Morley, Murray Rothbard, Leonard Read, Rose Wilder Lane, Henry Grady Weaver, and Henry Hazlitt.[55] Embittered by the experience of having narrowly lost out on a major financial windfall, Fifield continued to badger Pew for contributions, but the oilman stuck to his guns, claiming that his position as "the principal contributor to *Christian Economics*" was bleeding him dry, and that any support beyond Sun Oil's $5,000 annual contribution would be impossible.[56]

By the fall of 1951 there were signs that Pew and his allies had succeeded in establishing a beachhead in enemy territory. With President Truman's approval rating in free fall—thanks to a stalled domestic agenda and the ongoing military quagmire on the Korean peninsula—it appeared likely that a Republican would soon occupy the White House for the first time in a generation. And as the national mood shifted rightward, the circle of ministers who had backed the Spiritual Mobilization reorganization effort sensed that the views of the clergy too were evolving. In an article published in the conservative opinion journal *The Freeman*—yet another Pew-funded venture—Stewart Robinson, who served on advisory boards to both Spiritual Mobilization and the CFF, informed readers that "the Protestant clergy [were] again awakening to the threat of statism," thanks to the efforts of "two groups that have formed to help them." Although neither Spiritual Mobilization nor CFF had "the financial power or political prestige that . . . belonged to the Federal Council of Churches," they had eternal truth on their side, and "more and more" clergymen were proving receptive to their message. The day was coming, it seemed, when America's pastors, remembering that "clerical income is entirely derived from capital," would finally stop "bit[ing] the hand that feeds them."[57]

As grounds for his soaring optimism, Robinson might well have cited the fact that Fifield's *Freedom Story* program was now airing on more than eight hundred stations.[58] He might have mentioned that thousands of clergymen were annually penning patriotic, antistatist sermons in the hopes of landing a check from Spiritual Mobilization. He might have noted that CFF's journal, *Christian Economics*, was reaching a reported ninety thousand readers every month, the bulk of them clergymen; or that Spiritual Mobilization's *Faith and Freedom* was reaching around twenty thousand. All of these claims were true. Yet upon closer examination, it was hard to say what, if anything, had really changed since the dark days of the early Truman administration. A pessimist would have noted, for example, that only a tiny percentage of the clergymen who received either *Christian Economics* or *Faith and Freedom* bothered to pay the voluntary subscription rate of one dollar annually; in the case of *Christian Economics*, the number of paid subscribers probably never topped a thousand. Moreover, a CFF-sponsored poll of three hundred Protestant ministers, conducted in 1953, revealed that only 15 percent relied "heavily" on *Christian Economics* for news about economic issues, and that most of those who read the magazine disagreed with its point of view.[59] Kershner, a talented speaker, did manage to organize a number of widely publicized conferences for Protestant clergymen, but his services were never exactly in high demand. The high point of an October 1950 speaking tour on behalf of the CFF, for example, was an address to the state convention of the Kansas Woman's Christian Temperance Union.[60]

Writing to Fifield in November 1951, Pew declared that the experiences of the past few years had left him even "more convinced that the ministers play the most important part in the formation of public opinion." Yet, even after the small fortune he had expended to educate them, America's religious leaders remained, on the whole, a sorry lot—a far cry indeed from their Founding-era forebears, who had fearlessly "ministered from the pulpit as to what it was that constituted liberty and why liberty should be preserved at all costs."[61]

Molding the Opinion Molders

While Pew was busy developing new organizations to sell libertarian economic ideas to the nation's ministers, his close friend Jasper Crane, recently retired after a long career with DuPont Chemical, took charge of NAM's long-standing clergy outreach program. The two men, who lived only a few miles apart, shared a great deal in common. Both were in their mid-sixties. Both came from engineering backgrounds. Both were devout Presbyterian laymen who would soon accept leadership roles in the National Council of Churches (the postwar successor to the Federal Council of Churches). Both spent their entire careers with companies that earned enormous profits doing business with the federal government— particularly during wartime—and yet both came away from the experience firmly convinced that Washington's burgeoning bureaucracies were hopelessly inefficient and a dire threat to traditional American freedoms.

There were also differences. Whereas Pew's intellectual interests ran to church history and the American Revolution, the mustachioed Crane spent most of his free time digesting the latest insights of the Austrian School economists. (He was, in fact, a major financial backer of the Mont Pelerin Society, the group responsible for bringing the works of Friedrich von Hayek and Ludwig von Mises to a wider audience.)[62] Moreover, Crane, unlike Pew, never claimed to be an expert on the origins of the Reformation or its contributions to the rise of capitalism. Still, he shared Pew's firm conviction that free-market capitalism and Christianity *were* somehow intertwined, even if the precise nature of the connection remained murky. No sooner had "the Pilgrims land[ed] upon these shores," he explained in a 1946 essay, than they had "set about the procurement of the necessities of life as individuals in their family groups, and thus . . . [had] established the beginnings of our economic system based upon individual enterprise."[63] (Not surprisingly, the Puritans' fixation on the economic sins of usury, oppression, and avarice went unmentioned.)

NAM's Committee on Cooperation with the Churches, which Crane headed from 1943 until the mid-1950s, represented one front in a larger, $400,000 campaign to enlist the leaders of voluntary associations—labeled "opinion moulders" in NAM's internal strategy memos—in the struggle against the regulatory state. Like other conservative business groups, NAM pushed a Janus-faced narrative concerning American civil society. On the one hand, church groups, women's groups, and educational entities were consistently described as hostile territory—a "source of enemy strength" that had been "strategically 'planted'" with collectivist ideas for "more than 25 years," in the words of the group's 1946 strategic plan.[64] On the other hand, civil society represented the highest ideals of American voluntarism, the counterpoint to the coercive regime of state-sponsored benevolence ushered in by the New Deal. And, assuming they could be disabused of their misguided economic ideas, there was reason to hope that volunteer groups might once again serve as a critical bulwark against the future growth of official authority. Thus, in the case of women's organizations, NAM's Public Relations Division developed an economics curriculum specially tailored to "the feminine mind," with its tendency to "react emotionally rather than logically." In practical terms, this meant plying women's groups with quizzes and skits that presented NAM's preferred policy positions as the only viable solution to the problems facing the typical American housewife, from the rising cost of food and clothing to the need for "new labor-saving devices." In theory, its internal reports stressed, every dollar invested in helping women's groups see the light would be repaid many times over, as civically active women would inevitably share their insights with friends and neighbors who were currently unaware of the creeping threat of democratic socialism.[65]

Converting clergymen would require an approach that was no less carefully tailored. In the winter of 1946–1947, Crane made it his mission to enlist the clergy in selling three policy proposals to the American people: the end of wartime price controls, eliminating a million and a half federal jobs to cut the deficit, and the reform of federal collective bargaining laws to strengthen the hand of management.[66] Yet he and other NAM officials were acutely aware that few clergymen would accept the arguments of a group with obvious business ties at face value. So he settled on a subtler strategy: claiming that labor groups were brimming with communists and exerting disproportionate influence over the nation's churches, he pleaded for equal time to tell management's side of the story.

The primary vehicle through which NAM conveyed its message was the clergy-industry conference. The format was simple. A committee of local

business leaders would invite all the Protestant, Catholic, and Jewish clergymen in a particular city to a luncheon or dinner meeting—or better yet, a series of meetings—at which they would be encouraged to exchange views on a
vaguely patriotic theme, such as "The Purpose of American Democracy" or "The
Purpose of American Science and Invention." Although the meeting could be
held in a hotel or restaurant, NAM officials stressed that the ideal spot was a local
factory. Upon arrival, each pastor, priest, or rabbi would be personally greeted
by the president of the company and invited to tour the facilities. Following the
tour, attendees would assemble in the company cafeteria or restaurant where
over dinner they would hear two addresses on the theme of the evening—one by
a leading clergyman, the other by a representative of business. The speeches were
followed by small-group discussions in which participants were encouraged to
"let their hair down," in the words of Robert L. Dieffenbacher, the Presbyterian
minister hired by NAM to administer the program. If all went smoothly—as
NAM insisted it almost always did—the conference would demonstrate that
the long history of tension between religion and business was all the result of
a simple misunderstanding. Desperate to retain their ideological hold over the
clerical mind, labor leaders had driven a wedge between ministers and company
heads. But now, thanks to the exclusion of the meddling "third party," it had at
last become possible to foster "better understanding and a spirit of cooperation
between leaders of industry and leaders of the church."[67]

The program sounded innocuous enough, but a trial run in the early 1940s
generated a good deal of controversy. Although dozens of conferences were successfully organized between 1940 and 1943, many clergymen refused to participate, arguing that any discussion of economic issues that did not include labor
representatives would amount to little more than a one-sided indoctrination
session. Others worried that their presence at lavish, NAM-funded dinners
would give the impression that religious leaders were in league with big business.[68] Some NAM officials apparently went so far as to falsely suggest that the
Federal Council of Churches had endorsed the program—a claim that enraged
the FCC's James Myers.[69] When ministers wrote to inquire about the rumors,
Myers reminded them that the FCC's policy was not to sponsor any event in
which "only manufacturers and ministers" would be present.[70] After he was
quoted in the press attacking NAM for not including labor representatives, consumer groups, and civil rights organizations in its conferences, Myers received
an invitation to discuss his concerns with NAM officials over dinner at the
Waldorf-Astoria. A frosty exchange of letters ensued in which Myers agreed to
meet with Jasper Crane and his associates, but only "on condition that I will pay
for my own dinner." Better yet, he suggested, the parties could meet in a conference room instead of the Waldorf. The proposed meeting apparently never took
place.[71]

NAM refined and expanded its clergy-industry program in the postwar period, hoping to gain a fresh hearing from ministers who had initially dismissed the effort as so much pro-business propaganda. With Crane at the helm, it developed a new curriculum—"Production is the Answer"—that was relentlessly positive in tone and carefully calibrated to create the impression of impartiality. Instead of beating ministers over the head with accounts of labor's sins or drawing dubious parallels between theology and economics, NAM's postwar conferences simply presented clergymen with statistics documenting the real-world effects of labor stoppages and price controls, leaving them to draw their own conclusions. The model dinner speech distributed by the Committee on Cooperation with the Clergy was light on religion and heavy on "facts"—that the recent GM strikes had cost workers $175 million in lost wages and auto dealers $113 million in lost commissions; that "75 cents out of each manufacturing sales dollar" was already going to pay workers' salaries (hence there was no need to raise the minimum wage); that new government programs and production shortages resulting from labor strife were the primary causes of inflation; and that price controls were useless in addressing these underlying problems. Speakers were also urged to concede that business was not entirely blameless. "In years gone by, some business leaders" had indeed engaged in "practices which were short-sighted and not in the public interest." But times had changed. The New Deal–era Wagner Act, with its rigid oversight of the collective bargaining process, had emboldened union bosses to the point that they were now the ones "flout[ing] the public interest" and making "unreasonable demands," confident that in the end "government would support them or take over the business operation in the event of a strike." The speech concluded with the reassuring observation that NAM's end goal was not a world without unions, but rather a society in which both labor and management would "approach the problem of wage rates intelligently" and "do their utmost to make collective bargaining work" so that America might "remain a land of freedom, steadily progressing toward an ever-higher living standard for all."[72]

The real genius of the new curriculum was that, unlike J. Howard Pew's various pedagogical projects, it did not challenge the importance of the "human factor" in industrial relations. Indeed, it readily conceded that ministers had an ethical duty to ask questions about the organization of the American economy and its impact on the day-to-day lives of their parishioners. But having conceded this much, it argued that the *means* favored by left-leaning propagandists—strong unions, price controls, the minimum wage—were bound to produce more human suffering rather than less.

Every facet of the program was strategically designed to ensure that both the attendees and the wider public got the point. To guide small group discussions, the Committee teed up a list of open-ended softball questions that invited businessmen to elaborate on the ways in which they were fighting to improve the lives of their employees—and on the ways in which their hands were tied by union bosses and current federal laws. ("Does management feel that [the current] interpretation [of the Wagner Act] has contributed to labor-management misunderstanding? What other changes in the Act does management believe are necessary?") At the conclusion of the discussion, participants were asked to write down their answers to a series of questions touching on the evening's theme. A committee of local businessmen would then tabulate the results and distribute them to the entire group, though not before "boiling down the comments to essentials." Finally, a press release, prepared at NAM headquarters far in advance, would be issued, its opening lines reading, "Labor and business should refrain from unfair practices, and do their utmost to make collective bargaining work if they really want the spiritual, intellectual and political blessings of America [name and title of speaker] declared last night at a [name of city] Church-Industry Conference." The impression that the assembled divines were monolithic in their condemnation of what the release described as labor's "unreasonable" tactics was clearly implied, even if never stated directly.[73]

Under the leadership of Crane and Noel Sargent (who took over in the mid-1950s), the Committee on Cooperation with the Churches copied what it understood to be the most successful tactic of its collectivist adversaries, working to "plant" free-market ideas deep within the institutional structure of American religion. It began with the seminaries. A 1949 strategic plan urged businessmen to request personal meetings with the deans or presidents of area seminaries to "discuss their cirriculums [sic] with a view to offering cooperation on any course which touches on economic or industrial practices." If administrators and faculty members proved receptive, they were supplied with speakers, pamphlets, and films. If they appeared "cold or hostile," they were to be given "special attention" in the hope that, through sheer persistence, they might be persuaded to cooperate. Businessmen were also encouraged to arrange factory tours for local seminary students and to offer interviews to the student editors of seminary newspapers. Offers of part-time employment were another useful means of persuasion, since many seminarians needed the money. Students should be reminded that by working in a factory during the summer months, they could simultaneously help pay for their education and "get first-hand experience in industrial methods and practice."[74]

By the late 1940s NAM had won the trust of many of the church officials who supervised the economic education of the nation's aspiring clergymen, including John C. Harmon, the Methodist Church's director of social and industrial relations, and Marshal Scott, dean of the Presbyterian Institute of Industrial Relations. Through these contacts NAM officials were in 1949 invited to participate in symposia and extension courses at Duke University Divinity School and the San Francisco Presbyterian Seminary. At Duke thirty divinity students were, in the words of Harmon, presented with their "first opportunity . . . to have a first-hand presentation of Management's task in conducting business," while management, in turn, got "its story across to those who expect to occupy positions of influence in the community." In San Francisco attendees of the NAM-sponsored extension course were addressed by a group of NAM officials before receiving tours at Standard Oil of California, General Motors' Oakland plant, and Oliver United Filters. Scott wrote NAM headquarters to inform the Committee that the program, which he judged "just about perfect," had made a significant impact on the students and clergy who attended.[75] NAM even managed to secure footholds in Union Theological Seminary and Yale Divinity School, two bastions of progressive Protestantism. Following a February 1955 meeting with Noel Sargent, Union Seminary's John C. Bennett, a social ethicist despised by Pew and other libertarians, agreed to permit NAM officials to address students on such topics as the guaranteed annual wage and state right-to-work laws. That same month NAM's Stanley Phraener reportedly received a positive reception when he presented parts of "How Our Business System Operates," a new economics curriculum NAM was developing for use in high schools and colleges, to a class of sixty-five Yale Divinity School students.[76]

Sargent, who took over the church-and-industry program in 1955, was perfectly suited to the task of cultivating relationships with mainline leaders. As a lay leader in the Episcopal Church and a board member of the National Council of Churches, he developed close friendships with a number of prominent Protestant thinkers and administrators. He was also a more systematic thinker than Pew or Crane, having earned economics degrees at the universities of Washington and Minnesota. And thanks to his educational background and his relative youth— he was about fifteen years younger than Pew and Crane—he had a generally sounder grasp of the arguments of his opponents. His most important strategic innovation as head of the clergy-industry program was to replace the original committee of businessmen with a new department that was to have four salaried regional directors. The reorganization bore fruit almost immediately as the regional directors launched themselves into the task of planting NAM's economic philosophy in the religious institutions of their respective jurisdictions. In the first four months of 1955, for example, the Eastern Division director, Warren Taussig, delivered addresses to the Manhattan Division of the Protestant Council of New York City, an industrial relations conference sponsored by the United Lutheran Church, and the Young Adult group of Newark's Second Presbyterian Church. He also met personally with the executive director of the Synagogue Council of America, the regional head of the Episcopal Church's Commission on Church and Industry, and the head of the United Lutheran Church's Board of Social Missions. And he successfully placed ghostwritten articles in several important periodicals, including the national Episcopal magazine *Forth*, the Catholic magazine *Jubilee*, and the Boy Scout publication *Scouting* (circulation 960,000). Taussig's greatest coup, however, was convincing the New York Archdiocese's superintendent of schools to adopt NAM's antiregulatory economics curriculum, "How Our Business System Operates," for use in the City's 102 parochial high schools. Henceforth NAM's church-and-industry department would assume responsibility for training thousands of New York parochial school teachers in the inexorable logic of market fundamentalism; the teachers, in turn, would impart NAM's economic wisdom to more than 38,000 schoolchildren.[77]

But the Eisenhower years would mark the high point of NAM's relationship with the mainline clergy. In the late 1950s, following Noel Sargent's retirement, the clergy-industry program shed many of the distinctive characteristics that had initially allowed it to reach a large audience. For Crane—and even more for Sargent—the secret to the program's success was the relentlessly upbeat and apolitical way in which it framed its economic message. When leadership passed to NAM vice president Charles "Chuck" Sligh, a close friend of J. Howard Pew, the message shifted to something resembling Pew's uncompromising brand of libertarianism. Sligh himself often parroted Pew's favorite line—"freedom of religion . . . and economic freedom are indivisible"—in his speeches to clergymen, and he helped launch a new periodical for ministers, *Dateline*, that adopted the far-right position on every major political issue of the day—from the minimum wage, to Social Security, to the Supreme Court's rulings ordering the states to correct the egregious imbalance between rural and urban representation in their legislatures.[78] The material presented at clergy-industry gatherings also grew more stridently ideological as NAM officials and their clerical allies embraced the arguments of Red-baiting zealots like Fred Schwarz, the Australian general practitioner whose Christian Anti-Communism Crusades filled stadiums in Southern California and elsewhere.[79] At times the group's tactics mirrored those of the secretive John Birch Society, as when Sligh, at Pew's suggestion, agreed to fund an investigation into the private lives of several National Council of Churches officials.[80]

Still, the fact remains that the NAM clergy-industry program, perhaps uniquely among the major conservative initiatives of the postwar period, succeeded in gaining a hearing for economic ideas that most mainline clergymen had long regarded as heretical. Whether many clergymen found the group's arguments in favor of deregulation, tax cuts, and right-to-work laws persuasive is an open question. But the group's programs, which reached tens of thousands of ministers over the course of the 1950s, may well have planted an ideological seed, even if the first signs of growth would not be evident for several years.

The Curious Failure of Christian Libertarianism

Over the course of the 1950s Pew, Crane, Sargent, and their allies at the National Association of Manufacturers spent a small fortune attempting to sell American clergymen on the idea that the welfare state was not supported by—indeed, was squarely in conflict with—the core theological commitments of their respective faiths. When all was said and done, however, they had little to show for their efforts. This fact was driven home by a 1958 survey of five hundred randomly selected Protestant ministers conducted by the Opinion Research Corporation, the same group whose 1949 poll of clergymen had set off alarm bells in the conservative ranks. Sponsored by *Christian Economics*—that is to say, by J. Howard Pew—the survey aimed to determine what impact, if any, the publication was having on the economic views of the clergy. The results were, to put it mildly, not encouraging. For starters, only about half of the respondents who appeared on the magazine's mailing list could recall ever having read it. Another "challenge for the editors" was that, even after eight years of receiving *Christian Economics*, only about half of ministers perceived any "connection between economic and religious freedom." Most troubling of all, however, was the most common reason that ministers gave for disliking *Christian Economics*—namely, that "the editorial fare [was] too narrowly and monotonously ultra-conservative."[81] Men like Pew, Crane, Fifield, and Kershner had long believed that simply putting libertarian arguments into the hands of pastors would be enough to turn the tide of public opinion against the welfare state. Now it was becoming increasingly clear that such arguments were, for many clergymen, a nonstarter.

What explains the relative impotence of well-funded and capably led conservative initiatives such as Spiritual Mobilization, the Christian Freedom Foundation, and the NAM clergy-industry program? Why did Pew and NAM get so little for their money? Surely one serious problem—the one identified in the 1958 poll—was that both Spiritual Mobilization and the CFF (though not NAM) embraced a version of libertarianism that was both extreme and dogmatic. Not content merely to critique the occasional excesses and inefficiencies of the welfare state, the principal contributors to *Faith and Freedom* and *Christian Economics* advanced the far more radical view that the *only* legitimate uses of state power were to protect citizens and their property from physical threats and to enforce contractual obligations. Social Security, federal aid to education, medical benefits for military veterans, farm subsidies, the Marshall Plan—all these programs were little better than theft, in that they used the coercive power of the state to mandate the shifting of resources from healthy and affluent Americans to their less fortunate neighbors, both at home and abroad. Such views were at least somewhat at odds with mainstream public opinion—polls showed that around 90 percent of Americans approved of the Social Security program's old-age pensions, for example—and they were likely even further from the mainstream of clerical opinion.[82]

A second problem was the libertarians' open disregard for religious authority. Suspicious of authority in general, they denounced the denominational hierarchies and the Federal Council of Churches as hotbeds of collectivism, and they cheered reports of dissension in the ranks. But for many clergymen, a faith without strong institutional backing—that is, without institutions capable of pronouncing and enforcing some theological, ethical, and procedural ground rules—was no faith at all. That Red-baiting politicians, including Senator Joe McCarthy, were beginning to train their fire on the churches only made ministers that much more sensitive to attacks on the institutional authority of the nation's religious bodies. Indeed, at the precise moment that Pew, Fifield, and NAM were ramping up their clergy education campaigns, the nation's state and local church councils were mounting a vigorous protest against House and Senate investigators, arguing that any attempt to force ministers to testify under oath about their past beliefs and associations would violate the First Amendment.[83] Fifield, in contrast, argued in the pages of *Faith and Freedom* that Congress's inquiry into the political beliefs of the nation's ministers represented a worthy first step toward exposing the "social action enthusiasts" who had "taken over extended control of the denominational machinery." The Spiritual Mobilization founder even went so far as to declare that it was not improper for "Congress, [when] investigating subversive activities, [to] examine suspect individuals—whatever robes they may be wearing or wherever they may be found."[84]

But the most serious problem was that, even with an array of talented libertarian commentators on the case, the precise nature of the connection between Christianity and libertarianism proved difficult to specify. To be sure, commentators like Edmund Opitz, an ordained Congregationalist minister who headed Spiritual Mobilization's New York office in the early 1950s, published scores of articles arguing that Christianity was incompatible with "altruism, the doctrine of putting the interests of others above the interests of yourself." Jesus's seemingly straightforward injunction to "love thy neighbor as thyself" contained "no suggestion that we ought to be our brother's keeper; nor is the brother's keeper idea contained in any part of Biblical teaching," Opitz opined. The key to the Christian libertarian's esoteric reading of the golden rule was the phrase "as thyself": only *after* believers had aroused themselves "to the need for a new direction . . . and orientation of *personal* life" could they possibly do anything worthwhile for their neighbors. And, indeed, acts of benevolence that were motivated by selfless love of one's fellow man rather than the personal quest for self-fulfillment were likely to do more harm than good, "betray[ing] us into smugness on the one side and resentment on the other," so that "the intended benefit rarely materializes." Though Opitz offered no explanation as to why Jesus had chosen to express himself in so opaque a manner, he never wavered from the conviction that the "true neighbor" respected the "rights of [his] fellow man" enough to leave him alone.[85]

Opitz's status as arguably the foremost theological defender of the libertarian policy agenda suggests that, while the postwar libertarian movement did not lack for serious thinkers, it did suffer from a dearth of serious *theological* ideas—or at any rate, ideas that were likely to strike orthodox clergyman as consistent with the core tenets of Christianity.

If inherited theological commitments provide some insight into why clergymen found the arguments of Fifield and Opitz easy to dismiss, they may also tell us something about why the Eisenhower-era iteration of Christian libertarianism did not catch on with the men and women in the pews. Indeed, to be a mainline Protestant in the 1950s was to be immersed in a religious culture that stressed service to humanity above all else, and that often viewed governmental and intergovernmental institutions as the most efficient way of aiding the needy. A striking example of this conviction can be seen in the mainline churches' multifaceted postwar campaign on behalf of the newly formed United Nations (a body despised by Pew and his allies). Perhaps the most popular manifestation of pro-U.N. sentiment took place on Halloween, when hundreds of thousands of Sunday school children participated in the annual "Trick or Treat for UNICEF" program; while canvassing their neighborhoods in search of candy, they carried small orange boxes in which they collected donations for impoverished families in foreign lands.[86] For older children, churches sponsored "Know Your United Nations" essay contests, as well as frequent trips to church youth seminars at U.N. headquarters in New York.[87] And in hundreds of American communities, including such out-of-the-way places as Terre Haute, Indiana, churches not only observed a "United Nations Sunday" (during which ministers were urged to incorporate material on the U.N. into their sermons) but also took the lead in organizing community-wide "U.N. Week" events at schools and other secular venues.[88]

Protestants who did not imbibe the ethic of service to humanity in their local churches likely encountered it in radio or television broadcasts. Sustaining-time programs such as *Frontiers of Faith*—broadcast nationally over the NBC television network—were often moderated by liberal church officials, such as the Presbyterian Eugene Carson Blake, who made no secret of their belief that Christians were obligated to combat social injustice wherever they encountered it.[89] In addition, most local church councils controlled significant blocks of radio air time; and while many of the programs they produced were purely spiritual in nature, others—with titles like *Churchmen Weigh the News* and *Religion Views the News*—interpreted current events in the light of the churches' broader commitment to aiding the downtrodden, both at home and abroad.[90]

Popular magazines also regularly informed their readers of the myriad ways in which mainline churchgoers were working to improve the world around them. In 1947 readers of *Life* learned that the "strength" of the Methodist church "lies in its great energy," that Methodists took pride in their commitment to "high social issues," that they were the first denomination to "openly oppose child labor and favor labor unions," and that the women of a "representative" 750-member Methodist church in Wilmington, Ohio, had organized nine separate committees dedicated to various facets of social reform.[91] Summing up the social teachings of the nation's largest denominations, the centerpiece essay of *Life*'s 1953 special edition on American Christianity reported that American believers were distinguished by their ability to hold two seemingly contradictory ideas in equipoise: the imperative to improve society and the reality of original sin. Americans knew in their bones that evil was woven into the fabric of human experience; but they also knew that God expected the citizens of the world's wealthiest nation to "do something about evil, both within [themselves] and in the world."[92]

This was more than wishful thinking on the part *Life*'s Presbyterian publisher, Henry Luce. In fact, although conservative activists like Pew and Fifield often talked of a divide between the pulpit and the pew—the idea being that the typical mainline clergyman was far more liberal than the typical layperson, at least on economic issues—the best contemporaneous studies found that laypeople were only marginally less supportive of social welfare and humanitarian programs than their ministers. A 1952 survey of Episcopalians, for example, revealed that even members of the nation's most affluent Protestant denomination strongly supported core elements of the New Deal/Fair Deal agenda, including federal protections for organized labor and robust taxes on corporate profits.[93] Similarly, a 1958 survey of middle-class white Protestants in the Detroit area found that only 16 percent believed that the government was currently doing "too much" in connection with "problems such as housing, unemployment, education," while 34 percent believed it was doing "too little" and 49 percent expressed support for the status quo.[94] Based in part on such findings, the Methodist minister and academic A. Roy Eckardt concluded in 1958 that the reason groups such as Spiritual Mobilization and the Christian Freedom Foundation were struggling was that their core principles were fundamentally at odds with the latent theological convictions of average churchgoers. American Protestants were lovers of freedom, he wrote, but many of them were also Calvinists at heart, and their Calvinism tended to manifest itself precisely when they were asked to subordinate reasonable communal obligations to an abstract, quasi-religious conception of individual liberty.[95]

The point can also be framed in terms of material self-interest. As we have seen, the postwar surge in church attendance was driven by men and women on the make—young and predominantly suburban-dwelling Americans who were seeking both a sense of community and a point of entry into "respectable" society. Mainline church membership was desirable in part because it marked a person as a solid citizen, as one who was committed to the common good and could therefore be trusted with authority in business and civic affairs. Those who sought it out were typically seeking *more* social ties and *more* social responsibility, not less. (Indeed, mainline church membership was strongly predictive of membership in other civic organizations.)[96] And in part for this reason, mainline churchgoers often exhibited a special affinity for the sorts of large, "establishment" institutions—from Protestant ecumenical bodies, to research universities, to federal bureaucracies, to the United Nations—that Pew and his small band of ideological allies viewed as dire threats to individual freedom.[97] It should come as no surprise, then, that relatively few mainline church members were drawn to writers who cast such institutions—or, for that matter, their own churches—as agents of the Kremlin.

5

Assaulting the Citadel

Some day there will no doubt emerge from the National Council [of Churches] a set of principles to which the Council will subscribe. . . . It is my conviction that if we lay people do our part in supplying the funds, that the Council will not neglect our views on what these principles should be.

—J. Howard Pew (1951)

The year 1952 witnessed one of the strangest unions in American history—that of J. Howard Pew and the National Council of Churches (NCC). Launched with great fanfare in 1950, the NCC was the product of a merger between the Federal Council of Churches and eleven small Protestant denominations that had previously remained aloof from ecumenical activities. The name change—from *Federal* Council to *National* Council—was part of a larger rebranding effort. In short, the NCC's founders envisioned an ecumenical organization that would carry on most of the FCC's major programs while shedding its left-of-center reputation. The FCC's staff and organizational structure were carried over largely intact, though some departments were renamed, probably in the hope of rendering them less offensive to potential donors.[1] Although the changes were largely cosmetic, the makeover proved a smashing success. During the early years of the Eisenhower administration, elected officials aligned themselves with the NCC at seemingly every opportunity. President Eisenhower and prominent members of his cabinet, such as John Foster Dulles, regularly chose Council gatherings as venues for major policy announcements, particularly ones touching on foreign policy or the nuclear threat. And in 1958, with thirty thousand spectators looking on, the president himself laid the cornerstone for the NCC's sparkling new headquarters at the Interfaith Center in Morningside Heights.[2]

Pew, of course, was by this point well-known for bankrolling a number of far-right organizations, several of which alleged that the NCC's forerunner, the FCC, had been thoroughly infiltrated by communist sympathizers. Beginning in the summer of 1950, however, the oilman abruptly reversed course and began exploring the idea of a partnership with many of the same religious leaders he had spent the previous decade defaming. As with many odd pairings, financial considerations helped bring Pew and the NCC together. The courtship began when the NCC's architects hatched the idea of a National Lay Committee—a body of prominent laymen and -women that would help the Council keep its finger on the pulse of lay opinion while also boosting the Council's budget. From Pew's perspective, the Lay Committee offered a potential backdoor into the citadel of the Social Gospel. The NCC needed money, and he was willing and able to supply it. In return, he asked only that the Council cease issuing pronouncements in favor of government aid to the less fortunate and instead transform itself into a champion of the free-enterprise system.

Pew's plan sounded simple enough on paper, yet it ultimately failed to accomplish its principal objective of prompting the NCC to abandon its commitment to a robust social welfare state. And, perhaps surprisingly, it was a group of prominent business leaders, not the alleged communists in the ranks of the clergy, who led the opposition to Pew's short-lived Lay Committee. Centered in the NCC's Department of the Church and Economic Life (DCEL), Pew's opponents, who included the former Studebaker CEO Paul G. Hoffman, the Cummins Engine CEO J. Irwin Miller, and the attorney and ecumenical leader Charles P. Taft (son of the late president), insisted that Christians should work toward the creation of a more just economic order. The men and women of the DCEL were not, as Pew often alleged, "collectivists" at heart; many of them were not even particularly fond of organized labor. But they did share a set of ethical convictions, derived from the mainline stewardship tradition, that made conflict with Pew's Lay Committee all but inevitable. The end result of Pew's attempt to infiltrate the National Council of Churches, then, was a clash of cultures—or, rather, a clash between the entrenched culture of the Protestant mainline and an upstart libertarian ideology that, as yet, had relatively few defenders in either the business community or the ranks of the clergy. Far more than a bureaucratic turf war, the struggle between the DCEL and Pew's Lay Committee came to be seen, not unreasonably, as a battle for the soul of American Protestantism.

We Seek No Glory, We Covet No Power

From the moment of its inception, the National Lay Committee provoked a good deal of opposition within the NCC. A number of vocal critics, including the Methodist Bishop G. Bromley Oxnam, a past president of the Federal Council of Churches, correctly surmised that Pew and his allies were aiming to undercut the moral authority of the denominational hierarchies. "Big business," he wrote, "has decided that the proper way to handle . . . progressive announcements on the part of the church is to get on the inside and control it." But other NCC officials, perhaps remembering the dire financial straits that had confronted the FCC in the 1930s and early 1940s, viewed Pew's offer of financial assistance as a godsend. The NCC's well-regarded general secretary, Samuel McCrea Cavert, even went so far as to suggest that it was Pew—and not the NCC—who was likely to be changed as a result of the partnership. In Cavert's estimation, Pew was less a devious schemer than an "old man" who longed for "the recognition he once had when he was directing a great enterprise." Perhaps ecumenical involvement would soften the retired executive's hidebound conservatism, leaving him with a genuine appreciation of the "social meaning of Christianity."[3]

In what can only be described as a case of motivated reasoning, most of the NCC's top brass sided with Cavert. Still, there were two practical sticking points that delayed the formal launch of the Lay Committee for several months. The first involved the selection of the men and women who would serve on the Committee: Who would decide who spoke for the laity? The second problem concerned the relationship of the Lay Committee to the NCC hierarchy. Was the Committee to be an advisory body only, or would it be afforded a formal role in Council affairs—for example, the right to influence personnel decisions or veto policy pronouncements?

In early 1952 the parties reached a compromise that granted Pew effective control over the Lay Committee's membership while denying him much of the formal authority he craved.[4] For the time being, the Lay Committee would be limited to an advisory role, with ten laypersons—five men and five women—authorized to sit on the Council's General Board as "consultants," meaning they would enjoy all the privileges of membership except for the right to vote. Pew was less than thrilled with the arrangement, but he remained confident—perhaps thanks to assurances from Cavert—that the Lay Committee's formal role would expand over time. As he explained to General Motors' Donaldson Brown in August 1951, if businessmen continued to "take an interest in the work of the Council and develop their budgets," they would soon find themselves in a position to veto NCC actions of which they disapproved. Henceforth church leaders would "think twice before . . . they allow . . . any such pronouncements as formerly were released by the Federal Council."[5]

Pew immediately set to work recruiting prominent business leaders for the newly created Committee. It soon became apparent, however, that he had little interest in assembling a broad or representative cross-section of American Protestants. He made no effort to ensure that all NCC member denominations were represented, nor to see that Committee slots were apportioned in accordance with the relative size of the denominations. His primary criterion, rather, was adherence to free-market orthodoxy. Among the Committee's charter members were Pew's close friends and fellow libertarians Jasper Crane and B. E. Hutchinson. Other early recruits included Harry A. Bullis of General Mills, Colby M. Chester of General Foods, Lem T. Jones of Russell Stover Candies, Olive Ann Beech of Beech Aircraft, H. W. Prentis of Armstrong Cork, Noel

Sargent of the National Association of Manufacturers (NAM), Charles E. Wilson
of General Electric, Charles R. Hook of Armco Steel, and Robert E. Wilson of
Standard Oil. To represent the views of organized labor, Pew tapped a group of
iconoclastic union heads, including Earl W. Jimerson of the Amalgamated Meat
Cutters and J. Scott Milne of the International Brotherhood of Electrical Workers,
who were best known for their efforts to root out suspected communists in the
union ranks.[6] In the end, the NCC's officers signed off on all of Pew's selections
save one. The choice of Donald J. Cowling, president of Carleton College and
cofounder of the conservative religious organization Spiritual Mobilization, to
serve as vice chair was apparently too much for Cavert to stomach.[7] In place of
Cowling, Pew settled on Lois Black Hunter, a former advertising executive who
had recently been appointed to the post of deputy industrial commissioner by
New York's Republican governor, Thomas Dewey.[8] Black soon took charge of the
Committee's day-to-day business, including monitoring affairs at NCC headquarters, informing Committee members of potentially adverse actions, and
formulating a strategic plan to enhance "lay" (read: conservative) representation
within the NCC ranks.

For roughly the first year and a half of the Lay Committee's existence, Pew's
plan to appropriate the institutional machinery of the NCC for his own purposes
seemed to be coming off without a hitch. First, he successfully pushed for the
creation of an ad hoc committee to study the question of whether the NCC
ought to be in the business of issuing policy statements on economic issues. To
no one's surprise, the committee reported back with the recommendation that
policy pronouncements should be kept to a minimum and addressed only to issues involving an "unmistakable ethical or religious concern." Next, as an added
layer of protection against "radical" pronouncements, the Pew forces arranged
for the creation of a Committee of Reference that would be tasked with reviewing
all materials published by individual departments to ensure that these were "of
such a character [as] may properly be issued by the authority of the division concerned." Finally, in December 1952 they secured the appointment of four laymen
to serve as voting members of the General Board, as well as the appointment of
three Lay Committee members to serve as vice presidents-at-large of the Council
(the latter group included Norman Vincent Peale's wife, Ruth Stafford Peale).[9]

These procedural triumphs, however, arguably paled in comparison to the
symbolic significance of the Lay Committee's annual gatherings—lavish affairs at which Committee members and top NCC officials, including Cavert
and NCC president Henry Knox Sherrill, were educated on the interdependence of Christianity and free-market economics. At the Committee's first annual meeting—held in Princeton, New Jersey, in April 1952—attendees were
treated to a gala dinner at the Princeton Inn, followed by a series of speeches
from J. Howard Pew's favorite libertarian thinkers. Vernon Orval Watts, chief

economist for the Pew-funded Foundation for Economic Education (FEE), took as his subject "The Meaning of Freedom." Howard Kershner, of the Christian Freedom Foundation, delivered a speech entitled "God, Gold and Government," which drew a direct line between FDR's Depression-era decision to abandon the gold standard and a host of contemporary social ills, from ballooning budget deficits to the erosion of traditional mores. Even the religious service that closed the weekend's festivities was tinged with political significance. Instead of recruiting a clergyman to deliver the Sunday morning sermon, Pew tapped Walter H. Judd, a former medical missionary and staunchly anticommunist Republican Congressman known for heaping scorn on Red China and the Fair Deal in roughly equal measure.[10]

That an entity so clearly at odds with the *Weltanschauung* of the mainline ecumenical project as Pew's Lay Committee actually got off the ground—that it did not provoke a full-blown revolt in the ranks of the denominational representatives who populated the NCC bureaucracy—was a testament to the diplomatic skills of Cavert and Sherrill. For a time, the two men successfully managed the delicate balancing act of convincing Pew that the NCC was open to incorporating the insights of free-market advocates into the organization's research programs and policy pronouncements while at the same time assuring nervous clerics and moderate lay leaders that Pew's aim was not, after all, to transform the NCC into a God-ordained bludgeon against the welfare state. But the deep philosophical divisions between the two camps could not be papered over forever. They burst to the surface in spectacular fashion in late 1952 and early 1953, when a pair of crises forced the NCC leadership to decide just how far down the libertarian path it was willing to travel.

The first crisis was sparked by the imminent publication of *Goals of Economic Life*, an NCC-sponsored volume that sought to provide a Christian perspective on modern economic problems.[11] In 1947 Cameron P. Hall, James Myers's successor as head of the FCC's Department of Industrial Relations—which would soon be reorganized and renamed the Department of the Church and Economic Life (DCEL)—had approached Paul Hoffman, the president of Studebaker, and Chester Barnard, head of New Jersey Bell, seeking input on the future direction of his department. Barnard, who served on the board of the Rockefeller Foundation, floated the idea of a book-length study that would explore some of the questions raised by the delegates to the FCC's 1947 Pittsburgh convention on the Church and Economic Life. The Foundation soon came through with a $100,000 grant, as well as a promise from Harper Brothers to publish the finished volume. The role of the FCC's research staff would be to formulate specific research questions and hire prominent academics to answer them.[12]

The resulting manuscript, unveiled by Hall's renamed department in July 1952, exceeded all expectations. The table of contents was packed with intellectual heavyweights, including the economists John Maurice Clark, Frank Knight, Kenneth Boulding, Eduard Heimann, and William Vickrey; the theologians John C. Bennett and Reinhold Niebuhr; the sociologist Robert Morrison MacIver; and the noted law professor Walton Hamilton. NCC officials were also pleased to discover that the book's substantive arguments, while occasionally provocative, remained well within the bounds of traditional mainline critiques of laissez-faire capitalism. Indeed, several commentators echoed the argument of Arthur Schlesinger's best-selling 1949 book, *The Vital Center*, which posited that the economic middle ground between communism and laissez-faire capitalism offered the surest foundation for liberal democracy. Even Knight, the only card-carrying conservative among the contributors, conceded that economic inequality was dangerous to democracy and often the result of factors beyond the control of individual citizens. Given that the "possession of economic capacity by an individual is determined largely by the position in society into which he is born . . . or by biological heredity . . . and only to a limited degree by his own efforts," Knight wrote, there could be no "serious opposition" to government initiatives, such as progressive taxation and Social Security, that provided citizens with a modicum of protection against the vicissitudes of the market.[13]

From Pew's perspective, of course, such claims were tantamount to heresy. Only a few days after receiving the galley proofs of the book, he penned a scathing letter to Cavert in which he derided the contributors as "economists [who are] without standing in their profession" and "totalitarian in their philosophy." (The sole exception, according to Pew, was Frank Knight, though one wonders whether Pew actually read his chapter.) That most of the contributors posited the existence of a placid middle ground between communism and market fundamentalism was, according to Pew, the strongest evidence of their treachery. For as everyone knew, the Bolshevik playbook instructed American advocates of communism to be subtle in their arguments, advocating only moderate-seeming half measures which, "if adopted, would inevitably lead to communism." Never one to shy away from hyperbole, Pew lamented that the book's publication would rank among the greatest humiliations of his life. As the public face of the Lay Committee, the appearance of such a volume under Council auspices would leave him "disgraced in the eyes of all my friends and associates."[14]

In a desperate attempt to discredit the *Goals of Economic Life*, Pew wrote the Christian Freedom Foundation's George Koether asking the CFF's research staff to conduct a thorough background check on the volume's thirteen coauthors.[15] Koether, who knew that Pew signed his paychecks, replied immediately with the news that most of the contributors were either "not sound in [their] economics" or "basically socialistic [in outlook]." Only Knight, who was vouched for by libertarian luminary Ludwig von Mises, was above suspicion, though Koether hastened to add that Mises did not necessarily "agree with Knight in every detail."

Koether promised to report back in a few weeks with additional "background" on all of the contributors, including any "Red affiliations."[16] He delivered his final report in early September 1952, accompanied by a letter announcing that the enclosed "biographical data" would give Pew "considerable ammunition with which to confront the . . . Council."[17] (Although the report is not preserved in Pew's papers, it presumably included the same sorts of sensational allegations that filled popular conservative books like John T. Flynn's *The Road Ahead* and Edgar C. Bundy's *Collectivism in the Churches*—for example, that Union Theological Seminary, where both Niebuhr and Bennett taught, was a hotbed of subversive activity.)[18]

Armed with this new information, Pew penned a much longer missive to Luther A. Weigle, the former dean of the Yale Divinity School, who was now chair of the NCC's Committee of Reference, and therefore theoretically in a position to recommend that the Council pull its support for the volume. This time Pew took aim at what he regarded as the book's most glaring flaw: the assumption, shared by nearly all of the contributors, that concentrated economic power was inherently threatening to human dignity, and ultimately to American democracy.[19] In fact, Pew insisted, the idea of "economic power" was little more than a "myth" invented by Marxist academics who hoped to "set [themselves] up as . . . judge[s]" over economic matters that they barely understood—or perhaps did understand, but were deliberately fudging in the service of the Soviets. In a remarkable inversion of the golden rule, Pew even went so far as to endorse the right of the wealthy to hoard their assets in the face of widespread human suffering. What Reinhold Niebuhr and the other contributors to *Goals of Economic Life* would call callous greed was in fact socially beneficial, he insisted, since it "tend[ed] to prevent a man from giving away the property he had worked hard to acquire, to the shiftless or incapable . . . and [thus to prevent] the demoralization that follows the gift of easy money."[20]

Unwilling to risk a public break with Pew and his allies, the NCC's leadership eventually proposed a compromise: The volume would be published, but it would not be described as an NCC-sponsored work. Instead, it would feature a foreword explaining that while Council staff members had helped facilitate the project, the contributors spoke only for themselves. This concession may have spared Pew from being "disgraced" in the eyes of his libertarian friends, but he was undoubtedly rankled by the volume of press coverage the book received—much of it engineered by NCC officials. A few months before the publication date, Charles P. Taft, who had recently accepted the chairmanship of the DCEL (with Hall remaining on as the head staff person), described the book in the *New York Times* as the "most significant" project ever attempted by the NCC, predicting that it would be "widely used in church groups, discussion classes, and other avenues of promotion."[21] A few months later Taft moderated a national NBC radio "discussion" that promoted *Goals of Economic Life* as mainline Protestantism's answer to postwar economic anxieties. The former FCC president was joined on the air by fellow DCEL members John C. Bennett, J. Kermit Eby, and Noel Sargent. Of the four, only Sargent, a NAM official, attempted a defense of "free society," and even he managed only the mealy-mouthed conclusion that "inequality is [not] evil per se," provided that private wealth was "used in a proper way in accordance with Christian ethics" (a perspective that would presumably rule out hoarding one's resources as a way of spurring the poor to redouble their labors). Taft, for his part, had nothing positive to say about those who claimed that the church should exit the economic field and "stick to religion." This, according to the DCEL's chairman, was precisely what Hitler had said to his country's clergymen: "You stick to preaching the Gospel on Sunday, and I'll take care of the economy and everything else."[22]

A second major challenge to Pew's worldview would prove even more difficult to turn back. Around the time the book controversy petered out, Pew received in the mail a copy of a statement of principles that had recently been approved—unanimously, no less—by the DCEL's membership. Entitled "Basic Christian Principles and Assumptions for Economic Life," the statement pulled no punches in laying out the traditional Protestant case against laissez-faire economics. Its opening section featured a classic summation of the stewardship ideal that might well have come from the pen of Lyman Beecher or Leonard Bacon: "All the re-sources of the earth . . . which under the laws of men become property . . . are gifts of God, and every form of ownership or control or use of such property must be kept under the most severe scrutiny so that it may not distort the purpose of God's creation. God is the only absolute owner. 'The earth is the Lord's, and the fullness thereof.' (Psalm 24:1)." After affirming the importance of laws to protect basic property rights, as well as the duty of every able-bodied man to work for the support of "himself and his family," the proposed statement, like the essays in the Rockefeller volume, flatly rejected the notion that redistributive programs were an affront to the personal freedom of the wealthy. Indeed, forms of property that gave "men power over others" stood "in special need of moral criticism," and might justifiably be limited—though certainly not abolished—in the name of mitigating human suffering.[23]

Pew found such sentiments hard enough to swallow when they appeared in a dense, scholarly volume that was bound to escape the notice of most Americans. But now they had found their way into a policy pronouncement that was up for consideration at the Council's next General Board meeting. If approved, the statement would inevitably be described in the press as the official position of the nation's largest Protestant ecumenical body. Not surprisingly, an irate Pew imme-diately fired off a letter to Cavert complaining that the proposed statement was "neither basic, [nor] Christian, nor does it enunciate a principle. . . . 'Erroneous Assumptions' might be a better title."[24]

Contrary to Pew's suspicions, the driving force behind both the Rockefeller volume and the statement of economic principles was no radical. Charles P. Taft was, rather, a prominent Republican politician and a major figure in the ecumenical movement, having served in the late 1940s as the first lay president of the FCC. By the time of the NCC's formation, he had scaled back his church activities to focus on politics; he would be the Republican party's 1952 nominee for governor of Ohio, and his brother, Senate Republican Leader Robert A. Taft, was an early favorite in the race for the 1952 presidential nomination. Still, Taft had agreed to remain with the reorganized Council as head of the DCEL, and he took the job quite seriously. Although he was sensitive to claims that the Council had become too closely linked to organized labor, and although he often worked to tone down official pronouncements that he deemed one-sided or overly critical of business (as in the case of the 1947 Pittsburgh Conference), he saw himself as a mediator whose primary responsibility was to identity ethical points on which the DCEL's labor and business representatives could reach agreement. More to the point, Taft never wavered in his conviction that the ultimate purpose of the ecumenical movement was to shine a light on those aspects of American society that tended to inhibit the spiritual flourishing of individual believers and their families—not the least of which was the lack of an adequate safety net to protect citizens who, through no fault of their own, found their lives upended by sickness or unemployment.[25]

With a public figure of Charles Taft's stature throwing his full weight behind the "Basic Principles" statement, Pew knew that burying the document would require more than back-channel pressure; it would require a public show of force. The Lay Committee's 1953 annual meeting, held in Hershey, Pennsylvania, provided the perfect occasion for such a display. With Cavert and other top NCC officials in attendance, Pew reserved four hours of the weekend's program for a discussion of the statement. One after another his handpicked representatives of lay opinion denounced the document as "communistic" and deserving of "the most severe criticism." The group then formed a subcommittee to draft an official response, which was to be presented at the May 1953 meeting of the General Board.[26] The resulting resolution deemed the "Basic Principles" statement "totally inadequate and basically defective both as to what it says and what it fails to say," claiming that "its adoption would offend the majority of people belonging to the Council's member churches."[27] Any economic statement endorsed by the General Board, the Lay Committee members insisted, should be "completely revised . . . [to] take cognizance of the contributions which the American [economic] system has made to human welfare, to the establishment of freedom, justice and order and in the implementation of Christian principles."[28] In addition, some Committee members wrote directly to Cavert threatening to withdraw financial support if the present version of the DCEL statement saw the light of day.[29]

The tactic worked. Faced with the unified opposition of the Lay Committee, Cavert pressured Taft and Cameron Hall to withhold the document from the upcoming General Board meeting and to revise it along the lines suggested by the Pew faction. The "Basic Principles" statement, Cavert now insisted, was "behind the times," and should be "oriented more to the situation of today, when people are deeply concerned to know whether it is possible to preserve our economic system . . . in the face of a worldwide conspiracy against it."[30] Taft defended his Department's work vigorously, taking particular umbrage at claims that the statement had been prepared by either economic amateurs or closet communists. He noted that "a very good group economists," none of whom were "generally described as Leftists," had participated in the drafting process, and that the resulting document "represented a middle-of-the-road view."[31] Nonetheless, he ultimately agreed that the Department should take a few months to "recast the statement in the light of [the] many comments of a constructive character" it had received.[32]

Pew regarded the tabling of the economic statement as a major victory for "freedom in the marketplace." And it was precisely for the purpose of defending this variety of freedom, he admitted to Cavert, that he had signed on with the NCC in the first place. But as usual, the defense of capitalism was mingled in the chairman's mind with the defense of Christianity. "When I accepted to serve on the Lay Committee," he wrote, "it was solely in the hope that I could render a service to the cause of Christianity. That is the spirit which permeates the minds and the hearts of all those who today constitute the Lay Committee. We seek no glory; we covet no power." [33] Given Pew's firm—if self-serving—belief that economic power was a myth, he well have been sincere in claiming that he and his ideological allies were uninterested in exercising earthly authority. In any event, they were about to discover that, at least within the confines of the NCC, religious authority was no myth. Stalling the statement of economic principles would be Pew's last significant triumph over his "collectivist" adversaries in the mainline ranks.

The Stewards and the Libertarians

Despite Pew's initial success at manipulating the NCC bureaucracy, it soon became apparent that his strategy of using financial leverage to engineer a top-down reorientation of the Council's economic philosophy suffered from two serious flaws. The first stemmed from the Council's highly democratic and decentralized decision-making structure. By design, individual departments such as the DCEL enjoyed a great deal of autonomy in formulating policy pronouncements and research projects. The General Board retained the authority to endorse or reject the end result—in short, veto power—but it lacked the ability to set the agenda. Nor was there much that either NCC officials or the General Board could do in the way of shutting down disfavored projects or lines of inquiry. As a result, Pew's crusade to prevent the NCC from weighing in on contemporary social and economic problems often resembled a game of Whack-a-Mole. More than once, he managed to cajole a recalcitrant department head into temporary submission, only to find that a different department was on the verge of issuing a closely related pronouncement that was no less offensive to his sensibilities.[34]

Pew's second—and more serious—error stemmed from his failure to recognize that his true enemy was not a tiny cadre of left-leaning clergymen, but rather a religious *identity* that was shared by a large swath of laymen and women, including a number of corporate leaders who were more than capable of exerting financial pressure of their own. The problem was not that the views of denominational leaders were increasingly remote from those of the laity; it was that the culture of American Protestantism as a whole cut against Pew's deeply held ideological convictions.

In fact, despite Pew's frequent assertions to the contrary, the NCC was not an elitist body ruled by out-of-touch clerical bureaucrats. Although the organization's upper echelons were dominated by clergymen, the Council's democratic structure was designed to ensure that the views of all American Protestants—or at least those in participating denominations—were fairly represented in the decision-making process. Important positions, such as seats on the General Board, were allocated in proportion to the size of the underlying denominations: the Methodists got more seats than the Presbyterians, who got more seats than the Congregationalists, and so on. Moreover, the individuals who filled these positions were selected by the denominations themselves, often through a democratically governed conclave such as a national assembly or convention. Pew's accusations of elite bias were more plausible when directed at lower-level bodies such as the departments, which were often composed of individuals recruited by NCC staff members (as opposed to being selected democratically by the denominations). But even here the selection process was constrained by guidelines that encouraged the allocation of seats on the basis of denominational size, and also by the fact that NCC officials were acutely aware that pronouncements issuing from ideologically or professionally homogenous bodies would never be accepted as truly representative of Protestant opinion.[35]

In the late 1940s, for example, Cameron Hall had restructured the Department of the Church and Economic Life for the explicit purpose of increasing business representation. One of the major weaknesses of the old Department of Industrial

Relations, as Hall explained in a later interview, was that it had included only "one employer . . . and he was a Quaker from Philadelphia"—an arrangement that made it all but impossible for the Department to present itself as the mouthpiece of Protestant opinion writ large.[36] The reorganized DCEL, in contrast, featured 125 members, including several prominent executives, a roughly equal number of labor officials, as well as representatives from agriculture, academia, and the clergy.[37] Early recruits from the business community included Studebaker's Paul G. Hoffman, J. Irwin Miller of the Cummins Engine Company, Chester I. Barnard of New Jersey Bell, W. Howard Chase of General Foods, J. Stanford Smith of General Electric, Robert E. Wilson of Standard Oil, John A. Stephens of U.S. Steel, John H. Hart of Goodrich Rubber, W. Walter Williams of Continental Mortgage, and S. Guernsey Jones, a prominent Newark banker.[38]

In terms of politics, the typical DCEL member was a moderate Republican, and several were close advisors of President Eisenhower; Williams and Chase would eventually occupy posts in Ike's Commerce Department, and Hoffman was largely responsible for persuading the retired general to pursue the Republican nomination in 1952.[39] Yet the group also included several active members whose views fell well to the left of the mainstream. One was Jerry Voorhis, the former California congressman who, after losing his seat to a Red-baiting Richard Nixon in 1946, became a leading figure in the cooperative movement. Another was J. Kermit Eby, a Brethren minister and theology professor who directed the research bureau of the Congress of Industrial Organizations (CIO) for several years. The Reuther brothers—Walter and Victor—who had risen through the ranks of the United Auto Workers to become, respectively, president and educational director of the CIO were also members, though in the early 1950s they rarely attended meetings. The DCEL even featured a number of representatives from the Far Right. Pew himself was a nominal member, and several of his allies, including the NAM's Noel Sargent and Lois Black Hunter, co-chairperson of the Lay Committee, were quite active in DCEL activities, if only for the purpose of keeping a close eye on their adversaries.[40] Looking back on his time with the DCEL, Voorhis was most impressed by the fact that the bulk of the group's members were able to set aside partisan differences and develop a "deep respect for one another around our common commitment to the Christian gospel." He had developed close friendships with both Taft and Jones, Voorhis told an interviewer in the late 1970s, "despite the fact that we were always on opposite sides of the fence politically" and locked horns "in almost every meeting."[41]

But for all its ideological diversity, the DCEL clearly contained an ethical center of gravity. In fact, as can be seen in Table 5.1, its core members shared several formative experiences, each of which tended to reinforce the Protestant ethic of stewardship. First, and most obviously, they were raised in, and in most cases continued to attend, mainline Protestant churches. Accordingly, they were

Table 5.1 Business representatives on the NCC's Department of the Church and Economic Life (DCEL)
( ) = Number of meetings attended between January 1951 and April 1953 (out of a total of 8 meetings)

Name	Employment	Denomination	College	CED?	YMCA?
Chester I. Barnard (0)	N. J. Bell	Congregational	Harvard		
W. Howard Chase (4)	General Foods	Reformed	U. of Iowa		
John N. Hart (4)	Goodrich Rubber	Congregational	Ohio State		
S. Guernsey Jones (1)	Banker	Congregational			
J. Irwin Miller (0)	Cummins Engine Co.	Disciples of Christ	Yale	X	
Frank W. Pierce (5)	Standard Oil (NJ)	Congregational	Cornell		
Wesley F. Rennie (1)	Committee for Economic Development	Methodist	Hillsdale College	X	X
Noel Sargent (3)	National Association of Manufacturers	Episcopalian	U. of Washington		
John A. Stephens (2)	U.S. Steel	Presbyterian USA	Wesleyan		
J. Stanford Smith (3)	General Electric	Methodist	DePauw		
Charles P. Taft (5)	Attorney	Episcopalian	Yale	X	X
W. Walter Williams (1)	Continental Mortgage	Congregational	U. of Washington	X	X
Robert E. Wilson (0)	Standard Oil (IN)	Presbyterian USA	College of Wooster	X	X

well aware of the churches' long-standing concerns with respect to issues such as systemic unemployment and economic inequality; and as lay leaders in their respective denominations, several had helped shape church pronouncements on these issues.[42] Second, most DCEL members had attended respected universities, typically Ivy League institutions or prestigious liberal-arts colleges, where they often held leadership roles in Protestant student organizations. Third, several had extensive experience in Protestant ecumenical work, typically through either the YMCA or (in the case of a small handful of female members) the YWCA. Indeed, at least three of the group's business representatives—Williams, Rennie, and Taft—were past presidents or board members of the YMCA, and two current YMCA officials, Dalton McClelland and Eugene E. Barnett, were also DCEL members.[43]

In addition to their similar religious and educational backgrounds, many of the DCEL's core members shared an additional characteristic: they were simultaneously active in the Committee for Economic Development (CED), an influential postwar think tank that advocated a center-left approach to the period's major economic and social problems. Indeed, the links between the CED and the DCEL ran deep. Studebaker chairman Paul Hoffmann was both a founding member of the DCEL and the first chairman (and cofounder) of the CED; when Hoffman resigned the CED chairmanship to accept a post in the Truman administration, W. Walter Williams, another DCEL member, was named as his replacement.[44] In addition, both Taft and J. Irwin Miller were CED trustees, and Wesley F. Rennie, another DCEL member, served as the CED's executive director.[45] The CED, in turn, enjoyed close relationships with the major New York–based foundations, as did several of the DCEL's core members: Chester Barnard served as president of the Rockefeller Foundation in the early 1950s, Hoffman was a past president of the Ford Foundation, and Miller was a longtime board member of the Ford Foundation.

Although dominated by businessmen, the CED—like the Ford and Rockefeller Foundations—had little use for Pew's brand of libertarianism. It was fervently internationalist, skeptical of austerity measures, supportive of moderate forms of state intervention in the economy (particularly in the area of monetary policy), enthusiastic about federal aid to education, and generally tolerant of organized labor. Above all, it aimed to ensure that the postwar period would not witness a return to the unstable economic conditions of the 1930s. Where mass unemployment and stagnant wages held sway, the CED's leaders believed, political instability—perhaps culminating in authoritarian rule—was sure to follow. Hence, it was in the business community's interest to treat workers fairly and to support government efforts to tame capitalism's inevitable excesses: wages should be kept as high as possible, collective bargaining encouraged, and a robust safety net put in place to aid workers displaced by the inevitable ebbs and flows of the economy. The CED's vision was hardly a master plan for a worker's paradise, but in contrast to Pew's doctrinaire libertarianism it at least conceded the stark reality of economic power. Workers really were at the mercy of forces beyond their control, Hoffman insisted, and there were things that the state could and should do to protect them from the inevitable "tendencies in the system toward booms and depressions."[46]

Given that the memberships of the CED and the DCEL overlapped to a substantial degree, it should come as no surprise that historians have sometimes characterized the DCEL as a body that provided religious cover for policies that its corporate members favored for purely secular reasons.[47] In reality, the question of ultimate motivations may be impossible to answer. For while the laymen who had the greatest role in shaping the DCEL's economic outlook undoubtedly had one eye on the corporate bottom line, most of their views on economic questions were easily squared with the mainline ethic of stewardship (something that could not be said of Pew's libertarian circle). Indeed, the stewardship ideal was second nature to the DCEL's centrist business representatives, and they invoked it constantly in their addresses to religious and civic groups. In a 1952 speech to a Denver church gathering, J. Irwin Miller explained that the DCEL's ultimate aim was to cure American society of its "tragic" tendency to "recognize Christ's role in individual life" while simultaneously promoting "irresponsible selfishness in its public and group life." This meant, among other things, making a case for "wages justly determined, for a concept of work that is dignified and rewarding, and [providing workers with] the voice in industry that Christian principles and democratic tradition demand."[48] Hoffman, who regularly addressed church groups, likewise couched his message in the language of "duty" and "responsibility." The very survival of free society, he told the Los Angeles Council of Church Women in 1951, depended on the cultivation of an "enlightened self-interest—a self-interest attuned to the times we are living in and not the kind of self-interest that would . . . wither on its outmoded prejudices."[49] Americans like Pew, who would gladly abolish the social safety net or eviscerate foreign aid programs in order to marginally lower their own tax bills, were in Hoffman's view doing the Soviets a giant favor.[50]

That Pew found it impossible to credit the religious motivations of businessmen like Miller and Hoffmann was probably due, at least in part, to his rather unusual upbringing. Pew's father, Joseph Newton Pew, managed the remarkable feat of raising his son as a devout Presbyterian while at the same time shielding him from the ethic of social service that pervaded mainline intellectual circles in the decades around the turn of the twentieth century. After amassing a small fortune in the oil and natural gas industries, the elder Pew moved his family to a fashionable Pittsburgh neighborhood and enrolled his three children in expensive private schools. But instead of launching young J. Howard on the usual path trod by the children of oil tycoons—namely, enrollment in an Ivy League institution—Pew's father sent his son, at the tender age of fourteen, to Grove City College, a small, nominally Presbyterian school located sixty miles north of Pittsburgh.[51] Although Grove City's curriculum was superficially similar to other colleges of the period, it was in fact tightly controlled by Joseph Newton Pew, who chaired the board of trustees. To prevent the germination of liberal religious or social theories, the elder Pew installed a close friend as president and forbade the granting of tenure. When it came to selecting faculty members, theological soundness trumped academic qualifications, and many instructors taught subjects in which they had little or no formal training.[52]

Hence, Pew almost certainly encountered no professors whose ideas ran contrary to his father's laissez-faire convictions. Nor was there any possibility of exposure to novel theories of social ethics through involvement with ecumenical student groups, since the teenager lived in a boardinghouse off campus, eschewed extracurricular activities, and was expected to return home every weekend to attend church.[53] After receiving his undergraduate degree, the eighteen-year-old Pew relocated to the Massachusetts Institute of Technology, where he sat in on a handful of courses in thermodynamics and structural design.[54] He left MIT a few months later, when he was still only nineteen, to accept an engineering position with his father's company, Sun Oil, where he would remain for the rest of his professional life.[55]

Lacking direct experience with either ecumenical groups or the larger mainline tradition of social ethics, Pew and his allies frequently mistook principled opposition for personal venality.[56] A case in point: in May 1953, J. Irwin Miller delivered an impromptu speech to the members of the NCC's General Board in which he attacked Pew's Lay Committee as a wolf in sheep's clothing. The Committee's sole aim, Miller suggested, was to "prevent the application of religion to economic affairs," a position that surely violated Christ's injunction that "the Gospel should be applied to all of life." All "groups in economic life need to have their consciences prodded and always will," Miller declared. If the General Board acceded to the demands of the Pew faction, it would "vacate one of its main fields of service to Christians everywhere." Pew and his circle were taken aback by the businessman's brazen accusation—and also by the fact that Miller's remarks were "promptly and vigorously applauded."[57] The only possible explanation for this turn of events, according to Jasper Crane, was a clerical conspiracy: the meeting must have been "pack[ed] . . . to carry through a particular programme," with Miller recruited to act as the stand-in for a bureaucratic cabal that was not "representative of the views of the ministers and lay people of the member churches."[58]

Crane made his allegation in a letter to Samuel McCrea Cavert, who was mystified by the charge. The NCC's general secretary nonetheless made inquiries with various department heads, only to find that the speech had been "Mr. Miller's own idea," and that NCC officials had "had nothing whatever to do with it."[59] At this point Crane posed the question directly to Miller, who reiterated his firm belief that the DCEL's "Basic Principles" statement was consistent with "the oldest and best of Christian traditions," reflecting as it did the core of Jesus's message to the young ruler, as well as his Sermon on the Mount.[60] Crane was eventually satisfied that Miller had acted of his own volition, and the two men in time developed a friendly rapport. Pew, in contrast, nursed an intense and lifelong hatred of Miller and the other left-leaning members of the DCEL, even going so far as to fund private investigations into their affairs in an apparently futile effort to dig up information that could be used discredit his old adversaries.[61] As late as 1968, when Miller was advising New York Governor Nelson Rockefeller in his long-shot bid for the Republican presidential nomination, Pew wrote to frontrunner Richard Nixon's finance chair, Maurice Stans, advising Stans to "investigate" Miller "as thoroughly as possible," for "I have never met a man for whom I hold as low an opinion as I do for Irwin Miller."[62]

The Pressure of Officialdom

By the fall of 1953 it was clear to Cavert and other top NCC officials, including the organization's new president, the Methodist Bishop William C. Martin, that they were caught between two irreconcilable factions. After Pew reiterated his firm opposition to the "Basic Principles" statement at the September General Board meeting, Cavert contacted the DCEL's executive secretary, Cameron Hall, urging him yet again to purge the document of any language that Pew and his allies might find offensive.[63] But Hall refused to back down. Instead, he pulled rank by soliciting a letter from Reinhold Niebuhr, the nation's most influential Protestant theologian (and a DCEL member), declaring that if the Department "went any further in the direction of condemning collectivism and exalting free initiative we would be under the suspicion of abdicating our function of prophetic criticism of culture."[64] Hall then scheduled a Department meeting for early October in which a slightly revised statement was approved with the recommendation that it be resubmitted to the General Board at its January 1954 meeting.[65] After learning of Hall's actions, Jasper Crane and Lois Black Hunter worked the phone lines, urging prominent Lay Committee members to write NCC headquarters with the aim of generating such a large "volume of protest" as would "throw the document into further study" and prevent the issuance of future "socialistic pronouncements."[66] Around twenty-five letters were secured, including one from Edwin Parsons, executive secretary of the National Council of Northern Baptist Men, who offered a succinct summary of the Lay Committee's guiding philosophy. "Laymen," he wrote, were "not interested in being handed down any more dilemmas. They have enough already."[67]

The two factions met face to face at the January General Board meeting, though major fireworks were avoided when Taft agreed to withdraw the statement yet again and to consider further revisions. This time, however, the DCEL's chairman drew a line in the sand. Indeed, the former FCC president delivered a lengthy prepared speech in which he laid out the "serious and perhaps insoluble" disagreement that had arisen between the Pew faction and much of the rest of the Council. In short, the Pew forces seemed to believe that "the supreme and unique Christian value and teaching is the dignity of the individual and his freedom and responsibility from which it follows inevitably that *any* (repeat *any*) interference by the state in the free-market economy is un-Christian because it limits the freedom and diminishes the responsibility of the individual. . . . [The free enterprise] system is, therefore, the only Christian economic system. . . . Our department cannot accept any such position in such terms and we doubt if many business men would put it that way."[68] To drive home the point that the DCEL would not be cowed into submission, J. Irwin Miller followed up Taft's speech with a letter to the NCC's associate general secretary, Roy G. Ross, declaring that the statement had "now become a test for the Council." If the General Board allowed Pew and his allies to block this "extraordinarily fair and well balanced" statement, Miller warned, it would send an unmistakable message that NCC policy pronouncements were now for sale to the highest bidder.[69]

Perhaps it was seeing two of the nation's most prominent lay leaders state the issue in such bald terms that at last rallied the Council's leaders to take a stand. Or perhaps the public's growing dissatisfaction with Senator Joseph McCarthy's communism investigations made Council officials less sensitive to accusations of "collectivist" infiltration in the churches, and thus more willing to risk a public break with one of the nation's chief Red-baiters. Or it may simply have been that the NCC's finances were in reasonably good shape by this point, leaving it less dependent on Pew's largesse. Whatever the reason, events in early 1954 quickly spiraled out of Pew's control.

The first sign of trouble came when the NCC's Committee on the Maintenance of American Freedom, an ad hoc body formed in response to the early 1950s Red Scare, publicly condemned Congress's increasingly aggressive efforts to root out suspected communist sympathizers in the nation's schools, churches, and bureaucracies. Upon being appointed to the Committee, Pew's close ally Jasper Crane had worked diligently to reorient its mission from defending the civil liberties of religious leaders to defending the free market. He urged that membership invitations be extended to such libertarian luminaries as Howard Kershner and Leonard E. Read, head of the Pew-funded Foundation for

Economic Education (FEE), and also suggested that "instead of feuding with the House Un-American Activities Committee," the Committee should consider "cooperat[ing] with them."[70] Instead, the Committee, under the leadership of former NCC president Henry Knox Sherrill, threw itself into the struggle against the phenomenon now known as McCarthyism.[71] In March 1954 it secured the General Board's endorsement for a statement accusing the House Un-American Activities Committee (HUAC) and McCarthy's Senate Committee of a range of procedural abuses.[72] Four months later Francis C. Harmon, a lawyer and Freedom Committee member who occasionally allied himself with the Pew forces, appeared before the Senate Committee on Rules and Administration, declaring in no uncertain terms that the National Council of Churches regarded congressional investigators' "improper conduct" as a "real and present danger to civil rights" and a threat to "our basic freedoms."[73] Crane later lamented that, instead of standing firm against the collectivists, the Freedom Committee had made common cause with them, describing the whole episode as "the most un-happy connection of my whole life."[74]

Adding insult to injury, the DCEL voted in late April to once again approve the "Basic Principles" statement, setting up yet another showdown at the General Board's September meeting. This last affront left Pew so discouraged that he wrote to Crane to announce that he was "finished with the National Council."[75] Crane, however, urged Pew not to go down without a fight. Convinced that the Lay Committee was, despite appearances, "going to win" in the end, he persuaded Pew and the rest of the Committee to coalesce around a three-pronged plan that, if successful, would at last wrest control of the Council from "left-wing church officialdom."[76] The first prong was to submit to the General Board a resolution requiring a supermajority (80 percent) vote of the Board in order to approve policy pronouncements. The second was a reso-lution that would bar the DCEL from considering further pronouncements or initiating studies without the explicit approval of the General Board.[77] Finally, the General Board would be asked to hold an up-or-down vote on a new state-ment of principles—informally known as the "Lay Affirmation"—that would admonish the Council for abandoning its "spiritual" and "evangelical" roots and attempting to "[sit] in judgment on current secular affairs."[78] What all this amounted to, of course, was a last-ditch attempt at a coup. If the Pew forces played their cards correctly at the Board's September meeting, Crane insisted, Charles Taft and his clerical allies would be "bereft of . . . support" and "the church . . . diverted from socialism and led over to the right side in the struggle for freedom."[79]

In the end, it was the pessimistic Pew who had the clearer view of the situation at NCC headquarters. By the late summer of 1954 even centrist NCC officials like President William Martin and Associate General Secretary Roy G. Ross wanted no part of Pew's "Lay Affirmation," which, if adopted, would have committed the Council to the dismantling of the welfare state.[80] Nor was there much interest in radically remaking the NCC's internal decision-making structure. Hence, instead of joining forces with the Pew faction to curb Taft's influence within the Council, Ross and Martin plotted strategy with the center-left forces, so that when the day of the General Board meeting finally arrived the Lay Committee's representatives found themselves outmaneuvered at every turn.[81] In a complex series of moves, the Board methodically dismissed each of Pew's three proposals. And then came the coup de grace: by a vote of seventy-seven to four, the Board adopted the "Basic Principles" statement as an official pronouncement of the Council.[82]

The final statement was, to be sure, a watered-down version of the one originally approved by the DCEL in 1952. The most significant changes concerned the communist threat. A passage that may well have originated with the NAM's Noel Sargent warned that "a thoroughgoing collectivism" that looked "to the state to remedy every evil creates its own evils. It may easily become a threat to freedom as well as to efficiency." Yet the core of the original message remained: the statement explicitly endorsed the stewardship principle, condemned excessive economic inequality, called for a basic standard of living, endorsed programs to aid the "sick, the aged, and the incapacitated," and advocated equality of opportunity for all Americans, including "equal access . . . to health, education, and employment."[83] What the Pew forces undoubtedly found most galling, however, was that the DCEL's economic manifesto received front-page coverage in the *New York Times*. Under a headline reading "Church Council Sets Social Code," readers were informed that the NCC's General Board—an entity representing the views of "35,000,000 persons"—had adopted the statement by an overwhelming margin, thereby overruling "a layman's group within the council that contended . . . that the church should . . . refrain from speaking out on political, social and economic issues that might tend to divide churchgoers." At the conclusion of the article, readers were directed to the last few pages of Section A, where they could read the four-thousand-word missive in its entirety.[84]

With rapprochement no longer a realistic possibility, the incoming NCC president, Eugene Carson Blake, began making plans to disband the Lay Committee, with the understanding that any members who so desired would be absorbed into other NCC departments that reflected their particular interests.[85] Pew, meanwhile, began making plans to engineer precisely the sort of messy public divorce the NCC's top brass most feared. In January 1956, after formally resigning his NCC post, he printed and distributed thousands of copies of a book-length collection of documents entitled *The Chairman's Final Report to the National Lay Committee*. Not surprisingly, the book's three hundred pages of text—including forty appendices—painted the Lay Committee in a highly positive light; the rest of the NCC, in contrast, came off as an elite-dominated, communist-friendly body that was utterly indifferent to the views of rank-and-file churchgoers. Characteristically, Pew lambasted the NCC for involving itself in "political" questions while at the same time insisting that Christian laymen were duty bound to oppose the "expanded state" and to support programs that fostered "the dignity and responsibility of the individual."[86]

Having lobbed his long-awaited bombshell, the ex-chairman sat back and awaited the press's reaction. He was undoubtedly pleased when his friend David Lawrence included a lengthy account of the Lay Committee's travails— complete with numerous verbatim quotations from *The Chairman's Final Report*—in a February 1956 issue of *U.S. News and World Report*.[87] But with the exception of reliably conservative outlets like Carl McIntire's *Christian Beacon*, Spiritual Mobilization's *Faith and Freedom*, and the *Southern Presbyterian Journal* (edited by Pew's friend—and Billy Graham's father-in-law—L. Nelson Bell), the widespread outrage he had hoped to provoke largely failed to materialize. And, indeed, left-leaning publications like *Christian Century* found his charges fairly easy to rebut. For if the Council were indifferent to lay opinion, as Pew claimed, then why did it reserve more than 100 of the seats on its 250-member General Board for laypeople? If it was true that the Council's policy pronouncements had alienated a large percentage of the laity, then why was it suddenly awash in cash, even receiving "help from contributors who would not have given" if "the church's representatives" had not stood up to the Pew forces? Was it not the case that the stiffest opposition to the Lay Committee had come from other laymen within the NCC ranks, including Charles P. Taft and J. Irwin Miller? And was it not, in fact, the Pew faction that had attempted to set itself up as a "House of Lords, with veto power of those actions of the officially appointed representatives of the churches which did not suit them"?[88]

Instead of directly rebutting the charge of elitism, Pew's small band of allies in the press embraced the characterization of the Lay Committee as a small and unrepresentative body—albeit a righteous one. According to *United Evangelical Action*, the house organ of the National Association of Evangelicals, these "titans of industry" were to be commended for fighting the good fight against "liberalism," which was "rampant in the whole structure" of the NCC. If Pew and his allies were guilty of anything, it was to have naively supposed that the bulk of "pastors . . . and . . . men who have been accorded high positions in denominational and inter-church organizations" were trustworthy, when they were in fact little more than a collection of "Communist-fronters, political meddlers of socialistic persuasion, [and] doubters of the faith."[89]

The Elusive Center

The fear that the Lay Committee's demise would transform the NCC into a bastion of radicalism was, of course, unfounded. In fact, the Council's economic orientation remained squarely in the vital center, as defined by Taft, Miller and the other powerful laymen who served as the organization's ideological rudder. But applying stewardship principles to politically charged economic problems remained a complicated business, even after Pew's departure. In the late 1950s and early 1960s, both labor and management expended a great deal of energy attempting to shape, promote, or block particular policy pronouncements, knowing that the mouthpiece of "the church," when it chose to speak, would receive wide coverage in the press. More than once the Council and its agencies found themselves caught up in political firestorms, attacked as ferociously from the left as from the right.

The controversy over right-to-work laws offers a case in point. The laws had their origin in the 1947 Taft-Hartley Act, a measure enacted over President Harry Truman's veto that effectively gutted the 1935 Wagner Act by, among other things, outlawing closed-shop agreements—arrangements that effectively forbade employers from hiring nonunion workers. (The law was cosponsored by Ohio Senator Bob Taft, one of organized labor's staunchest foes in the Senate.) In addition, Section 14(b) authorized individual states to take the further step of outlawing union-shop and agency-shop agreements, or arrangements that left hiring decisions in the hands of management while requiring newly hired workers to either join a union or contribute to the cost of union representation.[90] During the late 1940s and early 1950s laws inspired by 14(b) were adopted by eighteen states, mostly in the South. Proponents of these right-to-work laws, including the National Association of Manufacturers and the U.S. Chamber of Commerce, argued that they simply protected the individual worker who, for whatever reason, preferred not to be affiliated with a union. But critics, including many church-affiliated groups, countered that the real purpose of 14(b) was to drain the coffers of organized labor by making it difficult for unions to collect dues from workers that they were in many cases legally obligated to represent. (Labor thus dubbed the measures "right-to-wreck" laws.) Moreover, the critics pointed out, the "right-to-work" moniker was highly misleading, since closed-shop arrangements—the type that actually gave unions control of the hiring process—were already illegal under federal law. Nor, it goes without saying, did the new laws give anyone a guarantee of a job. As the Ohio Conference of the Methodist Church explained in an official pronouncement, "The term 'right-to-work' is an incorrect description of the proposed legislation since it would neither give the worker the right to demand a job of any employer nor would it prevent the employer from discharging him."[91]

The issue remained very much alive in the mid-1950s, as right-to-work supporters were pushing to ban union and agency shops in several Western and Midwestern states while organized labor was simultaneously launching a campaign to roll back right-to-work laws in the states where they had been adopted. It was at this point that the NCC's Department of the Church and Economic Life entered the fray. In early 1955, at the urging of Cameron Hall, the Department began work on a right-to-work statement. By early 1956 it had approved a lengthy document which, after dutifully laying out both sides of the argument, came down squarely against right-to-work laws, calling them "not in the public interest." In an attempt to be evenhanded, the document also contained a lengthy section listing the "democratic safeguards" to which workers in union shops were entitled. Among other things, unions were not to require "excessive initiation fees and dues," nor were they to discriminate on the basis of "race, creed, color, national origin, [or] sex." They were to hold "free and regular elections of union officials, with ample provision for free and secret expression of opinion on nominations, elections, and policy issues." And they were to provide adequate "protection against arbitrary or discriminatory treatment" of those who, for reasons of conscience or otherwise, "cannot participate in all the conditions of membership."[92]

Predictably, the Council's remaining conservative business leaders were less than pleased by the Department's actions. In early spring both S. Guernsey Jones and Robert E. Wilson wrote to Mildred McAfee Horton, the Council vice president whose jurisdiction covered Hall's department, to request that she quash the statement before it could be voted on by the General Board. Although Jones and Wilson had defended the Council's right to address economic questions during the "Basic Principles" kerfuffle, both men now blasted the DCEL for incorrectly applying Christian "moral and ethical" principles to the issue at hand. Instead of protecting the freedom and dignity of the individual worker, Jones complained, the Department had "violate[d] the principle of an individual's freedom of choice so flagrantly" as to risk alienating "a great segment of our church membership."[93] Nor was this an innocent mistake. According to Wilson, the whole point of the statement was to aid labor-friendly candidates in the November election. Organized labor's representatives in the Department had even admitted as much, he alleged, warning that if the Council did not quickly approve a right-to-work statement, "it would be too late for most of this winter's state legislative sessions where vigorous attempts at repeal are again being made."[94]

The woman who would ultimately determine the fate of the right-to-work document, Mildred McAfee Horton, was very much a product of the mainline establishment. The daughter and granddaughter of Presbyterian clergymen, Horton was both a respected academic and a pioneering government administrator. Her academic career began at Vassar, where she studied economics, sociology, and

English while also serving as president of the college's chapter of the Young Women's Christian Association (YWCA). After earning a master's degree in sociology from the University of Chicago, she served briefly as an administrator at Centre College, then, at the age of thirty-six, accepted the presidency of Wellesley. During World War II she left academia for a government position as chief administrator of Women Accepted for Volunteer Emergency Service (WAVES), an organization of eighty thousand female volunteers that aided the Navy war effort on the home front. Her leadership of the WAVES—a highly unusual organization in the context of the 1940s—made her something of a national celebrity, and in 1945 she appeared on the cover of *Time*. Shortly thereafter she married Douglas Horton, dean emeritus of the Harvard Divinity School and a leading Congregational official.[95]

Horton's economic philosophy was shaped by her Presbyterian upbringing, as well as her long association with—and academic study of—the YWCA. (Her master's thesis examined the organization's growth and development.) She later recounted that her parents had raised her "to believe in the essential worth of every human being, including myself," and to view even the lowliest of citizens as "children of God." Perhaps for this reason, she oversaw the integration of the WAVES, and also secured federal legislation ensuring that female volunteers received the same benefits as men. And while certainly no radical, she was a consistent and vocal advocate for the rights of organized labor. During her tenure at Wellesley she backed a controversial unionization drive by the college's maintenance employees. When the college's director of personnel complained that labor-management meetings were consuming time that would be better spent on other projects, Horton reportedly replied that "democracy takes time, but it is never a waste of time."[96]

It was this conviction that led Horton to oppose all attempts to unravel the New Deal–era system of collective bargaining. She thus informed Jones and Wilson that she intended to move forward with the DCEL's right-to-work statement, both for procedural reasons—she believed it was not the place of a divisional vice president to veto statements approved by a Department—and because she was "inclined to disapprove of laws which . . . make the state the arbiter on union membership rather than letting free bargaining determine the outcome of negotiations." At the same time, she made it clear that she was open to editorial revisions, particularly ones that would prevent "sentences [from being] quoted out of context" for political purposes.[97] Horton's support all but ensured that the statement would appear on the General Board's agenda. True to her word, however, she first backed an amendment that cut the phrase "not in the public interest" from the document, so that the critical paragraph now ended with the less inflammatory—though still unequivocal—statement that decisions about union and agency shops "should be left to agreement by management and labor through the process of collective bargaining."[98]

This concession was not enough to satisfy the right-to-work advocates on the General Board, however. At the group's June 1956 meeting, Pew's friend B. E. Hutchinson proposed amending the document to recognize that "dedicated Christians" held "highly diverse opinions" on the right-to-work question. In addition, Hutchinson moved that the document's policy recommendation be cut altogether, leaving only the background section and the list of "democratic safeguards" that unions were not to violate. Before this could be voted on, however, Horton proposed a compromise, which was immediately approved: Hutchinson's "highly diverse opinions" language would remain in the document, but so would the policy recommendation. At this point, the statement appeared destined for final approval. During a brief lunch break, however, the more moderate members of the opposition coalesced around a plan to delay a formal statement by the General Board and to instead authorize Horton's Division of Christian Life and Work to publish and distribute the document as "study material" for the purpose of soliciting feedback from relevant constituencies—provided, however, it was made clear that "any such document thus circulated has neither been approved nor disapproved by the General Board." This new proposal passed by the unusually close vote of forty to thirty-two, presumably because it drew opposition from both labor-friendly members (who desperately wanted a General Board pronouncement) and militantly pro-business members (who opposed the publication of *any* anti-right-to-work pronouncement, even one designated as study material, under NCC auspices).[99]

Watered down or not, the statement was more than provocative enough to spark a major row in the press. The National Right to Work Committee, while accurately noting that the Council had not taken an official position on the issue, nonetheless deemed it "strange, ironic and bewildering to find [a division of the NCC] approving of compulsion in a country where religious freedom is a basic tenet and where freedom of religion is protected by the Constitution." It went on to ask, rhetorically, how William Penn, Roger Williams, and other pioneers of religious liberty would feel about the idea of requiring workers to contribute to organizations whose political aims they opposed.[100] The *Southern States Industrial Council Bulletin* shifted the focus from religion to subversion, detecting in the document "the philosophy of socialism and communism."[101] The *National Review*, William F. Buckley's newly launched conservative journal, echoed the latter assessment, adding the novel allegation that the National Council of Churches had been bought off by a grant it had received from the Congress of Industrial Organizations in 1954.[102] (The question of why the Lay Committee's contributions, which dwarfed those of the CIO, had failed to corrupt the Council was not addressed.)

Labor papers, in contrast, trumpeted the statement as an unequivocal blow to the right-to-work cause. More problematically, many of them characterized it as an official pronouncement of the Council, which it plainly was not. The headline in the AFL-CIO *News* was fairly typical: "Council of Churches Opposes 'Wreck' Laws."[103] When a copy of the story reached NCC headquarters, Council president Eugene Carson Blake immediately contacted the paper's editor, Saul Miller, to demand a retraction.[104] Miller complied, though his retraction was hardly less provocative than the original story.[105]

In any event, Blake's attempt to correct the record came too late to prevent the Council from becoming a punching bag in several of that fall's most closely contested elections. In early October, for example, the general secretary of the Seattle Council of Churches contacted NCC headquarters with the news that Washington state's official voter guide listed the Council as formally opposing a right-to-work proposition that was set to appear on the November ballot. Whether this was an honest mistake or an attempt by labor to sway the election was unclear. Regardless, NCC officials worked feverishly to set the record straight.[106]

The most serious controversy, however, came in Kansas, where the right-to-work issue had become a major focus of the state's gubernatorial election. Fred Hall, the Republican incumbent, was a labor-friendly Methodist layman who had recently vetoed a right-to-work bill. Now several of the state's largest employers, including Boeing Airlines and Cessna Aircraft, were out for revenge, and Hall found himself facing a primary challenge from a right-to-work supporter named Warren Shaw. When the two men met face to face in a televised debate, Shaw attacked Hall's veto of the right-to-work measure, leading Hall to respond that his position was identical to that of the National Council of Churches, which, he claimed, had recently issued an unequivocal statement condemning right-to-work legislation. Shaw's campaign manager, James Pratt, immediately contacted NCC headquarters to verify the governor's claim, forcing Eugene Carson Blake to dispatch a telegram stating that the Council had "taken no official position whatever relative to" the right-to-work question.[107] After Shaw defeated Hall in the primary, Pratt again contacted the Council, this time to ask for copy of President Blake's letter to Saul Miller, which he hoped to distribute to prospective voters. He explained that his candidate was now locked in a tight race with Democrat George Docking, and he feared that the "erroneous report" in the AFL-CIO *News* would sway voters—particularly those who weren't able to tell the difference between the Council and its subsidiary units.[108] Once again Blake immediately dispatched a telegram authorizing the request.[109]

Despite the initially high hopes of business groups such as the U.S. Chamber of Commerce and NAM, 1956 was not a banner year for the right-to-work movement. The Washington ballot proposition failed by the overwhelming margin of sixty-eight percent to thirty-two percent, and Warren Shaw was defeated by his pro-labor Democratic rival in the Kansas governor's race.[110] And although

Kansas voters did eventually, in 1958, approve a right-to-work amendment to the state's constitution, no other state would adopt such a provision for the remainder of the decade, and only two would do so in the 1960s.

As business leaders began to contemplate the causes of their poor performance at the ballot box, several pointed the finger directly at Mildred McAfee Horton and her Division of Church, Life and Work. In late November 1956 J. Stanford Smith, CEO of International Paper, sent the members of the NCC's General Board a lengthy letter alleging that Horton and her staff had deliberately passed the right-to-work statement off as an official pronouncement of the Council. Among other things, Smith pointed out that the "study" booklet was printed in a format that was virtually identical to statements that had received the General Board's imprimatur. Moreover, he complained that the all-important caveat to the reader—that the document contained only study material and had not been endorsed by the General Board—had not appeared on the front of the booklet but on the inside cover, making it easy for the casual observer to miss. Smith closed his litany of complaints with a pair of rhetorical questions: Was the Council "letting itself be manipulated for propaganda purposes?" And was the "confusion resulting from the release of the document accidental," or had it been "deliberately contrived" by Horton's Division?[111]

Smith's allegations didn't sit well with NCC President Blake, who immediately redirected his fire from labor to business. Indeed, without naming names, he informed the Board at its December meeting that he "resent[ed]" Smith's "implications" that there had been "either on the staff or in any of the divisions of the Council any bad faith" with respect to the statement. Although Blake acknowledged that there was "room for difference as to the wisdom [of] what [Horton's Division] actually decided, any implication that they did that without either the authority or the best of intentions . . . ought to be resented by all the members of the General Board quite aside from whether you happen to like either the position they took or the action that they took."[112] The Council's president did agree, however, that in order to prevent such controversies in the future, a committee should be appointed to revisit the rules concerning the publication of study documents.[113]

Precisely how much impact the Council's pronouncements had on the larger debate concerning right-to-work laws is difficult to determine. (Although labor emerged triumphant in the 1956 state campaigns, its broader effort to roll back existing right-to-work laws never gained traction.)[114] Still, the episode provides clear evidence that Eisenhower-era politicians and interest groups *believed* that the NCC's views on public policy carried considerable weight with rank-and-file voters. Moreover, it offers a good example of the Council's fundamentally centrist orientation in the realm of economic policy—an orientation that is partly explained by the balance of forces within the NCC and its agencies, but was also broadly consistent with the core convictions of its most influential lay leaders, including Charles Taft, Mildred McAfee Horton, and J. Irwin Miller. Having spent their formative years immersed in institutions that stressed the duty of responsible stewardship, these men and women could only perceive J. Howard Pew's doctrinaire brand of libertarianism as antithetical to the message of the Gospel. If the "right-to-work" controversy drove a wedge through the ranks of the Council's business representatives, it was because the question of agency fees represented a borderline case—that is, a case where stewardship principles could not definitely settle the matter one way or the other.

Pew and his small band of allies naturally rejoiced at the resulting discord, viewing it as further proof that the mainline churches had strayed from their primary mission of saving souls. But many DCEL members, including J. Irwin Miller, would continue to defend the substance of the 1956 right-to-work statement, arguing that it had sketched a valid "third way" in the debate over the union shop (namely, leaving the parties free to negotiate whatever arrangements they wished, while simultaneously guaranteeing that workers would enjoy all the rights necessary to ensure the internal democracy of the resulting system). Unfortunately, Miller wrote in 1965, this approach had not yet "received the thoughtful attention it deserves."[115]

6

Inventing the Old-Time Religion

> It would be interesting to know how many of those attracted by
> [Billy Graham's] evangelistic Christianity are attracted by the ob-
> vious fact that his new evangelism is much blander than the old. For
> it promises a new life, not through painful religious experience but
> merely by signing a decision card. Thus a miracle of regeneration is
> promised at a painless price by an obviously sincere evangelist. It is
> a bargain.
>
> —Reinhold Niebuhr (1957)

In the mid-1950s, at a time when groups like the National Association of
Evangelicals (NAE) were suffering defeat after defeat in their struggle against
the Protestant mainline, at least one conservative Protestant was riding a wave
of popular acclaim. Billy Graham first captured the nation's attention in 1949
when his Los Angeles crusade—launched the same week it was discovered
that the Soviets had successfully detonated an atomic bomb—produced record
crowds, accompanied by several celebrity conversions and a wave of positive
coverage from the Hearst newspaper chain. Raised a Presbyterian and ordained
in the Southern Baptist denomination, the tall, lanky Graham displayed a rare
talent for presenting the Gospel message in simple and entertaining terms,
along with an intuitive sense of the ways in which the novel technologies of
radio and television could be used to breathe new life into the revival format.[1]
By 1954 he had delivered his straightforward message of sin and redemption to
at least eight million Americans in twenty-five cities. His radio program, "The
Hour of Decision," reached another fifteen million in the United States and elsewhere, and his syndicated column, "My Answer," could be read in seventy-three
newspapers.[2] And as if all this weren't enough, he was also in frequent contact
with both President Eisenhower and Vice President Nixon, having won both
men's appreciation for his implicit endorsement of the Republican ticket during
the 1952 campaign.[3]

But it was during the summer of 1957 that Graham cemented his place as
the greatest evangelist of his era. During his New York City crusade, which ran
from May to September, more than two million people heard Graham preach
at Madison Square Garden, while several times that number watched ABC's

televised broadcasts of the services. The crusade closed with an open-air evening service in Times Square that drew at least 75,000 people, and possibly as many as 200,000. A *New York Times* reporter who attended the event described a surreal scene in which the "orderly throng, standing shoulder-to-shoulder in the deep trough between towering buildings" and illuminated by the "lights from the Broadway theaters" and a "brilliant half-moon," listened reverently as Graham spoke from a makeshift speaker's platform constructed from "two trailer truck[s]" that "straddle[d] Broadway just below Forty-second Street." Never before had "Broadway been host to a quieter crowd."[4]

The New York City Crusade seemed to many commentators—then and now—to mark the arrival on the national scene of a new strand of Protestantism, an evangelical or neo-evangelical third way between the strident, separatist, doctrine-obsessed fundamentalism of preachers like Carl McIntire, Bob Jones, and John R. Rice, on the one hand, and the ecumenical, social justice–oriented liberal Christianity that held sway in the National Council of Churches and most of the large Northern denominations, on the other. In terms of theology, Graham was undoubtedly closer to the fundamentalists, but he saw his life's purpose as saving souls, not scoring debating points against theological opponents, and for this reason he often coordinated his evangelistic efforts with liberal clergymen and ecumenical bodies. This was too much for fundamentalists such as Jones and Rice, who, upon learning that Graham's New York crusade had been conducted with the aid of liberal bodies like the New York Protestant Council, denounced the revivalist as an apostate. But the overwhelming majority of American Protestants clearly welcomed Graham's ecumenical streak, as did the popular press. Indeed, Graham's overflowing revival meetings and budding media empire—not to mention the rapid growth of like-minded and apparently apolitical evangelistic groups such as Youth for Christ, Campus Crusade for Christ, and Inter-Varsity Christian Fellowship—seemed to augur an era of tranquility in the Protestant ranks, an age in which believers would finally abandon the arcane doctrinal disputes of the past for the more productive business of cooperative evangelistic endeavors.

But at least one prominent theologian wasn't buying it. In a series of opinion pieces and interviews conducted in the months before the opening of Graham's New York City crusade, the nation's most prominent living theologian, Reinhold Niebuhr, argued that Graham's apparently anodyne evangelicalism was anything but the panacea for Protestantism's ills: it was a dangerous solvent that, given time, would inevitably eat away at the sense of social obligation that mainline leaders had been carefully cultivating in their flocks for the better part of a century. Although he judged Graham to be a "personable and honorable" exponent of the Gospel, Niebuhr maintained that two aspects of his presentation—his sharp distinction between the saved and unsaved and his belief that bringing people to Christ was the sure and only cure for social evils—were fundamentally at odds with the theological heritage of the Reformation. Only someone ignorant of both the insights of modern psychology and Calvin's writings on original sin, Niebuhr argued, could believe that winning converts for Christ would bring an end to such thorny and intractable problems as racism, economic inequality, and nuclear proliferation. In fact, as Calvin saw all too clearly, the converted were at least as prone to temptation as the unrighteousness, and just as likely to turn a blind eye to the ways in which their own actions contributed to larger social evils. If anything, assuring people of their eternal salvation via the march to the altar and the signing of a decision card was likely to have the perverse effect of inuring them against prophetic criticism of their own culture. "It would be interesting to know how many of those attracted by [Graham's] evangelistic Christianity are attracted by the obvious fact that his new evangelism is much blander than the old," Niebuhr wrote. "For it promises a new life, not through painful religious experience but merely by signing a decision card. Thus a miracle of regeneration is promised at a painless price by an obviously sincere evangelist. It is a bargain."[5]

The general consensus in 1957—and today, for that matter—was that Niebuhr's attacks on the genial Graham were in bad taste. Given that the revivalist had graciously joined forces with his theologically liberal and neo-orthodox counterparts in organizing the New York City crusade, the thinking went, he surely deserved better than the outright scorn he was receiving from Niebuhr. But while the condescending tone of Niebuhr's editorials did their author no favors, the substance of his critique proved prescient. Graham's revivals and their myriad offshoots did, in fact, represent a serious threat to the mainline ideals of stewardship and collective accountability for sin—and the threat was not accidental.

In fact, Graham had spent a good deal of time in the months leading up to the New York City crusade planning the launch of a new periodical, *Christianity Today*, that would soon be doing everything in its power to convince ministers and average churchgoers alike that the social justice programs of the mainline churches were not only profoundly misguided but positively blasphemous. With financial backing from J. Howard Pew, and in the capable editorial hands of the evangelical theologian Carl F. H. Henry, *Christianity Today* soon gained a large paying circulation and a degree of influence with journalists and politicians that far exceeded the size of its readership. To a much greater extent than either Pew's previous projects or the clergy outreach program of the National Association of Manufacturers, Graham's journal succeeded in making opposition to the welfare state and federal civil rights programs respectable—a point of view to which a genuine believer could in good conscience subscribe. And although Graham and Henry, unlike Pew, were not unconcerned about social problems such as racism and poverty, the end result of their efforts was more or less what

Niebuhr predicted. By casting themselves as modern-day Luthers—by encouraging fellow believers to liberate themselves from the illegitimate authority and extrabiblical pronouncements of the mainline churches—the revivalist and the evangelical theologian helped create a world in which it would be possible for white middle-class believers to relieve themselves of responsibility for the fates of their less privileged neighbors, all while remaining assured of their own essential righteousness.

The Milk and the Meat

Billy Graham enjoyed being close to power. Over the course of his long public career, he forged friendships with numerous presidents, including Eisenhower, Johnson, Nixon, Reagan, and Clinton. The journalist Nancy Gibbs once remarked that Graham "came with the [Oval O]ffice like the draperies."[6] That he managed to occupy the role of spiritual counselor to presidents for nearly six decades testifies to his public reputation for nonpartisanship. Although he often found subtle ways to signal support for a preferred candidate—as when he invited Richard Nixon to sit on the speaker's platform at his revivals—he was careful never to issue formal endorsements, even when he had a strong preference for a particular candidate. On those occasions when his man came up short, he was unfailingly gracious to the winner, and usually found himself invited to the White House as a result.

In private, however, Graham was not shy about discussing politics, and the views he expressed were more or less indistinguishable from those of James Fifield and Norman Vincent Peale. He believed that "godless" communism posed a grave threat to humanity and that communists were everywhere on the march, searching for ways to undermine American institutions. He believed that free-market capitalism was the only economic program that was consistent with the nation's founding ideals. And he believed that liberals who admitted doubts about the benevolent workings of the market were, whether they knew it or not, guilty of abetting the Kremlin. This included, presumably, the leaders of the Protestant mainline. As Graham told an interviewer from U.S. News and World Report in 1957, far too many well-intentioned politicians and religious leaders had been duped by Marx's claim that establishing "social justice and [giving] every man . . . equal material goods . . . will change the individual and make him a better man." Such activists, Graham alleged, were guilty of putting the cart before the horse. Had they read and understood the Gospel message, they would know that society was "made up of individuals, and until the individuals have been changed, it is impossible to have a better society."[7]

Graham was hardly the first theologically conservative minister to draw a dichotomy between the church's "true" mission of soul saving, on the one hand, and social reform on the other. Nor was he the first to suggest that the mainline churches now found themselves on the wrong side of this divide. But he *was* arguably the first prominent fundamentalist to carry the argument through to its logical conclusion. Whereas the early fundamentalists were greatly troubled by orthodox Protestantism's rapidly diminishing influence within the broader culture, Graham had relatively little to say on such subjects as evolution and Catholicism.[8] Nor did he pine for the days when Prohibition Bureau agents had roamed the nation's cities in search of illicit liquor. He seemed genuinely to believe that, by finding Jesus, believers could save themselves from such worldly temptations as the saloon and the secular college campus, with or without the help of lawmakers.

From the point of view of the wealthy, conservative businessmen who provided the financial backing for his crusades—men such as Pew and the Texas oilman Sid Richardson—this was a crucial concession.[9] It removed the most significant barrier to cooperation between conservative Protestants and libertarians—and, indeed, it suggested that the two groups were natural allies. For if the Bible was silent on questions of social ethics, then the countless mainline clerics who were busy providing religious cover for government social programs were guilty of heresy. And if the core of the Christian message, properly understood, concerned individual autonomy and responsibility—that is, the individual sinner's responsibility to hear and respond to Christ's offer of forgiveness, as spelled out in the Gospels—then what business did *anyone* have invoking the coercive power of the state to remedy alleged social ills? Did not such efforts inevitably impinge upon the sovereignty of the individual conscience, subordinating some citizens' notions of right and wrong to those of their more numerous or better connected neighbors? Surely private philanthropy, not bureaucracy and forced economic redistribution, was the proper Christian response to social problems such as poverty.[10]

Graham could not say all of this himself, of course—at least not publicly. He needed a mouthpiece, and it was for this purpose that he launched what would become the most influential religious periodical of the second half of the twentieth century. The idea for *Christianity Today* originated in a series of conversations Graham had with his father-in-law, L. Nelson Bell, in late 1954 and early 1955.[11] Bell, a physician and former missionary, was staunchly conservative in both politics and theology. He was also experienced in the magazine business, having founded and edited the *Southern Presbyterian Journal*, an outlet for conservative Southern Presbyterian voices. By late 1954 both Graham and Bell had become concerned that the cities visited by the evangelist were not able to sustain the religious enthusiasm unleashed by his crusades.

As Graham wrote to a supporter, his campaigns tended to "thrill and excite the clergy for a short period and show them what God can do with old-fashioned theology." But when the crusade left town, ministers inevitably neglected the old-time religion and reverted to what they knew best, namely, the liberal theology of their seminary days and the social justice causes championed by the denominational hierarchies. The best way to prevent this scenario, Graham concluded, would be to "follow through with a periodical" that would reinforce his conservative theological perspective and "give [ministers] a reason for the hope that is in them."[12]

In public Graham portrayed *Christianity Today*'s aims as purely spiritual, but in private he acknowledged that the magazine would have a good deal to say about politics. Whereas most existing religious periodicals, such as the *Christian Century*, were "liberal," *Christianity Today* would be "conservative, evangelical, and anti-Communist."[13] The critical difference between the new magazine and existing right-wing religious periodicals, such as *Faith and Freedom* and *Christian Economics*, would be the order of presentation: theological questions and practical ministerial concerns, not libertarian polemics, would take center stage. Politics would be discussed only in moderation, and only when the subject in question could be credibly linked to theology. The basic strategy was designed to mimic the careful staging of Graham's evangelistic crusades. Graham had learned the hard way that launching a direct assault on a minister's theological or political convictions rarely yielded positive results. The trick, he wrote to an early financial backer of *Christianity Today*, was to

> give milk instead of meat. You have to feed many ministers with a spoon and nurse them along until they are able to take more. For example, in the first ministers' meetings in a campaign I hold my big stick behind my back and give a talk which liberals and evangelicals alike could accept. After the campaign has progressed a month, my last message to the ministers is that of a shouting fundamentalist—and they take it. Why? Because I slipped up on them and used strategy of love, courtesy, graciousness, and above all, tolerance toward their point of view. When they gained confidence in me they would take anything I had to say, no matter how strongly it was put. *I think of the strategy of the magazine should be along similar lines.*[14]

Graham and Bell were well aware that the project they envisioned would need to be massive in scale. Indeed, they hoped to send the magazine to "every Protestant minister" in America, with the aim of "chang[ing] the entire course of the American Protestant church within two years."[15] Launching such an enterprise would require the help of wealthy investors, and it was for this reason that they turned to an old friend: J. Howard Pew.

By the mid-1950s Pew had developed a close relationship with Bell, whose *Southern Presbyterian Journal* was a frequent beneficiary of Pew's financial support.[16] It is not clear exactly when Pew befriended Graham, but the two were well acquainted by late 1954, when Pew cut a $25,000 check to the Billy Graham Evangelistic Association. By early 1955 Graham and Pew were carrying on a lively correspondence, and the following year Pew went so far as to contribute $5,000 to the construction of a new home for the evangelist outside Montreat, North Carolina.[17] Notwithstanding his close friendships with the two men, Pew likely harbored doubts about the wisdom of backing yet another conservative religious periodical. But after receiving several pleading letters from Graham, he eventually signed on to the project, agreeing to front the estimated $250,000 to $300,000 that would be necessary to get the publication off the ground.[18] Graham, naturally, was elated. "When you stand before the Master," he wrote the oilman, "He will say to you that [this] was the greatest investment that you made in your entire life."[19]

All parties knew that the choice of editor would be crucial to the magazine's success. The challenge would be to find a respected religious intellectual who was reliably conservative in matters of theology and politics but not so polarizing as to alienate potential converts. The Presbyterian minister Marcellus Kik, who was seriously considered for the post, was inoffensive enough, but he was rejected when Graham concluded that his postmillennial convictions rendered him theologically suspect. (Kik would eventually join the magazine as an assistant editor.) As Graham wrote to Bell, postmillennialists, who believed that human agency would play some role in preparing the world for Christ's return, were not true evangelicals. Kik was undoubtedly a talented writer and thinker, but if appointed editor-in-chief there was a real danger that he would "have the ability of swaying various articles in the light of his [Postmillennial] convictions." Readers might even be left with the false impression that they were religiously obligated to address specific social ills.[20]

In the end, Graham and Bell secured the services of Carl F. H. Henry, a widely respected theologian whose influential 1943 book, *The Uneasy Conscience of Modern Fundamentalism*, had urged conservative Protestants—presumably in retreat since the prohibition debacle and the Scopes "monkey trial" of 1925—to reengage with mainstream American culture.[21] The crucial difference between Henry and Kik was that Henry was an unambiguous Premillennialist; the ultimate aim of his hoped-for cultural mission was to save souls, not solve the world's problems. To be sure, Henry allowed that God might occasionally prick the believer's conscience, alerting him to such worldly evils as war and starvation. But the only lasting solutions to such problems were redemptive in nature, proceeding from the salvation of individual souls rather than the fallible dictates of human reason. In the realm of social policy, the job of the culturally engaged evangelical was to remind secular policy makers and religious liberals that their utopian schemes were bound to fail, since they addressed the symptoms rather than the underlying disease. The modern evangelical, in Henry's telling, joined the United Nations in "condemning aggressive warfare" while at the same time "disputing the frame of reference by which the attempt is made to outlaw such warfare." He joined the civil rights activist in condemning "racial hatred and intolerance, while at the same time protesting the superficial view of man which overlooks the need of individual regeneration." And he agreed with labor organizers on the need to address "industrial problems, while protesting the fallacy that man's deepest need is economic."[22] This was Billy Graham's understanding of the relationship between religion and politics in a nutshell. And, crucially, it was a perspective to which no card-carrying libertarian could possibly object.

Henry's tenure at *Christianity Today* would be tumultuous, but he was nonetheless an inspired choice. For one thing, he was very well connected in academic circles, and he secured a steady stream of interviews and articles from the world's leading theologians, thus lending *Christianity Today* the intellectual heft that eluded openly polemical publications like *Faith and Freedom* and *Christian Economics*. The tall, burly seminary professor was also an experienced journalist who had worked as a newspaper reporter prior to enrolling in seminary. He was therefore comfortable in the halls of power, and from the magazine's inception he cultivated close relationships with potential political backers, from the up-and-coming Oregon politician Mark O. Hatfield to Richard Arens, counsel for the House Un-American Activities Committee.[23]

With the combined Rolodexes of Graham and Pew at their disposal, Henry and Bell had little difficulty arranging for positive press coverage of the magazine's launch. In May 1955, five months before the first issue of *Christianity Today* was scheduled to roll off the presses, the Associated Press distributed a glowing story about a new magazine that was the brainchild of the nation's most famous evangelist. In contrast to existing religious periodicals, which regularly entangled themselves in insoluble political dilemmas, *Christianity Today* would confine itself to the nuts and bolts of the Gospel. In the words of the editor-in-chief, the new magazine "was not anti-anything. We are pro-Christian, and pro-God in a world that is rapidly drifting in the humanistic direction."[24] A few weeks later the conservative radio commentator Paul Harvey, whose program reached some twenty million Americans every week, offered his own endorsement. Harvey was a longtime friend of Graham's, but subtlety was not his strong suit, and he apparently missed the memo about the magazine's purportedly apolitical outlook. "The pastor's study has been plentifully supplied [in] recent years with reading material from way out in left field," he barked. "Sermons reflect what the preacher reads. The pinkish propagandists have tried hard to capture the pulpit for the dissemination of their twisted truth. . . . A new magazine is soon to be published which will stress unadulterated, unconfused Christianity. Why don't you subscribe for your pastor. Of whatever faith. Believe me, he is being flooded with the other stuff."[25]

The critical question, of course, was how to pique the interest of the hundreds of thousands of clergymen who were regularly discarding their free copies of *Faith and Freedom* and *Christian Economics*. And it was on this front that Billy Graham's involvement was particularly critical. Graham, who regularly appeared near the top of Gallup's annual ranking of most-admired Americans, would serve as the magazine's public face and author the lead article in the first issue. And thanks to Pew's generosity, Graham's introductory message could be sent, free of charge, to every Protestant minister in America whose name could be gleaned from public sources or from Pew and Graham's existing mailing lists. At the same time, well-off laymen would be encouraged to follow Paul Harvey's advice and purchase gift subscriptions for ministers who were unable to afford the annual subscription price of $5. With any luck, the founders believed, the enterprise would be self-sufficient within two years.[26]

The magazine's inaugural issue, which hit newsstands in October 1956, was perfectly tailored to the needs and interests of the typical Protestant minister. Its forty pages of forty-pound eggshell paper included reviews of recent books on religion, a Bible "Book of the Month" column featuring sermon-ready insights on Matthew's Gospel, an essay by the Dutch seminarian C. G. Berkouwer that translated recent European theological trends into ordinary English, a humor column recounting one pastor's embarrassing slip of the tongue while delivering an invocation at a political convention, and a current events section summarizing the latest news from around the world. The careful reader, however, would instantly sense that *Christianity Today* was more than a how-to manual for busy pastors, for nestled within all the pages of practical advice was a message with obvious political salience: American Protestants, the magazine argued, were obeying the wrong master. They had put their faith in denominational leaders, celebrated theologians, and ambitious programs of social reform, all while ignoring the revealed Word of God. It was time to return to the only true source of authority in the reformed Protestant tradition, namely, the Bible. *Sola scriptura.*

Billy Graham introduced the argument in his centerpiece essay, "Biblical Authority in Evangelism," which told the story of a young English communist who had accompanied some friends to a Graham revival expecting to hear a presentation filled with "sociology, politics, psychology, or philosophy." To their great surprise, the woman and her companions found themselves enraptured by a speaker who had nothing more to offer than the unadorned Word of God— and this, it turned out, was enough to "br[eak] open their hearts." Renouncing godless communism, they immediately "surrendered their lives to Christ."[27]

Carl Henry developed the theme in a more explicitly political piece titled the "Fragility of Freedom," which castigated Western intellectuals for engaging in a futile search for a secular justification for democracy and human rights. No satisfactory "antithesis of the totalitarian world's philosophy of the enslavement of the individual spirit" would be forthcoming, Henry declared, until Western thinkers realized that orthodox Christianity was the only "purveyor of human freedom . . . adequate to repel the Communist revolution."[28] The magazine's inaugural editorial, entitled "Why 'Christianity Today'?," closed the deal. The nation was intellectually and spiritually adrift, it proclaimed, and the reason was that "theological liberalism had failed to meet the moral and spiritual needs of the people." American Protestantism now found itself lost in pointless "speculation that neither solves the problem of the individual nor of the society of which he is a part." The remedy was straightforward: a return to the only book capable of "light[ing] the pathway of life, the record of the One Who alone meets our needs for now and eternity."[29]

Making Peace with Mammon

The founders of *Christianity Today*—J. Howard Pew included—were from the outset determined to broaden the magazine's base of financial support beyond the Pew family. Pew, they knew, was hardly the only wealthy businessman who harbored dreams of severing the church from the welfare state. And Bell and Graham, at least, were well aware that relying solely on Pew's generosity was a risky proposition, not only because the mercurial businessman was known to sour on his pet projects without warning, but also because it fueled accusations that *Christianity Today* was just another vehicle for Pew's extremist political views, albeit a cleverly disguised one.[30]

In order to recruit a network of wealthy backers, however, it would be necessary for the three men to walk a fine line. On the one hand, they would need to convince potential donors that a periodical dominated by *theological content* could succeed in shifting the *political* orientation of America's ministers to the right. On the other hand, if they wanted to gain a hearing from skeptical ministers, they would have to ensure that whatever political content did appear in the magazine was sufficiently subtle—and sufficiently related to theology—as to avoid the appearance of propaganda. Pew and Bell, who took charge of the magazine's early fundraising efforts, responded to the first problem by selling potential donors on the idea that Henry's brand of *sola scriptura* Protestantism was not only theologically sound, but also the most effective way of advancing the libertarian economic program. As Bell put the point in a letter to a prominent Houston attorney, all of the "wild economic, political and social ideas abroad today stem from man trying to work things out himself without God. It is our conviction that if we can win many of our ministers back to preaching the simple Gospel and winning men to Christ (not to new social concepts), we will have made the greatest single contribution possible to not only helping individuals but also our nation and the world."[31] In short, ministers who focused solely on matters of individual salvation would be inclined to leave economic problems where they belonged: in the hands of wealthy businessmen like Pew.

This way of framing the magazine's aims convinced a number of conservative businessmen to cut checks to *Christianity Today*. In June 1956 a fundraising letter touting a new "Christian magazine" that would counter the current "socialist" drift of the mainline churches yielded several donations in the $500-to-$1,000 range.[32] Among the magazine's earliest supporters were Howard E. Butt, Jr., a devout Southern Baptist and heir to a Texas supermarket empire who would soon quit the family business to launch a series of evangelistic enterprises; John Bolten, a Massachusetts manufacturer who had recently sold his operation to General Tire and Rubber at a healthy profit with the aim of launching a second career in religious publishing; and C. Davis Weyerhaeuser, heir to a Minnesota timber fortune, who also donated heavily to religious causes. Others included Walter Harnischfeger, president of a Milwaukee-based heavy equipment manufacturer; Walter Bennett, head of a Chicago-based advertising agency that assisted with Graham's revival campaigns; Earl Hankamer, a wealthy Texas oilman and soon-to-be benefactor of Baylor University's business school; and Jeremiah Milbank, Jr., a New York City investor and part-time political operative who came from one of the oldest families in Greenwich, Connecticut.[33]

From the outset, however, it was apparent that the magazine's fate would hinge on the support of a handful of big donors, "men of great Christian vision" who, as L. Nelson Bell put it, "sense[d] the worldwide significance" of *Christianity Today* and would therefore be willing consider donations in the five- to six-figure range.[34] Two such men soon materialized: W. Maxey Jarman and Harold Luhnow. Jarman was CEO of Genesco, a Nashville-based shoe manufacturer, while Luhnow, a wealthy businessman from Kansas City, managed the William Volker Fund, arguably the most important funder of libertarian causes in the middle decades of the twentieth century.[35] (Among other projects, the Volker Fund underwrote the academic salaries of Ludwig von Mises at New York University and Friedrich Hayek at the University of Chicago.) In 1959 Jarman contributed $18,000 to *Christianity Today*, while Luhnow's Volker Fund pitched in $25,000. These amounts paled in comparison to Pew's contributions, but they were enough to generate hope that the magazine might one day wean itself from his largesse.

Aside from their personal wealth, most of *Christianity Today*'s financial backers shared at least four characteristics in common. First, with the exception of Milbank—who seems to have lost interest in the magazine by the early 1960s—their ties to the Eastern establishment were few and far between. Second, most of them came from money, though certainly not old money. In most cases their fathers or grandfathers—many of whom were immigrants—had founded successful companies, which the son or grandson now controlled. Like Pew, they were raised on stories of the family patriarch pulling himself up by his bootstraps, succeeding against all odds by the sheer force of an undaunted entrepreneurial spirit. Third, most of them bore lasting grudges against the twin scourges of entrepreneurship, unions and government bureaucrats; Jarman in particular regularly made headlines for his battles with union organizers and antitrust regulators.[36] Finally, and not surprisingly, they were mostly Republicans who leaned strongly in the direction of libertarianism. This was obviously true of Luhnow and the Volker Fund, but it was also true of Jarman, who unsuccessfully sought the Republican nomination for governor of Tennessee; of Hankamer, who helped lay the groundwork for a Republican insurgency in traditionally Democratic Texas; and of Milbank, who was a driving force behind Arizona Senator Barry Goldwater's rise to national prominence.[37] By and large, these were wealthy cultural outsiders who, despite appearances to the contrary, believed that the proverbial deck was stacked against them—and that the social justice activists in the mainline churches were at least partly to blame for their problems.

Christianity Today's attempts to forge financial linkages with establishment business types mostly ended in failure—but not for lack of trying. In 1957 Pew and Billy Graham organized a luncheon fundraiser at the Waldorf-Astoria with the aim of recruiting prominent New York executives to their cause. The guest list included the chairman or presidents of IBM, General Motors, Tiffany & Co., the New York Stock Exchange, Union Carbide, J. C. Penney, Georgia-Pacific, the Dixie Cup Company, Vick Chemical, and the brokerage firms E. F. Hutton and Harris Upham & Company. Also invited were such pillars of New York society as the publisher Henry Luce, the philanthropist Cleveland E. Dodge, the Pan Am executive S. F. Pryor, and Maurice T. Moore, a prominent attorney (and Luce's brother-in-law) who had helped administer the Marshall Plan. Several of the most prominent invitees claimed previous engagements—one even begged off because of "labor troubles"—but several, including Luce and top executives from Union Carbide, Georgia-Pacific and Tiffany & Co., agreed to attend. [38] Pew, who personally supervised preparations for the event, spared no expense, treating his guests to broiled filet mignon of Blue Ribbon beef with sauce béarnaise, souffléd potatoes, asparagus tips with hollandaise sauce, chocolate soufflé, and hot vanilla sabayon. Although no alcohol was served (out of respect for the teetotaling Graham), each gentleman was offered "a good imported cigar" following dinner.[39]

While the cigars were being passed around, Pew introduced the keynote speaker, joking that for once he would spare the audience his thoughts on the "Philosophy of Freedom and the interdependence of Freedom and Christianity."[40] Graham's precise words to the assembled crowd of power players are lost to history, but follow-up letters from Bell and Pew suggest that the evangelist made Pew's argument for him. In short, it was "Mr. Graham's thesis" that the present "trend toward Socialism in America" would never be stopped until the nation's preachers abandoned the "Socialistic and Humanistic fields" and returned to the "old Gospel."[41] Investing in *Christianity Today* was thus a logical move for any businessman who hoped to roll back the myriad social programs that were presently "carry[ing] this country toward a totalitarian state."[42]

For all the careful planning that went into the fundraiser, it yielded few new supporters. The underlying problem was that the message was a poor fit for the audience, most of whom had little interest in mounting the sort of full-blown assault on the welfare state that so obsessed Pew and his band of libertarian allies. But if being spurned by the Northeastern establishment left *Christianity Today* dangerously dependent on a small handful of financial backers, it also meant that the magazine's editorial stance would be unaffected by the need to appease politically moderate Protestants—the kind of people, in short, who had sunk Pew's effort to infiltrate the National Council of Churches. And indeed, the magazine would frequently serve as a launching point for the former Lay Committee chairman's attacks on his old adversaries in the NCC's Department of the Church and Economic Life. (Although Pew frequently denied the charge, there is ample evidence that this was, in fact, his major motivation in agreeing to underwrite the magazine.)[43] In June 1959, for example, *Christianity Today* published Pew's review of *Goals of Economic Life*, the Rockefeller-sponsored volume he had tried and failed to suppress during his brief affiliation with the NCC. Not surprisingly, Pew panned the book, claiming that "Marxist overtones seep[ed] insidiously through" every one of its chapters, and that it seemed designed to convey "Kremlin instructions to Party workers in our country to cast doubt on the efficacy of the free market system of economics."[44]

With Pew's encouragement, the editors continued their assault on the Council through the early 1960s, alleging in a pair of articles that NCC officials had intentionally stacked the DCEL with leftist academics and labor leaders, thus ensuring that its pronouncements would follow the union line.[45] Around the same time, the magazine launched an ill-considered attack on J. Irwin Miller, another longtime adversary of Pew's and a major benefactor of the National Council of Churches. In this case the complaint was that Miller was single-handedly propping up the finances of the *Christian Century*, the unofficial voice of the ecumenical movement. This may well have been true, but as at least one reader pointed out in a letter to the editor, it was also a case of the pot calling the kettle black.

Clearly someone was footing the bill for the hundred thousand or more free copies of *Christianity Today* that were being mailed to American ministers every two weeks, and word on the street was that the magazine's "sole angel" was none other than the "wealthy layman J. Howard Pew."[46]

The Bureaucratic Critique of Mainline Authority

Christianity Today was far more than a mouthpiece for Pew's many grievances, however. In fact, a straightforward review of the magazine's editorial positions— many of which were identical to earlier Pew-funded publications—tends to obscure its editor's greatest achievement, which was to develop a theologically plausible critique of mainline social involvement. When it came to teasing out the elusive connection between libertarian economics and Christianity, Carl Henry was hardly more successful than James Fifield or Howard Kershner. Where Henry and his colleagues did enjoy a degree of success was in sowing theological doubts about the appropriateness of *the church* involving itself in the business of social reform. If they could not convincingly cast the welfare state as a demonic invention, they could at least argue that its clerical backers in the mainline denominations were claiming authority that was not rightfully theirs. And in so doing, they could deprive the welfare state of one of its most important sources of popular legitimacy.

Hardly an issue of *Christianity Today* went by that did not include one or more articles attacking religious authority as it existed in mid-century America. Following Martin Luther, the editors asserted that the vitality of a given faith was inversely proportional to the extent of the bureaucratic apparatus that had grown up around it. The clear implication was that the mainline denominational and ecumenical hierarchies, far from aiding the cause of the Almighty, were draining the very life from American Protestantism. After all, bodies such as the NCC and World Council of Churches spent much of their time on activities that had little to do with saving souls, and they consumed vast amounts of resources that would have been better spent on evangelistic work. Worst of all, they were staffed by unaccountable bureaucrats who appeared not to understand that the only valid source of authority in the Protestant tradition was the revealed Word of God. All in all, the situation resembled the one that had confronted Luther in the sixteenth century; and as Luther had rightly pointed out, there was only one remedy when religious institutions became so unresponsive, inept, or corrupt that they actively hindered efforts to perpetuate the faith. In such cases ministers and average churchgoers alike had no choice but to throw off the yoke of ille-gitimate clerical authority and "bow once more before the Word of God, and in faithful service to it proclaim the presence of the free grace of God in the Word that became flesh, died for our sins, arose for our justification, now lives to make intercession for us, and shall one day return to judge the world, and through judgment, redeem it."[47]

This was not an original line of argument. Conservative Protestants from James Fifield to Howard Kershner to the more combative Carl McIntire had been deriding the mainline bureaucratic apparatus since the 1940s, often drawing implicit or explicit analogies to the Medieval papacy. What was novel about *Christianity Today*'s critique was that it skillfully linked Reformation-era theological arguments to a series of popular postwar books that likewise called attention to the dangers of "organized bigness." Indeed, it is striking that the year of *Christianity Today*'s birth, 1956, also witnessed the publication of William H. Whyte's *The Organization Man* and C. Wright Mills's *The Power Elite*.[48] Both books sold well, and both drew attention to the fact that power in postwar America had become dangerously concentrated in large institutions, such as corporations and government bureaucracies. Concentrated power, they suggested, was dangerous not only because it was often beyond the reach of democratic controls, but also because the institutions that possessed it were inherently destructive of individual initiative, creativity, and personality. To be sure, neither Whyte nor Mills had much to say about the organizational structures of the nation's churches, but as *Christianity Today*'s editors clearly recognized, the basic thrust of the argument was easily adapted to the current state of American Protestantism. After all, if secular bureaucracies were inherently soul crushing, then the same could surely be said of the byzantine denominational and ecumenical bodies that seemed to be playing an increasingly dominant role in the nation's religious life.

This bureaucratic critique of religious authority took center stage in the magazine's October 1961 issue, much of which was devoted to applying the insights of *The Organization Man*—which had by this point sold more than two million copies—to the overgrown bureaucracies of the Protestant mainline. Although the author of the lead article, a Presbyterian minister and Wheaton College graduate named William Henry Anderson, acknowledged that "organized bigness" was a necessary fact of modern life, he lamented that national religious organizations were increasingly resembling "big government" and "big business" in their tendency to "regulate and override both the individual and the [local] church." The seminaries, instead of tutoring future ministers in the art of saving souls, were busy "produc[ing] interchangeable cogs to maintain smooth operation of [the] machinery." Students who showed signs of independent thought—the future "Luthers and Wesleys" of the world—were quickly shown the door. Once ensconced in a pulpit, new ministers obsequiously followed orders from on high, hoping one day to be rewarded with a cushy, well-paying administrative position. (The truly lucky seminary graduates, from the perspective of the modern organization men, were the reported 20 percent who landed administrative jobs right off the bat.) And the most alarming thing was that average American churchgoers showed so little concern about the increasingly regimented nature of the nation's religious life. Whereas "previous generations" had "found their religious authority in the Bible, in the creed, or in both," postwar Americans seemed perfectly content to turn over the "functions once controlled by the [local] church governments" to large-scale religious organizations and the bureaucrats who ran them. As a result, the individual minister now found himself in much the same position as the "organization man" described on the dust jacket of Whyte's best-selling book. Caught "between the individual beliefs he is supposed to follow and the collective life he actually lives," he searched in vain "for a faith to bridge the gap."[49]

But while citations to secular studies like *The Organization Man* lent Henry's critique of mainline religious authority a veneer of intellectual sophistication, *Christianity Today*'s editor knew that his argument, if it was to win over rank-and-file ministers, would ultimately have to be grounded on theological premises. And it was surely in part for this reason that *Christianity Today* devoted hundreds of pages to the works of the world's most famous living theologian, Karl Barth. A genuine intellectual superstar, the Swiss-born Barth packed auditoriums during his 1962 visit to the United States, and *Christianity Today*, which had been touting Barth's works since its founding, provided its readers with breathless coverage of his every utterance. At first glance, it may seem curious that a theologically conservative periodical would give pride of place to a theologian who was in no sense a biblical literalist, but Barth's emphasis on divine revelation as the only legitimate source of religious authority resonated with Henry's antiestablishment instincts. So too did Barth's devastating critique of the liberal theological tradition, with its tendency to reduce theology to a form of rational inquiry akin to philosophy or social ethics. According to Barth, this disastrous wrong turn, which could be traced back to nineteenth-century German liberal theologians such as Friedrich Schleiermacher, was both wrong-headed and blasphemous: wrong-headed, in that it supposed that fallible human beings, using fallible human methods, could somehow reason their way to genuine knowledge about the Almighty; blasphemous, in that it attempted to pass off the inevitably flawed insights of particular human thinkers as the revealed Word of God.[50]

If one ignored the question of biblical inerrancy, Barth's theology was uniquely well suited for use as a battering ram against the American mainline power structure, and the editors of *Christianity Today* regularly invoked it for this purpose. Although Barth himself was not averse to social involvement—part of his appeal surely derived from his protests against German militarism in the years preceding the two world wars—he nonetheless insisted that social ethics and theology were two distinct enterprises, with the former ultimately grounded in human reason and the latter dependent solely on divine revelation. In the hands of Henry and his team of contributing writers, this insight provided the basis for a powerful indictment of mainline social activism. Indeed, when one examined the administrative apparatus of a typical mainline denomination—with its myriad divisions, departments, committees and councils, each staffed by a roster of policy experts and devoted to a different facet of social reform—what was this but a misguided attempt to reduce the revealed Word of God to a secular social science? Precisely as Barth had foreseen, the liberals in the mainline churches had substituted the study of humanity and its well-being for the worship of the Almighty, with the result that "the gospel" had been reduced to little more than "left-wing sociology and politics."[51] Or as one *Christianity Today* correspondent put the point, Barth's learned tomes merely confirmed what Billy Graham had been saying all along: that "the God of philosophy is always an idol."[52]

Carl Henry's overtly partisan editorials no doubt seemed less polemical—indeed, less political—when framed by the insights of such respected and generally apolitical thinkers as Barth and William Whyte. Take, for example, a 1958 essay entitled "Can We Salvage the Republic?," easily the most explicitly political piece to appear in the magazine's first few issues. Henry began his cri de coeur with a familiar recounting of the welfare state's many sins. A "cancerous collectivism" had infected the federal government, he wrote, and the newly minted social programs issuing from Washington—Social Security, unemployment insurance, socialized medicine—were directly responsible for the country's ballooning budget deficit, its worrisome inflation rate, and what seemed an "endless spiral of punitive taxation." But why, the reader might wonder, should a religious magazine concern itself with political problems? Henry's answer was twofold. First, he insisted that Protestants ought to acknowledge and repent for their role in creating a "power-state" that was largely beyond the reach of democratic controls and whose activities had little to do with religion. Second, he argued that the unchecked growth of bureaucratic authority posed dire spiritual problems in the present. The centralizing trends that had begun in the government agencies, unions, and corporations had now spread to the Protestant denominational hierarchies—massive institutions that desired nothing so much as to subordinate the individual conscience to their own organizational imperatives. And the spiritual costs of submission were steep: each "unprotested misrepresentation of one's beliefs, each unprotested identification with groups that do not express one's convictions, weakens and finally destroys an individual's character." If average churchgoers and ministers did not speak out against the unchecked authority of denominational leaders and their allies in government, they would soon discover what the Russian Orthodox Church already knew: that those who clung to influence by flattering despotic bureaucrats ultimately enjoyed "only as much 'freedom' . . . as serves the tyrant's whim!"[53]

Here at last was a critique of mainline social activism that seemed genuinely to flow from theological premises, as opposed to being reverse engineered to support the libertarian policy preferences of a wealthy backer like J. Howard Pew. Instead of directly stating what its patrons actually believed—that mainline leaders were secret communists, or at least fellow travelers—*Christianity Today* simply lamented the loss of a mythical "old-time" religion, a pristine faith unsullied by association with secular power brokers. Instead of asserting that Christian principles, properly understood, *demanded* free market economic policies, it asked that mainline leaders stop providing religious cover for divisive social policies that found no direct support in the text of the Bible. And instead of directly disputing the notion that the wealthy were religiously obligated to aid the downtrodden, it pointed out the soul-crushing real-world effects of well-intended government programs that transferred resources from well-off citizens to their less fortunate neighbors. The problem wasn't that Christianity was unconcerned with the fate of the poor or disadvantaged, Henry insisted; it was that American Christians, under the direction of false prophets, had channeled their social concern into a dead-end program of coercive benevolence that attempted—and typically failed—to supply citizens' material needs, all while worsening the spiritual condition of the nation.

The Kennedy administration's early experiments in socialized medicine were a case in point. For years, the magazine insisted, most American doctors had gladly treated poor patients free of charge. But now the New Frontiersmen in the White House had decided to throw money at a nonexistent problem. The new scheme would force doctors, under threat of legal penalty, and at vast expense to the taxpayer, to do something most of them were already doing voluntarily. Even if the new system achieved marginal increases in health coverage, there was no getting around the fact that it had unwisely substituted "compulsion" for "compassion."[54] Another sign of the times was "Big Labor's" fierce opposition to right-to-work laws. Once upon a time the labor movement had been motivated by such noble goals as securing an honest wage for an honest day's work. Sadly, it was now a "cause with . . . a waning conscience" whose "big . . . bosses" were shamelessly selling out workers in order to pad their own salaries with forced union dues.[55] Or consider the administration's threat to impose price controls on the steel industry. What at first glance seemed a technical question of economic policy was in fact a great moral test for the nation: if allowed to go unchallenged, Kennedy's steel policy would establish the precedent that "the decision of a tiny handful of men in the White House" was sufficient to override even the most basic legal and constitutional rights. The end result would be to cement "the image of omnipotent government."[56]

Carl Henry's jaundiced view of the New Frontier and the Great Society yielded a number of incisive editorials, but it also produced at least a few spectacular misfires. In the spring of 1964, for example, *Christianity Today* published a shocking exposé of corruption in the Peace Corps, alleging that the Corps's activities in West Cameroon were stoking sectarian tensions and threatening to undo decades of evangelistic work by Protestant missionaries. Although West Cameroonian officials hadn't even requested Peace Corps volunteers, the Kennedy administration had pressured them to participate in the program. Once inside the country, Peace Corps officials had immediately joined forces with Roman Catholic educators to help staff dozens of new Catholic schools, thus provoking fears of prosecution in the Protestant population. (It would not have escaped readers' notice that the Corps was led by the Catholic Sargent Shriver.) Meanwhile, Corps volunteers assigned to Protestant schools—virtually all of the country's schools were run by missionaries—mocked their students' religious convictions, urging them to skip chapel, and even organizing drinking parties "that lasted almost until dawn." Here, Henry believed, was a perfect illustration of why well-intentioned liberal programs almost always went awry. As "Big Government" spread "into more and more arenas" of life, it inevitably produced "deplorable religio-political mergers" while "penaliz[ing] religious groups that conscientiously refuse[d] to compromise with increasing government subsidy."[57]

There was only one problem with Henry's big scoop: it was a work of fiction. Henry had gotten his information from a young Baptist missionary who turned out to possess a vivid imagination and who later recanted virtually all of his allegations. As the director of the Peace Corps, Sargent Shriver, and other Corps officials immediately pointed out in letters to *Christianity Today*, Cameroonian officials had eagerly accepted the Corps's offer to aid their badly understaffed schools, and the rumors about a Catholic-school building boom were just that—rumors. Moreover, Baptist and other Protestant missionary groups lavished praise on the Peace Corps volunteers, few of whom seemed to be engaged in a secret program of promoting atheism.[58] In the end Henry had no choice but to publish a full retraction along with a "frank apology" to the Peace Corps volunteers, who were "making a worthy contribution in many lands."[59] Perhaps it was possible for the New Frontiersmen to do something right after all.

The occasional misstep notwithstanding, Henry's novel editorial perspective, with its emphasis on the rapidly shrinking domain of the individual conscience, was well calibrated to appeal to the moral sensibilities of rank-and-file Protestant ministers and their middle-class congregants. Whereas most issues of *Faith and Freedom* and *Christian Economics* were tossed, unread, into the trashcan of a minister's study, private polls commissioned by *Christianity Today* indicated that most of the ministers who received the magazine—even those who didn't ask for it—actually read it. Indeed, in less than two years *Christianity Today* became the magazine most read by ministers, and the largest circulation Protestant religious magazine in the United States. And although a good many readers complained about the magazine's political slant, few of them asked to have their names removed from the mailing list—presumably because they still valued the magazine's religious content. Just as Billy Graham had predicted, most readers seemed to like the milk well enough, even if a few grumbled about the meat.

The Uneasy Conscience of Carl Henry

Although Carl Henry shared J. Howard Pew's instinctual hatred of the welfare state, there were other important matters on which the two men did not see eye to eye. One involved the strategic problem of how best to reach the tens of thousands of "liberal" ministers who had not previously considered the evangelical view of theology or politics worthy of their attention. Pew's initial position was that *Christianity Today* should give no quarter to liberalism. In fact, before the magazine's official launch, he argued that all articles and editorials should be approved by the board prior to publication—an idea that was scrapped only when Billy Graham intervened to second Henry's view that no self-respecting journal of opinion would adopt such a policy.[60] The best way to reach across the ideological divide, Henry insisted, no doubt correctly, was to occasionally open the magazine's pages to liberal writers, whose views could then be rebutted in hard-hitting editorials. Moreover, Henry insisted that *Christianity Today* would do well to avoid too close an association with "right-wing Republicanism," even though "that is where most of us stand." In order to ensure "the fullest possible hearing for [our] theological priorities," political content should be kept to a few pages per issue, and explicit endorsements of candidates and policies avoided.[61]

There was also a serious theological disagreement between Pew and Henry, though it was initially obscured by the two men's shared disdain for the liberal do-gooders that staffed the National Council of Churches and the mainline denominational hierarchies. At its core, the disagreement stemmed from Pew's idiosyncratic belief that the fundamental precepts of Christianity were indistinguishable from the fundamental precepts of libertarian economics. As he put it in a letter to Henry, "freedom was a theological concept," and from this it followed that Christianity demanded maximum scope for human freedom in all "areas of human activity." Henry, in contrast, was no libertarian. He did not believe, nor did he see how any self-respecting theologian could possibly believe, that the free market was a divinely ordained institution whose operations always worked to the benefit of humanity. When Pew sent Henry a stack of Howard Kershner's writings on natural law, *Christianity Today*'s editor-in-chief made no effort to hide his distaste for the editorial perspective of *Christian Economics*. Like "much . . . right wing economic writing today," Kershner's expansive claims about the Christian foundations of libertarianism were pitched at a high level of "generality." When it came to theology, "details and specific illustrations" were few and far between, as were "examples from the pages of the Holy Writ." And indeed, Kershner seemed never to consider that the will of the Almighty might "sometimes run counter to our immediate likes and dislikes."[62]

Although Henry's editorial decisions, particularly his willingness to give (very limited) space to liberal perspectives, frequently provoked howls of protest from Pew, Maxey Jarman, and other board members, all agreed that the celebrated theologian was on balance a boon to the magazine's prospects. This would change during the tumultuous years of 1963 and 1964, when the movement for African American civil rights drove a wedge between *Christianity Today*'s editor and its major financial backers.

As a periodical that promised to offer a Christian perspective on current events, *Christianity Today* could hardly avoid discussion of the civil rights movement. Its earliest editorials took the view—apparently shared by Billy Graham and L. Nelson Bell—that while racial segregation was a moral evil, it was one that was best addressed through spiritual renewal.[63] Aggressive federal action on the civil rights front, the magazine insisted, was a cure worse than the disease. Like other grandiose liberal reforms, civil rights legislation would inevitably erode the constitutional rights of the Southern states and their white citizens, thus handing the forces of "authoritarianism" yet another victory over the forces of "freedom."[64] The magazine was also highly critical of the "radical integrationists" in the mainline churches—those ministers who, as Carl Henry wrote in a private letter to Pew, would force integration on the South even at the cost of tearing "the churches . . . to shreds."[65] Henry allowed that individual Christians should feel free to speak out or protest if the spirit moved them, so long as they did not engage in civil disobedience. And the magazine offered warm praise for Billy Graham's integrated revivals, which, it claimed, demonstrated the power of prayer to overcome long-standing barriers to racial harmony. Still, the editors were adamant that the mainline denominations and ecumenical bodies had no business entangling themselves in an issue as complex and divisive as desegregation; individual action was one thing, but formal policy pronouncements were something else altogether.

Like many white Northerners who were appalled by the violent repression of civil rights demonstrators during the spring of 1963, however, Carl Henry would eventually change his mind—as would some of his close associates on the staff of *Christianity Today*. Although never an enthusiastic proponent of federal civil rights enforcement, Henry nonetheless became convinced that the civil rights bill that became law in July 1964 was a genuine manifestation of Christian principles. He even went so far as to write President Lyndon Johnson to congratulate him on his civil rights message to Congress, telling the president that the speech was his finest hour (an act that surely would have rankled Pew, had he known about it).[66] Another member of the magazine's editorial staff, Frank Gaebelein, experienced an even more dramatic crisis of conscience. In early 1964, while Henry was on sabbatical in Europe and Africa, Gaebelein penned an editorial offering an unqualified endorsement of the federal civil rights bill, only to have it spiked by L. Nelson Bell (who served as Pew's unofficial representative on the editorial staff). The following year, when he was dispatched to cover the brutal attacks on civil rights demonstrators in Selma, Alabama, Gaebelein dropped his notebook and joined hands with the marchers.[67]

Of course, if there was one thing J. Howard Pew could not abide, it was clergymen who engaged in social activism. It was perhaps inevitable, then, that Henry and Gaebelein's show of support for civil rights, measured as it was, would eventually provoke a rift between *Christianity Today*'s editors and its principal financial backer. In June 1964 Pew's simmering displeasure finally boiled over into full-blown rage. The fireworks began when the United Presbyterian Church in the U.S.A.—Pew's own denomination—adopted a raft of pro–civil rights resolutions at its 176th General Assembly in Oklahoma City. With the stated clerk and former NCC president Eugene Carson Blake at the helm, the Presbyterians elected an African American moderator (for the first time in the denomination's history), barred local churches from discriminating on the basis of race, abolished racially segregated presbyteries, encouraged local and regional church bodies to form alliances with civil rights organizations, approved of nonviolent civil disobedience in the furtherance of racial equality, and—last but not least—shot down a motion from the presbytery of West Tennessee that would have condemned Blake for his recent arrest during a civil rights demonstration.[68]

Not surprisingly, Pew immediately contacted Gaebelein, who was serving as acting editor-in-chief while Henry was on sabbatical, to demand that *Christianity Today* expose the General Assembly for the heretical body it undoubtedly was. Instead, the magazine ran a news feature that, while accurately summarizing the Assembly's actions, also seemed to cast them in a generally positive light.[69] At this point Pew took matters into his own hands, penning an essay entitled "The Mission of the Church," which he demanded that Gaebelein run as the lead article in the next issue of *Christianity Today*. Although the essay barely mentioned civil rights, it lambasted the General Assembly for entangling itself in "civil affairs" and neglecting the church's "spiritual mission," even going so far as to claim that "the moral corruption and spiritual poverty of our day" was directly attributable to the "social gospel" that Blake and others had substituted for the unvarnished doctrines of John Calvin.[70] (Gaebelein, for his part, agreed to publish Pew's missive, but he did not run it as the lead article.)

Then, at a *Christianity Today* board meeting in late June, while Henry was still on sabbatical, Pew launched into a lengthy diatribe, the thrust of which was that the magazine had "failed of its mission [of defending our Protestant heritage]. Its failure was not due to a shortage of money or personnel; it was due to editorial incompetence. Incompetence in that the members of the editorial staff failed to challenge the erroneous acts of our leading denominations in forthright, unequivocal language." Why, he wondered aloud, should he continue to support a religious magazine whose editors were such poor theologians that they could not recognize rank heresy when they saw it?[71] When Gaebelein, who was in regular contact with Henry, objected that all of his actions were in keeping with magazine's well-established editorial policies, Pew reportedly turned to Billy Graham and declared: "We've got to get rid of Carl."[72]

Following his return to the *Christianity Today* offices in early July, Henry went out of his way to repair relations between the editorial staff and Pew, even going so far as to compose a special editorial statement declaring that the magazine's editors and board of directors were united in their opposition to religious leaders who would entangle "the Church" in a "secular, controversial issue."[73] (Although no mention was made of civil rights, the use of the singular "issue" was telling.) Pew was sufficiently appeased as to withdraw his threat to cut ties with the magazine. But the appearance later that month of Henry's latest book, a collection of lectures on social ethics, reignited the controversy.

On the one hand, Henry's *Aspects of Christian Social Ethics* landed some solid blows against mainline social ethicists such as Reinhold Niebuhr and John C. Bennett. Henry made a strong case that mainline leaders often put forward confused and even contradictory theological justifications for particular policy stances; that they ignored or downplayed tragic value tradeoffs that resulted from using the state as an instrument of benevolence (for example, restrictions on religious liberty); and that forming alliances with particular interest groups (read: organized labor) left the church vulnerable to being tarnished by the sins of its allies. And yet Henry reserved some of his harshest words for his fellow evangelicals, most of whom were sitting out the struggle for African American civil rights. Here, Henry now believed, was a case where the Bible provide a clear mandate for social action, and yet far too many evangelicals were ignoring biblical injunctions concerning the equal worth and dignity of every human being. Even if it was true that the mainline churches had at times been overly zealous in their civil rights advocacy, and even if they were prone to self-righteous demonization of their critics, this did not excuse evangelical inaction. "The conservative clergy," Henry wrote, had been

> wrong in minimizing the importance of the Church's witness to the social order. . . . In the matter of expounding biblical principles of social justice, of exposing unsound theories to open shame, of openly challenging race discrimination and civil rights compromises, the evangelical churches ought to have been *in the vanguard*. . . . Too often evangelical pulpits have neglected to

emphasize those very divine principles of social life which they professed to defend in the face of liberal and neo-orthodox theological defection. Hence, in the absence of relevant preaching, indignation over statute-breaking ran deeper in the Bible Belt than a sense of guilt concerning the injustice of their own local laws.[74]

Pew, naturally, was outraged by Henry's fairly unambiguous call for evangelicals to assume their rightful place at the forefront of the civil rights struggle—all the more so because he had provided Henry with a detailed list of criticisms of an early draft of the manuscript, few of which had been incorporated into the finished text.[75] Upon reading the volume, L. Nelson Bell, who had been playing the role of intermediary between Pew and Henry for several years, finally agreed with Pew that Henry's thinking on "social issues" had become hopelessly "fuzzy" and "confused," and that his days at the magazine were probably numbered. Together with Billy Graham, Pew and Bell settled on an arrangement whereby Henry would turn over the writing of editorials touching on current events to Harold Lindsell, a resolutely conservative theology professor whom the three men hoped to groom as Henry's eventual successor.[76] For his part, Henry, who was much in demand as a lecturer and who nursed a long list of grievances concerning his salary and other administrative matters, was not exactly hostile to the idea of a separation. Although he would remain on the editorial staff of *Christianity Today* through 1967, his attention was increasingly focused on other projects.[77]

If there is a lesson to be learned from Carl Henry's tumultuous tenure at *Christianity Today*, it is that critiquing mainline Protestant social activism was a much simpler endeavor than crafting a viable alternative perspective. Like Billy Graham, Henry was undoubtedly sincere in his belief that the official leaders of American Protestantism were perverting the Gospel message, claiming a biblical warrant for many policies that, well intentioned or not, could find no clear support in the Bible. In theory, both Graham and Henry accepted that individual Christians ought to point out social evils when they saw them, but they insisted that neither denominational leaders nor the National Council of Churches had any business orchestrating religious activism from on high. Authentic acts of Christian protest, the two men maintained, sprang directly from the only authority that mattered: the revealed Word of God. But as subsequent generations of well-intentioned evangelical reformers would soon discover, stating the matter in this way only gave rise to a new and thorny set of problems. Would individual believers even recognize social evils without a "prophetic voice" to point the way? Did not exclusive reliance on the Bible as the sole judge of social obligations imply the need for disinterested and authoritative—or at least highly influential—interpreters? And if the answer was "no"—if "the priesthood of the believer" principle was now to be taken literally as a guide to Christian social ethics—then what was to stop individual believers from reading their own prejudices and material interests into the Bible's famously pliable text? For libertarians like Pew, who desired nothing so much as the dismantling of established religious authority, these questions were of secondary importance. But for a genuine theologian, they were very troubling indeed.

7

The Last Hurrah

The Civil Rights Act of 1964

Oldtimers on Capitol Hill have never seen anything like it. . . . Not since Prohibition has the church attempted to influence political action in Congress as it is now doing on behalf of President Johnson's civil rights bill.

—Rowland Evans and Robert Novak (1964)

On June 10, 1964, Georgia Senator Richard B. Russell, the dean of the upper chamber's Southern delegation, stood to address his colleagues. The sixty-six-year-old appeared tired, and his genteel drawl was tinged with bitterness. For the past fifty-four days, Russell, a diehard segregationist, had led a filibuster against what would become the Civil Rights Act of 1964. But now, as the senator himself admitted, "the jig [was] up."[1] For the first time in history, supporters of civil rights had mustered the necessary supermajority to overcome a Southern filibuster—a move that all but ensured that the bill would eventually make its way to the White House for the president's signature. Adding insult to injury, the man who would sign the bill into law was none other than Russell's onetime protégé, Lyndon Baines Johnson.

There was little Russell could do at this point except assign blame. Why had the filibuster—a procedural tool that had proved so successful in eviscerating previous civil rights bills—failed to work its magic in the spring and summer of 1964? Why were so many senators, including many conservatives who were generally skeptical of novel federal regulations, supporting a bill that promised to extend government oversight to hotels, restaurants, and a range of privately owned businesses? Perhaps surprisingly, Russell did not train his fire on venerable civil rights leaders, such as Martin Luther King, Jr., nor did he target up-and-coming civil rights groups like the Student Non-Violent Coordinating Committee (SNCC). Rather, he laid most of the blame at the feet of the nation's white religious leaders:

I have observed with profound sorrow the role that many religious leaders have played in urging passage of the bill, because I cannot make their activities jibe with my concept of the proper place of religious leaders in our national life. During the course of the debate, we have seen cardinals, bishops, elders, stated clerks, common preachers, priests and rabbis come to Washington to press for the passage of the bill. . . . Day after day, men of the cloth have been standing on the Mall and urging a favorable vote on the bill. They have encouraged and prompted thousands of good citizens to sign petitions supporting the bill. . . . This is the second time in my lifetime that an effort has been made by the clergy to make a moral question of a political issue. The other was prohibition. We know something of that.[2]

If taken literally, Russell's account of how the civil rights bill had managed to reach the floor of the Senate was wildly inaccurate. White religious leaders were far from the only ones working to enact civil rights legislation, and they likely would not have entered the fight if not for the unrelenting prodding of thousands of African American activists. And yet Russell was certainly correct on two points: the lobbying campaign that white religious leaders mounted on behalf of the 1964 civil rights bill was truly unprecedented, and these "men of the cloth" had indeed convinced hundreds of thousands of their parishioners to write, call, send telegrams to, and personally visit their representatives to urge passage of the Civil Rights Act. Never before—or at least not since Prohibition—had so many religious people expended so much time, money, and energy in support of a single piece of legislation. Indeed, there was much anecdotal evidence to suggest that religious activists were largely responsible for winning over the handful of wavering Midwestern and Mountain-state senators whose votes had provided the winning margin in the fight for cloture.[3]

But why did white northern churchgoers, who had in the past avoided serious engagement with racial issues, suddenly throw themselves into the struggle for a meaningful civil rights bill in 1963–1964? Although Russell seems to have viewed this burst of religious activism as a kind of collective madness, it is more properly seen as an example—the very last, in fact—of the power that religious institutions exerted over rank-and-file churchgoers in the middle decades of the twentieth century. For while the most dramatic of the religious demonstrations on behalf of civil rights often appeared spontaneous, they were in fact carefully choreographed endeavors, often planned months in advance by denominational leaders and ecumenical bodies. An examination of the push for the Civil Rights Act therefore provides a unique opportunity to observe the mechanisms through which mainline churches—as well as Catholic and Jewish religious bodies— shaped the ethical sensibilities of their members and mobilized them for political action. Though no one knew it at the time, religious authority was about to begin a steep and irreversible decline. But to understand that decline, we must first understand how religious authority was constructed, maintained, and exercised during the heady days of the civil rights movement.

To that end, this chapter draws on the records of the National Council of Churches, the denominational civil rights bodies, and the state and local councils of churches to document the specific mechanisms that allowed church officials to mobilize large numbers of churchgoers on behalf of civil rights reform. Although the general arc of the story will be familiar to those who have read prior histories of the Civil Rights Act, the focus here is on religious authority and its role in shaping the views and actions of average believers. With that in mind, the chapter concludes with a section in which I use data from the 1964 National Election Study to test whether church involvement affected white Protestants' views concerning the Civil Rights Act. As we shall see, the public opinion data generally confirm the picture that emerges from the archival record—namely, that the churches' educational efforts were, in fact, a critical factor in building northern white support for a meaningful civil rights bill.

Laying the Groundwork

In truth, the notion that white Protestants had been largely silent on the issue of race prior to the debate over the 1964 Civil Rights Act was not entirely accurate. By the early 1960s the mainline denominations were fully committed to integrating public schools, and most had expressed at least qualified support for the civil disobedience campaigns that were beginning to gain momentum in a number of Southern and border states. The NCC was also actively, if cautiously, promoting civil rights initiatives through its Department of Racial and Cultural Relations. Led by the African American minister and scholar J. Oscar Lee, the Department regularly spoke out on issues such as lynching and fair housing, while also organizing annual interracial "institutes" that brought together white and black church leaders to discuss proposals for combating the effects of discrimination in American life.[4] In addition, every February Lee secured air time and newspaper coverage for a brief Race Relations Sunday message that expressed the Council's views on the state of race relations. And while these sermons on racial harmony tended toward the anodyne, the idea of using biblical arguments to challenge entrenched racial hierarchies was more than offensive enough to provoke the ire of conservative white Protestants. In fact, Lee's department compiled a fat file of "Questionable Inquiries" consisting almost entirely of letters from angry citizens who had heard a Race Relations Sunday message delivered from the pulpit or over the airwaves.[5]

But if the churches' engagement with civil rights was not entirely new, the *nature* of their engagement undoubtedly changed in early 1963. That spring the mainline denominations began for the first time to devote serious resources to programs that aimed to integrate congregations and communities, as well as to mobilize rank-and-file believers to support civil rights legislation. In May, shortly after the *New York Times* published the iconic photograph of a police dog tearing into the midriff of a young participant in the Birmingham Children's March, the Northern branch of the Presbyterians (UPC-USA) pledged $500,000 for an emergency committee to support the civil rights movement.[6] The United Church of Christ (UCC) created its own civil rights commission a few weeks later, authorizing the group to "mobiliz[e] the whole membership of the Church" to "press for . . . civil rights legislation."[7] In early June the NCC, which represented the largest mainline denominations, followed suit, creating an emergency Commission on Religion and Race (CORR) that soon established itself as the unofficial coordinator of the Protestant churches' civil rights activities.[8]

In addition to that spring's unprecedented acts of civil disobedience, there was another catalyst for the churches' more aggressive brand of civil rights activism: for the first time in modern history, a president had thrown the full weight of his office behind a push for meaningful civil rights legislation. On June 11, two days after the NCC established its Commission on Religion and Race, President John F. Kennedy delivered a nationally televised address calling on Congress to enact legislation that would secure African American voting rights, speed the integration of public schools, and give "all Americans the right to be served in facilities which are open to the public." Six days later Kennedy invited an interracial group of Protestant, Catholic, and Jewish leaders to the White House to form an ad hoc religious advisory committee under the chairmanship of the NCC's president, J. Irwin Miller. President Kennedy began his opening remarks by noting that the "whole matter" of civil rights had "accelerated" in recent weeks, so that it was "fair to say that the Negro community is determined that in 1963 they will go a long way towards achieving equality of opportunities and equality of rights." He acknowledged that his proposed bill was bound to stoke "resentments against Washington," and that he could not "say with certainty what its fate will be." The greatest service religious leaders could perform, therefore, would be to tamp down the white backlash by stressing the legislation's religious roots: "The more we can make this . . . a community action, with moral overtones and not merely a political effort, the better off we will be."[9] Miller followed up the meeting by releasing a public letter pledging that Protestant church leaders would work hand in hand with Jews and Catholics to "accomplish the goals, common to both the nation and each of the religious groups, of human dignity and equal opportunity."[10]

CORR, which would be tasked with upholding Protestantism's end of the bargain, was up and running by late June. As important as the size of the group's budget—which was roughly seven times the amount that Oscar Lee's department

received for its civil rights initiatives—was the fact that it was designed to operate entirely outside the NCC's bureaucratic chain of command.[11] Indeed, the
General Board, in the act of creating the Commission, took the highly unusual
step of authorizing it to "to make commitments, call for actions, [and] take risks"
in order to advance the NCC's declared principles "in the area of religion and
race."[12] CORR's leaders would report directly to the General Board, and in practice the only man whose approval was needed for even the most consequential
decisions was J. Irwin Miller. In fact it was Miller, the president of the Cummins
Engine Company and the NCC's first lay president, who, along with the former
NCC president Eugene Carson Blake, led the push for an independent commission that would trade the Council's traditionally cautious stance on race relations
for a more direct approach. As Blake bluntly informed the General Board, it was
high time that some white, middle-class Christians "got on the wrong end of a
fire hose."[13] The soft-spoken Miller lacked Blake's flair for the dramatic, but he
privately told CORR staffers that he, too, was "prepared to go to jail or anything"
if it would help to advance the cause.[14]

CORR's members, who were selected by Miller in consultation with NCC
officials, included prominent black and white clergymen, as well as representatives from business, labor, and academia. For the role of chairman, Miller initially selected Arthur C. Lichtenberger, presiding bishop of the Episcopal
Church; when Lichtenberger fell ill, Eugene Carson Blake eagerly stepped into
the role. Robert W. Spike, a United Church of Christ minister and theologian
with a record of promoting interracial cooperation between New York City–area
churches, was brought on board as executive director. Other key staff members
included the pioneering African American activist and political operative
Anna Arnold Hedgeman, who served as coordinator of special projects; James
Hamilton, a young Washington lawyer who coordinated the group's lobbying
efforts; John Pratt, a recent Columbia Law School graduate and former seminary
student, who took charge of legal issues; Jon L. Regier, a Presbyterian minister
and NCC official with a background in settlement house work, who served as li-
aison to ecumenical groups and the Council bureaucracy; and J. Oscar Lee, who
took a leave of absence from the Department of Racial and Cultural Relations to
serve as CORR's associate director.[15]

At its initial meetings the group hammered out a three-pronged strategy.[16]
The first prong called for religious leaders to organize massive public displays of
support for the president's bill; ideally these would be staged at critical moments
in the legislative process—for example, if the bill passed the House but faced a
filibuster in the Senate. The second called for a behind-the-scenes lobbying effort in which religious leaders and prominent lay people would be assigned to
pressure specific members of Congress with whom they had some previous connection. The final—and undoubtedly most crucial—prong called for mobilizing

large numbers of Midwestern churchgoers to support the administration's bill. Victor Reuther, the Methodist layman and union official who chaired CORR's working group on legislation, persuaded his colleagues that the religious forces should focus their efforts on rural states and districts where the bill's other major supporters—namely, labor unions and African American civil rights groups— exerted little influence. The focus on the Midwest was also dictated by simple math: With Southern lawmakers monolithically opposed to the president's bill and most urban Northeasterners likely to support it, it stood to reason that the measure's fate rested with the largely Republican Midwestern bloc.[17]

Whether significant numbers of Midwestern churchgoers could be mobilized to support the civil rights bill was anyone's guess, but at least two prominent pundits judged the job a fool's errand. According to Rowland Evans and Robert Novak, rural and small-town whites "had little personal contact with Negroes," and many were in thrall to Far-Right groups who were tarring the president's bill as a communist-inspired assault on the rights of white Americans. Having carefully examined the mail of a "Republican from a Midwestern state," the pair concluded that "heart-felt" anti–civil rights letters were "pouring in from the rural districts"—a development that did not bode well for the president's signature domestic initiative.[18]

Perceptions in Washington began to shift, however, following the August 28 March on Washington. The brainchild of the union leader A. Phillip Randolph and the freelance civil rights organizer Bayard Rustin, the March for Jobs and Freedom, as it was formally known, aimed to highlight the breadth and depth of support for federal action by uniting African American civil rights activists, union members, and white churchgoers in a massive demonstration on the National Mall. The NCC became involved with the event in early July, when civil rights groups secured a commitment from Blake to help supply at least "30,000 white people" for the planned demonstration.[19] The decision was not without controversy. Francis Harmon, a prominent NCC lay leader and informal advisor to CORR, urged J. Irwin Miller to steer clear of the march on the grounds that Washington was a "tinder-box" where an "an unexpected incident could start a terrible holocaust" for which the NCC would be blamed.[20] Several Southern and border-state church groups offered similar assessments. The editor of the *Virginia Methodist Advocate*, for example, claimed to have inside information that the event was being organized by communist agitators who hoped to capitalize on the "highly emotional nature of the Negro" by inciting a riot in the nation's capital.[21] In the end Miller deferred to the judgment of Blake and Spike, both of whom strongly favored participation.

The job of organizing a white religious delegation fell to Anna Hedgeman, CORR's director of special projects, who immediately went to work promoting the event through denominational and conciliar channels.[22] In late July CORR staffers distributed thousands of flyers summarizing the March's objectives to state and local church councils, as well as to churches and individuals on the NCC's myriad mailing lists. An organizing manual, which offered travel tips and logistical information, went out in early August.[23] Law-and-order concerns were never far from Hedgeman's mind. Each local church delegation was instructed to choose a captain, and each captain was required to maintain a list, to be surrendered to the police upon request, of the names and addresses of everyone in his or her delegation.[24] NCC staff members who would be making the trip to Washington were subjected to lectures on such topics as psychological preparation and inner group discipline.[25] Worries about the potential for a riot may also have prompted CORR to assume the burden of feeding the marchers. On August 27, the day before the march, hundreds of CORR-recruited volunteers gathered at New York City's Riverside Church to prepare eighty thousand sack lunches, which were transported to Washington overnight in refrigerated trucks.[26]

In the end, of course, the march proved both peaceful and highly effective in mobilizing public support for the cause of racial equality. In all, Hedgeman's efforts helped secure the participation of forty thousand white marchers—roughly ten thousand more than the amount originally pledged by Blake and about one-sixth of the total attendance. (Significantly, the Midwestern states seem to have been well represented; Indiana's churches, for example, sent 225 white marchers, most of them ministers and denominational officials).[27] For Robert Spike, CORR's executive director, the moment when the interracial religious delegation began its slow procession toward the Lincoln Memorial marked a transformative juncture in the history of American Christianity. "When the NCC delegation, over 100 strong, moved into the stream of marchers," Spike wrote in his official report to the Commission, "and we began to sing the song of victory, one of the deepest longings of my ministry was for a moment fulfilled—the longing that the Church of Jesus Christ be in the midst of human struggle, not on the sidelines. And we were there—in an act so full of symbolism that no one could escape it, and with the satisfaction that we were no longer token representatives. The power of Protestantism was marching with us, and we had a right to be there at long last, because we were bearing some of the far reaching burdens of the struggle."[28] Eugene Carson Blake, who shared the speaker's platform with King, Randolph, John Lewis, and other giants of the movement, used his moment in the spotlight to apologize for white Protestants' years of reticence on civil rights and to promise that they would do everything in their power to make up for lost time. Although they "came late" to the struggle, the mainline churches came in a "reconciling and repentant spirit," and they were determined "to be found on God's side" in the coming push for a strong civil rights bill.[29]

The unusual presence of so many white religious leaders at a civil rights gathering caught the attention of political handicappers, including the *New York*

Times's longtime Washington bureau chief, James "Scotty" Reston, who laid out the new conventional wisdom concerning the president's bill in an August 30 column. "If the preachers said what they really thought about this racial crisis and even half of those who heard and believed them wrote their honest convictions for or against racial equality to Capitol Hill, the political balance on racial equality might easily be transformed," he predicted. "For while the politicians here are not saying much about the march, they are listening."[30] The syndicated columnist Marquis Childs agreed, observing that

> religious support for integration covers the whole religious spectrum. The question is whether this support will be translated into concerted effort to convince the waverers [in Congress] that a majority of Americans of every kind and color and not just the leaders of a few pressure groups want action. In many states—in the Midwest, in the plain and Rocky Mountain states—the proportion of negroes [*sic*] to white[s] is small. Unless [congressmen] from these regions hear from the folks back home who have a real conviction of the need to correct ancient wrongs they may get the impression that no one cares very much.[31]

The challenge confronting CORR and the bill's other supporters, as the pundits foresaw, was that the typical Midwestern church member had little direct experience with the evils of segregation, let alone with the minutiae of the proposed civil rights bill. And uninformed citizens, as more than one columnist pointed out, were unlikely to make great sacrifices on behalf of a piece of legislation from which they could expect few direct benefits. Even James Hamilton, CORR's legislative strategist, was forced to admit that foot-dragging Midwestern congressmen were probably "doing a good job of representing their constituents," most of whom were themselves undecided about the merits of the bill.[32]

In order to assuage Midwesterners' fear of the unknown, CORR and civil rights advocates within the denominations launched a massive educational and grassroots mobilization effort. Two critical features of the mid-century religious landscape worked to their advantage. First, as Figure 7.1 makes clear, the two most aggressively pro–civil rights of the mainline denominations, the United Presbyterian Church in the U.S.A. and the United Church of Christ, were very well represented in the Midwest and Plains states. Although virtually all of the large mainline denominations contributed to the NCC's civil rights program—at least in the beginning—the northern Presbyterians and the UCC were the first to develop serious civil rights bodies within their own churches. And in states such as North and South Dakota, the ratio of these churches to total population ran as high as one church for every 2,200 residents.[33]

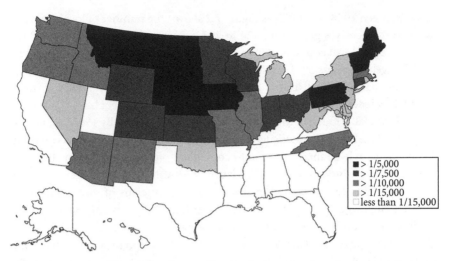

Figure 7.1 Combined density of United Presbyterian Church in the U.S.A and United Church of Christ churches, 1952

Second, and arguably more important, the church federation (or "conciliar") movement was particularly strong in the Midwest. With the encouragement of the Federal Council of Churches (the forerunner of the NCC), dozens of cities and states had founded Protestant ecumenical bodies—typically called councils or federations of churches—in the 1920s and 1930s. Many of the functions performed by church councils, such as conducting neighborhood surveys, facilitating pulpit exchanges, and coordinating church placement, were purely ecclesiastical. But they also provided a powerful vehicle for mainline clergymen and lay leaders to express what they believed to be the Christian position on public issues ranging from legalized gambling to capital punishment to civil rights. Moreover, they were from their inception intended to serve as "clearing-house[s] of information." They allowed NCC officials to distribute material to ministers and lay leaders in even the most remote parts of the country while simultaneously encouraging local church leaders to supply NCC headquarters with valuable intelligence concerning the views of the men and women in the pews.[34] Indeed, most state and local councils modeled their organizational structures on that of the NCC, the better to facilitate the flow of information to and from Council headquarters.[35]

As late as the 1930s, professional church councils—that is, councils with paid executives and other staff members—were common only in the nation's largest cities. This changed in the immediate postwar period, when the mainline denominations found themselves inundated with new members and flush with cash. Between 1958 and 1965, as Figure 7.2 shows, the number of local councils with paid executives grew from 220 to 293—an expansion of 33 percent.[36] By 1959 state and local councils employed nearly 700 people and commanded annual budgets in excess of $13 million ($115 million in 2019 dollars).[37] Moreover, an additional 650 small towns and counties had by the early 1960s formed councils or federations of churches that operated on a volunteer basis.[38]

And, crucially, much of this growth came in the Midwest. By 1963, as Figures 7.3 and 7.4 make clear, states such as Illinois, Indiana, and the Dakotas boasted far more church councils and paid ecumenical officials per citizen than the average state.[39] Indeed, ten of the eleven Midwestern states targeted by the pro–civil rights forces ranked in the top twenty in terms of number of paid council employees per white Protestant resident.[40] Equally important, many of these state and local councils featured Human Rights or Racial and Cultural Relations Departments that were already fully engaged on the civil rights front. For example, church councils in Nebraska and Indiana were by 1962 actively lobbying for the repeal of their states' antimiscegenation statutes and for the adoption of state laws prohibiting discrimination in public accommodations. And dozens of local councils had by this point launched hands-on initiatives in areas such as fair housing, employment discrimination, and urban renewal. These efforts naturally brought white church officials into contact with African American civil rights activists, and many local councils had already forged

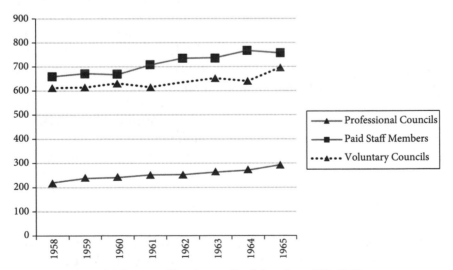

Figure 7.2 Growth of state and local councils of churches, 1958–1965
Source: Yearbooks of American Churches, 1958–1965

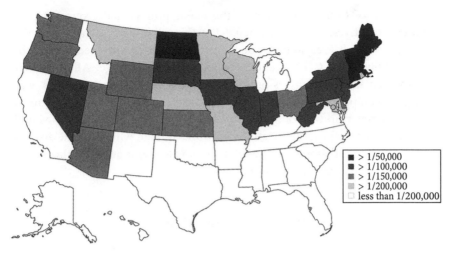

Figure 7.3 State and local church council density, 1963
Source: Yearbook of American Churches

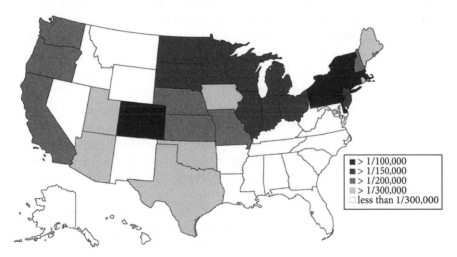

Figure 7.4 State and local church council staff density, 1963
Source: Yearbook of American Churches

close ties with local chapters of the Urban League, the NAACP, and other civil rights organizations.[41]

Realizing that local council cooperation would be essential to CORR's grassroots mobilization efforts, J. Irwin Miller and Oscar Lee traveled to Wisconsin's Lake Geneva in June 1963 to address the annual meeting of the

Association of Council Secretaries, the major professional group for paid council executives. After Lee briefed the three hundred attendees on the nuts and bolts of President Kennedy's proposal, the group pledged to "cooperate fully" with CORR's efforts to aid the bill's passage. Among other commitments, the executives promised to seek "face-to-face meetings with Congressmen in home districts" and to promote letter-writing campaigns in local churches.[42] In the coming months, the state and local councils would provide the critical communications network through which CORR distributed legislative bulletins, educational tracts, and lobbying advice to thousands of congregations across the country.[43]

The Battle for the Midwest

The battle for the Midwest kicked off in earnest in early September when CORR, in cooperation with state and local church councils, organized a series of statewide "legislative conferences." These gatherings brought together clergymen, church officials, and lay leaders to discuss the specifics of the president's bill and also the theological basis for the church's involvement. At the first conference, held in Lincoln, Nebraska, attendees listened to pro–civil rights pleas from a list of dignitaries that included the state's governor and two members of Congress, as well as Victor Reuther and the NAACP's Washington bureau director, Clarence Mitchell. The basic formula was repeated in Colorado, Illinois, Ohio, and Minnesota.[44]

The point of these statewide gatherings was to create a vanguard of informed elites who would be equipped to persuade their coreligionists of the merits of the civil rights bill. But CORR staffers also worked to arrange small gatherings in local churches with the aim of promoting face-to-face encounters between average Midwesterners and civil rights activists. In September four-person teams composed of local church officials, trained theologians, student representatives of the major African American civil rights groups, and legislative experts fanned out across Nebraska, Indiana, Iowa, South Dakota, Illinois, and Ohio. They organized as many as twenty meetings in each state, with an average attendance of around a hundred people; costs were split among CORR, local church councils, and the mainline denominations. Anna Hedgeman, who oversaw the operation, judged it an unqualified success, noting in particular the "excellent newspaper, television, and radio coverage" the sessions received. Some of the team members, including the Southern Christian Leadership Conference's (SCLC) Annell Ponder, offered more measured—though still generally positive—assessments. Although Ponder, who was a member of the Iowa team, found the white church members she addressed to be woefully uninformed "about the Negro situation," she nonetheless sensed that many of them were genuinely convinced of "the need for . . . strong civil rights legislation."[45]

These were not empty words. Many of the Midwestern church members who attended the CORR-sponsored sessions seemed to be deeply moved by what they heard, including Ponder's account of the brutal beating she had suffered in a Mississippi jail only weeks before traveling to Iowa.[46] When Prathia Hall, an African American member of the South Dakota team, was subsequently arrested during a demonstration in Georgia, a group of concerned South Dakota church members contacted NCC headquarters to inquire about her well-being and to offer assistance.[47] In Boone, Iowa, a delegation of women from the First Presbyterian Church wrote denominational officials with an offer to take "several young Negro staff persons of SNCC into our homes for a few weeks of rest and relaxation."[48] (SNCC leaders regretfully reported that they could find no takers for the offer, since all of the group's activists preferred to remain on the front lines.)

Carefully planned educational sessions likely produced a number of converts to the cause of racial equality, yet their impact was clearly augmented by the horrific events of September 15. That morning a group of Ku Klux Klan members dynamited Birmingham's Sixteenth Street Baptist Church, killing four young African American girls and injuring more than twenty other people. Religious leaders across the nation sprang into action. In New York the Protestant Council ordered thousands of black mourning bands emblazoned with the words "BIRMINGHAM CHILDREN" and distributed them free of charge to the city's congregations. Presbyterian church officials in New York, Chicago, and other major cities asked ministers to incorporate a moment of silence, as well as a plea for a strong civil rights bill, in their Sunday sermons.[49] CORR's Robert Spike responded to the bombing by sending the nation's state and local church councils a list of practical suggestions for action, including stocking church pews with paper, envelopes, and pencils to facilitate letter writing; having churches pay the cost of postage for letters to local members of Congress; collecting letters in the offering plate; and ensuring that commemorative activities were thoroughly covered by "local news media—press, radio, and television."[50]

Within days of the bombing, Midwestern members of Congress were reporting a sharp uptick in pro–civil rights mail. Based on yet another examination of congressional mailbags—albeit one conducted the day after the bombing, well before the full weight of the tragedy had registered with white Northerners—the *Wall Street Journal's* Jerry Landauer concluded that the bill's supporters now had the upper hand, and that "roughly half" of supportive letters "reveal[ed] church inspiration." One source for Landauer's story was Kansas Senator James B. Pearson, who reported that his mail was now running "heavily for civil rights." Letters were pouring in from such tiny hamlets as Pretty Prairie, Alma, Pittsburg,

Fredonia, and Parsons, and most of the "letterheads [seemed to] indicate a church-inspired campaign."[51] Never one to rest on his laurels, Spike responded to the *Journal* story by urging participants in CORR's recent legislative conferences to redouble their efforts. Now that the avalanche of "mail from the Midwest" had caught the attention of the pundits, it was time to "concentrate" specifically "on the . . . House Judiciary Committee," where the bill was awaiting action.[52]

By late October developments in the Judiciary Committee too were trending in a positive direction. On October 2, with the encouragement of Chairman Emanuel Celler of New York, a Judiciary subcommittee approved a civil rights bill with considerably more teeth than the one originally proposed by the president. Liberal church groups were elated. More astute legislative analysts, on the other hand, realized that the subcommittee's bill would never pass the full House. Thus began three weeks of intense negotiation among Kennedy's inner circle, the Committee's liberal Democrats, and House Republican leaders. The end goal, from the president's perspective, was to water down the bill just enough to make House passage possible, but not so much as to alienate liberal supporters of civil rights. Because Southern Democrats controlled a large bloc of seats on the Judiciary Committee, Kennedy leaned heavily on Republicans, including Ranking Member William McCulloch and Minority Leader Charles Halleck, to provide the votes necessary to get a revised bill out of committee. By the last week of October the parties had hammered out a compromise that fell roughly halfway between the subcommittee version and the president's original proposal. Although the new version scaled back voting rights guarantees and limited the Justice Department's authority to initiate desegregation suits, it nonetheless retained a robust public accommodations section, which required owners of restaurants, theaters, hotels and similar business to serve all customers without regard to race. On October 29 the revised bill passed the full Committee on a vote of twenty to fourteen.

At this point attention shifted to the Rules Committee—the last body capable of preventing H.R. 7152 from reaching the House floor. Unfortunately for civil rights backers, the Committee was chaired by "Judge" Howard W. Smith, a Virginia Democrat and staunch segregationist. Smith's Committee had a well-earned reputation as a burying ground for liberal reform proposals of all kinds, but particularly those that threatened to upend the South's system of racial subordination. Knowing that Smith was highly unlikely to schedule hearings on H.R. 7152 absent outside pressure, the bill's supporters weighed a pair of rarely used procedural maneuvers, both of which could in theory force the chairman's hand. The first procedure, known as Rule 11, allowed a simple majority vote of the Committee's members to override the will of the chairman. The second procedure, known as the discharge petition, discharged a bill from Committee consideration, bringing it directly to the House floor once a majority of the House's

435 members signed a petition to that effect. The problem with both tactics was that they would require significant Republican support to overcome the monolithic opposition of Southern Democrats. And the Republican leadership, which had so recently saved the Democrats from political disaster in the Judiciary Committee, was far from eager to play this role a second time.

Before civil rights proponents could settle on a definite strategy, fate intervened. On November 22, 1963, John F. Kennedy was assassinated in Dallas, and Lyndon B. Johnson was sworn in as the nation's thirty-sixth president as he returned to Washington aboard Air Force One. Five days later, in a nationally televised address to a joint session of Congress, Johnson pledged his support for the late president's civil rights bill. The new president, a former Senate Majority Leader, was unrivaled in his mastery of the dark arts of legislative arm-twisting. Quietly at first, and then openly, he let it be known that he backed the discharge petition plan, though he was well aware that the tactic was a long shot. (Since 1932, when the discharge rule was adopted, only fourteen bills had reached the House floor by this method, and only two had become law.)[53] The problem was that the Southern delegation would ignore the petition, which meant that some sixty to seventy Republican signatures would be needed to reach a majority—an impossible number unless Republican leaders pressured rank-and-file members to sign, which they seemed highly unlikely to do. At the same time, and probably with Johnson's blessing, pro–civil rights members of the Rules Committee, including Ohio Republican Clarence Brown, the Committee's Ranking Member, tentatively explored the possibility of invoking Rule 11.[54]

Religious lobbying activity, which had tapered off somewhat as H.R. 7152 languished in Judge Smith's Rules Committee, ramped up once again when news of the discharge petition reached the press. As fate would have it, the National Council of Churches was holding its triennial General Assembly in Philadelphia at the precise moment that the discharge plan took shape. Robert Spike, who was in frequent contact with civil rights supporters in the House, used his spot on the program to inform the delegates about the discharge petition, which offered the only real "hope of prying the civil rights bill out of the House Rules Committee this year." If the Assembly's four thousand delegates were serious about passing a civil rights bill, they should consider planning a side trip through Washington on their way home. Better yet, he suggested, why not charter buses to take a group of nonvoting delegates directly from the convention hall to Capitol Hill to lobby on behalf of the petition? (Even at this moment of national crisis, apparently, voting delegates were expected to remain at their posts).[55]

At eight o'clock in the morning on December 6, two busloads of ministers and laypeople departed Philadelphia for Washington. The mostly white delegation, whose members hailed from twenty different states, arrived shortly after noon and immediately set about cornering representatives who had not yet staked out a clear position on the discharge petition. Seven church people from Ohio buttonholed Republican Representatives William McCulloch, Paul Schenck, Frances Bolton, and Charles Mosher, with mixed results. McCulloch, who, despite a strong voting record on civil rights, was a great respecter of institutional tradition, flatly refused to back the contentious discharge tactic. The other three Republicans said they would sign, but only if Judge Smith did not schedule hearings in a reasonable amount of time.[56] Although the NCC group garnered relatively few firm commitments, its dramatic gesture made headlines across the country, generating stories in the *New York Times*, the *Washington Post*, the *Los Angeles Times*, and other major papers.[57]

Less publicized tactics also proved effective in mobilizing church people to support the petition. Marshal Scott, who headed the Presbyterian Commission on Religion and Race (CORAR), telegraphed synods and presbyteries across the Midwest with news of the discharge plan. Within days local and regional Presbyterian leaders were contacting CORAR headquarters to report on their lobbying activities. On December 8, a day before the petition was formally filed, the Southeast Iowa Presbytery's newly formed civil rights commission wrote to say it had already sent telegrams to all of the state's Congressmen.[58] By December 11 the group had disseminated a thousand flyers to local congregations and dispatched special delivery packages with specific instructions for contacting members of Congress to every "minister, clerk, and women's association in the Presbytery."[59] A few hundred miles to the southwest, the head of the Wichita-area synod responded to Scott's request by providing all of the city's ministers and sessions—local church governing bodies—with information on how to support the discharge process.[60] In the southeastern corner of that state, the head of the Neosho presbytery proudly reported that five of its congregations had already contacted their Congressman about the petition.[61]

At first this flurry of lobbying activity seemed to be bearing fruit. On December 9, the day the petition was filed, over 130 members journeyed to the well of the House to sign it. Momentum then stalled, owing mainly to a lack of enthusiasm among moderate Republicans. Majority Leader Carl Albert privately informed Johnson that he expected to pick up no more than thirty Republicans—less than half of the number needed. Still, the fact that the petition garnered 150 signatures within days of its filing—and that many more members had pledged to sign if they saw no action from the Rules Committee—sent a strong signal to Judge Smith that civil rights proponents would not go quietly. An even stronger signal was sent by Clarence Brown, who informed Smith that a coalition of Northern Democrats and Republicans was prepared to invoke Rule 11 if hearings on H.R. 7152 were not scheduled, and soon. Whether because of the discharge threat or the Rule 11 threat, Smith relented. In mid-December the chairman acknowledged "the facts of life around here"—namely, that the bill's supporters had the votes "to take [the bill] away from me, and they can do it any minute they want to."[62] Hearings began on January 9.

H.R. 7152 reached the House floor on January 31, 1964. It passed the lower chamber ten days later by a vote of 290 to 130. Despite the lopsided margin, the days before final passage were not without drama. Several round-the-clock monitoring operations were necessary to ensure that enough supportive House members were always on hand to block the introduction of hostile amendments and attempts to refer the bill back to committee.[63] In the end, however, the only bloc of representatives whose position on the bill was ever in serious doubt—the Midwestern Republicans—stood firm. Between them, the states most heavily targeted by CORR and the other religious groups—Illinois, Indiana, Iowa, Nebraska, Ohio, and South Dakota—sent sixty-seven representatives to Washington; of these, only five voted against final passage.[64]

The Fight for Cloture

At this point attention shifted to the Senate, where civil rights foes enjoyed an institutional advantage that was potentially even more valuable than the chairmanship of the Rules Committee: the filibuster. Under then-current Senate rules, sixty-seven votes were needed to cut off debate by invoking cloture. Cloture was a contentious procedure, however, and many longtime members, including many racial moderates, considered the tactic an affront to the upper chamber's august tradition of unlimited debate. If one assumed that a dozen or so Northern traditionalists would refuse to cut off debate, it followed that the chamber's twenty or so diehard segregationists had an outside chance of talking H.R. 7152 to death, or at least seriously weakening it via the amendment process.

However, Richard Russell, the leader of the segregationist bloc, was a realist who was well aware that his opponents had all the momentum. Those closest to the Georgian knew that his real aim was to draw out the debate as long as possible in the hope that fate would somehow intervene. Northern white opinion might turn against the bill, Russell thought, if the hot summer months brought racial unrest to the nation's cities. Or perhaps groups such as the shadowy Coordinating Committee for Fundamental American Freedoms (CCFAF), which were spending a small fortune tarring the bill as an affront to the rights of white Americans, would succeed in fomenting enough grassroots opposition to dissuade Northern moderates from joining the cloture effort. With these contingencies in mind, Russell divided his troops into three shifts and prepared to grind the legislative process to a halt.

As in the House, it was widely understood that only the churches were well positioned to apply pressure to the twenty or so senators whose votes would ultimately decide the outcome of the cloture fight. Joe Rauh of the Legislative Conference on Civil Rights (LCCR), the umbrella group that coordinated the lobbying activities of the civil rights forces, declared that the push for cloture would have "to rely primarily on the [Protestant churches]," since the wavering senators were for the most part "Wasps—white, Protestant, Anglo-Saxon Americans." In fact, several of the critical Midwestern senators were Catholic, but Rauh's basic point—that the churches were better situated to exert influence than the unions and civil rights groups—was undoubtedly correct.[65] As CORR's chief legislative strategist, James Hamilton, informed NCC officials in mid-January, "The critical geographic areas in which support must be generated and sustained are the midwest and the west. . . . If the church cannot develop the necessary concern and commitment in these areas, Congress will not pass a meaningful civil rights bill, for other groups committed to the enactment of the legislation do not have sufficient strength there to make the necessary impact."[66]

Of all the Midwesterners who might be persuaded to support the bill, none was more critical than Everett Dirksen of Illinois, the Senate's Minority Leader. The sixty-eight-year-old Dirksen, with his signature shock of curly white hair, was not averse to bipartisan cooperation, and he possessed a reasonably progressive record on racial issues. In fact, although Dirksen came from a relatively humble background, he was in many ways a product of the same mainline intellectual culture that had shaped the worldviews of J. Irwin Miller, Charles P. Taft, and countless other mid-century elites. Growing up in tiny Pekin, Illinois, he served as president of his Reformed Church's Christian Endeavor Society for several years; following service in World War I, he honed his rhetorical skills filling the church's pulpit on Sunday nights.[67] But Dirksen was also unpredictable and, like his counterparts in the House, resented being asked to save his partisan rivals from political debacles of their own making. Even though Dirksen would likely vote "yes" should the bill ultimately come up for a vote, he was almost certain to introduce weakening amendments, if for no other reason than to save face with conservative Republicans, many of whom already doubted their leader's partisan bona fides. Nor could anyone say for certain, when the Senate began formal consideration of H.R. 7152 on February 17, where the minority leader stood on the issue of cloture.

The bill's religious supporters had, of course, been preparing for the eventuality of a filibuster for more than six months.[68] As in the House, their plan involved three components. The first was to once again stir up a groundswell of grassroots lobbying activity. As early as June 1963 the nation's state and local council executives had hatched a plan to respond to the anticipated filibuster by organizing a letter-writing quota system under which individual churches would be expected to produce an amount of pro–civil rights mail corresponding to the size of their membership. [69] To this end, on January 16 CORR dispatched a formal Call to Action to local church councils and the NCC's thirty-plus member denominations. Noting that "time" was "now the critical factor in the struggle for civil rights legislation," the missive asked church members to contact their senators with instructions to oppose all attempts at "delay and obstruct[ion]."[70] In early March, as the Senate debate got under way in earnest, CORR staffers once again fanned out across the Midwest in an effort to stimulate a second round of letters and phone calls. James Hamilton journeyed to South Dakota, where he joined officials from the state council of churches on a two-day barnstorming tour that was designed to put pressure on Karl Mundt, a key undecided vote on cloture.[71] Anna Hedgeman discussed the bill with church groups in North Dakota, Wisconsin, and Michigan.[72] In Iowa—home to Senators Bourke Hickenlooper and Jack Miller, both formally undecided on cloture—the state council of churches worked with NCC officials to organize a series of civil rights workshops that drew representatives from 230 congregations.[73]

Around the same time, CORR officials made arrangements to inundate Senate offices with church delegations, which were to be dispatched to Washington in waves over the course of the spring. The first delegation, consisting of a hundred representatives of the United Church of Christ (UCC), arrived on Capitol Hill on March 16. Dubbed the Washington Witness, the group was composed of carefully chosen UCC ministers and laymen from the eighteen states whose senators were deemed most crucial to the cloture fight. Denominational officials made a special effort to recruit minor dignitaries, such as a state Republican party chairman and a state judge, who personally knew the senators they would be lobbying. To ensure maximum publicity, several state delegations recorded their interviews with senators for use on the radio and prepared press releases for hometown papers. Although the Illinois delegation was disappointed by Dirksen's noncommittal remarks on cloture, Hubert Humphrey, the bill's floor manager and a UCC member himself, greeted his coreligionists warmly, declaring that final passage was all but assured "if the church people of America will really rise up." The group capped off its day on the Hill by recording a five-minute film, made with the help of Humphrey's staff, which was distributed to television stations in each of the eighteen states.[74]

In addition to highly publicized episodes such as the Washington Witness, church officials worked to initiate informal, behind-the-scenes contacts between religious leaders and undecided senators. A favorite CORR tactic was to monitor senators' travel schedules so that prominent religious leaders could "just happen" to be present when they landed at their hometown airports. In the case of Nebraska Senator Roman Hruska, CORR had help from the senator's administrative assistant, who phoned the LCCR whenever his boss left the nation's capital.[75] The leadership of the Nebraska Council of Churches also kept in constant contact with Hruska, meeting with him multiple times, both in Nebraska and

Washington.[76] Catholic civil rights advocates were at least as persistent as their Protestant counterparts. Iowa Senator Jack Miller, another key undecided vote, endured a near-constant stream of appeals from the archbishop of Dubuque.[77] In South Dakota, Catholic leaders badgered Senator Karl Mundt relentlessly. When Mundt opposed the segregationists on a key procedural vote, he was heard to say, "I hope that satisfies those two goddamned bishops that called me last night!"[78]

Such complaints, coupled with the constant presence of church delegations in the Senate office building, sent the Washington press corps into a frenzy. "Oldtimers on Capitol Hill have never seen anything like [it]," proclaimed Evans and Novak. "Not since Prohibition has the church attempted to influence political action in Congress as it is now doing on behalf of President Johnson's civil rights bill."[79] According to the New York Times's E. W. Kenworthy, many pro–civil rights senators were now cautiously optimistic about breaking the filibuster. The key difference between 1964 and the largely failed civil rights pushes of 1957 and 1960, his anonymous sources said, was that the white churches, not "professional" (read: black) civil rights groups, were now taking the lead on the lobbying front.[80]

The anti–civil rights forces, too, sensed the ground shifting beneath their feet. Fearing that the churches might well succeed where African American civil rights groups and labor unions had not, militant segregationists including South Carolina Senator Strom Thurmond struck back, arguing that the UCC and like-minded religious groups were violating federal law by lobbying lawmakers and should therefore be stripped of their tax-exempt status. (It was not an accident that pro–civil rights religious groups described themselves as "witnessing" rather than "lobbying.")[81] At the same time, the pro-segregation CCFAF launched a massive public relations blitz in the North and West. In early March, with financial backing from conservative Northerners, including the publisher William Loeb III and the industrialist Wickliffe Preston Draper, the group ran a full-page advertisement in two hundred small and medium-sized Midwestern papers. Under the headline "Billion Dollar Blackjack—The Civil Rights Bill," the ads made the case that H.R. 7152 amounted to little more than a costly handout to undeserving blacks. In early April, when Alabama Governor George Wallace shocked the nation by winning 34 percent of the vote in the Wisconsin Democratic primary, many commentators concluded that the CCFAF's propaganda was finding a receptive audience in rural hamlets and white ethnic enclaves across the Midwest.[82]

In the end, however, the "Billion Dollar Blackjack" campaign did not fundamentally alter the dynamics of the Senate debate. And its failure was due in no small part to the efforts of countless state and local church councils who worked diligently to counter the segregationists' disinformation campaign. In Illinois and Iowa, for example, church councils supplied local congregations with a steady stream of books and articles rebutting CCFAF's claims that communist agents were behind the civil rights push.[83] In Ohio the state council distributed a brief section-by-section summary of the civil rights bill to aid ministers in combating the arguments of the bill's opponents.[84] In sparsely populated north-central Kansas, the Religion and Race Commission of the local presbytery de-voted large parts of its monthly newsletter to a line-by-line rebuttal of CCFAF's sensational claims and an exposé of the group's shady financial practices.[85] Finally, in Indiana, where George Wallace was viewed as a serious threat in the state's early-May primary, the state council of churches "prepared materials to aid pastors and parishioners in meeting the [Alabama governor's] arguments" while also arranging for Jewish, Catholic, and Protestant leaders to issue a joint statement in favor of the civil rights bill. When Wallace received a somewhat smaller share of the vote than some pundits had predicted—albeit a still robust 30 percent—the state council credited the churches' educational efforts for the governor's comparatively poor showing.[86]

It was at precisely this moment—as Wallace's insurgent campaign was throwing a scare into national Democratic leaders—that the nation's three lar-gest faiths launched the final phase of their plan to quash the filibuster. Beginning with a massive interfaith rally at Georgetown University on April 28, Protestant, Catholic, and Jewish leaders staged a series of dramatic public displays in the nation's capital. The Georgetown rally, which had been in the planning stages since January, was formally announced in early April. The response exceeded all expectations. Ministers, priests, and rabbis from all parts of the country poured into the nation's capital. The crowd of 6,500 was so large that it overflowed the university's Gymnasium, spilling out into and filling an adjacent auditorium. Once seated, the assembled divines heard from an all-star cast of religious leaders, including the archbishops of Baltimore and Washington, CORR's Eugene Carson Blake, Rabbi Uri Miller of the Synagogue Council of America, and Bishop Julian B. Smith of the Christian Methodist Episcopal Church. "Our task as churchmen is not to be expert in legislation [or] to tell the Congress how to legislate," Blake told the racially mixed crowd. "But it is our task and it is our competence to cut through the fog of immorality that threatens every American home and every church and synagogue." Although only four senators attended the gathering—all of them staunch supporters of the bill—the Interracial Convocation on Civil Rights made news broadcasts and headlines across the country, and the *New York Times* ran a four-column-wide photo of the event on its front page.[87]

A less publicized—but arguably more powerful—display of religious support took place the following morning, when the National Council of Churches con-vened the first of a long-planned series of daily religious services at the Lutheran Church of the Reformation, located just a block from the Capitol. The idea was to provide a dramatic counterpoint to the Southerners' round-the-clock speechmaking: While Thurmond, Russell, and the rest of the segregationist contingent waxed eloquent about states' rights and "freedom of association," Christian pilgrims from across the country would gather next door to read Scripture, hear sermons, and pray before heading to the Capitol to "witness" in person.[88] At the suggestion of CORR's Robert Spike, no benediction would be offered until the Senate voted on H.R. 7152. Not to be outdone, Protestant, Jewish, and Catholic seminary students from seventy-five different institutions began their own round-the-clock vigil at the Lincoln Memorial. From April 20 until the day the Senate acted on the bill—assuming it did act—three-person teams, operating in three-hour shifts, would stand in silent prayer before a banner reading, "Night and Day as witness to our common effort to help secure Justice and equal rights for all our citizens by passing the Civil Rights Bill as it came from the House."[89]

A final dramatic public display took place on May 18, when an interracial group of 270 Protestant clergymen marked the ten-year anniversary of the *Brown v. Board of Education* decision by marching from the Church of the Reformation to the steps of the Supreme Court. As the ministers, who hailed from forty-one states, knelt in front of the marble edifice, Spike led them in a simple prayer: "Help all who consider legislation to hear the voice of the oppressed rather than the complaints of the comfortable." Then, led by a seminarian "dressed in a maroon robe and bearing a gilded cross from the Washington National Cathedral," the clergymen marched two by two, in a procession stretching nearly a block, to the steps of the Senate. (Ever conscious of congressional protocol, Spike had the cross put away before the group reached the Senate steps so as not to "run afoul of regulations against holding sectarian religious services.")[90] There they were met by Senators Kenneth Keating and Hubert Humphrey, who praised the nation's ministers for their unceasing efforts to ensure that America "fulfilled [its] obligations with respect to human dignity.'"[91]

These highly publicized religious demonstrations in the nation's capital had a galvanizing effect on church groups in the hinterlands—including many that had previously remained aloof from the struggle for racial equality. On May 3, a thousand Methodist students staged a "kneel-in" that briefly blocked the entrance to the Pittsburgh Civic Arena, where the denomination was holding its quadrennial general conference. A reporter on the scene observed that many of the conference's nine hundred voting delegates appeared "disturbed" as they attempted to navigate their way through the throng of praying young people. Disturbed or not, they quickly approved a resolution calling for a strong civil rights bill, which was immediately transmitted to all one hundred senators.[92] Two weeks later the Illinois Synod of the Lutheran Church in America—a body representing some 350 congregations and 255,000 church members—voted overwhelmingly to request that the state's senators "use their full powers to bring the civil rights bill substantially unchanged to a vote." Because the state's senior senator, Paul Douglas, was a diehard liberal on civil rights, the message could only have been aimed at Dirksen.[93] On May 26 another important Dirksen constituency, the Chicago Federation of Churches, teamed up with the Urban League to sponsor a pro–civil rights rally at Soldier Field, to be held at the end of June. The event, which was expected to draw 100,000 people, would be headlined by Martin Luther King, Jr., and feature a five-thousand-voice choir. [94] Finally, in early June, the General Synod of the Reformed Church in America—Dirksen's denomination—adopted its own resolution urging swift action on H.R. 7152.[95]

Whether religious pressure played a significant role in the minority leader's decision to negotiate an end to the Senate stalemate is difficult to say. In all likelihood, this abundance of religious "witnessing" only stiffened Dirksen's resolve in pursuing the course he had known he would follow from the beginning. In any event, on May 5, he sat down with representatives from the Johnson administration and the Senate Democratic leadership to begin the painstaking process of negotiating a series of mostly technical changes to the bill's language. Although no one could be sure of his motivations at the time, it soon became apparent that Dirksen's aim was not to gut the bill but rather to provide a degree of political cover for wavering Republicans who were taking fire from both sides. By May 13 the parties had hashed out an agreement that offered a handful of concessions to conservatives while leaving in place most of the bill's critical antidiscrimination protections. (The most significant change limited the Justice Department's ability to independently initiate lawsuits against discriminatory employers and business owners.) There was some doubt about whether Dirksen could sell his own troops on the agreement, but in the end—and with considerable help from activist groups—he succeeded in rounding up the necessary support to force consideration of H.R. 7152. The coup de grace came on June 7, when, in an inspired tactical maneuver, the pro–civil rights forces permitted a vote on a series of amendments favored by a bloc of Midwestern conservatives under the leadership of Iowa's Hickenlooper, thus splitting the Senate's conservative coalition. When the most significant of the amendments, whose only real purpose was to allow Hickenlooper's faction to save face with conservative constituents, were soundly defeated, it became clear that the cloture push would probably succeed.[96]

On June 10, seventy-one senators—four more than necessary—voted to cut off debate and proceed to consideration of the civil rights bill. In the end, only one senator from a state in which religious groups had invested serious resources—Milton Young of North Dakota—voted against the motion. Indeed, a number of hidebound traditionalists, including Hickenlooper and Miller of Iowa, Roman Hruska and Carl Curtis of Nebraska, Frank Carlson of Kansas, and Karl Mundt of South Dakota, supported a cloture motion for the first time in their careers.[97] Nine days later the Senate passed the amended version of

H.R. 7152 by the lopsided margin of seventy-three to twenty-seven. Of the senators targeted by religious groups, only Hickenlooper, the leader of the Senate's conservative Republican faction, opposed final passage. On July 2 the House passed the amended bill, and President Johnson signed it into law in a nationally televised ceremony the same day.

Gauging the Impact of Mainline Mobilization Efforts

As we have seen, contemporary observers from Richard Russell to the syndicated columnists Evans and Novak attributed the civil rights bill's passage to a groundswell of religious enthusiasm. Yet the evidence cited in support of this thesis was often anecdotal: journalists' haphazard examinations of congressional mailbags, representatives' self-reported tallies of constituent phone calls, rumors of church delegations roaming the halls of the House and Senate office buildings. There were, moreover, at least a few contrarians who suspected that talk of grassroots enthusiasm for the bill was little more than wishful thinking. If Northern white churchgoers were so committed to the cause of racial equality, then why was George Wallace racking up 30 percent or more of the vote in Northern Democratic primaries? Did this not suggest a divide between the pulpit and the pews? Perhaps the "cardinals, bishops, elders, stated clerks, common preachers, priests and rabbis" that Senator Russell blamed for the bill's passage spoke only for themselves.[98]

Perhaps the best way of gauging the effectiveness of the churches' educational efforts is to turn to contemporaneous public-opinion data. More specifically, we can use the early 1960s American National Election Studies (ANES)—which contained a number of questions on both religious behavior and civil rights—to assess whether religious elites' pro–civil rights messages reached their intended audiences and, if so, whether they influenced the views of average churchgoers. The first important takeaway from the ANES data is that religious elites' pro–civil rights pleas did not go unnoticed. In the 1964 study, more than two out of three (68 percent) Northern white Protestants who belonged to a church reported that "problems of race relations" had been discussed at their places of worship. And of those who had encountered civil rights–related messages, a remarkable 91 percent reported that their "minister[s]" believed that "religion or the Bible favor[s] . . . integration."[99] This finding is particularly noteworthy because most churchgoing respondents reported that discussion of political campaigns and issues was *not* something they usually encountered in church. Indeed, only 10 percent of Northern white Protestant church attenders could recall ever hearing an "election campaign" discussed from the pulpit.[100]

But were average churchgoers actually *persuaded* by these clerical appeals to racial equality? One way to test whether pro–civil rights messages resonated with the men and women in the pews is to compare the views of regular churchgoers to those who attended less frequently. It stands to reason that the impact of religious educational efforts would be more pronounced in the case of individuals who had the greatest exposure to them—namely, regular church attendees. And in fact, this is precisely what we find, at least in the case of Northern white Protestants.

Figures 7.5 and 7.6 illustrate the relationship between religious attendance and support for federal civil rights initiatives among three groups: Northern white Protestants, Southern and border-state white Protestants, and white Catholics. In the case of Northern white Protestants, the major takeaway of Figure 7.5 is that support for the 1964 Civil Rights Act rises in tandem with frequency of church attendance. Whereas only 45.5 percent of respondents who reported that they "seldom" or "never" attended services expressed support for the bill, 50.6 percent of those who attended church "often" did so; and among "regular" churchgoers support rose to 58 percent.[101] The ANES data also indicate that the impact of church attendance on racial views extended beyond support for the Civil Rights Act. As Figure 7.6 makes clear, regular Protestant

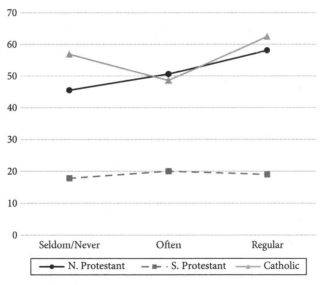

Figure 7.5 Support for the 1964 Civil Rights Act by religious tradition and frequency of church attendance (whites only)

Source: ANES 1964 Time Series Study

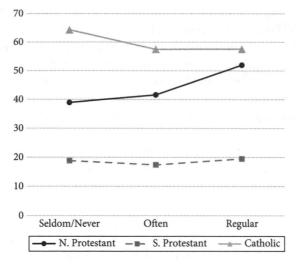

Figure 7.6 Support for public school integration by religious tradition and frequency of church attendance (whites only)
Source: ANES 1964 Time Series Study

churchgoers were also more supportive of federal efforts to integrate public schools than those who attended sporadically or not at all. Whereas only 38.9 percent of respondents who "seldom" attended services expressed support for federal school integration efforts, 52 percent of those who "regularly" attended services did so.[102]

If church attendance had a significant impact on the racial views of Northern white Protestants, it does not seem to have affected Jews and Catholics in the same way. This is not surprising. Jewish Americans had long been overwhelmingly supportive of civil rights initiatives (83 percent of those contacted for the ANES study endorsed the 1964 Civil Rights Act), their views seemingly stemming less from specifically religious concerns than from long and bitter experience with exclusionary policies.[103] It is also likely that partisan loyalties played some role in motivating Jewish and Catholic support for the bill. Both groups were reliable members of the New Deal coalition and would therefore be expected to give at least nominal support to the major domestic initiatives of Democratic presidents. President Kennedy was particularly popular with his fellow Catholics, and Catholic voters likely viewed the civil rights bill as the martyred president's most important legacy. Not surprisingly, the 1964 ANES found that a substantial majority of Northern white Catholics expressed support for the Civil Rights Act, but as Figures 7.5 and 7.6 make clear, attendance at mass was not systematically correlated with greater support for civil rights initiatives.[104] In the case of the Civil Rights Act, observant and nonobservant Catholics exhibited roughly equal levels of support, while in the case of school integration less observant Catholics were somewhat more likely to express liberal views (though the sample size may be too small to permit any firm conclusions on the nature of the relationship). Finally, Figures 7.5 and 7.6 indicate that white Southerners overwhelmingly opposed both the Civil Rights Act and school integration regardless of their level of religious engagement—no surprise, since relatively few white Southern clergymen spoke out against segregation.[105]

Still, it remains to be seen whether the relationship between regular church attendance and support for the Civil Rights Act holds up when controlling for other well-known predictors of racial liberalism. The results from two logistic regression models—reported in the appendix in Table A.1—controlling for education, party identification, age, gender, and union membership suggests that it does.[106] Specifically, the first model indicates that regular church attenders were about 1.7 times as likely as other northern white Protestants to express support for the bill, all else being equal.[107] (Respondents were asked whether they approved or disapproved of the recently enacted federal law giving "Negroes . . . the right to go to any hotel or restaurant they can afford, just like white people.")[108] The second model indicates that regular church attenders were also significantly more likely to express support for federal school integration efforts, all else being equal. In both cases, the relationship between regular church attendance and support for federal civil rights enforcement meets or exceeds conventional levels of statistical significance.[109]

Of course, it may be objected that opinions are less significant than actions. It is therefore worth asking whether regular church attendees were also more apt to engage in pro–civil rights activism during the period when the Civil Rights Act was debated in Congress. Although the 1964 ANES did not include any questions asking about civil rights engagement in particular, it did ask whether respondents had written to a public official to give an "opinion about something that should be done." Because letter-writing campaigns were at the heart of the mainline churches' lobbying strategy, it is reasonable to suspect that regular churchgoers would be more likely than others to have engaged in this activity.

And in fact, this is precisely what the data suggest. As can be seen in Table A.2, regular churchgoers were more than twice as likely as other citizens to report having contacted a public official, all else being equal. Not surprisingly, college graduates and respondents with relatively high incomes were also more likely to report having written to their representatives. But even after controlling for these well-known predictors of political engagement, church attendance remains both substantively and statistically significant. Interestingly, regular church attendance was *not* significantly predictive of other, more overtly partisan forms of political engagement, such as displaying a campaign button or sticker or attending a political meeting.. Also noteworthy is that the relationship between regular church attendance and having written to an elected official only holds for Northern white Protestants. Among Catholics and Southern white Protestants, similar regression models (results not shown) reveal no relationship between church or mass attendance and contact with elected officials. Admittedly, there is no way to say how many of the letters written by churchgoing Northern Protestants concerned the Civil Rights Act, but the fact that these respondents were more likely to have contacted an elected official, coupled with the regionally limited nature of the correlation, is at least consistent with the hypothesis that the mainline churches' educational efforts succeeded in compelling a significant number of churchgoers to contact their representatives.

Still, correlation does not equal causation, and it may be objected that racial liberals were self-selecting into Northern Protestant churches during the 1950s and 1960s. In this case, the ANES data are telling us less about the effectiveness of the churches' educational efforts than about the types of people who found these churches appealing. Although this possibility cannot be completely discounted, there is a good deal of suggestive evidence indicating that pro-civil rights appeals from religious elites, not self-selection, was driving the results reported in Table A.1. Most importantly, regular attendance does *not* appear to be correlated with racial liberalism prior to the initiation of the mainline churches' civil rights push in the summer and fall of 1963. Indeed, as can be seen in Table A.3, neither the 1960 nor the 1962 ANES indicate any relationship between church attendance and support for school integration. (Because the school integration question was the only civil rights question that appeared in all the early ANES studies, I rely on it here as a proxy for racial liberalism more generally.)[110] Not until the 1964 ANES do we see a strong correlation between attendance and support for integration, and—what is equally significant—the relationship appears to weaken in the years after 1964, when the mainline churches' civil rights bodies began diverting resources from educational initiatives to other activities (as discussed in Chapter 9). In 1966, church attendance remains positively correlated with support for integration among northern white Protestants, but no longer at a statistically significant level.

Hence, it appears likely that many northern white Protestants *became* racial liberals at the precise moment that their religious leaders began pressing the case for civil rights reform, then either lost interest in the subject or returned to a more conservative stance after the 1963–1964 civil rights push concluded. If this interpretation is accurate, then white mainline churchgoers were not immersing themselves in church activities because they held preexisting liberal convictions on race; rather, their (short-lived) racial liberalism was likely due, at least in part, to information and arguments encountered while attending church.

PART III

FROM REVELATION
TO RATIONALIZATION

8

Revolt in the Suburbs

[T]he Goldwater revolution . . . include[s] . . . many young suburbanite executives. [They] have themselves profited greatly from the
delicate balances of our democratic order, but are afraid that some
other group, such as the Negro—perhaps the only genuine American
proletarian—also will profit.
                    —Reinhold Niebuhr, "Goldwater vs. History" (1964)

In June 1964 religious leaders celebrated the Senate's historic action on civil
rights by holding an interfaith service of "prayer and thanksgiving" on the lawn
of the Methodist Building—an imposing edifice, located just across the street
from the Capitol, that had once housed the offices of the nation's most powerful
prohibitionists. Standing under a hot sun, representatives from the National
Council of Churches, the National Catholic Welfare Conference, and the Union
of American Hebrew Congregations thanked God for a political triumph that,
only a year before, had seemed no less improbable than the early twentieth-century push for a constitutional amendment to ban the sale and manufacture of
alcohol. Now, having achieved the impossible, the clergymen vowed that the passage of the civil rights bill would not mark the end of their interfaith activism but
rather the dawn of a new era in which Jewish, Catholic, and Protestant leaders
would work hand in hand to awaken average Americans to the myriad social
injustices in their midst. "The religious forces represented here have no inten-
tion of dissolving or even weakening the ties that have bound them so closely in
recent months and years," declared Father John Cronin of the NCWC. "We seek
to wipe out from our society every trace of discrimination and overt prejudice."[1]

Within a few short years, however, it would become clear that Cronin, Robert
Spike, and the other speakers at the noontime service were badly mistaken about
what the future held for progressive religious leaders. Although there would be
many more attempts at interfaith political activism, the mechanisms necessary
to translate prophetic visions into political realities were by 1964 beginning to
decay, the victims of social and economic changes that few observers sensed,
though they were already well under way. Like the Eighteenth Amendment, the
Civil Rights Act of 1964 marked the end of an era.

Indeed, by the late 1960s the mainline denominations—so recently hailed as the conscience of the nation—appeared to be on the brink of extinction. Pollsters reported that weekly church attendance had plummeted to levels not seen since the Great Depression. Newspapers relayed this information under such dire headlines as "Church Attendance Lagging," "Church-Interest Decline Continuing," and "More Empty Pews Loom in '70."[2] Even holiday-season puff pieces were tinged with gloom. "The central theme of Christmas is hope in the midst of despair, and no one may need this message more . . . [in] 1970 than the churches themselves," ran the opening sentence of a Christmas Day 1969 *New York Times* feature on the state of religion in America.[3]

And if the news concerning church attendance was bad, the news concerning the ecumenical movement was worse. Fewer people in the pews meant fewer dollars in the offering plates, and many congregations were forced to reduce their contributions to their parent denominations and local ecumenical bodies. The denominations, in turn, naturally prioritized their own administrative bureaucracies over funding the activities of the National Council of Churches. Starved for resources, state and local church councils began disbanding departments and laying off employees at an alarming rate. The NCC, for its part, began "spinning off" many of its key programs— essentially transforming them into self-financing entities, few of which were likely to survive for long—and contemplating a variety of radical restructuring proposals.

The debate over the causes of mainline Protestantism's sudden and unanticipated decline is now nearly fifty years old. The most common explanation links the collapse to the unprecedented social and political upheavals of the late 1960s. On this view, white Americans abandoned the mainline churches largely out of disgust at their parent denominations' increasingly left-wing stances on issues such as civil rights, the Vietnam War, gender equality, and economic justice. Writing in 1969, the sociologist Jeffery Hadden argued that the mainline denominations were being torn apart by a "struggle over the meaning and purpose of the church." The problem, according to Hadden, was that many clergymen felt compelled to address divisive social questions, while most lay people simply wanted their ministers to provide spiritual guidance, not solve the world's problems.[4] This perspective soon hardened into conventional wisdom, even finding expression in popular works such as Richard Ford's 1986 novel *The Sportswriter*. Looking back on his college days in the 1960s, the protagonist, Frank Bascombe, recalled attending a mainline Protestant church where "the preacher . . . aimed his mumbled sermons toward world starvation, the UN and [the Southeast Asia Treaty Organization], and . . . seemed embarrassed when it came time to stand up and pray. Christianity . . . in those times was . . . factual and problem-solving oriented. The spirit was made flesh too matter-of-factly.

Small-scale rapture and ecstasy (what I'd come for) were out of the question given the mess the world was in. Consequently I loathed going."[5]

There is, to be sure, a grain of truth in this old story. Newspapers from the period contain no shortage of stories about believers irked by their ministers' left-wing activism, and of whole congregations working to separate from denominations they now regarded as "too political"—by which they usually meant "too liberal." And yet, there are at least two gaping holes in the familiar politicization-of-the-churches narrative. First, the mainline churches did not suddenly discover politics in the mid-1960s; they had been intimately involved with questions of economic redistribution, civil rights, and war and peace for nearly six decades. Second, with the notable exception of gender issues, the churches did not move appreciably to the left in the mid-1960s. The public stances so often cited to explain the unrest in the pews—for example, calls for increased aid to the inner cities and for peace talks in Vietnam—were broadly consistent with what denominational elites had been saying for decades.

So why did average Protestants desert their churches in droves? And what, if anything, did the conservative backlash of the late 1960s and early 1970s have to do with religion? This chapter and the next will argue that the reigning conventional wisdom gets the causal relationship between declining religious engagement and the rightward drift of American politics backlash exactly backward. In other words, the erosion of mainline religious authority—which was well under way by the early 1960s—was as much a cause as a consequence of the conservative turn in American politics. The waning of religious authority liberated upwardly mobile white Americans to follow their own inclinations and interests, not only in their personal lives but also in their thinking about politics and society. And it was at precisely this point that many of them developed a sudden affinity for the extreme libertarian view that the use of state power to correct systemic injustice or redirect resources to the less fortunate was fundamentally illegitimate, a violation of natural rights. J. Howard Pew's one-man crusade was about to find its army. The irony was that for all the money Pew had poured into "educating" the nation's clergymen, it was the *collapse* of clerical authority that at last allowed his perspective to find a large audience.

The Erosion of Religious Authority before the 1960s

The first flaw in the familiar narrative linking the decline of the mainline churches to the political upheaval of the late 1960s concerns the issue of timing. Simply put, the postwar religion boom petered out in the late 1950s and early 1960s, that is, well before the rise of the various left-wing political movements—antiwar, black power, women's liberation—that are often blamed for driving a wedge between mainline leaders and average white churchgoers. As Figure 8.1 shows, the percentage of Americans who told Gallup interviewers they had attended religious services in the previous week shot up from 39 percent in 1950 to an all-time high of 51 percent in 1957. Thereafter weekly attendance declined by roughly one percentage point per year, falling to 45 percent by 1964 and to 42 percent by 1970. Looking only at Protestants, weekly attendance peaked in 1957–1958 at 44 percent. By 1964 it had fallen to 38 percent, where it would remain more or less unchanged for the rest of the decade.

Although we lack reliable weekly attendance figures for specific Protestant denominations, there are ample data to suggest that attendance patterns in the largest mainline churches followed the national trend. For example, Sunday school enrollment began to decline for the Presbyterians in 1960, for the Methodists in 1961, and for the Episcopalians in 1962. In part, this was a function of slowing birth rates, but as Figure 8.2 makes clear, Sunday school enrollment declined at a much faster pace than did the under-eighteen population. For both Protestants and the general population, then, the steepest decline in weekly attendance occurred between 1957 and 1964. In this brief, seven-year period roughly 12 percent of the nation's weekly church attenders (and nearly 14 percent of Protestant attenders) found ways to spend their Sunday mornings that did not involve listening to sermons or singing hymns.[6]

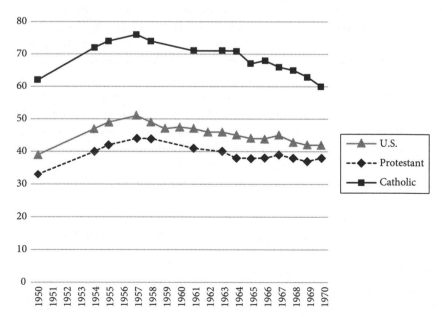

Figure 8.1 Percentage of weekly church attendees, 1950–1970
Source: Gallup Organization

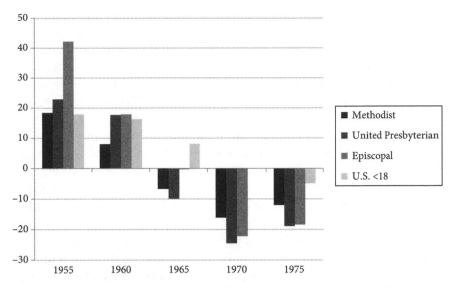

Figure 8.2 Percentage change in Sunday school enrollment over previous five years
Source: Doyle and Kelly, "Comparison of Trends in Ten Denominations"

Another sign of declining religious authority was that many white middle-class Americans were beginning to regard their churches' official teachings on a range of issues as advisory rather than binding. Rates of religious intermarriage, for example, increased significantly for mainline Protestants who reached marrying age in the mid-1950s or later—a clear indicator that the differences between, say, Lutheran and Presbyterian doctrine, or even Lutheran and Catholic doctrine, held less significance for Eisenhower-era Americans than for their counterparts in earlier periods.[7] Moreover, many Protestants were by the late 1950s openly flouting long-standing religious prohibitions against gambling, Sabbath breaking, and other personal vices. As late as the 1960s, most Protestant clergymen—mainline as well as fundamentalist—condemned all forms of gambling as sinful, and Protestant church councils devoted a good deal of time and energy to defending legal prohibitions in this area. And yet their parishioners increasingly had other ideas. The percentage of Americans who told pollsters that they had played cards for money during the previous year increased from 21 percent in 1938 to around 44 percent in 1954 (and 64 percent in the case of men).[8] By 1951 Gallup found that Americans favored the legalization of lottery gambling—a practice banned in most states since the Civil War era—by a margin of fifty-one percent to thirty-nine.[9]

Ministers were well aware of their growing inability to police their parishioners' private lives. A 1965 Detroit-area survey of nearly three hundred Presbyterian, Methodist, and United Church of Christ ministers found that many clergymen had all but given up condemning personal vices, such as drinking and gambling. One Methodist minister reported that church members displayed "open resentment" toward the denomination's long-standing prohibition against alcohol use. A Presbyterian reported that most churchgoers tuned out their ministers "the moment they get on [the subject of] gambling." Of the ministers surveyed, only 20 percent believed that the pronouncements of their parent denominations had a "great" impact on the views and conduct of local church members.[10] Small-town ministers seem to have enjoyed barely more clout than their big-city counterparts. In an influential 1958 study of everyday life in "Springdale," New York, the sociologists Arthur J. Vidich and Joseph Bensman recounted the sad tale of the town's newly installed Methodist minister, who had "upset both his congregation and the community with a strict, almost fanatical approach against the ordinary 'sins'—smoking, drinking and card playing—which are so much a part of the everyday fabric of community life." The minister was soon forced to abandon his crusade, but the damage had been done. The town's residents still regarded him as a pariah, and even his own parishioners made every effort to avoid him outside of formal services.[11]

Not surprisingly, proposals to relax or repeal long-standing morals laws— particularly in the area of gambling—proliferated in the 1950s and early 1960s. As early as 1953, New Jersey voters overwhelmingly approved a proposal to permit bingo games and raffles. The New York state legislature followed suit in 1957, amending the state constitution to legalize bingo. In 1964 lawmakers in New Hampshire established the first legal lottery since the 1890s, and two years later a statewide referendum to bring lottery gambling to New York passed by a margin of nearly two to one.[12] In each case Protestant church councils mounted sustained campaigns to prevent the repeal of existing criminal prohibitions, and in each case they suffered a humiliating defeat.[13]

This is not to suggest that mainline religious authority had completely evaporated by the early 1960s. To the contrary, as the successful push for the 1964 Civil Rights Act makes clear, the churches were still more than capable of educating and mobilizing their members on a large scale, particularly when their goals were humanitarian in nature and not aimed at their parishioners' personal lives. And yet, with the benefit of hindsight, declining rates of church attendance and the proliferation of minor vices clearly signaled that the social dynamics that had long undergirded mainline religious authority were beginning to crumble.

What explains the sudden erosion of religious authority at the end of the Eisenhower era? One troubling development, from the perspective of the churches, was a generational turn away from organized religion affecting citizens who came of age around 1960 or later. As Figure 8.3 makes clear, much of the sharp decline in weekly church attendance was driven by the behavior of young Americans. In 1957 more than 50 percent of citizens between the ages of twenty-one and twenty-nine attended church on a weekly basis; by 1964 only 39 percent did so; and by 1970 less than one third were regular church attenders. Scholars of religion had long speculated that individual religiosity followed a natural life-cycle pattern, in which young people drifted away from the church in their late teens and early twenties, only to return to the fold when they married and had children. But if this was true for members of the World War II generation, it did not hold for their children. Instead, many baby boomers left organized religion as young adults and never returned.[14]

Even more worrisome was the fact that young, upwardly mobile Protestants—long the demographic backbone of the mainline—seemed to be leading the exodus from the churches. As late as the 1950s academic studies indicated that up-wardly mobile Protestant men were both more likely to switch denominations—typically to become Episcopalians, Presbyterians, or Congregationalists—and to become highly active in their new churches.[15] Sometime around 1960, however, the "pull" that the more prestigious mainline denominations had long exerted on aspiring members of the middle and upper classes began to weaken, and then it disappeared altogether. By the mid-1960s sociologists of religion were finding

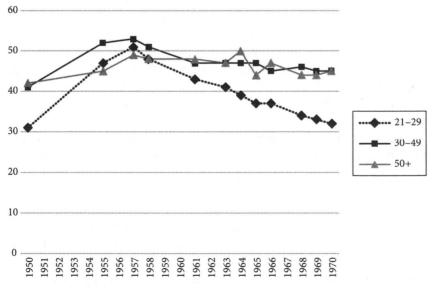

Figure 8.3 Weekly church attendance by age, 1950–1970
Source: Gallup Organization

that neither occupational nor educational mobility was predictive of church switching.[16]

The sociologists Rodney Stark and Charles Glock hypothesized that a new social dynamic was emerging in which highly educated professionals, after moving "up" the denominational ladder, were within a few years leaving organized religion altogether.[17] They did not provide a great deal of empirical evidence for this "up-and-out" dynamic, but data from the American National Election Studies provides some support for their hypothesis (though it is perhaps better described as a singular shift toward secularism rather than a novel pattern of church switching). Whereas college-educated Americans were traditionally more likely than other citizens to be regular church attendees, this long-standing pattern disappeared over the course of the 1960s and early 1970s, so that by 1976 the two groups' rates of church attendance were roughly identical. Significantly, the rate of regular church attendance by *young* college-educated Americans (defined as those under thirty-five) fell below the attendance rate of the overall white population as early as 1964.

But merely pointing out that young, upwardly mobile Protestants who came of age after about 1960 felt increasingly free to eschew organized religion begs the question. Why were baby boomers less incentivized than their parents to pursue church membership and adhere to the moral codes of their chosen denominations? One popular explanation points to the subjective experiences and self-perception of the baby-boom generation itself. Perhaps it was the sudden and unprecedented material affluence of the postwar years. Perhaps it was the influence of television. Perhaps it was the advent of rock and roll. Or perhaps it was a general reaction against the role of formerly venerable elites and institutions in misleading the public about the atrocities of the Vietnam War (and later Watergate). Whatever the reason, many Americans who came of age in the 1960s and early 1970s seem to have rejected not only their parents' specific religious affiliations but the very idea of external moral or spiritual authority itself.[18]

There is undoubtedly some truth in such accounts, though it is notoriously difficult to document empirically the effects of a force as nebulous as generational self-perception. In part for this reason, one suspects that the Baby Boomer *Weltanschauung* was, like the stewardship ethic before it, at least partly the product of profound changes in the socioeconomic environment. Two new social dynamics in particular almost certainly contributed to the budding revolt against external moral authority. First, developments in higher education and the labor market greatly reduced the social and economic significance of church membership (as well as other forms of group membership), thereby sounding the death knell for Max Weber's "sect spirit." As college enrollments skyrocketed, as more and more students pursued degrees in science and engineering, and as massive corporations consumed an ever-larger percentage of the labor market, informal social networks and markers of respectability—like Weber's lapel pin—became less and less important as stepping-stones to the middle and upper classes.[19] Large employers such as General Electric, General Motors, and Boeing were interested in technical expertise, not family connections or religious orthodoxy. Many corporations now relied on standardized tests—often administered by third parties—to guide hiring decisions.[20] Needless to say, these employers did not know, let alone care, how their workers spent their Sunday mornings.[21]

Second, the postwar period witnessed an unprecedented surge in residential mobility. In the decades preceding World War II, the percentage of Americans who reported having relocated to a new state within the previous five years averaged around 6.5 percent. This figure more than doubled, to around 14 percent, in 1950, where it remained, more or less unchanged, through 1980.[22] To put this figure in context, around twenty-three million Americans told census takers in 1960 that they had relocated to a new state within the past five years.

It is only natural to speculate that people who relocate to a new state or region will experience some difficulty in recreating the social ties, including religious ties, they enjoyed in their old hometowns. And yet, the best sociological studies of the subject suggest that geographic mobility by itself is rarely fatal to religious commitment. A far more important consideration is the religious culture of the destination region. In short, uprooted citizens tend to accommodate themselves to the religious habits of their new neighbors. Those who move from a region with high levels of religious commitment to a less pious area will tend to become less involved in religious activities, and vice versa.[23]

It matters a great deal, then, that the regional "winner" in the relocation sweepstakes of the 1950s and 1960s was the West. Drawn by the promise of good jobs in the aerospace and defense industries, millions of Americans relocated from the Midwestern, Southern, and border states to the growing cities of the western Sunbelt. Southern California, in particular, experienced explosive growth. Between 1940 and 1970 the population of Orange County, home to a number of large defense contractors and aerospace companies, grew from 130,000 to more than 1.4 million—an astonishing annual growth rate of 8.3 percent.[24] By 1960 fully 50 percent of Americans living in California had come from elsewhere, and only 8 percent had relocated from elsewhere in the West. Setting to one side the 9 percent who emigrated from foreign countries, the bulk of the remaining 6.7 million Californians had relocated from the Midwest or the South; both regions lost about 2.7 million residents to the Golden State over the preceding decades.[25]

Figure 8.4 Weekly church attendance by region, 1950–1970
Source: Gallup Organization

As Figure 8.4 makes clear, citizens who journeyed westward from the Midwest or South left behind regions with historically high levels of religious commitment for areas with comparatively low levels of commitment. More to the point, Americans who relocated to California and other parts of the western Sunbelt seem to have distanced themselves from organized religion as they adjusted to their new environments. (The opposite dynamic seems to have been at work for the much smaller number of citizens who moved from the West to the South and Midwest.)[26] As we shall see, there was no shortage of thriving Protestant churches in California in the 1950s and 1960s. But these churches claimed a much smaller share of the white Protestant population as members than similar churches located elsewhere in the United States, and their authority—judged in terms of their ability to shape their members' ethical sensibilities and mobilize them on behalf of specific causes—was even weaker than church membership and attendance figures would suggest. Indeed, at the very moment that Midwestern clergymen were launching their successful campaign on behalf of federal civil rights legislation, their California counterparts were struggling in vain to arrest the growth of a grassroots conservative insurgency that viewed the civil rights movement as a communist plot. Not for the first time, events in California offered a preview of what lay in store for the rest of the country.

The Conservative Insurgency in California

After working for more than a decade to mobilize a grassroots rebellion against the horrors of the welfare state, the aging pioneers of the Far Right, including James Fifield and J. Howard Pew, watched with a mixture of satisfaction and disbelief as hundreds of thousands of white, middle-class Californians suddenly declared war on the nation's centrist political establishment. In hindsight, it was probably the short-lived 1960 Goldwater-for-president boom that signaled the beginning of a genuine grassroots conservative movement in the Golden State. During the summer months thousands of California suburbanites formed Goldwater clubs and canvassed their neighborhoods in a quixotic bid to prevent Vice President Richard Nixon, a man they regarded as an unprincipled political chameleon, from clinching the Republican nomination. In the end, the hardline anticommunist senator from Arizona decided not to challenge his party's presumptive nominee, but his supporters were undeterred.[27]

The following year thousands of them welcomed the Australian physician and lay preacher Fred Schwarz and his Christian Anti-Communism Crusade to Southern California. A born salesman who combined "missionary zeal, political enthusiasm and Madison Avenue deftness," Schwarz's message was simple: the nation's institutions—from the big Washington bureaucracies to your local mainline church—had been thoroughly penetrated by Red sympathizers. (One of his stump speeches was entitled "Why Millionaires, College Professors, and Ministers of Religion Become Communists.") For several consecutive nights in late August and early September, capacity crowds of sixteen thousand packed the Los Angeles Sports Arena, where they heard Schwarz and other self-proclaimed experts on the communist menace call for the United States to withdraw from the United Nations, cut diplomatic ties with the Soviets, and purge that notorious nest of pinkos, the State Department. On "Youth Night," when celebrities including Ronald Reagan, Roy Rogers, Pat Boone, and John Wayne gave testimonials, the crowd overflowed the venue, and more than a thousand young people listened to their heroes over loudspeakers in the parking lot.[28]

Momentum continued to build through the fall, when more than two thousand Southern Californians, newly trained in the art of spotting communist agents, protested President John F. Kennedy's November 18 appearance at the Hollywood Palladium. Bearing signs that read "Get the Reds Out of the State Department" and "Thank God for Right-Wing Patriots," the "shouting, milling pickets overflowed the sidewalk and lined the street on both sides as bumper-to-bumper traffic was snarled" for blocks along Sunset Boulevard. (Kennedy, for his part, devoted part of his speech to denouncing unnamed conservative groups that saw "treason in our churches, in our highest court, in our treatment of water.")[29] Strom Thurmond, the arch-segregationist senator from South Carolina who visited the region a few days after Kennedy, received a much warmer welcome. In Santa Monica a capacity crowd of two thousand roared its approval when Thurmond demanded that Congress rein in the State Department's "pussyfooting diplomats" and launch a formal investigation into the alleged "muzzling" of General Edwin Walker, a proud John Birch Society member who had recently been disciplined for distributing right-wing propaganda to his troops.[30] When the general himself visited Los Angeles in January at the invitation of James Fifield's Freedom Club, more than thirteen thousand diehard conservatives attended the event, most of them no doubt hoping to hear Walker tell them what they already knew: that his superiors at the Department of Defense were dangerously lacking in patriotism and likely in cahoots with the Kremlin. They were not disappointed.[31]

Fifield, who had been warning Southern Californians of the communist threat for decades, did everything in his power to fan the flames of insurgency. And yet he could claim little direct credit for the sudden upsurge of interest in conservative causes. At the forefront of the region's burgeoning conservative movement were a new generation of right-wing organizations, including Schwartz's Christian Anti-Communism Crusade (CACC), the John Birch Society (JBS), and the United Republicans of California (UROC). At first glance these organizations bore a strong resemblance to Spiritual Mobilization, the Christian Freedom Foundation, and the other would-be grassroots groups that were kept afloat by J. Howard Pew's largesse during the lean years of the 1950s. The key difference, however, was that the JBS, the CACC, and UROC were not top-heavy organizations that existed for the purpose of disseminating libertarian propaganda, most of which went unread. Rather, they were populated by tens of thousands of living, breathing citizens who genuinely believed that Soviet agents had infiltrated the highest levels of the U.S. government, and that the very existence of social welfare programs like Social Security constituted a dire threat to the American way of life.

The JBS paved the way, demonstrating that the views of the Far Right were no longer anathema to white middle-class suburbanites. Following its founding in 1958 by the Massachusetts-based candy manufacturer Robert Welch, the group grew quickly, swelling to some 80,000 to 100,000 members by the mid-1960s. (Exact membership figures were a closely guarded secret.) Believing that the best way to defeat the communists was to copy their allegedly secretive tactics, Welch insisted that members organize themselves into cells that were small enough to meet in private homes. Individual cells took orders from a centralized command structure, headed by Welch, and carried out "assignments," such as letter-writing campaigns, literature distribution, and recruiting candidates to run for state and local offices. Although the JBS claimed members in most states, academic studies concluded that the group enjoyed its strongest support in Southern California—a fact Welch himself confirmed. By the early 1960s roughly 30 percent of Birchers hailed from Golden State, most of them from rapidly growing suburban communities in Los Angeles, Orange, and San Diego Counties. In Orange County alone, 38 chapters were operating by 1962, and Los Angeles County would claim nearly 150 chapters by the middle of the decade.[32]

The United Republicans of California, though organized with the seemingly modest aim of pushing the state's Republican party apparatus to the right, was in many ways similar to the JBS—and in fact, there was probably a good deal of overlap in membership. The group was launched in 1962 by a coterie of far-right activists who were irate that their party had once again nominated the milquetoast Richard Nixon for high office—this time for governor of California. UROC's principal founder, a political operative named Rus Walton, envisioned an organization that would be "run on the grassroots," with small "units" dedicating themselves to purging nearby officeholders and party functionaries who refused to adopt a hardline stance on communism and commit to the dismantling of the welfare state. Within a few weeks of the 1962 gubernatorial primary, Walton later recalled, the group had "more than five hundred units," with new ones popping up "wherever there were people gathered in a living room."[33]

In contrast to the JBS and UROC, Schwartz's Christian Anti-Communist Crusade did not claim a large grassroots membership in the traditional sense. Rather, its principal activity—facilitated by donations from wealthy conservative activists, including the Los Angeles millionaire Patrick Frawley—was organizing "Schools of Anti-Communism."[34] Combining "educational" programming with the atmosphere of a pep rally, Schwarz's schools aimed to alert large audiences to the creeping communist menace, and to equip them with the knowledge necessary to know a communist-inspired program (e.g., Medicare) when they saw one. If there were no CACC chapters per se, the group nonetheless owed its existence to the hundreds of thousands of average citizens who flocked to its public programs. And like the JBS, the CACC enjoyed its greatest success in California. At the height of its popularity in 1962 and 1963, its events filled stadiums and arenas from Anaheim to Oakland, often aided by local officials who issued formal declarations of approval and even closed public schools for the occasion.[35]

Perhaps the most striking thing about the insurgent conservative groups of the early 1960s is that they managed to build large popular bases of support even though—or perhaps because—they espoused views that were far to the right of those held by the average Republican elected official. The JBS, of course, became a national punch line after some of its founder's more extreme views—for example, that President Eisenhower was a communist agent—became public knowledge. But UROC's program was hardly less extreme. In the area of foreign policy, it regularly passed resolutions demanding that high-ranking federal officials be censured for their weak-kneed responses to alleged Soviet provocations; on the domestic front, it made common cause with racists, decorating the podium at its first statewide convention with a Confederate flag. Not surprisingly, the group's moderate Republican opponents claimed it was little more than a JBS front group.[36]

Regardless of whether this was true, UROC's views soon spread from the margins to the mainstream of California politics. In early 1964 it engineered a hostile takeover of the California Republican Assembly (CRA), a grassroots organization of moderate Republicans founded by the former governor Earl Warren. Far from destroying the fourteen-thousand-member CRA, the takeover expanded its membership as more than six thousand new recruits came aboard in the latter half of 1964.[37] By mid-1964 a group that had once been synonymous with anodyne, "country club" Republicanism was calling for a formal investigation of communist subversives in the State Department and—in a rebuke to those who labeled the JBS an extremist group—declaring that the "true extremists" were to be found in such center-left groups as Americans for Democratic Action, the California Democratic Council, and the American Civil Liberties Union (ACLU), groups whose "militant philosophies" were "compatible with totalitarian forms of government as practiced under Socialism and Communism."[38]

The sudden realization that hundreds of thousands of middle-class Californians actually *believed* the JBS's propaganda—whether or not they were dues-paying members—spawned a cottage industry of academic studies on the rise of "right-wing extremism" or "ultra-conservatism." As it turned out, compiling a demographic profile of the new conservative activists was a relatively straightforward matter. Though the details varied slightly from group to group, analyses based on survey data, internal group records, and letters to the editor all agreed that the types of citizens who were attracted to groups like the JBS and UROC were generally young, white, well-educated, professional or white-collar workers (and their wives). A disproportionate number were engineers who worked in the aerospace industry, but doctors, dentists, and other professions were also well represented. And, at least in California, conservative group members tended to be concentrated in areas that had experienced rapid population growth in the 1950s, including Los Angeles, Orange County, and San Diego County. Most of them—like most of their neighbors—had relocated to the West Coast from the Midwest or South within the previous few years.[39]

Coming up with a causal theory to explain why these particular young professionals, out of millions of similarly situated citizens, had embraced the views of the Far Right proved a much bigger challenge. The popular theory that

Birchers and other conservative activists were suffering from "status inconsistency" or "status anxiety"—in essence, that they were not afforded the degree of professional or social respect they believed they deserved—found little empirical support. In fact, most conservative group members seemed to hold down well-paying jobs that were appropriate to their educational backgrounds.[40] Neither were the new activists particularly alienated from modern society, as another theory had it. On the contrary, most seemed to be thoroughly integrated into their communities: they were involved with multiple civic organizations, they volunteered for political campaigns, and they possessed a fairly strong sense of political efficacy.[41] Some scholars speculated that fundamentalist churches were behind the surge of right-wing activism. Southern California was home to many large fundamentalist congregations, and surveys showed that the percentage of fundamentalists was slightly higher among members of far-right groups than in the general population. Yet the same surveys also showed that most conservative group members—or at least a solid plurality—were technically mainline Protestants, not fundamentalists. Moreover, as many as a quarter of JBS members were Catholics—something one would hardly expect to find in a movement founded on fundamentalist theological precepts.[42]

It seems likely that the authors of the earliest studies of the modern conservative movement were drawn to psychological explanations for the simple reason that they found the views espoused by Far Right groups morally repulsive. Reasonable people could disagree about the appropriate size of the federal budget or the details of the nuclear test ban treaty, the thinking went. But only someone in the grips of a psychological malady would advocate abolishing the federal income tax, withdrawing from the United Nations, or radically ramping up production of nuclear weapons. And yet, as several more recent studies of Southern California conservatism have pointed out, one need not resort to elaborate psychological theories to account for the substantive positions adopted by groups like the JBS and the UROC. In fact, for all their fascination with paranoid conspiracy theories, the new conservative groups' policy positions were generally in keeping with the material self-interest of their members. For example, most of the new activists were economically dependent on federal defense spending and thus had every reason to fear the consequences of a sudden thaw in U.S.-Soviet relations.[43] Being better situated financially than most Americans, they had little need of social welfare programs—unless one puts federal defense spending in this category—and they naturally opposed paying taxes to fund them. And they were overwhelmingly homeowners, which, in addition to fueling animus toward high property-tax rates, generated opposition to civil rights initiatives that might result in integrated neighborhoods and reduced property values.[44] Viewed from this angle, the mystery is not why white middle-class Californians launched a revolt against their state's—and the nation's—center-left political establishment;

it is why similarly situated citizens in other parts of the country were so slow to join them.

The Missing Churches

One possibility, largely overlooked in the existing literature, is that California's rapid population growth resulted in a relatively weak religious infrastructure, which in turn liberated Protestant citizens from the normative commitments that continued to bind their coreligionists in other states. For despite a never-ending a program of church construction, the mainline denominations were unable to match California's explosive growth rate. The 1936 census—the last one to investigate Americans' religious affiliations—revealed that there were nearly twice as many Methodist churches in Iowa (population 2.5 million) as in California (population 6.3 million). The Baptists, Lutherans, and Congregationalists gained a somewhat firmer foothold on the West Coast, but even these denominations had by this point barely managed to match the number of churches they had constructed in the less populous Midwestern states.[45] All told, the six largest mainline denominations claimed only about one church for every 4,100 California residents. In Iowa, by comparison, the ratio was one church for every 1,175 residents. One might object that California's unusually large Catholic population skewed the state's Protestant church-to-total-population ratio. And yet the percentage of Catholics in Iowa was nearly as high as in California.[46] (Nor does California's relatively urbanized population account for the discrepancy, since congregation sizes in the two states were roughly comparable).[47] The problem, in short, was not the number of Catholics, but rather the logistical challenges posed by an unanticipated and seemingly never-ending population boom on the western edge of the continent.

And this was the situation *before* the great population explosion of the 1940s and 1950s. The National Council of Churches' comprehensive 1952 survey of American religious bodies revealed that California's mainline churches were falling even further behind in their effort to keep pace with the exponential growth rates of the postwar years. By this point, the state's ratio of mainline churches to residents exceeded only two other states—Alaska and (heavily Mormon) Utah.[48] Millions of new California residents thus found themselves in an environment where mainline religious institutions were spread unusually thin, and a significant percentage of them, perhaps in part because they found no church of their preferred denomination within easy driving distance, drifted away from organized religion. In 1957 a survey of Los Angeles County and its environs, carried out by some six thousand church volunteers, revealed that only about one in three Southern California residents who claimed a Protestant affiliation was a church member—and this at a time when the percentage of church members in the total U.S. population was over 60 percent.[49]

To be sure, the mainline denominations and church councils conducted countless evangelistic campaigns and worked diligently to ramp up church construction in the Golden State. They also labored to impose a sense of order on the process by, for example, negotiating informal agreements that divided up neighborhoods and subdivisions in such a way as to avoid unnecessary competition.[50] But this was undoubtedly part of the problem. Conducting formal surveys of a community's religious needs took time (and money), as did negotiating with the developers whose cooperation was necessary to secure prime real estate for church construction. Even as hundreds of thousands of new residents poured into the state every year, church bureaucrats were bogged down in endless debates over whether particular subdivisions had too many (or too few) churches of a particular denomination. In 1958 the Research and Planning Committee of the Southern California Council of Churches, whose jurisdiction covered the entire southern part of the state as well as southern Nevada, reported that its nine member denominations had between them put in 221 requests for "allocations," or new churches; of these, only 35 were in the process of being built.[51] In that year's annual report, the department all but begged for more funding for "map development and church building information," noting that "lack of time and budget" had become a serious "handicap."[52] Not until 1961, however, did mainline church officials pony up funds to hire a full-time director of research and planning.[53]

Orange County, whose citrus groves and grazing lands were largely paved over in the 1950s and early 1960s, offers a particularly striking illustration of the general problem. The county's population more than quintupled between 1950 and 1970, as more than 1.2 million new residents settled into newly constructed tract homes in cities such as Fullerton, Anaheim, Santa Ana, and Irvine. Yet, in this same period, the total number of Episcopal, Methodist, Presbyterian, American Baptist, and United Church of Christ churches increased by barely 90 percent. Together, these five denominations constructed fifty-five new churches—or one for every 22,000 new residents.[54] Ecumenical bodies, too, were sparse in the West, particularly in California. Although the state boasted some twenty-five professional church councils and another twenty-seven volunteer ones, its ratio of church councils to white Protestant residents was still among the lowest in the nation. Indeed, with one council for every 210,000 white Protestants, California's church council density ranked below that of every non-Southern state except for New Mexico, Idaho and Maryland.[55] In some Midwestern and Northeastern states, in contrast, this ratio ran as high as one council for every 25,000 residents.[56]

Given the low ratio of church officials to population and the broader decline of church membership as a marker of social respectability, it should come as no surprise that California developed a uniquely lax religious culture. In 1950, for example, Ronald Reagan informed readers of *Modern Screen* that he worshipped at Hollywood Beverly Christian Church in part because the church had "little hard and fast dogma" and did not stress the concepts of sin or hell.[57] (One suspects that many prominent Los Angeles ministers turned a blind eye to their celebrity parishioners' personal lives.) Reagan was hardly a typical California suburbanite, of course, but like his less famous neighbors he was an infrequent churchgoer who had little interest in committing serious time or energy to religious pursuits. Indeed, California clergymen regularly complained about church members who prioritized recreational activities over attending services. When asked in the mid-1960s why attendance rates were declining among the young, a Presbyterian minister in the wealthy Los Angeles neighborhood of Pacific Palisades speculated that it was because so many Protestant young people had been raised to view their churches as little better than daycare centers. "So often I see the guy who drives up to church in his Cadillac and says, 'OK, kids, everybody out!' He's wearing Bermuda shorts, has his golf clubs in the back, and away he goes. The kids pick up the idea that church is not something for adults."[58]

There were, to be sure, many middle-class Californians who still felt strongly the pull of organized religion. But thanks to the weakness of the mainline infrastructure, these believers were uniquely free to seek out churches that catered to their preexisting beliefs, prejudices, or whims. At the same time, charismatic preachers were freer than elsewhere to follow their entrepreneurial instincts; all an aspiring evangelist needed was a message that appealed to the state's Southern and Midwestern transplants and a plot of land not governed by strict zoning laws.[59]

The explosive growth of Anaheim's Central Baptist Church offers a case in point. Founded in 1956 by a tent revivalist named Bob Wells, the congregation had by the early 1960s grown to more than three thousand members. A transplanted Alabamian, Wells's message was equal parts biblical literalism, hardline anticommunism, and J. Howard Pew–style libertarian economics. The church's mission statement, while light on theology, endorsed "the free enterprise system" and condemned "Modernism, Socialism, Communism, and every form of 'One Worldism'" as inventions of the devil. Far from shrinking from explicit engagement with political issues, Wells embraced a range of causes that were popular with Orange County suburbanites: He railed against organized labor, warned of subversion in the State Department, and praised the John Birch Society from the pulpit. And the more political he became, the more new members poured into his ever-expanding sanctuary. Within ten years of its founding, the church would claim four thousand members, with weekly attendance often exceeding total membership.[60]

Coming in a close second in the competition for Orange County churchgoers was Robert Schuller's Garden Grove Community Church, located just down the street from Central Baptist, near Disneyland. A Chicago native, Schuller moved west in 1955 and began conducting Sunday services from the top of a drive-in movie theater snack bar. The idea of enjoying a religious service from the comfort of one's car caught on with Orange County suburbanites, and by 1961 Schuller's congregation had moved to a permanent building with seating for a thousand. (A mechanical glass door on one side of the sanctuary opened to a five-hundred-space parking lot for congregants who preferred the drive-in experience.) In terms of theology (and temperament), Schuller, who was ordained in the Reformed Church, was closer to James Fifield and Norman Vincent Peale than Bob Wells. But his politics were well within the parameters of the Central Baptist mission statement. He maintained close ties to Schwartz's Christian Anti-Communist Crusade, for example, and joined several local campaigns that aimed to root out suspected communists in local government. Most important, Schuller viewed the free enterprise system in quasi-religious terms, reminding his congregants that "wealth is no crime" and that the profit motive was perfectly compatible with Christian teaching.[61]

By the early 1970s Southern California would boast ten of the nation's one hundred largest congregations, most them located in the suburbs around Los Angeles and San Diego.[62] A majority of these "megachurches" were Southern Baptist; others, like Garden Grove Community Church, were nominally mainline or nondenominational. Some of them, like Anaheim's Central Baptist and Tim LeHaye's Scott Memorial Church near San Diego, viewed political activism as a natural extension of conservative theology; others preferred to focus on spiritual matters, keeping overt political appeals to a minimum. Regardless of denomination or theological orientation, however, the region's largest and fastest-growing congregations were alike in that they eschewed the traditional mainline ethic of stewardship in favor of paeans to patriotism, freedom, and capitalism—the sorts of themes, in other words, one encountered in nearly every issue of *Christianity Today*. Not surprisingly, the concentration of churches affiliated with the National Association of Evangelicals (NAE) was higher in Orange County than almost anywhere else in the nation.[63]

Still, it is probably a mistake to claim, as some early students of the conservative movement did, that fundamentalist (or evangelical) churches were the primary *cause* of the conservative insurgency. For one thing, the best contemporary studies of the movement found that the typical conservative activist was a mainline Protestant, not a fundamentalist (or evangelical), and often one with rather weak ties to organized religion.[64] But the larger point is that, in sharp contrast to the situation in the Midwestern and Eastern mainline churches, there is little evidence that California's suburban megachurches possessed the authority necessary to shape the worldviews of their members. Having relocated to a region where religious authority was comparatively weak and secured jobs with large corporations on the basis of their educational qualifications and technical expertise, the state's middle-class suburbanites had little reason to fear that leaving— or even failing to seek out—a particular congregation would seriously diminish their social standing or economic prospects.[65] The churches that flourished in this climate of lax religious authority were, naturally, those that tended to reinforce, rather than challenge, the preexisting interests and prejudices of their members (and potential members). Thus, while conservative churches often served as staging grounds for the early 1960s conservative movement, a major factor in the rise of these NAE-affiliated congregations was the existence of a Protestant population that had already been liberated from traditional forms of religious authority. Stated otherwise, it was the weakness of California's mainline Protestant infrastructure, more than the strength of its conservative churches, that paved the way for a grassroots conservative insurgency.

"The Soundest Defeat for Religious Forces in Years"

Despite their relative numerical weakness, California's mainline church leaders did not shy away from expressing what they believed to be the Christian position on controversial public issues. Beginning in the mid-1950s, the state council of churches—which was divided into Northern and Southern branches—issued an annual "Statement of Legislative Principles" that combined humanitarian concern for the poor and disabled with a moralistic aversion to all forms of legalized vice. Year after year mainline leaders urged state lawmakers to abolish the death penalty, increase funding for mental health programs, prohibit discrimination in housing and employment, protect the right of workers to organize, and maintain strict criminal prohibitions against all forms of gambling.[66] These goals, however, were largely aspirational. Aside from mailing their recommendations to elected officials and ministers, church officials made little effort to secure their enactment.[67]

In late 1963, however, a direct challenge to one of the churches' core principles—the right to fair housing—convinced mainline leaders that they had little choice but to enter the political arena en masse. In April church officials had cheered when Governor Edmund G. "Pat" Brown signed legislation empowering the state's Fair Employment Practices Commission (FEPC) to investigate claims of racial discrimination in the purchase or rental of homes and apartments. Although the Rumford Act—named after the pioneering African

American assemblyman William Byron Rumford, its chief sponsor—was a relatively modest measure that contained no shortage of loopholes, it nonetheless represented a significant intervention in the state's real estate market, and this was more than enough to provoke howls of protest from the powerful California Real Estate Association (CREA), an organization that had long supported the use of restrictive covenants and other measures to prevent minorities from purchasing homes in all-white enclaves. Almost as soon as Brown signed the Rumford Act into law, CREA began laying plans to nullify it by means of a statewide ballot initiative. By early 1964 the Realtors and their allies had secured enough signatures to guarantee a statewide vote on what came to be known as Proposition 14—a constitutional amendment guaranteeing the property owner's unfettered right to "sell, lease or rent any part or all of his real property, [or] to decline to sell, lease or rent such property to such person or persons as he, in his absolute discretion, chooses." Not content merely to repeal the Rumford Act, CREA hoped to bar future legislatures from taking any steps whatsoever to curb housing discrimination.[68]

From the perspective of mainline church leaders, who had long complained about the state's segregated housing patterns, it was difficult to imagine a clearer affront to the Christian ideals of racial equality and human dignity. As the Methodist bishop for Los Angeles, Gerald Kennedy, informed a *Los Angeles Times* reporter in December 1963, the appalling result of passing Prop 14 would be to enshrine a "sin"—housing discrimination—in the state constitution.[69]

To prevent this from happening, the leaders of the Northern and Southern Councils hashed out a three-pronged plan of attack. First, to ensure that voters knew precisely where the churches stood on the issue of fair housing, they would launch a public relations push combining press releases, newspaper advertisements, television and radio appearances, and high-profile public events, including rallies headed by Martin Luther King, Jr., and Eugene Carson Blake. At the congregational level, a variety of educational programs—including a "Keep California Fair Week," slated for October—would give ministers a chance to explain their reasons, both practical and spiritual, for opposing the proposed amendment. Finally, church members would be asked to canvass their communities, making the case against Prop 14 in face-to-face encounters with their neighbors. Funded primarily by designated denominational contributions, the campaign's initial budget was modest—around $15,000 in the case of the Southern California effort—but church leaders were confident that more funds would materialize once rank-and-file churchgoers were fully informed of Prop 14's diabolical purpose.[70]

On paper, the SCCC's tactics bore a close resemblance to those that mainline church groups were employing to great effect in their push for a federal civil rights bill. From early on, however, it was clear that the California campaign faced obstacles that made success less likely than in the case of the Washington lobbying campaign. The national push, as we have seen, hinged on a coordinated lobbying campaign in the Midwest that faced little in the way of organized opposition. The major anti–civil rights group, the Committee for Fundamental American Freedoms, was essentially a front group for Southern elected officials and a handful of eccentric Northern allies that did little more than place newspaper advertisements. The mainline churches, in contrast, were well organized, influential, and capable of acting through a variety of interlocking instrumentalities, from state and local denominational bodies to the various councils of churches. Although the total number of church members who wrote or called their members of Congress was probably small relative to the size of the relevant electorate, these highly motivated activists were in some respects pushing against an open door. Stated otherwise, there was a significant intensity gap in the Midwestern states that worked to the advantage of the Civil Rights Act's supporters.[71]

In California this situation was reversed. The state had by this point developed a vibrant network of grassroots conservative groups, many of which were more than happy to join forces with the deep-pocketed CREA to nullify a measure they regarded as a socialist assault on the rights of property owners. Mainline religious authority, in contrast, was comparatively weak and certainly untested. Because of the low ratio of active church members to Protestant identifiers, church educational efforts were bound to reach a much smaller percentage of the population than in the Midwestern states where the fate of the federal civil rights law was decided. Moreover, while several cities and counties had active church councils, the density of ecumenical bodies was far lower than in the Midwestern and Northeastern states.[72] Nor were California's church councils situated geographically in such a way as to maximize their influence. Some relatively small hamlets, such as Redlands and Glendale, boasted fully staffed councils, while other densely populated areas, such as the newly built suburban communities of Orange County, had no professional ecumenical bodies whatsoever.[73]

The first sign that religious opponents of Prop 14 were facing an uphill battle came in early February, when CREA and its allies presented state officials with more than 700,000 signatures in support of its proposed amendment—some 300,000 more than were necessary under state law to put the matter to the voters. The large number of signatures must have come as a particular shock to the state's councils of churches, which had in December circulated a letter urging Protestant ministers to request that their flocks *not* sign the petition.[74] Not surprisingly, most of the signers were from Southern California: between them, Los Angeles, Orange, and San Diego Counties produced half a million signatures.[75] Remarkably, Prop 14's sponsors accomplished this feat without the aid of paid signature gatherers. The bulk of the labor came from CREA's 45,000 dues-paying members, in conjunction with grassroots conservative groups, including the United Republicans of California (UROC), which resolved at its November convention to join CREA in "seek[ing] restoration to each individual person of full property rights as intended in the Constitution."[76] When state Republican party chairman Caspar Weinberger reminded the group's leaders that the state GOP platform had long contained a fair housing plank, they brushed him off. "Principle," they told the *Times*, was "more important than blind conformity" to party orthodoxy.[77]

From the perspective of mainline religious leaders, the hugely successful petition drive was a serious blow—but hardly a fatal one. Given that their own mobilization effort was still in the planning stages, they could at least comfort themselves with the thought that many signers had been duped into supporting a measure they barely understood. The real test would come when church officials launched their long-awaited campaign to educate churchgoers and the general public on the spiritual dimensions of the fair housing debate.

That effort was under way by the summer, and early reviews were positive, even glowing. Indeed, longtime observers of the California political scene agreed that never before in the state's history—or at least not since prohibition—had so many ministers expended so much time and energy to influence the outcome of an election. Every week brought a new batch of pronouncements from local church councils and ministerial associations urging a "no" vote on Prop 14.[78] By late summer more than a thousand ministers had agreed to sign their names to a full-page, anti–Prop 14 ad that would run in the *Los Angeles Times* shortly before Election Day.[79] Members of the clergy were also well represented in the hundreds of town halls that the Coalition Against Prop 14 (CAP-14)—an umbrella group representing unions, civil rights groups, and Democratic grassroots organizations—was conducting across the state.[80] In the city of Redlands (population 26,000), for example, representatives of the local council of churches addressed no fewer than thirty public meetings "directed at defeat of the anti–fair housing amendment."[81] Ministers even threw themselves into the task of fundraising, making calls and organizing dinners to help CAP-14 raise the $1 million it had pledged to spend in defense of the Rumford Act (though only about half of this amount was actually raised). As one crusty politico remarked to the syndicated columnists Evans and Novak, it wasn't every day that you found yourself surrounded by preachers "at a $50-a-plate supper."[82]

The campaign to educate the laity also seemed to be coming off more or less as planned. The Presbyterians and Episcopalians organized traveling educational teams that addressed dozens of congregations every week.[83] At the same time, the state and local church councils busied themselves with distributing thousands of "Local Church Plans"—informational packets containing all the materials a congregation would need to mobilize opposition to Prop 14, from "No on 14" bumper stickers to handy summaries of the mainline denominations' positions on fair housing to tips on organizing coffee klatches to contact information for the CAP-14 speakers' bureau.[84] Perhaps the most important item in the packet was "The Church Says No on Proposition 14," a slick, professionally produced pamphlet summarizing what mainline officials believed were the strongest arguments for fair housing legislation. "The right of every person to acquire, rent and sell property," it declared, "is basic to human dignity and freedom as conceived in the Bible, and is a moral issue which religious people cannot dodge." Signed by all of the state's largest Protestant denominations except the Baptists, more than half a million copies of the pamphlet were distributed to churchgoers in late summer and early fall.[85]

Then a strange thing happened. With each new poll released by the Field organization, it became clear that Protestant support for Prop 14, far from dissipating, was solidifying. Between May and October the overall percentage of voters who told pollsters that they intended to vote "yes" on the measure climbed from 48 percent to 57.5 percent. Protestant support increased even more—from 49 percent in May to nearly 63 percent in October.[86] The official pronouncements, educational teams, and Local Church Plans that so impressed political commentators were, it seemed, disappearing into a void.

Part of the problem was that the well-funded "yes" forces used every means at their disposal to suppress the arguments of the opposition. In some cities local elected officials, presumably fearing for their political futures, refused to provide church officials with the necessary permits to hold anti–Prop 14 rallies on city property.[87] When a renegade Southern California realtor named Richard Hallmark began working with church leaders to form an anti–Prop 14 group called California Realtors for Fair Housing (CRFH), he suddenly encountered difficulty getting his license renewed.[88] (Adding insult to injury, a conservative student group decided to make a cute point about the sanctity of private property by caravanning from UCLA to Covina to picket Hallmark's home, inviting reporters along for the ride.)[89] At least one prominent Prop 14 supporter, who was also a former Los Angeles County treasurer and tax collector, threatened to have the tax exemption of any church whose minister spoke out against the initiative revoked, though state officials insisted this was unlikely to happen.[90]

The cumulative impact of such threats on the battle for public opinion was probably marginal, however. The more serious concern, from the perspective of religious leaders, was that the anticipated groundswell of church-based opposition to Prop 14 simply never materialized. Indeed, a large percentage of local pastors either didn't share their nominal superiors' commitment to fair housing, or else did share it but were fearful of provoking a backlash from politically conservative parishioners affiliated with CREA, UROC, or the CRA. As a member of the Southern California task force put it, the group's message seemed not to be "filtering down to the pews." In some populous areas, including Orange County, there was "no evidence of any action" whatsoever on the part of local ministers.[91] Further north, in the Bay Area, the head of the Contra Costa County Council of Churches likewise lamented that "only a small percentage of our member-churches" seemed to be "get[ing] involved at the local level with this as a moral issue."[92] One problem, as Julius Keiser, who led the Southern California campaign, noted, was that there was "no facility in many churches to deal at the local level with this kind of issue." His point was that few California congregations, in contrast to their counterparts in the Midwest and Northeast, featured social action or human rights committees—the congregation-level bodies that were providing much of the infrastructure for the federal civil rights lobbying campaign. If many congregations weren't "follow[ing] the Plan provided for action," it was at least in part because they had "no organizational machinery to tackle a job of this kind."[93]

But lack of organizational machinery was only part of the problem. The deeper issue was that many middle-class church members simply had no interest in being educated about the religious or ethical dimensions of the Prop 14 fight. Many of them, in fact, were determined to do the educating themselves—and, failing this, to show their ministers the door. When the pastor of Los Angeles's First Baptist Church sent his congregation a letter laying out the Christian case for fair housing laws, conservative church members responded with a congregational letter of their own, then threatened to cut off financial support.[94] In Glendale, a wealthy suburb of Los Angeles, a group of Methodist laymen took out a full-page ad in the city paper to protest their ministers' support for the "socialistic" Rumford Act.[95] In the same city the pastor of the First Methodist Church complained to the *Los Angeles Times* about the volume of anonymous hate mail that was pouring into his office daily.[96] Meanwhile, in nearby Burbank, the Reverend Paul Peterson of the First Baptist Church deemed it wiser to pander to his congregation's prejudices. After polling church members on Prop 14 and finding them overwhelmingly opposed, he began preaching against fair housing laws, then resigned—or was fired from—his position as head of the local ministerial association.[97]

No group, however, suffered greater internal dissension than the Episcopalians. Almost as soon as the bishops declared their opposition to the initiative, a dissident group of laymen and women led by Barbara Taylor of Santa Ana formed an anti–fair housing organization called—perversely enough—"Episcopalians for Christ." The group's first official act was to arrange for the Reverend T. Robert Ingram, rector of St. Thomas Episcopal Church of Houston, to speak at a posh Santa Monica hotel. Perhaps the foremost Episcopal defender of segregation, Ingram contributed essays to *The Citizen*, the official outlet of the White Citizens' Councils, where he argued that God himself had ordained the separation of the races.[98] Bishop Eric Bloy of Los Angeles worked to spread the word that Ingram's visit had not been approved by the church hierarchy, and that the views of Episcopalians for Christ were "in sharp conflict with the position of this diocese and that of the Episcopal Church." In all likelihood, however, the resulting *Los Angeles Times* story only increased public interest in the intrachurch feud.[99]

Lay opposition intensified in September, when California's bishops arranged to send every Episcopalian in the state a copy of a special issue of the denominational periodical *Church and Race* that was entirely devoted to condemning Prop 14.[100] One article singled out the nearly all-white enclave of Glendale to illustrate the pernicious effects of housing discrimination. Needless to say, the membership of the city's fashionable St. Mark's Church was less than pleased. Much to the chagrin of their priest, a cautious but committed Prop 14 supporter, the entire vestry signed a letter opposing the bishops' stance on Prop 14, which it then read to the congregation during Sunday services.[101] The episode prompted Taylor to complain in her *Episcopalians for Christ* newsletter that church members were being "pummeled with periodicals, leaflets, 'Christian' publications, forums, panel discussions, plays and sermons, all telling us how to vote [on Proposition 14]." It was high time for laypeople to remind their priests that the property owner had a "God-given right to choose for himself" whether or not to sell to a particular buyer.[102] CREA, vigilant as always for opportunities to exacerbate the divide between pulpit and pew, reworked Taylor's missive and blasted it out to the state's major newspapers in the form of a press release.[103] In response, the bishops took to the pages of the *Times* to condemn both CREA and Taylor's group for their "callous, cynical and irreverent attitude toward the rights and obligations of bishops and clergy to speak on moral issues."[104] At this point the conservative activists, far from falling into line, responded by hitting the church hierarchy where it really hurt: by year's end thirty California parishes had either delayed or refused to pay their annual diocesan assessments, most of them in protest of the parent denomination's stance on Prop 14.[105]

When Election Day finally arrived, California voters, as predicted, overwhelmingly backed the idea of a constitutional right to discriminate in the sale or rental of real estate. In the end, fully 65 percent of voters supported Prop 14. In Los Angeles County voters broke two to one in favor; Orange County voters did them one better, voting three to one in favor. The vote was much closer in the Bay Area: Prop 14 received only bare majority support in the counties of San Francisco (52.9 percent), Marin (52.2 percent), and Santa Clara (53.1 percent). Supporters of fair housing legislation could take some comfort in the fact that the amendment faced a serious challenge in the courts—and, in fact, the U.S. Supreme Court would strike it down on Equal Protection grounds in 1966. But for Protestant religious leaders there was no avoiding the fact that "the church" had suffered a shocking blow to its prestige. The conservative *Los Angeles Times*, which had endorsed Prop 14, called its passage "the soundest defeat for religious forces in recent years."[106]

Of course, California was not the only place where religious leaders suffered humbling defeats on the fair housing question. In fact, virtually all of the fair housing proposals that were put to city- or statewide votes went down to defeat in the 1960s, notwithstanding religious elites' strong support for reform. Yet the Prop 14 result was arguably unique both in its lopsidedness and in the apparent futility of religious mobilization. In the Northeast and Midwest, where the religious infrastructure was comparatively well developed, votes were typically closer and the effects of religious messaging more evident.[107]

Still, some California religious leaders, pointing out that the state's percentage of churchgoing residents was small relative to other regions of the country, argued that Prop 14's passage was not the humiliating setback it first appeared. As Harry McKnight of the Los Angeles Federation of Churches observed in an interview with the *Los Angeles Times*, it was unreasonable to expect California's clergymen to carry a statewide election on a highly controversial subject when only about 33 percent of Californians were church members—and many of those were not regular attenders.[108] In almost his next breath, however, McKnight admitted that many Los Angeles–area churchgoers had simply defied their spiritual leaders and voted for the proposition. When asked what this portended for the future of mainline Protestantism in California, the minister disputed the implication that white believers might "bolt the churches" over their opposition to fair housing. "Where else do they have to go?" he demanded. "Unless the church leadership is divided, as they were not in this case, they have no other place to go. After they cool off, they will be back."[109]

9

The Twilight of the
Protestant Establishment

Many months ago, planners of the [National Council of Churches']
eighth triennial assembly selected as [their] theme 'Therefore
Choose Life,' from Deuteronomy. . . . They may or may not have
realized that the organization might actually face a life-or-death
situation.

—*Christianity Today* (1969)

As late as 1964 mainline Protestant leaders could take comfort in the fact that the
conservative insurgency appeared unlikely to spread beyond the Golden State.
To be sure, the churches' prominent role in the push for federal civil rights legislation prompted a fresh round of communist accusations against the National
Council of Churches and its constituent denominations. And there was some
evidence that the audience for right-wing attacks on the mainline churches was
growing: the number of radio stations airing hardline conservative preachers
such as Carl McIntire and Billy James Hargis, for example, expanded rapidly in
the mid-1960s, notwithstanding the NCC's efforts to force them off the air. And
yet, the results of the 1964 presidential election—in which conservative icon and
Civil Rights Act opponent Barry Goldwater carried only the Deep South and
his home state of Arizona—seemed to indicate that the mainline churches were
more or less in tune with the zeitgeist. In fact, when one considered that Lyndon
Johnson had won handily even in California, it was possible to conclude that the
Prop. 14 defeat was not quite the catastrophe it first seemed. Clearly, many of the
same right-leaning voters who had turned out to oppose fair housing regulations
nonetheless viewed Goldwater as a step too far.

By 1968, when the next presidential election was held, the picture looked very
different. Polls conducted four short years after the civil rights push revealed that
a solid majority of churchgoers now disapproved of churches and ministers who
engaged in "social action." Reports of mainline churches attempting to withdraw
from their parent denominations proliferated in the press, typically accompanied by complaints that church officials were too preoccupied with political
questions such as civil rights and the widening war in Southeast Asia. Some large

NCC member denominations, including the Southern Presbyterians, narrowly defeated motions to withdraw from the Council altogether. Most troubling of all, many conservative donors began to withhold funds from denominations and ecumenical bodies that they now regarded as "too political," thus exacerbating the churches' long-standing financial woes.

As we have seen, the widespread view that the churches' political activities *caused* the downward trend in mainline attendance and giving is mistaken; both trends began in the closing years of the Eisenhower administration, long before the social and political upheavals of the late 1960s. Still, it is undeniable that the late 1960s witnessed an upsurge in lay opposition to religious political activism, particularly when such activism was directed at left-leaning causes such as urban economic development and ending the Vietnam War. Moreover, the decline in attendance and giving accelerated noticeably after 1969, largely, it seems, because of lay opposition to the churches' outspoken stances on civil rights and Vietnam.

Which brings us to the central question of this chapter: why did so many rank-and-file believers, after years of embracing—or at least acquiescing in—the "prophetic" political stances of denominational leaders, discover a sudden aversion to religious social action in the late 1960s? One possibility, the one usually suggested by laypeople at the time, is that the churches did, in fact, become more "political" in the late 1960s. And yet, as I demonstrate below, there is little evidence to support such claims: the number of political pronouncements issuing from religious bodies remained roughly on par with past years, and church policy pronouncements actually received somewhat less press coverage than in the past.

So why did so many average churchgoers *believe* that their nominal religious leaders had suddenly become too political? The answer can be traced to three factors. First, as large numbers of young, college-educated whites abandoned the mainline churches, the median age of regular churchgoers shot upward, leaving churches filled with older believers who were more likely than their younger counterparts to adopt conservative positions on questions of foreign policy and race. By the late 1960s, and as a direct result of this demographic shift, church pronouncements that were even mildly critical of the Vietnam War (for example) risked sparking a backlash among a churchgoing population that was aging by the year. Meanwhile, many younger believers argued that the churches were not doing enough to combat the evils of militarism and racism. Confronted with an aging membership, yet desperate to win back upwardly mobile young parishioners, the churches faced an insoluble demographic dilemma.

Second, the post-1960 decline in attendance and giving triggered a rapid unraveling of the mainline churches' local infrastructure. Confronted with shrinking budgets, church officials made painful cuts to the very institutions—the local church councils, the college ministry, media and broadcasting commissions—that represented their most vital links to the grass roots. As a result, elites' efforts to educate and stimulate discussion among local churchgoers met with little success. At the same time, average believers increasingly complained, with good reason, that church policy statements were formulated with little, if any, input from the laity.

Finally, the mainline churches' relationships with the business community began to deteriorate in the years around 1970. When the leading lights of the postwar economic establishment began to retire from public life, they were replaced by a younger cohort of executives who saw little reason to engage in time-consuming deliberations about Christianity's implications for labor relations or monetary policy. Lacking strong ties to the mainline denominations, and disdainful of the stewardship ethic, the new cohort shifted resources away from deliberative entities like the NCC's Department of the Church and Economic Life, pouring them into newly created think tanks that could be counted on to advocate for lower taxes and deregulation. In addition to exacerbating the churches' budgetary woes, the loss of business support deprived church policy pronouncements of an important source of legitimacy, significantly diminishing their sway in the political sphere.

Explaining the Perception of a Newly Politicized Church

We have seen that mainline church leaders engaged with social and political issues with great regularity in the period between the New Deal and the civil rights movement. But did they become even more political in the late 1960s? The question is difficult to answer, in part because there is no objective way of defining whether a given pronouncement or action should be classified as political rather than spiritual. One way to make the question less subjective is to look for variance in the number of policy pronouncements issued by leading ecumenical bodies over time. Figure 9.1 displays the yearly number of pronouncements by the NCC's General Board on which votes were recorded. As late as the late 1960s the NCC was still widely regarded as the unofficial voice of the Protestant mainline, notwithstanding reports of dissension at the grassroots level. If mainline churchgoers sensed that the church was becoming more political, it may have been because the nation's most prominent ecumenical body was staking out positions on contemporary political questions more frequently than in the past.

But the data offer only modest support for this hypothesis. Between 1953 and 1969, the annual number of pronouncements ranged between zero and eight; the average number issued per year was three. In support of the idea that the churches grew more political in the late 1960s, it may be pointed out that the annual average was slightly higher in the 1960s (3.3) than in the 1950s (2.6), and

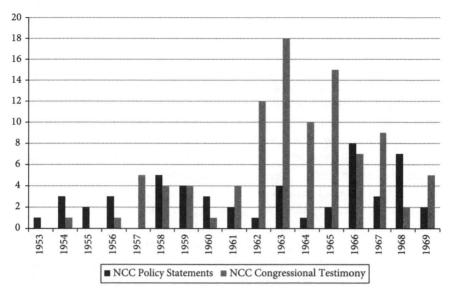

Figure 9.1 Frequency of NCC policy pronouncements and Congressional testimony, 1953–1969

Source: Dean M. Kelley, *The National Council of Churches and the Social Outlook of the Nation* (New York: National Council of Churches, 1971)

the two years with the highest number of pronouncements occurred after 1965. Yet it would be a mistake to read too much into the post-1960 figures, since many of the pronouncements issued in this period dealt with uncontroversial issues (such as adult literacy programs and religious tax exemptions) and thus likely escaped the notice of most churchgoers. Moreover, aside from 1966 and 1968, the number of statements issued per year during the late 1960s was roughly on par with that in earlier periods.[1]

One type of political activity that clearly did become more common in the 1960s was testifying before Congress. NCC officials, after offering only occasional testimony in the 1950s, became regular contributors to congressional hearings beginning in the middle of the following decade; indeed, there were four years during the mid-1960s in which Council officials submitted or gave live testimony on at least ten different occasions. Any churchgoer who monitored congressional hearing schedules would therefore have been fully justified in concluding that the Council was becoming "more political." In reality, however, much of this testimony concerned relatively uncontroversial issues (e.g., the census, agriculture policy, Indian land claims, African refugees), meaning it was barely covered in the press (if at all) and almost certainly failed to filter down to the men and women in the pews.[2]

Another possible explanation for the widespread perception of an increase in political activism is that the churches' policy pronouncements were receiving more media coverage than in the past. Figure 9.2, which tracks the annual number of articles in the *New York Times* and *Washington Post* that referenced the National Council of Churches, offers some support for this hypothesis: 1966 in particular was a banner year for press coverage of the Council, as both the *Times* and the *Post* devoted significant space to the Council's initial pronouncements concerning the Vietnam War, its embattled civil rights initiative in the Mississippi Delta (the Delta Ministry), and the leadership changes consummated at its 1966 triennial General Assembly in Miami.

And yet, the overall trend in press coverage during the 1960s clearly pointed downward. Particularly after 1966, when it became clear that mainline attendance and fundraising had entered a downward spiral, major media outlets began to discount the Council's claim to speak for the bulk of American churchgoers. News items concerning NCC policy pronouncements were pushed to the back pages and sections of the major papers, eventually disappearing altogether. Moreover, front-page references to the NCC, which were quite common in the early 1960s (in part because of the churches' prominent role in the civil rights movement), declined markedly in the latter years of the decade. After 1966 the stories that did appear in the front portions of major papers tended to focus on declining attendance figures, budget shortfalls, and reports of dissension in the ranks—which may offer a partial explanation for the perception of a newly "politicized" church. Average churchgoers may have been unaware of the details

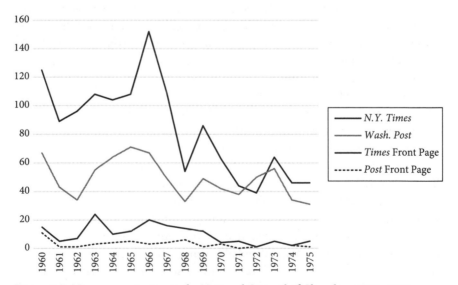

Figure 9.2 Newspaper stories on the National Council of Churches, 1960–1975

of NCC policy pronouncements or congressional testimony, but they probably were aware that the Council's political actions were generating their fair share of controversy.

But this brings us back to the key question: why all the controversy? Shifting the focus from the actions of church leaders to the changing composition of the average congregation provides an important clue. In short, the post-1960 exodus of upwardly mobile twenty- and thirtysomethings from the mainline churches created, almost overnight, an elderly churchgoing population. (As we saw in the last chapter, the percentage of 18–29 year-olds who attended weekly services plummeted from around 50 percent in 1957 to a little over 30 percent in 1970.)[3] The defection of younger, more educated citizens—most of whom left organized religion altogether, at least for the time being—left the pews filled with believers who were far more likely than younger Americans to adopt conservative positions on major social and political issues and also more likely to disapprove of "the church" involving itself in politics. The 1968 American National Election Study (ANES), for example, revealed that, among Northern Protestant identifiers, the percentage approving of the Civil Rights Act was nearly twenty points higher among respondents under thirty-five as compared to those over thirty-five.[4]

At least initially, then, many young white Protestant identifiers remained sympathetic to the values and issue positions espoused by their childhood churches, even as they increasingly distanced themselves from organized religion. Hence, when Gallup reported in 1968 that the overall percentage of Americans who believed that the church should "stay silent" on social and political issues had risen nine points in the past decade (to 53 percent), it was essentially reporting the emergence of a generational split.[5] Given that older churchgoers tended to be more politically conservative, they naturally tended to object when their overwhelmingly left-leaning religious leaders engaged in political activism. Indeed, polls conducted in the late 1960s found that, while 60 percent of churchgoers over fifty-five believed that the "clergy should stick to religion and not concern themselves with social, economic, and political questions," only 39 percent of those under thirty-five agreed.[6] The same polls showed that young, highly educated citizens—the very people who were abandoning the mainline churches in droves—made up the group most likely to support clerical activism.[7]

The Collapse of the Mainline Infrastructure

The emergence of this demographic bind—which, as we shall see, was greatly exacerbated by the provocations of young activists on the left—was undoubtedly the single most important factor motivating the lay reaction against religious political involvement in the late 1960s. Still, it is possible that the mainline churches might have weathered the storm had it not been for the simultaneous collapse of the local-level infrastructure that had long connected denominational and ecumenical officials to the men and women in the pews. Perhaps the most consequential instance of institutional decay involved the state and local councils of churches. As we have seen, the local councils remained fairly vibrant into the mid-1960s; indeed, they were arguably the most important institutional actors during the churches' push for the 1964 Civil Rights Act. Following passage of the Civil Rights Act and the Voting Rights Act, many state and local councils turned their attention to such thorny problems as segregated housing patterns, community-police relations, and discrimination in employment, all of which were believed to be fueling unrest in the nation's urban centers. Unfortunately for the churches, however, 1965 marked the peak year for local council financing and staffing. In 1966 many churches and denominations, alarmed by the downward trends in attendance and giving, began reducing their contributions to ecumenical initiatives. As a result, and as Figure 9.3 makes clear, council heads had no choice but to begin eliminating departments and laying off staff. Between 1965 and 1971 the number of paid council officials declined by more than 20 percent. More sobering still, statistics unveiled at the 1969 meeting of the Association of Council Secretaries (ACS), the major professional organization for local church council workers, showed that four times as many ministers had left local council

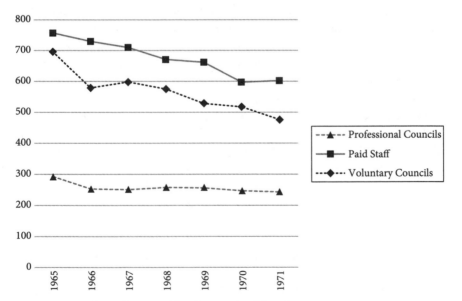

Figure 9.3 Decline of state and local councils of churches, 1965–1971
Source: Yearbooks of American Churches, 1958–1965

employment (whether voluntarily or because of layoffs) as had been hired during the previous year.[8] By 1970 the ACS was confronting a budget shortfall of more than 50 percent.[9] The number of voluntary local councils—that is, councils staffed by unpaid local ministers or lay leaders—also declined sharply: more than two hundred (nearly 32 percent) ceased operations the six-year period beginning in 1965.[10]

The rapid erosion of the conciliar network occurred at a particularly inopportune time for the mainline churches. At the very moment that religious leaders, fresh from their victory in the fight for the Civil Rights Act, were attempting to facilitate a national religious dialogue on a new round of divisive policy questions, they chose, or perhaps were forced, to eviscerate one of the only agencies that might have made such a dialogue possible. As a result, many churchgoers encountered the National Council of Churches' pronouncements on the Vietnam conflict (for example) not in the context of a local workshop or conference, but rather in the secular press, or perhaps in a denominational periodical. Conservative laypeople had complained for years about religious elites who seemed determined to dictate policy from on high, and without considering the views of rank-and-file churchgoers. Following the unraveling of the church council system, such complaints were not without merit. Even the president of the ACS was forced to acknowledge in 1970 that a combination of funding cuts, layoffs, and political controversies had created a "gulf" between "the local church and the councils"—one that was rapidly becoming a "bottomless pit."[11]

The collapse of the church council network was, however, only one facet of a broader decline of mainline institutional authority. Two additional examples of the decline of mainline dominance—in religious radio broadcasting and in university campus ministries—will suffice to demonstrate the point. For much of the twentieth century the mainline churches were the major beneficiaries of federal licensing requirements that encouraged broadcasters to set aside certain time slots for free (or sustaining time) public service programing, a category that included religious broadcasts. Through its Broadcasting and Film Commission (BFC), and in close cooperation with mainline denominational officials, the National Council of Churches effectively controlled the content of most Protestant religious programming. In its role as gatekeeper the Council regularly prevented preachers it deemed charlatans, or whose political views it deemed too extreme, from gaining access to the airwaves. (State and local councils often performed a similar role at the regional level.) Thus, while mainline religious broadcasts rarely featured explicitly political commentary (which risked running afoul of FCC regulations), it is no stretch to assume that the bulk of religious radio programming was broadly sympathetic to the mainline churches' policy priorities. Anyone who heard a radio sermon from Eugene Carson Blake (for example), would surely be left with little doubt about where the churches stood with respect to issues such as civil rights and arms control—even if the Presbyterian leader refrained from mentioning these issues by name.

In the early 1960s, however, two developments converged to break the mainline stranglehold on religious broadcasting and unleash a tidal wave of right-wing radio sermonizing, much of it explicitly critical of the mainline churches and the NCC. First, the Federal Communications Commission issued a policy directive declaring that stations could henceforth use *commercial* religious broadcasts to fulfill their public-interest obligations. The 1960 rule change produced a nearly instantaneous boom in conservative radio preaching as stations that had previously shunned paid religious programming rushed to consummate deals with fundamentalist syndicators like Carl McIntire and Billy James Hargis.[12] Between 1960 and 1964 the number of stations airing McIntire's *Twentieth-Century Reformation Hour* increased by more than 400 percent, from 108 to 460. By the time the debate over the Civil Rights Act reached its climax, McIntire's conspiratorial take on the civil rights movement—he believed it had been orchestrated by Moscow with the aim of subverting property rights and ushering in a socialist state—could be heard in every state, with the possible exceptions of Nevada and parts of upper New England.[13]

A fierce critic of the National Council of Churches, McIntire stepped up his attacks in 1965, when the NCC began tentatively exploring ways of addressing the socioeconomic roots of black poverty. Indeed, the fundamentalist Presbyterian organized a special initiative—"Project Truth"—for the express purpose of fomenting grassroots religious opposition to the NCC's desegregation and poverty relief efforts in the Mississippi Delta.[14] Initially NCC officials played down the significance of their chief radio critic, insisting that McIntire was a marginal figure whose popularity was largely confined to the Deep South (where the concentration of stations airing his program was highest). This strategy became untenable, however, after a handful of prominent Northern congregations began acting on McIntire's advice to separate from the parent denominations.[15] By 1966 NCC President Rueben H. Mueller had little choice but to acknowledge, in a press conference at the group's triennial assembly, that "grassroots [church] members" were being unduly influenced by a "flood" of "bombastic radio broadcasts purveying accusations against the national council"—broadcasts that seemed designed to "squeeze more dollars out of the pockets of gullible people."[16]

The second factor that broke the mainline broadcasting monopoly was money, or rather the lack thereof. Confronted in 1966 with an annual deficit of $140,000, the NCC's Broadcasting and Film Commission began closing regional offices and laying off staff, thus undercutting its ability to coordinate activities with state and local church officials.[17] To be sure, the fact that the NCC and its local counterparts were forced to reduce broadcasting budgets did not stop them from pressing federal regulators to take action against fundamentalist firebrands—a tactic that eventually succeeded in unraveling McIntire's media empire.[18] But this was a relatively minor victory in a larger battle that the mainline churches were destined to lose. By the late 1960s mainline officials lacked the resources to purchase significant blocks of airtime, particularly after competition between fundamentalist syndicators began to drive up the cost of premium time slots; nor were many station managers interested in giving away airtime that was increasingly valuable on the open market. Conservative—if not always explicitly political—religious broadcasting proliferated, and the sustaining-time religious program, a staple of the midcentury broadcasting landscape, soon disappeared from the scene entirely.[19]

By the mid-1960s a similar challenge to mainline authority was playing out on the nation's college campuses, where mainline chaplains and university ministers had long exercised a controlling interest in the religious life of the student community. The modern campus ministry was born in the years around 1900, when church leaders awoke to the fact that mandatory religious training had largely disappeared from the standard curriculum at top-tier universities. Convinced that impressionable young men (and later women) should not be left to their own devices in matters of faith, most Protestant-affiliated private universities created a chaplain's office, whose functions included counseling students, advising student religious groups, and coordinating religious services and educational programming. At roughly the same time, to address the needs of public university students, the large mainline denominations began hiring and training "campus ministers," who were typically based in churches or offices within easy walking distance of the campus. Although campus ministers were not salaried university employees, they enjoyed close relations with university administrators and were often treated as de facto university staff members. Significantly, the number of chaplains and campus ministers exploded in the immediate postwar period as the mainline churches, suddenly flush with cash, assumed the responsibility of ministering to the hundreds of thousands of G.I. Bill–funded students who were inundating the nation's campuses.[20]

Postwar campus clergymen often took a special interest in social ethics and in many cases were explicitly instructed to do so by their parent denominations. The Methodists, for example, advised campus ministers to bear "prophetic witness" to the nation's students and to "foster a Christian community" that would prepare students to confront injustice in the wider world.[21] Surveys of campus clergymen indicated that most eagerly embraced the assignment. Researchers noted that university ministers and chaplains were on average better educated than parish pastors and were also significantly more liberal in their views on race relations, economic inequality, and foreign policy.[22] It was perhaps only natural, then, that campus ministers' offices and student ecumenical groups such as the campus YMCAs became hubs of the mid-1960s student movement. As one sociologist observed in 1966, "The best visiting lecture series or the most experimental theater can [usually] be found under the aegis of the campus ministry. At other schools, the programs of social action or of welfare service to surrounding neighborhoods are conducted out of the chaplain's office or the denominational foundations ringing the campus. At still other campuses, these foundations serve as open forums, allowing theological speakers who might otherwise be denied hearings."[23]

By the time these words appeared in print, however, they were already out of date. As the student movement grew more uncompromising in its demands, left-leaning students increasingly abandoned mainline-affiliated student organizations in favor of militantly secular groups such as Students for a Democratic Society (SDS). Typical of the new activists were the leaders of the NCC-backed University Christian Movement (UCM), who voted their organization out of existence to protest the mainline churches' insufficient opposition to the Vietnam War.[24]

But the more serious threat to the mainline campus ministry originated on the Right. By the early 1960s a growing cadre of evangelical groups, most of which viewed the mainline churches' social teachings as heretical, were making inroads on campuses from coast to coast. By far the largest and most influential of the new groups was Campus Crusade for Christ. Founded in 1951 by a former candy salesman named Bill Bright and his wife, Vonette, Campus Crusade presented itself as a purely evangelistic endeavor with no broader political agenda. In interviews, however, Bright sometimes acknowledged that his decision to launch the group had been motivated in part by his belief that university campuses were hotbeds of communism and that mainline campus ministers, with their ubiquitous social action programs, were exacerbating the problem.[25] His plan to displace the pink-tinged mainline campus ministry centered on a new version of the Gospel—one that reduced the entirety of the Bible and Christian teaching to four "spiritual laws," all of which concerned the individual's relationship with God, and none of which so much as hinted at the possibility of broader religious or ethical obligations toward one's neighbors.[26] For fairly obvious reasons, this message proved popular with many of the same millionaires who were backing *Christianity Today* and other right-leaning evangelical endeavors. It also proved popular with students. Following its initial success at UCLA— where 250 students, including the student body president, the editor of the student newspaper, and the quarterback of the football team signed up in the first year—Campus Crusade quickly spread to hundreds of campuses. By 1961 the group had acquired sufficient resources to purchase an abandoned resort, together with eighteen hundred acres in the San Bernardino Mountains, to serve as its international headquarters.[27] Far from resting on his laurels, however, Bright focused his energies on an aggressive expansion drive, urging supporters such as the Texas oilman (and John Birch Society backer) Bunker Hunt to cut even larger checks to the only campus Christian group that—as he put it in a fundraising appeal—was taking the fight to "thousands" of "communist professors" and depriving "radical groups" of "their influence in student government and with campus newspapers."[28]

Mainline campus ministers were not amused. Many of them fired back with essays and op-eds accusing Christian Crusade of spreading a blatantly false gospel—one that seemed designed, in the words of a chaplain at Southern Methodist University, to lure "insecure, self-doubting, lonely teenagers" away from their home churches, replacing a Methodist faith rich in "theology and tradition" with a cultlike focus on Bright's four extrabiblical laws.[29] On many campuses mainline clergymen used every tool at their disposal to block Campus Crusade's requests for recognition as an officially sanctioned student organization. At the University of Miami four mainline campus ministers joined together to produce a report that accused Crusade workers of defaming the existing campus ministries and of "violating student privacy" by witnessing, uninvited, in the dormitories.[30] In Arkansas the Presbyterian synod likewise advised against granting recognition, arguing that Campus Crusade aimed to pull students "away from their natural communities into [an exclusively] Christian grouping" and to foster a purely individualistic faith that was concerned "with the soul at the expense of the whole of life."[31] However, such pleas did little to slow Campus Crusade's explosive growth. At a time when university administrators were everywhere in the process of dismantling unpopular restrictions on student speech and organizing, the idea of barring an outwardly benign evangelistic group from proselytizing on campus was a nonstarter. Free to witness at will, Campus Crusade thrived in the increasingly deregulated campus environment of the late 1960s. By the end of the decade the group boasted more than three thousand workers spread across 250 institutions of higher learning.[32]

In some ways strikingly out of tune with the zeitgeist—its workers typically dressed conservatively, and men were required to keep their hair short—Bright's individualistic, antiestablishment brand of Christianity was in other respects of a piece with the late-1960s obsession with unmediated forms of spirituality and self-discovery. The group's rapid growth was probably also aided by the fact that Bright mostly confined his political musings to fundraising letters and to discussions with a small circle of advisors.[33] Many Crusade workers—and certainly most student members—were likely unaware of the group's role in a broader struggle over the social meaning of Christianity. And yet it would be difficult to overstate their contribution to the collapse of the university ministries that the mainline churches had so carefully constructed over the preceding six decades. By the end of the 1970s, as mainline officials struggled to scrape together funds for an increasingly skeletal campus ministry, the entrepreneurial

Bright would be expanding on every front—launching a billion-dollar fund-raising drive, forming dozens of new campus chapters, initiating a massive phone bank–based evangelistic crusade, opening a "Christian Embassy" to minister to Washington politicians, and even forming lucrative new partnerships with such corporate giants as Mobil, Pepsico, and Coca-Cola.[34]

Vietnam, Black Power, and the Growing Generational Divide

The emergence of a generational divide in the churches, coupled with the erosion of mainline authority at the grassroots, did more than doom the churches' post-1964 attempts at political advocacy, however. It also produced a tragic dynamic in which political advocacy tended actually to exacerbate the underlying demographic and other problems that were driving the mainline's decline.

In the case of Vietnam, most mainline religious leaders were by late 1965 convinced that the Johnson administration's plans for escalation raised ethical questions that the churches could not in good conscience ignore. In early December the NCC's General Board overwhelmingly approved a statement, drafted by Eugene Carson Blake, calling for a unilateral halt to the U.S. bombing of North Vietnam and the replacement of U.S. forces by United Nations peacekeepers. With remarkable foresight, the statement predicted that the failure to take these steps—particularly in the face of grave doubts about the competence and human rights record of the South Vietnamese regime—would only generate additional "distrust and hatred" of American servicemen, whom many Vietnamese already viewed as an occupying force.[35]

Over the next two years the NCC, together with the Presbyterians, Congregationalists (United Church of Christ), and Methodists, launched a variety of educational programs that aimed to carry this message to the men and women in the pews. In sharp contrast to the 1963–1964 civil rights campaign, however, the churches' Vietnam program appears to have had little impact on lay opinion—except, perhaps, to widen the chasm between average churchgoers and denominational leaders. One problem was funding. Faced with rapidly shrinking resources, church leaders struggled to find money for antiwar initiatives, and the effort was poorly financed in comparison to the civil rights campaign. As a result, the NCC's outreach efforts in particular often appeared hilariously ham-handed: the centerpiece of its 1966–1967 education campaign was a "multimedia packet" whose entire contents consisted of printed copies of NCC pronouncements on Vietnam, together with a voice recording of a church official reading the very same statements. In the words of a Presbyterian media consultant, it was highly unlikely that such "dull, elitist, and outdated" material prompted many churchgoers to rethink their convictions concerning the war.[36]

A more serious problem concerned the nature of the audience: older Americans, as we have seen, were both overrepresented in the churchgoing population and more likely than other citizens to oppose antiwar activism. Particularly during a time of budgetary crisis, many elderly churchgoers resented even the relatively modest sums their denominations were devoting to the antiwar cause. If the Methodist Church was really facing a financial crunch, as church officials alleged in their emergency fundraising appeals, then why was it allocating $100,000 to a Vietnam Education Project that seemed far removed from the church's core mission?[37] Finally, the churches had done little to lay the groundwork for a major antiwar mobilization. Compared to civil rights, Vietnam was an unfamiliar subject; most churchgoers were barely aware of the conflict prior to the first large-scale troop deployments in the summer and fall of 1965. And now denominational leaders were asking them not only to take time to study the issue but also to consider steps that seemed likely to result in a communist takeover of an American ally. Not surprisingly, many ministers simply ignored their superiors' requests to organize Vietnam discussion groups and to integrate NCC materials into their Sunday morning sermons.[38]

Church officials, for their part, were well aware that the nation's college campuses, not its churches, comprised the beating heart of the antiwar movement. For this reason they worked diligently to forge alliances with the movement's young leaders. Among other steps, they authorized liaisons to meet with the youth-dominated antiwar groups, including the National Mobilization Committee to End the War in Vietnam (the Mobe); provided antiwar groups with office space in local churches; and encouraged clergymen to participate in antiwar marches and protests. From a public relations standpoint, these efforts backfired spectacularly. For one thing, they exacerbated congregational tensions, as younger and older churchgoers debated the wisdom and propriety of using church facilities as bases for antiwar organizing. Several previously thriving university congregations either split or saw their memberships decimated by the defection of students (or else older churchgoers) who decided that they could not in good conscience worship with war supporters (or opponents).[39] But the larger problem was that student activists gave church leaders little credit for their committed, if cautious, antiwar advocacy. In fact, many young people, noting the Council's close ties to the Johnson administration, were determined to keep it at arm's length.[40] From this perspective the NCC's reluctance to endorse more radical forms of protest confirmed suspicions that the group was, at bottom, an establishment body whose leaders would never truly break ranks with their friends in Washington.

These simmering tensions boiled over at the NCC's 1969 General Assembly, generating headlines from coast to coast. By this point the Council was already on record as a staunch opponent of the war. Moreover, it had recently taken a number of steps designed to afford students and young people greater influence in its decision-making structures. And it had agreed to provide student activists with ample time on the assembly agenda with which to make the case for an even more aggressive antiwar stance. None of this prevented a disaster in Detroit.[41] Not content with the space provided them on the official program, young activists staged several impromptu protests in the convention hall, from a mock draft of convention delegates to the reading of a manifesto whose demands included immediate amnesty for draft resisters, as well as the payment of $300 million to "the youth of Amerika" as reparations for "the lies we've been forced to listen to."[42] A more serious request came from James Rubin, a twenty-one-year-old Hope College student who asked that the Council hold his draft card "in trust" and provide him with legal counsel to fight charges of draft dodging. Council officials immediately agreed to put the proposal to a vote, and it was backed by a solid majority of delegates (228 to 184). And yet, because NCC rules required a two-thirds majority for official pronouncements of the General Assembly, Rubin's request was denied. At this point a minister from the Free Church of Berkeley leapt onto the speaker's platform and emptied a can of blood-red paint, drenching both the speaker's table and the Council's incoming president, Arthur Flemming.[43] Watching—or reading about—these events from afar, many conservative churchgoers no doubt applauded themselves for accurately predicting how the Council's dalliance with the student movement would end.

After 1965 a similar dynamic played out in the field of civil rights. That fall, following the disastrous riots in Watts, the mainline churches and the NCC began gradually shifting the focus of their "race and religion" programs from protecting African American civil rights to addressing what they believed to be the underlying socioeconomic causes of urban poverty and crime. Initially the Council experimented with a series of short-lived pilot programs that attempted to promote economic development and interracial cooperation in cities such as Detroit and Cleveland.[44] In 1967, following the outbreak of racial violence in Newark, Detroit, and other cities, these programs were abandoned in favor of a more ambitious initiative. That fall thirteen Protestant denominations, together with Jewish and Catholic groups, launched the Interreligious Federation for Community Organization (IFCO) with the aim of channeling religious funds into projects designed to stimulate economic development in minority communities across the country. Within the first eighteen months of its existence the group had issued grants totaling $1.5 million, with the bulk of the money (96 percent) coming from the mainline Protestant churches.[45]

The impetus for the shift in emphasis came from black church officials, who argued that the riots were being fueled by the frustrations of urban blacks who lacked meaningful opportunities for economic advancement. Many of these officials, including Benjamin F. Payton, the African American academic and minister who in 1966 replaced Robert Spike as director of the NCC's Commission on Religion and Race (CORR), favored diverting funds from existing educational and outreach programs in order to address the deepening crisis in the nation's inner cities. How, Payton asked, could the churches justify devoting significant funds to educational programs for primarily white congregations at a time when many of the nation's urban centers were literally on fire? Preferring action to dialogue, Payton condemned such long-standing programs as Brotherhood Week and Race Relations Sunday, both of which dated to the 1920s, as "little aspirins by which we salve our consciences."[46] These programs withered under his direction (and that of his successors), and the Council thereby deprived itself of yet another vehicle that might have facilitated constructive engagement between African American church leaders and middle-class whites who were skeptical of the churches' new focus on economic empowerment.[47]

Still, as late as 1968 relatively few white churchgoers registered serious objections to their churches' antipoverty programs. Although the decision to allocate funds to such programs during a time of declining resources no doubt rankled some believers, the reaction against the churches' antiwar programs was at this point far more pronounced. This changed in April 1969, when a Student Non-Violent Coordinating Committee (SNCC) executive secretary named James Forman unveiled his "Black Manifesto." Speaking at the National Black Economic Development Conference (NBEDC), an event organized by IFCO, Forman demanded that the nation's white churches pay $500 million—a sum later increased to $3 billion—in reparations for their role in perpetuating systemic racial inequality.[48] As if Forman's demands were not provocative enough, his strategies for publicizing them generated even more controversy. In early May he and his followers interrupted a Sunday morning communion service at Riverside Baptist Church, long viewed as the unofficial hub of the ecumenical movement, causing the church's pastors, together with fifteen hundred worshipers, to walk out of their own sanctuary in protest. He then moved across the street to the Interchurch Center, home to the National Council of Churches and dozens of mainline Protestant agencies, where he staged sit-ins in various offices. Then, in early June, he announced a "general strike" whose aim was to shut down all twenty-eight agencies (and 2,200 workers) located within the building.[49]

As church officials struggled to contain the Forman controversy—at one point they secured an injunction blocking him from the Interfaith Center—prominent black church leaders began pressing the NCC to radically increase minority representation in its upper echelons. As in the case of the antiwar movement, events came to a head at the NCC's December 1969 General Assembly in Detroit. Highly sensitive to their critics' well-founded complaints, Council officials secured the nomination and election of an African American man as the Council's vice president, two others as program vice presidents, three more as vice presidents at large, and the appointment of an African American woman, Theressa Hoover, to head the powerful nominating committee. And yet the more radical critics, led by Reverend Albert Cleage, Jr., pastor of a Detroit church called the Shrine of the Black Madonna (formerly the Central Congregational Church), dismissed these moves as half measures, insisting that they would accept nothing less than Cleage's election as NCC president. When the post went instead to Cynthia Wedel, a white woman and longtime leader in the ecumenical movement (and the Council's first female president), Cleage demanded that the Council's president-elect step aside, declaring that "the women's liberation movement must not stand in the way of the black liberation movement." When Wedel ignored this advice, he called down vengeance from heaven, denouncing the NCC as "the antichrist in this generation."[50]

The press, naturally, had a field day with the drama in Detroit. Yet the most important long-term effect of Cleage's and Forman's demonstrations (Forman also made it onto the General Assembly program) was to exacerbate the already worrisome divide between Protestant elites and rank-and-file churchgoers. Within days of Forman's "strike" against the Interchurch Center, the Gallup organization began polling Americans on the idea of reparations. To no one's surprise, 92 percent of white churchgoing respondents disapproved of them, as did 90 percent of the overall sample.[51] When mainline denominational officials pledged roughly $1 million to a fund, to be administered by IFCO, that would advance some of the manifesto's proposals, the news did not sit well with the nation's rapidly aging white churchgoers.[52] Hostile mail poured into NCC headquarters accusing the Council of submitting to "blackmail" and "extortion."[53] Methodist church officials were inundated with letters declaring, "One penny for Forman and not another for you."[54] *Christianity Today* and other evangelical publications fanned the flames, gleefully reporting on every detail of Forman's campaign and proclaiming him the "new hero" of the "religious liberals."[55]

So widespread was the outrage that several NCC-affiliated denominations had little choice but to reduce their contributions to the Council. Although the Council's revenues had been declining for years, the falloff in denominational contributions between 1969 and 1971 was particularly steep (nearly 15 percent) and could well be attributable to the Forman controversy.[56] In any event, the end result of the churches' encounter with the black power movement was to force radical cutbacks to the churches' initiatives in the area of religion and race. Designated contributions to these programs fell off even more sharply than overall contributions to the Council, and the fall of 1969 witnessed the first of several rounds of layoffs within the NCC's Department of Social Justice (which housed the Office of Religion and Race).[57] Thus, as in the case of Vietnam, the churches' post-1965 efforts to address the pressing social problems of race

relations and black poverty were not only hamstrung by a decaying infrastructure and a deepening generational (and racial) divide; they also had the tragic
effect of accelerating the very forces that were already driving the mainline's
decline.

The Demise of the Corporate Stewardship Tradition

At the same time that much of the laity was revolting against clerical activism
on Vietnam and race relations, an equally troubling rift was developing between
the mainline churches and their corporate supporters. The National Council
of Churches, as we have seen, had from its inception enjoyed close ties to the
business community; indeed, it was partly for the purpose of cultivating such
relationships that the old Federal Council of Churches had been reorganized and
renamed. Although the NCC was not without corporate critics—a small circle of
conservative executives, led by J. Howard Pew, spent the 1950s attempting to foment lay opposition to what they regarded as the NCC's "collectivist" economic
program—such efforts met with little success, and as late as the mid-1960s the
upper ranks of the Council were well stocked with center-left business leaders: J.
Irwin Miller, head of Cummins Engine, served as president of the NCC from
1960 to 1963; several well-known executives served on the Council's finance
committee, or else in its Department of the Church and Economic Life (DCEL);
others served on its primary governing body, the General Board.

Corporate support worked in two distinct ways to bolster the Council's reach
and influence. First, the participation of prominent executives in the DCEL
and other Council bodies lent gravitas to the NCC's policy pronouncements,
allowing church officials to claim, accurately, that their missives were formulated
with input from ethically minded labor *and* business leaders. Absent the active
participation of executives such as Miller, Robert E. Wilson (Standard Oil), and
Charles R. Hook (Armco Steel), it is unlikely that the NCC's policy reports and
statements would have merited frequent coverage in papers such as the *New York
Times* and *Washington Post*.

Second, and perhaps more obvious, business leaders played a critical role in
propping up the Council's finances. Executives such as Miller were naturally
well connected, and their Rolodexes allowed the NCC to tap into networks of
wealthy elites from coast to coast. One particularly important fundraising network centered around the Committee for Economic Development (CED), the
influential postwar think tank whose corporate membership overlapped to a significant extent with the DCEL.[58] In addition, NCC-affiliated executives regularly
organized regional fundraising drives focused on their own companies' supply
chains. Miller, for example, solicited large donations from a long list of mid-sized

manufacturers in the Midwest, most of whom did business with Cummins Engine (or hoped to). In 1960 he secured sizable contributions from dozens of toolmakers and engine-part manufacturers, several of whom took the opportunity to ask if Cummins might consider upping its order for the coming year.[59] Other executives, including Melvin H. Baker (National Gypsum Company), Leon Hickman (Alcoa), and David Cassat (Commercial Credit Corporation), spearheaded similar regional fundraising drives in other parts of the country.[60] The amount of money derived from such efforts was not huge, but it was significant. In 1962 the Council took in about 6 percent of its total income (or $1.2 million) from corporate sources and wealthy individuals; in some years this figure ran as high as 12 percent.[61]

Why did prominent executives devote time, energy, and money to a religious group whose pronouncements often cut against the corporate bottom line? In Miller's case, deep-rooted religious convictions seem to have been the dominant factor; in other cases, more mundane motives were probably at work. That is to say, the Council's politically conservative backers—including Hook, Wilson, and the NAM's Noel Sargent—likely recognized that the NCC's statements on current affairs carried weight with policymakers and the public, and they sought a seat at the table for the purpose of heading off, or at least watering down, unfavorable pronouncements. Indeed, it bears emphasizing that many economically conservative business leaders stood by the NCC even in the face of repeated and sometimes humiliating defeats on matters of policy. Roger Blough, the CEO of U.S. Steel, continued to make donations to the Council even after the NCC issued a report endorsing labor-friendly revisions to the Taft-Hartley Act that were strongly opposed by the steel industry.[62] In a letter accompanying one such contribution, Blough complained to Miller that the Council's recent assessment of labor relations in his industry had been "less than objective and constructive." Nevertheless, Blough acknowledged that "the Council does a useful job," and "for that reason" he would continue to support it. A more plausible explanation was that Blough simply feared the consequences of severing relations with a respected religious organization whose ethical pronouncements regularly garnered front-page coverage in major newspapers.[63]

Beginning in the late 1960s, three developments conspired to unravel the Council's seemingly robust connections to the corporate world. First, the core group of executives that had guided the NCC's financial program from its inception began to retire or succumb to ill health. Charles Hook, the longtime chair of the finance committee, died in 1963.[64] Hook's successor, the lawyer Charles Parlin, was already sixty-five at the time of his appointment. The NCC's associate treasurer, a Kraft Foods executive named John Platt, retired from church activities the same year.[65] By 1965 nearly all of the executives who were most active in

Council fundraising activities during the 1950s had reached retirement age, and most would be dead by the mid-1970s.[66]

Of course, the fading of the founding generation would have been of little consequence had it been followed by the rise of a new crop of like-minded executives. But this was not to be. To the contrary, the late 1960s and early 1970s witnessed the emergence of a new generation of corporate leaders who were less willing than their predecessors to accept ethical guidance from religious groups like the NCC, or even from center-left secular organizations like the Committee for Economic Development. Joseph Coors, the CEO of Coors Brewing, offers a somewhat extreme example of the general trend. A CED trustee, Coors angrily resigned from the organization in 1972 after publicly denouncing its support for "the one-world philosophy which I abhor and which would destroy the United States of America."[67] From this point forward the beer magnate lavished funds on upstart "New Right" organizations, such as the Heritage Foundation and the Committee for the Survival of a Free Congress, that characterized virtually all forms of government intervention in the economy as communist inspired. Coors's agent in Washington, a former television news director and part-time congressional staffer named Paul Weyrich, displayed a rare talent for wrangling donations from the types of corporate executives who in an earlier era might have been expected to lend support to the NCC's economic program. His appeal was straightforward: business leaders who supported "anti–free enterprise candidates in the vain hope that this will make them less hostile to business" were "simply bankrolling their own destruction."[68] Instead of worrying about public perception, businessmen should demand that their trade organizations wage open war on taxes and regulations; they should be more like the labor unions, civil rights organizations, and environmental groups—interest groups that looked out for number one, and let the chips fall where they may.[69]

To be sure, Joseph Coors's abrupt decision to sever all connections to the moderate, establishment types in the CED was somewhat atypical. But by the mid-1970s many less ideologically driven executives had come to agree with Coors and Weyrich regarding the potential benefits of adopting a more self-interested approach to issue advocacy. By this point dozens of prominent CEOs and large corporations were quietly steering funds to trade groups (such as the Business Roundtable and the U.S. Chamber of Commerce) and think tanks (for instance, the American Enterprise Institute and the Cato Institute) that focused on eliminating taxes and regulations, as opposed to deliberating with other economic actors about policies that might be expected to advance the common good.[70] By way of justification, the conservative advocacy groups claimed that debate on economic issues had for too long been dominated by center-left entities like the CED, the Ford Foundation, and the Brookings Institution, and that an infusion of fresh ideas would only invigorate public discourse. "To break up this monopoly," the American Enterprise Institute's (AEI) William Baroody explained, would require "a calculated, positive, major commitment—one which will insure that the views of other competent intellectuals are given the opportunity to contend effectively in the mainstream of our country's intellectual activity. . . . But . . . that can hardly happen without reordering priorities in the support patterns of corporations and foundations—at least by those corporations and foundations concerned with preserving the basic values of this free society and its free institutions."[71] As more and more executives followed the advice of Baroody, Weyrich, and Coors—shifting their donations and energies from the older, establishment foundations to doctrinaire free-market groups such as AEI and the Heritage Foundation—entities like the CED began to wither. By the end of the decade the mainline churches' most important link to the corporate world would be reduced to the role of bit player in the epoch-defining debates over energy, monetary, and tax policy.[72]

A second problem was that the passing of the NCC's founding generation launched the Department of the Church & Economic Life—the vehicle through which corporate leaders had traditionally attempted to influence NCC policy pronouncements—into a budgetary tailspin. Lacking funds to pay its full-time research staff, the DCEL was in the mid-1960s downgraded from a department to a program.[73] Around the same time the NCC stopped paying the expenses of the executives who were expected to travel to New York City three times per year to serve as advisors to its economic program, a step that greatly reduced participation from outside the New York region.[74] By the late 1960s the Council's financial problems were so severe that it could no longer afford a single full-time staffer to oversee its initiatives in the economic realm.[75] Few businessmen, understandably, saw much point in devoting time or money to an organization that was no longer regarded as the authoritative voice of American Protestantism, and that was in any case no longer capable of marshaling the resources necessary to undertake academically rigorous studies of economic problems. By 1969 all that remained of the once-formidable DCEL was an "economic program committee," which rarely met and whose membership featured not a single CEO or president of a major or even mid-sized corporation.[76]

Third, as the DCEL faded into oblivion, the task of applying ethical scrutiny to big business passed to a pair of semiautonomous, NCC-affiliated bodies that regularly adopted an openly antagonistic stance toward the corporate world (often for justifiable reasons). Launched in the early 1970s, both the Corporate Information Center (CIC) and the Interfaith Center for Corporate Responsibility (ICCR) were led by young activists who viewed themselves as foot soldiers in the Ralph Nader–led consumer movement, and who were determined to foment a grassroots rebellion against corporations that degraded the environment, exploited the natural resources of developing countries, or did business with the apartheid regime in South Africa.[77] Although the groups were poorly funded (they would be forced to merge in the mid-1970s), they succeeded in persuading the NCC and several mainline denominations to protest ethically dubious corporate practices by, among other things, restructuring their investment portfolios.[78] But these were minor victories (the amount of stock involved was relatively small), and they came at a steep cost. In the first half of 1972, shortly after the CIC published a trio of reports attacking the corporate behemoths Gulf Oil, Honeywell, and Union Carbide, corporate donations to the Council plummeted by 50 percent. NCC officials concluded that the drop was directly attributable to "corporations refusing to contribute to the National Council of Churches because of their expressed dissatisfaction with the program of the Corporate Information Center here."[79]

An incident from 1980 vividly illustrated how much things had changed since the days when corporate giants like U.S. Steel meekly submitted to the "prophetic" judgments of church officials. That summer, in an effort to repair the Council's badly damaged links to corporate America, NCC President M. William Howard, Jr., asked the seventy-one-year-old J. Irwin Miller to lead a series of dinner meetings to be attended by prominent CEOs and the heads of the mainline churches. Miller, who was now retired from Cummins Engine but still active in church and foundation activities, readily agreed to host the group at the Century Club. Between them, the two men wrote to around thirty executives, inviting them to participate in a "frank" discussion with the aim of "understand[ing] what the world, its problems, and its needs looks like to the other fellow," and, if possible, "find[ing] areas for constructive and beneficial cooperation." Possible discussion topics would include "South Africa and its official policy of apartheid," the "continuing high unemployment rate of inner city youth," and the problem of "world hunger" in an age of "food surpluses."[80]

Within a few weeks, executives from four companies—AT&T, Monsanto, Pfizer, and Koppers (a Pittsburgh-based chemical company)—had accepted the invitation. But these were the exceptions. Executives from Ford, General Motors, DuPont, Corning Glass, Ralston Purina, Aetna, J. C. Penney, and several other companies formally declined to participate; their counterparts at John Deere, Levi-Strauss, Gulf Oil, Caterpillar, Citibank, First National Bank of Boston, and GTE did not even bother to respond. Only by including executives from Cummins Engine and Chemical Bank (where Miller served on the board) were Miller and Howard able to bring the total number of businessmen up to half a dozen.[81]

Miller prepared for the dinner meeting by filling a series of notecards with relevant Bible verses and excerpts from past NCC pronouncements on economic issues, no doubt hoping to rekindle the ideals that had motivated the Council's corporate backers during the 1950s and 1960s. The unifying theme of his presentation was that American business leaders were increasingly shirking their responsibilities toward workers, the environment, and developing nations. One card declared that "in the past few years . . . our collective stewardship of the planet has been wasteful and destructive and our transactions in the marketplace are often of the kind the prophet denounced." This was followed by a quotation from the book of Amos that read in part:

> . . . that we may buy the poor for silver
> And the needy for a pair of sandals,
> And sell the refuse of the Wheat.[82]

Miller seems not to have realized that the language of stewardship, which had been second nature to so many postwar executives, had by 1980 all but vanished from the corporate vocabulary. Or perhaps he did realize it but—like the prophet—refused to make even token concessions to the self-centered spirit of the age.

Not surprisingly, the ensuing discussions were cordial but yielded little in the way of tangible results, likely because the executives in attendance were well aware of two facts: first, that evangelicals, not mainline Protestants, were now the dominant force in American Protestantism; and, second, that a longtime critic of the Protestant stewardship tradition now resided at 1600 Pennsylvania Avenue.

10

Why the Prophetic Torch Wasn't Passed

I am persuaded [that] evangelical[ism] . . . disadvantageously walks
on crutches if it does not, along with the banner of grace, carry the
flag also of truth, and of righteousness or justice, in the name of the
Living God of revelation.
—Carl F. H. Henry to Harold Lindsell (1972)

The late 1960s and early 1970s witnessed a flurry of popular commentary on the
resurgence of American evangelicalism. With the benefit of hindsight, it appears
that the reported explosion of evangelical religiosity was somewhat exaggerated.[1]
But at a time when most mainline Protestant churches were shrinking, the fact
that many conservative Protestant denominations were holding steady relative
to population growth was certainly newsworthy. And, indeed, at least a few of
these denominations—the Southern Baptists, the Missouri Synod Lutherans, the
Churches of Christ, the Assemblies of God—were actually growing at a healthy
clip. This last realization led *Time* magazine to declare in 1969 that a "hidden
majority" of evangelical churchgoers were the "new pacesetters" of American
Protestantism. Between them, the article noted, the four fastest-growing conservative churches boasted almost half as many members (nineteen million) as the
thirty or so denominations that comprised the National Council of Churches.
Add to this the eight million Protestants who belonged to smaller conservative
denominations or independent churches, and also the thirteen million or so
mainline church members who were believed to harbor conservative theological convictions, and it becomes clear that "a significant majority" of America's
sixty-seven million Protestants now held "a distinctively traditional view of
Christianity."[2]

But what did the rise of theologically conservative Protestantism portend for
American politics? Perhaps surprisingly, nothing in the *Time* article indicated
that the evangelical resurgence was likely to bolster the fortunes of political
conservatives. In fact, the event that occasioned the essay, the Billy Graham–
sponsored U.S. Congress on Evangelicalism, suggested precisely the opposite.
Over the course of six days in a Minneapolis convention center, 4,600 representatives of theologically conservative churches had listened sympathetically as
speaker after speaker made the case for a biblically grounded program of social

reform. The African American evangelist Tom Skinner had urged audience members to "go to the cross in repentance" for their inaction on civil rights. The civil rights leader Ralph Abernathy had explained that social problems such as "war, racism and poverty" were interconnected, and that combating them was very much the business of the church. Oregon Senator Mark Hatfield, a fierce critic of the war in Vietnam, had declared that true evangelicalism entailed "orienting one's life to the purpose of His peace."[3] All of these speakers—and many others who offered similar unvarnished accountings of the nation's moral failings—received enthusiastic ovations. Perhaps for this reason, Skinner informed reporters that the gathering had witnessed the birth of "a new [evangelical] model of Christian piety," one that would focus less on minor vices such as the wearing of miniskirts and more on the question of "whether you are available to your fellow man." The *New York Times*'s religion reporter echoed this assessment, declaring the Congress indicative of "a new liberal mood among fundamentalist Protestants."[4]

The 1969 U.S. Congress on Evangelicalism serves as a reminder that the marriage of theological conservatism and political conservatism was not foreordained. As late as the mid-1970s, most evangelicals defined themselves in opposition not to political liberalism, but rather to the theological liberalism, hierarchical organizational forms, and general snobbishness that they considered the hallmarks of the Protestant mainline. Although evangelical groups such as the National Association of Evangelicals and publications such as *Christianity Today* had long complained about the "social action" agendas of the mainline churches, the movement's leading thinkers had always insisted that the disagreement concerned means rather than ends. Racism, poverty, and war were indeed problems that ought to trouble Christians, they acknowledged. But these and other social ills were too complex, and too rooted in spiritual blindness, to admit of straightforward political solutions. For this reason, dragging "the church" into politics was often counterproductive: it exposed clergymen to all the temptations of worldly power, alienated potential converts who found themselves politically at odds with church leaders, and generally undercut the church's primary mission of saving the lost. The point was not that Christians should withdraw from politics; it was that they should seek the guidance of the Holy Spirit—not denominational bureaucrats—when considering the proper response to social problems.

In 1976 this strand of socially conscious, politically moderate evangelicalism was widely credited with powering Jimmy Carter's successful bid for the presidency. A devout Southern Baptist who—somewhat incongruously—professed a deep appreciation for the writings of Reinhold Niebuhr, Carter insisted that Christian principles required believers to concern themselves with social injustice, whether it be in the form of "racial discrimination, . . . injustice in tax programs, . . . [or] injustice in our criminal justice system."[5] At the time such views seemed well within the evangelical mainstream. But by the early 1980s Carter's brand of evangelicalism—like the pronouncements of Billy Graham's 1969 Congress—would be reduced to a historical footnote. Thanks to the efforts of Jerry Falwell's Moral Majority and other so-called Religious Right groups, most of which took shape in the waning months of Carter's presidency, the evangelical label became synonymous with a political perspective whose social vision was primarily concerned with combating abortion and sexual immorality. Subjects like poverty, militarism, and environmental degradation gradually disappeared from the agendas of prominent evangelical organizations and thinkers—and from the political calculations of rank-and-file churchgoers. Once an ideologically diverse faith tradition, evangelicalism became monolithically conservative.

How did this happen? Conventional wisdom holds that evangelicalism's political valence was transformed by the sexual revolution, and by the political parties' respective reactions to it. If many evangelicals in the late 1960s and early 1970s embraced *both* moral traditionalism and social justice concerns, it was because the Republican and Democratic parties had yet to stake out clear positions on issues such as abortion and homosexuality. During Carter's single term in office, however, the parties began to embrace starkly different philosophies on moral issues, with the Republicans endorsing "traditional" values and the Democrats advocating greater personal autonomy in the moral realm. In consequence, evangelicals were forced to choose between moral traditionalism and social justice. Most opted for the former, aligning themselves with the Republicans and embracing that party's positions, not only on moral issues but even on subjects seemingly far removed from personal morality, such as welfare, deregulation, and taxes. In so doing, they cemented an alliance that would shape the course of American politics for decades to come.

This familiar story is largely true—but only when it is used to describe the behavior of a relatively small cohort of elite activists. When applied to the millions of Americans who were filling evangelical churches, its claims are less persuasive. In fact, there is much evidence to suggest that racial animus and economic anxieties played a larger role than so-called moral issues in driving white evangelicals to become conservative Republicans. The distinction is important because it speaks to the power—or, rather, the weakness—of religious ideas and institutions in modern American politics and society. If specifically religious concerns pushed white evangelicals to the political Right, then what I have framed as a story of declining religious authority is perhaps more properly conceived as a "changing of the guard," with the years around 1980 marking the point at which conservative evangelical churches and leaders began to fill the political space previously occupied by their mainline Protestant adversaries.

Religious ideas and institutions, it may be said, still retain their hold over a sizable part of the citizenry; it's just that today's religious voters prefer conservative policies to liberal ones, and Republicans to Democrats. On the other hand, if white evangelicals drifted to the political Right for essentially secular reasons—and often in the face of counterpressures from prominent evangelical leaders and institutions—then we have further confirmation of religion's limited ability to shape political behavior in an age of religious autonomy. In that case it is the weakness of evangelical institutions, not their strength, that best explains why the term "conservative evangelical" has come to seem redundant.

Beyond Miniskirts: The Short-Lived Era of Evangelical Social Concern

The era of evangelical social concern was brief but real, and it touched every facet of the evangelical movement—from the intellectual circles of the seminaries and theological periodicals to ecumenical bodies such as the National Association of Evangelicals to the evangelical prayer groups and Bible studies that were proliferating in the nation's capital. Perhaps no single figure better illustrates the comparatively liberal spirit of the age than Carl Henry, the influential theologian and former *Christianity Today* editor, who, after his departure from the magazine business, divided his time between theological writing, lecturing, and penning intentionally provocative essays for the religious press. Since the late 1940s Henry had vehemently disputed claims that evangelicalism lacked a meaningful conception of social ethics, or that its social vision was simply the sum total of white middle-class fears and resentments. To the contrary, Henry insisted that refocusing believers' attention on the Bible and the individual's personal relationship with Christ—subjects allegedly neglected by the mainline churches—would necessarily usher in an era of deep and sincere deliberation concerning what he called "intractable pockets of social injustice" in American society.[6] Now that the evangelical churches had finally surpassed their mainline rivals in size and cultural influence, he was keen to see this prophecy fulfilled.[7]

And yet, by the early 1970s Henry was beginning to worry that prominent evangelicals such as Billy Graham and Bill Bright would squander the evangelical movement's newfound cultural clout either by ignoring social problems of a nonsexual nature or else by embracing the shortsighted and self-serving solutions put forward by politicians such as Graham's close friend Richard Nixon. In 1972, when Bright organized (and Graham addressed) a massive youth gathering known as "Explo' '72," Henry was initially enthusiastic about the event, believing that the organizers would use the opportunity to alert young evangelicals to the myriad social injustices in their midst.[8] But after examining a preliminary program and discovering little more than a bland admixture of patriotic and evangelistic appeals—and nothing whatsoever concerning the "social righteousness which God demands"—Henry backed out of the event.[9] As he wrote in a letter explaining his decision, the time had come for evangelicals, if they hoped to develop "a legitimate biblical non-socialist definition of justice, ... [to] flesh it out not with clichés but with substantive content."[10] Evangelicalism, he warned, would "walk on crutches if it does not, along with the banner of grace, carry the flag also of truth, and of righteousness or justice, in the name of the Living God of revelation."[11]

The list of social ills to which Henry hoped to apply biblical principles of truth and justice was long: it included not only familiar "family values" issues such as abortion, divorce, and pornography, but also race relations and "big business disregard of automobile safety, cigarette advertising, [and] ecological pollution."[12] To be sure, the theologically conservative Henry remained suspicious—and at times overtly critical—of the evangelical movement's left fringe, represented by figures like Jim Wallis and Ron Sider. With roots in the late 1960s student protest movements, Wallis and Sider advanced class-based conceptions of social justice that struck Henry as both unbiblical and dangerously close to Marxism.[13] And yet, as late as 1973 he joined them and other self-described Young Evangelicals in drafting and signing the Chicago Declaration of Evangelical Social Concern, a document urging rank-and-file believers to tackle social problems ranging from entrenched poverty to the unequal treatment of women in church and society (while largely dodging the question of government's role in advancing these aims).[14]

Henry was far from the only mainstream evangelical who found a good deal of merit in the causes, if not necessarily the candidates, of the political Left. Francis Schaeffer, the era's leading popularizer of evangelical theological ideas, likewise insisted that evangelicals could not in good conscience ignore issues like poverty and environmental degradation. In *Pollution and the Death of Man* (1970), Schaeffer lamented that the modern secular worldview had deprived "Western man" of his sense of "awe" and "wonder," leading him to view the natural world not as a divinely created order, but as a domain to be exploited for material gain and short-term pleasure. Evangelicalism, in contrast, promised to liberate believers from a "plastic culture" and "the mechanistic worldview [of] university textbooks," ultimately restoring a sense of divine obligation to preserve God's creation for the use of future generations.[15] Three years later Schaeffer sent his publisher a manuscript on economics advocating what he called "compassionate capitalism." While unsparing in his attacks on Marxism, Schaeffer found no shortage of flaws in the American economic order, beginning with its failure to honor the biblical injunction to "care for the poor and the stranger." Citing Old Testament passages concerning usury, timely payment of wages, and the treatment of debtors, he heaped scorn on the theory that "Christianity is for capitalism," full stop. In fact, the Bible was replete with commands concerning "economic justice," and to subordinate these to the single-minded pursuit of profit was to succumb to a kind of materialism that was incompatible with the law of the scriptures.[16]

Perhaps surprisingly, such perspectives made their way into the evangelical movement's flagship periodical, *Christianity Today*, with some regularity. Although Harold Lindsell, who replaced Henry as editor in 1967, was certainly no liberal (either in theology or politics), neither was he at this point a doctrinaire conservative. Over the opposition of the magazine's staunchly conservative financial backers, he permitted positive coverage of left-leaning evangelical activists' pronouncements against the Vietnam War and food shortages in the developing world, and in favor of the Nixon administration's short-lived push for a universal basic income.[17] And in 1971, following the publication of Schaeffer's *Pollution and the Death of Man*, he devoted an entire issue to fleshing out a biblical case for immediate action to combat manmade threats to the environment. Rejecting the view, which he attributed to the Jesus movement, that evangelicals should devote the entirety of their energies to winning souls, Lindsell argued that believers were both duty bound to prevent the destruction of God's creation and uniquely suited to combating the materialistic assumptions that had launched the human race on a suicidal quest for "an ever higher standard of living."[18]

As these remarks make clear, the major evangelical writers on social ethics were at this point united by their shared alarm at the rampant materialism that they saw as the defining feature of post-1960s American culture. Like "secular humanism," "materialism" was a catchall term that could be applied to virtually any theory, program, or lifestyle that did not proceed from biblical presuppositions. At least initially, however, the label was an equal-opportunity pejorative that was useful in highlighting the spiritual blind spots of both liberals and conservatives. If writers like Henry and Schaeffer believed that liberalism's great sin was its belief that government could—and should—cure social ills while ignoring the needs of the soul, they also faulted conservatives for their inability to perceive the ways in their major objectives, including the pursuit of military power and the promotion of ever greater corporate profits, tended to undercut Americans' spiritual well-being.

The evangelical social vision thus cut across the period's major ideological divide; and, at least for a few years in the early 1970s, the same could be said of the movement's most important institutions. Within the National Association of Evangelicals, left-leaning believers housed in the Evangelical Social Action Committee (ESAC) churned out a steady stream of proclamations against militarism, environmental degradation, and world hunger, several of which were endorsed by the parent organization.[19] The Southern Baptist Convention's

Christian Life Commission (CLC) likewise insisted on placing problems such as war and poverty on a par with more traditional moral concerns, such as drinking and divorce. As Foy Valentine, the CLC's chairman, explained in 1971, the "Jehovah God . . . portrayed by the prophets" would be as, if not more, alarmed by the nation's unsavory "military alliances, racial segregation, [and] the unconscionable profits of the [pharmaceutical] industry" than by the more familiar evils of illegal drug use and "family fragmentation."[20]

Such proclamations did not disappear into a vacuum. Rather, they garnered a sympathetic hearing from dozens of moderate and left-leaning evangelicals serving in Congress—lawmakers such as John B. Anderson, a lay leader in the NAE-affiliated Evangelical Free Church, who occupied the number three spot in the House Republican leadership for most of the 1970s. A Goldwater supporter in 1964, Anderson's politics drifted leftward after he became convinced of the need for federal action to dismantle the nation's racial caste system. By 1969, when he joined the Republican leadership, he was perhaps best known for his support of federal open housing laws. In the years that followed he earned a reputation for fiscal conservatism (based in part on his opposition to what he regarded as wasteful defense projects), but he also adopted moderate-to-liberal stances on social issues such as the Equal Rights Amendment (ERA) and abortion.[21] His social liberalism notwithstanding, Anderson was a fixture at NAE events: he was named the group's Layman of the Year shortly after he joined the House, and in 1975 he keynoted the group's annual convention.[22]

If Anderson was the most prominent evangelical in the House, his counterpart in the Senate was Mark Hatfield (R-OR), another Rockefeller Republican who combined fiscal moderation with center-left stances on foreign policy and social issues. A devout Baptist, Hatfield was an early and eloquent opponent of the Vietnam War, a champion of environmental regulation, and a staunch supporter of the Equal Rights Amendment (though not of abortion rights). Such left-of-center views frequently caused tensions with Hatfield's fellow Republicans—his anti-Goldwater address to the 1964 GOP convention was interrupted by a bomb threat but did not seriously diminish his standing in the evangelical community. Though the early 1970s he sat on the boards of Campus Crusade for Christ and several other evangelical institutions, and he maintained friendships with a long list of evangelical leaders, including Billy Graham and Carl Henry.[23] The Oregon senator was particularly popular with younger evangelicals. In 1970, when he delivered the commencement address at Fuller Seminary, many of the graduates donned black armbands in support of the senator's antiwar stance.[24] Four years later, when Wheaton College administrators, fearing a backlash from conservative donors, discouraged Hatfield from visiting campus, he showed up anyway. School officials responded by scheduling a mandatory chapel service at the same time as his appearance, a ham-fisted attempt at censorship that most

students simply ignored. A headline in the student newspaper summed up the
student body's reaction to the Hatfield's address: "He Came; He Spoke; and We
Were Conquered."[25]

Hatfield and Anderson were, however, only the most celebrated representatives of a much larger cohort of center-left evangelicals in Congress. In fact, an
exhaustive 1974 profile of Congress's evangelicals compiled by journalists affiliated with *Christianity Today* concluded that doctrinaire proponents of "rugged
individualism" such as Jesse Helms (R-NC) and John Conlan (R-AZ) were now
outnumbered by evangelical politicians whose Christian convictions pointed
in the direction of "compassion . . . [and] reaching out to the helpless."[26] Many
of the Rockefeller Republicans who comprised the latter group were active in a
Capitol Hill prayer cell whose leaders included John Dellenback (R-OR), a bow
tie–wearing evangelical Presbyterian who exhibited a quasi-religious passion for
battling corporate malfeasance and protecting the environment; John Buchanan,
Jr., a moderate Alabama Republican and ordained Southern Baptist clergyman
who strongly supported the ERA and Title IX, and who helped lead the fight to
sanction the apartheid regimes in South Africa and Rhodesia; and Albert Quie,
a moderate Republican and part-time farmer from Minnesota who championed
the Pell Grant program in the House.[27]

Even before Jimmy Carter's surprising 1976 triumph, then, the growing
visibility of center-left evangelicals in Congress, coupled with evangelical
intellectuals' newfound interest in environmental and social justice, led many
commentators to speculate that the evangelical resurgence was having a moderating effect on the American polity—that it was tempering, rather than exacerbating, the social and political divisions of the late 1960s. This was the conclusion
reached, for example, by John B. Anderson in his address to the NAE's 1975 annual convention.[28] And it was also a major theme of countless books and articles documenting the rapid growth of prayer groups and Bible studies on Capitol
Hill.[29]

But there were at least two major flaws in this line of reasoning. The first was
the assumption that evangelicals constituted a relatively cohesive voting bloc
whose members took their political cues from elites such as Henry, Anderson,
and Hatfield. In reality, white evangelicals, far from coalescing under the banner
of a single, politically moderate program, were deeply divided by geography.
While the political convictions of Northern white evangelicals typically fell
somewhere in the middle of the ideological spectrum, Southern evangelicals
were overwhelmingly conservative, even relative to other white Southerners,
and particularly on the subject of race. If many Southern evangelicals voted for
the proudly "born again" Carter in 1976, careful analysis of the 1972 or 1976
American National Election Studies would have revealed that many of them
did so in spite of what was known about the Georgian's substantive policy views

on issues such as civil rights (about which Carter was, as a candidate, famously cagey).[30]

The second problem with the evangelicalism-as-moderating-force thesis concerned the evangelical movement's institutional foundations, or lack thereof. In short, evangelical leaders, in sharp contrast to mid-century mainline Protestant clergymen, exerted little real authority over their flocks, nor did they possess a well-developed infrastructure for disseminating arguments and information. This was in part by design, since evangelicals had long defined their faith tradition in opposition to what they perceived as the overly hierarchical and bureaucratized structures employed by their mainline rivals. Hence, the Southern Baptist Convention (SBC), the largest of the newly thriving evangelical denominations, disavowed any claim whatsoever to "authority" over individual congregations or believers; and indeed, its organizational structure, which dispersed national-level power across numerous semi-autonomous boards and agencies while leaving state conventions in charge of the purse strings, effectively foreclosed large-scale efforts to shape the political convictions of average churchgoers.[31]

But if evangelicalism's lack of centralized direction sprang in part from principled motives, it also reflected a basic fact of American religious life following the demise of Max Weber's sect spirit—a reality that shaped the nation's burgeoning ranks of nondemonizational "megachurches" as much as its Southern Baptist congregations. In short, in the new age of religious autonomy, when church membership no longer functioned as an important marker of social status, religious leaders who pursued political agendas contrary to the interests or prejudices of their coreligionists were not likely to survive for long. As a result, left-leaning evangelical elites were left highly vulnerable to external influences, whether in the form of shifts in mass opinion or targeted pressure from small bands of ideologically driven political operatives. Those who sought to marry theological conservatism with support for racial reconciliation, ecological concern, and arms reduction were about to discover just how bleak the prospects for "prophetic" leadership had become.

Evangelicals in the Age of Racial Realignment

The era of widespread evangelical social concern did not survive Jimmy Carter's single term in office. By the summer of 1980, many of the same pundits who had credited evangelicals with powering Carter's 1976 run were predicting that the "evangelical vote" would again be a major factor on Election Day—and that it would almost certainly benefit Carter's Republican opponent, Ronald Reagan. Front-page articles with headlines like "Religious Right Marches Into Politics" and "Evangelical Whites Rally to Reagan" proliferated in the press.[32] Newspaper readers learned that right-leaning religious interest groups—the Moral Majority, Christian Voice, the Religious Roundtable—were springing up at an incredible rate, each one seemingly larger and better funded than the last. Dubbed the "Religious Right" by the media, the new groups backed only candidates who pledged to oppose abortion and gay rights, return prayer to the public schools, adopt a hard line against the Soviets, and reduce spending on social welfare programs. After a brief flirtation with former Texas governor John Connally, they threw their support to Reagan, and the Republican nominee returned the favor by showering them with praise. "I want you to know that I endorse you and what you are doing," he told a large gathering of conservative ministers in August.[33] Not surprisingly, when Reagan, as expected, won a convincing victory in November, many analysts concluded that highly motivated evangelical voters had propelled him to victory.[34]

Why did so many evangelicals, in the span of barely four years, turn from the center-left social vision of Jimmy Carter to the rigid conservatism of Ronald Reagan—a candidate whose ideological commitments counseled against serious efforts to address systemic racism, environmental degradation, and the other social problems that had captured the imagination of early 1970s evangelicals? At the time many pundits concluded that Carter had lost the evangelical vote by ignoring the "moral" or "family" issues that had long occupied a prominent place on the evangelical social agenda. In particular, the leaders of such groups as Christian Voice and the Moral Majority faulted Carter for appointing prominent feminists to White House posts; for endorsing the ERA; for not supporting legislation to return prayer to the public schools; and for ignoring the scourge of legalized abortion.[35] Perhaps most of all, they faulted him for not reining in the Internal Revenue Service when it issued new rules demanding that private Christian schools demonstrate good-faith efforts to enroll minority students or else be stripped of their tax-exempt status. (The new rules were hugely unpopular with evangelical and fundamentalist pastors, many of whom operated predominantly white religious schools that were now at risk of going broke.)[36] Implicit in this version of events was the claim that things might have turned out differently if only Carter had paid more attention to the policy concerns of his coreligionists.

There are, however, at least two serious problems with this familiar story. First, there is little evidence that the political behavior of evangelicals during the Carter and Reagan years differed meaningfully from that of other white citizens. In fact, white voters as a group had been trending conservative since the late 1960s (though this fact was obscured by the Watergate-dominated elections of 1974 and 1976), and virtually all subsets of the white electorate—not just evangelicals—moved further toward the GOP during the early 1980s.

Second, it does not appear that "moral" issues such as abortion and school prayer played a particularly important role in the rightward drift of the white electorate. Issues like abortion were undoubtedly important to such conservative evangelical elites as the televangelists Jerry Falwell and Pat Robertson, and also to thousands of rank-and-file activists affiliated with the Moral Majority, the National Right to Life Committee, and like-minded organizations. But evidence that these issues altered the political allegiances of large numbers of average evangelicals—let alone nonevangelicals—is surprisingly hard to come by. Upon close inspection, it seems likely that race-based antipathy toward federal social welfare programs, not outrage at the decline of traditional mores, was the driving factor behind the partisan realignment of the early 1980s.

That white voters were trending conservative on racial issues and federal welfare spending was evident as early as 1969, when a twenty-nine-year-old Republican operative named Kevin Phillips published *The Emerging Republican Majority*, a deeply researched study that situated the 1968 election in the broader sweep of American political history. What most impressed Phillips about the recent presidential contest was not Richard Nixon's narrow victory over Hubert Humphrey, but rather the fact that former Alabama Governor George Wallace, running as an independent, had captured more than 13 percent of the popular vote. That Wallace, a man best known for his pledge to maintain "segregation forever," had not only carried the Deep South but also siphoned crucial votes from Humphrey in the border states and traditionally Democratic areas of the North, suggested to Phillips that the post–New Deal party system was fracturing along racial lines. In the 1930s white voters in the industrial North had flocked to the Democratic party because of its focus on bread-and-butter issues and its promise to rein in the plutocrats whose economic mismanagement had led to the Great Depression. In recent years, however, the party had shifted its attention to the plight of disadvantaged racial minorities, embracing the "Negro socioeconomic revolution" and pouring resources into the "urban ghetto." And this, according to Phillips, had been a disastrous strategic error. Redirecting wealth from millionaires to white farmers and factory workers was one thing; shifting it from middle-class taxpayers to programs that benefited urban blacks—particularly at a time when cities were burning and real wage growth was beginning to stagnate—was something else entirely. The upshot was that the Democrats, by inadvertently triggering a white backlash against their own programs, had handed the Republicans a golden opportunity. So long as Republicans kept issues like civil rights, busing, and welfare at the forefront of the national debate, there was a good chance that disaffected Southern and working-class whites would desert the Democrats for good, cementing the GOP's position as the nation's dominant party for decades to come.[37]

Phillips' prediction proved remarkably prescient—in part because Republican operatives took it as their playbook for the 1970s. Richard Nixon's political team, in particular, trained its sights on wavering white Democrats in the Sunbelt and the blue-collar suburbs of the industrial North.[38] If many of the latter were Catholic "white ethnics," the majority of Sunbelt residents were, as Phillips noted, "solidly Anglo-Saxon and Protestant (often Baptist)."[39] But the important point was that both groups were believed to share the same resentments. Having endured the cultural and political turmoil of the late 1960s, the "silent majority"—as Nixon famously dubbed them—desired nothing so much as a return to a time before elites began lavishing attention on black-power activists, feminists, antiwar protestors, and other malcontents who seemed bent on undermining the tranquility of middle-class suburban life. Nixon's advisor Pat Buchanan, who greatly admired Phillips's work, agreed that the Democratic party was now divided between "the loafing classes (welfare, students) and the working classes," and he devised a number of strategies to widen the fissure. These ranged from fairly anodyne (framing administration initiatives in ways likely to appeal to "the working men and women, white and blue collar") to outright skullduggery (such as secretly pushing busing legislation and covertly promoting controversial African American Democratic candidates).[40]

When Watergate derailed Nixon's plan to effect a racial realignment of the party system, the independent conservative operatives of the so-called New Right took up the cause. Frequent critics of the Nixon and Ford administrations, which they viewed as too accommodating of Republican moderates, New Right operatives such as Paul Weyrich and Richard Viguerie were less interested in cobbling together Electoral College majorities than in building a monolithically conservative Republican party. Yet, no less than Nixon and Buchanan, they believed that the GOP's path to majority status ran through the white working class; and to this end, they made every effort to foment an us-versus-them mindset in the white electorate, often using thinly veiled racial appeals that lacked the subtlety of Nixon's paeans to the silent majority. Viguerie, a direct-mail pioneer who raised funds for Wallace's 1976 presidential bid, believed that citizens who donated time or money to political causes were typically not out "to win friends, but to defeat enemies."[41] Weyrich, the part-time congressional staffer and professional organizer who oversaw the formation of the Committee for the Survival of a Free Congress (CSFC) and several other New Right groups, likewise urged conservative candidates to focus their campaigns on "emotional issues" that resonated with middle-class voters at a very personal level—issues like welfare, busing, crime, and gun control.[42] Politicians who accepted campaign help from Weyrich and the New Right—including Helms, Conlan, Bob Dornan (R-CA), and Larry McDonald (D-GA)—tended to follow this script, warning potential supporters that liberal elites were diverting their hard-earned tax dollars to expensive and wasteful programs that primarily benefited shiftless minorities.[43]

Whether it was the New Right's efforts to stoke racial resentment or (as Phillips suspected) an inexorable process set in motion by the Democratic party's embrace of civil rights (or perhaps some combination of the two), white voters tacked sharply rightward on racial issues over the course of the late 1970s and early 1980s. As late as 1972, as can be seen in Figure 10.1, roughly one-third of Northern whites expressed support for federal programs designed to improve the "social and economic position" of "blacks and other minorities."[44] (Another 42 percent claimed to have no opinion on the issue, and 25 percent expressed opposition.) However, Northern white support for federal civil rights programs fell sharply in the late 1970s, then rebounded slightly in the mid-1980s, only to plunge to less than 10 percent (for evangelicals) and 15 percent (for nonevangelicals) by the mid-1990s. And as Figure 10.2 makes clear, the shift was not limited to members of a single religious tradition. Over the time frame depicted in the figure, support for federal civil rights programs decreased by roughly the same amount among evangelicals, Catholics, and even nonbelievers. (White mainline Protestants also became more conservative on racial issues, though the shift was less pronounced than in the case of the other groups.) Only white Southerners, who were already staunchly conservative on race, were unaffected by the general trend.[45]

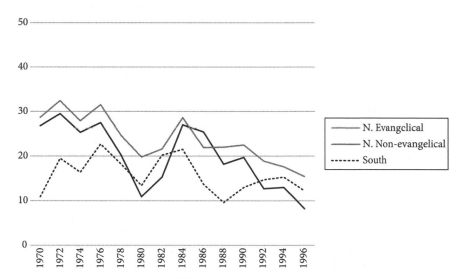

Figure 10.1 White support for federal civil rights initiatives, 1970–1996
Source: ANES Cumulative Data File

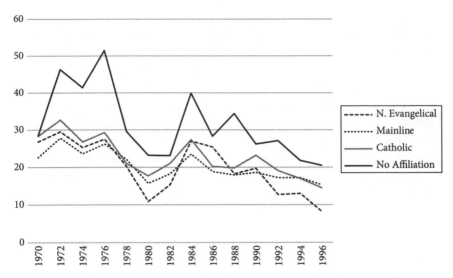

Figure 10.2 White support for federal civil rights initiatives by religious tradition, 1970–1996
Source: ANES Cumulative Data File

At the same time that Northern white voters were becoming more conservative on race, both they and Southern whites became more likely to identify as Republicans. Figure 10.3 documents the extent of the Republican gains, as measured by ANES respondents' self-reported party identification. At the beginning of the 1970s, Catholics and white Southerners—two pillars of the New Deal coalition—were far more likely to identify as Democrats than Republicans. By the end of Reagan's two terms in office, however, the Democratic party's forty-point identification advantage with Catholics had shrunk to zero, while its advantage with Southern evangelicals had decreased by nearly thirty points. (Although not pictured, the party's advantage with white Southerners as a whole decreased by a similar amount.) Republicans also made significant gains with Northern white evangelicals, a group that had traditionally been about evenly divided between the two parties. As late as 1978, with Carter still in the White House, Northern evangelicals were slightly more likely to identify as Democrats than Republicans; but by 1988 the Republicans' identification advantage with this group had swelled to more than thirty points. Finally, lest one suppose that secularizing trends in the wider society were the major forces pushing white voters to the right, it is worth noting that white citizens with no religious affiliation, another traditionally Democratic constituency, also turned away from the party, becoming nearly thirty points more Republican between 1978 and 1988.[46]

Figure 10.3 Democratic party identification advantage by religious tradition, 1972–1988 (whites only)

Source: ANES Cumulative Data File

That the white exodus from the Democratic party occurred simultaneously with an uptick in racial conservatism does not, of course, prove that racial animus was the primary cause of the early-1980s realignment. Other factors, including economic anxieties stemming from a deepening recession, undoubtedly played a role in pushing white voters toward the Republican party. Nor is it necessarily true that the various subsets of the white electorate discussed above all moved toward the GOP for the same reasons. Many contemporary observers, as we have seen, claimed that white evangelicals were uniquely concerned with moral issues such as abortion and school prayer, and that they embraced the Republican party only after it became clear that the Carter administration had thrown in its lot with the women's movement and other alleged foes of traditional morality. White evangelicals acted strategically, on this view, embracing the wider agenda of the newly conservative GOP only because doing so would tend to advance their more fundamental goals of restricting abortion, restoring school prayer, and preventing Internal Revenue Service scrutiny of private religious schools.[47]

The idea that white evangelicals followed a unique path into the modern conservative coalition will not withstand serious scrutiny, however. One reason to doubt such claims is that evangelicals' views concerning abortion and the role of women in society—issues that are often said to have launched the Religious Right—either remained constant or moved slightly to the left during the Carter and Reagan years, even as their views on racial issues shifted sharply rightward. To be sure, evangelicals' views on abortion became more conservative relative to those of other groups within society, as can be seen in Figures 10.4 and 10.5. Yet it does not appear that abortion became significantly more salient for evangelicals as they diverged from other white voters on the issue. When asked to name the most important issues facing the country in the pivotal election year of 1980, less than 1 percent of evangelicals mentioned any of the "moral" issues that are often blamed for Carter's defeat.[48] Nor did large numbers of white evangelicals grow significantly more concerned about abortion as the decade progressed. As late as 1988, only 1.4 percent of them mentioned abortion when asked to name the most important problem facing the country (while another 2.5 percent mentioned a generalized fear of "moral or religious decay").[49]

To further test the relative salience of moral concerns and white-backlash issues, we can ask whether average evangelicals, at the time they began moving toward the GOP, perceived a clear difference between the major parties' stances on abortion and civil rights—and, if so, whether they found the Democratic party's stance more off-putting in one case as opposed to the other. To answer these questions, we can draw on ANES questions asking respondents to situate both themselves and the two parties on a numerical scale describing a range of possible positions on the two issues. On the issue of civil rights, ANES studies prior

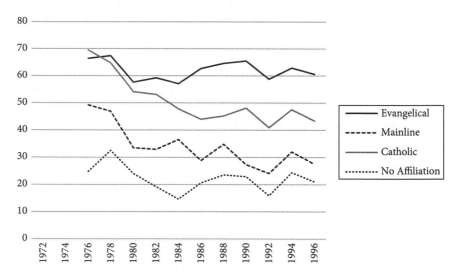

Figure 10.4 Opposition to abortion by religious tradition (whites only)
Source: ANES Cumulative Data File

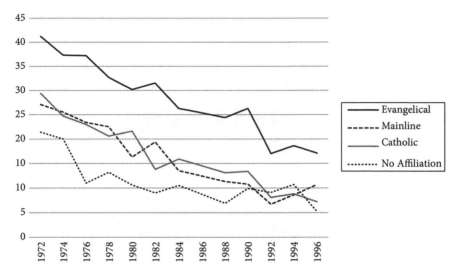

Figure 10.5 Support for traditional gender roles by religious tradition (whites only)
Source: ANES Cumulative Data File

to 1980 found that most voters perceived only moderate differences between the Republican and Democratic positions, likely because both parties harbored a mix of racial liberals and conservatives. By 1980, however, the New Right's laserlike focus on busing, welfare, and crime—all of which featured prominently in the party's 1980 platform—combined with Ronald Reagan's states'-rights rhetoric and campaign-trail references to "welfare queens" had transformed public perception of the GOP position with respect to federal programs benefiting racial minorities. As can be seen in Figure 10.6, white evangelicals (like other white respondents) were by this point well aware that the parties had staked out starkly different positions. On average, evangelicals judged the Republicans 1.72 points more conservative on civil rights than the Democrats on a seven-point scale—an increase of more than 240 percent from the 1976 figure.[50]

Abortion was another cross-cutting issue on which the two parties were slow to adopt strongly distinguished positions. The Republicans did not include anti-abortion language in their platform until 1976, and not until 1980 did the two parties adopt something like their modern positions, with the Republicans endorsing the reversal of *Roe v. Wade* and the Democrats promising to protect access to legalized abortion. Figure 10.6 indicates that at least some evangelicals were aware of these developments, as most reported in 1980 that the Republicans were more conservative on abortion. Significantly, however, the perceived partisan "gap" with respect to abortion—0.38 point on a four-point scale—was much smaller than in the case of civil rights. (For purposes of comparison, the

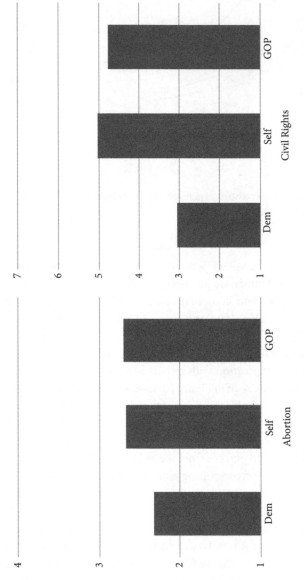

Figure 10.6 Evangelical self-placement and perception of party stances on civil rights and abortion, 1980

Source: ANES 1980 Time Series Study

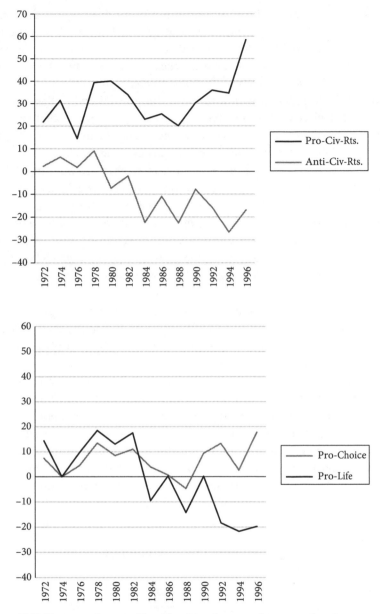

Figure 10.7 Democratic party identification advantage by respondent issue position on civil rights and abortion (whites only)

Source: ANES Cumulative Data File

perceived partisan gap is about 29 percent of the possible range in the case of civil rights, and about 13 percent in the case of abortion.) But it isn't just that evangelicals believed the parties to be further apart on civil rights than on abortion; Figure 10.6 also indicates that evangelicals were on average far more dissatisfied with the Democratic party's stance on civil rights. On both issues, the average evangelical placed herself closer to the Republicans, but the gap between the self-placement of the average respondent and her perception of the Democratic party's stance was about three times as large in the case of civil rights.

Figure 10.7 presents a final piece of evidence suggesting that "moral" concerns played at best a supporting role in the white electorate's rightward drift. In short, it shows that a partisan cleavage emerged with respect to racial issues years before a similar cleavage emerged with respect to abortion. As early as 1972 the Democrats' party identification advantage among white voters who supported federal civil rights initiatives, relative to those who opposed them, was twenty percentage points. By the late 1980s, the party-identification gap with respect to civil rights views had widened to forty points, and by the mid-1990s it would grow to more than seventy points.

Now note the very different situation with respect to abortion. As late as 1982 pro-life voters were, on average, slightly *more Democratic* than their pro-choice adversaries. And while antiabortion voters did shift sharply toward the Republicans in 1984, the two groups would remain roughly similar in terms of party identification through the rest of the decade. Not until the early 1990s do we see the emergence of a durable partisan cleavage on the issue of abortion. Hence, it seems highly unlikely that large numbers of white voters spent the Carter and Reagan years strategically adjusting their positions on racial and economic issues in deference to the GOP's hardline stance against abortion. More likely, the opposite occurred: many white voters, including white evangelicals, became pro-life only *after* some combination of racial animus and economic anxiety drew them into the GOP fold.[51]

Baptizing the White Backlash

For all the scholarly and media attention lavished on Religious Right groups like the Moral Majority, the evidence presented above suggests that their role in facilitating white evangelicals' rightward ideological drift was modest at best. A number of recent political science studies have reached similar conclusions. Ryan Claassen reports that contemporary claims of a vast "mobilization" of previously disengaged evangelical voters were largely unfounded.[52] Michele Margolis has marshaled an impressive array of evidence to show that the flourishing of conservative evangelical churches in the late 1970s and early 1980s is better understood as an effect, rather than a cause, of white voters' growing political conservatism.[53] Perhaps the simplest way of illustrating the general thrust of these studies is simply to point out that, across a host of issues, the evolution of white evangelical opinion tracked almost perfectly the broader drift of white non-college opinion, as can be seen in Figure 10.8. (As late as 1994 the average white evangelical had no formal education beyond high school, making evangelicals the least educated of major white religious groups.)[54] Far from marching into politics under the command of celebrity preachers—as so many contemporaneous accounts had it—evangelicals overwhelmingly behaved like other working-class whites, their political behavior shaped as much by race and class as by specifically religious motivations.[55]

The Religious Right's great achievement, then, was not the defeat of Jimmy Carter; nor was it elevating issues such as abortion and gay rights to a central place in the nation's public discourse. Rather, it was providing cross-pressured voters with a religious rationale to justify their growing antipathy toward the egalitarian domestic agenda that had long enjoyed the enthusiastic support of the nation's mainline Protestant churches, as well as the tacit support of many prominent evangelical thinkers and institutions. And indeed, there is ample evidence that Weyrich, Viguerie, and the other political strategists who helped launch the Moral Majority began lavishing attention on conservative Protestant clergymen for precisely this reason: they worried that center-left evangelicals like John B. Anderson and Mark Hatfield, who gave social justice concerns equal billing with personal morality, were muddying the New Right's message that middle- and working-class whites were the real victims of systemic inequality. Weyrich, in particular, sensed that if the public meaning of Christianity were reduced to a set of litmus tests on issues like abortion and school prayer, and if social welfare programs were reconceived as attacks on the nuclear family, then Hatfied, Anderson, and like-minded evangelicals could no longer credibly present themselves as Christian public servants; on the contrary, they would now appear as lackeys of the secular left.[56]

To ensure that average churchgoers got the message, the major Religious Right groups, working in tandem with Weyrich and other New Right strategists, created voter guides that melded "pro-family" and white backlash appeals into a seamless whole.[57] Candidates who hoped to win the backing of groups like Christian Voice, the Moral Majority, and the Religious Roundtable were required not only to declare their opposition to abortion and gay rights, but also to oppose busing, welfare, arms reduction negotiations, the creation of the Department of Education, and efforts to sanction the apartheid regimes in Southern Africa.[58] Predictably, this formula often tarred centrist lawmakers as enemies of the faith while simultaneously elevating far-right candidates with dubious religious credentials to the status of Christian statesmen. The Maryland Congressman

(a)

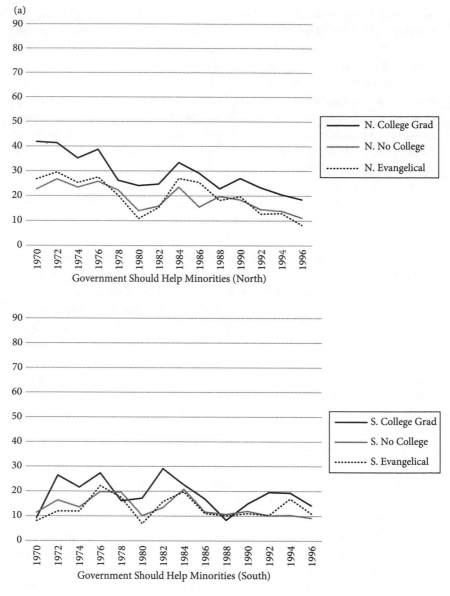

Figure 10.8 Evangelical opinion tracks non-college-educated white opinion on multiple issues

Source: ANES Cumulative Data File

(b)

Figure 10.8 Continued

and longtime New Right operative Robert Bauman received a 94 rating from Christian Voice shortly after his arrest for soliciting an underage male prostitute; and the same group awarded Barry Goldwater, whose commitment to the pro-life cause was far from ironclad, a perfect score of 100.[59] Such discoveries provided fodder for countless op-eds denouncing Falwell and other Religious Right leaders as shills for big business, or else for the conservative wing of the Republican party. But in the context of the white-backlash politics of the late 1970s and early 1980s, the claim that Christian principles mandated support for candidates who opposed busing, welfare, and détente made perfect sense. Many believers longed for a religious perspective that would reconcile their racial and economic anxieties with their sense of themselves as compassionate, God-fearing church members, and the Religious Right, with its dark warnings about "hardcore socialists" who were working in tandem with "the women's liberation movement" to "break down the traditional family," provided exactly that.[60]

In 1978 a New Right–backed primary challenge to John B. Anderson made clear that, with the proper messaging, evangelicals could be convinced to turn on their own. Weyirch, who masterminded the effort, had nursed an intense dislike of the Illinois Republican since 1976, when the two had tangled at that year's Republican convention. Like other conservative Reagan supporters, Weyrich had arrived in Kansas City determined to use what leverage he possessed to shift the GOP platform rightward, thus drawing a sharp contrast to what his ally Jesse Helms called the "Democratic welfare-state platform."[61] In the end the New Right forces, working closely with socially conservative delegates led by the Catholic activist Phyllis Schlafly, won a number of important victories, including planks critical of gun control, welfare, abortion, and the Ford Administration's policy of détente toward the Soviets. But not all of their demands were met, and Anderson, who was a Ford delegate, was a major reason why. From his perch on the platform committee, the chair of the House Republican Conference made every effort to block the New Right's pet proposals, including two that were of particular interest to Weyrich.[62] The first, introduced by Weyrich's benefactor, Jospeh Coors, would have excised platform language supporting child-care assistance for working parents. Anderson was happy to compromise on the form such assistance should take—whether tax credits or direct federal funding—but he vehemently rejected the idea that federal action on child care was inherently pernicious. "Working mothers need some day care aid," he reasoned.[63] In addition, Anderson was largely responsible for torpedoing a New Right–backed amendment that would have committed the party to zeroing out federal funding for education.[64]

For his troubles, Anderson was awarded the top spot on the New Right's mid-term hit list.[65] Although the idea of attempting to unseat a member of the House GOP leadership generated opposition from a number of New Right–aligned

House members, Weyrich pressed ahead with his plan, and by early 1978 a long list of New Right groups were actively aiding Don Lyon, the forty-six-year-old televangelist and Christian school administrator who was challenging Anderson in the Republican primary.[66] Aided by Viguerie's direct mail apparatus, Lyon soon outraised his better-known opponent.[67] More to the point, he did everything in his power to paint Anderson as a tool of godless secular humanism. Likely acting on the advice of his New Right advisors, Lyon zeroed in on one vote in particular: in the summer of 1977 Anderson had voted against a poison-pill amendment, introduced by the New Right stalwart (and proud John Birch Society member) Larry McDonald (D-GA), that would have prohibited the federally funded Legal Assistance Corporation from providing legal aid to homosexuals. As Anderson later explained, he had voted against the amendment "because I thought it was a cheap shot—the kind of thing a politician offers and then charges off to the mimeograph machine to tell the world what a hero he is for saving public morals."[68] Cheap shot or not, the vote became a staple of both Viguerie's mailings and Lyon's stump speech, as did Anderson's past votes in support of the Equal Rights Amendment—a measure that, as Lyon informed his audiences, was not designed to secure "equal rights for women," but rather to "help the lesbian, the homosexual."[69] After months of such attacks, even long-time Anderson supporters began to admit that they now harbored doubts about whether their congressman still stood for "Midwest thinking."[70]

The seventeen-year House veteran ultimately survived Lyon's challenge, though most analysts concluded that he owed his narrow victory to a significant Democratic crossover vote (something Anderson had encouraged by sending mailings to registered Democrats in the weeks before the primary).[71] But 1978 would be Anderson's last race for Congress. In 1980, when his name again appeared atop the New Right's list of potential targets, he resigned his congressional seat to pursue a long-shot bid for the presidency—a quixotic campaign designed in part to draw attention to what he regarded as the un-Christian agenda of conservative preachers such as Jerry Falwell, who had by this point endorsed the full panoply of New Right causes. Hoping to attract press coverage for his flagging presidential campaign, Anderson took his message directly to hostile audiences, warning a National Religious Broadcasters convention that "the political marriage of the Moral Majority and the New Right" threatened to "inject unbending rigidity and intolerance into church pew and polling booth alike."[72] Religious Right groups returned the favor, awarding Anderson failing grades in their 1980 campaign materials.[73] In the end, the former NAE Evangelical of the Year captured less than 7 percent of the popular vote, and perhaps 5 percent of the white evangelical vote.[74]

Other center-left evangelicals did not survive even their initial encounters with the Religious Right. One such casualty was John Buchanan, a moderate

Alabama Republican and ordained Southern Baptist clergyman who appeared on Weyrich's target list in 1980.[75] Like Anderson, Buchanan had won election to Congress in 1964 as a Goldwater Republican but moved almost immediately to the left. He integrated his congressional staff, helped lead a congressional investigation of the Ku Klux Klan, nominated African Americans to the military service academies (becoming the first member of the Alabama delegation to do so), and focused attention on human rights abuses in South Africa and Rhodesia.[76] By the early 1970s he was widely viewed as a progressive on racial and gender issues, though his efforts to trim federal spending continued to earn him at least middling grades from conservative interest groups.[77] Like his fellow Baptist Jimmy Carter, Buchanan was a New South politician who hoped to bury the racially charged politics of his region's past, and as late as 1978 it appeared that most of his constituents shared this sentiment. Indeed, the Republican regularly won reelection by wide margins, often facing only token Democratic opposition in the general election.[78]

This changed in 1980, when the New Right groups joined forces with the Moral Majority to support Buchanan's primary challenger, a Birmingham insurance agent and John Birch Society member named Albert Lee Smith.[79] In what promised to be a low-turnout election, the conservative insurgents trained their fire at Buchanan's allegedly liberal voting record on school prayer.[80] In reality Buchanan was anything but a diehard church-state separationist; while in Congress he had authored a proposed constitutional amendment loosening some court-imposed restrictions on school prayer, and he had even signed his name to a discharge petition that would have forced the full House to vote on a more conservative prayer proposal. Neither move, however, stayed the hand of his opponents. Jerry Falwell, speaking at a Birmingham rally, tarred Buchanan as a school prayer opponent; and the Alabama chapter of the Moral Majority blanketed the district with mailers highlighting the incumbent's alleged support for the Supreme Court's antiprayer rulings, as well as his "soft" stances on busing, defense spending, and welfare. When asked to reconcile the group's campaign messaging with Buchanan's voting record, the executive director of the Alabama Moral Majority demurred, saying that "he looked for a general attitude, not just votes." Buchanan "may have voted for [school prayer] somewhere," he admitted, "but basically he [is] against it."[81] On Election Day Buchanan was defeated by the not particularly close margin of ten points. "I'd say they did a rather thorough job of beating my brains out with Christian love," he said of the Moral Majority in the wake of the loss.[82]

Largely forgotten today, the primary challenges to John B. Anderson and John Buchanan serve as reminders that the secular drift of American liberalism in the 1970s and 1980s was as much the work of conservative activists as liberal ones. Stated otherwise, the rapid disappearance of devout center-left evangelicals from the national political scene did not, for the most part, result from any innate dislike of religion on the part of left-leaning voters or party officials; more often such figures were driven from office, or else relegated to back-bench status, through the efforts of New Right groups and their allies in the Religious Right. By the mid-1980s most of the moderate evangelicals who had captured the attention of Capitol Hill reporters a decade earlier were no longer in elective office. Of the very small handful that remained, some were fortunate to represent constituencies that resisted the broader white electorate's rightward shift; others survived by reinventing themselves as across-the-board conservatives.[83]

The Shrinking Evangelical Conscience

The increasingly conservative mood of the white electorate did not go unnoticed by the evangelical movement's intellectual leaders. Although writers such as Harold Lindsell and Francis Schaeffer did not have to worry about being defeated at the ballot box, they did have to worry about donors, book sales, and magazine readerships; and for this reason they too came under serious pressure to renounce the center-left positions they had espoused during the early 1970s. In Lindsell's case, the most immediate source of pressure was W. Maxey Jarman, the apparel company head who became *Christianity Today*'s most important benefactor following the death of J. Howard Pew. A failed Republican candidate for Tennessee governor, Jarman shared Pew's politics, and like Pew he did not hesitate to badger the magazine's editor about content that ran counter to his convictions.[84] Whether because of Jarman's unrelenting criticism, or perhaps because he sensed a shift in his readers' ideological leanings, Lindsell grew both more conservative and more dogmatic in his politics as the decade progressed. In 1974, shortly before Richard Nixon resigned the presidency, Lindsell delivered a speech at the annual convention of the National Religious Broadcasters in which he linked the Watergate scandal to the rise of a broader culture of moral permissiveness—a culture that was particularly evident on the nation's college campuses, where illegal drugs were rampant, and where swimming pools were increasingly "used by both sexes in the nude at the same time."[85] Via a curious twist of logic, the address concluded that Nixon's moral compass had been damaged by the loose morals of the college leftists he had spent the better part of his presidency attacking.

Shortly thereafter, the former theology professor turned his attention to the question of biblical inerrancy, launching a crusade to expose as "false evangelicals" all those who doubted that the Bible was historically accurate in all respects or who dismissed certain passages as not binding upon modern-day believers. Although the bulk of *The Battle for the Bible* (1976) and *The*

Bible in the Balance (1979) consisted of point-by-point critiques of theologians Lindsell regarded as heretics (several of whom were his former Fuller Seminary colleagues), political considerations were never far from the surface.[86] The question of gender relations featured prominently in both works, and Lindsell was particularly critical of scholars who dared to interrogate the Pauline injunction that women be subordinate in all things to men.[87] But his larger theme was anti-elitism: he believed that the evangelical movement had been infiltrated by academics whose egalitarian values bore an alarmingly close resemblance to those of secular liberals. The sooner average evangelicals learned that "impeccable academic pedigrees" were more often a sign of "corruption" than genuine spiritual insight, the better off the movement would be.[88]

Finally, around the time of Ronald Reagan's victory in the 1980 presidential election, Lindsell reinvented himself as a champion of the free enterprise system. In the early 1970s, when he had expressed sympathy for the aims of the environmental movement, he had blamed most of the nation's problems on the rise of an acquisitive, secular culture in which the pursuit of more and cheaper "material things" increasingly "compensate[ed] for lack of spiritual fulfillment."[89] But by 1982, when *Free Enterprise: A Judeo-Christian Defense* hit bookstores, the call to subordinate material desires to spiritual development had been replaced by "the mandate to create wealth." Formerly a sign of spiritual decay, the quest for "an ever higher level of material well-being" was now taken as a given, an ineradicable aspect of human nature that only a fool or tyrant would attempt to alter. To the killjoys, such as E. F. Schumacher, who asked why consumers needed "fifty kinds of perfume, [or] thirty kinds of deodorant," Lindsell replied that, far from jeopardizing the nation's moral foundations, those who "created demand" for new and different types of products were to be celebrated as the guarantors of American freedom. "Small" was no longer beautiful; it was a step on the road to socialism. [90]

Schaeffer's ideological transformation was no less striking. After spending the early part of the decade advocating "compassionate capitalism" and concern for the environment, the Swiss-based writer pivoted in the late 1970s to biblical literalism and abortion. Accompanied by a book of the same name, his 1976 film *How Shall We Then Live?* warned believers to be on their guard against the march of a secular, humanistic worldview—reflected, for example, in the Supreme Court's recent abortion rulings—that would lead inexorably to infanticide and euthanasia. Three years later Schaeffer partnered with the future Surgeon General C. Everett Koop to produce *Whatever Happened to the Human Race?*, a four-hour epic devoted almost entirely to abortion, and culminating with a scene in which Koop "inveighed against abortion while standing in the midst of hundreds of abandoned baby dolls strewn across the banks of the Dead Sea."[91] Both films—and the accompanying books—were hugely influential in evangelical circles; Jerry Falwell, who regularly distributed Schaeffer's writings to Moral Majority members and contributors to the *Old-Time Gospel Hour*, credited them with inspiring his decision to enter the political realm.[92]

Coincidence or not, Schaeffer's shift to "moral" or "family" issues occurred at the precise moment that he gained admission to the halls of power. Like Billy Graham, Schaeffer felt called to minister to those in high office, but in the early 1970s his attempts to secure an audience with President Nixon had been rebuffed by White House aides.[93] Nixon's successor proved more accommodating, however, and by 1976 Schaeffer had developed a close relationship with Gerald Ford and his family.[94] From this point forward Schaeffer became a regular speaker at Republican gatherings, and—more to the point—he now had ready access to funding for his ambitious film and book projects.[95] As befitted his new role as spiritual advisor to Capitol Hill Republicans and their donors, Schaeffer's final books, written in the midst of a losing battle with cancer, made no mention of capitalism's ethical blind spots, nor of the duty of care for the environment. Rather, both *A Christian Manifesto* (1984) and *The Great Evangelical Disaster* (1984) painted a Manichean vision of a culture divided between agents of good (who endorsed both the absolute authority of the Bible and the full range of conservative political causes) and agents of evil (who wrongly believed that human reason could play a meaningful role in developing moral standards and solving social problems). Evangelicals who advocated dismantling "unjust social structures" belonged in the latter camp. Though their message sounded "at first . . . close to . . . what Scripture teaches on justice and compassion," this was only because they were careful to use "all the right evangelical words and avoid any red-flag rhetoric." Dig deeper and it became clear that they were preaching a false gospel, one spawned by an unholy union of Marxism and secular humanism.[96]

The ecological crisis, too, became in Schaeffer's later writings a stalking horse for the anti-Christian agenda of the political left. Although there was nothing wrong, in theory, with caring for the environment, Schaeffer now warned that most proponents of environmental regulation were guilty of placing the lesser orders of creation on an equal plane with human beings, who alone had been created in God's image. And once a thinker had taken this fateful step, it became perilously easy to justify "kill[ing] children in the womb, and then if one does not like the way they turn out, to kill children after they are born. And then it goes on to the euthanasia of anyone who becomes a burden or inconvenience. After all, . . . [if] human life is not intrinsically different from animal life . . . why should it be treated differently?"[97] By a leap of logic that rivaled Harold Lindsell's account of the Watergate scandal, Schaeffer thus arrived at the view that those who insisted on caring for the lesser orders of creation were logically committed to exterminating the higher.[98]

•

Such claims were not only difficult to reconcile with Schaeffer's prior writings on capitalism and the environment; they were borderline nonsensical. And to Carl Henry, who had long preached that a revival of theological orthodoxy would tend to broaden the average believer's sense of social concern, they were nothing short of tragic. To be sure, Henry sympathized with parts of the Religious Right's agenda. As early as 1970 he had warned against the legalization of "abortion on demand," and he agreed with Schaefer and Lindsell that a "secular humanistic" worldview had permeated the nation's educational institutions, to disastrous effect. Observing events in the mid-1980s, however, he could only lament that his life's work of forging a coherent evangelical perspective on social ethics— one that would address not only issues of personal morality but also broader social problems such as poverty and race relations—had proved a failure. The problem, Henry candidly acknowledged, was that evangelicals possessed neither a coherent "vision" with respect to "socio-cultural concerns" nor "organizations" with sufficient strength to mount a "comprehensively coordinated" program.[99] Plenty of evangelicals were engaged in political activism, but the largest and most visible religious interest groups were money-hungry operations whose aims were derived as much from the prejudices of potential donors as from than the revealed Word of God. All too often, groups like the Moral Majority embraced policies, such as support for apartheid South Africa, that were not only unbiblical but demonstrably immoral.[100] And on those rare instances when they turned their attention to problems such as world hunger, their efforts were typically scattershot, ineffective, and self-serving, amounting to little more than a "rush for the media limelight."[101]

Hence, at the end of his long public career, the evangelical movement's most important theologian was forced to acknowledge a tension that had haunted the margins of most of his writings on social ethics. In short, top-down, bureaucratic authority drained the life from the Gospel message; but in the absence of strong denominational and ecumenical bodies there was little anyone could do to prevent the "entrepreneurs" of the Religious Right from "exploit[ing]" the "evangelical movement's hard-won prominence . . . in view of constituency appeal and in quest of potential funding."[102] Having led a successful assault on mainline clerical authority, Henry now discovered that shockingly few of his newly liberated coreligionists were interested in a conception of social ethics that called for self-sacrifice in the name of addressing "intractable pockets of social injustice" in American society.[103] For most evangelicals, the message of the Religious Right, which suggested that hard-working whites were the real victims of unjust social structures, was far more appealing.

Conclusion

On one level, this book's subtitle is grossly unfair to modern-day American Protestants. Although white churchgoers have, as a rule, gravitated to the political right in the years since 1980, many individual congregations remain deeply involved in humanitarian projects—from feeding the homeless to promoting interracial and interfaith understanding. The nation's mainline Protestants, while comparatively few in number, remain as committed as ever to aiding those on the margins of society. And there are even signs of a revival of social justice activism in the evangelical churches, as many evangelical elites are demonstrating a renewed interest in causes such as global poverty, comprehensive immigration reform, and climate change. In light of these facts, it may be said that white Protestants have not, in fact, stopped loving their neighbors; if church-based progressive activism is a less powerful social force than in decades past, it is nonetheless far from dead.

But to put the matter this way is to evade the critical question of whether organized Protestantism retains the capacity to change minds. Does the fact that respected religious leaders or organizations have endorsed a given cause make it more likely that rank-and-file believers will do the same, even in cases where self-interest, prejudice, or ingrained ideological commitments would counsel a different course? For much of the twentieth century, the answer to this question was obviously "yes." Today, I believe, it is "no."

By way of illustration, consider the much-discussed revival of elite-level evangelical social concern that began shortly after the turn of the twenty-first century. After years of focusing almost exclusively on opposing abortion, same-sex marriage, and other alleged threats to traditional morality, many prominent evangelicals shifted gears in the early 2000s, urging Christians to reflect on a wider array of social problems. The leaders of the National Association of Evangelicals, representing some forty-five thousand churches and thirty million church members, made a serious push to mobilize evangelicals in support of efforts to combat climate change, as did the editors of *Christianity Today*.[1] Megachurch pastor and best-selling author Rick Warren lobbied the George W. Bush administration to increase funding for humanitarian aid programs and combating the HIV/AIDS epidemic abroad.[2] Immigration reform, too, made its way onto the evangelical agenda, as the NAE, the Southern Baptist Convention (SBC), the Council for Christian Colleges and Universities (CCCU), and a long list of evangelical elites launched an initiative called Evangelical Immigration Table (EIT) for the purpose of promoting a moderate but compassionate approach to illegal immigration.[3]

In many ways these initiatives resembled the postwar mainline Protestant campaigns that successfully alerted rank-and-file churchgoers to social problems, such as racial segregation, that they might have preferred to ignore—but with one major difference: Relatively few twenty-first-century evangelicals were swayed by the impassioned appeals of their purported leaders. In the case of climate change, efforts by the NAE and other groups to mobilize average churchgoers were soon derailed by opposition from SBC officials and conservative clergymen who deemed the subject beyond the church's purview. Remarkably, the main opponents of the effort—who, somewhat perversely, labeled their organization the Interfaith Stewardship Alliance—candidly acknowledged that they feared the consequences of staking out a position that ran counter to the views of most churchgoers.[4] In the case of foreign aid, polls conducted during Rick Warren's push for increased funding found that white evangelicals, far from heeding his prophetic pronouncements, remained more likely than members of other faiths to *oppose* altruistic aid programs—and their views changed little over subsequent years. That the George W. Bush administration managed to increase funding for anti–HIV/AIDS and other foreign aid programming was likely due not to the support of rank-and-file evangelicals, but rather to the fact that the issue was of such little consequence to most evangelicals that they remained unaware of the administration's initiatives in this area.[5]

But it is the failed push for immigration reform that perhaps best illustrates evangelical elites' impotence in the realm of social ethics. Believing that—in the words of the NAE's government affairs director—God had "brought [undocumented immigrants] here for a purpose," officials from the NAE and a host of other evangelical groups spent much of 2013 and 2014 targeting churchgoers with the message that Christian principles, properly understood, favored a comprehensive immigration reform plan that would include a path to citizenship for most undocumented immigrants.[6] The EIT spent $400,000 on a Christian-radio ad campaign, rented billboards in fifty-six critical congressional districts, launched blogs, organized conferences, and staged numerous rallies and marches. In interviews EIT organizers insisted that there existed "a silent majority of evangelicals in support of immigration reform"; reach these churchgoers with a compelling biblical message, the thinking went, and they might well turn the political tide in favor of a comprehensive reform bill.[7]

No such bill emerged from Congress, of course. But, more to the point, the "silent majority" of evangelical reform supporters never materialized. In fact, far from mobilizing in support of comprehensive immigration reform, white evangelicals continued to exhibit far more hostility toward the idea than members of other religious groups. Polls conducted at the height of the EIT's 2013–2014 advertising blitz found that a whopping 62 percent of evangelicals agreed with the statement "We should make a serious effort to deport all illegal immigrants back to their home countries."[8] Moreover, while a few noted mega-church pastors actively supported the immigration reform push, clergy opinion polls found that most evangelical ministers, like their parishioners, were un-moved by the EIT's pleas. Surveyed in 2017, most Southern Baptist pastors who reported having spoken about immigration to their congregations said they had opposed the relatively tolerant policies favored by denominational leaders.[9] At the outset of the immigration reform push, the SBC's Richard Land had con-fidently predicted that Southern Baptists overwhelmingly favored "a Christian and . . . compassionate" approach to immigration reform, and were therefore unlikely to be swayed by the alarmist rhetoric of "anti-immigration folks" like "Rush Limbaugh and Sean Hannity."[10] The poll numbers, however, painted a very different picture.

In the winter of 2015–2016, when Donald Trump emerged as a serious con-tender for the Republican nomination, commentators were split on whether churchgoing evangelical voters could be persuaded to support a profane, thrice-married former casino owner. Many observers suspected that Trump would win the evangelical vote, but by a smaller margin than other recent GOP nominees, and that a mediocre showing with evangelicals might well cost the GOP the election.[11] Obviously such predictions proved to be wildly off the mark. But the larger point is that they rested on assumptions that, at least in hindsight, should have been jettisoned following the unsuccessful elite-led reform campaigns of the early 2000s. Long before 2016, in other words, it should have been clear that religious institutions and arguments exert at most a modest influence on white evangelicals' political behavior, meaning that evangelicals were likely to vote like similarly situated nonevangelicals, regardless of whatever objections their pur-ported religious leaders might raise to the idea of a Trump presidency.

And this is precisely what happened. Although many evangelical elites—from the SBC's Russell Moore to the editors of Christianity Today to the best-selling author Max Lucado—strongly condemned Trump's rhetoric and aspects of his policy agenda, their pleas mostly escaped the notice of rank-and-file churchgoers. In fact, one post-election study found that around 45 percent of evangelicals believed that both Moore and Christianity Today had endorsed Trump.[12] The story was much the same at the congregational level, where cues from ministers seem to have exerted little influence over the electoral choices of average evangelicals. Only about 23 percent of evangelicals reported that their pastors had expressed an opinion about candidate Trump; and of the mi-nority of evangelicals who did encounter Trump-related messages at church, most reported that their ministers had simply echoed the sentiment of the wider community: those in conservative areas offered praise, while those in liberal areas raised concerns. Summing up these findings, a pair of political scientists have concluded that "most evangelicals were left to their own devices in evaluating the candidates."[13]

In light of such evidence, it makes little sense to blame (or credit) evangelical religiosity with fueling the rise of either Donald Trump or the broader strain of conservative populism he represents. For in contrast to the mainline churches in their prime, today's evangelical elites possess neither the intrinsic religious authority nor the institutional resources necessary to meaningfully shape their followers' views on major social and political questions. On the contrary, evangelical elites tend to take their marching orders from the men and women in the pews—men and women who overwhelmingly identify as conservative Republicans.

This is not to deny that evangelical religiosity is a useful predictor of individual-level ideology and partisanship. Rather, it is to say that evangelicalism appears increasingly epiphenomenal to other, more fundamental demographic determinants of political behavior. White voters who lack college degrees, or who reside in sparsely populated exurbs or rural areas, tend to exhibit comparatively high levels of enthusiasm for Trump's nativist agenda, regardless of where they fall on the religiosity spectrum.[14] And while evangelical religiosity may not be the primary *cause* of such sentiments, neither is it particularly effective at mitigating them.[15]

The present-day situation in the mainline churches is only superficially different. To be sure, the typical mainline church member's views on issues like immigration and economic redistribution fall somewhat to the left of the typical evangelical's. And yet, as in the evangelical case, there is little reason to believe that the mainline churches are changing many minds. For one thing, mainline congregations tend to contain more individuals whose professional and educational backgrounds are predictive of political liberalism—meaning that, even if we knew nothing about their religious habits, our expectations concerning their political views would be roughly the same.[16] Where such citizens are in short supply, the shrinking number of mainline churches that still exist often survive by adapting to their surroundings. Although it is true that some clergymen and church leaders continue to perform the "prophetic" role of challenging prevailing political beliefs in the name of religious truth, such instances appear to be the exception rather than the rule. More often than not, ministers who dare to raise controversial issues from the pulpit are careful to couch their critiques in highly abstract terms;[17] in other cases, contentious issues on which the parent denomination has adopted a point of view at odds with congregational opinion are avoided altogether.[18]

There is an irony here that Reinhold Niebuhr, who had much to say about the ironic twists and turns of American history, would surely have appreciated. In short, the collapse of Protestant religious authority has not liberated the religious sphere from the taint of the political—the result predicted by so many of the postwar establishment's critics. Instead, it has bound the two spheres ever more closely together. Left to their own devices, believers increasingly self-select into congregations populated by fellow partisans, and ministers increasingly mirror the ideological convictions of their congregants. And as congregations grow more ideologically homogeneous by the day, it becomes increasingly difficult to say what distinguishes a religious act (or conviction) from a political one. That believers on both sides of the present cultural divide are sincerely committed to their respective visions of righteousness only exacerbates the problem. For as Niebuhr pointed out nearly seven decades ago, in a passage that might well have come from the pen of James Madison, our "notions of justice" are inevitably "touched by interest and passion. They always contain an ideological element, for they tend to justify a given equilibrium of power in a given historical situation."[19]

Acknowledgments

I have accumulated many debts in the process of researching and writing this book. I am enormously grateful to Karen Orren for steering me toward the study of religion and politics, and for her invaluable advice and encouragement over the years. In a sense *The End of Empathy* is an outgrowth of our many conversations about the role of religion in American political development. Although we have not always seen eye to eye on this endlessly fascinating topic, this book could not have been written without her.

I am also grateful to David Campbell, Anthony Chaney, Elesha Coffman, Paul Djupe, Ben Gaskins, Mirya Holman, Joanna Tice, Janelle Wong, Molly Worthen, and several anonymous reviewers for providing feedback on various parts of the manuscript, and to Marty Cohen, Lori Cox Han, and Paul Matzko for generously sharing early drafts of works in progress. I thank Howard Bauleke for sharing his encyclopedic knowledge of the U.S. House, Natalie Davis for speaking with me about one of the Moral Majority's first successful interventions in electoral politics, and David Karol for pointing out a pair of potentially embarrassing factual errors.

Several of my colleagues at Chapman University, including Gordon Babst, Ann Gordon, Nubar Hovsepian, Andrea Molle, Crystal Murphy, Michael Pace, David Shafie, Robert Slayton, and Justin St. P. Walsh generously served as sounding boards for some of the ideas developed in the book. I am especially grateful for a fall 2018 sabbatical, which gave me time to finish the manuscript, and to Stephanie Takaragawa for organizing a works-in-progress event where I presented the book's final chapter (and where Paul Djupe served as discussant).

I am grateful to Erin Berthon and Talisa Flores for processing the paperwork required for various research trips and conference presentations, and to several outstanding student research assistants, including Jace Jenican, Muhammad Karkoutli, Connor Kridle, Lindsey Narkchareon, Claire Norman, Andrew Perez, and Mallory Warhurst, for helping with various aspects of the manuscript's preparation. Connor, who worked on the project the longest, and who endured many long conversations about it, deserves special thanks.

I benefited enormously from the assistance of the librarians, archivists, and staff of several libraries and historical societies, including the Library of Congress; the Presbyterian Historical Society; the Hagley Museum and Library; the Billy Graham Center Archives; the Indiana Historical Society; the Roosevelt, Eisenhower, and Nixon Presidential Libraries; and the special collections departments at Union Theological Seminary, Fuller Theological Seminary, Wheaton College, and the Claremont Colleges.

Finally, this book could not have been written without the love and support of my family. My children, Eleanor and William, inspire me every day. My hope is that they will grow to live in a world where concern for the marginalized is once again at the heart of American Christianity. I owe my parents an incalculable debt for always encouraging my love of learning. My wife's parents deserve special thanks for joyfully providing thousands of hours of child care, countless delicious meals, and many other forms of assistance to make our busy lives possible. Most of all, I am blessed to be married to a woman who is everything a person could ask for in a companion and then some.

Heidi Hyun, this book is for you.

Table A.1 Predicting support for federal civil rights initiatives in 1964, Northern White Protestants only (logistic regression model; standard errors in parentheses)

	Model 1: Predicting support for 1964 Civil Rights Act		Model 2: Predicting support for school integration	
	B	Exp(B)	B	Exp(B)
Party ID	−.106*	.900	.024	1.024
	(.044)		(.043)	
Female	.072	1.075	.101	1.106
	(.184)		(.180)	
Age	−.009	.991	−.004	.996
	(.006)		(.006)	
Union household	.005	1.005	.260	1.297
	(.214)		(.213)	
Education level	.188	1.207	.231*	1.259
	(.101)		(.098)	
Church attendance	.524**	1.688	.470*	1.599
	(.194)		(.188)	
Constant	−.076	.927	−1.120**	.326
	(.416)		(.407)	
Pseudo R-square	.053		.043	
N	522		563	

Source: ANES 1964 Time Series Study. ***$p \leq 0.001$; **$p \leq 0.01$; *$p \leq 0.05$

Table A.2 Predicting political engagement in 1964, Northern White Protestants only (logistic regression model; standard errors in parentheses)

	Model 1: Written to Official		Model 2: Displayed Button or Sticker		Model 3: Attended Political Meeting	
	B	Exp(B)	B	Exp(B)	B	Exp(B)
Strong partisan	.084	1.088	.851**	2.343	1.068**	2.909
	(.057)		(.264)		(.354)	
Female	.369	1.447	.132	1.141	-.002	.998
	(.243)		(.266)		(.349)	
Age	.007	1.007	-.022*	.978	.019	1.019
	(.008)		(.009)		(.012)	
Union household	.271	1.311	.100	1.105	.425	1.529
	(.284)		(.302)		(.417)	
Education level	.648***	1.911	.260*	1.297	.966***	2.627
	(.123)		(.132)		(.170)	
Church attendance	.598*	1.819	.072	1.074	.348	1.417
	(.238)		(.275)		(.351)	
Constant	-3.926***	.020	-1.862**	.155	-6.300***	.002
	(.575)		(.582)		(-.893)	
Pseudo R-square	.151		.043		.214	
N	522		563		523	

Source: ANES 1964 Time Series Study. ***$p \leq 0.001$; **$p \leq 0.01$; *$p \leq 0.05$

Table A.3 Predicting support for school integration, 1960–1966, Northern White Protestants only (logistic regression model; standard errors in parentheses)

	1960		1962		1966	
	B	Exp(B)	B	Exp(B)	B	Exp(B)
Party ID	−.009	.991	−.057	.944	−.088	.916
	(.045)		(.051)		(.048)	
Female	.032	1.033	−.054	.948	.397*	1.488
	(.197)		(.220)		(.193)	
Age	−.021**	.979	.007	1.007	−.009	.991
	(.007)		(.007)		(.006)	
Union household	−.159	.853	—	—	.240	1.271
	(.223)				(.221)	
Education level	.122	1.130	.289*	1.335	.175	1.191
	(.093)		(.131)		(.117)	
Church attendance	.100	1.105	−.063	.939	.297	1.346
	(.211)		(.235)		(.203)	
Constant	.632	1.881	−.019	.981	−.354	.702
	(.452)		(.529)		(.496)	
Pseudo R-square	.041		.020		.049	
N	440		397		480	

Source: ANES 1960, 1962, and 1966 Time Series Studies. ***$p \leq 0.001$; **$p \leq 0.01$; *$p \leq 0.05$

Archival Sources and Abbreviations

CCC   City Council of Churches Records, William Adams Brown Ecumenical Library Archives, Burke Library, Union Theological Seminary, New York, New York

CTI   Records of Christianity Today International, Billy Graham Center Archives, Wheaton College, Wheaton, Illinois

FCC   Federal Council of Churches Records, William Adams Brown Ecumenical Library Archives, Burke Library, Union Theological Seminary, New York, New York

FDR—PPF President's Personal File, Franklin D. Roosevelt Presidential Library & Museum, Hyde Park, New York

FES   Francis and Edith Schaeffer Papers, Special Collections, Buswell Library, Wheaton College, Wheaton, Illinois.

GNL   Good Neighbor League Papers, Franklin D. Roosevelt Presidential Library & Museum, Hyde Park, New York

HJV   H. Jerry Voorhis Papers, Claremont Colleges Library Special Collections, Claremont, California

ISM   Irwin-Sweeney-Miller Family Collection, Indiana Historical Society, Indianapolis, Indiana

JGW   John G. Winant Papers, Franklin D. Roosevelt Presidential Library & Museum, Hyde Park, New York

JHP   J. Howard Pew Papers, Hagley Museum and Library, Wilmington, Delaware

NAE   National Association of Evangelicals Records, Special Collections, Buswell Library, Wheaton College, Wheaton, Illinois

NAM   National Association of Manufacturers Records, Hagley Museum and Library, Wilmington, Delaware

NCC   National Council of the Churches of Christ in the United States of America Records, Presbyterian Historical Society, Philadelphia, Pennsylvania

PGH   Paul G. Hoffmann Papers, Harry S. Truman Presidential Library, Independence, Missouri

RMN-AF   Alphabetical Name Files, White House Central Files, Richard M. Nixon Presidential Library and Museum, Yorba Linda, California

RMN-RM Religious Matters Series, White House Central Files, Richard M. Nixon Presidential Library and Museum, Yorba Linda, California

SCC   State Council of Churches Records, William Adams Brown Ecumenical
            Library Archives, Burke Library, Union Theological Seminary,
            New York, New York
SCE   Southern California Ecumenical Council Records, David Allan
            Hubbard Library Archives, Fuller Theological Seminary, Pasadena,
            California
UPC   United Presbyterian Church in the U.S.A. Council on Church and Race,
            Presbyterian Historical Society, Philadelphia, Pennsylvania

Notes

Introduction

1. Tobin Grant, "Polling Evangelicals: Cut Aid to World's Poor, Unemployed," *Christianity Today*, February 18, 2011; Tara Isabella Burton, "Polls Suggest White Evangelicals Will Still Back Trump after Family Separation Controversy," Vox.com, June 27, 2018; Philip Bump, "The Group Least Likely to Think the U.S. Has a Responsibility to Accept Refugees? Evangelicals," *Washington Post*, May 24, 2018; Paul Djupe, "Evangelicals and Immigration—A Sea Change in the Making?" www.prri.org; Robert P. Jones, Daniel Cox, Juhem Navarro-Rivera, E. J. Dionne, Jr., and William A. Galston, "What Americans Want from Immigration Reform in 2014," www.prri.org; Michael O. Emerson and Christian Smith, *Divided by Faith: Evangelical Religion and the Problem of Race in America* (New York: Oxford University Press, 2000); Melissa Deckman, Dan Cox, Robert Jones, and Betsy Cooper, "Faith and the Free Market: Evangelicals, the Tea Party, and Economic Attitudes," *Politics and Religion* 10 (2016): 82–110; Baxter Oliphant, "Support for Death Penalty Lowest in More than Four Decades," http://www.pewresearch.org/fact-tank/2016/09/29/support-for-death-penalty-lowest-in-more-than-four-decades.
2. Recall, for example, his promise to "bring back" waterboarding and other, unnamed forms of torture that were "a hell of a lot worse." Or his promise to "punish" women who sought abortions. Or his frequent depictions of undocumented immigrants as dangerous criminals. Or his characterization of refugees as a serious threat to national security.
3. Ryan P. Burge, "The 2016 Religious Vote," March 10, 2017, https://religioninpublic.blog/2017/03/10/the-2016-religious-vote-for-more-groups-than-you-thought-possible.
4. Gregory A. Smith and Jessica Martinez, "How the Faithful Voted," www.pewresearch.org; Sarah Pulliam Bailey, "White Evangelicals Voted Overwhelmingly for Donald Trump, Exit Polls Show," *Washington Post*, November 9, 2016.
5. See, for example, Michael Massing, "How Martin Luther Paved the Way for Donald Trump," *Nation*, April 19, 2018, pp. 14–26; John Ehrenreich, "White Evangelicals' Continued Support of Trump Feels Surprising. It Shouldn't," Slate.com, May 7, 2018; Nancy D. Wadsworth, "The Racial Demons That Help Explain Evangelical Support for Trump," Vox.com, April 30; Corey Robin, "The Triumph of the Shill," *n + 1*, Fall 2017; Katha Pollitt, "Why Evangelicals—Still!—Support Trump," The Nation.com, March 22, 2018; Jim Newell, "Trump Answers Prayers," Slate.com, May 3, 2018; Jim Newell, "Why Evangelicals Are Smart to Support Trump," Slate.com, October 19, 2016.
6. Michael Gerson, "The Last Temptation," *Atlantic*, April 2018, pp. 42–52; Peter Wehner, "Why I Can No Longer Call Myself an Evangelical Republican," *New York*

Times, December 9, 2017; John Fea, "Evangelical Fear Elected Trump," TheAtlantic. com, June 24, 2018. Also see Ross Douthat, "Save the Mainline," *New York Times*, April 15, 2017, p. SR 11.

7. Studies that attribute the rise of the Religious Right to the unraveling of traditional sexual mores and/or the advent of legalized abortion include Michael J. McVicar, *Christian Reconstruction: R. J. Rushdoony and American Religious Conservatism* (Chapel Hill: University of North Carolina Press, 2015); Donald T. Critchlow, *Phyllis Schlafly and Grassroots Conservatism: A Woman's Crusade* (Princeton, NJ: Princeton University Press, 2005); J. Brooks Flippen, *Jimmy Carter, the Politics of Family, and the Rise of the Religious Right* (Athens: University of Georgia Press, 2011); Seth Dowland, *Family Values and the Rise of the Christian Right* (Philadelphia: University of Pennsylvania Press, 2015); Marjorie J. Spruill, *Divided We Stand: The Battle over Women's Rights and Family Values That Polarized American Politics* (New York: Bloomsbury, 2017); Daniel K. Williams, *Defenders of the Unborn: The Pro-Life Movement before* Roe v. Wade (New York: Oxford University Press, 2016), 205–242.

8. Studies that stress the role of federal civil rights initiatives, including the aggressive push to integrate private religious schools, include Joseph Crespino, "Civil Rights and the New Religious Right," in Bruce J. Shulman and Julian E. Zelizer, eds., *Rightward Bound: Making America Conservative in the 1970s* (Cambridge, MA: Harvard University Press, 2008); Randall Balmer, *Redeemer: The Life of Jimmy Carter* (New York: Basic Books, 2014), 102–108; William Martin, *With God on Our Side: The Rise of the Religious Right in America* (New York: Broadway Books, 1996), 171–173; Lisa McGirr, *Suburban Warriors: The Origins of the New American Right* (Princeton, NJ: Princeton University Press, 2001), 182–185. For a subtle and provocative variation on this theme, see David Hollinger's argument that mainline Protestant leaders, by publicly concerning themselves with the plight of marginalized groups, effectively undermined their own ability to speak for white middle-class churchgoers. David Hollinger, *After Cloven Tongues of Fire: Protestant Liberalism in Modern American History* (Princeton, NJ: Princeton University Press, 2013), 18–49.

9. For studies that emphasize the role of the conservative business community as well as the economic motivations of white middle- and upper-class voters, see Kevin Kruse, *One Nation Under God: How Corporate America Invented Christian America* (New York: Basic Books, 2016); Robert O. Self, *All in the Family: The Realignment of American Democracy since the 1960s* (New York: Hill and Wang, 2012); Bethany Moreton, *To Serve God and Mammon: The Making of Christian Free Enterprise* (Cambridge, MA: Harvard University Press, 2009); Darren E. Grem, *The Blessings of Business: How Corporations Shaped Conservative Christianity* (New York: Oxford University Press, 2016).

10. On the influence of identity-based considerations relative to specifically religious commitments, see, for example, Robert D. Putnam and David E. Campbell, *American Grace: How Religion Divides and Unites Us* (New York: Simon and Schuster, 2012), Chapter 12; Christopher H. Achen and Larry M. Bartels, *Democracy for Realists: Why Elections Do Not Produce Responsive Government* (Princeton, NJ: Princeton

University Press, 2016); David E. Campbell, Geoffrey C. Layman, John C. Green, and Nathanael G. Sumaktoyo, "Putting Politics First: The Impact of Politics on American Religious and Secular Orientations," *American Journal of Political Science* 62 (2018): 551–565; Michele F. Margolis, "How Politics Affects Religion: Partisanship, Socialization, and Religiosity in America," *Journal of Politics* 80 (2017): 30–43.

11. The literature on the role of religious institutions in shaping individual believers' political views, and in motivating particular forms of political action, is vast. Some important works in this vein include Putnam and Campbell, *American Grace*; Paul A. Djupe and Christopher P. Gilbert, *The Prophetic Pulpit: Clergy, Churches, and Communities in American Politics* (Lanham, MD: Rowman and Littlefield, 2003); Paul A. Djupe and Christopher P. Gilbert, *The Political Influence of Churches* (New York: Cambridge University Press, 2009); David E. Campbell, John C. Green, J. Quin Monson, *Seeking the Promised Land: Mormons and American Politics* (New York: Cambridge University Press, 2014).

12. My conception of religious authority is indebted to the work of Mark Chaves. See in particular, "Secularization as Declining Religious Authority," *Social Forces* 72 (1994): 749–774, 756.

13. Consider, for example, the uneasy relationship between the modern-day Catholic Church and Catholic elected officials who reject the Church's teachings on such issues as abortion, same-sex marriage, and the death penalty—an issue discussed in Kenneth D. Wald and Allison Calhoun-Brown, *Religion and Politics in the United States*, 6th ed. (Lanham, MD: Rowman and Littlefield, 2011), 256–259; and John C. Green, *The Faith Factor: How Religion Influences Americans Elections* (Westport, CT: Praeger, 2007), 143.

14. Laurence R. Iannaccone, "Why Strict Churches Are Strong," *American Journal of Sociology* 99 (1994): 1180–1211. Also see Dean M. Kelley, *Why Conservative Churches Are Growing: A Study in the Sociology of Religion* (Macon, GA: Mercer University Press, 1972).

15. Iannaccone, "Why Strict Churches Are Strong"; Paul A. Djupe and Christopher P. Gilbert, "Politics and Church: Byproduct or Central Mission?," *Journal for the Scientific Study of Religion* 47 (2008): 45–62; James Q. Wilson, *Political Organizations* (New York: Basic Books, 1973). For the original formulation of the "selective benefits" thesis, see Mancur Olson, *The Logic of Collective Action: Public Goods and the Theory of Groups* (Cambridge, MA: Harvard University Press, 1965).

16. Max Weber, "'Churches' and 'Sects' in North America," in Peter Baehr and Gordon C. Wells, eds., *Max Weber: The Protestant Ethnic and the "Spirit of Capitalism" and Other Writings* (New York: Penguin, 2002), 203–220, 210. I am also indebted to Stephen Kalberg's insightful discussion of Weber's writings on American civil society. Stephen Kalberg, *Searching for the Spirit of American Democracy: Max Weber's Analysis of a Unique Political Culture, Past, Present, and Future* (Boulder, CO: Paradigm, 2014).

17. Weber, "Churches and Sects," 213. Although Weber's description of the sect was likely based on the early American Methodists and Baptists, most of the nation's large Protestant denominations were by the mid-nineteenth century operating in the manner of sects, in the sense that they rigorously screened potential members,

monitored the conduct of those admitted to the fellowship, and no longer conceived of themselves as universal churches.

18. Ibid., 207.
19. Ibid., 205.
20. "If I discover that a client doesn't go to church, then I wouldn't trust him with fifty cents," the man declared. Ibid., 205.
21. Ibid., 207–208. Emphasis in the original.
22. Ibid., 206.
23. Ibid., 213.
24. See, for example, Rodney Stark and Charles Y. Glock, *American Piety: The Nature of Religious Commitment* (Berkeley and Los Angeles: University of California Press, 1968), 167, 186–203; David O. Moberg, *The Church as a Social Institution* (Englewood Cliffs, NJ: Prentice-Hall, 1962); W. Seward Salisbury, *Religion in American Culture: A Sociological Interpretation* (Homewood, IL: Dorsey Press, 1964), 454–457; Richard F. Curtis, "Occupational Mobility and Church Participation," *Social Forces* 38 (1959): 308–314; Seymour Martin Lipset, "Religion and Politics in the American Past and Present," in Robert Lee and Martin E. Marty, eds., *Religion and Social Conflict* (New York: Oxford University Press, 1964), 69–126; Benton Johnson, "Ascetic Protestantism and Political Preference," *Public Opinion Quarterly* 26 (1962): 35–46. Also see William C. Whyte, *The Organization Man* (New York: Simon and Schuster, 1956), 368; Vance Packard, *The Status Seekers* (New York: David McKay, 1959), 200.
25. Hadley Cantril, "Educational and Economic Composition of Religious Groups," *American Journal of Sociology* 47 (1943): 574–579; Liston Pope, "Religion and the Class Structure," *Annals of the American Academy of Political and Social Science* 256 (1948): 84–91; Mabel Newcomer, *The Big Business Executive: The Factors That Made Him, 1900–1950* (New York: Columbia University Press, 1955), 47–48; Beverly Davis, "Eminence and Level of Social Origin," *American Journal of Sociology* 59 (1953): 11–18.
26. The rationalization or bureaucratization of American corporations and professions— including hiring and promotion decisions—is discussed at length in C. Wright Mills, *White Collar: The American Middle Classes* (New York: Oxford University Press, 1953). Also see Newcomer, *The Big Business Executive*, 145–148.
27. For two particularly influential versions of this argument, see Jeffrey K. Hadden, *The Gathering Storm in the Churches* (Garden City, NY: Doubleday, 1969); Dean M. Kelley, *Why Conservative Churches Are Growing* (New York: Harper & Row, 1972).
28. Dietrich Bonhoeffer, *The Cost of Discipleship* (1937; New York: Touchstone, 1959), 49.
29. On the etymology of "mainline Protestantism," see Elesha J. Coffman, *The Christian Century and the Rise of the Protestant Mainline* (New York: Oxford University Press, 2013), 5, 213–215.
30. Terms such as *liberal* or *ecumenical* might have substituted for *mainline*, but both come with their own problems. *Liberal* was of course a freighted and contested term at the time and one that would have been unceremoniously rejected by many mainline church members (including many who supported these churches' broader humanitarian agendas.) *Ecumenical* is problematic for the simple reason that the doctrinally

and politically conservative Protestants who called themselves "evangelicals" also celebrated the virtues of interdenominational cooperation. Hence, mainline it is.

Chapter 1

1. Kelley, for example, seems to have modeled the National Consumer League's guiding philosophy on the stewardship ideals of the her abolitionist ancestors, who had argued that consumers of cotton, sugar, and other slave-produced commodities (which was to say, virtually all Northerners) were complicit in the evil of slavery. Addams, for her part, regularly interpreted the settlement movement, of which her Hull House was the shining American example, not as a radical break with the past but as a return to "that wonderful fellowship, that true democracy of the early church," in which "the Gospel message, a command to love all men," had been received and obeyed "with a certain joyous simplicity." Landon R. Y. Storrs, *Civilizing Capitalism: The National Consumers' League, Women's Activism, and Labor Standards in the New Deal Era* (Chapel Hill: University of North Carolina Press, 2003), 15; Kathryn Kish Sklar, *Florence Kelley and the Nation's Work: The Rise of Women's Political Culture, 1830-1900* (New Haven, CT: Yale University Press, 1995) 22, 85; Jane Addams, "The Subjective Necessity for Social Settlements," in Jean Bethke Elshtain, ed., *The Jane Addams Reader* (New York: Basic Books, 2002), 14-28, 23.
2. Winthrop, "A Model of Christian Charity"; full text available online at https://history.hanover.edu/texts/winthmod.html.
3. On the origins and development of the jeremiad, see Perry Miller, *The New England Mind: From Colony to Province* (Cambridge, MA: Harvard University Press, 1953); Sacvan Bercovitch, *The American Jeremiad* (Madison: University of Wisconsin Press, 1978); Andrew R. Murphy, *Prodigal Nation: Moral Decline and Divine Punishment from New England to 9/11* (New York: Oxford University Press, 2009), 17-43.
4. Genesis 2:15 reads: "And the Lord God took the man, and put him into the garden of Eden to dress it and to keep it." And see Mark R. Stoll, *Inherit the Holy Mountain: Religion and the Rise of American Environmentalism* (New York: Oxford University Press, 2015), 69.
5. Stoll, *Inherit the Holy Mountain*, 75-76. The quotation is from Increase Mather, in Matthew G. Hall, *The Last American Puritan: The Life of Increase Mather, 1639-1723* (Middletown, CT: Wesleyan University Press), 98.
6. Mark Valeri, *Heavenly Merchandise: How Religion Shaped Commerce in Puritan America* (Princeton, NJ: Princeton University Press, 2010), 69-71; Perry Miller, *The New England Mind: From Colony to Province* (Boston: Beacon Press, 1953), 36-37, 41; Sumner Chilton Powell, *Puritan Village: The Formation of a New England Town* (Middletown, CT: Wesleyan University Press, 1963); Increase Mather, *An Earnest Exhortation to the Inhabitants of New-England* (Boston, 1676), 11, 12, 14, available online at http://digitalcommons.unl.edu/etas.
7. On the evolving attitudes of the clergy, see, for example, Valeri, *Heavenly Merchandise*, 102-110. Max Weber famously traced the broader cultural shift with respect to

commercial activities to the Puritans' anxiety concerning the afterlife: taught that they could neither know nor affect the eternal fate of their souls, they began to interpret commercial success as a sign that they were laboring in a God-ordained calling, and thus probably among the elect that the Almighty had, for mysterious reasons of his own, spared from eternal damnation. Max Weber, *The Protestant Ethic and the Spirit of Capitalism*, ed. Stephen Kalberg (1905; New York: Oxford University Press, 2011), 78–82.

8. As Alan Heimert put the point, many clergymen believed that "the outbreak of the Revolution was not an affliction but . . . an unadorned blessing, and that if God had a controversy with His American people it was presumably because they had delayed too long in acting on behalf of their own general welfare." Heimert, *Religion and the American Mind: From the Great Awakening to the Revolution* (Cambridge, MA: Harvard University Press, 1966), 296–297. Also see Murphy, *Prodigal Nation*, 41–43.

9. For an insightful discussion of how early nineteenth-century reformers revived, and in some cases altered, Puritan ideas and rhetorical forms, see Robert H. Abzug, *Cosmos Crumbling: American Reform and the Religious Imagination* (New York: Oxford University Press, 1994), 144.

10. Young, *Bearing Witness Against Sin: The Evangelical Birth of the American Social Movement* (Chicago: University of Chicago Press, 2007), 54–85; John W. Compton, *The Evangelical Origins of the Living Constitution* (Cambridge, MA: Harvard University Press, 2014), 29–35.

11. The legal obstacles that confronted the antebellum reform movements are discussed at length in Compton, *Evangelical Origins*, 52–72.

12. "We are all alike guilty," declared William Lloyd Garrison in 1829. "New-England money has been expended in buying human flesh; New-England ships have been freighted with sable victims; New-England men have assisted in forging the fetters of those who groan in bondage." Quoted in Abzug, *Cosmos Crumbling*, 144.

13. Leonard Bacon, *The Duties Connected with the Present Commercial Distress* (New Haven, CT: Hitchcock & Stafford, 1837), 15.

14. W. J. Rorabaugh, *The Alcoholic Republic: An American Tradition* (New York: Oxford University Press, 1979), 76–92; Daniel Okrent, *Last Call: The Rise and Fall of Prohibition* (New York: Simon & Schuster, 2010), 8.

15. Indeed, several antebellum prohibition measures were struck down by judges who deemed them incompatible with state or federal constitutional provisions that protected vested property rights. See Compton, *Evangelical Origins*, 52–72.

16. Lyman Beecher, *Six Sermons on the Nature, Occasions, Signs, Evils and Remedy of Intemperance* (New York: American Tract Society, 1827), 68.

17. Ibid., 66, 67, 59. Beecher's ideas quickly attained the status of orthodoxy within the broader movement. For similar arguments condemning the liquor traffic for its misuse of God-given resources, see *Permanent Temperance Documents of the American Temperance Society* (Boston: Seth Bliss, 1835), 273, 277, 300, 301, 302, 314.

18. See, for example, Philip Gorski, *American Covenant: A History of Civil Religion from the Puritans to the Present* (Princeton, NJ: Princeton University Press, 2017, 88–92);

Robert N. Bellah, *The Broken Covenant: American Civil Religion in Time of Trial*, 2nd ed. (Chicago: University of Chicago Press, 1975), 52–55.

19. Abraham Lincoln, "Second Inaugural Address," in Conrad Cherry, ed., *God's New Israel: Religious Interpretations of American Destiny* (Chapel Hill: University of North Carolina Press, 1998), 201–202, 202.

20. On the Northern clergy's providential understanding of the war, see Harry S. Stout, *Upon the Altar of the Nation: A Moral History of the Civil War* (New York: Viking, 2006); Mark A. Noll, *The Civil War as a Theological Crisis* (Chapel Hill: University of North Carolina Press, 2006), 75–94. As both Stout and Noll point out, Southern minsters developed their own, very different providential understanding of the conflict.

21. Horace Bushnell, "Our Obligations to the Dead," in Cherry, *God's New Israel*, 203–214, 212, 214.

22. See, for example, Charles C. Cole, Jr., *The Social Ideas of the Northern Evangelists, 1826–1860* (New York: Columbia University Press, 1964); Henry F. May, *Protestant Churches and Industrial America* (New York: Harper, 1949); Chris Lehman, *The Money Cult: Capitalism, Christianity, and the Unmaking of the American Dream* (Brooklyn, NY: Melville House, 2016); see Stewart Davenport, *Friends of the Unrighteous Mammon: Northern Christians and Market Capitalism, 1815–1860* (Chicago: University of Chicago Press, 2008); David Sehat, *The Myth of American Religious Freedom* (New York: Oxford University Press, 2011), 183–192; Richard W. Pointer, "Philadelphia Presbyterians, Capitalism, and the Morality of Economic Success," in Mark A. Noll, ed., *God and Mammon: Protestants, Money, and the Market, 1790–1860* (New York: Oxford University Press, 2002), 171–191.

23. Employing his usual flair for metaphor, Beecher likened European industrial workers to trees that were "band[ed] with iron" and deprived of "the light and the rain of heaven." Lyman Beecher, *The Memory of Our Fathers* (Boston: T. R. Marvin, 1828), 8–9.

24. Ibid. Such arguments were frequently echoed in the political economy literature of the period. See Davenport, *Friends of the Unrighteous Mammon*, 97–105.

25. On the early Social Gospel theologians' work among poor and immigrant congregations, see Gary Dorrien, *Social Ethics in the Making: Interpreting an American Tradition* (Malden, MA: Wiley-Blackwell, 2009), 36–44, 61–69, 84–92.

26. Walter Rauschenbusch, *Christianity and the Social Crisis* (New York: Macmillan, 1907), 234. This aspect of Rauschenbusch's thought is discussed in Susan Curtis, *A Consuming Faith: The Social Gospel and Modern American Culture* (Columbia: University of Missouri Press, 2001), 18–19. On the role of empirical evidence in persuading both elites and average citizens of the legitimacy of industrial laborers' complaints, see, for example, Robert H. Bremner, *From the Depths: The Discovery of Poverty in the United States* (New York: New York University Press, 1956).

27. Helen Stuart Campbell, *Prisoners of Poverty: Women Wage-Workers: Their Trades and Their Lives* (1887; Boston: Little, Brown, 1900), 152.

28. Josiah Strong, *Our Country: Its Possible Future and Its Present Crisis* (New York: American Home Missionary Society, 1885), 106.

29. As Washington Gladden put the point in 1893, whatever material wealth such men "produced with [their] machinery" was surely "a paltry contribution to society when compared with the social capital which [they] destroyed in [their] unsocial relations with [their] workmen." Gladden, *The Tools and the Man: Property and Industry under the Christian Law* (Boston: Houghton, Mifflin, 1893), 104.

30. To be sure, the leaders of the Social Gospel movement drew inspiration from a variety of sources, including the various religiously inspired variants of socialism that were beginning to gain traction in England and elsewhere. Yet the movement's lodestar was the long-standing American Protestant conception of citizens as stewards or trustees who were duty bound to prevent the misappropriation of God-given resources to economic activities that profited from or perpetuated human suffering. Gladden, *Tools and the Man*, 74, 79, 90; Richard T. Ely, *Social Aspects of Christianity and Other Essays* (New York: Crowell, 1889), 31; Walter Rauschenbusch, *The Social Principles of Jesus* (New York: Young Women's Christian Associations, 1916), 128; *Christianizing the Social Order* (New York: Macmillan, 1912), 101. For an insightful discussion of the intermingling of religious and secular ideas in the broader Social Gospel movement (and its English equivalent), see James T. Kloppenberg, *Uncertain Victory: Social Democracy and Progressivism in European and American Thought, 1870-1920* (New York: Oxford University Press, 1986), 205-212 and passim.

31. To have any hope of reaching the working man, Rauschenbusch wrote, the evangelist must first "try to understand his peculiar sin and failure from his own point of view, and see by what means salvation can effectively be brought to him." *Christianizing the Social Order*, 114.

32. Ibid., 112. Finney's quote concerning the "spirit of the reformer" can be found in William G. McLoughlin, *Revivals, Awakenings, and Reform* (Chicago: University of Chicago Press, 1978), 128-129.

33. Rauschenbusch, *Christianizing the Social Order*, 113.

34. *The Federal Council of Churches of Christ in America, A Record of Development and Progress* [pamphlet] (New York, 1912). Presbyterian Historical Society, RG 18, Box 81, Folder 20.

35. Aaron Ignatius Abell, *The Urban Impact on American Protestantism, 1865-1900* (London: Archon, 1962), 230-231.

36. "Institutional Churches," in W. D. P. Bliss, ed., *The New Encyclopedia of Social Reform* (New York: Funk and Wagnalls, 1908), 629-631; Bremner, *From the Depths*, 59-60; Matthew Bowman, *The Urban Pulpit: New York City and the Fate of Liberal Evangelicalism* (New York: Oxford University Press, 2014), 127-133, 140-151.

37. Elias B. Sanford, ed., *Report of the First Meeting of the Federal Council* (New York: Revell Press, 1909), 238-239.

38. Frank Mason North, "The Church and Modern Industry," in *Report of the First Meeting of the Federal Council* (New York: Revell Press, 1909), 228-229, 238-239. Press accounts quoted in Curtis, *A Consuming Faith*, 17.

39. In *Christianity and the Social Crisis*, Rauschenbusch singled out Roosevelt as one of the few political leaders who seemed to grasp the core insights of the Social Gospel. After Rauschenbusch's book became a runaway bestseller, Roosevelt sought the

theologian's advice on domestic policy (as did Woodrow Wilson and other leading politicians). On Roosevelt's relationship with Rauschenbusch (as well as Gladden), see, for example, William R. Hutchison, *Religious Pluralism in America: The Contentious History of a Founding Ideal* (New Haven, CT: Yale University Press, 2003), 107–108; Sidney M. Milkis, *Theodore Roosevelt, the Progressive Party, and the Transformation of American Democracy* (Lawrence: University Press of Kansas, 2009), 112–113, 127, 153. Rauschenbusch discusses Roosevelt in *Christianity and the Social Crisis*, 255–256, 272, 386.

40. Theodore Roosevelt, "The New Nationalism," in Gordon Hutner, ed., *Selected Speeches and Writings of Theodore Roosevelt* (New York: Vintage, 2013), 85–102, 97.

41. Theodore Roosevelt, "Who Is a Progressive?," in Ronald J. Pestritto and William J. Atto, eds., *American Progressivism: A Reader* (Lanham, MD: Lexington Books, 2008), 35–45, 44.

42. "The Progressive Convention," *The Outlook*, August 17, 1912, pp. 857–864; "Hail New Party in Fervent Song," *New York Times*, August 6, 1912, p. 1. For insightful analyses of the proceedings, see Robert M. Crunden, *Ministers of Reform: The Progressives' Achievement in American Civilization, 1889-1920* (New York: Basic Books, 1982), chap. 7; Sidney M. Milkis, *Theodore Roosevelt, the Progressive Party, and the Transformation of American Democracy* (Lawrence: University Press of Kansas, 2009), 147–156.

43. It perhaps goes without saying that the reformers' understanding of the immigrant worker's plight suffered from a number of blind spots, beginning with a paternalistic and ethnocentric conception of American citizenship. Still, it is worth noting that many of the policies championed by middle-class groups such as the GFWC and the Congress of Mothers enjoyed strong support from the working-class populations they were designed to aid. With the notable exception of Prohibition, Protestant reformers could on most issues credibly present themselves as allies rather than antagonists.

44. Lorine Swainston Goodwin, *The Pure Food, Drink, and Drug Crusaders, 1879-1914* (Jefferson, NC: McFarland, 1999), 232–240; Richard F. Hamm, *Shaping the Eighteenth Amendment: Temperance Reform, Legal Culture, and the Polity* (Chapel Hill: University of North Carolina Press, 1995); Walter I. Trattner, *Crusade for the Children: A History of the National Child Labor Committee and Child Labor Reform in America* (Chicago: Quadrangle Books, 1970), 126–127; Jan Doolittle Wilson, *The Women's Joint Congressional Committee and the Politics of Maternalism, 1920-1930* (Urbana: University of Illinois Press, 2007), 104–108; Julie Novkov, "Historicizing the Figure of the Child in Legal Discourse: The Battle over the Regulation of Child Labor," *American Journal of Legal History* 44 (2000): 369–404.

45. For example, Southern textile manufacturers hired W. W. Kitchin, brother of House floor leader Claude Kitchin, to serve as their point man in the fight against a federal child labor law. The liquor industry could usually count on the aid of such reliable "wets" as House Speaker James "Champ" Clark and Minority Leader James Mann. Finally, the Democrats' stranglehold on the South, coupled with Congress's use of the seniority system to select committee chairs, ensured that Southern Democrats

would be overrepresented in congressional leadership posts. Trattner, *Crusade for the Children*, 126; Okrent, *Last Call*, 71.

46. Richard W. Leeman, *"Do Everything" Reform: The Oratory of Frances E. Willard* (New York: Greenwood Press, 1992), 3–44, 171, 159; Theda Skocpol, *Protecting Soldiers and Mothers: The Political Origins of Social Policy in United States* (Cambridge, MA: Belknap Press, 1992), 329–333, 337–340, 359–361, 364–365, 396–401, 414–416, 442–445; Elisabeth S. Clemens, *The People's Lobby: Organizational Innovation and the Rise of Interest Group Politics in the United States, 1890–1925* (Chicago: University of Chicago Press, 1997), 197–202, 309; Goodwin, *The Pure Food, Drink, and Drug Crusaders*, 131–151; Susan Crawford and Peggy Levitt, "Social Change and Civic Engagement: The Case of the PTA," in Theda Skocpol and Morris P. Fiorina, eds., *Civic Engagement in American Democracy* (Washington, DC: Brookings Institution, 1999), 249–296, 256; Molly Ladd-Taylor, *Mother-Work: Women, Child Welfare, and the State, 1890–1930* (Urbana: University of Illinois, 1994), 51–55.

47. C. Howard Hopkins, *History of the YMCA in North America* (New York: Association Press, 1951), 388–389, 477–479; Christopher H. Evans, *The Social Gospel in American Religion: A History* (New York: New York University Press, 2017), 118. It is also noteworthy that group's railroad associations became a nexus for labor organizing activity (with local secretaries sometimes taking up the cause). Thomas Winter, *Making Men, Making Class: The YMCA and Workingmen, 1877–1920* (Chicago: University of Chicago Press, 2002), 83–85.

48. Launched in 1881 by the Congregationalist minister Francis E. Clark, the Christian Endeavor movement aimed to provide an environment of mutual support for young men and women—typically defined as those over eighteen who were not yet married—seeking to cultivate a deeper commitment to the Christian faith. Each Young People's Society was affiliated with a specific Protestant congregation, and members were strictly required to attend monthly devotional meetings at which all participants took an active part, whether "through a simple sentence, a prayer, a song, a testimony, or a verse from the scripture." George Thomas Kurian and Mark A. Lamport, eds., *Encyclopedia of Christian Education*, vol. 3 (Lanham, MD: Rowman and Littlefield, 2015), 1170; Christopher Coble, "The Role of Young People's Societies in the Training of Christian Womanhood (and Manhood), 1880–1910," in Margaret Lamberts Bendroth and Virginia Lieson Brereton, eds., *Women and Twentieth-Century Protestantism* (Urbana: University of Illinois Press, 2002), 74–92; Francis E. Clark, *The Christian Endeavor Manual* (Boston: University Society of Christian Endeavor, 1903), 192–195, 251–253; *The Story of the Seattle Convention: The Official Report of the Twenty-Third International Christian Endeavor Convention* (Boston, MA: United Society of Christian Endeavor), 97–99. Francis E. Clark, *The Christian Endeavor Manual* (Boston: University Society of Christian Endeavor, 1903), 192–195, 251–253; *Official Report of the Twentieth International Christian Endeavor Convention* (Boston, MA: United Society of Christian Endeavor, 1901), 3–4, 28–32, 74–81.

49. Table 1.2 includes only groups that required membership dues and additional commitments above and beyond membership in the parent denomination.

50. Because auxiliary groups tended to be organized in a highly decentralized manner, the causes championed varied not only from group to group but even across local chapters of the same group. One Baptist group whose activities went beyond anti-liquor activism was the Woman's Missionary Union, which also joined campaigns for child labor laws. On the Epworth League, see, for example, the broad range of petitions submitted by the Wisconsin League in *Journal of the House of Representatives of the United States* (54th Congress, 1st Session) (Washington, DC: Government Printing Office, 1896), 369. On the women's auxiliary groups, see Paul Harvey, "Saints but Not Subordinates: The Woman's Missionary Union of the Southern Baptist Convention," in Margaret Lamberts Bendroth and Virginia Lieson Brereton, *Women and Twentieth-Century Protestantism* (Urbana: University of Illinois Press, 2002), 4–24; Oliver S. Baketel, ed., *Methodist Year-Book for 1921* (New York: Methodist Book Concern, 1921), 261; Storrs, *Civilizing Capitalism*, 142.

51. The idea that the nation's mainline churches and Protestant-dominated membership groups, together with its more prestigious universities and leading progressive intellectuals, functioned as a kind of informal religious establishment is explored in Hutchison, *Religious Pluralism in America*, chap. 3; and Eldon J. Eisenach, *The Next Religious Establishment: National Identity and Political Theology in Post-Protestant America* (Lanham, MD: Rowman & Littlefield, 2000), chap. 2.

52. The quoted passage is from an address by Sarah Platt Decker, an early and influential leader of the GFWC. Sarah S. Platt Decker, "Response to Address of Welcome," in Mrs. John Dickinson Sherman, ed., *The General Federation of Women's Clubs: Eighth Biennial Convention* (Chicago: General Federation of Women's Clubs, 1906), 23.

53. On the decline of grassroots political activism and the subsequent rise of top-down interest groups that make relatively few demands of their members (at least in terms of time and energy), see Theda Skocpol, *Diminished Democracy: From Membership to Management in American Civic Life* (Norman: University of Oklahoma Press, 2003).

54. Both Eldon Eisenach and Charles Taylor have argued persuasively that reform-oriented group activity was an important component of the nineteenth-century American Protestant identity. Eisenach, *The Next Religious Establishment*, 37, and *The Lost Promise of Progressivism* (Lawrence: University Press of Kansas, 1994); Charles Taylor, *A Secular Age* (Cambridge, MA: The Belknap Press of Harvard University, 2007), 446–448.

55. Kevin Butterfield, *The Making of Tocqueville's America: Law and Association in the Early United States* (Chicago: University of Chicago Press, 2015), 35. Indeed, most denominations seem to have viewed policing the conduct of one's fellow church members as a religious duty. As an 1835 manual on Congregational church discipline explained, any man who failed to report the sin of a fellow congregant was himself guilty of sin, since he had thereby deprived the sinner of the opportunity to reflect on and correct his immoral ways. John Mitchell, *The Practical Church Member: Being a Guide to the Principles and Practice of the Congregational Churches of New England* (New York: Leavitt, Trow, 1835), 7.

56. Individuals who applied to join the former group were reminded that a YWCA facility was "not designed to be a reformatory" and that "no one will be admitted whose

references in regard to character are not perfectly satisfactory." Members of Christian Endeavor chapters were excommunicated following three unexcused absences; public sins, if not confessed, were treated no less harshly. Daphne Spain, *How Women Saved the City* (Minneapolis: University of Minnesota Press, 2001), 92; Kurian and Lamport, *Encyclopedia of Christian Education*, 1170.

57. See, for example, William F. Mohr, ed., *Who's Who in New York (City and State) 1914: A Biographical Dictionary of Contemporaries* (New York: Who's Who in New York City and State, 1914). An examination of the "H" section—a letter chosen at random—of the 1914 edition of Who's Who in New York City and State reveals no fewer than 109 professionals (or about 17 percent of the total) claiming to be church members: 40 lawyers, 16 bankers, 13 doctors, 9 merchants, 8 manufacturers, 6 engineers, 5 insurance executives, 4 real-estate brokers, 2 architects, 2 "brokers," 2 advertising managers, 1 "capitalist," and 1 "financier." The overwhelming majority of those claiming religious affiliation in this particular volume were Protestants; the most common affiliations were Presbyterian, Episcopalian, and Methodist. (Clergymen and theologically trained educators and writers were excluded from the list.)

58. Weber observed that there was "hardly [an American] small businessman with ambitions who does not wear some [group's] badge in his buttonhole." "'Churches' and 'Sects' in North America (1906)," in Peter Baehr and Gordon C. Wells, eds., *Max Weber: "The Protestant Ethic and the 'Spirit' of Capitalism"; and Other Writings* (New York: Penguin, 2002), 203–220, 210.

59. Mary I. Wood, "The Woman's Club Movement," *Chautauquan* 59, no. 1 (June 1910): 13.

60. Also see Nettie F. Bailey, "The Significance of the Woman's Club Movement," *Harper's Bazaar*, March 1905, 204–209, 204, 205, 207.

61. In 1908, for example, the Maine Union featured departments for Work among Foreign Speaking Peoples, Young Woman's Work, Hygienic Reform, Medical Temperance, Scientific Temperance, Sunday School Work, Temperance Literature, the Press, Anti-Narcotics, Bible Reading and Evangelistic Work, Prison and Jail Work, Reformatories for Women, Almshouse Work and Charities, Securing Homes for Homeless Children, Work among Railroad Employees, Work among Soldiers and Sailors, Work among Lumbermen and Quarrymen, Work among Light Stations, Sabbath Observance, Purity in Literature and Art, Schools Savings Bank, Legislation and Petition, Christian Citizenship, the Franchise (or Suffrage), and Peace and Arbitration. *Thirty-Fourth Annual Report of the Woman's Christian Temperance Union of Maine* (Rockland, ME: Press of the Courier Gazette, 1908),7–8, 54.

62. *Forty-Third Annual Report of the Young Women's Christian Association of Dayton, Ohio* (Dayton, OH: J. W. Johnson, 1914), 7–16.

63. Thomas St. Clair Evans, "Student Association Work at the University of Pennsylvania," *Religious Education* 5, no. 5 (December 1910): 518–520. The one-in-seven figure is found in George M. Marsden, *The Soul of the American University: From Protestant Establishment to Established Nonbelief* (New York: Oxford University Press, 1994), 343.

64. *Thirty-Fourth Annual Report of the Woman's Christian Temperance Union of Maine*, 82–84.

65. *Forty-Sixth Annual Report of the Young Women's Christian Association of Dayton, Ohio* (Dayton, OH: McBride Printing, 1917), 28.

66. Henriette Greenbaum Frank and Amalie Hofer Jerome, eds., *Annals of the Chicago Woman's Club* (Chicago: Chicago Woman's Club, 1916), 278.

67. *Fifty-First Annual Report of the Young Woman's Christian Association of Dayton, Ohio* (Dayton, 1922), 10.

68. Ladd-Taylor, *Mother-Work*, 52.

69. Wood, "The Woman's Club Movement," 13.

70. Skocpol, *Protecting Soldiers and Mothers*, 393. Also see Storrs, *Civilizing Capitalism*.

71. The leaders of these bodies cultivated close relationships with policy experts at the NCLC, the NCL, and the federal Children's Bureau, who were more than happy to supply hard data for use in Sunday sermons, Sunday-school materials, and denominational periodicals. See, for example, Robin Muncy, *Creating a Female Dominion in American Reform, 1890–1935* (New York: Oxford University Press, 1991), 57; Harry F. Ward, *A Yearbook of the Church and Social Service in the United States* (Boston: Pilgrim Press, 1914), 110, 105, 107, 98.

72. The FCC had by this point cultivated a small network of wealthy donors that included John D. Rockefeller and the copper magnate Cleveland Dodge. The Commission's initial budget was around $5,000. Charles S. MacFarland, *Christian Unity in the Making: The First Twenty-five years of the Federal Council of the Churches of Christ in America, 1905–1930* (New York: Federal Council of Churches, 1948), 57, 60–63, 116.

73. See, for example, *Proceedings of the Annual Conference* (American Academy of Political and Social Science, 1906), 114, 121–122. A fairly complete collection of Labor Sunday materials from the early twentieth century can be found in NCC, RG 18, Box 25, Folder 4.

74. *Uniform Child Labor Laws: Proceedings of the 7th Annual Conference* (New York: National Child Labor Committee, 1911), 195. For lists of churches observing Child Labor Sunday in specific cities, see "Earnest Attacks on Child Labor," *Chicago Daily Tribune*, January 25, 1909, p. 9; "Child Labor Sunday Here," *New York Times*, January 23, 1916, p. 13; "Child-Labor Sunday Today," *New York Times*, January 28, 1917, p. 18. The figure of thirty thousand is from John A. Hutchison, *We Are Not Divided* (New York: Round Table Press, 1941), 117, 108.

75. Worth M. Tippy and F. Ernest Johnson, "The Church and Women in Industry" [pamphlet] (New York: Commission on the Church and Social Service of the FCC), 1918. PHS, RG 18, Box 52, Folder 3.

76. Ibid.

77. Skocpol, *Protecting Soldiers and Mothers*, 393; Storrs, *Civilizing Capitalism*, 26–27.

78. Skocpol, *Diminished Democracy*, 25–30, 40–43.

79. George Hall et al., "Reports from State and Local Child Labor Committees and Consumers' Leagues," *Annals of the American Academy of Political and Social Science* 29 (1907): 142–183, 150, 163, 173; Oliver C. Bryant et al., "Reports from State and

Local Child Labor Committees," *Annals of the American Academy of Political and Social Science*, 35 (1910): 160–194, 160, 175–176, 188.

80. The description is from Skocpol, *Protecting Soldiers and Mothers*, 393.

81. For example, lawmakers' fear of the "woman vote" was clearly a factor in the Oregon Congress of Mothers' successful 1913 push for a statewide mothers' pension plan. In accounting for the measure's passage, the *Portland Oregonian* observed that the state had recently enfranchised women, and that "neither Senators nor Representatives [were] opposing any measures which will tend to be of assistance to women." Quoted in Mark H. Leff, "Consensus for Reform: The Mothers'-Pension Movement in the Progressive Era," *Social Service Review* 47 (1973): 397–417, 408.

82. Wilson, *The Women's Joint Congressional Committee*, 9–17; Clemens, *The People's Lobby*, 293–295; Skocpol, *Protecting Soldiers and Mothers*, 319–320.

83. Muncy, *Creating a Female Dominion*, 47; Skocpol, *Protecting Soldiers and Mothers*, 488–489.

84. Jacqueline K. Parker and Edward M. Carpenter, "Julia Lathrop and the Children's Bureau," *Social Service Review* 55 (1981): 60–77, 62. On Lathrop's GFWC membership, see Muncy, *Creating a Female Dominion*, 58.

85. Skocpol, *Protecting Soldiers and Mothers*, 488–489; Parker and Carpenter, "Julia Lathrop and the Children's Bureau," 68–69; Muncy, *Creating a Female Dominion*, 60.

86. Quoted in Skocpol, *Protecting Soldiers and Mothers*, 497. The Bureau also received a reputational boost from the fact that the FCC and mainline denominational bodies regularly plugged its activities in their official publications. See, for example, Tippy and Johnson, "The Church and Women in Industry." Also see Muncy, *Creating a Female Dominion*, 57.

87. See Skocpol, *Protecting Soldiers and Mothers*, 504–506; Jan Doolittle Wilson, *The Women's Joint Congressional Committee and the Politics of Maternalism, 1920–1930* (Urbana: University of Illinois Press, 2007), 43–49, 69–74.

88. See, for example, Ladd-Taylor, *Mother-Work*, 173; Skocpol, *Protecting Soldiers and Mothers*, 515–517.

89. Quoted in Skocpol, *Protecting Soldiers and Mothers*, 505.

90. *Uniform Child Labor Laws: Proceedings of the 7th Annual Conference* (New York: National Child Labor Committee, 1911), 195–196.

91. "Eleventh Report of the General Secretary of the National Child Labor Committee," *Child Labor Bulletin* 4, no. 3 (November 1915): 144.

92. Kriste Lindenmeyer, "Keating-Owen Act," in Melvyn Dubofsky, ed., *The Oxford Encyclopedia of American Business, Labor, and Economic History* (New York: Oxford University Press), 1:417.

93. On mainline Protestant bodies' support for the measure, see Robert Moats Miller, *American Protestantism and Social Issues, 1919–1939* (Chapel Hill: University of North Carolina Press, 1958), 217–218.

94. The law was invalidated in *Bailey v. Drexel Furniture Co.*, 259 U.S. 20 (1922).

95. "The Children's Amendment" [pamphlet] (Washington, DC: Trade Unionist, 1924). NCC, RG 18, Box 82, Folder 7.

96. Miller, *American Protestantism and Social Issues*, 217–219.

97. The vote in the House was 297 to 69; in the Senate it was 61 to 23.

98. Robert T. Handy, *A Christian America: Protestant Hopes and Historical Realities* (New York: Oxford University Press, 1971), 129.

99. The group sent shock waves through the political system in 1906 when, after a seemingly minor dispute over the wording of a local option law, it backed a relatively unknown challenger to Ohio's popular and well-connected incumbent Republican governor, Myron Herrick. Despite having few credentials beyond the League's endorsement, the Democratic challenger won, and the ASL's reputation as the nation's premier pressure group was sealed. On Herrick's defeat, see Okrent, *Last Call*, 39–40; Ann-Marie E. Szymanksi, *Pathways to Prohibition: Radicals, Moderates, and Social Movement Outcomes* (Durham, NC: Duke University Press, 2003), 140–141.

100. Ernest H. Cherrington, *The Evolution of Prohibition in the United States* (1920; Montclair, NJ: Patterson Smith, 1969), 284; Gaines M. Foster, *Moral Reconstruction: Christian Lobbyists and the Federal Legislation of Morality, 1865–1920* (Chapel Hill: University of North Carolina Press, 2002), 185–189.

101. Cherrington, *The Evolution of Prohibition*, 320.

102. Quoted in Roger A. Bruns, *Preacher: Billy Sunday and Big-Time American Evangelicalism* (Urbana: University of Illinois Press, 1992), 130.

103. Christians, Riley wrote in *Messages for the Metropolis*, his 1906 indictment of the city's political machine, were "especially charged with civic reform." Quoted in William Vance Trollinger, Jr., *God's Empire: William Bell Riley and Midwestern Fundamentalism* (Madison: University of Wisconsin Press, 1990), 63.

104. Quoted in Matthew Avery Sutton, *American Apocalypse: A History of Modern Evangelicalism* (Cambridge, MA: Belknap Press, 2014), 232.

105. Riley quoted in Trollinger, *God's Empire*, 65; Straton quoted in Sutton, *American Apocalypse*, 114. On the origins of MBI's pro-business worldview, see Timothy W. Gloege, *Guaranteed Pure: The Moody Bible Institute, Business, and the Making of Modern Evangelicalism* (Chapel Hill: University of North Carolina Press, 2015).

106. Straton trained most of his fire on theater owners, whom he accused of profiting from "sensualism" and "the passion for pleasure." Quoted in J. Terry Todd, "New York, the New Babylon? Fundamentalism and the Modern City in Reverend Straton's Jazz Age Crusade," in John M. Gigge and Diane Winston, eds., *Faith in the Market: Religion and the Rise of Urban Commercial Culture* (New Brunswick, NJ: Rutgers University Press, 2002), 74–87, 75.

107. This point is discussed in more detail in chap. 3.

108. Quoted in Sutton, *American Apocalypse*, 37.

109. Michael Kazin, *A Godly Hero: The Life of William Jennings Bryan* (New York: Alfred A. Knopf, 2006).

110. For a good example of Bryan's thinking on this point, see the 1905 commencement address entitled "Man," in William Jennings Bryan, *Speeches of William Jennings Bryan*, vol. 2 (New York: Funk & Wagnalls, 1909), 291–314, 301–307.

Chapter 2

1. Daniel Okrent, *Last Call: The Rise and Fall of Prohibition* (New York: Simon and Schuster, 2010), 118.
2. Walter Lippmann, *A Preface to Morals* (New York: Macmillan, 1929), 4, 20. The Aristophanes quotation is from *The Clouds*.
3. 128. According to Riesman, the notion of feeling sympathy for labor organizers never occurred to the profit-driven industrial titans of the Gilded Age, nor even to later industrial innovators such as Henry Ford. The modern executive, in contrast, was greatly influenced by "the expectations the public has, or is thought to have of them." David Riesman, Nathan Glazer, and Reuel Denney, *The Lonely Crowd: A Study of the Changing American Character* (New Haven, CT: Yale University Press, 1961 [1950]), 128, 134.
4. William H. Whyte, Jr., *The Organization Man* (New York: Simon and Schuster, 1956), 365–381.
5. "Dry Regime Inquiry by Churches Shows Outcome in Doubt," *New York Times*, September 14, 1925, p. 1; "Finds Dry Law Aids Economic Advance; Alcoholism Rising," *New York Times*, September 15, 1925, p. 1; "Prohibition Fails to Reduce Crime," *New York Times*, September 16, 1925, p. 27; "Alcohol Diversion Chief Dry Act Foe," *New York Times*, September 17, 1925, p. 25; "Prohibition Report Holds Mellon Law in Dry Enforcement," *New York Times*, September 18, 1925, p. 1; "Blames Public for 'Dry' Troubles," *New York Times*, September 19, 1925, p. 1.
6. "Dr. Wilson Assails Report," *New York Times*, September 20, 1925, p. 2.
7. "Scores Dry Report by Church Council," *New York Times*, October 25, 1925, p. 18.
8. "Refuses to Divide Enforcement Work," *New York Times*, October 31, 1925, p. 1.
9. "Church Council Held in Dry Leash," *New York Times*, December 12, 1925, p. 18.
10. See https://prohibition.osu.edu/american-prohibition-1920/federal-council-churches. Accessed July 10, 2017.
11. Kenneth D. Rose, *American Women and the Repeal of Prohibition* (New York: New York University Press, 1996), 61–62.
12. On the evolution of Protestant elites' thinking on matters of religious and ethnic diversity, see, for example, Eric P. Kaufmann, *The Rise and Fall of Anglo-America* (Cambridge, MA: Harvard University Press, 2004); David A. Hollinger, *Protestants Abroad: How Missionaries Tried to Change the World but Changed America* (Princeton, NJ: Princeton University Press, 2017).
13. "Church Council Held in Dry Leash," *New York Times*, December 12, 1925, p. 18.
14. For examples of cities where the Klan functioned as a de facto arm of government, see Lisa McGirr, *The War on Alcohol: Prohibition and the Rise of the American State* (New York: Norton, 2016), 133–135.
15. George M. Marsden, *Fundamentalism and American Culture: The Shaping of Twentieth-Century Evangelicalism, 1870–1925* (New York: Oxford University Press, 1980), 190–191; Matthew Avery Sutton, *American Apocalypse: A History of Modern Evangelicalism* (Cambridge, MA: Belknap Press, 2014), 128–130. Straton eventually turned against the Klan and attempted to force Haywood out of the church. See, for

example, "Ku Klux Klan Denounced from Many Pulpits," *New York Times*, December 1, 1922, p. 2; "Ku Klux Klan Must Go, Says Dr. Straton," *New York Times*, December 4, 1922, p. 4.

16. "The Ku Klux Klan Disowned by the Churches" (press release), September 29, 1922, NCC Record Group 18, Box 12, Folder 9.

17. Robert Moats Miller, "A Note on the Relationship between the Protestant Churches and the Revived Ku Klux Klan," *Journal of Southern History* 22 (1956): 355–368, 366–367. Indeed, even the Southern branches of the Baptists and Methodists adopted strongly worded resolutions denouncing the KKK as an un-Christian organization. Samuel McCrea Cavert to Howard Agnew Johnson, September 15, 1922, NCC Record Group 18, Box 12, Folder 9; Miller, "A Note on the Relationship," 363–365.

18. Kaufmann, *Rise and Fall of Anglo-America*, 127–128; Kelly J. Baker, *Gospel According to the Klan: The KKK's Appeal to Protestant America, 1915–1930* (Lawrence: University Press of Kansas, 2011), 66–67.

19. Linda Gordon, *The Second Coming of the KKK: The Ku Klux Klan* (New York: Liveright, 2017), 79–80.

20. Arguably the most notorious demonstration of Klan power occurred at the 1924 Democratic Convention in New York City, where pro-Klan forces not only helped sink the nomination bid of New York's Catholic governor, Al Smith, but also managed to defeat (by a single vote) a resolution condemning the organization as a threat to "religious liberty" and "civic rights." The spectacle was a public relations disaster for the Democratic party, but it also dealt a serious black eye to the prohibition cause, not least because William Jennings Bryan, the nation's leading dry crusader, spoke against the anti-Klan resolution. (Though Bryan privately despised the Klan, he was apparently unwilling to risk alienating a group of delegates who were certain to oppose the nomination of a wet candidate at the head of the ticket.) Michael Kazin, *A Godly Hero: The Life of William Jennings Bryan* (New York: Random House, 2006), 281; McGirr, *The War Against Alcohol*, 168–169; Okrent, *Last Call*, 245–246.

21. See, for example, Miller, "A Note on the Relationship," 363–365; Kaufmann, *Rise and Fall of Anglo-America*, 127–128; Kenneth T. Jackson, *The Ku Klux Klan in the City, 1915–1930* (1967; Chicago: Ivan R. Dee, 1992), 34, 99, 247. For additional examples of anti-Klan resolutions, see "Federal Church Council Condemns Ku Klux Klan," *Christian Science Monitor*, October 16, 1922, p. 5; "'Blue Sabbath' Society Ignored by Church Body," *Chicago Daily Tribune*, October 23, 1923, p. 19; "Pastors Condemn Mob Acts," *Los Angeles Times*, May 1, 1922, p. 12; "M.E. Pastors Vote Against Race Hostility," *Chicago Daily Tribune*, October 9, 1923, p. 4.

22. See, for example, Gordon, *Second Coming of the KKK*, 112–113 and passim.

23. On the decline of the 1920s Klan, see ibid., 191–197.

24. See, for example, Wendy L. Wall, *Inventing the "American Way": The Politics of Consensus from the New Deal to the Civil Rights Movement* (New York: Oxford University Press, 2008), 80–81.

25. Kaufmann, *Rise and Fall of Anglo-America*, 127–134.

26. Kevin M. Schultz, *Tri-Faith America: How Catholics and Jews Held Postwar America to Its Protestant Promise* (New York: Oxford University Press, 2011), 26–35.

27. William L. Marbury, "The Nineteenth Amendment and After," *The Woman Patriot* 4 (December 25, 1920): 8.
28. Jan Doolittle Wilson, *The Women's Joint Congressional Committee and the Politics of Maternalism, 1920–30* (Urbana: University of Illinois Press, 2010), 169–170.
29. David E. Kyvig, *Repealing National Prohibition*, 2nd ed. (Kent, OH: Kent State University Press, 2000), 118–119, 120, 126.
30. Quoted in Wilson, *The Women's Joint Congressional Committee*, 149–150.
31. The DAR even went so far as to organize a sophisticated spying operation that worked to infiltrate the LWV and other allegedly subversive groups. Ibid., 166; Kristen Marie Delegard, *Battling Miss Bolsheviki: The Origins of Female Conservatism in the United States* (Philadelphia: University of Pennsylvania Press, 2012), 136–137.
32. Delegard, *Battling Miss Bolsheviki*, 129–131, 132, 134–135.
33. Quoted in Molly Ladd-Taylor, *Mother-Work: Women, Child Welfare, and the State, 1890–1930* (Urbana: University of Illinois Press, 1994), 122. Also see Wilson, *The Women's Joint Congressional Committee*, 155–157.
34. Quoted in Wilson, *The Women's Joint Congressional Committee*, 156–159.
35. On the Bureau's corrupt hiring practices and incompetent administration, see Okrent, *Last Call*, 131–135; McGirr, *The War on Alcohol*, 189–229. The Hearst newspaper chain's sensationalized—though factually accurate—coverage of botched enforcement efforts is discussed in Okrent, *Last Call*, 318–319.
36. Quoted in Wilson, *The Women's Joint Congressional Committee*, 129.
37. Ladd-Taylor, *Mother-Work*, 187.
38. Ibid., 188.
39. See, for example, George Marsden, *Fundamentalism and American Culture*, 2nd ed. (New York: Oxford University Press, 2006), 171–178 and passim.
40. H. Paul Douglass, *The Springfield Church Survey: A Study of Organized Religion with Its Social Background* (New York: George H. Doran, 1926), 224–226, 403.
41. C. Luther Fry, *The U.S. Looks at Its Churches* (New York: Institute of Social and Religious Research, 1930), 2–3, 5, 90; H. Paul Douglass, *St. Louis Church Survey: A Religious Investigation with a Social Background* (New York: George H. Doran, 1924), 309.
42. See, for example, E. Digby Baltzell, *Philadelphia Gentlemen: The Making of a National Upper Class* (1958; Chicago: Quadrangle, 1971), 223–261.
43. Quoted in Jerome Davis, "The Minister and the Economic Order," *Journal of Educational Sociology* 10 (1937): 269–279, 274.
44. James K. Wellman, Jr., *The Gold Coast and the Ghetto: Christ and Culture in Mainline Protestantism* (Urbana: University of Illinois Press, 1999), 60.
45. Quoted in ibid., 59.
46. Robert S. Lynd and Helen Merrell Lynd, *Middletown: A Study in Modern American Culture* (New York: Harcourt Brace, 1929), 355 n. 14, 383, 369, 333 n. 3.
47. Ibid., 333 n. 3.
48. See, for example, Raymond H. Hinkel, "Basic Social Pronouncements of Representative Protestant Churches, 1925–1935," (Ph.D. diss., University of Southern California, 1935), chap. 3.
49. Glenn T. Miller, *Piety and Profession: American Protestant Theological Education, 1870–1970* (Grand Rapids, MI: William B. Eerdmans, 2007), 162.

50. On the *Christian Century*'s rising national profile in the 1920s, see Elesha J. Coffman, *The "Christian Century" and the Rise of the Protestant Mainline* (New York: Oxford University Press, 2013), 59–110. The 1920s witnessed other significant innovations in the realm of religious print culture, including a popular mail-order book club—modeled on the Book-of-the-Month Club—that aimed to provide middlebrow readers with the latest and best books on religion. Matthew S. Hedstrom, *The Rise of Liberal Religion: Book Culture and American Spirituality in the Twentieth Century* (New York: Oxford University Press, 2013), 61–71.

51. See, for example, *The Coal Strike in Western Pennsylvania* (New York: Federal Council of Churches of Christ in America, 1928); *The Twelve Hour Day in the Steel Industry* (New York: Federal Council of Churches of Christ in America, 1923). Both pamphlets can be found in NCC, Record Group 18, Box 72, Folder 23. The Council also joined with the National Catholic Welfare Council to formally oppose the aims of the Open Shop movement. John A. Hutchison, *We Are Not Divided: A Critical and Historical Study of the Federal Council* (New York: Round Table Press, 1941), 111.

52. Charles S. MacFarland, *Christian Unity in the Making: The First Twenty-Five Years of the Federal Council of the Churches of Christ in America* (New York: Federal Council of Churches, 1948), 209, 217. Also see *Mob Murder in America: The Challenge Which Lynching Brings to the Churches* (New York: Federal Council of Churches, 1923).

53. The Committee on Goodwill, after being reorganized as the National Conference of Christians and Jews, would continue its lobbying efforts on behalf of domestic social programs and interfaith tolerance for several decades. MacFarland, *Christian Unity in the Making*, 266–267, 281–282.

54. See, for example, Federal Council of the Churches in Christ in America, Department of Research and Education; National Catholic Welfare Conference, Social Action Department; Central Conference of American Rabbis, Social Justice Commission, *The Centralia Case: A Joint Report on the Armistice Day Tragedy at Centralia, Washington* (New York: Brooklyn Eagle Press, 1930).

55. Robert A. Schneider, "Voice of Many Waters: Church Federation in the Twentieth Century," in William R. Hutchison, ed., *Between the Times: The Travail of the Protestant Establishment in America* (New York: Cambridge University Press, 1989), 95–121, 108–109.

56. "Industrial Program of Churches Commended," *Federal Council Bulletin* 4 (June-July 1921): 75. Also see MacFarland, *Christian Unity in the Making*, 206–207.

57. MacFarland, *Christian Unity in the Making*, 253.

58. Indeed, it was a $50,000 gift from Hoover that allowed the FCC's most overtly political subunit, the Commission on the Church and Social Service, to carry out its most controversial research programs. *Directory of Charter Associates of the Federal Council of Churches of Christ in America* (New York: Federal Council of Churches, 1930), NCC, RG 18, Box 82, Folder 13.

59. Schneider, "Voice of Many Waters," 109.

60. Ross W. Sanderson, *Church Cooperation in the United States* (New York: Association of Council Secretaries, 1960), 106–107.

61. H. Paul Douglass, *Protestant Cooperation in American Cities* (New York: Institute of Social and Religious Research, 1930), 51.

62. Ibid., 449. Douglass reports that the median federation budget was $11,000, and that fully one-fourth of federations had annual budgets of $30,000 or more.
63. Douglass reports the participation rates in some representative cities as Chicago, 43 percent; Detroit, 52 percent; Pittsburgh, 54 percent; and St. Louis, 90 percent. H. Paul Douglass, *Protestant Cooperation in American Cities* (New York: Institute of Social and Religious Research, 1930), 95; *The St. Louis Church Survey* (New York: George H. Doran Co., 1924), 174.
64. Roy B. Guild, *Community Programs for Cooperating Churches: A Manual of Principles and Methods* (New York: Association Press, 1920), 20.
65. H. Paul Douglass, *Church Comity* (New York: Institute for Social and Religious Research, 1929).
66. Douglass, *Protestant Cooperation in American Cities*, 379, 372.
67. Ibid., 247.
68. Ibid., 380–381.
69. William Adams Brown, *The Church in America: A Study of the Present Condition and Future Prospects of American Protestantism* (New York: MacMillan, 1922), 219.
70. Like the federated women's groups, the nation's church councils tended to be organized along parallel lines, so that each local, state, and national body featured departments dedicated to comity, evangelism, social service, religious education, and the like. Sanderson, *Church Cooperation in the United States*, 143.
71. Douglass, *Protestant Cooperation in American Cities*, 490–494; Hutchison, *We Are Not Divided*, 117, 108.
72. Quoted in Douglass, *Protestant Cooperation in American Cities*, 253.
73. A survey of some three thousand "constituents" of local church federations conducted in the late 1920s found high levels of support for the Council-backed industrial relations and interracial comity programs, with 67 and 65 percent of respondents, respectively, rating them "highly" important. Yet, because the sample was composed disproportionately of clergymen and lay leaders, these findings must be taken with a grain of salt; ibid., 418. A separate 1929 study—with an admittedly small sample size—found that Northern clergymen expressed overwhelmingly positive views of the church federation movement, while those in the South tended to oppose it. Archer B. Bass, *Protestantism in the United States* (New York: Thomas Y. Crowell, 1929), 125–128.
74. Douglass, *Protestant Cooperation in American Cities*, 390.
75. C. Luther Fry, *The U.S. Looks at Its Churches* (New York: Institute of Social and Religious Research, 1930), 4, 64.

Chapter 3

1. For an early version of this claim, see Elizabeth Kirkpatrick Dilling, *The Roosevelt Red Record and Its Background* (Chicago, 1936), 231. For an overview of the "Red" accusations leveled at the Council during the 1920s and early 1930s, see John A. Hutchison, *We Are Not Divided: A Critical and Historical Study of the Federal Council* (New York: Round Table Press, 1941), 122–125.

2. The claim that FDR's program was too radical for the electorate was the lesson that some Republicans—perhaps desperate for signs of hope—drew from the unexpected victories of conservative Republicans in a handful of late September primary elections. See, for example, "Republicans Hail LaFollette Defeat as Trend to Hoover," *New York Times*, September 22, 1932, p. 1.

3. "Address of Governor Franklin D Roosevelt, Naval Armory, Belle Isle Bridge, Detroit Michigan, October 2, 1932," Master Speech File, 1898–1945, Series 1, Box 11, FDR Presidential Library and Museum, available online at http://www.fdrlibrary.marist.edu/archives/collections/fdrspeeches.html; "Roosevelt Pleads for Social Justice in Detroit Address," *New York Times*, October 3, 1932, p. 1.

4. Merlin Gustafson and Jerry Rosenberg, "The Faith of Franklin Roosevelt," *Presidential Studies Quarterly* 19 (1989): 559–566; Gary Scott Smith, *Faith in the Presidency: From George Washington to George W. Bush* (New York: Oxford University Press, 2006), 193–199. On Hopkins and Perkins, see, for example, Christopher H. Evans, *The Social Gospel in America: A History* (New York: New York University Press, 2017), 147.

5. As the General Conference of the Congregational Church declared in 1934, church members should do everything in their power to ensure that the current "profit-seeking system of economics," which had produced so much "human misery and want in the midst of abundance," was replaced by "a new social order characterized by cooperation and effort for the common good." Quoted in Raymond H. Hinkel, "Basic Social Pronouncements of Representative Protestant Churches, 1925–1935" (Ph. D. diss., University of Southern California, 1935), 33–34.

6. Important exceptions include Ronald Isetti, "The Money Changers of the Temple: FDR, American Civil Religion, and the New Deal," *Presidential Studies Quarterly* 26 (1996): 678–693 and Donald Meyer, *The Protestant Search for Political Realism, 1919–1941*, 2nd ed. (Middletown, CT: Wesleyan University Press, 1988); and Paul A. Carter, *The Decline and Revival of the Social Gospel: Social and Political Liberalism in American Protestant Churches, 1920–1940* (Hamden, CT: Archon Books, 1971). More recent works that discuss how Protestant elites and lay people related to the Roosevelt administration and its policies include, Alison Collis Greene, *No Depression in Heaven: The Great Depression, the New Deal, and the Transformation of Religion in the Delta* (New York: Oxford University Press, 2015); Elesha J. Coffman, *The Christian Century and the Rise of the Protestant Mainline* (New York: Oxford University Press, 2013); Michael Janson, "A Christian Century: Liberal Protestantism, the New Deal, and the Origins of Post-War American Politics" (PhD Dissertation, University of Pennsylvania, 2007); and John F. Woolverton, *A Christian and a Democrat: A Religious Biography of Franklin D. Roosevelt* (Grand Rapids, MI: William B. Eerdmans, 2019). I regret that I did not learn of the Woolverton book in time to incorporate its insights into this chapter.

7. For a recent critical review of the literature on the New Deal–era party realignment, see Christopher Achen and Larry Bartels, *Democracy for Realists: Why Elections Do Not Produce Responsive Government* (Princeton, NJ: Princeton University Press, 2017), chap. 9.

8. Quoted in William Finley McKee, "The Attitude of the Federal Council of the Churches of Christ in America to the New Deal: A Study in Social Christianity" (Ph. D. diss., University of Wisconsin, 1954), 89–90.

9. In addition to participating in the President's Emergency Committee for Unemployment (later renamed the President's Organization for Unemployment Relief), FCC officials busied themselves with identifying concrete steps that local congregations could take to aid the hungry and jobless. A November 1930 directive, for example, urged "every church to establish an employment committee to canvass church members to find part-time work for the unemployed, to promote the use of the church plant for shelter or educational programs for the unemployed, to support the relief drives of charitable organizations, [and] to cooperate with the Salvation Army and YMCA in providing food and shelter." The Council also encouraged churches to plant subsistence gardens, undertake canning drives, and organize study groups to examine potential policy remedies. Quoted in McKee, "The Attitude of the Federal Council," 87–88.

10. By December 1930, when the FCC's Executive Committee adopted a series of resolutions advocating the creation of public employment agencies, public works programs, and a system of unemployment insurance, it was apparent that an un-bridgeable philosophical divide separated the Quaker President from mainline de-nominational leaders. Ibid., 87–90.

11. On federated women's clubs and the New Deal, see, for example, Sarah Wilkerson-Freeman, "From Clubs to Parties: North Carolina Women in the Advancement of the New Deal," *North Carolina Historical Review* 68 (1991): 320–339. On the Townsend clubs' use of religious appeals, see Edwin Amenta, *When Movements Matter: The Townsend Clubs and the Rise of Social Security* (Princeton: Princeton University Press, 2006), 119–120; Aaron Q. Weinstein, "Onward Townsend Soldiers: Moral Politics and Civil Religion in the Townsend Crusade," *American Political Thought* (2017): 228–255. The female-dominated National Consumers' League also provided critical support for the New Deal, though the League remained an elite organiza-tion with modest grassroots support. Landon R. Y. Storrs, *Civilizing Capitalism: The National Consumers' League, Women's Activism, and Labor Standards in the New Deal Era* (Chapel Hill: University of North Carolina Press, 2000).

12. "Protestant Gifts $378,000,000 in Year," *New York Times*, September 28, 1933, p. 23.

13. Myers describes some of his more interesting experiences on the picket lines in "Notes from the Diary of a Modern Circuit Rider," *Forum and Century*, October 1937, p. 175. For an overview of his career, see Elizabeth Fones-Wolf and Ken Fones-Wolf, "Lending a Hand to Labor: James Myers and the Federal Council of Churches, 1926–1947," *Church History* 68 (1999): 62–86.

14. On the genesis of the Wisconsin plan, see Daniel Nelson, *Unemployment Insurance: The American Experience, 1915–1945* (Madison: University of Wisconsin Press, 1969), 118–128.

15. Grace Abbott, "Compulsory Unemployment Insurance – Why?" *Church and Society* 3 (January 1931): 1.

16. Charles K. Gilbert and James Myers to Presidents of Ministers Associations, February 20, 1932, NCC, RG 18, Box 52, Folder 25. "Unemployment Reserves: Questions Answered," NCC, RG 18, Box 52, Folder 25.

17. Elizabeth S. Magee to James Meyer [sic], January 24, 1931, NCC RG, 18, Box 55, Folder 13.

18. Although the first draft of his letter was prepared by the Conference, Myers insisted on adding a paragraph reminding the ministers that the delegates to the Federal Council's 1932 quadrennial had committed themselves to securing "social insurance against sickness, accident, want in old age and unemployment." Draft of Letter Submitted to Mr. William Myers [sic], Federal Council of Churches, NCC, RG 18, Box 55, Folder 13 (n.d.); James Myers [form letter to ministers], February 28, 1933, NCC, RG 18, Box 55, Folder 13.

19. C. Lawson Willard, Jr., to The Hon. Herbert H. Lehman, March 22, 1933, NCC, RG 18, Box 15, Folder 13; Robert Hastings Nichols to James Myers, March 11, 1933, NCC, RG 18, Box 15, Folder 13.

20. Paul Raushenbush changed the traditional spelling of his surname.

21. The Wagner-Lewis bill, whose primary drafter was Raushenbush's husband, Paul, relied on a novel system of federal tax offsets to incentivize the creation of unemployment insurance systems in the states. It imposed a nationwide payroll tax on all employers, but employers in states that adopted unemployment insurance would have their federal tax bill reduced by whatever amount they paid into the state system. Elizabeth Brandeis Raushenbush to James Myers, February 5, 1934, NCC Record Group 18, Box 55, Folder 13. On the origins of the Wagner-Lewis bill, see Nelson, *Unemployment Insurance*, 198–202.

22. James Myers to Elizabeth Brandeis Raushenbush, February 10, 1934, NCC, RG 18, Box 55, Folder 13; James Myers to Samuel McCrea Cavert (memorandum), February 10, 1934, NCC, RG 18, Box 55, Folder 13; Elizabeth Brandeis Raushenbush to James Myers, February 15, 1934, NCC, RG 18, Box 55, Folder 13.

23. James Myers (draft form letter), February 10, 1934, NCC, RG 18, Box 55, Folder 13.

24. See, for example, "Conference Backs Social Security," *New York Times*, April 9, 1935, p. 9.

25. Quoted in Hinkel, "Basic Social Pronouncements," 83, 67, 89, 60.

26. "Episcopalians Ask End of Child Labor," *New York Times*, May 9, 1934, p. 21; "Episcopal Group Urges a Job Fund," *New York Times*, October 13, 1934, p. 9; "Church Acts Against War," *Los Angeles Times*, October 23, 1934, p. 5.

27. A full list of the members of Roosevelt's Committee on Economic Security is available at https://www.ssa.gov/history/reports/ces/ces6.html. On Witte's outreach efforts to the denominational social service agencies, see "Conference Backs Social Security," *New York Times*, April 9, 1935, p. 9.

28. "Report of the Committee on Economic Security," available at https://www.ssa.gov/history/reports/ces/ces5.html. On the genesis of the Committee on Economic Security, and its role in securing the adoption of a federal unemployment insurance law, see Nelson, *Unemployment Insurance*, 204–211.

29. Sydney E. Goldstein to John G. Winant, February 12, 1936, JGW, Box 155, "Churches, Conferences with Religious Leaders"; Memo; R. Huse to John G. Winant, March 30, 1936, JGW, Box 155, "Churches, Conferences with Religious Leaders."

30. "The National Social Security Program," *Information Service*, September 5, 1936, p. 1; in JGW, Box 155, "Churches, Conferences with Religious Leaders."

31. Memo; R. Huse to John G. Winant, March 30, 1936, JGW, Box 155, "Churches, Conferences with Religious Leaders."

32. Henry Sloane Coffin to John G. Winant, February 10, 1937, JGW, Box 155, "Co General."

33. Quoted in Arthur M. Schlesinger, *The Coming of the New Deal: 1933–1935, The Age of Roosevelt* (1958; Boston: Mariner, 2003), 114–115.

34. The symbol first appears on the inside cover of the September 13, 1933 issue of *Christian Century*. This is not to suggest that the periodical was uncritical in its attitude toward the New Deal. Only a week after it first displayed the Blue Eagle, it excoriated NRA administrators for ignoring the plight of Southern blacks. "Negro Workers and the NRA," *Christian Century*, September 23, 1933, p. 1165. On pastors displaying the Blue Eagle, see Alison Collis Greene, "A 'Divine Revelation'? Southern Churches Respond to the New Deal," in Andrew Preston, Bruce J. Schulman, and Julian E. Zelizer, eds., *Faithful Republic: Religion and Politics in Modern America* (Philadelphia: University of Pennsylvania Press), 56–70, 60.

35. James Myers to Rev. R.A. McGowan, June 20, 1933, NCC, RG 18, Box 52, Folder 25; James Myers to Edward L. Israel, June 23, 1933, NCC, RG 18, Box 52, Folder 25; James Myers to Rev. R.A. McGowan, June 23, 1933, NCC, RG 18, Box 52, Folder 25.

36. James Myers to Samuel McCrea Cavert, June 28, 1933, NCC, RG 18, Box 52, Folder 25; "Joint Statement of Three Religious Bodies," NCC, RG 18, Box 52, Folder 25.

37. [News clipping, no title], *Washington Herald*, July 19, 1933. NCC, RG 18, Box 52, Folder 25.

38. "Important Memorandum to Councils of Churches, Ministers Associations, and Denominational Commissions," July 11, 1933, NCC, RG 18, Box 52, Folder 25.

39. Wilbur E. Saunders to James Myers, August 13, 1933, NCC, RG 18, Box 52, Folder 25.

40. Wilbur E. Saunders to James Myers, August 13, 1933, NCC, RG 18, Box 52, Folder 25; James Myers to John A. Vollenweider, October 26, 1933, NCC, RG 18, Box 52, Folder 25; John A. Vollenweider to James Myers, September 6, 1933, NCC, RG 18, Box 52, Folder 25.

41. See, for example, the following documents in FDR-PPF, Folder 811: Lindley H. Miller to Franklin D. Roosevelt, September 15, 1933; Franklin D. Roosevelt to Lindley H. Miller, September 22, 1933; and Memo re: "Mr. Harold Baxter," January 5, 1934.

42. "Clergy Back N.R.A. Drive," *Los Angeles Times*, September 26, 1933, p. 1; "Drive Endorsed by Roosevelt," *Los Angeles Times*, September 27, 1933, p. 1; "Hair-Cut Price Fight Brewing," *Los Angeles Times*, September 30, 1933, p. 1.

43. Quoted in McKee, "Attitude of the Federal Council of the Churches of Christ," 169–170.

44. Quoted in ibid., 170. The mainline denominations, too, were by this point issuing a steady stream of pronouncements characterizing the New Deal as the natural outgrowth of Christian stewardship principles. Sydney E. Ahlstrom, *A Religious History*

of the American People (New Haven, CT: Yale University Press, 1972), 922; Hinkel, "Basic Social Pronouncements," 60–61, 73, 79–80, 85; "Episcopalians Ask End of Child Labor," *New York Times*, May 9, 1934, p. 21.

45. Roosevelt's address was reprinted in full in "Roosevelt Rallies Churches to Defend Social Justice," *Christian Science Monitor*, December 7, 1933, p. 2; and "Roosevelt Address to Church Group," *New York Times*, December 3, 1933, p. 2.
46. "Strikes in Prosperity and Depression," *Information Service* 12 (June 2, 1934): 2. Quoted in McKee, "The Attitude of the Federal Council of the Churches," 246.
47. *A. L. A. Schechter Poultry Corporation v. United States*, 295 U.S. 495 (1935).
48. The Roosevelt Administration, too, had its doubts about the need for new federal labor laws, at least until the Supreme Court invalidated Section 7(a) in the spring of 1935. On organized labor's initial opposition to the bill, see, for example, Laura Weinrib, *The Taming of Free Speech: America's Civil Liberties Compromise* (Cambridge, MA: Harvard University Press, 2016), 201–207; Janson, "A Christian Century," 138–144.
49. James Myers to Robert F. Wagner, May 10, 1934, NCC, RG 18, Box 52, Folder 25.
50. Fones-Wolf and Fones-Wolf, "Lending a Hand to Labor," 77–78.
51. James Myers to R. A. McGowan, February 18, 1935, NCC, RG 18, Box 55, Folder 16; R. A. McGowan to James Myers, February 19, 1935, NCC, RG 18, Box 55, Folder 16; James Myers to Robert F. Wagner, February 20, 1935, NCC, RG 18, Box 55, Folder 16.
52. Press release [no title], March 22, 1935, NCC, RG 18, Box 55, Folder 16.
53. James Myers to Executive Committee, March 1, 1935, NCC, RG 18, Box 55, Folder 16.
54. James Myers to Arthur Hays Sulzberger, March 21, 1935, NCC, RG 18, Box 55, Folder 16.
55. "Three Faiths Back Wagner Labor Bill," *New York Times*, March 26, 1935, p. 12. Myers also disseminated the statement to the labor papers, hoping to sway wavering union members to support the bill. Janson, "A Christian Century," 148.
56. James Myers to Leon H. Keyserling, March 5, 1935, NCC, RG 18, Box 55, Folder 16; James Myers to Robert F. Wagner, March 5, 1935, NCC, RG 18, Box 55, Folder 16; David I. Walsh to James Myers, March 22, 1935, NCC, RG 18, Box 55, Folder 16.
57. Myers' testimony before the Committee is summarized in McKee, "The Attitude of the Federal Council of the Churches," 237–238; and Janson, "A Christian Century," 149–150. On the Southern delegation's role in shaping the final text of the legislation, see Ira Katznelson, *Fear Itself: The New Deal and the Origins of Our Time* (New York: Liveright, 2013), 259–260.
58. Robert C. Albright, "Senate Votes Wagner Bill to Aid Labor," *New York Times*, May 17, 1935, p. 1.
59. James Myers to Secretaries of Councils of Churches, May 17, 1935, NCC, RG 18, Box 55, Folder 16.
60. Harlan M. Frost to James Myers, May 23, 1935, NCC, RG 18, Box 55, Folder 16, PHS; Fletcher D. Parker to James Myers, May 23, 1935, NCC, RG 18, Box 55, Folder 16; Elim A. E. Palmquist to James Myers, May 23, 1935, NCC, RG 18, Box 55, Folder 16.
61. "Wagner Bill," *New York Times*, June 20, 1935, p. 1; "Measure on Labor Disputes Adopted after House Debate," *Washington Post*, June 20, 1935, p. 1.

62. "Roosevelt Signs the Wagner Bill as 'Just to Labor,' " *New York Times*, July 6, 1935, p. 1.

63. See, for example, ibid.; "Labor Measure Is Made Ready for Roosevelt," *Washington Post*, June 28, 1935, p. 3.

64. Katznelson, *Fear Itself*, 258; David Brian Robertson, *Capital, Labor and the State: The Battle for American Labor Markets from the Civil War to the New Deal* (Lanham, MD: Rowman and Littlefield, 2000), 199–200.

65. Although the interfaith organization included a number of prominent Jews and Catholics, its primary focus was Northern Protestants. The League's chairman, Stanley High, was the former editor of the *Christian Herald* and a prominent supporter of prohibition; its honorary directors included such luminaries as the Presbyterian reformer Charles Stelzle, the social worker Lillian Wald, the suffragist Carrie Chapman Catt, and the Methodist bishop of Detroit. "Drive Is Begun for Roosevelt Independents," *Christian Science Monitor*, April 25, 1936, p. 1; "Church, Dry Unit Formed," *Washington Post*, April 25, 1936, p. 1; William Edward Leuchtenburg, *The FDR Years: On Roosevelt and His Legacy* (New York: Columbia University Press, 1997), 129.

66. Rev. John Evans, "Clergy Resents New Deal Plot to Dictate Vote," *Chicago Daily Tribune*, May 28, 1936, p. 9; Samuel McCrea Cavert to Charles Stelzle, April 15, 1936, GNL, Box 9, "Manifestos and Publicity." The League's outreach to the black churches was apparently more successful, and may well have succeeded in convincing many African American voters to abandon the party of Lincoln. See Eric Schickler, *Racial Realignment: The Transformation of American Liberalism, 1932–1965* (Princeton, NJ: Princeton University Press, 2016), 50–51.

67. Although the League would cling to life for another two years, playing a minor role in the failed push to ratify the Child Labor Amendment, it disbanded for good in 1939.

68. David W. Wills, "Black Americans and the Establishment," in William R. Hutchison, ed., *Between the Times: The Travail of the Protestant Establishment in America, 1900–1960* (New York: Cambridge University Press, 1989), 168–192, 178–179.

69. Ward's views are accurately summarized in John A. Vollenweider to James Myers, October 23, 1933, NCC, RG 18, Box 52, Folder 25; and James Myers to John A. Vollenweider, October 26, 1933, NCC, RG 18, Box 52, Folder 25.

70. A 1938 survey of more than one thousand Protestant ministers from the Baltimore area, for example, found that 80 percent supported their churches' efforts to "oppose sweat-shop conditions, child labor, [and] long hours of work," while only 24 percent agreed with the statement that ministers should "preach the gospel and let the problems of the world take care of themselves as individuals are made better." Norman L. Trott and Ross W. Sanderson, *What Church People Think about Social and Economic Issues* (New York: Association Press, 1938), 16.

71. Monroe Billington and Cal Clark, "Clergy Reaction to the New Deal: A Comparative Study," *Historian* 48 (1986): 509–524. Also see Billington and Clark, "Nebraska Clergymen, Franklin D. Roosevelt, and the New Deal," *Nebraska History* 72 (1991): 78–88; "The Episcopal Clergy and the New Deal: Clerical Responses to Franklin D. Roosevelt's Letter of Inquiry," *Historical Magazine of the Protestant Episcopal Church* 52 (1983): 293–305.

72. Quoted in Billington and Clark, "Clergy Reaction to the New Deal," 510–511.
73. Ibid., 514. Because the poll was designed for internal White House use, there is little reason to suspect that Mills manipulated the results; it does not appear that the findings were ever released to the press, or otherwise used for campaign purposes.
74. One study of responses from a representative sample of nine states, conducted by the historians Monroe Billington and Cal Clark, found that about 60 percent of responses were either "favorable" or "highly favorable" in their evaluations of the administration's domestic program, while 17.6 percent were "unfavorable" and 3.9 percent "highly unfavorable." In terms of substantive issues, the two programs singled out in the President's letter—Social Security and the public works programs—garnered the most support, with about 85 percent approving of the first and 74 percent approving of the second. Ibid., 511, 515.
75. As Billington and Clark have pointed out, however, Catholic and Jewish clerics were underrepresented in the overall sample. Ibid., 513.
76. John M. Newsom to Franklin D. Roosevelt, October 12, 1935, FDR-PPF, 21A, Box 8.
77. R.W. Everroad to Franklin D. Roosevelt, October 10, 1935, FDR-PPF, 21A, Box 8.
78. Fred S. Leathere to Franklin D. Roosevelt, October 2, 1935, FDR-PPF, 21A, Box 5.
79. C.C. Martin to Franklin D. Roosevelt, October 2, 1935, FDR-PPF, 21A, Box 2.
80. See, for example, Charles Chval to Franklin D. Roosevelt, January 19, 1936, FDR-PPF, 21A, Box 8; Herbert L. Miller to Franklin D. Roosevelt, September 26, 1935, FDR-PPF, 21A, Box 8.
81. See, for example, Alison Collis Greene, *No Depression in Heaven: The Great Depression, the New Deal, and the Transformation of Religion in the Delta* (New York: Oxford University Press, 2015), 114.
82. Quoted in Matthew Avery Sutton, *American Apocalypse: A History of Modern Evangelicalism* (Cambridge, MA: Belknap Press, 2014), 232.
83. Quoted in ibid., 239. Also see the critical letters to FDR quoted in Billington and Clark, "Nebraska Clergymen, Franklin D. Roosevelt, and the New Deal," 86.
84. Ahlstrom, *A Religious History of the American People*, 927–928.
85. Robert Wuthnow, *Red State Religion: Faith and Politics in America's Heartland* (Princeton, NJ: Princeton University Press, 2012), 173–175; Daniel Levitas, *The Terrorist Next Door: The Militia Movement and the Radical Right* (New York: Thomas Dunne, 2002), 27.
86. Quoted in George M. Marsden, *Fundamentalism and American Culture: The Shaping of Twentieth-Century Evangelicalism, 1870–1925* (New York: Oxford University Press, 1980), 210.
87. Barry Hankins, *God's Rascal: J. Frank Norris and the Beginnings of Southern Fundamentalism* (Lexington: University Press of Kentucky, 1996), 100.
88. For Roosevelt's share of the Protestant vote in 1932 and 1936, see James L. Sundquist, *Dynamics of the Party System: Alignment and Realignment of Political Parties in the United States* (Washington, DC: Brookings Institution, 1983); James A. Reichley, *Religion in American Public Life* (Washington, DC: Brookings Institution, 1985), 225; Leuchtenburg, *The FDR Years*, 156–157. One reason for Roosevelt's improved performance was, of course, that the 1928 Democratic nominee, Al Smith, was a Catholic.

89. For all their proto-libertarian commitments, the League's organizers were not averse to clothing their appeals in the language and symbolism of Christianity. For example, the conservative publisher David Lawrence penned a pro-League pamphlet entitled "Tenth Commandment," implying that Roosevelt's supporters were guilty of coveting resources that rightly belonged to the wealthy. See, for example, George Wolfskill, *The Revolt of the Conservatives: A History of the American Liberty League, 1934–1940* (Boston: Houghton, Mifflin, 1962), 283. I thank an anonymous reviewer for alerting me to this connection.

90. On the origins of the American Liberty League and its relation to the AAPA, see ibid., 54–55; David E. Kyvig, *Repealing National Prohibition*, 2nd ed. (Kent, OH: Kent University Press, 2000), 191–196.

91. As usual, J. Frank Norris went further than most, informing his flock—in what is surely one of the most bizarre accusations in the history of American political rhetoric—that the Liberty League was "one of the two principal Russian communistic organizations in this country," the other being the League for Industrial Democracy. Quoted in J. Frank Norris, *Inside History of First Baptist Church, Fort Worth and Temple Baptist Church: Life Story of J. Frank Norris* (Eugene, OR: Wipf and Stock, 1988), 233. Also see Hankins, *God's Rascal*, 143.

92. The Liberty League's benefactors did provide some financial support to Southern organizations opposed to the New Deal, such as the short-lived Southern Committee to Uphold the Constitution. These efforts mostly came to naught, however, when the openly racist tactics employed by the Southern Committee were exposed in the Northern press. See, for example, Wolfskill, *Revolt of the Conservatives*, 176–178.

93. Kevin M. Kruse, *One Nation Under God: How Corporate America Invented Christian America* (New York: Basic Books, 2015), 12; Kim Phillips-Fein, *Invisible Hands: The Businessmen's Crusade against the New Deal* (New York: Norton, 2009), 70–73; Brian Doherty, *Radicals for Capitalism: A Freewheeling History of the Modern American Libertarian Movement* (New York: Public Affairs, 2007), 271–272.

94. Kevin M. Kruse, "How Corporate America Invented Christian America," *Politico*, April 16, 2015, available online at http://www.politico.com/magazine/story/2015/04/corporate-america-invented-religious-right-conservative-roosevelt-princeton-117030.

95. Spiritual Mobilization's public relations efforts and fundraising activities are discussed in more detail in chap. 5.

96. Kruse, *One Nation Under God*, 19.

97. Fifield's most popular book, *The Single Path*, was essentially a self-help book in the vein of Norman Vincent Peale's Eisenhower-era best sellers. Like Peale, Fifield was possessed of an unshakable confidence in the essential goodness of the American businessman. ("Have you ever noticed how friendly the top men in a business organization are? Did it ever occur to you that this friendliness emanated from a deep sense of love toward their fellow men?") Also like Peale, Fifield arrived, via circular reasoning, at the view that the capitalist system had been created by God to improve the human condition. ("I hold that the blessings of capitalism come from God. A system that provides so much for the common good and happiness must

flourish under the favor of the Almighty. This could not be so if capitalism were essentially immoral, if the system of reinvesting capital in one's own enterprise was basically inconsistent with good.") James Fifield, *The Single Path* (Englewood Cliffs, NJ: Prentice-Hall, 1957), 91, 87.

98. The relationship between the State Department and the Federal Council of Churches was a major concern of both J. Elwin Wright and Ralph T. Davis, two of the principal founders of the National Association of Evangelicals. See, for example, J. Elwin Wright to Harry A. West, December 30, 1941, in NAE Box 1, Folder marked "Pre–St. Louis Convention Letters and Materials"; Ralph T. Davis to T. Roland Philips, November 26, 1941, NAE Records, Box 1, Folder marked "Pre–St. Louis Convention Letters and Materials."

99. Daniel Williams, *God's Own Party: The Making of the Christian Right* (New York: Oxford University Press, 2010), 16–17; Joel A. Carpenter, *Revive Us Again: The Remaking of American Fundamentalism* (New York: Oxford University Press, 1997), 130–131, 147–150; Paul Matzko, "Radio Politics, Origins Myths, and the Creation of Evangelicalism," *Fides et Historia* 48 (2016): 61–90.

100. The meeting's organizers repeatedly cited access to the radio airwaves as the most important reason for launching the NAE. See, for example, J. Elwin Wright to R. J. Bateman, May 12, 1942, NAE Box 1, Folder marked "Pre–St. Louis Convention Letters and Materials"; Harold Ockenga to Ralph T. Davis, February 11, 1941, NAE Box 1, Folder marked "Pre–St. Louis Convention Letters and Materials"; Ralph T. Davis to T. Roland Philips, November 26, 1941, NAE Box 1, Folder marked "Pre–St. Louis Convention Letters and Materials"; J. Elwin Wright to Mrs. F. Cliffe Johnston, January 7, 1942, Ralph T. Davis to T. Roland Philips, November 26, 1941, NAE Box 1, Folder marked "Pre–St. Louis Convention Letters and Materials"; J. Elwin Wright to Harry A. West, December 30, 1941, in NAE Box 1, Folder marked "Pre–St. Louis Convention Letters and Materials."

101. David Otis Fuller to [unknown], March 23, 1942, NAE Box 1, Folder marked "Pre–St. Louis Convention Letters and Materials."

102. Harold Ockenga to J. Elwin Wright, March 28, 1942, NAE Box 1, Folder marked "Pre–St. Louis Convention Letters and Materials."

103. For Ockenga's battles with the Boston Council over access to airtime on Boston station WBZ, see Harold Ockenga to Ralph T. Davis, February 11, 1941, NAE Box 1, Folder marked "Pre–St. Louis Convention Letters and Materials."

104. There was a definite undercurrent of anti-Catholic bigotry at the initial NAE meeting. Ockenga, for example, warned his audience to beware of "Romanism in its growth, power and political influence." Harold Ockenga to J. Elwin Wright, March 28, 1942, NAE Box 1, Folder marked "Pre–St. Louis Convention Letters and Materials."

105. J. Elwin Wright to R. J. Bateman, May 12, 1942, NAE Box 1, Folder marked "Pre–St. Louis Convention Letters and Materials."

106. One factor that aided the NAE's recruiting efforts was the decision to eschew the word *fundamentalism*—which had by this point become firmly linked in the public mind with factionalism, bigotry, and anti-intellectualism—in favor of the less

freighted term *evangelical*. Also shrewd was the NAE's decision to admit individual churches from denominations that remained affiliated with the Federal Council, thus providing an organizational home for conservative congregations that, for whatever reason, did not wish to separate from their denominational hierarchies. For a profile of some of the NAE's major financial backers, including the Chicago businessman Herbert J. Taylor, who served as group's founding treasurer, see Sarah Ruth Hammond, "God's Business Men: Entrepreneurial Evangelicals in Depression and War" (Ph.D. diss., Yale University, 2010).

107. Frances FitzGerald, *The Evangelicals: The Struggle to Shape America* (New York: Simon and Schuster, 2017), 164. One major obstacle to the NAE's recruiting drive was the existence of a competing fundamentalist umbrella group, the militantly separatist American Council of Christian Churches (ACCC). Fearing that the NAE would draw members away from his own organization, the ACCC's combative founder, Carl McIntire, spread the rather implausible—but it appears, widely believed—rumor that the NAE's ultimate aim was to create an FCC-style "superchurch" that would enforce doctrinal uniformity among its member churches. A second problem was the NAE's failure to snag the eight-million-member Southern Baptist Convention. Although the SBC's theology leaned strongly fundamentalist, its real calling card was congregational independence, and its leaders tended to look askance at ecumenical projects of all stripes—even ones that promised to take the fight to liberal Protestantism. See for example, Molly Worthen, *Apostles of Reason: The Crisis of Authority in American Evangelicalism* (New York: Oxford, 2016), 37–39; FitzGerald, *The Evangelicals*, 162–164.

Chapter 4

1. On NAM's legislative agenda in the winter of 1947, see, "FTC Witch Hunt Is Feared by NAM," *New York Times*, February 25, 1947, p. 43; "NAM Urges Laws to Bar Strikes," *New York Times*, January 5, 1947, p. 4; "New Labor Laws Vital, Mosher Says," *New York Times*, February 19, 1947, p. 50; "NAM Says Truman Fails to Economize," *New York Times*, February 6, 1947, p. 16. On the drafting of what became the Taft-Hartley Act, see, for example, Rick Wartzman, *The End of Loyalty: The Rise and Fall of Good Jobs in America* (New York: Public Affairs, 2017), 61–65.

2. Alfred P. Haake to J. Howard Pew, February 26, 1947, JHP, Box 12. "Alfred P. Haake," in *Who's Who among Association Executives* (New York: Institute for Research in Biography, 1935), 213, 612. On Haake's involvement with Spiritual Mobilization, see Kevin M. Kruse, *One Nation Under God: How Corporate America Invented Religious America* (New York: Basic Books, 2015), 17–19.

3. C. Kirk Hadaway and Penny Long Marler, "Growth and Decline in the Mainline," in Charles H. Lippy, ed., *Faith in America: Changes, Challenges, New Directions: Volume I: Organized Religion Today* (Westport, CT: Praeger, 2006), 1–24, 3–4; Robert T. Handy, "The American Religious Depression, 1925–1935," *Church History* 29 (1960): 3–16; Sydney E. Ahlstrom, *A Religious History of the American People* (New

Haven, CT: Yale University Press, 1972), 918–931; Robert D. Putnam, *Bowling Alone: The Collapse and Revival of American Community* (New York: Simon and Schuster, 2000), 70–71; Matthew S. Hedstrom, "The Commodification of William James: The Book Business and the Rise of Liberal Spirituality in the Twentieth-Century United States," in Jan Stievermann, Philip Goff, and Detlef Junker, eds., *Religion and the Marketplace in the United States* (New York: Oxford University Press, 2015), 125–144, 131.

4. Hadaway and Marler, "Growth and Decline in the Mainline," 8.

5. William C. Whyte, *The Organization Man* (New York: Simon and Schuster, 1956), 367–368, 380; Vance Packard, *The Status Seekers* (New York: David McKay, 1959), 195. Packard emphasizes the importance of social and professional connections in driving the surge in church membership: "Many still kneel in fervent prayer at night. For the majority of American Christians, however, going to church is the nice thing that proper people do on Sundays. It advertises their respectability, gives them a warm feeling that they are behaving in a way their God-fearing ancestors would approve, and adds (they hope) a few cubits to their social stature by throwing them with a social group with which they wish to be identified." Social scientists also found extensive evidence to suggest that church membership—particularly mainline Protestant membership—provided many upwardly mobile Americans with an entry point into "respectable" society. See, for example, Rodney Stark and Charles Y. Glock, *American Piety: The Nature of Religious Commitment* (Berkeley and Los Angeles: University of California Press, 1968), 167, 186–203.

6. Also significant was an increase in churchgoing by young men, a group that traditionally lagged far behind women in this department. Rates of weekly church attendance by men between the ages of twenty-one and thirty-four spiked from 28 percent in 1952 to 44 percent in 1964. Robert D. Putnam and David E. Campbell, *American Grace: How Religion Divides and Unites Us* (New York: Simon and Schuster, 2012), 83–86.

7. Stark and Glock, *American Piety*, 167, 186–203; Michael Hout, Andrew Greeley, and Melissa J. Wilde, "The Demographic Imperative in Religious Change in the United States," *American Journal of Sociology* 107 (2001): 468–500; Darren E. Sherkat, "Tracking the Restructuring of American Religion: Religious Affiliation and Patterns of Religious Mobility, 1973–1998," *Social Forces* 79 (2001): 1459–1493; Wade Clark Roof and William McKinney, *American Mainline Religion: Its Changing Shape and Future* (New Brunswick, NJ: Rutgers University Press, 1987), 162.

8. The Presbyterian Church USA, for example, which had suffered a decline relative to the rate of population growth in the 1930s, grew by some 36 percent in the 1950s (when the U.S. population grew by 18 percent). The only exception to the general trend of relative growth was the Methodist Church, which grew at about the same rate as population in the postwar period. Hadaway and Marler, "Growth and Decline in the Mainline," 14. Also see Robert Wuthnow, *The Restructuring of American Religion: Society and Faith since World War II* (Princeton, NJ: Princeton University Press, 1988), 18.

9. William M. King, "The Reform Establishment and the Ambiguities of Influence," in William R. Hutchinson, ed., *Between the Times: The Travail of the Protestant Establishment in America, 1900–1960* (New York: Cambridge, 1989), 122–140,

127–130. Also see Andrew Preston, *Sword of the Spirit, Shield of Faith: Religion in American War and Diplomacy* (New York: Anchor Books, 2012), 484–485.

10. Wuthnow, *The Restructuring of American Religion*, 81.

11. Quoted in Jonathan J. Golden, "From Cooperation to Confrontation: The Synagogue League of America," (Ph.D. diss., Brandeis University, 2008), 85. Alfred P. Haake to J. Howard Pew, February 6, 1947, JHP, Box 12.

12. David Lawrence, "Sniping at Profit-and-Loss System," *United States News*, December 27, 1946, pp. 24–25.

13. Alfred P. Haake to J. Howard Pew, February 26, 1947, JHP, Box 12.

14. Alfred P. Haake to J. Howard Pew, February 26, 1947, JHP, Box 12.

15. Alfred P. Haake to Jasper Crane, March 3, 1947, JHP, Box 12.

16. Alfred P. Haake to J. Howard Pew, February 26, 1947, JHP, Box 12; Alfred P. Haake to Jasper Crane, JHP, Box 12; "Meeting Ground," *Time*, March 3, 1947, p. 94.

17. Alfred P. Haake to J. Howard Pew, February 26, 1947, JHP, Box 12; Alfred P. Haake to Jasper Crane, March 3, 1947, JHP, Box 12.

18. Alfred P. Haake to J. Howard Pew, February 6, 1947, JHP, Box 12; Alfred P. Haake to J. Howard Pew, February 26, 1947, JHP, Box 12; Alfred P. Haake, "Impressions of the Conference on Economics held by the Federal Council of Churches of Christ in America," February 26, 1947, JHP, Box 12; Alfred P. Haake to Jasper E. Crane (copy to J. Howard Pew and James W. Fifield), March 3, 1947, JHP Box 12. On Pew's plan to retire, see J. Howard Pew to Alfred P. Haake, March 10, 1947, JHP, Box 12.

19. "The Public Relations Program of the National Association of Manufacturers," JHP, Box 146.

20. Doherty, *Radicals for Capitalism*, 157–158; Allan J. Lichtman, *White Protestant Nation: The Rise of the American Conservative Movement* (New York: Atlantic Monthly Press, 2008), 207–208.

21. Quoted in Mary Sennholz, *Faith and Freedom: The Journal of a Great American, J. Howard Pew* (Grove City, PA: Grove City College, 1975), ix, 43.

22. J. Howard Pew to B.E. Hutchinson, November 13, 1952, JHP, Box 146.

23. In 1948, for example, a NAM-sponsored poll revealed that 45 percent of clergymen believed that NAM's tax cut proposals were designed to "favor manufacturers," while only 39 percent believed they were "fair to everybody." 53 percent of clergymen surveyed believed that NAM looked out for the interests of "big companies," while only 33 percent thought that the group represented the "views of all manufacturers." And only 37 percent of clergymen believed that the organization's views on labor questions were "up to date," as compared to 43 percent who judged them "out of date" or gave qualified responses. Summary of Survey included in Holcombe Parkes to J. Howard Pew, September 21, 1950, JHP, Box 30.

24. Opinion Research Corporation, "Business and the Clergy: A Report of the Public Opinion Index for Industry" (Princeton, NJ: Opinion Research Corporation, 1949), JHP, Box 23.

25. Although the ORC's summary report does not indicate whether African American churches were included, the sources consulted to generate the sample do not seem to have included the major African American denominations.

26. J. Howard Pew to Claude Robinson, January 7, 1949, JHP, Box 23. Pew seems to have gotten the idea for this question from Norman Vincent Peale. See Norman Vincent Peale to J. Howard Pew, January 4, 1949, JHP, Box 23.

27. Liston Pope, "Religion and the Class Structure," *Annals of the American Academy of Political and Social Science* 256 (1948): 84–91, 87. Also see Hadley Cantril, "Educational and Economic Composition of Religious Groups," *American Journal of Sociology* 47 (1943): 574–579; Mabel Newcomer, *The Big Business Executive: The Factors That Made Him, 1900–1950* (New York: Columbia University Press, 1955), 47–48; Beverly Davis, "Eminence and Level of Social Origin," *American Journal of Sociology* 59 (1953): 11–18.

28. See, for example, Richard F. Curtis, "Occupational Mobility and Church Participation," *Social Forces* 38 (1959): 308–314; Seymour Martin Lipset, "Religion and Politics in the American Past and Present," in Robert Lee and Martin E. Marty, eds., *Religion and Social Conflict* (New York: Oxford University Press, 1964), 69–126; Benton Johnson, "Ascetic Protestantism and Political Preference," *Public Opinion Quarterly* 26 (1962): 35–46; Stark and Glock, *American Piety*, 167, 186–203; David O. Moberg, *The Church as a Social Institution* (Englewood Cliffs, NJ: Prentice-Hall, 1962); W. Seward Salisbury, *Religion in American Culture: A Sociological Interpretation* (Homewood, IL: Dorsey Press, 1964), 454–457. Also see Whyte, *The Organization Man*, 368; Vance Packard, *The Status Seekers* (New York: David McKay, 1959), 195–202.

29. Packard, *The Status Seekers*, 195, 197.

30. Alfred P. Haake to Jasper E. Crane (copy to J. Howard Pew and James W. Fifield), March 3, 1947, JHP, Box 12.

31. Patsy Peppers to J. Howard Pew, May 24, 1948, JHP, Box 19; James W. Fifield, Jr., to J. Howard Pew, September 23, 1948, JHP, Box 19. On Spiritual Mobilization's sermon contests, see Kruse, *One Nation Under God*, 20.

32. *Spiritual Mobilization: Monthly Bulletin* 14:11 (November 1948), JHP, Box 19.

33. Carey McWilliams, "Battle for the Clergy," *Nation*, February 1947, pp. 151–153.

34. Norman Vincent Peale to J. Howard Pew, September 23, 1948, JHP, Box 19.

35. Indeed, Pew claimed to have personally witnessed the man he now considered "the greatest minister in America" convert an audience of social gospel–minded clergymen at a 1944 FCC convention in Philadelphia. By the end of Peale's speech to the convention, "the audience got up and cheered him," Pew reported, "although I am sure a large percentage of his audience came there believing in a philosophy quote different from that which [he] expounded." J. Howard Pew to Herbert Stockham, September 9, 1948, JHP, Box 19.

36. Although Peale led a Dutch Reformed congregation, he was raised in the Methodist tradition, the son of an Ohio minister. As one historian has noted, "Peale's gospel of optimism departed from the usual strict Calvinism of the Reformed Church and drew more from his own brand of Methodism, although John Wesley would have hardly recognized Peale's Methodism. Peale's view of sin was the telltale sign that he had little use for either Calvin or Wesley. For him, sin was not an intractable condition, but a defect in personality that could be improved upon by positive patterns of

thought." Andrew S. Finstuen, *Original Sin and Everyday Protestants: The Theology of Reinhold Niebuhr, Billy Graham, and Paul Tillich in an Age of Anxiety* (Chapel Hill: University of North Carolina Press, 2009), 22.

37. Clarence Woodbury, "God's Salesman," *American Magazine*, June 1949, pp. 36–41. On Peale's Religio-Psychiatric Clinic, see, for example, Christopher Lane, *Surge of Piety: Norman Vincent Peale and the Remaking of American Religious Life* (New Haven, CT: Yale University Press, 2016).

38. Peale's statement of purposes was drafted as a letter to Pew's friend and fellow conservative B. E. Hutchinson but was apparently sent only to Pew. Norman Vincent Peale to J. Howard Pew, September 19, 1948, JHP, Box 19; Norman Vincent Peale to J. Howard Pew, September 23, 1948, JHP, Box 19.

39. J. Howard Pew to Ira Mosher, June 21, 1948, JHP, Box 19; J. Howard Pew to James D. Francis, October 1, 1948, JHP, Box 19.

40. Wesley Goodson Nicholson to Ralph Walker, July 22, 1948, JHP, Box 19.

41. J. Howard Pew to James W. Fifield, Jr., October 29, 1948, JHP, Box 19.

42. H. C. Stockham to J. Howard Pew, September 7, 1948, JHP, Box 19.

43. J. Howard Pew to James D. Francis, May 3, 1948, JHP, Box 19.

44. Don G. Mitchell to J. Howard Pew, May 26, 1948, JHP, Box 19.

45. Ministers who agreed to serve included Lester Clee, a Presbyterian clergyman and Republican party activist who had recently lost a bid for governor in New Jersey; George W. Cooke, pastor of Rochester's West Avenue Methodist Church; John W. Christie, Jasper Crane's pastor at Wilmington's Westminster Presbyterian Church; Frederick Schweitzer, president of Bloomfield College; Stewart M. Robinson, pastor of the Second Presbyterian Church of Elizabethtown, New Jersey; and Lee Beynon, pastor of the First Baptist Church of Montclair, New Jersey.

46. On Kershner's relief work, see, for example, Eckard V. Toy, "Christian Economics," in Ronald Lora and William Henry Longton, eds., *The Conservative Press in Twentieth-Century America* (Westport, CT: Greenwood Press, 1999), 163–169, 164.

47. Norman Vincent Peale to J. Howard Pew, March 16, 1949, JHP, Box 23; also see Norman Vincent Peale to J. Howard Pew, January 4, 1949, JHP, Box 23; Norman Vincent Peale to Jasper Crane, January 13, 1949, JHP, Box 23; Norman Vincent Peale to James W. Fifield, Jr., March 17, 1949, JHP, Box 23.

48. George W. Cooke to Norman Vincent Peale, May 23, 1949, JHP, Box 23; Norman Vincent Peale to J. Howard Pew, June 4, 1949, JHP, Box 23.

49. J. Howard Pew to Norman Vincent Peale, June 6, 1949, JHP, Box 23.

50. Lichtman, *White Protestant Nation*, 174.

51. "Minutes of a Meeting of the Executive Committee of Christian Freedom Foundation, Inc.," October 12, 1950, JHP, Box 180, Hagley; Toy, "Christian Economics," 165.

52. Toy, "Christian Economics," 165. On Pew's relationship with the American Economic Foundation, see Mark R. Wilson, *Destructive Creation: American Business and the Winning of World War II* (Philadelphia: University of Pennsylvania Pres, 2017), 95.

53. J. Howard Pew to Percy L. Greaves, Jr., October 19, 1950, JHP, Box 180.

54. Spiritual Mobilization, "Annual Report to Contributors, 1952–3," JHP, Box 36; James W. Fifield, Jr., to J. Howard Pew, November 9, 1951, JHP, Box 30; Kruse, *One Nation Under God*, 33.

55. Eckard V. Toy, "Faith and Freedom," in Ronald Lora and William Henry Longton, eds., *The Conservative Press in Twentieth-Century America* (Westport, CT: Greenwood Press, 1999),153–161, 156. If there was a meaningful difference in the perspective of the two journals, it was that *Faith and Freedom* had comparatively little interest in theology. Over the course of the 1950s it drifted ever further in the direction of full-blown libertarianism, while Kershner never gave up on bridging the gap between libertarians and fundamentalists (who still supported enforcement of Protestant mores). See Toy, "Ideology and Conflict in American Ultra-Conservatism, 1945–1960," 64.

56. J. Howard Pew to James W. Fifield, Jr., July 6, 1949, JHP, Box 24, Hagley; J. Howard Pew to James W. Fifield, Jr., October 27, 1953, JHP, Box 36.

57. Stewart M. Robinson, "Clergymen and Socialism," The *Freeman*, August 13, 1951, pp. 717–720.

58. Kruse, *One Nation Under God*, 23.

59. Toy, "Christian Economics," 163–169.

60. Memo, n.d.; Howard E. Kershner to the Board of Directors of the Christian Freedom Foundation, JHP, Box 180.

61. J. Howard Pew to James Fifield, November 30, 1951, JHP, Box 30.

62. Phillips-Fein, *Invisible Hands*, 46–52.

63. Jasper Crane, "Church and Industry Face a Common Foe," *Understanding: A Quarterly Devoted to Cooperation between Clergymen and Business* 1:1 (September, 1936): 8.

64. "The Public Relations Plan of the National Association of Manufacturers," 1946, in JHP, Box 146. A pamphlet published by the U.S. Chamber of Commerce in the early 1950s listed no less than fifteen types of "local groups" that had been infiltrated by Communists and fellow travelers, including women's organizations, youth organizations, Negro organizations, churches, "character-building groups," schools, recreational groups, "clubs and fraternal groups of all sorts," "rent and consumer groups," and labor unions. Quoted in Eckard Vance Toy, Jr., "Ideology and Conflict in American Ultra-Conservatism, 1945–1960 (Ph.D. Dissertation, University of Oregon, Department of History, 1965), 48.

65. NAM Public Relations Division, "Review of NAM's Women's Program and Suggestions for Strengthening the Association's Activities in this Area," June 3, 1956, NAM Series 1, Box 223.

66. "The Public Relations Plan of the National Association of Manufacturers," 1946, JHP, Box 146.

67. "Trying to Indoctrinate the Clergy? Nothing To It," *Protestant Voice*, April 16, 1943 (NCC Record Group 18, Box 52, Folder 24).

68. Pro-labor papers, not surprisingly, had a field day with the news. See, for example, "NAM Tries to Hit the Sawdust Trail, Shouting Hallelujah, Free Enterprise!" *PM*, January 3, 1945, p. 6 (NCC Record Group 18, Box 52, Folder 24).

69. James Myers to Samuel McCrea Cavert, July 16, 1942, NCC Record Group 18, Box 52, Folder 24.

70. Roswell P. Barnes to Arthur E. Wilson, March 10, 1944, NCC Record Group 18, Box 52, Folder 24.

71. Robert L. Dieffenbacher to James Myers, March 23, 1943, NCC Record Group 18, Box 52, Folder 24; James Myers to Robert L. Dieffenbacher, March 24, 1943, NCC Record Group 18, Box 52, Folder 24.

72. "Production Is the Answer: Suggested remarks for Businessmen at Local Church and Industry Conference," (n.d., 1946), NAM Series 1, Box 270.

73. "Newspaper Release for Local Church and Industry Conference" (n.d.), NAM Series 1, Box 270; "Production Is the Answer: Highlights for Roundtable Discussion at Local Church and Industry Conference," (n.d., 1946?), NAM Series 1, Box 270; "Clergymen Look at the Facts: A Program for Church and Industry Cooperation in the Community," (n.d.), NAM Series 1, Box 270.

74. "Toward Clergy-Industry Understanding," NAM Series 1, Box 270.

75. "Industrial Panels for Church Organizations," in NAM Series I, Box 270. Harmon and Scott are quoted on pp. 11-12.

76. Warren J. Tausig to Ransom P. Rathbun, March 4, 1955, NAM Series I, Box 163. Even as the Committee focused much of its energy on the seminaries, it maintained that no church affiliated group was too small or insignificant as to be unworthy of instruction in the principles of free market capitalism. The 1949 strategic plan observed that "young people's meetings, Bible classes, and other church groups" provided excellent opportunities for informing average Americans "about the economic system and how industry operates." "Toward Clergy-Industry Understanding," NAM Series 1, Box 270.

77. Warren J. Taussig, "Report of the Clergy and Industry Relations Program in the Eastern Division, January 1-31, 1955," NAM Series 1, Box 163; Warren J. Taussig, "Report of the Clergy and Industry Relations Program in the Eastern Division, February 1-28, 1955," NAM Series 1, Box 163; Noel Sargent to Harvey Frye, Warren Taussig, John Harmon, and Don Mallery, March 16, 1955 (Memorandum Re: Church-Industry Relations), NAM Series 1, Box 163; Warren J. Taussig, "Report of the Clergy and Industry Relations Program in the Eastern Division, March 1 to April 30," NAM Series 1, Box 163

78. In Dateline, September 1965, see "Help or Hindrance?" (p. 2); "Reapportionment: Who's to Decide . . . the People or the Courts?" (pp. 3-4); and "Paddle Your Own Canoe" (p. 4). On the periodical's launch, see Memo; Kenneth R. Miller to Members of the NAM House Staff, February 14, 1957, NAM Series I, Box 163.

79. See, for example, "Sharing the Wealth," Address by D. Hayes Murphy to the NAM Clergy-Industry Advisory Committee, June 19, 1958, NAM Series I, Box 163

80. J. Howard Pew to Pauline Baker, February 11, 1961, JHP, Box 72, Hagley; J. Howard Pew to Charles R. Sligh, Jr., February 27, 1961, JHP, Box 72; Charles R. Sligh, Jr. to Pauline M. Baker, March 7, 1961, JHP, Box 72; J. Howard Pew to Charles R. Sligh, Jr., March 27, 1961, JHP, Box 72.

81. Opinion Research Corporation, "What Protestant Clergymen Think of Christian Economics," (Princeton, NJ: Opinion Research Corporation, 1958), JHP, Box 183.

82. Sally R. Sherman, "Public Attitudes Towards Social Security," *Social Security Bulletin* 52 (1989): 2–16, 3.

83. See, for example, "A New Birth of Freedom: An Editorial," *Ohio Christian News*, November 1953, p. 4, SCC, Box 7, Folder 5; "Assembly Takes Stands on Six Vital Issues," *Ohio Christian News*, November 1952, p. 8, SCC, Box 7, Folder 5.

84. James W. Fifield, "The Director's Page," *Faith and Freedom*, April 1953, p. 19. On the public reaction to HUAC's questioning of Bishop G. Bromley Oxnam and other clergymen, see Angela M. Lahr, *Millennial Dreams and Apocalyptic Nightmares: The Cold War Origins of Political Evangelicalism* (New York: Oxford University Press, 2007), 46–47.

85. Edmund A. Opitz, "Live a New Kind of Life," *Faith and Freedom*, February 1955, p. 10. Emphasis in the original. To his credit, Opitz relished the chance to match wits with the intellectual heavyweights of the Protestant mainline, though there is little evidence that either side's views were altered by the resulting exchanges. In 1953, for example, he debated the merits of the welfare state with Union Theological Seminary's John C. Bennett—a man long despised by libertarians, and one of Opitz's former teachers—in the pages of *Faith and Freedom*. Edmund A. Opitz and John C. Bennett, "Dear Mr. Bennett: Dear Mr. Opitz," *Faith and Freedom*, April 1953, pp. 3–6; Emund A. Opitz and John C. Bennett, "Dear Mr. Bennett: Dear Mr. Opitz: Part Two," *Faith and Freedom*, May 1953, pp. 10–15.

86. In many cities, the program was spearheaded by the United Church Women or the local council of churches. In other cities, a wide range of civic and religious groups—including the Girl and Boy Scouts, as well as Jewish and Catholic groups—joined together to form a coordinating committee. *Annual Meeting of the Assembly, Massachusetts Council of Churches, 1956*, p. E23, SCC, Box 9, Folder 5; "Indiana Council of United Church Women," *Indiana Church Councilor*, January–February, 1960, p. 2, SCC, Box 2, Folder 5.; "Constructive Halloween," *News-Letter (Council of Churches of Buffalo and Erie County)*, October, 1957, p. 2, CCC, Box 1, Folder 16.

87. The Federation of Churches of Christ in Albany and Vicinity, "United to Serve: Annual Dinner Meeting, 1951," p. 10, CCC, Box 1, Folder 2; "Know Your United Nations," *The Churches Working Together (Newsletter of the Federation of Churches of Christ in Albany and Vicinity)*, March 1950, p. 2, CCC, Box 1, Folder 3; "Essay Contest on Point IV Set," *Ohio Christian News*, November 1952, p. 7, SCC, Box 7, Folder 5; Hundreds of Ohioans Launch 28th Annual Prince of Peace Contest," *Ohio Christian News*, November 1952, p. 7, SCC, Box 7, Folder 5; "Annual Report: Christian Youth Council," in *The Annual Meeting of the Greater Portland Area Council of Churches, 1946*, n.p., SCC, Box 2, Folder 6.

88. "Council United Nations Workshops Successful," *Indiana Church Councilor*, July–August, 1955, p. 3, SCC, Box 2, Folder 5; The Federation of Churches of Christ in Albany and Vicinity, "United to Serve: Annual Dinner Meeting, 1951," p. 10, CCC, Box 1, Folder 2; The Church Federation of Los Angeles, *Fall Bulletin*, 1955, p. 1, SCC, Box 1, Folder 2; "Human Rights Day December 10," *The Church at Work (the Bulletin*

of the Metropolitan Church Federation of St. Louis, December 1951, p. 2, CCC, Box 5, Folder 5; "United Nations Service Held," *The Church at Work (the Bulletin of the Metropolitan Church Federation of St. Louis*, December 1952, p. 7, CCC, Box 5, Folder 5; "Protestant Churches Celebrate UN Day," *The Church at Work (the Bulletin of the Metropolitan Church Federation of St. Louis*, October 1952, p. 8, CCC, Box 5, Folder 5; "Human Rights Day Observed," "United Nations Service Held," *The Church at Work (the Bulletin of the Metropolitan Church Federation of St. Louis*, December 1952, p. 7, CCC, Box 5, Folder 5; "Plan to Observe UN Day, Oct. 24," *Oregon Church News*, September 1954, p. 4, SCC, Box 9, Folder 5.

89. "Dr. Blake Council Speaker," *The Pittsburgh Protestant*, September 1955, p. 1, CCC, Box 5, Folder 1; *The Bulletin (Publication of the Southern California–Nevada Council of Churches)*, September 1961, n.p., SCC, Box 1, Folder 2.

90. *Massachusetts Council of Churches Annual Convention, 1949*, p. 4; *Massachusetts Council of Churches Annual Convention, 1951*, p. 15, SCC, Box 2, Folder 8; *Albany Federation of Churches Annual Dinner, 1947–1948*, p. 6, CCC, Box 1, Folder 2.

91. "The Methodist Church: Its Strength Lies in Its Great Energy," *Life*, November 10, 1947, pp. 113–128. Similarly, a 1951 *Life* profile of the nation's twelve most successful churches (as determined by a poll of 100,000 Protestant ministers) featured a rural Baptist congregation whose minister advocated federally sponsored soil conservation methods while serving as chaplain of the state grange. "Great American Churches," *Life*, January 1, 1951, pp. 80–86.

92. John Knox Jessup, "The World, the Flesh, and the Devil," *Life*, April 6, 1953, pp. 140–143, 143.

93. By a 65 percent to 21 percent margin, Episcopal churchgoers supported federal protections for workers who sought to organize (the margin among priests was 89 to 9). By a 72 percent to 19 percent margin, lay people supported federal action to curb excessive corporate profits (the margin among priests was 85 to 9). At the same time, most Episcopal church members opposed compulsory unionism (73 percent to 18 percent) and government "interference" with "private enterprise" during peacetime (85 percent to 8 percent). Charles Y. Glock, Benjamin B. Ringer, and Earl R. Babbie, *To Comfort and to Challenge: A Dilemma of the Contemporary Church* (Berkeley, CA: University of California Press, 1967), 157, 158, 160, 161. (Although this study was published in 1967, it was based on survey data collected in 1958).

94. Gerhard Lenski, *The Religious Factor: A Sociologist's Inquiry*, Rev. Ed. (New York: Anchor Books, 1963), 151–152.

95. In Eckardt's words, "The 'common man' has just enough Calvinism left inside to remember that people who come around and, in the name of the life of the 'spirit,' chat friendly-like about the dignity of the individual, may actually have their eye on his wallet more than his soul." A. Roy Eckardt, *The Surge of Piety in America: An Appraisal* (New York: Association Press, 1958), 130.

96. A 1962 study, for example, revealed that an astonishing 91 percent of Congregationalists and 90 percent of Methodists belonged to at least one non-church organization—such as a fraternal group or service club—and more than half belonged to *four or more* such organizations. Among non-mainline Protestant

denominations, in contrast, 30 percent of churchgoers belonged to *no* non-church organizations, and only 17 percent belonged to four or more. Bernard Lazerwitz, "Membership in Voluntary Associations and Frequency of Church Attendance," *Journal for the Scientific Study of Religion* 2 (1962): 74–84. Lazerwitz's findings are summarized in Stark and Glock, *American Piety*, 170.

97. The abovementioned 1952 survey of Episcopal church members, for example, revealed that a whopping 64 percent believed that "the church" should "actively encourage its members to support the U.N." And as late as 1964, an astonishing 69 percent of mainline churchgoers, when asked how often the federal government could be trusted to "do what is right," answered "always" or "most of the time." Glock, Ringer, and Babbie, *To Comfort and to Challenge*, 145; American National Election Study (NES), 1964. ANES respondents were asked: "How much of the time do you think you can trust the government in Washington to do what is right—just about always, most of the time, or only some of the time."

Chapter 5

1. The Department of Industrial Relations, for example, became the Department of the Church and Economic Life. Richard P. Poethig, "Cameron Hall, Economic Life, and the Ministry of the Laity," *American Presbyterians* 72 (1994): 33–47, 39–40. In the case of the DCEL, the name change was initiated in 1948, at a time when planning for the NCC was well under way but before the new organization's formal launch.

2. See, for example, "Eisenhower Urges Atomic Stockpiles for Defense of U.S.," *New York Times*, October 7, 1953, p. 1; "Excerpts from Dulles Message to Council of Churches of Christ," *New York Times*, December 12, 1952, p. 18; "Excerpts from Dulles Speech on Foreign Policy," *New York Times*, November 19, 1958, p. 6. For an account of the cornerstone-laying ceremony, see James F. Findlay, *Church People in the Struggle: The National Council of Churches and the Black Freedom Movement, 1950–1970* (New York: Oxford University Press, 1993), 11–12.

3. Oxnam and Cavert are quote in Elizabeth A. Fones-Wolf, *Selling Free Enterprise: The Business Assault on Labor and Liberalism, 1945–60* (Champaign: University of Illinois Press, 1994), 238–239.

4. For Pew's demand that he be authorized to select the Lay Committee's members, see Lem T. Jones to Samuel McCrea Cavert, February 19, 1951, NCC, RG 4, Box 3, Folder 23. Also see Samuel McCrea Cavert to J. Howard Pew, February 20, 1951, NCC, RG 4, Box 3, Folder 23; Samuel McCrea Cavert to J. Howard Pew, March 7, 1951, NCC, RG 4, Box 3, Folder 23; Samuel McCrea Cavert to Luther A. Weigle, April 5, 1951, NCC, RG 4, Box 3, Folder 23.

5. Quoted in Fones-Wolf, *Selling Free Enterprise*, 239. Also see Henry J. Pratt, *The Liberalization of American Protestantism: A Case Study in Complex Organizations* (Detroit, MI: Wayne State University Press, 1972), 88–89.

6. "Earl W. Jimerson, A Union Head, Dies," *New York Times*, October 6, 1957, p. 85; Thomas F. Brady, "British Labor Gets U.S. View on Reds: A.F.L. Spokesmen Given

Mild Heckling on Menace Theme," *New York Times*, September 9, 1953, p. 11. For a full list of members as of March 1952, see enclosure in J. Howard Pew and Lois B. Hunter to J. Irwin Miller, March 21, 1952, in ISM, Series 2, Box 341, Folder 4.

7. J. Howard Pew to B. E. Hutchinson, October 27, 1953, JHP, Box 168.

8. "Many Women Named, Dewey Backers Say," *New York Times*, October 17, 1946, p. 12; "Sales Force Found in Public Inquiry," *New York Times*, June 23, 1937, p. 46.

9. Pratt, *The Liberalization of American Protestantism*, 90-92.

10. "National Laymen's and Laywomen's Committee of the National Council of the Churches of Christ in the U.S.A., Meeting at Princeton Inn, Princeton, New Jersey, Saturday and Sunday, April 5th and 6th," in NCC Papers, RG 4, Box 3, Folder 24, Presbyterian Historical Society. For his speech on the gold standard Kershner would soon receive a $1,000 prize from the Freedoms Foundation, a Pennsylvania-based group that rewarded citizens and officials for highlighting threats to economic liberty. See Eckard Vance Toy, Jr., "Ideology and Conflict in American Ultraconservatism, 1945-1960" (Ph.D. diss., University of Oregon, 1965), 131 n. 6.

11. Alfred Dudley Ward, ed., *Goals of Economic Life* (New York: Harper and Brothers, 1953).

12. Poethig, "Cameron Hall, Economic Life, and the Ministry of the Laity," 39. After the formation of the NCC, the Rockefeller Foundation would pledge an additional $125,000 to fund a total of six volumes.

13. Frank H. Knight, "Conflict of Values: Freedom and Justice," in Alfred Dudley Ward, ed., *Goals of Economic Life* (New York: Harper and Brothers, 1953), 204-230, 224, 227, 229.

14. J. Howard Pew to Samuel McCrea Cavert, July 23, 1952, JHP, Box 146. Bennett and Niebuhr, two figures long hated by Pew, were singled out for special criticism. So perfectly did their "double talk" and "wild assumptions" mirror the Bolshevik line, he wrote, that "one wonders" whether they were not "associated with the Party."

15. J. Howard Pew to George Koether, July 17, 1952, JHP, Box 146.

16. George Koether to J. Howard Pew, July 23, 1952, JHP, Box 146; George Koether to J. Howard Pew, July 28, 1952, JHP, Box 146.

17. George Koether to J. Howard Pew, September 5, 1952, JHP, Box 146.

18. Edgar C. Bundy, *Collectivism in the Churches* (Wheaton, IL: Church League of America, 1958), 209; John T. Flynn, *The Road Ahead: America's Creeping Revolution* (New York: Devin-Adair, 1949), 112-113.

19. Reinhold Niebuhr, for example, used his *Goals of Economic Life* essay to lament American liberalism's "strange blind[ness] to the factor of [economic] power in man's social life." Reinhold Niebuhr, "The Christian Faith and the Economic Life of Liberal Society," in Alfred Dudley Ward, ed., *Goals of Economic Life* (New York: Harper and Brothers, 1953), 433-459, 435.

20. J. Howard Pew to Luther A. Weigle, October 15, 1952, NCC, RG 4, Box 4, Folder 34.

21. George Dugan, "Church Study Due on Economic Life," *New York Times*, February 24, 1952, p. 66.

22. "The Goals of Economic Life: An NBC Radio Discussion by John Bennett, Kermit Eby, Noel G. Sargent, and Charles P. Taft," *University of Chicago Roundtable* 778 (1953): 1-11, 4, 11.

23. Quoted in J. Howard Pew, *The Chairman's Final Report to the Members of the National Lay Committee* (1950), 128–136.

24. J. Howard Pew to Samuel McCrea Cavert, April 2, 1953, NCC, RG 4, Box 1, Folder 21.

25. In 1936, he had even published a slim anti-FDR tract arguing that one of the New Deal's most glaring flaws was its lack of government-funded health insurance. Charles P. Taft, *You and I—and Roosevelt* (New York: Farrar and Rinehart, 1936), 77, 81.

26. Pew, *Chairman's Final Report*, 138.

27. See "Resolution III," enclosure in J. Howard Pew and Lois B. Hunter to Members of the National Lay Committee, March 17, 1953, in ISM, Series 2, Box 341, Folder 4.

28. See enclosure in J. Howard Pew and Lois B. Hunter to Members of the National Lay Committee, March 17, 1953, in ISM, Series 2, Box 341, Folder 4.

29. Charles R. Hook of Armco Steel, for example, announced that he would "not want to continue as a member of the. . . Council" if a sentence condemning "one-sided support of either economic individualism or economic collectivism" was not "stricken from the report." Charles R. Hook to Samuel McCrea Cavert, April 24, 1952, NCC, RG 4, Box 1, Folder 21.

30. Samuel McCrea Cavert to Cameron P. Hall, April 8, 1953, NCC, RG 4, Box 1, Folder 21; Samuel McCrea Cavert to Cameron P. Hall, April 14, 1953, NCC, RG 4, Box 2, Folder 32.

31. Charles P. Taft to Jasper E. Crane, April 9, 1953, JHP, Box 146; Charles P. Taft to Jasper E. Crane, April 29, 1953, JHP, Box 146.

32. Charles P. Taft to Jasper E. Crane, April 29, 1953, JHP, Box 146.

33. J. Howard Pew to Samuel McCrea Cavert, May 8, 1953, NCC, RG 4, Box 1, Folder 21.

34. Around the time he succeeded in tabling the DCEL's economic policy statement, for example, Pew was irate to discover that a pronouncement on the rights of welfare recipients issuing from the Department of Welfare had just been approved. J. Howard Pew to Samuel McCrea Cavert, January 29, 1953, NCC, RG 4, Box 4, Folder 34.

35. The officers of the NCC's divisions—the upper echelon of the bureaucracy, beneath only the General Board—were elected by the delegates to the NCC's triennial General Assemblies. The divisions, in turn, were given considerably leeway in the formation of subordinate departments, though their organizational structures had to be approved by the General Board. "By-Laws of the Division of Christian Life and Work," HJV, Box 39, Folder AA-1 6.

36. Poethig, "Cameron Hall, Economic Life, and the Ministry of the Laity," 39–40.

37. Ibid.

38. To be sure, some business representatives were members in name only, but most took their duties quite seriously. Between January 1951 and April 1953 Chase, Hart, Smith, and Stephens attended at least two meetings, as did Halbert Jones, a North Carolina industrialist, and Frank W. Pierce, personnel director at Standard Oil of New Jersey. Williams and Jones attended only one meeting. Some members who apparently never attended a meeting in this period—for example, J. Irwin Miller and Paul Hoffmann— were nonetheless in regular contact with the DCEL's executive director. (Miller would become more active in 1954, as we shall see). "Study of Attendance at Eight Meetings

of the General Committee, Department of the Church & Economic Life," NCC, RG 4, Box 1, Folder 21. As Hall later recalled, the Department's lay members were "bears for work." They typically held three two-day meetings per year, and their sessions often stretched into the late evening. Poethig, "Cameron Hall, Economic Life, and the Ministry of the Laity," 40.

39. On Hoffman's courtship of Eisenhower, see Alan R. Raucher, *Paul G. Hoffman: Architect of Foreign Aid* (Lexington: University Press of Kentucky, 1985), 92–95.

40. Ibid.; "Study of Attendance at Eight Meetings of the General Committee, Department of the Church & Economic Life," NCC, RG 4, Box 1, Folder 21.

41. Jerry Voorhis to J. Edward Carothers, December 17, 1976, HJV, Box 39, Folder AA-1 18.

42. Both Charles P. Taft and Noel Sargent (of NAM) were prominent Episcopal lay leaders; in addition, Taft had earlier served as the first lay president of the FCC (see chap. 4).

43. Charles Taft served a stint as president of the YMCA following his graduation from Yale Law School. Wesley F. Rennie served as YMCA general secretary from 1933 to 1947, and W. Walter Williams was president of the group's National Council. Mildred McAfee Horton, the NCC official whose jurisdiction covered the DCEL, had a long and fruitful association with the YWCA. While an undergraduate at Vassar, she led the college's association; later she launched a successful academic career with a master's thesis examining the YWCA's structural features and organizational dynamics. On Rennie's YMCA experience see "Wesley F. Rennie Appointed," *New York Times*, September 18, 1949, p. 74; John Nurser, *For All People and All Nations* (Washington, DC: Georgetown University Press, 2005), 75–76. On Williams, see his biography on the History Link website at http://historylink.org/File/7193. On Horton, see "Mildred McAfee Horton (1900–1994): Portrait of a Pathbreaking Christian Leader," *Journal of Presbyterian History* 76 (1998): 159–174, 161–163; "Mildred McAfee Horton Dies; First Head of WAVES Was 94," *New York Times*, September 4, 1994.

44. Karl Schriftgiesser, *Business Comes of Age: The Impact of the Committee for Economic Development, 1942–1960* (New York: Harper & Brothers, 1969), 139.

45. Rennie is listed as a DCEL member in "Study of Attendance at Eight Meetings of the General Committee, Department of the Church & Economic Life," NCC, RG 4, Box 1, Folder 21.

46. Quoted in Rick Wartzman, *The End of Loyalty: The Rise and Fall of Good Jobs in America* (New York: Public Affairs, 2017), 18. On the CED's formation and economic philosophy, see, for example, Mark S. Mizruchi, *The Fracturing of the American Corporate Elite* (Cambridge, MA: Harvard University Press, 2013), 37–44, 55–62, 67–76; John B. Judis, *The Paradox of American Democracy: Elites, Special Interests, and the Betrayal of the Public Trust* (New York: Routledge, 2000), 66–71.

47. See, for example, Fones-Wolf, *Selling Free Enterprise*, 232–233.

48. Loose documents included with J. Irwin Miller to Cameron P. Hall, January 14, 1953, ISM, Series 2, Box 308, Folder 2.

49. Speech to Los Angeles Council of Church Women, November 2, 1951, PGH, Box 123.

50. Paul G. Hoffman, "Address Before the Men's Forum of the Congregational Church, Benton Harbor, Michigan," February 3, 1946, PGH, Box 109.

51. To appreciate the unusual nature of Pew's upbringing, one need only consider the contrasting case of John D. Rockefeller, Jr., another devout son of a self-made oil tycoon who was an almost exact contemporary of Pew's. When it came time to select a college, young John was steered by his father and family friend William Harper Raines toward Brown University, the only Baptist-affiliated institution in the Ivy League. While at Brown he became an enthusiastic joiner of mainline Protestant organizations, such as the YMCA, where he learned the creed of stewardship. (In a typical address to the University's YMCA chapter he urged his audience to "aid the unfortunate" in the name of Christ, and to remember that one "cannot serve God and mammon.") Also while at Brown, Rockefeller studied with prominent social scientists including Elijah Benjamin Andrews and Henry B. Gardiner, who took seriously the proposition that property was a gift from God, held in trust for the advancement of his kingdom. It should come as no surprise, then, that Rockefeller entered adulthood convinced that the family fortune was not something to be hoarded in the name of preventing sloth, but rather a divine blessing he was obligated to share with the less fortunate. Albert F. Schenkel, *The Rich Man and the Kingdom: John D. Rockefeller, Jr., and the Protestant Establishment* (Minneapolis: Fortress Press, 1995), 18–19.

52. During the late 1880s and early 1890s, for example, the college's primary instructor in physics and chemistry (who also taught courses in psychology and literature) was a minister who successfully lobbied to have the Bible adopted as a textbook for his science courses. David M. Dayton, *'Mid the Pines: An Historical Study of Grove City College* (Grove City, PA: Grove City College Alumni Association, 1973), 41, 46, 52–55; Mary Sennholz, *Faith and Freedom: The Journal of a Great American* (Grove City, PA: Grove City College Press, 1975), 14–20.

53. He was, according to one classmate, "a rather shy and quiet boy who didn't play any sports or participate in any extracurricular activities. He didn't even have a girlfriend." Senholz, *Faith and Freedom*, 19.

54. Dayton, *'Mid the Pines*, 52.

55. Sennholz, *Faith and Freedom*, 19–20.

56. To be sure, several members of the Pew faction, including Jasper Crane and B. E. Hutchinson, attended elite institutions, where they almost certainly encountered ideas they would later come to regard as "socialist" or "un-American." Jasper Crane, for example, studied chemistry at Princeton, while B. E. Hutchinson took engineering classes at MIT (though, like Pew, he apparently left without earning a degree). Yet, like Pew, Crane and Hutchinson claimed to be largely self-taught in matters of economics and religion. Vincent Curcio, *Chrysler: The Life and Times of an Automotive Genius* (New York: Oxford University Press, 2001), 289; Jasper Crane to J. Howard Pew and Lois Black Hunter, June 6, 1955, JHP, Box 168; J. Howard Pew to B. E. Hutchinson, November 13, 1952, JHP, Box 146.

57. Jasper Crane to Samuel McCrea Cavert, May 25, 1953, NCC, RG 4, Box 17, Folder 31. Also see the account in "General Board Meets," *Christian Century,* June 3, 1953, pp. 654–656.
58. Jasper Crane to Samuel McCrea Cavert, May 25, 1953, NCC, RG 4, Box 17, Folder 31.
59. Samuel McCrea Cavert to William C. Martin, NCC, RG 4, Box 17, Folder 31.
60. J. Irwin Miller to Jasper E. Crane, July 9, 1953, NCC, RG 4, Box 1, Folder 21.
61. J. Howard Pew to Pauline Baker, February 11, 1961, JHP, Box 72; J. Howard Pew [secretary] to M. G. Lowman, February 15, 1961, JHP, Box 72; J. Howard Pew to Charles R. Sligh, Jr., February 27, 1961, JHP, Box 72; Charles R. Sligh, Jr. to Pauline M. Baker, March 7, 1961, JHP, Box 72; J. Howard Pew to M. G. Lowman, March 27, 1961, JHP, Box 72; J. Howard Pew to Charles R. Sligh, Jr., March 27, 1961, JHP, Box 72.
62. J. Howard Pew to Maurice H. Stans, July 3, 1968, JHP, Box 94.
63. Samuel McCrea Cavert to Cameron P. Hall, September 24, 1953, JHP, Box 146.
64. Reinhold Niebuhr to Cameron P. Hall, October 2, 1953, NCC, RG 4, Box 1, Folder 21.
65. Although Pew alleged that Hall had single-handedly "ram[med] through" the revised statement, Hall made clear in his internal communications with Cavert that he had acted with the full support of several influential business representatives, including not only Taft and Miller, but also John A. Stephens of U.S. Steel, John H. Hart of Goodrich Rubber, and the banker S. Guernsey Jones. J. Howard Pew to Jasper Crane, September 24, 1953, JHP, Box 168; Cameron P. Hall to Samuel McCrea Cavert, November 19, 1953, NCC, RG 4, Box 1, Folder 21.
66. Jasper Crane to Lois Black Hunter, December 12, 1953, JHP, Box 168.
67. Jasper Crane to J. Howard Pew, February 4, 1954, JHP, Box 146; Edwin W. Parsons to Roswell P. Barnes, January 19, 1954, NCC, RG 4, Box 7, Folder 8. On Parsons's professional background, see "Sails Today as Delegate to Laymen's Conference," *New York Times,* April 12, 1949, p. 58; "President Urges Modern Crusade: Asks Baptists in Convention to Fight Once Again with Courage of Forefathers," *New York Times,* June 13, 1951, p. 17.
68. "Remarks of Charles P. Taft at the General Board, National Council of the Churches of Christ, January 20, 1954," JHP, Box 146. Emphasis in the original.
69. J. Irwin Miller to Roy G. Ross, February 1, 1954, NCC, RG 4, Box 7, Folder 8.
70. Jasper E. Crane to William C. Martin, March 13, 1953, NCC, RG 4, Box 3, Folder 33; Jasper E. Crane to Roswell P. Barnes, June 20, 1957, NCC, RG 4, Box 17, Folder 31; Jasper E. Crane to Roswell P. Barnes, June 20, 1957, NCC, RG 4, Box 17, Folder 31.
71. The term appears, for example, in the minutes of the Committee's January 19, 1954 meeting. "Minutes of the Committee on the Maintenance of American Freedom," NCC, RG 4, Box 8, Folder 12.
72. "Statement on Behalf of the National Council of the Churches of Christ in the U.S.A. before the Subcommittee on Rules of the Senate Committee on Rules and Administration, July 6, 1954," NCC, RG 4, Box 8, Folder 12.
73. Ibid.
74. Jasper E. Crane to Roswell P. Barnes, June 20, 1957, NCC, RG 4, Box 17, Folder 31.
75. As usual, Pew painted himself as the innocent victim of a communist-led conspiracy. With the purest of motives, he had agreed to aid the Council in its time of need, only

to find himself exploited by a body of clerics who were bereft of "integrity" and "intellectual honesty" and who "employ[ed] the same techniques as the Communists." J. Howard Pew to Jasper Crane, July 2, 1954, JHP, Box 168.

76. Jasper Crane to J. Howard Pew, July 14, 1954, JHP, Box 168.

77. Pratt, *The Liberalization of American Protestantism*, 96–97.

78. As was often the case with Pew's attacks on the Council, the affirmation immediately undercut its own rationale by defining a "Christian society" as one in which "economic decisions are arrived at in a free market," without the interference of meddling politicians. Pew, "The Chairman's Final Report," 186–188.

79. Jasper E. Crane to J. Howard Pew, August 9, 1954, JHP, Box 168.

80. Although the "Lay Affirmation" had the support of a substantial majority of the Lay Committee's members, a number of prominent members, when polled on the matter, either voted "no" or abstained. The first group included not only J. Irwin Miller and Charles P. Taft, but also John Nuveen, Jr., head of a prominent Chicago-based municipal bond firm; Sadie T. M. Alexander, the first African American woman to receive a Ph.D. in economics in the United States; and Helen Kenyon, a pioneering female leader in higher education. Abstainers included Robert E. Wilson of Standard Oil and—perhaps surprisingly—Noel Sargent of NAM. See "National Lay Committee Members Voting Disapproval of the Affirmation" [loose document] in ISM, Series 2, Box 341, Folder 5.

81. Roy G. Ross to William C. Martin, September 10, 1954, JHP, NCC, RG 4, Box 7, Folder 8.

82. Instead of approving the "Lay Affirmation," the Board voted merely to "receive" the document without in any way endorsing its contents. The proposal to require supermajority support for policy pronouncements was referred to an unfriendly committee where it was all but certain to remain interred for the foreseeable future. Finally, the proposal to curb the autonomy of the Department of the Church and Economic Life was sufficiently watered down as to ensure that it would have no practical effect. Pratt, *The Liberalization of American Protestantism*, 98–99.

83. Pew, *The Chairman's Final Report*, 194–202.

84. "Churches Council Sets Social Code," *New York Times*, September 16, 1954, p. 1; "'Norms' Adopted to Guide Christians," September 16, 1954, p. 26. The Pew forces could at take comfort in the fact that the *Times* article emphasized the document's anticommunist language, noting that it "oppos[ed] collectivism and back[ed] free enterprise."

85. Significantly, several of Pew's closest allies, including Hutchinson and Crane, elected to retain their seats on the General Board rather than cut ties with the NCC altogether. But while Hutchinson and Crane made clear that their sympathies lay with Pew, other members of the Lay Committee were just as convinced that Pew's efforts to dictate Council policy had crossed a line. For example, Robert E. Wilson of Standard Oil, a Lay Committee member who was also affiliated with the DCEL, was so disgusted by Pew's actions that he agreed to join J. Irwin Miller in spearheading a December 1954 fundraising drive for the very department that Pew had hoped to eviscerate. The resulting form letter, far from downplaying the controversial "Basic Principles"

statement, placed it front and center, touting it as an example of the Department's unique ability to achieve "unity of spirit in [the] highly complex area ... of economic life." [Form letter], J. Irwin Miller to [blank], November 1954, ISM, Series 2, Box 308, Folder 4; Cameron P. Hall to J. Irwin Miller, December 6, 1954, ISM, Series 2, Box 308, Folder 4; J. Irwin Miller to Cameron P. Hall, December 9, 1954, ISM, Series 2, Box 308, Folder 4; C.L. Corban to Robert E. Wilson, December 10, 1954, ISM, Series 2, Box 308, Folder 4; P.F. Prince to J. Irwin Miller, December 15, 1954, ISM, Series 2, Box 308, Folder 4.

86. Pew, *The Chairman's Final Report*, vi–vii.

87. "Laymen and Clergy at Odds on Role of Church in Politics," *U.S. News and World Report*, February 3, 1956, 43–48.

88. "Mr. Pew and the Clergy," *Christian Century*, February 22, 1956, JHP, Box 160.

89. "A Startling Report," *United Evangelical Action*, March 15, 1956, JHP, Box 160.

90. In a union shop, employees are required to become full-fledged union members. Agency-shop employees may decline to join the union but must pay the union an amount equivalent to the cost of collective bargaining representation.

91. "Excerpts from Church Group Pronouncements on Right-to-Work Laws," ISM, Series 2, Box 335, Folder 1.

92. "Proposed Statement on Union Membership as a Condition of Employment," NCC, RG 4, Box 16, Folder, 22.

93. S. Guernsey Jones to Mrs. Douglas Horton, May 1, 1956, NCC, RG 6, Box 3, Folder 12; Robert E. Wilson to Mrs. Douglas Horton, May 8, 1956, NCC, RG 6, Box 3, Folder 12; Robert E. Wilson to Mrs. Douglas Horton, May 18, 1956, NCC, RG 6, Box 3, Folder 12; Robert E. Wilson to the Members of the Executive Board of the Division of Christian Life and Work, May 18, 1956, NCC, RG 6, Box 3, Folder 12.

94. Robert E. Wilson to the Members of the Executive Board of the Division of Christian Life and Work, May 18, 1956, NCC, RG 6, Box 3, Folder 12.

95. "Mildred McAfee Horton: Portrait of a Pathbreaking Christian Leader," 161–163; "Mildred McAfee Horton Dies; First Head of WAVES Was 94," *New York Times*, September 4, 1994.

96. "Mildred McAfee Horton: Portrait of a Pathbreaking Christian Leader," 161–163.

97. Mrs. Douglas Horton to S. Guernsey Jones, May 10, 1956, NCC, RG 6, Box 3, Folder 12.

98. Meeting Minutes, June 5, 1956, Executive Committee of the Division of Christian Life and Work, NCC, RG 6, Box 3, Folder 12. The amendment was introduced by Charles Taft at the June 1956 meeting of the Division of Christian Life and Work's executive committee.

99. Minutes of the General Board Meeting, June 6–7, 1956, NCC, RG 6, Box 3, Folder 12. Nelson Cruikshank, an AFL-CIO official who was also a member of the DECL, was particularly aggrieved by the last-minute changes to the text. Shortly after the General Board meeting he penned a hyperbolic letter to Horton alleging that the combined effect of cutting the "not in the public interest" language and adding Hutchinson's paragraph acknowledging the existence of "highly diverse opinions" among committed Christians was "tragic," as it had "the carefully designed effect of ... negat[ing]

completely the position expressed by both the Department and the Division." But Horton pushed back forcefully against the allegation that she had somehow sold out organized labor. The new language, she insisted, had not "alter[ed] in any degree the intent" of the original document. Rather, it had merely stated a fact: "Moral problems are involved [in the question of right-to-work laws]. The answer is not simple since so many Christians disagree on it." But the critical point was that the statement then proceeded to make clear, in Horton's words, that as "for [the Division of Christian Life and Work], we have come to an answer [on the right-to-work question] and here it is." Nelson H. Cruikshank to Mrs. Douglas Horton, June 28, 1956, NCC, RG 6, Box 3, Folder 12. Also see Nelson Cruikshank to Arild Olsen, June 28, 1956, NCC, RG 6, Box 3, Folder 12; Mrs. Douglas Horton to Nelson H. Cruikshank, July 7, 1956, NCC, RG 6, Box 3, Folder 12.

100. "Religious Freedom?" Newsletter of the National Right to Work Committee, July 1956 [clipping], ISM, Series 2, Box 335, Folder 1.

101. Editorial, Southern States Industrial Council Bulletin, September 1, 1956 [clipping], ISM, Series 2, Box 335, Folder 1.

102. "Easy," National Review, August 25, 1956 [clipping], ISM, Series 2, Box 335, Folder 1.

103. "Council of Churches Opposes 'Wreck' Laws," AFL-CIO News, June 16, 1956 [clipping], ISM, Series 2, Box 335, Folder 1. Also see "National Council of Churches Hits 'Right-to-Work' Laws," United Rubber Worker, July 1954 [clipping], ISM, Series 2, Box 335, Folder 1.

104. Eugene Carson Blake to Saul Miller, July 17, 1956, NCC, RG 6, Box 3, Folder 12.

105. Under the headline "Church Council Division Issued 'Wreck' Law Blast," the new story repeated the claim—technically true—that the General Board had authorized the statement's distribution, while largely avoiding the problem of the original story's misleading headline. "Church Council Division Issued 'Wreck' Law Blast," AFL-CIO News, June 16, 1956 [clipping], NCC, RG 4, Box 16, Folder 22.

106. Gertrude L. Apel to Roy G. Ross, October 2, 1956, NCC, RG 4, Box 16, Folder 22; Wilbur C. Parry to Gertrude L. Apel, October 8, 1956, NCC, RG 4, Box 16, Folder 22. For background on the 1956 ballot proposition, see Gilbert J. Gall, The Politics of the Right to Work: The Labor Federations as Special Interests, 1943–1979 (New York: Greenwood Press, 1988), 82–83.

107. Western Union telegram from Eugene Carson Blake to James V. Pratt, August 6, 1956, NCC, RG 4, Box 16, Folder 22.

108. James V. Pratt to Eugene Carson Blake, October 24, 1956, NCC, RG 4, Box 16, Folder 22.

109. Western Union telegram, Roy G. Ross to James V. Pratt, October 30, 1956, NCC, RG 4, Box 16, Folder 22. For background on the right-to-work debate in Kansas, see Gall, The Politics of Right to Work, 115–117.

110. For the results of the Washington referendum, see Gall, The Politics of Right to Work, 70.

111. J. Stanford Smith to Roswell P. Barnes, November 30, 1956, NCC, RG 4, Box 16, Folder 22.

112. "Minutes of the General Board, Excerpt," NCC, RG 4, Box 16, Folder 22. The excerpt is included in Roy G. Ross to Eugene Carson Blake, December 28, 1956.

113. Roy G. Ross to Harold W. Conant, October 17, 1956, NCC, RG 4, Box 16, Folder 22; Roy G. Ross to Charles R. Hook, October 3, 1956, NCC, RG 4, Box 16, Folder 22; Roy G. Ross to Charles E. Wilson, October 3, 1956, NCC, RG 4, Box 16, Folder 22.

114. The NCC's General Board, for its part, did eventually approve a version of the 1956 statement, incorporating it into a much broader 1959 pronouncement entitled "Ethical Issues in Industrial Relations of Concern to Christians." By this point, however, the labor unions had been knocked on their heels by Senator John McClellan's Select Committee on Improper Activities in Labor and Management, whose inquiries into Jimmy Hoffa's Teamsters Union revealed a host of shadowy practices, including links to organized crime. The NCC responded to the Committee's findings by issuing a sharply worded condemnation of the unions in question. Stanley Rowland, Jr., "Churches Assail Union Corruption," *New York Times*, October 4, 1957, p. 11; "The Moral Crisis in the Labor Union Movement and in Labor-Management Practices," in HJV, Box 39, Folder AA-1 8.

115. J. Irwin Miller to C. P. Von Herzen, October 25, 1965, ISM, Series 2, Box 335, Folder 3.

Chapter 6

1. Elesha Coffman, "'You Cannot Fool the Electronic Eye': Billy Graham and Media," in Andrew Finstuen, Anne Blue Wills, and Grant Wacker, eds., *Billy Graham: American Pilgrim* (New York: Oxford University Press, 2017), 197–215.

2. Frances FitzGerald, *The Evangelicals: The Struggle to Shape America* (New York: Simon and Schuster, 2017), 177.

3. See, for example, William Martin, *A Prophet with Honor: The Billy Graham Story* (1991; Grand Rapids, MI: Zondervan, 2018), chap. 9.

4. "Graham's Farewell Packs Broadway," *New York Times*, September 2, 1957, p. 1.

5. Reinhold Niebuhr, "Literalism, Individualism, and Billy Graham," *Christian Century*, May 23, 1956, pp. 640–642; R. N., "Editorial Notes," *Christianity and Crisis*, March 5, 1956, pp. 18–19. The final quotation is from a *Life* magazine interview quoted in Mark Silk, *Spiritual Politics: Religion and America since World War II* (New York: Simon and Schuster, 1988), 105.

6. Quoted in Grant Wacker, *America's Pastor: Billy Graham and the Shaping of a Nation* (Cambridge, MA: Belknap Press, 2014), 205.

7. "Does a Religious Crusade Do Any Good?," *U.S. News & World Report*, September 27, 1957, pp. 72–81, 78.

8. During the 1960 presidential campaign, for example, when Norman Vincent Peale and other prominent Protestants openly opposed the idea of a Catholic President, Graham never raised the issue of John F. Kennedy's religion in public (though he found other ways to signal his support for his close friend Richard Nixon). Wacker, *America's Pastor*, 208–209.

9. On Graham's relationship with Richardson, see ibid., 154–155, 207; Kevin M. Kruse, *One Nation Under God: How Corporate America Invented Christian America* (New York: Basic Books, 2015), 50–51, 54, 58–59.

10. In his largely sympathetic biography, Wacker observes that Graham admired J. Howard Pew, Sid Richardson, and his other wealthy benefactors for their work ethic and "affinity for personal responsibility, private philanthropy, and meritocratic capitalism." Wacker is equivocal on the extent to which Graham shared Pew's libertarian economic views. As explained below, however, the revivalist's correspondence in the months preceding the launch of *Christianity Today* leaves little doubt that he was generally sympathetic to Pew's point of view. Wacker, *America's Pastor*, 156.

11. See, for example, L. Nelson Bell to J. Howard Pew, January 14, 1955, JHP, Box 41; L. Nelson Bell to J. Howard Pew, April 20, 1952, JHP, Box 52.

12. Billy Graham to J. Howard Pew, April 13, 1955, JHP, Box 42.

13. Billy Graham to J. Howard Pew, March 26, 1955, JHP, Box 42.

14. Billy Graham to J. Howard Pew, April 13, 1955, JHP, Box 42.

15. Billy Graham to J. Howard Pew, March 26, 1955, JHP, Box 42.

16. L. Nelson Bell to J. Howard Pew, March 27, 1954, JHP, Box 52; L. Nelson Bell to J. Howard Pew, June 30, 1954, JHP, Box 52; L. Nelson Bell to J. Howard Pew, December 12, 1954, JHP, Box 52.

17. J. Howard Pew [secretary] to Fred Dynert, March 22, 1956, JHP, Box 48; Billy Graham to J. Howard Pew, April 18, 1956, JHP, Box 48.

18. Billy Graham to J. Howard Pew, February 8, 1955, JHP, Box 42; Billy Graham to J. Howard Pew, March 26, 1955, JHP, Box 42; Billy Graham to J. Howard Pew, April 2, 1955, JHP, Box 42; J. Howard Pew to Billy Graham, April 7, 1955, JHP, Box 42.

19. Billy Graham to J. Howard Pew, April 13, 1955, JHP, Box 42.

20. Billy Graham to L. Nelson Bell, June 9, 1955, JHP, Box 42.

21. To remain aloof from public discourse, Henry argued in *The Uneasy Conscience*, only ceded control of national institutions to the liberals, thus ensuring that millions of Americans would be indoctrinated into a flawed worldview that subordinated the saving power of individual faith to the false gods of secular reason, amoral science, and a never-ending program of government-sponsored social reforms. Carl F. H. Henry, *The Uneasy Conscience of Modern Fundamentalism* (1947; Grand Rapids, MI: William B. Eerdmans, 2003).

22. Ibid., 87–88.

23. Carl F. H. Henry to Richard Arens, August 13, 1956, CTI, Series I, Box 16, Folder 27. Henry carried on a long-running correspondence with Hatfield, a self-proclaimed evangelical whose political convictions generally ran to the left of Henry's. See, for example, Mark Hatfield to Carl F. H. Henry, June 22, 1956, CTI, Box 17, Folder 65; Carl F. H. Henry to Mark Hatfield, November 11, 1960, CTI, Box 17, Folder 65; Carl F. H. Henry to Mark Hatfield, May 17, 1963, CTI, Box 17, Folder 65; Mark Hatfield to Carl F. H. Henry, May 21, 1963, CTI, Box 17, Folder 65.

24. Associated Press, "New Magazine Planned to Stress Christianity," May 10, 1956, JHP, Box 46.

25. "Excerpt from *Paul Harvey News*," September 27, 1956, JHP, Box 46. On the reach of *Paul Harvey News*, see "Paul Harvey, Homespun Radio Voice of Middle America, Is Dead at 90," *New York Times*, March 2, 2009, p. A16.

26. Billy Graham to J. Howard Pew, March 26, 1955, JHP, Box 42; Billy Graham to J. Howard Pew, February 8, 1955, JHP, Box 42; Associated Press, "New Magazine Planned to Stress Christianity," May 10, 1956, JHP, Box 46.

27. Billy Graham, "Biblical Authority in Evangelism," *Christianity Today*, October 1956, p. 6.

28. Carl F. H. Henry, "The Fragility of Freedom in the West," *Christianity Today*, October 1956, pp. 8, 11, 17.

29. "Why 'Christianity Today'?," *Christianity Today*, October 1956, p. 20.

30. Billy Graham to J. Howard Pew, May 29, 1956, JHP, Box 48.

31. L. Nelson Bell to Paul E. Wise, JHP, Box 47.

32. Many of the magazine's early backers were mid-sized manufacturers from the South or Midwest. Ernest M. Sims, owner of the Elkhart, Indiana–based Metal Forming Corporation, sent $500, along with a note declaring that the upcoming launch of *Christianity Today* was "the most heartening forward development that has occurred in the field of religious activity in many years." F. N. Bard, chairman of Chicago's Barco Manufacturing Company, contributed $100 to help expose the machinations of religious organizations, like the National Council of Churches, who were "getting into politics and economic matters about which they know very little, and on which they seem to be badly guided." Ernest M. Sims to J. Howard Pew, June 12, 1956, JHP, Box 47; F. N. Bard to J. Howard Pew, June 27, 1956, JHP, Box 47.

33. "Meeting of the Board of Directors of Christianity Today," September 13, 1956, JHP, Box 46; List of Contributors, December 1957, JHP, Box 58; List of Contributors, 1959, JHP, Box 67.

34. L. Nelson Bell to J. Howard Pew, JHP, Box 41.

35. The Billy Graham Evangelistic Association (BGEA) also made large, regular donations to *Christianity Today*, though Grem suggests that Pew was the ultimate source of the money. See Darren E. Grem, *The Blessings of Business: How Corporations Shaped Conservative Christianity* (New York: Oxford University Press, 2016), 74.

36. See ibid., 91–92.

37. On Hankamer, see Darren Dochuk, "There Will Be Oil: Presidents, Wildcat Religion, and the Culture Wars of Pipeline Politics," in Brian Balogh and Bruce J. Schulman, eds., *Recapturing the Oval Office: New Historical Approaches to the American Presidency* (Ithaca, NY: Cornell University Press, 2015), 93–107, 101–103.

38. "Acceptances for Luncheon on Monday, June 10th," in JHP, Box 53.

39. C. C. Philippe to J. W. Pew [*sic*], June 3, 1957, JHP, Box 53.

40. J. Howard Pew's handwritten notes for the *Christianity Today* fundraiser are found in JHP, Box 53.

41. L. Nelson Bell to J. G. Davidson, June 13, 1957, JHP, Box 53.

42. Ibid.; L. Nelson Bell to Joseph Adamsen, June 12, 1957, JHP, Box 53.

43. Prior to the official launch of *Christianity Today*, Pew sent potential donors copies of his *Chairman's Final Report* and other NCC documents, thus implying that the

magazine would continue the work of the recently disbanded Lay Committee. See, for example, George Stoll to J. Howard Pew, June 28, 1956, JHP, Box 47; J. Howard Pew to C. M. Goethe, July 10, 1956, JHP, Box 47. For Pew's denial of ulterior motives, see J. Howard Pew to Paul E. Wise, June 21, 1956, JHP, Box 47.

44. J. Howard Pew, Review of "Goals of Economic Life," *Christianity Today*, June 22, 1959.

45. "The NCC and Economic Planning," *Christianity Today*, February 1961, JHP, Box 72. For Pew's encouragement of such attacks, see J. Howard Pew to Carl F. H. Henry, January 12, 1959, JHP, Box 63; J. Howard Pew to Carl F. H. Henry, February 2, 1961, JHP, Box 72; J. Howard Pew to Carl F. H. Henry, February 6, 1961, JHP, Box 72.

46. Robert P. Montgomery to Carl F. H. Henry, March 13, 1961, JHP, Box 72.

47. The quoted passage is from "The Shape of the Church," *Christianity Today*, October 27, 1961, pp. 20–21. Also see William Henry Anderson, Jr., "Business and Control: The Organization in the Church," *Christianity Today*, October 27, 1961, pp. 3–5; Geoffrey W. Bromiley, "Ecumenism and Authority," *Christianity Today*, April 27, 1962, pp. 11–12; J. Howard Pew, "Calvin's Influence in Church Affairs," *Christianity Today*, May 11, 1962, pp. 9–11; Arthur A. Rouner, Jr., "Gathered Church, Great Church," *Christianity Today*, May 25, 1962, pp. 9–11; "Presbyterians Depart from Geneva in Headlong Flight," *Christianity Today*, June 22, 1962, p. 21; "WCC Approves a Trinitarian Basis," *Christianity Today*, December 22, 1961, pp. 22–23.

48. William C. Whyte, *The Organization Man* (New York: Simon and Schuster, 1956); C. Wright Mills, *The Power Elite* (New York: Oxford University Press, 1956). *The Man in the Gray Flannel Suit*, an important fictional work that advanced similar themes, had appeared the year before, with a film based on the novel following in 1956. Sloan Wilson, *The Man in the Gray Flannel Suit* (New York: Simon and Schuster, 1955).

49. William Henry Anderson, Jr., "Business and Control: The Organization in the Church," *Christianity Today*, October 27, 1961, pp. 3–5. Also see the issue's lead editorial, "The Shape of the Church," *Christianity Today*, October 27, 1961, pp. 20–21.

50. For representative articles on Barth, many of which were penned by Carl Henry's undergraduate philosophy professor, Gordon Clark, see Gordon H. Clark, "Barth's Critique of Modernism," *Christianity Today*, January 5, 1962; Gordon H. Clark, "Special Report: Encountering Barth in Chicago," *Christianity Today*, May 11, 1962, pp. 35–36; H. Daniel Friberg, "Almost Oracular: Reflections on Karl Barth's Lectures," *Christianity Today*, May 25, 1962, pp. 23–25; "Highlights of Barth's Visit to the United States," *Christianity Today*, May 25, 1962, p. 26. For criticism of Barth's views on biblical inerrancy, see "The Enigma in Karl Barth," *Christianity Today*, June 8, 1962, pp. 24–25; "The Dilemma Facing Karl Barth," *Christianity Today*, January 4, 1963, pp. 26–27.

51. "The Enigma in Barth," *Christianity Today*, June 8, 1962, pp. 24–25.

52. Gordon H. Clark, "Special Report: Encountering Barth in Chicago," *Christianity Today*, May 11, 1962, pp. 35–36.

53. "Can We Salvage the Republic?" *Christianity Today*, March 3, 1958, pp. 3–7.

54. "Compulsion, Not Compassion—That Is the Question," *Christianity Today*, May 25, 1962, p. 22.

55. "Big Labor Favors Featherbedding and Assails the Right to Work," *Christianity Today*, December 21, 1962, p. 27.

56. "Stock Market Tumbles in Confused Economic Climate," *Christianity Today*, June 22, 1962, p. 23.

57. "Religion and the Peace Corps," April 24, 1964, *Christianity Today*, April 24, 1964, pp. 27–28; "Peace Corps Aids Sectarian Expansion," *Christianity Today*, August 28, 1964, p. 31.

58. Sargent Shriver, "The Peace Corps" [letter to the Editor], *Christianity Today*, July 31, 1964, p. 31; Sargent Shriver to Carl F. H. Henry, October 9, 1964, *Christianity Today*, October 9, 1964, Christianity Today Papers, Box 16, Folder 10, BGCA; William E. Bozarth to Christianity Today, October 20, 1964, CTI, Box 16, Folder 10; Carl F. H. Henry to Ben Lawrence, October 21, 1964, CTI, Box 16, Folder 10; Carl F. H. Henry to Charles Caldwell, October 23, 1964, CTI, Box 16, Folder 10; Ben Lawrence to Carl F. H. Henry, October 23, 1964, CTI, Box 16, Folder 10; Carl F. H. Henry to Charles Caldwell, October 26, 1964, CTI, Box 16, Folder 10; Carl F. H. Henry to Ben Lawrence, October 29, 1964, CTI, Box 16, Folder 10; Charles C. Woodard, Jr. to Carl F. H. Henry, November 13, 1964, CTI, Box 16, Folder 10; Carl F. H. Henry to Dr. E. K. Martin, November 17, 1964, CTI, Box 16, Folder 10; Carl F. H. Henry to Charles C. Woodard, Jr., November 17, 1964, CTI, Box 16, Folder 10; Ben Lawrence to Carl F. H. Henry, November 21, 1964, CTI, Box 16, Folder 10; Carl F. H. Henry to A. D. Mengot, November 30, 1964, CTI, Box 16, Folder 10; Carl F. H. Henry to Ben Lawrence, November 30, 1964, CTI, Box 16, Folder 10; Carl F. H. Henry to Rev. S. Uteff, November 30, 1964, CTI, Box 16, Folder 10; Richard Schilke to Christianity Today, December 2, 1964, CTI, Box 16, Folder 10.

59. "Peace Corps in West Cameroon," *Christianity Today*, January 1, 1965, p. 29.

60. As Graham explained to Pew: "I do not think that our three editors are going to allow anything to appear in the magazine that will conflict with our views on economics and socialism. However, I do not believe we can expect them to submit to us as a board, the magazine each issue before it goes to print. It would be like a minister submitting his manuscript to his elders before preaching it. No self-respecting editor would submit to what he would consider a humiliation or a lack of confidence." Billy Graham to J. Howard Pew, September 27, 1957, JHP, Box 48. Also see L. Nelson Bell to J. Howard Pew, September 14, 1956, JHP, Box 52; J. Howard Pew to Billy Graham, October 1, 1956, JHP, Box 48.

61. Carl F. H. Henry to J. Howard Pew, December 2, 1958, JHP, Box 58.

62. Carl F. H. Henry to J. Howard Pew, October 8, 1957, JHP, Box 53.

63. Graham's complicated history on the issue of racial segregation is discussed in Daniel K. Williams, *God's Own Party: The Making of the Christian Right* (New York: Oxford University Press, 2010), 28–31; FitzGerald, *The Evangelicals*, 202–206; and Steven P. Miller, *Billy Graham and the Rise of the Republican South* (Philadelphia: University of Pennsylvania Press, 2009).

64. "Color Line in State University a Wobbly Defense of Freedom," *Christianity Today*, October 12, 1962.

65. "Slavery and Segregation," Draft Editorial, [n.d., 1958], JHP, Box 58; Carl F. H. Henry to J. Howard Pew, April 25, 1960, JHP, Box 67.

66. Quoted in David R. Swartz, *Moral Minority: The Evangelical Left in an Age of Conservatism* (Philadelphia: University of Pennsylvania Press, 2012), 23.
67. Carl F. H. Henry, *Confessions of a Theologian: An Autobiography* (Waco, TX: Word Books, 1986), 227.
68. "Presbyterians Press Social Claims," *Christianity Today*, June 19, 1964.
69. Ibid.
70. J. Howard Pew, "The Mission of the Church," *Christianity Today*, July 3, 1964, pp. 11–14.
71. Christianity Today Board Meeting Minutes, June 25, 1964, JHP, Box 83.
72. Henry, *Confessions of a Theologian*, 251.
73. "The Mission of the Church," *Christianity Today*, July 17, 1964, p. 3.
74. Carl F. H. Henry, *Aspects of Christian Social Ethics* (Grand Rapids, MI: W. B. Eerdmanns, 1964), 122–123. Emphasis in the original.
75. J. Howard Pew to Carl F. H. Henry, October 15, 1962, JHP, Box 77; J. Howard Pew to Carl F. H. Henry, October 19, 1962, JHP, Box 77.
76. L. Nelson Bell to J. Howard Pew, July 27, 1964, JHP, Box 83; J. Howard Pew to L. Nelson Bell, August 3, 1964, JHP, Box 83; L. Nelson Bell to J. Howard Pew, August 16, 1964, JHP, Box 83.
77. Henry, *Confessions of a Theologian*, 252–301.

Chapter 7

1. Quoted in Beschloss, *Taking Charge: The Johnson White House Tapes, 1963–1964* (New York: Simon and Schuster, 1997), 331–332.
2. Quoted in Charles Lloyd Garrettson III, *Hubert H. Humphrey and the Politics of Joy* (New Brunswick, NJ: Transaction Publishers, 1993), 143–144; *Congressional Record*, June 10, 1964, p. 13309.
3. By one tally, twenty-two of the twenty-six senators targeted by religious groups had supported the cloture motion. James L. Adams, *The Growing Church Lobby in Washington* (Grand Rapids, MI: William B. Eerdmans), 33.
4. James F. Findlay, Jr., *Church People in the Struggle: The National Council of Churches and the Black Freedom Movement, 1950–1970* (New York: Oxford University Press, 1993), 28–29.
5. In 1957 a group of South Carolina Lutherans contacted NCC headquarters to demand that the Council cease disseminating the writings of "Martin Luther King . . . or any other person favoring the integration of the races." Other correspondents, including a Methodist layman from Michigan, were more creative. Instead of giving a platform to racial agitators, he insisted, the NCC should instead ensure that black churches were adequately funded, so that their members would not be tempted to invade white congregations. This would serve God's purpose of "keep[ing] the white race white." Donald L. Crolley, Secretary of St. Luke's Lutheran Church Council, Summerville, South Carolina to Secretary of Race Relations, National Council of Churches, January 22, 1957, NCC, RG 6, Box 45, Folder 15; L. A. Putnam to the Department of Racial and Cultural Relations, October 18, 1960, NCC, RG 6, Box 45,

Folder 15. By the mid-1950s around two hundred radio stations were airing a con-
densed version of the message. "Report on the Thirty-Second Annual Observance of
Race Relations Sunday, February 14, 1954," NCC, RG 6, Box 45, Folder 10.

6. Taylor Branch, *Pillar of Fire: America in the King Years, 1963–65* (New York: Simon &
Schuster, 1998), 104.

7. "Action for Racial Justice Now," ISM, Series 2, Box 299, Folder 4.

8. CORR's budget for the remainder of 1963 was set at a robust $175,000, with most
of the money coming in the form of designated contributions from the Council's
member denominations. In contrast, the NCC's Department of Racial and Cultural
Relations—which had worked to promote interracial harmony since the 1920s—
received a paltry $25,000 annually for its work to combat Jim Crow. Minutes: National
Council of Churches Commission on Religion and Race, June 28, 1963, NCC, RG 6,
Box 47, Folder 30; Findlay, *Church People in the Struggle*, 24, 34.

9. "Meeting of the President with Religious Leaders, June 17, 1963," 1, 2, 5, 6, JFK
Library. Available online at https://www.jfklibrary.org/Asset-Viewer/Archives/
JFKPOF-097-011.aspx.

10. The first draft of Miller's letter was composed by the Kennedy advisor Louis
Oberdorfer. Jon L. Regier to J. Irwin Miller, July 11, 1963, NCC, RG 6, Box 48, Folder
1; Jon L. Regier to J. Irwin Miller, July 19, 1963, NCC, RG 6, Box 48, Folder 1; J. Irwin
Miller to President John F. Kennedy (Draft), July 15, 1963, in NCC, RG 6, Box 48,
Folder 1.

11. Findlay, *Church People in the Struggle*, 24, 34.

12. Minutes: National Council of Churches Commission on Religion and Race, June 28,
1963, NCC, RG 6, Box 47, Folder 30.

13. Robert Spike, "Summer of Significance," NCC, RG 6, Box 48, Folder 2.

14. Miller never saw the inside of a jail cell, but Blake would soon be arrested along with
other religious leaders during an attempt to integrate a Baltimore-area amusement
park. Jon L. Regier to Robert W. Spike, July 14, 1963, NCC, RG 6, Box 48, Folder 1.

15. Anna Arnold Hedgeman, *The Gift of Chaos* (New York: Oxford University Press,
1977), 79; Branch, *Pillar of Fire*, 123–124, 128.

16. Minutes: National Council of Churches Commission on Religion and Race, June 28,
1963, NCC, RG 6, Box 47, Folder 30; "June 18, 1963 Meeting of Staff of Commission
on Race," NCC, RG 6, Box 48, Folder 2.

17. Minutes: National Council of Churches Commission on Religion and Race, June 28,
1963, NCC, RG 6, Box 47, Folder 30; Minutes: Commission on Religion and Race,
National Council of Churches, July 26, 1963, NCC, RG 6, Box 47, Folder 30. A fourth
prong, which caused a good deal of friction with the Kennedy administration, called
for various forms of aid to the thousands of demonstrators who were risking their
lives in direct action campaigns in the Southern and border states. The group established an emergency fund for bailing out jailed demonstrators and also arranged to
dispatch emergency response teams to hot spots such as Albany, Georgia, where civil
rights organizations were engaged in a prolonged battle with white city officials. On
tensions with the Kennedy administration, see Jon L. Regier to Robert Spike, July 14,
1963, NCC, RG 6, Box 48, Folder 1.

18. Rowland Evans and Robert Novak, "Civil Rights Barrier Rising in the Midwest," *Los Angeles Times*, August 21, 1963, ISM, Series 2, Box 301, Folder 1.

19. Jon L. Regier to Robert Spike, July 14, 1963, NCC, RG 6, Box 48, Folder 1.

20. Francis Stuart Harmon, "Report" [n.d.], p. 16, in NCC, RG 6, Box 48, Folder 5.

21. George S. Reamy to Robert W. Spike, August 14, 1963, ISM, Series 2, Box 301, Folder 1.

22. For an overview of Hedgeman's work with the NCC's Commission on Religion and Race, see Jennifer Scanlon, *Until There Is Justice: The Life of Anna Arnold Hedgeman* (New York: Oxford University Press, 2016), 155–188. I regret that I did not discover Scanlon's biography in time to incorporate its many insights into this chapter.

23. March on Washington for Jobs and Freedom, Organizing Manual No. 1, [n.d.], NCC, RG 6, Box 48, Folder 1; "Church Assembly, Washington, DC, August 28, 1963" [pamphlet, n.d.], NCC, RG 6, Box 48, Folder 1; Robert W. Spike to "Friends" [form letter], August 2, 1963, ISM, Series 2, Box 301, Folder 1.

24. Minutes: Commission on Religion and Race, National Council of Churches, July 26, 1963, NCC, RG 6, Box 47, Folder 30; Hedgeman, *The Gift of Chaos*, 82.

25. Steering Committee Task Force to All N.Y. Staff, NCCC, August 19, 1963, NCC, RG 6, Box 48, Folder 1.

26. Robert Spike, "Report of the [CORR] Executive Director," September 5, 1963, ISM, Series 2, Box 301, Folder 1; Jon L. Regier to Staff of the Division of Home Missions, August 21, 1963, NCC, RG 6, Box 48, Folder 2; James MacCracken to Church World Service Administration Committee, August 29, 1963, NCC, RG 6, Box 48, Folder 2.

27. "Indiana Churches Confront Racial Issues," *Indiana Church Councilor*, November 1963, p. 2, SCC, Box 2, Folder 5.

28. Robert Spike, "Report of the [CORR] Executive Director," September 5, 1963, ISM, Series 2, Box 301, Folder 1.

29. Quoted in Michael B. Friedland, *Lift Up Your Voice like a Trumpet: White Clergy and the Civil Rights and Antiwar Movements, 1954–1973* (Chapel Hill: University of North Carolina Press, 1998), 89.

30. James Reston, "The First Significant Test of the Freedom March," *New York Times*, August 30, 1963.

31. Marquis Childs, "Churches Have Civil Rights Task" [clipping], *Lincoln Star*, September 6, 1963, ISM, Series 2, Box 299, Folder 4.

32. Minutes, National Council of Churches of Christ in the USA Commission on Religion and Race, October 22, 1963, NCC, RG 6, Box 47, Folder 30.

33. Data on church density are from the National Council of Churches 1952 Survey on Churches and Church Membership in the United States, available online at the Association of Religion Data Archives, http://www.thearda.com. Figures for the UCC were arrived at by combining the totals of the Congregational Christian Churches and the Evangelical and Reformed Church, the two denominations that in 1959 merged to form the UCC.

34. William Adams Brown, *The Church in America: A Study of the Present Condition and Future Prospects of American Protestantism* (New York: MacMillan, 1922), 219. For an example of the upward flow of information, see the 1962 survey of state and

local council officials conducted by the NCC's Department of Racial and Cultural Relations. [No title], NCC, RG 6, Box 46, Folder 25.

35. Like the NCC, the typical local council featured departments dedicated to research and planning, Christian education, Christian life and work, publicity, legislation, and the like (though there was some variation from council to council).

36. Benson Y. Landis, ed., *Yearbook of American Churches* (New York: National Council of Churches, 1965). Also see Ross W. Sanderson, *Church Cooperation in the United States* (New York: Association of Council Secretaries, 1960), 205–211.

37. Sanderson, *Church Cooperation*, 205–211.

38. Benson Y. Landis, ed., *Yearbook of American Churches* (New York: National Council of Churches, 1963).

39. Council density data from ibid. Both tables exclude councils of religious education and their employees.

40. Data on the numbers of church councils and paid staff members are found in Landis, *Yearbook of American Churches*. Data on percentage of Protestant residents are drawn from the 1952 and 1971 Churches and Church Membership in the United States Studies, conducted by the National Council of Churches and the Department of Research and Statistics of the Lutheran Church—Missouri Synod, respectively. Both datasets are available at the Association of Religion Data Archives, www.thearda. com. African American residents and total population based on 1960 census figures.

41. Between 1959 and 1962 councils in Toledo, Wichita, Terra Haute, St. Paul, Kalamazoo, Fort Wayne, Decatur (Illinois), and Kenosha (Wisconsin) organized workshops to smooth the way for the adoption of fair housing laws. And in Flint, Michigan, the local church council sponsored neighborhood meetings to prevent the "panicked selling" that often greeted the arrival of black residents in formerly all-white enclaves. In Lincoln, Omaha, Cleveland, Topeka, and Port Huron (Michigan) local councils worked with elected officials to combat employment discrimination, in some cases spearheading initiatives to ramp up the hiring of minority applicants in the public sector. These examples are drawn from a 1962 survey of state and local council executives conducted by the National Council of Churches' Department of Racial and Cultural Relations. An untitled summary of the responses can be found in NCC, RG 6, Box 46, Folder 25.

42. "Association of Council Secretaries, National Conference, June 16–22, 1963" [brochure], NCC, RG 24, Box, Folder 30; "Association of Council Secretaries, Twenty-Second Annual Conference," Exhibit K, NCC, RG 24, Box, Folder 30; "Association of Council Secretaries, Twenty-Second Annual Conference," Exhibit M, NCC, RG 24, Box 1, Folder 30.

43. Hedgeman, *The Gift of Chaos*, 99–100.

44. "Midwest Conference on Civil Rights Legislation," ISM, Series 2, Box 299, Folder 5; Robert W. Spike to Participants in the Civil Rights Legislative Conference, September 19, 1963, ISM, Series 2, Box 299, Folder 5; Jerry Landauer, "Church Pressure Aids Changes for a Strong Civil Rights Measure," *Wall Street Journal*, September 17, 1963, p. 1; Findlay, *Church People in the Struggle*, 51; "Civil Rights Legislation Now," *Illinois Church Councilor*, September 1963, p. 2, SCC, Box 2, Folder 1; "Indiana Churches

Confront Racial Issues," *Indiana Church Councilor*, November 1963, p. 2, SCC, Box 2, Folder 5; "Civil Rights Consultations Held in Ohio," *Ohio Christian News*, November 1963, p. 17, SCC, Box 8, Folder 5.

45. Tom Brown, a Student Non-Violent Coordinating Committee (SNCC) field secretary and member of the Indiana team, found that state's white residents to be similarly ignorant about the problems facing "Negroes in Indiana," yet he was impressed that audience members "asked questions" and "said they would write to senators and would send funds to the south." Anna A. Hedgeman, "Summary Report—October 22, 1963 to January 9, 1964," NCC, RG 6, Box 47, Folder 31; Minutes, National Council of Churches of Christ in the USA Commission on Religion and Race, October 22, 1963, NCC, RG 6, Box 47, Folder 30; "Indiana Churches Confront Racial Issues," *Indiana Church Councilor*, November 1963, p. 2, SCC, Box 2, Folder 5; "Civil Rights Consultations Held in Ohio," *Ohio Christian News*, November 1963, p. 17, SCC, Box 8, Folder 5.

46. Charles M. Payne, *I've Got the Light of Freedom: The Organizing Tradition and the Mississippi Freedom Struggle*, 2nd ed. (Berkeley and Los Angeles: University of California Press, 2007), 227–228.

47. Anna A. Hedgeman, "Summary Report—October 22, 1963 to January 9, 1964," NCC, RG 6, Box 47, Folder 31; Hedgeman, *The Gift of Chaos*, 99.

48. Mrs. S. N. Tompkins to Robert Stone, March 18, 1964, UPC, Box 4, Folder 19.

49. "Clergy in City to Make Plea on Civil Rights," *Chicago Tribune*, September 21, 1963, p. A25; George Dugan, "Birmingham Stirs Faiths to Action," *New York Times*, September 21, 1963, p. 24. Not to be outdone, Methodist church leaders announced plans for a massive civil rights rally that would in late September draw five thousand clergy and laypeople to the New York Hilton to "express public support of President Kennedy's civil rights program." "5,000 Methodists Urged at Rally to Press for Civil Rights Action," *New York Times*, September 30, 1963, p. 42.

50. Robert W. Spike to NCC General Board, September 18, 1963, ISM, Series 2, Box 299, Folder 5.

51. Jerry Landauer, "Church Pressure Aids Changes for a Strong Civil Rights Measure," *Wall Street Journal*, September 17, 1963, p. 1.

52. Robert W. Spike to Participants in the Civil Rights Legislative Conference, September 19, 1963, ISM, Series 2, Box 299, Folder 5.

53. Todd S. Purdum, *An Idea Whose Time Has Come: Two Presidents, Two Parties, and the Battle for the Civil Rights Act of 1964* (New York: Henry Holt, 2014), 165.

54. Clay Risen, *The Bill of the Century: The Epic Battle for the Civil Rights Act* (New York: Bloomsbury, 2014), 142–145; Purdum, *An Idea Whose Time Has Come*, 163–166.

55. Quoted in "Churchmen Urge Rights Bill Drive," *Washington Post*, December 6, 1963, p. A17.

56. Robert E. Baker, "Church Leaders Lobby for Rights Bill Petition," *Washington Post*, December 7, 1963, p. A1.

57. Dan L. Thrapp, "Church Council Plans Civil Rights Caravan," *Los Angeles Times*, December 6, 1963, p. 28; George Dugan, "Churchmen Urge Action on Rights,"

New York Times, December 7, 1963, p. 15; "Churchmen Urge Rights Bill Drive," *Washington Post,* December 6, 1963, p. A17.

58. "Commission on Religion and Race, Southeast Iowa Presbytery, December 8, 1963," UPC, Box 4, Folder 19.

59. Joan J. Bott to Robert Stone, December 11, 1963, UPC, Box 4, Folder 19.

60. Wilmer N. Thornburg to Robert Stone, December 5, 1963, UPC, Box 4, Folder 21.

61. Ralph D. Mitchell to Commission on Religion and Race, January 14, 1964, UPC, Box 4, Folder 21.

62. Quoted in Risen, *The Bill of the Century,* 149–150.

63. Findlay, *Church People in the Struggle,* 53; Risen, *The Bill of the Century,* 156–158.

64. Findlay, *Church People in the Struggle,* 54.

65. Quoted in Adams, *The Growing Church Lobby in Washington,* 27.

66. James A. Hamilton, "Report on Civil Rights Legislation, January 16, 1964," NCC, Record Group 6, Box 47, Folder 31.

67. Everett McKinley Dirksen, *The Education of a Senator* (Urbana, IL: University of Illinois Press, 1998), 6, 49.

68. Indeed, NCC officials had informed local church council executives as early as mid-June that the "crucial test" in the push for civil rights would "come in connection with a vote for cloture to prevent [a] filibuster," and that the success of the cloture tactic would likely "depend on the effectiveness of the action taken by members of the religious community." "Association of Council Secretaries, Twenty-second Annual Conference," Exhibit K, NCC, RG 24, Box 1, Folder 30.

69. Ibid.

70. "Call to Action," January 16, 1964, NCC, RG 6, Box 47, Folder 30.

71. "South Dakota Council of Churches, Annual Assembly, 1964," NCC, RG 10, Box 10, Folder 27.

72. Minutes, National Council of Churches of Christ in the USA, Commission on Religion and Race, June 29, 1964, Exhibit D: Report of the Coordinator for Special Events, NCC, RG 6, Box 47, Folder 30.

73. "Annual Meeting, Iowa Council of Churches, January 22, 1965," p. 2, NCC, RG 10, Box 8, Folder 20.

74. James E. Clayton, "Churchmen Comb Senate for Rights Support," *Washington Post,* March 18, 1964, p. A8; "Church Leaders Will Lobby in Washington for Rights Bill," *New Pittsburgh Courier,* March 14, 1964, p. 20; Robert C. Albright, "Rights Backers Needled with Relocation Proposal," *Washington Post,* March 17, 1964, p. A2; Jerry Landauer, "After the Filibuster . . . ," *Wall Street Journal,* March 9, 1964, p. 1; Adams, *The Growing Church Lobby in Washington,* 27–29.

75. Risen, *The Bill of the Century,* 194–195.

76. "Nebraska Council of Churches, Annual Report, January 25, 1965," NCC, RG 10, Box 9, Folder 12.

77. Purdum, *An Idea Whose Time Has Come,* 297.

78. Quoted in ibid., 288. Also see Risen, *The Bill of the Century,* 195.

79. Rowland Evans and Robert Novak, "Inside Report: Rights and Religion," *Washington Post,* March 20, 1964, p. A19.

80. E. W. Kenworthy, "Churches Termed Key to Rights Bill," *New York Times*, March 21, 1964, p. 14.

81. Joseph Hearst, "Church Rights Lobby Seen as Tax Violation," *Chicago Tribune*, March 13, 1964, p. 7.

82. Risen, *The Bill of the Century*, 98–99, 178–179.

83. "The Church Through the Churches: The Annual Meeting of the General Assembly of the Illinois Council of Churches," January 12–13, 1965," p. 9, NCC, RG 10, Box 8, Folder 16; "1964 Annual Reports: Cedar Rapids–Marion Area Council of Churches," NCC, RG 10, Box 8, Folder 20.

84. "Analysis of the Civil Rights Act of 1964," *Ohio Christian News*, May 1964, p. 8, SCC, Box 8, Folder 5.

85. Untitled news item, *News Notes* (Solomon Presbytery, Commission on Religion and Race), pp. 1–2, April 1964, UPC, Box 4, Folder 19.

86. "Broad Social Concerns Reflected in Year's Work," *Indiana Church Councilor* 73, no. 4 [1964 Annual Report Issue]: 5, NCC, RG 10, Box 8, Folder 17.

87. Minutes, National Council of Churches of Christ in the USA, Commission on Religion and Race, March 26, 1964, p. 7, NCC, RG 6, Box 47, Folder 30; Minutes, National Council of Churches of Christ in the USA, Commission on Religion and Race, June 29, 1964, Exhibit D: Report of the Coordinator for Special Events, NCC, RG 6, Box 47, Folder 30; James A. Hamilton, "Report on Civil Rights Legislation, January 16, 1964," NCC, Record Group 6, Box 47, Folder 31; Ben A. Franklin, "Interfaith Rally in Capital Backs Civil Rights Bill," *New York Times*, April 29, 1964, p. 1; Risen, *The Bill of the Century*, 211.

88. Anna Arnold Hedgeman, "Report of the Coordinator of Special Events," June 29, 1964, NCC, RG 6, Box 47, Folder 30; Risen, *Bill of the Century*, 193; Findlay, *Church People in the Struggle*, 55–56. As James Hamilton, who had pitched the plan as early as January, explained, holding "round-the-clock watch services in a church close to Capitol Hill" would serve to "demonstrate and dramatiz[e] the concern of millions of Christians across the nation about the fate of the bill." James A. Hamilton, "Report on Civil Rights Legislation, January 16, 1964," NCC, Record Group 6, Box 47, Folder 31.

89. The vigil would not have been possible without the support of local churches' women's groups, who pitched in to feed the visiting seminarians, and the Church of the Holy Comforter, which housed them in its basement. Jerry Doolittle, "Rain Fails to Deter Start of Prayer Vigil on Rights," *Washington Post*, April 20, 1964, p. A3; Ben A. Franklin, "Interfaith Rally in Capital Backs Civil Rights Bill," *New York Times*, April 29, 1964, p. 1; Risen, *The Bill of the Century*, 205–206.

90. "Capitol Hill Crusade," *New Pittsburgh Courier*, May 30, 1964, p. 11; Elsie Carper, "Rights Passage Prayer Offered by Churchmen," *Washington Post*, May 19, 1964, p. 1.

91. "200 Clergymen Urge Passage of Rights Bill," *Los Angeles Times*, May 19, 1964, p. 2.

92. George Dugan, "Methodist Backs Rights Protests," *New York Times*, May 4, 1964, p. 25; Richard Philbrick, "Methodists Want Strong Bill on Rights," *Chicago Tribune*, May 9, 1964, p. 3.

93. Richard Philbrick, "Lutherans Pass Two Rights Resolutions," *Chicago Tribune*, May 20, 1964, p. A5.

94. "Rights Rally Scheduled in Soldier Field," *Chicago Tribune*, May 27, 1964, p. 7.
95. "Reformed Church Backs Rights Bill and Integration," *New York Times*, June 11, 1964, p. 33.
96. Risen, *The Bill of the Century*, 224–225.
97. The final tally can be found in the online version of the Congressional Quarterly (CQ) Almanac, https://library.cqpress.com/cqalmanac/document.php?id=cqal64-1304621.
98. Two influential books, both published after the 1964 civil rights debate, popularized the notion that mainline Protestant leaders were far more liberal on civil rights than their parishioners: Jeffrey K. Hadden, *The Gathering Storm in the Churches* (Garden City, NY: Doubleday, 1969); Dean M. Kelley, *Why Conservative Churches Are Growing* (New York: Harper & Row, 1972).
99. 1964 National Election Study, VAR 640411.
100. 1964 National Election Study, VAR 640412.
101. Because only a very small number of Protestant- and Catholic-identifying respondents reported that they "never" attended religious services, I have collapsed the "never" and "seldom" categories into a single category. Percentages are based on number of respondents who reported holding an opinion. Including respondents who reported "no interest" in these questions lowers the overall levels of support for civil rights initiatives, but does not change the underlying relationships between attendance and racial liberalism. The overall sample sizes for Figure 7.5 were as follows: Northern Protestant = 457; Southern/border state Protestant = 262; Catholic = 272. And for Figure 7.6: white Protestant = 494; Southern/border state Protestant = 286; Catholic = 287.
102. That overall support for school integration was fairly tepid may be due to the wording of the question, which asked whether "the government in Washington" should "see to it" that "white and Negro . . . children go to the same schools." Although the controversy over "forced" busing did not reach fever pitch until later in the decade, it seems likely that many white suburbanites were by 1964 reacting negatively to the thought of federal bureaucrats policing the racial composition of local schools.
103. See, for example, Eric Schickler, *Racial Realignment: The Transformation of American Liberalism, 1932–1965* (Princeton, NJ: Princeton University Press, 2016), 93–94, 101, 126, 152, 170–174; Michael R. Gardner, *Harry Truman and Civil Rights: Moral Courage and Political Risks* (Carbondale: Southern Illinois University Press, 2002), 56–57, 174–177. Although the number of Jews included in the ANES study is too small to allow for statistically meaningful generalizations, Jewish respondents who attended synagogue "regularly" or "often" registered levels of support virtually identical to the levels of support expressed by those who attended "seldom or never."
104. The role of the Catholic hierarchy in encouraging support for the Civil Rights Act is discussed in Lawrence J. McAndrews, *What They Wished For: American Catholics and American Presidents, 1960–2004* (Athens: University of Georgia Press), 65–67; Findlay, *Church People in the Struggle*, 48, 55, 58, 71 n. 41.

105. There were, of course, exceptions to the rule. For a discussion of Southern clergymen who joined the civil rights struggle, see David L. Chappell, *A Stone of Hope: Prophetic Religion and the Death of Jim Crow* (Chapel Hill: University of North Carolina Press, 2004).

106. The role of union educational efforts—particularly those of the Congress of Industrial Organizations (CIO)—in boosting white support for civil rights enforcement is discussed, for example, in Eric Schickler, *Racial Realignment: The Transformation of American Liberalism, 1932–1965* (Princeton: Princeton University Press, 2016); and Christopher Baylor, *First to the Party: The Group Origins of Political Transformation* (Philadelphia: University of Pennsylvania Press, 2018).

107. I have excluded respondents from the Deep South and border states. The eleven states of the Confederacy comprise the Deep South category. The border states are defined as Kentucky, Maryland, Oklahoma, and West Virginia. Owing to the 1964 ANES's rather primitive method of measuring denominational affiliation, there is no reliable way of separating mainline and evangelical respondents. The most serious flaw in the study's treatment of denominational affiliation is that it does not distinguish between the conservative and liberal branches of the Baptist and Lutheran faiths. Treating all Northern-state Baptists or Lutherans as either "mainline" or "evangelical" would be highly misleading. Although the American Baptist Convention was firmly within the mainline family (and strongly supportive of civil rights programs), large numbers of Northern-state Baptists belonged to smaller, fundamentalist-linked denominations, or else attended independent churches with fundamentalist leanings. Similarly, the Northern Lutherans contained both conservative (Missouri synod) and liberal (e.g., American Lutheran Church, Lutheran Church in America) branches. Rather than exclude all Baptists and Lutherans, I have treated Northern white Protestants as a single group.

108. VAR640408.

109. Partisan identification was measured on a 7-point scale, with strong Democrats coded as 0 and strong Republicans coded as 6. Hence, the negative coefficient indicates a negative relationship between Republican partisanship and support for the law. Education level was recoded to group respondents into four categories: those with less than a high school degree; high school graduates; some college attendance; and college graduates and above.

110. The question underwent slight wording questions from year to year. In 1960, respondents were asked whether they agreed or disagreed with the claim that "[t]he government in Washington should stay out of the question of whether white and colored children go to the same school." In 1964 and 1966, respondents were asked whether they believed that the "government in Washington" should "see to it that white and . . . colored children are allowed to go to the same schools," or whether "this is not the government's business." The list of possible responses also changed. In 1960, respondents were given the option of expressing strong or weak support/opposition to school integration; in later years, their only options were to agree or disagree. I have recoded the 1960 responses to conform to the options available in later studies.

Chapter 8

1. "Jubilant at Civil Rights Victory, Religious Heads Vow to Fight On," *Washington Post*, June 23, 1964, p. A8.

2. Lynn Lilliston, "Church Attendance Lagging but Not Religious Interest," *Los Angeles Times*, August 17, 1966, p. D1; George Gallup, "Church-Interest Decline Continuing, Poll Shows," *Washington Post*, December 26, 1964, p. B7; Louis Cassels, *Washington Post*, December 27, 1969, p. E7.

3. Edward B. Fiske, "Christmas, 1970: Church Crisis," *New York Times*, December 25, 1970, p. 40.

4. The sociologist Jeffrey Hadden put the matter starkly: the mainline denominations were being torn apart by a "struggle over the meaning and purpose of the church." The clergy believed that the churches should attempt to mediate the great social questions of the day, while the bulk of the laity insisted that the minister's job was to provide spiritual guidance, not solve the world's problems. Jeffrey K. Hadden, *The Gathering Storm in the Churches* (Garden City, NY: Doubleday, 1969), 17.

5. Richard Ford, *The Sportswriter* (1986; New York: Vintage, 1995), 104.

6. Between 1960 and 1965, for example, Presbyterian Sunday school enrollment declined by about 10 percent, and Methodist enrollment by more than 6 percent, even as the national population of children under 18 grew by more than 8 percent. Data on Sunday school enrollments and baptism rates are found in Ruth T. Doyle and Sheila M. Kelly, "Comparison of Trends in Ten Denominations," in Dean R. Hoge and David A. Roozen, *Understanding Church Growth and Decline* (New York: Pilgrim Press, 1979), 145–159, 153–158. Dean M. Kelley's data on church school enrollment differ slightly from Hoge and Roozen's; he reports that both Episcopalian and Methodist church school enrollment peaked in 1959. Dean M. Kelley, *Why Conservative Churches Are Growing* (New York: Harper & Row, 1972), 4–5.

7. One study found that the percentage of "liberal Protestants" marrying within their own faith decline from about 26 percent in the pre-1933 birth cohort to about 18 percent for the post-1933 birth cohort. For "moderate Protestants" the decline was from 40 percent to 28 percent. For Episcopalians specifically, the decline was from 20 percent to a little over 10 percent. Darren E. Sherkat, "Religious Intermarriage in the United States: Trends, Patterns, and Predictors," *Social Science Research* 33 (2004): 606–625.

8. The figure of 44 percent was determined by averaging the responses of men and women (which Gallup reported separately). In this same time span the percentage of Americans who said they had recently bet on a horse race increased from 10 percent to 34 percent (in the case of men) and 21 percent (in the case of women). George H. Gallup, ed., *The Gallup Poll, 1935-1971* (New York: Random House, 1972), 126–127, 918–919, 1288, 1820–1821, 1876–1877. Attitudes toward Sunday shopping underwent a similarly rapid transformation, as pointed out in Alan Petigny, *The Permissive Society: America, 1941-1965* (New York: Cambridge University Press, 2009), 64–65.

9. Gallup, *The Gallup Poll*, 126–127, 918–919, 1288, 1820–1821, 1876–1877.

10. Hobart A. Burch, "Denominations and Councils of Churches: Competitive or Complementary" (Ph.D. diss., Brandeis University, 1965), 299–302.

11. Arthur J. Vidich and Joseph Bensman, *Small Town in Mass Society: Class, Power and Religion in a Rural Community* (1958; Princeton, NJ: Princeton University Press, 1968), 235.

12. "Churches in Jersey Differ on Bingo Vote," *New York Times*, October 31, 1953; George Dugan, "Protestants Launch Drive Against Bingo," *New York Times*, September 23, 1957; Emanuel Perlmutter, "Future of Bingo Up to the Voters," *New York Times*, October 27, 1957; James V. Healion, "New Hampshire Lottery Fight Looms," *Chicago Tribune*, May 12, 1963; Frank L. Prial, "Lottery's Muddy Track," *Wall Street Journal*, December 28, 1966; Mary Hornaday, "New York Lottery Foes Line Up," *Christian Science Monitor*, July 27, 1966; George H. Favre, "N.Y. Church Group Musters Lottery Foes," *Christian Science Monitor*, February 18, 1966.

13. To be sure, many clergymen claimed that they had not been ignored so much as outnumbered: Catholics comprised a large share of the electorate in northeastern states such as New York and New Jersey, and polls showed that they were more supportive of legalized gambling than Protestants. Yet the same polls also showed that average Protestants were at best lukewarm supporters of the status quo. And, indeed, many of them openly favored the legalization of activities, such as bingo and raffles, that they were already enjoying in private thanks to the widespread indifference of state officials. Egan, "Democrats Weigh State Bingo Issue," *New York Times*, May 19, 1953; George Gallup, "Gallup Poll," *Los Angeles Times*, June 2, 1964; Paul L. Montgomery, "Proposal for Lottery Seems to Be Winner," *New York Times*, November 9, 1966; Douglas Robinson, "Voters Approve a Proposition and 8 Amendments," *New York Times*, November 10, 1966.

14. Robert D. Putnam and David E. Campbell, *American Grace: How Religion Divides and Unites Us* (New York: Simon and Schuster, 2012), 98. As Michele F. Margolis has shown, however, life-cycle effects continued to exert influence over Americans' religious behavior, albeit in a somewhat different way than in the past. In the case of the evangelical resurgence of the late 1970s and 1980s, it appears that young parents with conservative political leanings returned to organized religion in large numbers; in contrast, young parents with liberal political leanings were more likely to turn away from organized religion altogether. Michele F. Margolis, *From Politics to the Pews: How Partisanship and the Political Environment Shape Religious Identity* (Chicago: University of Chicago Press, 2018).

15. Richard F. Curtis, "Occupational Mobility and Church Participation," *Social Forces* 38 (1959): 308–314; Seymour Martin Lipset, "Religion and Politics in the American Past and Present," in Robert Lee and Martin E. Marty, eds., *Religion and Social Conflict* (New York: Oxford University Press, 1964), 69–126; Rodney Stark and Charles Y. Glock, *American Piety: The Nature of Religious Commitment* (Berkeley and Los Angeles: University of California Press, 1968), 167, 186–203; Benton Johnson, "Ascetic Protestantism and Political Preference," *Public Opinion Quarterly* 26 (1962): 35–46. Also see Whyte, *The Organization Man*, 368; Mabel Newcomer, *The Big Business Executive: The Factors That Made Him, 1900–1950* (New York: Columbia

University Press, 1955), 47–48; Vance Packard, *The Status Seekers* (New York: David McKay, 1959), 200.

16. Darren E. Sherkhat and John Wilson, "Preferences, Constraints, and Choices in Religious Markets: An Examination of Religious Switching and Apostasy," *Social Forces* 73 (1995): 993–1026; Michael Hout, Andrew Greeley, and Melissa J. Wilde, "The Demographic Imperative in Religious Change in the United States," *American Journal of Sociology* 107 (2001): 468–500; Robert H. Lauer, "Occupational and Religious Mobility in a Small City," *Sociological Quarterly* 16 (1975): 380–392.

17. Stark and Glock, *American Piety*, 167, 186–203. Also see Robert H. Lauer, "Occupational and Religious Mobility in a Small City," *Sociological Quarterly* 16 (1975): 380–392.

18. As the sociologists Wade Clark Roof and William McKinney have written, the baby boomers' "commitment to personal freedom and choice, individual autonomy, and personal quest, as well as tolerance of diversity and openness, tended to erode loyalty to the religious establishment. . . . Not just religious attitudes and values but notions of duty to nation, family values and sexuality, and the inherent good or evil in the democratic capitalist state came up for review. Ideas about authority and moral decision making generally were caught up in new and changing constellations of cultural values." Wade Clark Roof and William McKinney, *American Mainline Religion: Its Changing Shape and Future* (New Brunswick, NJ: Rutgers University Press, 1987), 61–62.

19. The percentage of eighteen-to-twenty-four-year-olds attending college increased from 17.8 percent to 33.5 percent between 1955 and 1974. David Goldfield, *The Gifted Generation: When Government Was Good* (New York: Bloomsbury, 2017), 330–331. The rationalization or bureaucratization of American corporations and professions—including hiring and promotion decisions—is discussed at length in C. Wright Mills, *White Collar: The American Middle Classes* (New York: Oxford University Press, 1953). Also see Newcomer, *The Big Business Executive*, 145–148.

20. William H. Whyte, Jr., *The Organization Man* (New York: Simon and Schuster, 1956), 200.

21. For more general discussions of the relationship between the higher-education boom and the post-1960 decline in religiosity, see Roof and McKinney, *American Mainline Religion*, 65–66; Robert Wuthnow, *The Restructuring of American Religion* (Princeton, NJ: Princeton University Press, 1988), 161–164.

22. Raven Molloy, Christopher L. Smith, and Abigail K. Wozniak, "Internal Migration in the United States," Working Paper, National Bureau of Economic Research, August 2011. Available online at: http://www.nber.org/papers/w17307. Also see James N. Gregory, "Internal Migration: Twentieth Century and Beyond," in Lynn Dumenil and Paul Boyer, eds., *Oxford Encyclopedia of American Social History* (New York: Oxford University Press, 2012), 540–545.

23. Robert Wuthnow and Kevin Christiano, "The Effects of Residential Migration on Church Attendance in the United States," in Robert Wuthnow, ed., *The Religious Dimensions: New Directions in Quantitative Research* (New York: Academic Press, 1979), 257–274; Roger W. Stump, "Regional Migration and Religious Commitment

in the United States," *Journal for the Scientific Study of Religion* 23 (1984): 292–303; Christian Smith, David Sikkink, and Jason Bailey, "Devotion in Dixie and Beyond: A Test of the 'Shibley Thesis' on the Effects of Regional Origin and Migration on Individual Religiosity," *Journal for the Scientific Study of Religion* 37 (1998): 494–506. Stump's data were gathered primarily in the 1970s, while Smith, Sikkink, and Bailey use data from the 1990s.

24. Richard L. Forstall, ed., *Population of States and Counties of the United States, 1790–1990* (Washington, DC: Bureau of the Census, 1996). Available online at https://www.census.gov/population/www/censusdata/PopulationofStatesandCountiesoftheUnitedStates1790-1990.pdf.

25. For U.S. census data on internal migration data, see ipums.org, operated by the University of Minnesota Population Center. Much of this data is summarized in an accessible visual form at www.nytimes.com/interactive/2014/08/13/upshot/where-people-in-each-state-were-born.html.

26. Wuthnow and Christiano, "The Effects of Residential Migration on Church Attendance"; Stump, "Regional Migration and Religious Commitment"; Smith, Sikkink, and Bailey, "Devotion in Dixie."

27. See, for example, Darren Dochuk, *From Bible Belt to Sunbelt: Plain-Folk Religion, Grassroots Politics, and the Rise of Evangelical Conservatism* (New York: Norton, 2011), 226; Mary C. Brennan, *Turning Right in the Sixties: The Conservative Capture of the GOP* (Chapel Hill: University of North Carolina Press, 1995), 33.

28. A mid-October encore performance featuring Reagan, Wayne, and Jimmy Stewart not only sold out the Hollywood Bowl but was broadcast live on thirty-four television stations across six Western states. Louis Fleming, "Anti-Red School Told Victory Plan," *Los Angeles Times*, September 2, 1961, p. 3; "School Against Communism Opens Monday," *Los Angeles Times*, November 6, 1960, p. 15; Louis Fleming, "New U.S. Foreign Policy Urged at Anti-Red School," *Los Angeles Times*, August 29, 1961, p. 2; "Probe into 'Muzzling' of Military Asked," *Los Angeles Times*, August 31, 1961, p. B1; "Anti-Red Rally Told to Seek 'Total Victory,'" *Los Angeles Times*, October 17, 1961, p. B1.

29. "2,000 Pickets Protest Aid to Red Nations," *Los Angeles Times*, November 19, 1961, p. A1; Kennedy quoted in Dochuk, *From Bible Belt to Sunbelt*, 236.

30. "Thurmond Assails Army 'Muzzling,'" *Los Angeles Times*, November 29, 1961, p. 2; "Thurmond Says Russia 'Ordered' U.S. Muzzling," *Los Angeles Times*, November 30, 1961, p. 26. Also see Joseph Crespino, "Strom Thurmond's Sunbelt: Rethinking Regional Politics and the Rise of the Right," in Michelle Nickerson and Darren Dochuk, eds., *Sunbelt Rising: The Politics of Space, Place, and Region* (Philadelphia: University of Pennsylvania Press, 2011), 58–81.

31. "Walker Carries His Crusade to the Southland," *Los Angeles Times*, January 11, 1962, p. B1; Dochuk, *From Bible Belt to Sunbelt*, 237.

32. Dochuk, *From Bible Belt to Sunbelt*, 265; Lisa McGirr, *Suburban Warriors: The Origins of the New American Right* (Princeton, NJ: Princeton University Press, 2001), 76–78; Kurt Schuparra, *Triumph of the Right: the Rise of the California Conservative Movement, 1945–1966* (Armonk, NY: M. E. Sharpe, 1998), 105.

33. By late 1963 it claimed six thousand dues-paying members; that number would climb as high as twenty thousand in mid-1964 as conservative suburbanites rallied to the presidential candidacy of Barry Goldwater. Rus Walton, Oral History Interview, Regional Oral History Office, Bancroft Library, University of California, Berkeley; "Council Backs, GOP Unit Hits Rumford Act," *Los Angeles Times*, January 1, 1964, p. A1; Michelle M. Nickerson, *Mothers of Conservatism: Women and the Postwar Right* (Princeton, NJ: Princeton University Press, 2012), 160.

34. Kevin M. Kruse, *One Nation Under God: How Corporate America Invented Christian America* (New York: Basic Books, 2015), 152.

35. "Mosk Blasts at Anti-Red Crusade School," *Los Angeles Times*, January 25, 1962, p. A13; "41 Mayors Proclaim Anti-Communism Week" [advertisement], *Los Angeles Times*, August 20, 1961, p. D12; McGirr, *Suburban Warriors*, 54–55; Dochuk, *From Bible Belt to Sunbelt*, 152, 222–225.

36. "United GOP Delegates Cheer for Goldwater," *Los Angeles Times*, February 3, 1964, p. 2; Rick Perlstein, *Before the Storm* (New York: Nation Books, 2009), 337.

37. McGirr, *Suburban Warriors*, 125.

38. Lawrence E. Davies, "Fair-Housing Law Assailed on Coast," *New York Times*, September 7, 1964, p. 6.

39. Several of the best contemporaneous studies of right-wing activism in the early 1960s are collected in Robert A. Schoenberger, ed., *The American Right Wing: Readings in Political Behavior* (New York: Holt, Rinehart and Winston, 1969). Also see Barbara Shell Stone, "The John Birch Society of California" (Ph.D. diss., University of Southern California, 1968). Many of these early studies are conveniently summarized and compared in Seymour Martin Lipset and Earl Raab, *The Politics of Unreason: Right-Wing Extremism in America, 1790–1970* (New York: Harper & Row, 1970), 295–326. McGirr's study of thirty-five conservative group leaders in Orange County confirmed many of the conclusions of the earlier studies. Her sample was dominated by engineers and professionals who had moved to their current cities within the past ten years. McGirr, *Suburban Warriors*, 83–84. Also see William B. Hixson, Jr., *Searching for the American Right Wing: An Analysis of the Social Science Record* (Princeton, NJ: Princeton University Press, 1992); Clyde Wilcox, "Sources of Support for the Old Right: A Comparison of the John Birch Society and the Christian Anti-Communism Crusade," *Social Science History* 12 (1988): 429–449.

40. See, for example, Raymond E. Wolfinger, Barbara Kaye Wolfinger, Kenneth Prewitt, and Sheilah Rosenhack, "America's Radical Right: Politics and Ideology," in Schoenberger, *The American Right Wing*, 9–47, 32–36; Hixson, *Searching for the American Right Wing*, 80–82; Lipset and Raab, *The Politics of Unreason*, 306–309, 311.

41. Wolfinger, Wolfinger, Prewitt, and Rosenhack, "America's Radical Right," 29–32; Hixson, *Searching for the American Right Wing*, 90–91; Sheilah Koeppen, "The Radical Right and the Politics of Consensus," in Schoenberger, *The American Right Wing*, 48–82, 56–57; Wilcox, "Sources of Support for the Old Right," 442.

42. For studies examining the religious backgrounds of members of Far Right groups, see Fred W. Grupp, Jr., "The Political Behavior of Birch Society Members," in Schoenberger, *The American Right Wing*, 83–118, 92–93; Stone, "The John Birch

Society of California," 92–93; David Clement Henley, "The Clerical Conservative: A Study of Conservative and Ultra-Rightist Protestant Ministers and Organizations of the Los Angeles Area," (Master's thesis, University of Southern California, 1964).

43. By 1964 fully 41.5 percent of manufacturing jobs in Los Angeles and Orange Counties—representing 354,700 employees—were in defense-related industries such as aircraft manufacturing and aerospace electronics. Dochuk, *From Bible Belt to Sunbelt*, 170.

44. See, for example, McGirr, *Suburban Warriors*, 163; Dochuk, *From Bible Belt to Sunbelt*, 170–172; Crespino, *Strom Thurmond's Sunbelt*; Daniel Martinez Hosang, "Racial Liberalism and the Rise of the Sunbelt West: The Defeat of Fair Housing on the 1964 California Ballot," in Michelle Nickerson and Darren Dochuk, eds., *Sunbelt Rising: The Politics of Space, Place, and Region* (Philadelphia: University of Pennsylvania Press, 2011).

45. Only the Episcopal Church, a relatively small denomination in terms of total membership, succeeded in replicating the churches-to-population ratio it enjoyed elsewhere.

46. Data on number of churches can be found in U.S. Department of Commerce, Bureau of the Census, *Religious Bodies: 1936*, 2 vols. (Washington, DC: Government Printing Office, 1941). In Iowa the percentage of the state's population identifying as Catholic was reported as 11.7 percent; in California it was 15.5 percent. The six mainline denominations included in this tally were the Congregationalists, Northern Baptists, Episcopalians, Methodists, Presbyterians, and the United Lutheran Church in America. State population figures for 1936 were arrived at by averaging the states' 1930 and 1940 populations.

47. One might object that California's relatively urbanized population allowed mainline Protestant leaders to meet demand while constructing fewer churches, which in turn housed comparatively large congregations. But according to the National Council of Churches' 1952 study of American religion (discussed below), the average California Methodist congregation was only slightly larger than the average Iowa congregation (384 members to 306). Stated otherwise, California's comparatively small number of churches was reflective of lower rates of church membership among Protestant identifiers; it was not an artifact of significantly larger congregation size.

48. National Council of Churches, Churches and Church Membership in the United States, 1952. Data may be downloaded at the Association of Religion Data Archives website: www.thearda.com.

49. "The Department of Research and Planning," in *History and Bylaws of the Southern California-Nevada Council of Churches, 1957*, 9–10, SCE, Box 24, folder labeled "Minutes—Annual Assembly, 1959–1962."

50. A brief but insightful overview of the mainline churches' response to the Southern California population boom can be found in Winston W. Crouch and Beatrice Dinerman, *Southern California Metropolis: A Study in Development of Government for a Metropolitan Area* (Berkeley and Los Angeles: University of California Press, 1964), 271–274.

51. "The Department of Research and Planning," in *History and Bylaws of the Southern California-Nevada Council of Churches, 1957*, 9–10, SCE, Box 24, folder labeled

"Minutes—Annual Assembly, 1959–1962." Also see Crouch and Dinerman, *Southern California Metropolis*, 272. The nine participating denominations were the Christian Church, Church of the Brethren, Congregational, Evangelical and Reformed, Evangelical United Brethren, Methodist, Presbyterian U.S.A., Reformed Church in America, and United Presbyterian.

52. Forrest C. Weir, "The General Secretary's Message, 48th General Assembly, Southern California–Southern Nevada Council of Churches, SCE, Box 24, folder labeled "Minutes—Annual Assembly, 1959–1962."

53. Ibid.

54. Data from the 1952 and 1971 Churches and Church Membership in the United States Studies, conducted by the National Council of Churches and the Department of Research and Statistics of the Lutheran Church—Missouri Synod, respectively. Both datasets are available at the Association of Religion Data Archives: www.thearda.com.

55. The white Protestant population was calculated by subtracting African American residents (based on the 1960 census), Jewish residents, Catholic adherents, and Mormon adherents (based on percentages reported in 1952 Church Membership Study for Jews and Mormons and 1971 Church Membership Study for Catholics) from the total population (based on the 1960 census).

56. See Figures 7.3 and 7.4.

57. Quoted in Gary Scott Smith, *Faith and the Presidency: From George Washington to George W. Bush* (New York: Oxford University Press), 327.

58. Lynn Lilliston, "Church Attendance Lagging but Not Religious Interest," *Los Angeles Times*, August 17, 1966, p. D1.

59. On the role of lax zoning laws in spurring the growth of fundamentalist and political conservative churches, see Dochuk, *From Bible Belt to Sunbelt*, 241–242.

60. Ibid., 167, 190–191, 245; McGirr, *Suburban Warriors*, 104.

61. Quoted in McGirr, *Suburban Warriors*, 106–107.

62. Elmer Towns, "100 Largest Sunday Schools," *Christian Life*, October 1974, pp. 18–19.

63. McGirr, *Suburban Warriors*, p. 342, n. 124.

64. Grupp, "The Political Behavior of Birch Society Members," 92–93; Stone, "The John Birch Society of California," 92–93. In Grupp's sample of JBS members, 49 percent described themselves as "liberal" Protestants and 20 percent as "fundamentalists." Of the liberal Protestants, 62 percent reported that they attended church "regularly" or "often," while 79 percent of the fundamentalists reported that they did so. Stone reported that "several" liberal Protestant members of her JBS sample were "searching for a new church," and that most cited disagreement with the "liberal" stances of the National Council of Churches as their primary reason for doing so. Stone's study was limited to California; Grupp's was national in scope but featured a high percentage of Westerners.

65. As Dochuk puts the point, in the "diffuse, democratized setting" of the California suburbs, "ministers gained authority by the strength of their personality and the marketability of their skills. Clerical authority . . . was no longer an assumed or assigned

right but a provisional dispensation awarded by people in the pews." Dochuk, *From Bible Belt to Sunbelt*, 178.

66. "Statement on Legislative Principles," in *History and Bylaws of the Southern California–Nevada Council of Churches, 1957*, 32–35, SCE, Box 24, folder labeled "Minutes—Annual Assembly, 1959–1962."

67. Although there was much talk of hiring a Sacramento-based legislative director to publicize the positions of the state-level church councils, funding was not forthcoming until 1967. "Our Man in Sacramento," *Ecumenical Concern* 4 (November 1966): 3, SCE, Box 4, folder labeled "Newsletter, 1955–1956."

68. On the origins of Proposition 14, see Hosang, "Racial Liberalism and the Rise of the Sunbelt West," 188–213, 190–195; Mark Brilliant, *The Color of America Has Changed: How Racial Diversity Shaped Civil Rights Reform in California, 1941–1978* (New York: Oxford University Press, 2010), 190–197.

69. "2 Clerics Urge Year's Trial of Housing Act," *Los Angeles Times*, December 14, 1963, p. B5.

70. Both bodies created special task forces, staffed by church officials on loan from the denominations, to put their plans into effect. On the planning of the churches' anti–Prop 14 campaign, see the minutes of the Southern California Council of Churches' Civil Rights Commission, as well as the minutes of the special Prop 14 task force of seconded denominational officials, in SCE, Box 24, folder labeled "Civil Rights Committee (Proposition 14)."

71. On the "intensity gap" concept, see, for example, Jennifer L. Hochschild and Katherine Levin Einstein, *Do Facts Matter? Information and Misinformation in American Politics* (Norman: University of Oklahoma Press, 2015),33.

72. In 1963 there were twenty-five local, county, or state councils of churches with paid staff members in the state of California, or about one for every 630,000 residents. Ohio, in comparison, claimed twenty-two such bodies, or about one for every 440,000 residents. Benson Y. Landis, ed., *Yearbook of American Churches, 1963* (New York: National Council of Churches of Christ in the U.S.A., 1963), 111–118, 164–169.

73. As of 1963 there were no Orange County–based local or county-level church councils listed in the *Yearbook of American Churches*. As a counterpoint to Orange County, consider that the small city of Redlands (population 26,000) boasted a well-funded local church council with a full-time executive director. *Yearbook of American Churches, 1963*, 116–118.

74. Carroll L. Shuster [form letter to "Dear Colleague"], December 23, 1963, CCC, Box 4, Folder 3.

75. "Anti-Rumford Petitions Get 700,000 Signatures," *Los Angeles Times*, February 5, 1964, p. A1; "Petitions Accepted" [standalone photo caption], *Los Angeles Times*, February 9, 1964, p. 2.

76. "Council Backs, GOP Unit Hits Rumford Act," *Los Angeles Times*, January 1, 1964, p. A1.

77. "GOP Group Rejects Plea on Rumford Act," *Los Angeles Times*, January 5, 1964, p. 18.

78. "League to Discuss Ballot Propositions: Political Notes," *Los Angeles Times*, October 18, 1964, p. Q7; "Clerics Plan Fight for Rumford Act," *Los Angeles Times*, January 12, 1964, p. N1; "Vote 'No' on Proposition 14," advertisement, *San Diego Evening Tribune*, October 31, 1964 [news clipping], SCC, Box 24, folder labeled "Civil Rights Committee (Proposition 14)," FTS.

79. "The Council of Churches in Southern California, 52nd General Assembly," NCC, RG 10, Box 7, Folder 53.

80. Dochuk, *From Bible Belt to Sunbelt*, 249; *1964 Annual Report*, Redlands Council of Churches, NCC, RG 10, Box 7, Folder 54.

81. 1964 Annual Report, Redlands Council of Churches, NCC, RG 10, Box 7, Folder 54.

82. Rowland Evans and Robert Novak, "Inside Report: California's Racial Vote," *Washington Post*, September 7, 1964, p. A17.

83. "Minutes, Secunded Denominational Staff for Civil Rights Program of Southern California Council of Churches, Minutes, September 29, 1964," SCE, Box 24, folder labeled "Civil Rights Committee (Proposition 14)"; "Episcopalians Map Fight to Defeat Prop 14," *Los Angeles Times*, September 17, 1964, p. 15.

84. Four thousand Local Church Plans were distributed in Southern California alone. "Local Church Plan to Defeat Proposition 14," SCE, Box 24, folder labeled "Civil Rights Committee (Proposition 14)."

85. "The Church Says No on Proposition 14" [pamphlet], SCE, Box 24, folder labeled "Civil Rights Committee (Proposition 14)"; "Report to the General Board of the Council of Churches . . . on the Civil Rights Committee's Effort to Defeat PROP 14," SCE, Box 24, folder labeled "Civil Rights Committee (Proposition 14)"; Northern California–Nevada Council of Churches, "Working Together in 1964" [1964 Annual Report], NCC, RG 10, Box 7, Folder 52.

86. Historical data for the field poll are available online at the University of California, Berkeley's Archive of Social Science Data: http://ucdata.berkeley.edu.

87. Becky M. Nicolaides, *My Blue Heaven: Life and Politics in the Working-Class Suburbs of Los Angeles, 1920–1965* (Chicago: University of Chicago Press, 2002), 311.

88. On the founding of CRFH, see "New Realty Group Backs Rumford Act," *Los Angeles Times*, December 3, 1963, p. A1; "CREA Vows New Fight on Housing Act," *Los Angeles Times*, December 4, 1963, p. H7. Hallmark's difficulties with the state licensing board are discussed in "Minutes, Civil Rights Committee, Council of Churches in Southern California, February 10, 1964," SCE, Box 24, folder labeled "Civil Rights Committee (Proposition 14)."

89. Harry Bernstein, "Union Leaders to Back Fight for Rumford Bill," *Los Angeles Times*, December 21, 1963, B3.

90. Bruce G. Merritt, "Faith and Fair Housing: An Episcopal Parish Church in the 1964 Debate over Proposition 14," *Southern California Quarterly* 95 (2013): 284–316, 298.

91. "Minutes, Civil Rights Committee, Council of Churches in Southern California, March 12, 1964," SCE, Box 24, folder labeled "Civil Rights Committee (Proposition 14)."

92. 1964 Annual Report, Council of Churches, Central Contra Costa County, NCC, RG 10, Box 7, Folder 54.

93. "Report to the General Board of the Council of Churches . . . on the Civil Rights Committee's Effort to Defeat PROP 14," SCE, Box 24, folder labeled "Civil Rights Committee (Proposition 14)"; "Minutes, Civil Rights Committee of the Council of Churches in Southern California, November 25, 1965 [sic]," SCE, Box 24, folder labeled "Civil Rights Committee (Proposition 14)."

94. Dan L. Thrapp, "Effects of Pulpit View on Prop 14 Analyzed," *Los Angeles Times*, November 22, 1964, p. G9.

95. Merritt, "Faith and Fair Housing," 298.

96. Thrapp, "Effects of Pulpit View on Prop 14 Analyzed."

97. "Charges Fly in Ouster of Unit Leader," *Los Angeles Times*, March 1, 1964, p. U1.

98. On Ingram's segregationist views, see, for example, David L. Chappell, *A Stone of Hope: Prophetic Religion and the Death of Jim Crow* (Chapel Hill: University of North Carolina Press, 2004), 110–111, 175 n. 55; Gardiner H. Shattuck, *Episcopalians and Race: Civil War to Civil Rights* (Lexington: University Press of Kentucky, 2000), 117; Neil R. McMillen, *The Citizens' Council: Organized Resistance to the Second Reconstruction, 1954–64* (Urbana: University of Illinois Press, 1994), 177.

99. "Bloy Refuses Backing for Texas Cleric's Talk," *Los Angeles Times*, December 2, 1963, p. A1.

100. "Minutes, Secunded Denominational Staff for Civil Rights Program of Southern California Council of Churches, Minutes, June 16, 1964," SCE, Box 24, folder labeled "Civil Rights Committee (Proposition 14)."

101. Merritt, "Faith and Fair Housing," 302.

102. "Prop 14 Attack by Episcopal Unit Deplored," *Los Angeles Times*, October 8, 1964, p. 18.

103. "Episcopal Churchman Hits CREA on Prop 14," *Los Angeles Times*, October 10, 1964, p. B7.

104. "Episcopal Churchman Hits CREA on Prop 14," *Los Angeles Times*, October 10, 1964, p. B7.

105. Merritt, "Faith and Fair Housing," 308.

106. Thrapp, "Effects of Pulpit View on Prop 14 Analyzed."

107. A study of voting behavior in a Toledo, Ohio, referendum found that white voters who attended church regularly supported fair housing at significantly higher rates than infrequent attenders (though overall white support was still tepid). As the study's author explained, "[religious] communication and exhortation were factors. . . The pro 'Fair Housing' campaign reached the churchgoers more than the public and the target was not entirely unreceptive." The author concluded that in California, in contrast, the fair housing campaign had unfolded along "party and class lines," with little evidence of religious influence. Howard D. Hamilton, "Voting Behavior in Open Housing Referenda," *Social Science Quarterly* 51 (1970): 715–729, 719, 718.

108. Thrapp, "Effects of Pulpit View on Prop 14 Analyzed." There is some evidence that Prop 14 fared better in areas of the state where there more men and women in the pews, and where the mainline infrastructure was comparatively well developed. Contra Costa County, in the East Bay, offers an interesting counterpoint

to Orange County. Both counties were relatively wealthy, overwhelmingly white, and featured high rates of home ownership. Both counties also experienced significant population growth in the postwar years, though Orange County's growth rate dwarfed that of Contra Costa County. Perhaps for this reason, the ratio of mainline churches to residents was much higher in Contra Costa County than in Orange County. Based on 1970 data, the four denominations that were most active in the anti–Prop 14 campaign—Episcopalians, Methodists, Presbyterians, and United Church of Christ—claimed sixty churches in Contra Costa County (or one for every 7,468 residents) and ninety-four in Orange County (or one for every 12,159 residents). And while Orange County lacked even a single paid ecumenical official, Contra Costa County boasted an active and fully staffed council of churches that oversaw a broad range of educational efforts in the area of fair housing. The other significant difference, of course, was that Orange County was overwhelmingly Republican, whereas Democrats enjoyed a significant numerical advantage in Contra Costa County (as they did in most of the Bay Area). Hence, while sorting out the relative significance of religion and party in shaping attitudes toward Prop 14 is no simple matter, it remains a striking fact that two counties that were virtually identical in every statistical category except for partisanship and density of mainline churches and officials differed so significantly in their rates of support for fair housing. Whereas only 22 percent of Orange County voters opposed Prop 14, nearly 39 percent of Contra Costa County voters did so. The Contra Costa County Council of Churches' activities in support of Prop 14 are summarized in 1964 Annual Report, Council of Churches, Central Contra Costa County, NCC Collection, RG 10, Box 7, Folder 54. Church density data can be found in the 1952 and 1971 studies of Churches and Church Membership in the United States, available online at the Association of Religion Data Archives website: wwwthearda.com. Demographic data for the two counties can be found in the 1960 census report, available online at https://www.census.gov/prod/www/decennial.html. A more accessible version of the census data for Contra Costa County is available online at http://www.bayareacensus.ca.gov/counties/ContraCostaCounty50.htm.

109. Dan L. Thrapp, "Effects of Pulpit View on Prop 14 Analyzed," *Los Angeles Times*, November 22, 1964, p. G9.

Chapter 9

1. All figures are from Dean M. Kelley, *The National Council of Churches and the Social Outlook of the Nation* (New York: National Council of Churches, 1971), 26–29.
2. Data from ibid., 19–25.
3. The mainline Protestant churches seem to have been hit particularly hard by this trend. Among ANES respondents, the median age of frequent mainline church attenders increased by a remarkable seven years between 1964 and 1972, from 48 to 55. (Figures based on weighted data for 1964 and unweighted data for the 1972 study, which did not include weights.) Because the ANES attendance question

underwent a wording change between 1964 and 1972, I am defining "frequent" church attenders as those who described themselves as "regular" attenders in 1964 and as "weekly" attenders in 1972.

4. The exact figures were 66.5 and 47.6 percent, respectively. A smaller, though still significant, gap was evident in questions dealing with school integration and employment discrimination. On school integration, 43 percent of respondents under thirty-five favored federal involvement (with 37 percent opposed), as compared to 36 percent of those over fifty-five (with 41 percent opposed). On employment discrimination, 45.3 percent of respondents under thirty-five favored federal action (with 37 percent opposed), as compared to 33.5 percent of those over fifty-five (with 40.3 percent opposed).

5. Jill K. Gill, *Embattled Ecumenism: The National Council of Churches, the Vietnam War, and the Trials of the Protestant Left* (DeKalb: Northern Illinois University Press, 2011), 261.

6. "Bloy Refuses Backing for Texas Cleric's Talk," Jeffrey K. Hadden, *The Gathering Storm in the Churches* (Garden City, NY: Anchor Book, 1969), 160–161, Table 60. As an NCC-funded study concluded in 1969, a "deep cleavage" had opened between increasingly secular college students and young professionals, on the one hand, and "a large majority of American Protestants," on the other. Louis Cassels, "Most Disapprove Church Social Action," *Washington Post*, September 6, 1969, p. D13.

7. Hadden, *Gathering Storm*, 160–163.

8. "Coming and Going of Council Personnel," *ACS Journal* 5, no. 1 (October 1969): iv–viii. In NCC Collection, RG 24, Box 2, Folder 27, PHS.

9. "Association of Council Secretaries, Minutes of the Board of Directors and Business Meetings," June 1970, NCC Collection, RG 24, Box 2, Folder 18, PHS.

10. Data from the *Yearbook of American Churches*, 1965–1971.

11. "Association of Council Secretaries, Minutes of the Board of Directors and Business Meetings," June 1970, NCC Collection, RG 24, Box 2, Folder 18, PHS.

12. See, for example, Jeffrey K. Hadden, "Religious Broadcasting and the Mobilization of the New Christian Right," *Journal for the Scientific Study of Religion* 26 (1987): 1–24, 16.

13. Although McIntire's show did not air on any stations based in Nevada, Maine, Vermont, or New Hampshire, it seems likely that at least some residents of these states were able to tune in to broadcasts from nearby cities, such as Boston and Los Angeles. Paul Matzko, *The Radio Right: How a Band of Broadcasters Took on the Federal Government and Built the Modern Conservative Movement* (forthcoming, Oxford University Press).

14. The task of integrating Southern society, McIntire told his followers, was beyond the church's purview, for the "Christian cannot condemn as sin what God has not defined as sin in Holy Scripture." Needless to say, church-led efforts to redistribute economic resources to needy blacks were a nonstarter—indeed, the opening wedge for communism. Markku Ruotsila, *Fighting Fundamentalist: Carl McIntire and the Politicization of American Fundamentalism* (New York: Oxford University Press, 2016), 164–166, 173–174.

15. See Matzko, *Radio Right*.
16. Richard Philbrick, "Church Council Leaders Uphold Critics," *Chicago Tribune*, December 6, 1966, p. B12.
17. Matzko, *Radio Right*.
18. Ibid.; Ruotsila, *Fighting Fundamentalist*, 249–250.
19. Hadden, "Religious Broadcasting and the Mobilization of the New Christian Right," 16–17.
20. Phillip E. Hammond, *The Campus Clergyman* (New York: Basic Books, 1966), 4–5.
21. Ibid., 14, 43–44.
22. An early 1960s survey of one thousand campus ministers found that 53 percent judged their own denominations "too conservative in the field of social action" (as compared to 17 percent of parish ministers). Ibid., 43.
23. Ibid., 10–11. Also see Doug Rossinow, *The Politics of Authenticity: Liberalism, Christianity, and the New Left in America* (New York: Columbia University Press, 1998), 93–133; Kenneth J. Heineman, *Campus Wars: The Peace Movement at American State Universities in the Vietnam Era* (New York: New York University Press, 1993), 88.
24. Gill, *Embattled Ecumenism*, 237.
25. John Dart, "Crusade for Christ Opens Hearts and Doors on Campuses," *Los Angeles Times*, August 8, 1971, p. B1.
26. In the two decades following the group's founding, Bright and his student organizers would distribute more than 125 million copies of the "Four Spiritual Laws" pamphlet. Russell Chandler, "Campus Crusade Looks to 'Great Awakening' in U.S.," *Los Angeles Times*, July 25, 1976, p. F1. The four spiritual laws are: "1) God loves you and has a wonderful plan for your life; 2) Man is sinful and separated from God, thus he cannot know and experience God's love and plan for his life; 3) Jesus Christ is God's only provision for man's sin. Through Him you can know and experience God's love and plan for your life; 4) We must individually receive Jesus Christ as Savior and Lord; then we can know and experience God's love and plan for our lives."
27. Dart, "Crusade for Christ Opens Hearts."
28. John G. Turner, *Bill Bright and Campus Crusade for Christ: The Renewal of Evangelicalism in Postwar America* (Chapel Hill: University of North Carolina Press, 2008), 107–108, 114. Turner observes that Hunt was Bright's major financial backer during the 1960s and 1970s. Other wealthy and politically conservative supporters included the construction mogul Guy Atkinson, the Holiday Inn cofounder Wallace E. Johnson, and the Chicago insurance executive W. Clement Stone. Doug McInnis, "The Gospel According to Bunker," *New York Times*, January 6, 1980, p. F5; Kenneth A. Briggs, "$1 Billion Drive Set by Evangelicals," *New York Times*, November 15, 1977, p. 19.
29. John Dart, "Growing Pains Plague Evangelical Movement," *Los Angeles Times*, September 2, 1972, p. 22.
30. Turner, *Bill Bright*, 73.
31. Ibid., 74.
32. Dart, "Crusade For Christ Opens Hearts," p. B1.

33. Bright was privately critical of the civil rights movement and strongly supportive of Barry Goldwater's 1964 presidential bid, warning that a Johnson victory would result in "the Communist flag. . . be[ing] hoisted over the White House." Quoted in Turner, *Bill Bright*, 111–112.

34. Tad Bartimus, "Wealthy Join Movement to Carry Gospel to the World," *Los Angeles Times*, June 7, 1980, p. B5; Chandler, "Campus Crusade Looks to 'Great Awakening' "; McInnis, "The Gospel According to Bunker"; Turner, *Bill Bright and Campus Crusade*, 168.

35. George Dugan, "Church Council Asks U.S. to Halt Vietnam Bombing," *New York Times*, December 4, 1965, p. 1; "Text of Council of Churches Policy Statement and Message," *New York Times*, December 4, 1966, p. 6.

36. Quoted in Gill, *Embattled Ecumenism*, 222.

37. James L. Adams, *The Growing Church Lobby in Washington* (Grand Rapids, MI: William B. Eerdmans, 1970), 221.

38. Gill, *Embattled Ecumenism*, 170–171. Gill notes that an NCC listening tour, organized in 1967, revealed six principal reasons for local ministers' and parishioners' lack of interest in the Council's antiwar program: "(1) It is confusing; (2) We don't know enough and Washington knows more; (3) Questions of loyalty and patriotism; (4) Resentment of protestors and unwillingness to be identified with them; (5) Fear of intimidation or reprisals; (6) Fear of causing dissension within church, family, etc."

39. In Lansing, Michigan, for example, a Methodist congregation that had in 1966 boasted an active student membership of eight hundred had by 1968 shrunk to fifty student members. Heineman, *Campus Wars*. Also see Mitchell K. Hall, *Because of Their Faith: CALCAV and Religious Opposition to the Vietnam War* (New York: Columbia University Press, 1990), 101.

40. In 1966, for example, reports that the Johnson advisor Bill Moyers had worked to water down an NCC pronouncement on Vietnam caused a major stir in the press. NCC officials, for their part, insisted that such contacts were essential to ending the war: how else but by persuading policymakers could one hope to effect a withdrawal? "Church Unit Reported Pressured on Vietnam," *Los Angeles Times*, February 25, 1966, p. 5.

41. Gill, *Embattled Ecumenism*, 265.

42. Quoted in ibid., 267.

43. Ibid., 270.

44. Findlay, *Church People in the Struggle*, 172–173.

45. Henry J. Pratt, *The Liberalization of American Protestantism: A Case Study in Complex Organizations* (Detroit: Wayne State University Press, 1972), 191.

46. Ibid., 182.

47. The decision to turn over leadership of the CORR to Payton, who was at this point perhaps best known for authoring a devastating critique of the Johnson aide Daniel Patrick Moynihan's report on the causes of breakdown within the African American family ("The Negro Family: The Case for National Action"), effectively severed the close relationship that CORR had previously enjoyed with the Johnson administration. Ibid., 180–182.

48. Pratt, *The Liberalization of American Protestantism*, 192. The money was intended to fund, among other things, a program to secure land for black farmers, programs to stimulate the growth of black-owned small businesses, the establishment of new black universities, new black-controlled media enterprises, and a program to develop cooperative economic business ventures between the United States and Africa.

49. Ibid., 189–190.

50. Gill, *Embattled Ecumenism*, 272.

51. Even black respondents were skeptical, with 52 percent registering disapproval. James F. Findlay, Jr., *Church People in the Struggle: The National Council of Churches and the Black Freedom Movement, 1950–1970* (New York: Oxford University Press, 1993), 205.

52. Ibid., 212.

53. Ibid., 205.

54. Louis Garinger, "Manifesto Causes Division," *Christian Science Monitor*, July 26, 1969, p. 7.

55. "The Churches and James Forman," *Christianity Today*, June 6, 1969, pp. 27–28.

56. William R. MacKaye, "Church Council Gets First Black President," *Washington Post*, December 8, 1972, p. B23.

57. Pratt, *The Liberalization of American Protestantism*, 201. The financial fallout from the Forman controversy was also probably responsible for the Council's decision to discontinue its Crisis in the Nation initiative, a major educational program that aimed to alert white churchgoers to the systemic causes of minority poverty and urban unrest (and that had no formal connection to Forman or IFCO). See Louis Garinger, "Manifesto Causes Division," *Christian Science Monitor*, July 26, 1969, p. 7; Findlay, *Church People in the Struggle*, 188.

58. In 1963, when J. Irwin Miller agreed to lead a "national appeal" to businessmen, Council officials prepared form letters targeting a long list of executives "with whom you have had personal association on C.E.D." Newton Hudson to J. Irwin Miller, October 10, 1963, ISM, Series 2, Box 297, Folder 9. Also see R. B. Stoner to J. Irwin Miller, October 11, 1963, ISM, Series 2, Box 297, Folder 9.

59. See 1960 and 1963 fundraising letters (and responses) in ISM, Series 2, Box 306, Folder 6; and Box 307, Folder 1. The head of a Detroit ball-bearing company included a postscript lamenting that he had unsuccessfully "solicited your account on any number of occasions to no avail" and asking for "suggestions" on how he might secure Cummins's business in the future. Jerome J. Frank to J. Irwin Miller, November 16, 1960, ISM, Series 2, Box 306, Folder 6.

60. See, for example, Memo, H. Leroy Brininger to Robert F. Burns, Jr., April 16, 1968, ISM, Series 2, Box 333, Folder 5; Donald F. Landwer to J. Irwin Miller, January 8, 1960, ISM, Series 2, Box 306, Folder 6.

61. National Council of Churches, Proposed National Appeal Committee, October 10, 1963, ISM, Series 2, Box 297, Folder 9; J. Irwin Miller to Walter Miller, January 17, 1961, ISM, Series 2, Box 306, Folder 7.

62. See, for example, Mary Hornaday, "Labor Law Change Urged by Clergy," *Christian Science Monitor*, November 25, 1960, p. 2; "Steel Strike Lessons," *New York Times*,

November 28, 1960, p. 30; "Wider U.S. Power in Strikes Urged," *New York Times*, November 26, 1960, p. 1. For Billy Graham's complaints about the NCC involving itself in the 1960 steel strike, see Richard Frohnen, "Graham Cites Church Moral Problem Issue," *Los Angeles Times*, December 1, 1960, p. B1.

63. Roger Blough to J. Irwin Miller, December 2, 1960, ISM, Series 2, Box 306, Folder 6.

64. Minutes, NCC General Business and Finance Committee, November 21, 1963, ISM, Series 2, Box 297, Folder 10.

65. Ibid.

66. Individuals who fit this description include Charles R. Hook, Sr. (1880–1963), Robert E. Wilson (1893–1964), Melvin H. Baker (1885–1976), Sidney D. Gamble (1890–1968), Francis S. Harmon (1895–1977), John Hervey Wheeler (1908–1978), Charles C. Parlin (1898–1981), David B. Cassat (1894–1982), Charles P. Taft (1897–1983), Chester Barnard (1886–1961), W. Walter Williams (1894–1983), and Paul G. Hoffman (1891–1974).

67. Stephen Isaacs, "Coors Beer—and Politics—Move East," *Washington Post*, May 4, 1975, p. A1.

68. Quoted in "Broadcast Commentary by Phil Nicolaides," PMW, Box 6, Folder 2.

69. See, for example, "Business Urged to Emulate Labor's Political Tactics" (newspaper clipping), PMW Box 8, Folder 2.

70. Mark S. Mizruchi, *The Fracturing of the American Corporate Elite* (Cambridge, MA: Harvard University Press, 2013), 148–149, 155–159; John B. Judis, *The Paradox of American Democracy: Elites, Special Interests, and the Betrayal of the Public Trust* (New York: Routledge, 2001), 120–126; Jason Stahl, "From Without to Within the Movement: Consolidating the Conservative Think Tank in the 'Long Sixties,'" in Laura Jane Gifford and Daniel K. Williams, eds., *The Right Side of the Sixties: Reexamining Conservatism's Decade of Transformation* (New York: Palgrave Macmillan, 2012), 101–120.

71. Quoted in Stahl, "From Without to Within the Movement," 113. Also see James A. Smith, *The Idea Brokers: Think Tanks and the Rise of the New Policy Elite* (New York: Free Press, 1991), 178–180.

72. By 1977 the unabashedly antiregulation American Enterprise Institute (AEI) was receiving fully twice as much coverage in the *New York Times* as its Keynesian predecessor, the CED. Mizruchi, *The Fracturing of the American Corporate Elite*, 174.

73. I have been unable to locate the exact date of the DCEL's demise. In 1969 the *Christian Century* described it as having happened "several years ago." "The Issue is Economic Justice," *Christian Century*, June 25, 1969.

74. Jane Carlton to Jerry Voorhis, December 10, 1968, HJV, Folder AA-1 19.

75. Memo, Roger L. Shinn to Members of the Program Committee on the Church and Economic Life, January 9, 1970, HJV, Folder AA-1 19.

76. Most of its members were ministers, academics, or labor officials. Minutes, Program Committee on the Church and Economic Life, November 20, 1969, HJV, Folder AA-1 19.

77. The origins of the CIC (and to a lesser extent the ICCR) are discussed in Dean M. Kelley to Herman Ellis, April 15, 1970, NCC, RG 6, Box 37, Folder 5; Bruce Hanson to Leslie Dunbar, July 10, 1970, NCC, RG 6, Box 37, Folder 5.

78. See, for example, Corporate Information Center, *Corporate Responsibility and Religious Institutions: Information and Action Documents* (New York: National Council of Churches, 1971); NCC Collection, Record Group 5, Box 18, Folder 21, PHS; "NCC Guidelines for Mission Investments," *Corporate Information Center Brief*, April 1973, p. 3A; NCC, RG 5, Box 18, Folder 21; A. Dale Fiers to R. H. Edwin Espy, May 27, 1970, NCC, RG 6, Box 37, Folder 5; James R. Gailey to R. H. Edwin Espy, May 20, 1970, NCC, RG 6, Box 37, Folder 5.

79. "Report of the Donor Support Committee," November 5, 1972, ISM, Box, 333, Folder 5. The CIC reports that may have triggered the decline are entitled: *The Union Carbide Case: A Center BRIEF for Information and Action* (New York: Corporate Information Center, 1971); *The Honeywell Case: A Center BRIEF for Information and Action* (New York: Corporate Information Center, 1971); *The Gulf-Angola Case: A Center BRIEF for Information and Action* (New York: Corporate Information Center, 1971). All found in NCC, RG 5, Box 18, Folder 21.

80. W. William Howard and J. Irwin Miller (form letter), n.d., ISM, Box 332, Folder 2.

81. John R. Collins to J. Irwin Miller, September 10, 1980, ISM, Box 332, Folder 2; Memorandum, John R. Collins to W. William Howard, September 10, 1980, ISM, Box 332, Folder 2; Memorandum, John R. Collins to W. William Howard, September 10, 1980, ISM, Box 332, Folder 2; John R. Collins to J. Irwin Miller, December 3, 1980, ISM, Box 332, Folder 2.

82. "Church Criticisms of Business," ISM, Series 2, Box 332, Folder 5. The quoted passage is from Amos 8:6.

Chapter 10

1. See, for example, Robert D. Putnam and David E. Campbell, *American Grace: How Religion Divides and Unites Us* (New York: Simon & Schuster, 2010), 105–106. As Putnam and Campbell point out, the percentage of Americans identifying as "evangelical Protestant" rose by about five points (23 to 28) between 1973 and the late 1980s—an increase that was "real and statistically significant," but which, in the end, added only about "one American in twenty to the ranks of the evangelicals." Hence, "despite the mountains of books and newspaper articles about the rise of the evangelicals, in absolute terms the change was hardly massive, except by comparison to the collapsing mainline Protestant denominations."

2. "U.S. Evangelicals: Moving Again," *Time*, September 19, 1969, pp. 64–65.

3. Ibid.

4. Edward B. Fiske, "New Liberal Mood Is Found among Fundamentalist Protestants," *New York Times*, September 14, 1969, p. 46. Also see Edward B. Fiske, "Evangelicals Learn about the Social Revolution," *New York Times*, September 21, 1969, p. E11. Skinner quoted in Fiske, "New Liberal Mood."

5. Quoted in Randall Balmer, *Redeemer: The Life of Jimmy Carter* (New York: Basic Books, 2014), 58.

6. Carl F. H. Henry to Harold Lindsell, September 26, 1970, CTI, Box 19, Folder 20.

7. See, for example, Carl F. H. Henry, "A Plea for Evangelical Demonstration," in *A Plea for Evangelical Demonstration* (Grand Rapids, MI: Baker Book House, 1971), 13–22; "What Is Man on Earth For?" in Carl F. H. Henry, ed., *Quest for Reality: Christianity and the Counter Culture* (Downers Grove, IL: InterVarsity Press, 1973), 155–161, 155.

8. Dubbed the "Christian Woodstock" by the media, Explo' '72 drew eighty thousand young people to Dallas, where over the course of a week they attended evangelism seminars during the day, then gathered each night at the Cotton Bowl for concerts and sermons.

9. Carl F. H. Henry to Harold Lindsell, May 19, 1972, CTI, Box 19, Folder 20.

10. Carl F. H. Henry to Harold Lindsell, May 25, 1972, CTI, Box 19, Folder 20.

11. Carl F. H. Henry to Harold Lindsell, May 19, 1972, CTI, Box 19, Folder 20.

12. Carl F. H. Henry to Harold Lindsell, May 19, 1972, CTI, Box 19, Folder 20; Carl F. H. Henry to Harold Lindsell, May 25, 1972, CTI, Box 19, Folder 20.

13. See, for example, Carl F. H. Henry, *Confessions of a Theologian: An Autobiography* (Waco, TX: Word Books), 349.

14. David R. Swartz, *Moral Minority: The Evangelical Left in an Age of Conservatism* (Philadelphia: University of Pennsylvania Press, 2012), 171, 178–184; Frances FitzGerald, *The Evangelicals: The Struggle to Shape America* (New York: Simon and Schuster, 2017), 252. The full text of the Chicago Declaration can be found at: https://www.evangelicalsforsocialaction.org/about-esa/history/chicago-declaration-evangelical-social-concern.

15. Francis Schaeffer, *Pollution and the Death of Man: The Christian View of Ecology* (Wheaton, IL: Tyndale House, 1979), 89, 24.

16. Francis A. Schaeffer, "Some Thoughts on Economics," FES, Series 2, Sub-Series 1, Box 3, Folder 1, pp. 3, 11, 15, 57.

17. "The President's Poverty Program," *Christianity Today*, September 12, 1969, pp. 34–35; Arthur Simon, "Hunger: Twenty Easy Questions, No Easy Answers," *Christianity Today*, July 16, 1976, pp. 19–22; Vernon C. Grounds, "Bombs or Bibles? Get Ready for Revolution!" *Christianity Today*, January 15, 1971, pp. 4–6.

18. "Terracide," *Christianity Today*, April 23, 1971, pp. 26–27.

19. Axel R. Schäfer, *Countercultural Conservatives: American Evangelicalism from the Postwar Revival to the New Christian Right* (Madison: University of Wisconsin Press, 2011), 116–117.

20. Quoted in Vernon C. Grounds, "Bombs or Bibles? Get Ready for Revolution!" *Christianity Today*, January 15, 1971, pp. 4–6, 6. It is a testament to the spirit of the times that Valentine felt free to join the deliberations that produced the 1973 Evangelical Declaration of Social Concern—and to sign his name to the resulting document. See, for example, Molly Worthen, *Apostles of Reason: The Crisis of Authority in American Evangelicalism* (New York: Oxford University Press, 2014), 189–190.

21. James C. Hefly and Edward E. Plowman, *Washington: Christians in the Corridors of Power* (Wheaton, IL: Tyndale House, 1975), 117–120; Geoffrey Kabaservice, *Rule and Ruin: The Downfall of Moderation and the Destruction of the Republican Party, from Eisenhower to the Tea Party* (New York: Oxford University Press, 2012), 234–235, 259, 359–360.

22. Randall Balmer, *God in the White House: A History; How Faith Shaped the Presidency from John F. Kennedy to George W. Bush* (New York: Harper-Collins, 2008), 109–110.

23. Swartz, *Moral Minority*, 77; Mark Hatfield to Carl F. H. Henry, June 22, 1956, CTI, Box 17, Folder 65; Carl F. H. Henry to Mark Hatfield, November 11, 1960, CTI, Box 17, Folder 65; Carl F. H. Henry to Mark Hatfield, May 17, 1963, CTI, Box 17, Folder 65; Mark Hatfield to Carl F. H. Henry, May 21, 1963, CTI, Box 17, Folder 65. In 1968 Graham even urged Richard Nixon to select Hatfield as his running mate—a suggestion that was given serious consideration until vetoed by the Republican convention's Southern contingent. Stephen P. Miller, *Billy Graham and the Rise of the Republican South* (Philadelphia: University of Pennsylvania Press, 2009), 133.

24. Swartz, *Moral Minority*, 80.

25. Ibid., 81.

26. James C. Hefley and Edward E. Plowman, *Washington: Christians in the Corridors of Power* (Wheaton, IL: Tyndale House, 1975), 123.

27. For the members of Dellenback's prayer cell, see John Dellenback to John Ehrlichman, October 15, 1971, RMN-RM, Box 2. Also see, "John R. Dellenback, 84, Former Republican Congressman," *New York Times*, December 11, 2002, p. C17; "John Buchanan, Once a Deep South Centrist in Congress, Dies at 89," *New York Times*, March 14, 2018, B14; "John Buchanan, Jr.," *Encyclopedia of Alabama* (http://www.encyclopediaofalabama.org/article/h-3286). On Quie's role in formulating the Pell Grant program, see John Brademas, *The Politics of Education: Conflict and Consensus on Capitol Hill* (Norman: University of Oklahoma Press, 1987), 33–37.

28. For a summary of Anderson's speech, see "Conservatives Are 'In': Shift in Religion in Capital," *Chicago Tribune*, July 12, 1975, p. 19.

29. See, for example, Hefley and Plowman, *Christians in the Corridors of Power*, 133; Wallace Henley, *Rebirth in Washington: The Christian Impact in the Nation's Capital* (Westchester, IL: Good News, 1977), 118–119.

30. For example, data from the 1972 ANES Times Series Study indicates that Northern white evangelicals supported federal efforts to aid minority groups (VAR 720629) at about the same rate as Catholics and mainline Protestants. In the South, in contrast, white evangelical support for such programs was about half that of Catholics and mainline Protestants.

31. Ellen M. Rosenberg, *The Southern Baptists: A Subculture in Transition* (Knoxville, TN: University of Tennessee Press, 1989), 52. The lone SBC agency responsible for promoting awareness of the denomination's public policy stances during the 1960s and 1970s, the Christian Life Commission (CLC), was chronically underfunded and regularly threatened with dissolution (in part because of its leaders' moderate views on civil rights). For most of this period it employed no more than five people, who were tasked with shaping the social convictions of more than 30,000 Southern Baptist congregations. John Lee Eighmy, *Churches in Cultural Captivity: A History of the Social Attitudes of Southern Baptists* (Knoxville: University of Tennessee Press, 1972), 179–185.

32. Bruce Buursma, "From Pews to Polls: Religious Right Marches into Politics," *Chicago Tribune*, October 2, 1980, A1; Godfrey Sperling, Jr., "Evangelical Whites Rally to Reagan," *Christian Science Monitor*, October 22, 1980, p. 1.

33. The remarks came at a National Affairs Briefing sponsored by the Religious Roundtable. The event, held in Dallas, was attended by seventeen thousand people, and a large percentage of the attendees were clergymen. Quoted in Donald T. Critchlow, *The Conservative Ascendancy: How the GOP Right Made Political History* (Cambridge, MA: Harvard University Press, 2007), 176.

34. The pollster Lou Harris, for example, estimated that the evangelical shift from Carter to Reagan had boosted the latter's popular vote margin by nearly seven points. Sara Diamond, *Roads to Dominion: Right-Wing Movements and Political Power in the United States* (New York: Guilford Press, 1995), 73.

35. For an overview of the Carter administration's increasingly rocky relationship with conservative religious leaders, see J. Brooks Flippen, *Jimmy Carter: The Politics of the Family and the Rise of the Religious Right* (Athens: University of Georgia Press, 2011).

36. Although the IRS's scrutiny of religious schools predated Carter, the issue generated little attention until 1978, when the agency issued new regulations requiring religious schools to demonstrate "good faith" efforts to enroll minority students. Balmer, *Redeemer*, 104–105; Joseph Crespino, "Civil Rights and the New Religious Right," in Bruce J. Shulman and Julian E. Zelizer, eds., *Rightward Bound: Making America Conservative in the 1970s* (Cambridge, MA: Harvard University Press, 2008), 90–105, 92–93, 98–104.

37. Kevin Phillips, *The Emerging Republican Majority* (1969; Princeton, NJ: Princeton University Press, 2015), 463.

38. Nixon and his advisors were also deeply impressed by the work of Ben Wattenberg and Richard Scammon, whose book *The Real Majority* (1970) offered a broadly similar analysis to that in Phillips's, albeit with the aim of helping the Democrats. Richard M. Scammon and Ben J. Wattenberg, *The Real Majority* (New York: Coward, McCan, and Geoghegan, 1970).

39. Ibid., 316.

40. Quoted passages are from: Memo, Pat Buchanan to Richard Nixon, November 18, 1970; and Memo, Pat Buchanan to John Mitchell and H. R. Haldeman, October 5, 1971, in Lori Cox Han, ed., *Advising Nixon: The White House Memos of Patrick J. Buchanan* (Lawrence: University Press of Kansas, 2019)). Also see: Memo, Pat Buchanan to Richard Nixon, March 24, 1971; Memo, Pat Buchanan to John Mitchell and H. R. Haldeman, September 8, 1971, in ibid.

41. Nick Thimmesch, "The Grass-Roots Dollar Chase—Ready on the Right," *New York Magazine*, June 9, 1975, pp. 58–63, 58.

42. Quoted in, *Conservative Digest*, September 1978, p. 16 (clipping), PMW, Box 7, Folder 2.

43. See, for example, Helms's speech to the platform committee of the 1980 Republican Convention, discussed below. Spencer Rich, "GOP Platform Panel Refuses to Support ERA," *Washington Post*, August 12, 1976, p. A3. Another way in which many of the early congressional supporters of the New Right appealed to voters' fears was by spinning elaborate conspiracy theories concerning the communist menace. Some, including John Roussellot (R-CA) and Larry McDonald (D-GA), openly touted their memberships in the John Birch Society. McDonald's car even sported vanity plates

reading "JBS 1." See, for example, Zach Dorfman, "The Congressman Who Created His Own Deep State," *Politico*, December 2, 2018. https://www.politico.com/magazine/story/2018/12/02/larry-mcdonald-communists-deep-state-222726.

44. All figures appearing in this chapter use the following coding scheme: The South is defined as the states that seceded to join the Confederacy. "Evangelical" and "mainline" are defined by denominational affiliation, using the scheme laid out in Brian Steensland, Lynn D. Robinson, W. Bradford Wilcox, Jerry Z. Park, Mark D. Regnerus, and Robert D. Woodberry, "The Measure of American Religion: Toward Improving the State of the Art," *Social Forces* 79 (2000): 291–318. The question used in Figures 10.1 and 10.2 (VCF0830) asks respondents to place themselves on a 7-point scale, with 1 indicating strong support for federal civil rights programs. I have recoded the data to group respondents into supportive, opposed, and neutral categories.

45. In the South, white evangelical support for civil rights programs was typically somewhat lower than the overall level of white support during this period. Because the differences were (with some exceptions) not especially large, and to avoid a visually cluttered presentation, the chart does not disaggregate Southern white opinion.

46. Only white mainline Protestants, traditionally the most Republican of all religious groups, did not move significantly toward the GOP during this period. Both mainline Protestants and secular whites would begin moving toward the Democrats in the early 1990s.

47. There is much evidence to suggest that elite religious activists during the late 1970s and early 1980s engaged in this sort of strategic calculation. My contention, however, is that their efforts had at best a modest impact on the political behavior of average evangelicals. On the strategic calculations of conservative religious elites, see, for example, Christopher Baylor, *First to the Party: The Group Origins of Political Transformation* (Philadelphia: University of Pennsylvania Press, 2018); Daniel Schlozman, *When Movements Anchor Parties: Electoral Alignments in American History* (Princeton, NJ: Princeton University Press, 2015); Daniel K. Williams, *Defenders of the Unborn: The Pro-Life Movement before* Roe v. Wade (New York: Oxford University Press, 2016), 239–253.

48. Data from the 1980 American National Election Study (ANES). When asked to list the "single most important problem the government in Washington should try to take care of," 28 percent of white evangelical respondents mentioned inflation; 17.1 percent mentioned the Iran hostages; 7.8 percent mentioned opposition to nuclear disarmament talks; 5.2 mentioned "preventing war" or "establishing peace"; and 4.1 percent mentioned unemployment. It is also noteworthy that the Reagan campaign, while giving Religious Right leaders virtual carte blanche in the drafting of the Republican platform, pointedly declined to emphasize issues such as abortion and the Equal Rights Amendment in its outreach efforts to evangelical churches—a decision based in part on polls showing that rank-and-file evangelicals were far more divided on these questions than their purported leaders. Balmer, *Redeemer*, 145.

49. Data from the 1988 American National Election Study (ANES).

50. Remarkably, between 1976 and 1980 white Southerners who were asked to rate the Republicans' stance on civil rights on a seven-point scale (with seven representing

the conservative extreme) revised their assessments upward by more than a full point, from 3.8 to 4.92. Northerners also noticed the Republicans' shifting rhetoric on race, revising their estimates of the party's racial conservatism upward by two-thirds of a point (from 3.92 to 4.63).

51. This is not to deny that anti-abortion and other socially conservative activists were an important force in many congressional districts. Focusing on the early 1990s, for example, Marty Cohen has shown that highly organized conservative religious activists effectively seized control of the Republican party machinery in several swing districts, and that their control of the nominating process was instrumental in shifting the GOP to the right on abortion and other "moral" issues. Marty Cohen, *Moral Victories in the Battle for Congress: Cultural Conservatism and the House GOP* (Philadelphia: University of Pennsylvania Press, 2019).

52. Ryan L. Claassen, *Godless Democrats and Pious Republicans? Party Activists, Party Capture, and the "God Gap"* (New York: Cambridge University Press, 2015), 82–87.

53. Michele F. Margolis, *From Politics to the Pews: How Partisanship and the Political Environment Shape Religious Identity* (Chicago: University of Chicago Press, 2018).

54. In the 1994 ANES the average level of educational attainment for white evangelicals was 3.69 on a seven-point scale, where 3 indicates a high school degree, 4 indicates some professional training beyond high school, 5 indicates having attended college but without attaining a four-year degree, 6 indicates a four-year college degree, and 7 indicates an advanced degree. In 1994, using this same scale, white Catholic respondents averaged 4.59, mainline Protestants averaged 4.71, and unaffiliated whites averaged 4.13.

55. The one exception (discussed above) is abortion; here white evangelicals were by the late 1980s expressing noticeably more conservative views than other working-class white voters.

56. See, for example, Paul Weyrich, "The Pro-Family Movement," *Conservative Digest*, May–June 1980, pp. 14–27, 15.

57. The New Right's role in launching and staffing the major Religious Right groups has been thoroughly documented. The Moral Majority, for example, was formed in May 1979 after a lengthy meeting between the televangelist Jerry Falwell and the New Right operatives Paul Weyrich, Richard Viguerie, and Howard Phillips. Robert Billings, a Christian school activist with extensive links to the New Right, became the group's executive director. Christian Voice's top lobbyist, Gary Jarmin, learned his craft while working for the New Right–aligned American Conservative Union. Christian Voice's congressional advisory board featured several New Right stalwarts, including Senators Gordon Humphrey, Roger Jepsen, Orrin Hatch, and James McClure, and Congressmen Phil Crane and Robert Dornan. The Religious Roundtable was organized by Ed McAteer, a longtime Weyrich associate who had also worked for both the Conservative Caucus and the Pew-funded Christian Freedom Foundation. Russell Chandler, "Lobby Seeks 'Born-Again' Vote," *Los Angeles Times*, August 5, 1979, p. A3; "Is Morality All Right?" *Christianity Today*, November 2, 1979, pp. 76–85; Robert C. Liebman, "Mobilizing the Moral Majority," in Robert C. Liebman and Robert Wuthnow eds., *The New Christian Right* (New York: Aldine, 1983), 50–74, 52; James L.

Guth, "The Politics of the Religious Right," in John C. Green, James L. Guth, Corwin E. Smidt, and Lyman A. Kellstedt, eds., *Religion and the Culture Wars: Dispatches from the Front* (Lanham, MD: Rowman & Littlefield, 1996), 7–29, 17–18; FitzGerald, *The Evangelicals*, 302–303, 310.

58. Nancy Lammers, ed., *The Washington Lobby*, 4th ed. (Washington, DC: Congressional Quarterly, 1982), 105–112; Robert C. Liebman, "Mobilizing the Moral Majority," in Robert C. Liebman and Robert Wuthnow, eds., *The New Christian Right* (New York: Aldine Publishing, 1983), 50–74, 52; "Evangelical Group Disagrees with 276 in Congress," *New York Times*, November 2, 1980, p. 34; Russell Chandler, "Lobby Seeks 'Born-Again' Vote," *Los Angeles Times*, August 5, 1979, p. A3.

59. "Michelle Magar, "Two Rights Make a . . . ," *Seven Days*, October 26, 1979 (clipping), PMW, Box 7, Folder 8; Deborah Huntington and Ruth Kaplan, "Whose Gold Is Behind the Altar? Corporate Ties to Evangelicals," *Contemporary Marxism* 4 (1981–1982): 62–94. Richard Kelley (R-FL), a staunch conservative who was embroiled in the ABSCAM scandal, also received a 94 rating from Christian Voice. "Evangelical Group Disagrees with 276 in Congress," 34. Goldwater did endorse a version of the Human Life Amendment in the midst of a closely contested 1980 Senate race, but he made no secret of his disagreements with dogmatic pro-lifers; together with his wife, Peggy, he was active in the Arizona chapter of Planned Parenthood for the duration of his Senate career. See, for example, Andrew E. Busch, "The Goldwater Myth," *Claremont Review of Books*, January 3, 2006, available online at https://www.claremont.org/crb/article/the-goldwater-myth.

60. The quote is from Paul Weyrich, "The Pro-Family Movement," *Conservative Digest*, May–June 1980, pp. 14–27, 15. Also see Lammers, *The Washington Lobby*, 105–112, 109.

61. Spencer Rich, "GOP Platform Panel Refuses to Support ERA," *Washington Post*, August 12, 1976, p. A3.

62. Over the vehement opposition of Reagan's camp, Anderson was named co-chair of a platform subcommittee on community affairs whose jurisdiction covered many issues of concern to the New Right. Richard L. Madden, "Ford Camp Loses Panel Chairmanship," *New York Times*, August 10, 1976, p. 14.

63. Spencer Rich, "School Prayer Plank," *Washington Post*, August 13, 1976, p. A1; Myra MacPherson, "Republican Women: 'Homemakers' and Some Quiet Causists," August 18, 1976, p. A15.

64. Spencer Rich, "Ford Rebuff Defeated in GOP Platform," *Washington Post*, August 14, 1976, p. A5. Anderson was not the only evangelical working to thwart the New Right agenda. Carl Henry's son Paul, a political science professor and local party official from Michigan, was a member of the convention rules committee. Interviewed by *Christianity Today* during the convention, he heaped scorn on fellow Republicans who demanded uncompromising "moral" language on subjects like abortion and the Soviets while simultaneously urging the GOP to withdraw its support for programs that aided the poor and marginalized. Such delegates, according to Henry, had "a lot of zeal without humanity—they don't realize how difficult these issues are." Tim

Miller and Tonda Rush, "God and the GOP in Kansas City," *Christianity Today*, September 10, 1976, pp. 59–60.

65. "My [decision] to do something about John Anderson came when I sat through the entire week of the Platform Hearings at the Republican National Convention in Kansas City and saw him perform," Weyrich informed the New Right publication *The Right Report*. "I knew at that point that if there was any way that he could be defeated he must be." "TRR Interview with Paul Weyrich," *Right Report*, February 16, 1978 (clipping), PMW, Box 6, Folder 8.

66. Several of Weyrich's closest congressional advisors objected that the Illinois congressman, in addition to being a member of the House GOP leadership, was not particularly liberal. Two congressmen, E. G. "Bud" Shuster (R-PA) and Robin Beard (R-TN), resigned from the board of Weyrich's Committee for the Survival of a Free Congress (CSFC) to protest the group's bid to oust Anderson. As Shuster, who held a 96 percent conservative rating from *Congressional Quarterly*, told reporters, Anderson "represents the mainstream of the Republican Party most of the time. He's a moderate fiscal conservative, no wild-eyed big spender. If people want to purge Republicans there is a long list we should go after before John B. Anderson." "Anderson Gets Added Support," *Rockford (IL) Register-Star*, January 29, 1978. In PMW, Box 6, Folder 8. In 1978, Anderson earned middling scores from both liberal and conservative groups. He voted with the left-leaning Americans for Democratic Action (ADA) on 51 percent of "scored" votes, and with the conservative Americans Constitutional Action (ACA) on 44 percent of such votes. "Anderson: Running on the GOP Left," *Congressional Quarterly*, November 3, 1979, pp. 2467–2472, 2471.

67. Jim Mason, *No Holding Back: The 1980 John B. Anderson Presidential Campaign* (Lanham, MD: University Press of America, 2011), 29, 33, 35.

68. Toni Carabillo, "Right-Wing Political Muscle-Flexing," *National NOW Times*, July 1978, p. 6.

69. Adam Clymer, "Right Wing Seeks to Unseat Rep. Anderson," *New York Times*, February 16, 1978, p. A18.

70. David S. Broder, "Rep. Anderson, a GOP Leader, in Tough Race for Reelection," March 16, 1978, p. A9.

71. David S. Broder, "Anderson Wins Illinois Race," *Washington Post*, March 22, 1978, p. A2.

72. Eleanor Randolph, "Anderson Assails Religious Politics," *Los Angeles Times*, September 30, 1980, p. 1.

73. John Dart, "Christians Score the Candidates," *Los Angeles Times*, November 1, 1980, p. C6.

74. The white evangelical figure is based on the 1980 American National Election Study, in which about 4.5 percent of evangelicals reported having voted for Anderson.

75. Broder, "Anderson Wins Illinois Race"; "Why the 'New Right' Isn't Doing Well at the Polls," *Business Week*, October 30, 1978, pp. 158–160.

76. Sam Roberts, "John Buchanan, Once a Deep South Centrist in Congress, Dies at 89," *New York Times*, March 12, 2018, B14.

77. In 1973, for example, the American Conservative Union (ACU) awarded him a 55. The group attacked his votes on wage and price controls, environmental regulation, and the minimum wage, while applauding his votes to trim the federal budget and grant more regulatory autonomy to the states. "1973 ACU Interim Ratings—House," PMW, Box 5, Folder 2.

78. During the 1970s Buchanan typically won about 60 percent of the vote in general elections. For precise figures, see Neal Wise, "Clergymen in the 95th Congress: A Case Study of Religion in Politics" (Ph.D. diss., Graduate Theological Union, 1982), 252.

79. On Smith's membership in the JBS, see, for example, Roberts, "John Buchanan."

80. I am grateful to Natalie Davis for pointing out that Alabama Republican primary contests were typically very low turnout affairs during this period. Davis, who worked as a pollster for the Buchanan campaign, was interviewed on February 19, 2019.

81. "Evangelical Group Quietly and Angrily Upsets Alabama Primary," *New York Times*, September 8, 1980, p. B10.

82. Quoted in Lammers, *The Washington Lobby*, 105.

83. To be sure, a handful of devout Rockefeller Republicans, including John Dellenback (R-OR) and William Hudnut (R-IN), had their careers ended by the Watergate-fueled Democratic wave of 1974. But their defeats had little if anything to do with their religious views. Some members of Dallenbeck's prayer circle, including Albert Quie (R-MN) and Guy Vander Jagt (R-MI), moved rightward to embrace the Reagan Revolution. Mark Hatfield, whose center-left views were more or less in keeping with the views of the Oregon electorate, would remain in the Senate until 1996.

84. Among other complaints, Jarman demanded explanations for why the magazine had published articles or editorials suggesting that the churches bore some responsibility for the nation's history of racial segregation, that Christian principles required the United States to provide aid to poorer nations, that there were ethical problems with the conduct of the war in Vietnam, and that Christians were religiously obligated to protect the environment. W. Maxey Jarman to Harold Lindsell, June 4, 1969, CTI, Box 19, Folder 23; W. Maxey Jarman to Harold Lindsell, September 12, 1969, CTI, Box 19, Folder 23; W. Maxey Jarman to Harold Lindsell, January 12, 1969, CTI, Box 19, Folder 23; W. Maxey Jarman to Harold Lindsell, April 12, 1971, CTI, Box 19, Folder 23.

85. Harold Lindsell, "NRB Address, 1974," CTI, Box 24, Folder 15.

86. Harold Lindsell, *The Battle for the Bible* (Grand Rapids, MI: Zondervan, 1976); *The Bible in the Balance* (Grand Rapids, MI: Zondervan, 1979).

87. Lindsell, *The Bible in the Balance*, 33–34.

88. Lindsell, *The Battle for the Bible*, 206.

89. "Terracide," *Christianity Today*, April 23, 1971, pp. 26–27.

90. Harold Lindsell, *Free Enterprise: A Judeo-Christian Defense* (Wheaton, IL: Tyndale House, 1982), 72–73.

91. Daniel K. Williams, *God's Own Party: The Making of the Christian Right* (New York: Oxford University Press, 2010), 155.

92. Schlozman, *When Movements Anchor Parties*, 106.

93. Memo, David Parker to Robert Finch, June 24, 1971, RMN-AF, Box 22.

94. Williams, *God's Own Party*, 141.
95. During the late 1970s Schaeffer's financial backers included the Pew trusts, the oilman Bunker Hunt, and Amway's Richard DeVos—all major funders of conservative political causes. Schlozman, *When Movements Anchor Parties*, 106; Williams, *God's Own Party*, 141.
96. Francis A. Schaeffer, *The Great Evangelical Disaster* (Wheaton, IL: Crossway, 1984), 114, 113. Also see Schaeffer, *A Christian Manifesto* (Wheaton, IL: Crossway Books, 1981), 124–125.
97. Schaeffer, *The Great Evangelical Disaster*, 104–105.
98. In his later writings Schaeffer was also convinced that leading liberals—including advocates of environmental regulation and economic redistribution—were bent on concentrating power in the hands of secular elites who would ultimately subvert American democracy. See, for example, *A Christian Manifesto*, 79–82.
99. Henry, *Confessions of a Theologian*, 397, 398.
100. "With prophetic self-assurance," Henry wrote, their leaders "counsel[ed] evangelicals . . . to invest in South African Krugerands [*sic*]" and to pledge their "uncritical" support for Israel, as if these nations could "do no wrong." The passage does not indicate which group Henry is targeting, but it appears shortly after a discussion of the Moral Majority. Ibid., 397–398.
101. Ibid., 397.
102. Ibid., 398.
103. Carl F. H. Henry to Harold Lindsell, September 26, 1970, CTI, Box 19, Folder 20.

Conclusion

1. Frances FitzGerald, *The Evangelicals: The Struggle to Shape America* (New York: Simon and Schuster, 2017), 551–553.
2. FitzGerald, *The Evangelicals*, 541.
3. Ruth M. Melkonian-Hoover and Lyman A. Kellstedt, *Evangelicals and Immigration: Fault Lines Among the Faithful* (Cham, Switzerland: Palgrave Macmillan, 2019), 58; Kevin R. den Dulk, "The GOP, Evangelical Elites, and the Challenge of Pluralism," in Paul A. Djupe and Ryan L. Claassen, eds., *The Evangelical Crackup? The Future of the Evangelical-Republican Coalition* (Philadelphia, PA: Temple University Press, 2018), 63–76, 68.
4. FitzGerald, *The Evangelicals*, 555–556; Robin Globus Veldman, *The Gospel of Climate Skepticism: Why Evangelical Christians Oppose Action on Climate Change* (Berkeley: University of California Press, 2019), 205–210.
5. See, for example, Robert Wuthnow and Valerie Lewis, "Religion and Altruistic Foreign Policy Goals: Evidence from a National Survey of Church Members," *Journal for the Scientific Study of Religion* 47 (2008): 191–209; Tobin Grant, "Polling Evangelicals: Cut Aid to World's Poor, Unemployed," *Christianity Today*, February 18, 2011. A 2011 poll by the Pew Research Center, discussed in the Grant article, found that 56 percent of evangelicals favored cutting foreign aid programs. as

compared to about 47 percent of non-evangelicals. Wuthnow and Lewis found a negative relationship between evangelical background and support for altruistic foreign aid programs, though the relationship did not reach statistically significant levels. For white evangelicals' relative lack of interest in foreign policy questions, see, for example, John C. Green, *The Faith Factor: How Religion Influences American Elections* (Westport, CT: Praeger, 2007), 138–139.

6. Quoted in Melkonian-Hoover and Kellstedt, *Evangelicals and Immigration*, 57.

7. Quoted in Ibid., 59.

8. Ibid., 101.

9. A plurality of 46 percent of Southern Baptist pastors disagreed with the view that immigration and diversity "strengthen" American society (only 31 percent agreed). Among the 41 percent of SBC pastors who reported that they "often" discussed immigration from the pulpit, a majority (51 percent) reported that they had called for reducing immigration levels (27 percent had called for raising them). Ibid., 150–151.

10. Quoted in Ibid., 54.

11. Darren Patrick Guerra, "Evangelicals Are Stopping Trump," *First Things*, April 16, 2016, https://www.firstthings.com/blogs/firstthoughts/2016/04/evangelicals-are-stopping-trump; Joseph N. Knippenberg, "Evangelicals Aren't Really That Keen on Donald Trump," *The Federalist*, March 23, 2016, https://thefederalist.com/2016/03/23/evangelicals-arent-really-that-keen-on-donald-trump/; Geoffrey C. Layman, "Where Is Trump's Evangelical Base? Not in Church," *Washington Post* (Monkey Cage Blog), March 29, 2016.

12. Paul A. Djupe and Brian R. Calfano, "Evangelicals Were On Their Own in the 2016 Election," in Paul A. Djupe and Ryan L. Claassen, *The Evangelical Crackup? The Future of the Evangelical-Republican Coalition* (Philadelphia: Temple University Press, 2018), 15–31, 22.

13. Ibid., 25.

14. On the emergence of the "diploma divide," see John Sides, Michael Tesler, and Lynn Vavreck, *Identity Crisis: The 2016 Presidential Campaign and the Battle for the Meaning of America* (Princeton, NJ: Princeton University Press, 2018), 26–29, 162–164, 178–179. On population density as a predictor of partisanship and ideology, see Jonathan A. Rodden, *Why Cities Lose: The Deep Roots of the Urban–Rural Political Divide* (New York: Basic Books, 2019), 86–91.

15. Paul Djupe and Ryan P. Burge, "Regular Churchgoing Doesn't Make Evangelicals More Moderate. It Makes Them More Enthusiastic for Trump," *Washington Post* (Monkey Cage Blog), October 9, 2018. A related line of experimental research has found that while religious arguments may succeed in moving pious evangelicals' attitudes to the left on issues such as immigration, exposure to such arguments has little, if any, impact on actual behavior, or even intended behavior. Michele F. Margolis, "How Far Does Social Group Influence Reach? Identities, Elites, and Immigration Attitudes," *Journal of Politics* 80 (2018): 772–785, 780.

16. Graham Reside, "The State of Contemporary Mainline Protestantism," in James Hudnut-Beumler and Mark Silk, eds., *The Future of Mainline Protestantism in America* (New York: Columbia University Press, 2018), 17–58, 33.

17. Paul A. Djupe and Christopher P. Gilbert, *The Political Influence of Churches* (New York: Cambridge University Press, 2009), 71–72.

18. On regional variation in the political and theological orientation of mainline Protestant churches, see Reside, "The State of Contemporary Mainline Protestantism," 50–51; David Bains, "The Beliefs and Practices of Mainline Protestants," in James Hudnut-Beumler and Mark Silk, eds., *The Future of Mainline Protestantism in America* (New York: Columbia University Press, 2018), 59–82, 67–68.

19. Reinhold Niebuhr, "The Christian Faith and the Economic Life of Liberal Society," in Alfred Dudley Ward, ed., *Goals of Economic Life* (New York: Harper and Brothers, 1953), 433–459, 440, 441–442.

Index

Tables and figures are indicated by *t* and *f* following the page number

For the benefit of digital users, indexed terms that span two pages (e.g., 52–53) may, on occasion, appear on only one of those pages.